Evaluating Empire and Confronting Colonialism in Eighteenth-Century Britain

This volume comprehensively examines the ways metropolitan Britons spoke and wrote about the British Empire during the short eighteenth century, from about 1730 to 1790. The work argues that following several decades of largely uncritical celebration of the empire as a vibrant commercial entity that had made Britain prosperous and powerful, a growing familiarity with the character of overseas territories and their inhabitants during and after the Seven Years' War produced a substantial critique of empire. Evolving out of a widespread revulsion against the behaviors exhibited by many groups of Britons overseas and building on a language of "otherness" that metropolitans had used since the beginning of overseas expansion to describe its participants, the societies, and polities that Britons abroad had constructed in their new habitats, this critique used the languages of humanity and justice as standards by which to evaluate and condemn the behaviors, in turn, of East India Company servants, American slaveholders, Atlantic slave traders, British political and military leaders during the American War of Independence, and abettors of British oppression in Ireland, including ministerial authorities, placemen, and pensioners, and rapacious Irish absentees and Protestant persecutors of Catholics. Although this critique represented a massive contemporary condemnation of British colonialism and manifested an impulse among metropolitans to distance themselves from imperial excesses, the benefits of empire were far too substantial to permit any turning away from it, and the moment of sensibility waned.

Jack P. Greene is the Andrew W. Mellon Professor Emeritus in the Humanities in the Department of History at Johns Hopkins University. Before retiring in 2005, he taught colonial British-American history for almost a half-century at Michigan State University, Western Reserve University, the University of Michigan, and Johns Hopkins University. Greene's publications are extensive, including eleven monographs, seven booklets, eight edited volumes, eight documentary editions, two anthologies, four encyclopedias, and one bibliography. He has also published nearly one hundred chapters in books, more than one hundred journal articles, and hundreds of book reviews. Additionally, he has supervised eighty-eight dissertations. Greene is a member of the American Historical Association, the American Philosophical Society, the American Academy of Arts and Sciences, the Royal Historical Society, and the British Academy.

Evaluating Empire and Confronting Colonialism in Eighteenth-Century Britain

JACK P. GREENE

Johns Hopkins University

CAMBRIDGE UNIVERSITY PRESS
Cambridge, New York, Melbourne, Madrid, Cape Town,
Singapore, São Paulo, Delhi, Mexico City

Cambridge University Press
32 Avenue of the Americas, New York, NY 10013-2473, USA

www.cambridge.org
Information on this title: www.cambridge.org/9781107682986

First published 2013

Printed in the United States of America

A catalog record for this publication is available from the British Library.

Library of Congress Cataloging in Publication Data

Greene, Jack P.
Evaluating empire and confronting colonialism in eighteenth-century Britain / Jack P. Greene.
    p. cm.
Includes bibliographical references and index.
ISBN 978-1-107-03055-8 (hardback) – ISBN 978-1-107-68298-6 (paperback)
1. Great Britain – Colonies – History – 18th century. 2. Great Britain – Colonies – Public
opinion – History. 3. Imperialism – Public opinion – History – 18th century. 4. Discourse
analysis – History – 18th century. I. Title.
DA480.G73 2013
325'.34109033–dc23   2012021362

ISBN 978-1-107-03055-8 Hardback
ISBN 978-1-107-68298-6 Paperback

Contents

Preface

Confronting Empire

During the American crisis between 1763 and 1783, the numerous critics of the British government's coercive policy were prone to ridicule those people who, although largely uninformed about the character and components of the overseas empire, nonetheless blindly supported Administration measures concerning them. Thus, in 1778, an anonymous wag calling himself a West India merchant published, in a series of letters in the *London Evening Post*, an alleged conversation among three members of Parliament. When one inquired of another whether he ever gave himself "the trouble of examining and considering the subject" of taxing the colonies, the second man declared: "Oh yes, that I've done in this case long ago.–I'm quite sartin that we are to tax the *West-Indies*, as well as the *West of England*." "You mean the *North-Americans*, I suppose, Sir?," asked the first man. "Why, you knows," the second answered, "its all the same thing:– *North-America, Bingal, Virginny, Jemaiky*, is all in the *Indies*, only the sea folks that loves to box the compass, calls things North and East and West ... and that makes it so puzzling to understand and to remember the name, and to know where all these *outlandish Colonies* are."[1] That the British public was content to be uninformed was the recurring complaint of people who had considerable experience living in or dealing with America, of whom John Fothergill, a prominent London Quaker, is a principal example. In a 1780 pamphlet, he remarked at length on the sad effects of this ignorance, which he took to be the principal explanation for "the madness and folly" of Britain's conduct of the American war. "Knowledge of AMERICA," he lamented, was "confined to the Merchants, and Traders chiefly. It was a country talked of, but no people, save those immediately interested in its produce, knew any thing about it."[2]

---

[1] *The West India Merchant. Being a Series of Papers Originally Printed under that Signature in the London Evening Post* (London, 1778), 15–17.

[2] John Fothergill, *An English Freeholder's Address to His Countrymen* (London, 1780), 2. See also Fothergill's earlier remarks along the same lines in *Considerations Relative to the North America Colonies* (London, 1765), 35–36.

If such ignorance actually existed, there was little excuse for it. During the previous three-quarters of a century, between roughly 1710 and the outbreak of the War for Independence, the American colonies had experienced a sustained period of growth and development in terms of every possible measure, including territorial expansion, population growth, and overseas commerce, trading not just with Britain but also with the Caribbean, southern Europe, Ireland, and Africa. Although this steady expansion led to the proliferation of economic treatises touting the colonies as "the principal *Cornucopia* of *Great-Britain's* Wealth,"[3] metropolitan Britons were, by and large, slow to recognize the colonies' growing economic and strategic importance. Between the mid-1730s and the early 1760s, however, this situation changed dramatically, as metropolitan officials and parliamentary leaders developed a deeper appreciation of the centrality of empire to Britain's economic well-being, naval power, and international standing, and with that, a growing recognition of the vulnerability of Britain's overseas settlements to attack from its principal imperial rivals, Spain and France, and the advisability of using state funds to protect them. The wars with Spain and France between 1739 and 1748 especially helped to focus attention upon France's growing capacity to rival Britain as a colonizing and maritime power and to underline, for metropolitan officials, the limits of metropolitan authority within the colonies. Efforts to shore up that authority began immediately in 1748, and the Seven Years' War from 1756 to 1763 eventually led to a massive increase in expenditures to support the naval and military forces required to check French expansion in the overseas colonial world from North America and the West Indies east to Bengal. The territories in America and India acquired in that war opened still further possibilities and created new problems for metropolitan involvement in imperial oversight. Thereafter, as P. J. Marshall has noted, a "determination to maintain a proper degree of British authority throughout the empire" and an "acceptance that government overseas might assume new powers and perform new functions" became dominant themes in the government's approach to empire. The only way to solve the empire's problems was to strengthen metropolitan control.[4]

Parallel to this growing official engagement with empire was a widening and deepening of public interest in all parts of the British overseas world. Over the past quarter-century, scholars have meticulously documented the expansion of print culture in Britain during the century following the Glorious Revolution and explored the impact of this development upon British domestic public life.[5] Although it is true, as Philip Lawson pointed out in 1989, that

[3] G. B., *The Advantages of the Revolution Illustrated, By a View of the Present State of Great Britain* (London, 1753), 30.

[4] P. J. Marshall, "Empire and Authority in the Later Eighteenth Century," republished in idem, *'A Free though Conquering People': Eighteenth-Century Britain and Its Empire* (Aldershot, U.K.: Ashgate, 2003), Chapter 2, 116.

[5] See especially Michael Harris and Alan Lee, eds., *The Press in English Society from the Seventeenth to the Nineteenth Centuries* (Cranbury, N.J.: Associated University Presses, 1986);

this scholarly literature contained little discussion of the imperial issues "that preoccupied so many contemporary writers in the Hanoverian period,"[6] several historians since the 1990s have abundantly remedied that deficiency. In her sweeping analysis of the centrality of empire in forging a national body politic after the union of England and Scotland, Linda Colley, in 1992, drew upon and thereby directed attention to a massive body of contemporary published writings about the empire and to the deep engagement with empire that those writings exhibited.[7]

Beginning in the 1730s and increasing exponentially over the next half-century, a wide variety of printed sources – histories, chorographies, economic treatises, political pamphlets, novels, plays, epic poems, sermons, improvement treatises, and magazine and newspaper articles – fed what was obviously a voracious appetite for information about the empire. Moreover, as Kathleen Wilson showed in her densely researched and thoroughly analyzed study of the intrusion of imperial considerations into British domestic political and cultural life, this public interest in empire was by no means confined to London and other major overseas trading centers such as Bristol, Liverpool, and Glasgow, but spread via provincial newspapers, printers, and booksellers over all of Britain.[8] By the 1750s and 1760s, information about the overseas empire was available to Britons wherever they resided, and the wide extent of the empire, as well as the distinctive character of each of its several parts, was well known to large segments of the metropolitan British population, many of whom were intimately involved with the colonies, whether producing items of export to them, exchanging goods with them, supplying them with labor and capital, processing colonial products, or participating in their defense. At the same time, parliamentary debates revealed on the part of the metropolitan political establishment increasing knowledge of and wider attention to imperial matters.

David Armitage and Eliga H. Gould have also contributed significantly to our understanding of the early modern British engagement with empire. Armitage has elegantly traced the gradual emergence among the politically literate, from the early sixteenth century through the age of Walpole, of an "ideology" of empire that by the 1740s proudly and aggressively depicted it in

---

Jeremy Black, *The English Press in the Eighteenth Century* (Philadelphia: University of Pennsylvania Press, 1987); Michael Harris, *London Newspapers in the Age of Walpole: A Study in the Origins of the Modern English Press* (Cranbury, N.J.: Associated University Presses, 1987); Robert Harris, *A Patriot Press: National Politics and the London Press in the 1740s* (Oxford: Clarendon Press, 1993); John Brewer, *Party, Ideology and Popular Politics at the Accession of George III* (Cambridge: Cambridge University Press, 1976), 139–60.

6 Philip Lawson, "'Arts and Empire Equally Extend': Tradition, Prejudice and Assumption in the Eighteenth Century Press Coverage of Empire," *Journal of History and Politics*, 7 (1989): 119.

7 Linda Colley, *Britons: Forging the Nation 1707–1837* (New Haven: Yale University Press, 1992).

8 Kathleen Wilson, *The Sense of the People: Politics, Culture, and Imperialism in England, 1715–1785* (Cambridge: Cambridge University Press, 1995).

contradistinction to the contemporary French and Spanish empires as, in his succinct characterization, "Protestant, commercial, maritime and free."[9] In his persuasive effort to explain the widespread popular support for the government's coercive colonial policies before and during the American War for Independence, Gould has thoroughly explored the extensive literature generated by the debate over the American question. In the process, he has illuminated the importance of empire within metropolitan political culture and the persistent public embrace of empire during the war and after the loss of thirteen American colonies.[10]

The central thrust of this literature has been to emphasize the growing metropolitan embrace of overseas empire after the 1730s, and embrace there certainly was. As P. J. Marshall aptly put it in the title of an important essay, late eighteenth-century Britain was to a remarkable extent a "Nation Defined by Empire."[11] This volume has a rather different emphasis. As the title suggests, it considers how metropolitan Britons spoke and wrote about the British Empire during the short eighteenth century, the early decades through the mid-1780s. Neither a history of ideas in the usual sense of that term nor a study of public opinion, it is rather an analysis of the many discourses or languages that metropolitan Britons used to assimilate, characterize, and evaluate the significance of the overseas empire and to debate the nature and dimensions of the myriad problems posed by empire in an era of rapid expansion and contraction after 1760. It uses the principal of those languages as analytic organizing categories.

This project relies primarily on an examination of two kinds of sources. The first are reports of parliamentary speeches; the second are contemporary metropolitan, including Irish, publications about or relating to the overseas portions of the empire. The vastness of such publications might seem to require some principle of selection, but, having never managed to find or invent one during more than a decade of research, I have simply proceeded by working through every relevant source I could find. Nevertheless, the fact that when I go online to check a quotation or a title I occasionally turn up yet another source suggests that I have missed a number of them. Unless they were originally printed somewhere in Britain or republished there, works that originated in America do not form part of the research base for this volume, and newspapers and magazines have been used sparingly and unsystematically.

The volume is very largely an exposition of my own analysis of the primary documents I have collected. References to the vast secondary literature are

---

[9] David Armitage, *The Ideological Origins of the British Empire* (Cambridge: Cambridge University Press, 2000). The quotation is from p. 173.

[10] Eliga H. Gould, *The Persistence of Empire: British Political Culture in the Age of the American Revolution* (Chapel Hill: University of North Carolina Press, 2000).

[11] P. J. Marshall, "A Nation Defined by Empire, 1755–1766," republished in idem, '*A Free though Conquering People*,' Chapter 5.

limited to those works that have most directly informed my understanding of the contexts of the many British debates over eighteenth-century empire. Focusing relentlessly on the public discussion of empire as contributors endeavored to define and debate the successive issues that having an empire raised, the volume deliberately adopts the expositional strategy of letting the contributors to this discussion speak, colorfully and forcefully, in their own words, proceeding on the assumption that authors and speakers in polemical arenas do not normally advance arguments that they think unlikely to persuade their audience. But I have not concerned myself with whether particular analyses of imperial problems were valid, or convincing, or actually won much of an audience, as interesting and important as those questions would be if this book were intended as a study of the battle for public opinion.[12] In the end, my concerns are far more modest: to analyze the ways in which people talked and wrote about empire as they tried to confront its unfolding problems in shifting contexts and to trace the gradual emergence after 1760 of a critique of empire on the grounds of humanity, justice, and liberty. This consciously limited objective has not required an explicit examination of questions of authorial identity, expertise, and intentions; the context and details of print production; or audience response – all important problems that this study implicitly raises and that call for further investigation.[13]

Extending to British behavior in India, America, Africa, and Ireland, this critique of empire was not the product of some general reassessment of empire by a few major analysts systematically applying or endeavoring to develop a coherent, much less uniform, set of principles to evaluate the morality of empire. Rather, it was a loose bundle of separate critiques by quite different and often unrelated groups arising out of attempts to diagnose, understand, and resolve specific problems associated with particular areas of the overseas empire. Earlier scholars have not entirely ignored these critiques. Wilson, Marshall, and Gould have all briefly drawn attention to them,[14] and a few specialized studies have investigated in some detail aspects of debates over specific problems or

---

[12] For illuminating considerations of these issues as they can be studied for the larger context of British writing, see the works cited in note 5, and, with specific reference to issues involving empire, Wilson, *Sense of the People*.

[13] Other interesting problems raised but not taken up in this volume also provide opportunities for further investigation. One involves the intellectual genealogy of the participants' ideas, which individual writers occasionally profess to have taken from one or the other of the pantheon of thinkers conventionally studied by historians of political thought. A second is the relationship between debate over empire and partisan politics, which, for instance, was especially important to the deeply partisan consideration of the American and Irish questions. A third is the link between evaluations of empire and the analysis of domestic problems within Britain, and a fourth is the relationship of this specifically British critique to the broader European intellectual context in which it took place.

[14] See Wilson, *Sense of the People*, 274–79; P. J. Marshall, "The Moral Swing to the East: British Humanitarianism, India and the West Indies," in idem, '*A Free though Conquering People*,' Chapter 9; and Eliga H. Gould, "Foundations of Empire, 1763–83," in Sarah Stockwell, ed., *The British Empire: Themes and Perspectives* (Oxford: Blackwell, 2008), 22.

practices.[15] This study, however, is the first to treat this subject comprehensively and in detail and to endeavor to explore and bring out the common elements in these parallel critiques.

Briefly put, the central argument of this volume is that, following several decades of largely uncritical celebration of the empire as a vibrant commercial entity that had made Britain prosperous and powerful, a growing familiarity with the character of overseas territories and their inhabitants during and after the Seven Years' War produced a substantial critique of empire deriving from a widespread and deep revulsion against the behaviors exhibited by many groups of British peoples overseas. Using the languages of humanity and justice as standards for evaluation, critics condemned, in turn, the behaviors of East India Company servants, American slaveholders, Atlantic slave traders, British political and military leaders and strategists during the American War of Independence, abettors of British oppressions in Ireland, including ministerial authorities, placemen, and pensioners, and rapacious Irish absentees and Protestant persecutors of Catholics.

Given the long-standing tendency of Europeans to view the world beyond Europe as a collection of essentially lawless and chaotic zones in which the norms "of European civil society did not apply" and "even British nationals were free to act in ways that the British would have viewed as unacceptable closer to home,"[16] the intensity and scope of this revulsion may at first seem surprising. But it was deeply rooted in a ubiquitous language of alterity or otherness that metropolitans had used since the beginning of overseas expansion to describe – and demean – the participants in that expansion and the societies and polities that they had built in their new habitats, a language that predisposed metropolitans to be antisettler. The continuing use of this language strongly belied the later eighteenth-century metropolitan conception of overseas settlers and traders as "brethren," a concept often employed by the Administration in its efforts to make subjecthood a device for the expansion of metropolitan authority in the overseas empire and subsequently invoked during the American crisis by opponents of coercion and exponents of reconciliation.[17] If the geographical situation of those operating beyond the line of European civility and law partially explained their many violations of metropolitan standards of

---

[15] Particularly, Nicholas B. Dirks, *The Scandal of Empire: India and the Creation of Imperial Britain* (Cambridge, Mass.: Harvard University Press, 2006); Tillman W. Nechtman, *Nabobs: Empire and Identity in Eighteenth-Century Britain* (Cambridge: Cambridge University Press, 2010); Christopher Leslie Brown, *Moral Capital: Foundations of British Abolitionism* (Chapel Hill: University of North Carolina Press, 2006); Srividhya Swaminathan, *Debating the Slave Trade: Rhetoric of British National Identity, 1759–1815* (Burlington, Vt.: Ashgate, 2009); and the essays in Kathleen Wilson, ed., *A New Imperial History: Culture, Identity and Modernity in Britain and the Empire 1660–1840* (Cambridge: Cambridge University Press, 2004).

[16] Gould, "Foundations of Empire, 1763–83," 22. Gould explores this subject at greater length in his influential "Zones of Law, Zones of Violence: The Legal Geography of the British Atlantic, circa 1772," *William and Mary Quarterly*, 3d ser., 60 (2003), 471–510.

[17] For a different perspective, see Stephen Conway, "From Fellow-Nationals to Foreigners: British Perceptions of the Americans, circa 1739–1785," *William and Mary Quarterly*, 3d ser., 59 (2002), 65–101.

justice and humanity, it certainly did not, for critics of the excesses of empire, excuse them.

Indeed, the continuing application of the language of alterity to participants in the on-site work of empire made it easy for critics to attribute responsibility for the behaviors they found offensive to those participants. In so doing, they defined colonials – settlers and traders – as demonstrably un-British and thereby manifested a powerful drive to distinguish and distance metropolitan Britons from overseas Britons and, in the name of British honor, civility, and humanity, to correct the worst excesses of British overseas colonialism by bringing colonial behaviors into line with metropolitan norms. In the meantime, they suggested that, notwithstanding powerful claims to the contrary by the objects of their scorn, the overseas portion of the British Empire was British only in the sense of being subject to metropolitan Britain and emphatically not because Britons abroad exhibited, much less shared, the same civil and humane values as Britons at home. Eventually, government inaction or ineffective action forced critics to acknowledge the stark facts of Britain's national responsibility for and complicity in each of the various evils they deplored.

In the process of confronting and coming to terms with empire in the wake of the Seven Years' War, metropolitan Britons thus displayed a deep ambivalence about it, at once embracing empire for the benefits that it brought to the home islands and condemning it for its excesses. Neither the critics nor the exponents of empire shared a political affiliation or formed an intellectually coherent group. Many in both categories wrote anonymously, and many were interested only in the problems of a single sphere of imperial activity. What the various critics had in common and what drew them into the national discussion of empire was their sense of shock, that the purportedly civilizing and humanizing tendencies of a great commercial empire could fail to prevent the excesses they detected in so many areas of British overseas activity, excesses they regarded as shameful, potentially embarrassing, and unworthy of a free, liberal, just, and humane people. Moreover, in expressing this sense of disappointment and shock about developments in specific areas, they contributed to the formation and widespread use of a common language that they could all use to identify what they regarded as the undesirable practices and costs of empire. Taken together, the many objections raised by these critics constituted a devastating assessment of the outcome of early modern British colonialism.

My use of the modern term *colonialism* here and in the title of this book is not meant to be polemical. The concept – indeed, the very word "colonialism" – was not part of early modern parlance on empire in Britain or elsewhere, but was invented by modern analysts to refer to and encompass the damaging effects of domination upon subject peoples in the fiduciary empires of the nineteenth and twentieth centuries and has more recently been applied to the expansion of settler societies under the aegis of both empires and nations.[18] I use it here because no other concept fully encapsulates the oppressive features

---

[18] On this point, see Jack P. Greene, "Colonial History and National History: Reflections on a Continuing Problem," *William and Mary Quarterly*, 3d ser., 64 (April 2007), 235–50.

of empire as its British critics identified them after 1760 and because I wish to call attention to their recognition of all the components of colonialism a century before the word was coined.[19]

The rather sudden emergence of the languages of humanity and justice and their antonyms as central tropes for the discussion and evaluation of empire requires an explanation. Whether or not this emergence was part of the broad Enlightenment disillusionment with empire that Sankar Muthu has studied through the writings of three prominent late eighteeenth-century continental philosophes,[20] it was to some extent influenced by a deepening penetration of humanistic and liberal ideas and sensibilities into British culture during the eighteenth century. The languages of improvement and civility, along with the associated languages of humanity, justice, and liberty, had of course been around for a long time, exponents of empire having used them from the start in both Ireland and America to conceptualize the colonial project.

But metropolitan analysts rarely applied such ideas to a consideration of the heavy price paid by indigenous peoples caught up in English expansion, and the important question is why not. Certainly, from the late sixteenth century onward, Britons – English and Scots – had openly committed oppressions of the sort conventionally associated with imperial expansion, more often than not with government sanction. In the oversettlement of the Irish plantations, they had managed to dispossess the indigenous Irish of the greater part of their land and, beginning in the 1690s, in an effort to force them to convert to Protestantism, had restricted their economic and educational opportunities, marginalized them socially, emasculated them civilly, and stifled their resistance by military force. In every American colony except Barbados and Jamaica, which had no indigenous peoples left at the time of English occupation, they had inadvertently spread European pathogens among the indigenes, inflicting a devastating mortality on the native inhabitants. The pattern of displacement settlement effectively drove the indigenes from their lands, and the labor systems they devised were characterized by the callous treatment of the laborers, many of whom were indigenous and many more imported. Their constant demand for slaves had contributed to interethnic violence in Africa, led to the capture and transportation of Africans by the thousand to areas of labor deficit in the New World, and condemned those who survived the lethal Atlantic crossing to a grim future with little prospect of regaining their liberty.

No doubt, the victims of these oppressions cried out against them, but few found an opportunity to voice their miseries and misfortunes in Britain. To be sure, by the closing decades of the seventeenth century a few articulate returning visitors, mainly clerics and merchants who had found the treatment of indigenous Americans and Africans in colonial contexts offensive, invoked

[19] Ania Loomba, *Colonialism/Postcolonialism* (London: Routledge, 1998), 1–20, provides a thoughtful and lucid definition.
[20] Sankar Muthu, *Enlightenment Against Empire* (Princeton: Princeton University Press, 2003).

the languages of justice and humanity in their efforts to inform metropolitans about the cruelties and human costs of the slave trade and slave systems that settlers were constructing in the Americas. But they objected, not to slavery per se, but to the excesses in the working, care, and punishing of the enslaved and, principally, to the failure to evangelize them. Such reports served mainly to fortify metropolitan reservations about the English-worthiness of American colonists and the societies they were building overseas and did little to sensitize them to the human and moral costs of empire. Indeed, insofar as they were aware of them, early observers of empire seem to have come to terms rather quickly with what later critics would identify as unacceptable oppressions, regarding them as the unavoidable concomitants of the noble work of building plantations and bringing civility to a raw, untamed, and savage New World and accepting as routine their consequences to indigenous and African peoples.

Several elements probably contributed to this insensitivity. First, for much of the first century of American colonization, the English imperial project was not yet a prominent arena of metropolitan engagement. Second, the Black Legend circulated by English and Dutch writers, with its lurid tales of alleged Spanish atrocities in the conquests of Mexico, Peru, and other areas of the New World, effectively deflected Britons from a close examination of their own behavior overseas. From that perspective, the English imperial project appeared comparatively benign, and metropolitans found it virtually unimaginable that their compatriots should descend to Spanish levels of cruelty and inhumanity. Third, a growing awareness of the economic, maritime, and strategic importance of the American empire in the early eighteenth century tended to focus attention on the benefits for Britons at home and in the colonies rather than upon the costs borne by non-British peoples. Fourth, religious and political animosities and fears growing out of the French and Spanish imperial challenge after 1730 and the wars of 1739 to 1763 further obscured any transgressions of metropolitan principles and standards.

As a result of all these and possibly other factors, the emergence of the languages of justice and humanity beginning in the early 1760s as a standard for the evaluation of British imperial behavior depended on several preconditions other than mere availability. First was the growing recognition from the early 1730s of the economic and strategic importance of the various components of overseas empire to Britain's commercial activities, its domestic economy, and its reliance for defense on naval superiority. Second, as a result of that recognition, was the development of an enhanced government and public interest in the empire in combination with government concern that most areas of the overseas empire could be much better monitored and managed. Third were the territorial acquisitions and consequent expansion of empire in combination with Britain's achievement of naval and military supremacy as a result of the Seven Years' War. Fourth was the Government's newfound confidence, a product of its new international dominance, in its ability to exert greater control over the empire. Fifth was the opening of opportunities for debate and criticism after 1763 as a result of Britain's ostensible imperial invulnerability. Britain had won the Seven Years' War, but in so doing it had also lost, at least in the short run, the enemies that had certifiably threatened its Protestant religious establishment and its vaunted free constitution. Unconstrained by formidable European opponents, British policymakers were suddenly impelled to try to enhance the economic potential of empire through closer imperial management, and imperial analysts of all persuasions were free to identify and condemn aspects of overseas involvement that violated British standards of humanity and justice.

What gave the languages of humanity and justice their new saliency, however, was their obvious relevance to the analysis and characterization of specific problems arising in the early 1760s with regard to both India and America, problems involving the plunder of India by East India Company servants and the resistance of the American colonies to metropolitan attempts to tax them and regulate their internal affairs. Those problems led to the identification of many specific concerns about the treatment of indigenous people and the moral worth of overseas settlers and Company representatives that quickly evolved into a standard by which long-standing practices and accepted institutions such as the slave trade, chattel slavery, and various Irish problems, as well as subsequent enterprises such as the American war, could be evaluated unfavorably and the legitimacy of the entire imperial project brought under scrutiny and into question. A temporary crisis of confidence as a result of Britain's inability to achieve its objectives in the American war, the withdrawal of thirteen American colonies from the empire, and the loss of Minorca and two colonies to Spain and a third colony to France as a result of military and naval defeats may have contributed to the further expansion of those languages as important elements in the discussion of empire within the larger British world.

In stressing the breadth and depth of the late eighteenth-century critique of empire, however, I do not mean to suggest that the critics carried the day. Scholars such as P. J. Marshall, C. A. Baily, Eliga H. Gould, and, most recently, Maya Jasanoff, among others, are certainly right in their contention that the British Empire, in the decades after its American losses, emerged stronger than ever and that Britain retained its powerful commitment to empire.[21] Relatively few of the critics cited in this volume ever hinted that Britain should withdraw or dissociate itself from empire. Rather, most of them shared with advocates of empire an appreciation of the economic and strategic importance of imperial commerce and a commitment to the maintenance of Britain's imperial grandeur. Moreover, aside from the regularization of British

---

[21] P. J. Marshall, *The Making and Unmaking of Empires: Britain, India, and America c. 1750–1783* (Oxford: Oxford University Press, 2005), and idem, *'A Free though Conquering People': Eighteenth-Century Britain and Its Empire*; C. A. Bayly, *Imperial Meridian: The British Empire and the World, 1780–1830* (London: Longman, 1989); Gould, *Persistence of Empire*; Maya Jasanoff, *Liberty's Exiles: American Loyalists in the Revolutionary World* (New York: Alfred A. Knopf, 2011).

administration in India, an accomplishment that fell far short of their demands, critics managed to achieve almost none of their policy objectives until the abolition of the slave trade almost two decades after this study concludes. Too many powerful interest groups were too deeply involved in empire, and empire was too economically and militarily successful and too thoroughly incorporated into Britain's national economic life and identity, to permit any turning away from it.

In this connection, it is also important to note that, as Muthu has cogently observed in reference to "prominent and innovative" political thinkers, the later decades of the eighteenth century were anomalous in their expression of serious reservations about empire. "Strikingly," he writes, "anti-imperialist sentiments," which he distinguishes from antislavery sentiment, "largely fell by the wayside as the eighteenth century came to a close" and as "later thinkers" failed to rally "to the cause of exposing imperial injustices, defending non-European peoples against imperial rule, and attacking the standard rationales for empire." By the middle of the nineteenth century, he concludes, "anti-imperialist thinking was virtually absent from Western European intellectual debates, surfacing only by way of philosophically obscure and politically marginal figures." Such "philosophically obscure" analysts have supplied the bulk of the evidence considered in this volume, but with the notable exception of the slave trade and slavery their influence appears to have had no more staying power than that of the prominent anti-imperial political thinkers Muthu analyzes.[22]

That the policy achievements of Britain's critics of empire were limited does not mean that they did not have a profound impact on how Britons spoke and thought about empire. In less than two decades, they managed to persuade a very large proportion of the British public that the slave trade and slavery were unacceptable evils unworthy of a humane and liberal nation, albeit it took them much longer to overcome the powerful opposition of the combined lobby of slave traders and West Indians and get concrete government action. Also importantly, the standard they developed forced subsequent proponents of empire to justify British rule in India and elsewhere in terms not only of economic and strategic considerations, but also of humanity, justice, improvement, and civility. In the short run, Britain, as a government and a nation, persisted in the embrace and celebration of empire, despite having been fully informed between 1764 and the late 1780s about its moral excesses, its suspect legal foundations, and the high costs it continued to exact from its numerous victims. Yet the fact that so many contemporaries were able to identify the destructive effects of colonialism and speak out at such length and with such forcefulness against them calls into serious question the position of modern scholars that to pass judgment on early modern colonialism is to be anachronistic, presentist, and beyond the scope of eighteenth-century sensibilities.

This volume consists of a Prologue, eight chapters, and an Epilogue. The Prologue uses the literature surrounding the Carib War in St. Vincent to introduce

[22] Muthu, *Enlightenment Against Empire*, 3–6.

the reader to metropolitan languages of empire and to call attention to the still relatively new use of the languages of humanity and justice to evaluate the behavior of Britons overseas. Constructed largely from my analysis of the growing volume of commercial treatises through the middle decades of the eighteenth century, Chapter 1 focuses on the languages of commerce and liberty as the primary vehicles for the celebration of empire as a principal source of Britain's wealth. The only chapter not built upon a discrete and well-defined body of literature, Chapter 2 uses examples from a wide range of genres to define and illustrate the flip side of the celebratory language of commerce: the language of otherness or alterity that from the beginning of English overseas empire metropolitans had employed to depict colonists as a new kind of other. Chapter 3 draws upon the literature growing out of the successful outcome of the Seven Years' War and the intensive debate over how Britain should respond to American resistance to metropolitan authority between 1764 and 1776 to illustrate the emergence of an old but newly prominent language of imperial grandeur as a principal language for speaking about empire. Throughout the debate over the American question, this was the Government's favorite language, wielded against the Opposition's insistence on describing the empire in the conventional languages of commerce and liberty, while both sides invoked the languages of humanity and justice to challenge the arguments of their opponents.

The next five chapters show how the languages of humanity and justice operated in a variety of settings to throw light on the undesirable by-products of empire. Chapter 4 treats the earliest extended use of those languages as markers for opposing the excesses of overseas empire during the debate, beginning in the mid-1760s and continuing for the next two decades, over the alleged plunder of India by East India Company servants. Chapter 5 describes how from the late 1760s some metropolitans, stimulated by the glaring contradiction between colonial claims to liberty and their enslaved labor forces and by a nascent antislavery movement, began to apply the same language to American slave owners and the societies in which they were predominant and eventually to African slave traders in the Atlantic and Britain. Chapter 6 considers how the continuing disagreements over the relative importance of the languages of imperial grandeur, on the one hand, and of commerce and liberty, on the other, shaped attitudes toward empire and war during the American War for Independence and the ways in which opposing sides used the languages of humanity and justice to score points against one another. Chapter 7 shifts the focus to Ireland, where long-standing Protestant Irish complaints about British commercial and political oppressions resurfaced during the American war and where from the perspective of the Quebec Act in 1774 the extent of Protestant discrimination against Catholics in Ireland, long represented by Irish Catholics as oppressive and inhumane, suddenly also became a subject of concern for metropolitan observers, who coupled that concern with an earlier condemnation of the Anglo-Irish regime for its irresponsible absenteeism and the corruption evident in its extensive pension list to bring that particular colonial regime under serious scrutiny. Chapter 8 explores British efforts to come to terms with the loss of thirteen of the American colonies and the continuing excesses of empire in India, Africa, the remaining American colonies, and Ireland in the decade after 1783. The Epilogue analyzes contemporary assessments of the costs and benefits of empire during the closing decades of the eighteenth century.

This book has been long in the making. My early career in studying the formation of colonial British America and the American Revolution made me thoroughly aware of some aspects of the underside of British imperial history in the early modern era, albeit my orientation then could be taken as little more than a protest against the effort to define the British imperial situation from the perspective of the metropolitan center. But my engagement from the late 1960s to the late 1980s with an Atlantic history initiative that laid heavy emphasis upon Caribbean, South American, and African engagement with the Atlantic world beginning in the fifteenth century profoundly impressed upon me the devastating effects upon native peoples and imported laborers of the colonial process throughout the Atlantic world, effects that called into question the self-celebrating attitude that colonial settlers took toward the expansion of Europe overseas and revealed that the colonial adventurers and settlers I wrote about were on the cutting edge of that devastation and the principal agents of it. In the late 1980s, during a planning session for some quincentennial celebration of Columbus's encounter with America, the late Wilcomb Washburn, in response to my suggestion that the costs as well as the benefits of that encounter needed to be considered and my mention of some Spanish examples to illustrate my point, accused me of still believing in the Black Legend. My quick reply that my only problem with the Black Legend was its being limited to the Spanish expressed my long-standing conviction that every expansionist early modern European power had its own record of injustice and inhumanity to account for and that the imperial and national narratives subsequently developed to celebrate – and excuse – the accomplishments of those who spearheaded the cultural transformation of so much of the world in pursuit of their expansionist aims have obscured the high price paid by those who lost their lands, lives, independence, and cultures in the process and, at the same time, helped those entities – empires and nations – to disguise from subsequent generations the shaky moral foundations on which they stand.

Although in a general way this book is an outgrowth of my engagement with Atlantic history, my interest in the specific subject it covers directly derives from an invitation by P. J. Marshall to contribute a chapter on imperial identity to a volume he was organizing on the eighteenth-century British Empire. This assignment took me into the realm of contemporary literature in which people articulated what it meant to be British and how empire affected British identity. Within this literature I found a significant pool of material by writers who, far from celebrating British imperial achievements, were appalled by the injustices and inhumanities that agents of empire had committed in pursuit of them – in India, in Africa, in the West Indies and North America, and in Ireland. Space limitations prevented me from pursuing this discovery at length in the chapter I wrote for Marshall's book. But when the History Department at the University of Western Ontario asked me to give the Joanne Goodman Lectures, I immediately thought of returning to this subject.

On October 24–26, 2000, I delivered three lectures under the title "Speaking of Empire: Celebration and Disquiet in Metropolitan Analyses of the Eighteenth-Century British Empire." Two of these lectures were early versions of Chapters 4 and 5, and the third was a greatly compressed combination of Chapters 1, 2, and 3. I presented a later version of Chapter 5 as a paper entitled "Creolean Despotism: The Humanitarian Critique of Slaveholders, and the Reassessment of Empire in Metropolitan Britain during the Eighteenth Century" at the Fifth Annual Conference of the Illinois Program for Research in the Humanities, University of Illinois, Urbana-Champaign, on April 5, 2003, and at the Department of History, University of Texas, Austin, on November 11, 2004, and Chapter 4 as a paper entitled "Arenas of Asiatic Plunder" at the Workshop on Early American History, University of Georgia, Athens, on August 22, 2003. I revised Chapter 3 and wrote the early drafts of Chapters 6 and 7 while I had a residency fellowship at the Rockefeller Foundation's Bellagio Conference and Study Center, in Bellagio, Italy, in August 2006, and I wrote Chapter 2 and revised much of the rest of the manuscript while I was a Fellow of the National Humanities Center during the academic year 2009–10.

Although most of the research was done at the John Carter Brown Library in Providence, Rhode Island, the British Library in London, and the Royal Irish Society Library in Dublin, several of my research assistants at Johns Hopkins University, including James Allegro, Ellen Holmes Pearson, Paul Tonks, Catheine Cardno, and Jessica Roney, have helped me gather material, as did my former student R. S. T. Stoermer. Maurice Bric, P. J. Marshall, Eliga H. Gould, Catherine Molineux, Peter S. Onuf, Alan Tully, Karin Wulf, Craig Yirush, and Nuala Zahedieh provided useful advice, as did two anonymous readers for Cambridge University Press. Brooke Newman offered a helpful critical reading of Chapter 5, and Eliga H. Gould of Chapters 3 and 6 and the Epilogue. Neil York generously read the entire manuscript and made many excellent suggestions for its improvement. Russell Hahn did yeoman work copyediting this substantial manuscript. I am grateful to all of these people and institutions and extend my special thanks to Professor Ian K. Steele, my principal host at the University of Western Ontario, and to my spouse, Amy Turner Bushnell, who read and criticized the manuscript at every stage and whose extraordinary copyediting skills greatly improved my text.

East Greenwich, Rhode Island
March 15, 2012

Prologue

"Scene of a Foul Transaction"

The Languages of Empire and the Carib War in St. Vincent

I

In 1772, the British government launched a military campaign against the so-called Black Caribs of the Windward Island colony of St. Vincent. In March, Wills Hill, earl of Hillsborough and secretary of state for the American colonies, ordered the royal navy to send several ships of the line and General Thomas Gage to dispatch two army regiments from Boston to St. Vincent. Under the command of newly promoted Major General William Dalrymple, the regiments arrived in the colony in early August. Throughout the fall, these forces, numbering more than a thousand but beset by disputes over command and extensive sickness among the soldiery, made little headway against the Caribs, who, though numbering only three to four thousand people and fewer than 500 fighting men, used guerrilla tactics to impede the British advance. By the end of the year, as the author of the most recent study of this expedition observes, "a comparatively vast military effort against a handful of Black Caribs had failed to exterminate them or even make them talk of peace."[1] As reports of this expedition and its problems filtered back to Britain in the late fall of 1772, they elicited a firestorm of criticism both in and out of Parliament. The ensuing debate over the justice of the war in St. Vincent provided a forum for the many discursive languages contemporary Britons used to speak about empire and revealed some of the earliest manifestations of a growing concern about the moral price of overseas colonialism, a price derived by weighing the economic and strategic benefits of empire against its ethical and moral costs.

---

[1] Robin F. A. Fabel, *Colonial Challenges: Britons, Native Americans, and Caribs, 1759–1775* (Gainesville: University of Florida Press, 2000), 186. Fabel's succinct study (pp. 134–205) provides by far the fullest and most balanced modern account of the Carib War. See also Bernard Marshall, "The Black Caribs – Native Resistance to British Penetration into the Windward Side of St. Vincent, 1763–1773," *Caribbean Quarterly*, 19 (1973): 4–20; J. Paul Thomas, "The Caribs of St. Vincent: A Study in Imperial Maladministration, 1763–73," *Journal of Caribbean History*, 18 (1983): 60–72; and Michael Craton's suggestive "The Black Caribs of St. Vincent: A Reevaluation," in Robert L. Paquette and Stanley L. Engerman, eds., *The Lesser Antilles in the Age of European Expansion* (Gainesville: University of Florida Press, 1996), 71–85.

II

St. Vincent was one of the prizes of the Seven Years' War, having been ceded by France to Britain in 1763 in the Treaty of Paris, along with Dominica, Grenada, and Tobago, three other islands in the Lesser Antilles. Shortly after this cession, Sir William Young, the first commissioner for land sales in the ceded islands, published a substantial tract designed to generate enthusiasm for their colonization and the sale of lands. "Since our conquest of Jamaica from the Spaniards" in the mid-1650s, said Young, waxing enthusiastic, "there has been no such opportunity of improving private fortunes" as the fertile lands of the ceded islands promised. Taking pains to praise colonizing activities as a means for individuals not just to acquire wealth but to contribute to national well-being, Young invoked the celebratory language of colonization, a subset of the related languages of improvement and civility that became increasingly prominent in early modern English social and economic discourse after the late sixteenth century and that remained pervasive well into the nineteenth century. Stretching back to Richard Hakluyt and other Elizabethan writers, the language of colonization had long been conventional in English and then British thinking about empire.[2] In using this language, Young associated the settlement of the ceded islands with the long and respectable tradition of overseas planting, a noble work that had brought fortune to colonial enterprisers, economic and social betterment to individual settlers, civility and a system of English law and governance to an expanding number of spaces in the New World and to some of the indigenous inhabitants of those spaces, and wealth and power to metropolitan Britain.

Colonization, Young suggested, was a grand enterprise of great national benefit, worthy of the exertions of Britain's most "publick spirited and enterprising men." "The establishment of colonies," he observed, "has in all ages and countries, and amongst men of the highest abilities and rank, been ever esteemed honourable and ornamental to the most exalted characters," and he expressed hope that "at the conclusion of a peace, by which so great an accession of territory hath been made to these kingdoms, . . . there will be found some men of eminence and spirit, who will deign to countenance by their example, and assist in perfecting, so noble a design" as the settlement of the four new colonies in the West Indies. "To nations supported principally by trade and navigation," he declared, employing the language of commerce, the principal language that eighteenth-century metropolitan Britons used to talk about empire,

the establishment of remote colonies (whose wants are constantly supplied by large exports from home, and whose returns of produce and manufactures greatly increase the revenue; and . . . have the further advantage of creating and connecting with it,

---

[2] See Richard Helgerson, *Forms of Nationhood: The Elizabethan Writing of England* (Chicago: University of Chicago Press, 1992), 153–91.

still other profitable branches of commerce and communication with Africa, and the continent of America) is particularly beneficial and important.

By catering to "the natural wants of men," stimulating men's "ingenuity and industry," and adding new sites for "that busy scene of submission and dependence . . . that compose[s] a great and commercial people," the establishment of colonies, he suggested, articulating what he called an "extensive view" of imperial enterprise, was overwhelmingly "productive of both national advantage and private interest." Such "useful and lucrative . . . undertaking[s]," he averred,

deserve[d] certainly to be considered as affectionately by the mother country, as if they were really so many remote counties, separated from it by seas, instead of rivers or land boundaries; and so far from our being jealous, or indifferent concerning their prosperity and contentment, we should acknowledge and cherish them as members of our own body, thus forming one vast Leviathon.

The reference to Leviathan called into play for the reader a third and relatively recent language of imperial grandeur or imperialism, prominent in metropolitan British discussions of empire since the middle of the eighteenth century.[3]

Young offered flattering portraits of all the ceded islands, but he especially touted St. Vincent for its excellent soil, luxuriant vegetation, and adequate water supply, predicting that it would "very soon be classed amongst the best, and most valuable of our sugar colonies." Young had to admit, however, that the eastern part of the island was already inhabited by a few thousand "natives" who owed their "tragic origins to a ship freighted with negroes from Africa to Barbadoes, and wrecked on these coasts." Rapidly adapting to the lush environment of St. Vincent, the survivors intermingled with the aboriginal Caribs, adopted many of their customs, "gradually extirpated, or reduced" the natives "to their obedience," and thus, Young wrote, "gave birth to a free republic." Dismissing reports that these Black Caribs were "turbulent and dangerous," Young depicted them "as a quiet and well disposed people, speaking French, and instructed by Roman catholic missionaries, in the principles of their religion." Observing that "many of them seemed disposed to quit their little cottages, and spots of provision ground, and to remove to" the French colonies of St. Lucia and Martinique, Young predicted that once they had been "duly apprized of the humanity and generosity of our gracious Sovereign, and assured of the enjoyment of their lands, freedom, favor and protection, they" would "be gained over to our cause, and even rendered useful."[4]

Specifically how the Caribs might be "rendered useful" Young did not say, but his emphasis upon the humanity of the British Crown called forth the

---

3 [William Young], *Considerations Which May Tend to Promote the Settlement of Our New West-India Colonies, By Encouraging Individuals to embark in the Undertaking* (London, 1764), 1–3, 11, 34–35.

4 Ibid., 9–10, 12; William Young, *An Account of the Black Charaibs in the Island of St. Vincent* (London, 1795), 6–8.

increasingly popular language of humanity that, as applied to British relations with subject peoples such as the Caribs, North American Indians, Catholics in Quebec and other former French possessions, Hindus and other natives in India, and finally, even persecuted Irish Catholics, would increasingly, in the decades following the Treaty of Paris in 1763, become in Britain an important ingredient of the discourse about overseas empire. The Crown having specifically directed that these "poor natives of St. Vincent" were "to remain undisturbed in their cottages and grounds," Young and the other commissioners took pains during the early years of British settlement in St. Vincent to observe the "humane caution" recommended by the Crown.[5]

As the commissioners for land sales and other new British settlers quickly discovered, however, the Carib lands, as Young reported in 1767, were "far more extensive, more level, and a finer country than" those available for British settlement, and the newcomers soon began to lay plans to open up the Carib territories for British settlement. But the Caribs, knowing that the Crown had ordered the commissioners "not to dispose of or survey any of the lands inhabited or claimed by them," kept a wary eye for any sign of British encroachment upon their territories, and when in early 1769 surveyors, supported by a small group of soldiers, began to lay out a road into Carib country, "a body of Indians upwards of 200, well armed, [and] firmly resolved, they said[,] to keep their freedom, and preserve their lands," took the surveyors and their escort prisoner and released them only after they had been assured that the surveying and road building would stop. "Apprehensive," as one St. Vincent official reported, that the whites were pursuing a design "not only of depriving them of their grounds, but also of reducing them into slavery," the Caribs made it abundantly clear during this incident that they were determined to avoid their subjection to the British Crown, to "preserve their independence," and to oppose by force "all interference within the country they called their own."[6]

In the face of such resistance, St. Vincent's white establishment quickly embarked upon a campaign to insure that the "fine cream part of this island" occupied by the Caribs should not remain entirely in Carib hands. From 1769 through early 1772, St. Vincent's land commissioners, executive officials, legislature, and agent peppered metropolitan authorities with letters, addresses, memorials, and reports intended to undermine metropolitan support for the Caribs and to enlist metropolitan aid in their designs on Carib lands. Applying the language of savagery that Europeans had long used to justify the dispossession of native peoples in the New World, they contrasted native savagery with English civility and denounced Carib resistance as a bar to the grand

---

[5] [Young], *Considerations*, 16; Young, *Account of the Black Charaibs*, 20.

[6] Memorial of William Young to Treasury, April 11, 1767, in William Cobbett et al., eds., *Parliamentary History of England from the Earliest Period to the Year 1803*, 36 vols. (London, 1806–20), 17: 578–79; President Harry Alexander to Lieutenant Governor Fitzmaurice, May 3, 1769, in ibid., 591–92; Fitzmaurice to Hillsborough, June 10, 1769, in ibid., 597; Memorial of Richard Maitland to Lord Hillsborough, [1769], in ibid., 594.

work of settlement and colonization. For such a "valuable and extensive tract of land" to remain "almost entirely uncultivated" and in the hands of "an erratic nation of savage warriors and hunters" seemed to whites to be, as a later writer declared, "[in]consistent with the common law of nations, with the general interest of the colony, or with the right of the British crown." For that reason, it appeared obvious to the settlers that, as the lieutenant governor put it in a dispatch to Hillsborough, as long as the Caribs were "permitted to occupy a large extent of country, without any mixture of white inhabitants, they [would] . . . retain their intractable nature, continue uncivilized, lawless, disaffected, and of no use; and that the rest of the colony" would "be in real danger, and constant apprehensions of sudden attack from them." As long as the Caribs continued "an armed force in actual rebellion in the heart of their country," he said, British colonists could scarcely be expected to continue "to hazard their fortunes and their persons, on the casual and capricious forbearance of lawless savages."[7]

Although the Black Caribs had been in St. Vincent for almost a century, since "about the year 1673," white interpreters took pains to deny that they were "the original and rightful possessors of the island of St. Vincent" or "an independent nation." Rather, they endeavored to paint them as "Negro *usurpers*," who, having been in the colony for only a generation or two, had early shown their true disposition by extirpating the original Carib population and, since the beginning of British settlement, had thumbed their noses at the British Crown's authority and menaced the lives and property of the settlers, pilfering their possessions, enticing away their slaves, and otherwise acting as the worst species of neighbors. Troublesome enough in peacetime, the Caribs, they predicted, would immediately go over to the French should France and Britain ever go to war. St. Vincent whites thought it obvious that, as the land commissioners wrote to the Crown in October 1771, it would "be impossible that so small an island" could "long continue divided between a civilized people and savages, who are bound by no ties of law or religion." Charging that the Caribs would neither submit to British government nor "yield up any part of the land they claim . . . without a sufficient force to terrify them to obedience," they called for military and naval aid "to force these people to obedience" and possibly even to bring about "their absolute and immediate removal" and transportation to some unoccupied island or even to Africa. Europeans had long used the language of civility to justify their actions in relation to indigenous peoples, and, more and more since the 1730s, British imperial projectors had often invoked a language of national security to justify state intervention in colonial projects. Calling upon both of these languages, an anonymous author laid out the essence of the settlers' plan in a pamphlet published in London in

---

[7] Alexander to Fitzmaurice, May 3, 1769, in ibid., 592; Address of the St. Vincent Council and Assembly, [1769], in ibid., 596; Fitzmaurice to Hillsborough, June 10, 1769, in ibid., 602–03; Memorial of Maitland to Hillsborough, [1769], in ibid., 594; Young, *Account of the Black Charaibs*, 21–22, 25.

1770 and written in the form of a dialogue between two Caribs: "though we well deserve it, for extirpating the natives, who gave us shelter in our distress," said Arioua, the "English Baccaras" were "not cruel," would "not extirpate us," and could be expected to "find us land somewhere," but "they must have possession of ours to secure the quiet of the island, in case of a war with the French Baccaras."[8] Through transportation, the writer implied, colonization could go forward without sacrificing the principles of humanity. In response to this mounting agitation, metropolitan authorities in the fall of 1771 ordered General Thomas Gage and the admiralty to dispatch a sufficient force to St. Vincent "to reduce the black Caribbs... to a due submission to his Majesty's authority and government." At the same time, however, Hillsborough, reemphasizing the Crown's continuing commitment to the principles of humanity, cautioned St. Vincent authorities to avoid "any unnecessary severities, that may have the appearance of cruelty or oppression."[9]

The British press followed the expedition with some interest, and news of the setbacks it experienced in the late summer and fall of 1772 soon reached Britain, where the justice of the venture came under immediate scrutiny. At the end of November, an anonymous author writing under the name "Probus" in the *Scots Magazine* reported that "an uncommon scene of cruelty" was "carrying on on the island of St. Vincent, against the innocent, natural inhabitants" for no greater crime than standing up for their own liberty and independence. Applying the well-worn English language of liberty that reached back to the common law theorists Sir John Fortescue and Sir Edward Coke,[10] "Probus" argued that the "cause of civil liberty... ought to be held sacred and inviolable in every part of the British Empire" and, using a language of rapacity or oppression usually associated with Turks or Spaniards, charged that by employing "British troops... to put these people to the sword," the British government was guilty of "reviving the Spanish cruelties at the conquest of Mexico, to gratify avaricious merchants, landholders, and venal commissioners.[11]

"Probus's" strictures were a preview of those articulated a few days later in the House of Commons. On December 9, Thomas Townshend, M.P. for Cambridge University, and three other members of the Opposition, including Barlow Trecothick, M.P. and alderman for London and a former New England and Jamaica merchant, Richard Whitworth, M.P. for Stafford, and Isaac Barré, M.P. for Wycombe and a former army officer with extensive experience in America during the Seven Years' War, subjected the Carib War to

---

[8] Young, *Account of the Black Charaibs*, 1, 6, 14; Memorial of Maitland to Hillsborough, [1769], in Cobbett et al., eds., *Parliamentary History*, 17: 595; Report of Commissioners for the Sale of Lands to Treasury, October 16, 1771, in ibid., 606–07; Memorial of Maitland to Hillsborough, [1771], in ibid., 612–14; *A New System of Fortification, Constructed with Standing Timber, &c. Or the Sentiments of a West-India Savage on the Art of War* (London, 1770), 13.

[9] Hillsborough to Admiralty, April 16, 1772, and to Governor Leybourne, April 18, 1772, in Cobbett et al., eds., *Parliamentary History*, 17: 522–34, 631.

[10] See Helgerson, *Forms of Nationhood*, 63–104.

[11] "Probus," in *Scots Magazine* (Edinburgh), 34 (1772): 588.

a scathing review. Using the ancient English language of justice, they called into question the essential justness of the war, denouncing it, in the words of Townshend, as "a breach of the national honour." Depicting the Carib insurgents as the descendants of shipwrecked slaves who had "incorporated with the natives," the "last remnants of the Aborigines of South America," Trecothick charged that the deployment of such a considerable force suggested that the Administration had decided that the "poor Caribbs ... should be totally extirpated," an objective that, if achieved, he said, echoing "Probus," would be a gross act of inhumanity comparable to "the barbarities of the Spaniards against the Mexicans." "While such a scene of iniquity and cruelty is transacting at St. Vincent's on the defenceless natives, under the authority of government," he declared, "I feel, Sir, for the honour of the British nation."[12]

Displaying a regard for the sanctity of native rights in the Americas that was, if not entirely unprecedented, certainly unusual among British commentators on empire, other speakers questioned not only the justice but also the legality of the undertaking and in the process employed the language of indigenous rights, one of the many extensions or branches of the language of humanity and one not often invoked in metropolitan discussions of empire before the late eighteenth century. "Before we pretend to extirpate those poor people," declared Whitworth, "we need to examine our right." Arguing that the French had lived in association with the Caribs only by treaty and had never owned or exercised jurisdiction over Carib lands, he denied that they had any right to cede those lands to the British. "To dispossess the unoffending natives of their country," he objected, was "nothing but the most wanton cruelty." When First Minister Frederick, Lord North, tried to head off further debate by suggesting that the Caribs' refusal to lay down their arms justified military measures, Barré asked the House whether any members would "pretend to say" that the Caribs were "not in the right?" Praising them for "fighting for liberty," he again appealed to the language of liberty, asserting that "every English heart must applaud them."[13]

When they turned their attention to the question of why these allegedly dishonorable measures had been undertaken in the first place, these speakers fixed upon what Townshend called "the rapacity of the planters in St. Vincent's." More and more after the mid-1760s, metropolitan analysts used the language of rapacity and oppression, a subset of the language of otherness that they employed to describe people whose behavior they considered morally inferior to their own, such as British nabobs in Bengal, planters in the New World, and slave traders on the African coast. Speaking in behalf of Administration, Welbore Ellis, M.P. for Petersfield, effectively acknowledged that planter demands were behind the expedition, but he traced them, not to their rapacity, but to their fear and vulnerability. Calling for "a word of sympathy for

[12] Thomas Townshend and Bartholomew Trecothick, speeches, December 9, 1772, in Cobbett et al., eds., *Parliamentary History*, 17: 568–69.
[13] Richard Whitworth, Lord North, and Isaac Barré, speeches, December 9, 1772, in ibid., 569–70.

the poor planters, who have quitted their country and friends, and at a great expence purchased plantations of the public," he contended that they were "entitled to protection also" and that it was "the duty of government to assist them with troops when their property" was "in danger." But the Opposition sniffed darker motives, charging, as Whitworth said, that "some of our traders or planters have taken a fancy to" the Carib "part of the island for country-houses to divert themselves" and that to gratify that or other sordid intentions of the St. Vincent establishment, "the British arms" were "to be employed, and the miserable natives ... to be cruelly dispossessed of their habitations, and driven from their families and friends."[14]

Demanding to know "the urgent reasons, which justify [such] a cruel outrage against humanity," Opposition speakers called for a parliamentary inquiry "to probe this foul transaction to the bottom." "Let us know the cause of those hostilities against a defenceless, innocent, and inoffensive people," insisted Trecothick. When the Carib fighting force consisted of fewer than 500 men, asked Lord George Germain, why are we "sending regiment after regiment to sacrifice, hunt down, and destroy these unfortunate people?" Why, asked Barré, should a force be sent "to attack a handful of men, the natives of the island, who have done you no injury?" Accusing the Administration of mismanaging the expedition, they further charged that the Administration's inhumanity extended beyond the Caribs to the British troops and demanded to know why soldiers had been "sent upon this disgraceful service" at "the worst season of the year, unprovided" with tents and camping equipment.[15]

When the Administration seemed to ignore these demands, Townshend rose again in the House on December 11 to ask for papers from the king that would provide the basis for "a general and impartial examination, that we may know why the poor Caribbs alone should be of consequence enough to engage the resentment of the British government, and employ the attention of the Ministry, when" it took "no notice ... of the conduct of other powers towards us."[16] Perhaps to Townshend's surprise, North offered no objection to this request. On December 23, the first minister provided the House with a lengthy set of documents, going all the way back to 1767 and illustrating the considerations that lay behind the decision to send troops to engage the Caribs.[17] As a measure of how much this expedition had captured the interest of a broader public, the London printer John Almon brought out early in 1773 an edition of these papers under the title *Authentic Papers Relative to the Expedition against the Charibbs, and the Sale of Lands in the Island of St. Vincent.*[18]

14 Thomas Townshend, Welbore Ellis, and Richard Whitworth, speeches, December 9, 1772, in ibid., 569, 572–73.
15 Thomas Townshend, Isaac Barré, Bartholomew Trecothick, and Lord George Germain, speeches, December 9, 1772, in ibid., 569–70, 572–73.
16 Thomas Townshend, speech, December 11, 1772, in ibid., 574–75.
17 These papers are printed in ibid., 575–639.
18 *Authentic Papers Relative to the Expedition against the Charibbs, and the Sale of Lands in the Island of St. Vincent* (London, 1773).

By the time the House took up these papers in mid-February 1773, the Carib War, as Barré declared in the House on February 12, had "engaged the attention of all Europe."[19] News emanating from St. Vincent continued to suggest that the Caribs had effectively stymied the British regulars.[20] As one correspondent from the West Indies reported in late January 1773, the regulars were sickly and, behaving as if they were "sensible that justice had not drawn the sword," seemed "to want that animation, which has hitherto, always appeared on more glorious occasions." If the British troops were hampered by the injustice of their cause, as this writer asserted in employing the language of justice, the Caribs continued "resolute and seem[ed] determined that the loss of liberty and property shall be accompanied with that of life." Such a "determination," he said, was "worthy of a Briton; and as such should be rever'd by one [a Briton], though found in the breast of a poor oppressed Carib." "The expedition was ill-judged," he concluded, and was "condemned by every rational being in the West-Indies."[21]

The House spent much of February 10 and 12 hearing testimony from people who had seen military service or held political office in the ceded islands and from generals who had not heard from the West Indies since mid-November. The Administration's principal witness, Henry Sharpe, speaker of the St. Vincent Assembly and lieutenant governor of the island, then in London, fully set out the rationale for metropolitan military intervention against the Caribs. Readily acknowledging himself as "the advisor of the project" for removing the Caribs from the island and transporting them to some nearby neutral island or to Africa, Sharpe used the language of security to contend that it "was impossible" for settlers "to live in safety" in St. Vincent as long as the Caribs "were suffered to live independent." As an important component of Britain's expanding and economically beneficial overseas empire, the success and integrity of the colonial effort in St. Vincent, he suggested, required state action to subdue any indigenous resistance that stood in its way. Depicting the Caribs in the most unflattering terms, he asserted that they

> were a faithless people; that while they continued in the island, neither the lives nor the properties of his Majesty's subjects could be secure; that murders and robberies were frequent; that his own negroes had been murdered in the field; and that no inducements were wanting to encourage negroes to desert; that the Caribbs were addicted to much drinking, and that their debaucheries were very cruel, and [that they were] abandoned to every species of vice.

At this point, Barré created a moment of levity when he interrupted Sharpe to inquire "what their vices were?" In reply, Sharpe cited their "love of a plurality of women" and their extreme "pleasure in . . . making themselves beasts by drinking," whereupon Barré inquired whether the Caribs did not also "love

---

[19] Isaac Barré, speech, February 10, 1773, in Cobbett et al., eds., *Parliamentary History*, 17: 724.

[20] *Gentleman's Magazine* (London), 43 (1773): 45–46, 152–53; *Lloyd's Evening Post* (London), April 2, 1773.

[21] "Extract of a Letter from a Gentleman in the West Indies, January 29, 1773," in *Pennsylvania Packet and General Advertiser* (Philadelphia), March 22, 1773.

liberty and property?" When Sharpe answered in the affirmative, Barré then elicited a roar of laughter by asking, "if they love women, wine, liberty and property, where is the difference, except in the colour, between them and Englishmen?" In this exchange, Barré used the language of English rights, a subset of the language of liberty that Britons used so extensively to identify their own national character, to underline the Caribs' essential humanity.[22]

A full-scale debate over the expedition followed three days later on February 15. Joined by Lord Folkestone, M.P. for Salisbury, and Charles Cornwall, M.P. for Grampound, Townshend, Barré, and Lord George Germain were again prominent in the Opposition attack. Townshend led off, dismissing Sharpe's testimony as that of "an interested planter," condemning the Administration's "almost instant resolution to extirpate those unhappy miserable Caribbs, whom it has become fashionable to call savages," and introducing two motions. The first declared that "the expedition against the Black Caribbs, in the island of Saint Vincent's," had been "undertaken without sufficient provocation on the part of those unhappy people, and at the instigation of persons interested in their destruction, and appears to be intended to end in the total extirpation of the said Caribbs." The second alleged that sending troops was unnecessary, would prove destructive of the lives of many soldiers, and was unlikely to succeed. The debate over the first resolution is what primarily concerns us here.[23]

As articulated by Germain, the Opposition's central contention was that the Caribs had "behaved themselves quietly as subjects till an attempt was made to reduce them to slavery, without even pretending any crime on their part." "Will any man in this House, at this time of day," asked Germain, "pretend to affirm, that standing on their own defence without even a crime imputed to them, was treason, and that they deserved to be extirpated merely to gratify a set of inhuman mercenary planters? No," he declared, employing the familiar British language of rights, "the constitution forbids such a violation of the rights of the poorest and meanest of society." Lord Folkestone agreed, arguing that the papers and testimony presented to the House made it "very evident that the first act of hostility was committed by us" through an "invasion of [Carib] property" and declaring that the Caribs were fully "justified in what they have done." "I should have thought, Sir, that our generosity, as Englishmen, would have taught us to consider the liberty and property of others as sacred, but if that was insufficient," Folkstone said, shifting from the language of rights to the language of humanity, "I should have thought that motives of humanity might have restrained us from wanton and premeditated acts of cruelty upon a defenceless people."[24]

---

[22] Testimony of Henry Sharpe, February 12, 1773, in Cobbett et al., eds., *Parliamentary History*, 17: 727.

[23] Thomas Townshend, speech, February 15, 1773, in ibid., 729–31.

[24] Lord George Germain and Viscount Folkestone, speeches, February 15, 1773, in ibid., 731, 735.

Even the Caribs' efforts to acquire French aid seemed to Opposition speakers to be defensible. As Charles Cornwall explained, the Caribs, having found "themselves in possession of certain rights and possessions," perceived "those rights attempted to be wrested from them, contrary to promises on which they imagined they might safely depend. Was it to be supposed," he asked, "that they could, on finding themselves, as they thought, so basely injured, forbear to resist?" Only "the measured language of mercenary planters or misinformed ministers," Cornwall declared, could condemn such behavior as "treason." Expressing his fear that "the unfortunate Caribbs" had "already [been] sacrificed to the avarice and inhumanity of a set of merciless planters and improvident ignorant ministers," Barré appealed to Lord North "in what manner he could extenuate the charge that would be made against a great, a powerful, and a more glorious nation, for this shameful outrage, this murder, extirpation, and robbery of a few harmless savages."[25]

However emphatic in presenting their case, these speakers made little headway against the Administration in this debate. At its conclusion, the Opposition lost the vote on both resolutions by a margin of more than two to one. But this vote did not immediately end the debate over the Carib War. In its immediate aftermath, the contest continued in the press. Bristling in response to Opposition charges that the St. Vincent settlers and the Ministry had behaved with injustice and inhumanity, "Candour," writing in the *London Chronicle*, an Administration newspaper, insisted that the settlers, in trying to live in "a state of amity," had always acted on the "fairest terms" with the Black Caribs, overlooking their many "insolent" transgressions and proving "ever ready to redress their complaints with the strictest justice." The Caribs, by contrast, had "frequently turned some of the settlers from their tables, plundered the house, and afterwards attempted to murder the owner, his family, and servants"; they had "secreted some slaves from their masters, and afterwards sold them with other runaways in the French islands"; they had destroyed "many mules, cattle, &c."; and, as the principal exhibition of their savagery, they had "almost totally extirpated the yellow Caribbs, aborigines of the Island, and murdered numbers in cold blood." Far from being innocent victims of planter inhumanity and of the Ministry's "arbitrary and oppressive" measures, "Candour" protested, using the language of colonization, the Caribs, having repeatedly interfered with the noble and civil work of colonization in St. Vincent, had shown themselves to be an intractable obstacle to this laudable enterprise being carried on to the national advantage. "Are not the black Caribbs, or more properly speaking those of African extract," he asked, resorting to the language of savagery, "a most cruel, bloody, revengeful, and perfidious set of people, can faith be held with them but at the point of a sword?"[26]

On the other side, "Homo Sum," writing in *The Gazeteer and New Daily Advertiser*, an Opposition newspaper, sought to rebut Government spokesman

---

[25] Charles Cornwall and Isaac Barré, speeches, February 15, 1773, in ibid., 733–34, 739–40.
[26] Essay by "Candour," in *London Chronicle* (London), February 20, 1773.

Hans Stanley's claim in parliamentary debate that the war was "founded in *natural* justice and *good faith*" and "supported by *sound policy*." The war could not be founded on natural justice, "Homo Sum" insisted, because it was "solely calculated to *desseize* and *banish* the Caribs from this island," when, according to "the laws of NATURAL *justice, the first occupants* of an *insular* territory acquire[d] the *dominion* of it." It could not be founded on good faith because the Crown had assured the Caribs "of the same protection that they had enjoyed under the French," who had always acknowledged them to be "a FREE people," while the war, having for "its principal object" the dispossession and expulsion of the Caribs, represented "a most notorious and glaring violation of that implicit confidence which the Caribbs had reposed in the royal" promise. As far as sound policy was concerned, "Homo Sum" admitted that "it would be *sound policy* in the Empress of Russia, in the quality of a *despotic* Monarch, to banish . . . any of her turbulent subjects into Siberia, or into any other parts of her own dominions." But he professed ignorance "of any *constitutional* law of this realm, or of any modern Act of Parliament which authorises the Sovereign Monarch of the British Empire to relegue any subjects of that Empire from *one* part of its dominion into *another*, much less to *banish* them out of ALL the dominions of the British Empire." As "SUBJECTS to the *Imperial* Crown of Great Britain," he maintained, the Caribs were "justly entitled to the same protection that every other *British* subject" enjoyed. Far from being sound policy, then, such an "*extra-dominial* [form of] banishment" as that seemingly intended by the Ministry, "Homo Sum" concluded, represented an "*inhuman* species of banishment" that was "neither warranted nor justified by the *constitutional* or *statutable* laws of the British Empire" and therefore represented "a violation not only of the laws of nations, but of the *constitutional* laws of this *realm*."[27]

But these pieces represented the last gasp for the participants in this debate, which did not survive the end of the Carib War. Late in February, the capitulation of the Black Caribs in St. Vincent concluded the war, with the Caribs agreeing to surrender a portion of their land, to permit roads to be built through their territories, and to extend allegiance to the British Crown in return for keeping most of their lands, and Caribs and settlers coexisted more or less peacefully until the mid-1790s, when a second Carib War ended in the Caribs' final subjugation and banishment to the island of Roatan, just off the coast of Honduras.[28]

III

This debate revealed a fundamental ambivalence within the British political nation about the nature and tendencies of imperial engagement. As one side stressed, in traditional terms, the economically beneficial and civilizing aspects

[27] Essay by "Homo Sum" in *The Gazeteer and New Daily Advertiser* (London), February 20, 1773.

[28] See Young, *Account of the Black Charaibs.*

of the colonizing process and evinced its impatience with "savage" resistance to it, the other emphasized the inhumanity, injustice, oppression, cruelty, and callous treatment suffered by the "natural" or native peoples caught up in it. The importance of the debate over the justice of the Carib War for the argument presented in this book is that by defending the Caribs on both legal and humanitarian grounds, the Opposition succeeded in bringing the intellectual foundations of early modern European colonization under serious scrutiny in the public sphere in metropolitan Britain.

Speaking on behalf of the Government, not the Opposition, Hans Stanley, M.P. for the borough of Southampton, found himself sufficiently moved by the Opposition's use of the languages of humanity and justice to defend the Caribs against the St. Vincent plantation establishment that he felt compelled, during the parliamentary debate of February 15, first to reconsider and then to condemn, not merely the military action against the Caribs, but the very "principles on which colonization was founded." "However current and prevalent the policy by which" colonies had been "established and supported might be among European powers," he observed, he confessed that he was "far from being satisfied with the notorious deviations from humanity and equity, by which they were upheld." Significantly, Stanley, in providing examples of the inhumanity of the colonizing process, turned, not to the casual dispossession of Caribs and other Amerindians, but to the high rate of mortality among Europeans and the proliferation of the African slave trade. "To think of the great number of his Majesty's European subjects, who daily fall victim to the noxious, and, one might almost say, the pestilential effects of the West India climates," he said, "was a matter of serious and melancholy consideration." "Upon the best computations," he lamented, "not one third of those who went to those islands to reside ever survived the seasoning." Moreover, he observed, "it was . . . a matter of which every man of common humanity must shudder, when he is informed that, upon the most accurate estimate of the numbers yearly enslaved, to gratify the thirst of gain and lucre of avaricious, unfeeling planters, they were proved by a learned author to be no less than 80,000." Although Stanley acknowledged that these "unhappy slaves were not brought to the market for slaughter," he expressed horror that "they were brought to market, if possible, for infinitely more cruel and iniquitous purposes," and he declared that

in his consideration of any matter of the nature of that now before him, he should not think of either the stature or complexion of any man, whether he was a pigmy or a Patagonian, or whether he was white, yellow, or black; he only looked at the present measure so far as it was founded on natural justice and good faith, and supported by sound policy.

In the case of the Administration's behavior in the Carib War, however, Stanley had no doubt of its propriety and justice. Not to have intervened militarily, he was persuaded, would have been for the government to suffer "the savages to murder our planters, and ravage their settlements" and ultimately to risk "the total destruction of the colony." The work of colonization, Stanley implied, ultimately trumped all considerations of humanity or native rights. Sir Richard Sutton, M.P. for St. Albans and another Administration spokesman, spoke similarly. While affirming his faith in the justice and necessity of the war, he nonetheless expressed, in a telling passage, his conviction that it would have "perhaps... been better, that our avarice had not led us to the discovery of America."[29]

Replying directly to Stanley, Charles Cornwall applauded Stanley's "general sentiments and reasonings" as doing "him honour as a man and a politician" and did not deny that they "might be extremely just as to the general scope of them," but he suggested that it was "erroneous" and unwise to move beyond immediate considerations of the justice of the Carib War to a general and far deeper reconsideration of the very "spirit of colonization and plantation, now carried on by the sovereigns and subjects of the several powers of Europe." Cornwall did not disagree that that spirit and the principles that supported it were "faulty in many respects, and perhaps in the end big with the most pernicious consequences." But he concluded, employing the language of reason of state, that they had "now become, in a great measure, [so] indispensably necessary to each separate state, considered individually, particularly to such whose rank and importance depended chiefly on commerce," that it would be impolitic and possibly dangerous to call any part of them into question.[30]

But the debate over the Carib War had already called them into question. By invoking, in the name of humanity, images of oppressed natives, cruel enslavement, and rapacious planters, the Opposition had precipitated a discussion of the very justice of early modern colonization. This was by no means an entirely new discussion. Indeed, it came more than two centuries after Spaniards, some of whom were appalled by the mistreatment of Amerindians in the mines and agricultural establishments of the New World, had thoroughly canvassed the subject.[31] Moreover, for at least a century and a quarter before the mid-1770s, a series of British writers, as Wylie Sypher showed fifty years ago in his path-breaking volume on the origins of the antislavery movement, had used the language of humanity to call attention to some of the darker aspects of colonization and empire, the callousness of settlers, and the barbarities of human slavery.[32] Yet within the larger British world, explicit discussions of the

---

[29] Hans Stanley and Sir Richard Sutton, speeches, February 15, 1773, in Cobbett et al., eds., *Parliamentary History*, 17: 731–32, 735.

[30] Charles Cornwall, speech, February 15, 1773, in ibid., 755.

[31] See Lewis Hanke, *The Spanish Struggle for Justice in the Conquest of America* (Philadelphia: University of Pennsylvania Press, 1949), and, for the continuing vitality of this debate into the seventeenth century, James Muldoon, *The Americas in the Spanish World Order: The Justification for Conquest in the Seventeenth Century* (Philadelphia: University of Pennsylvania Press, 1994).

[32] Wylie Sypher, *Guinea's Captive Kings: British Antislavery Literature of the XVIIIth Century* (Chapel Hill: University of North Carolina Press, 1952). For an excellent modern work touching

legitimacy of empire had for the first two centuries of English colonizing activity been relatively rare.[33] With regard to the situation of Amerindians, for instance, "expressions of sympathy," according to one recent study, "were largely absent from the public printed discourse" in Britain.[34]

Perhaps in association with the enhanced interest in the empire during and after the Seven Years' War, a few Britons did raise questions about the justice of European dispossession of indigenous peoples in America, in the process implicitly challenging traditional representations of colonization as a civilizing process and explicitly calling attention to its deleterious effects upon native societies. Thus, in 1755, the political writer John Shebbeare opened his four-volume novel *Lydia* with a portrait of Cannassatego, a young Indian warrior who, "much smitten with the Accounts of former Times; before the *Europeans*, these faithless Invaders, had reached the Shores of *America*," regarded the Europeans, French and English, as responsible for "the fallen Condition of his native Land" and lamented that his own and other nations had been "driven from the Ocean's Shores[,] our ancient Territories" and "held a Prey to *English* Perfidy, our Numbers lessened, our Country ravaged, our Wives borne off in Slavery, [and] our Children massacred." Denouncing these "Violators of our just Possessions" as "the exiled Caitiffs of the Land they came from," Cannassatego, parroting the metropolitan language of otherness, developed the theory "that those who had landed on the *American* Coast were Exiles from their native Land, doomed to that Punishment for Crimes which they had committed" there. Admitting that their oppressors had become too powerful "to be opposed by our exhausted Nations" and observing that "their Hearts [had become] too harden'd to feel Compassion at the Tales of Woe and Sufferings of the *Indian* Race," he resolved to go to Britain to "lay the Story of our Woes" before its "great King" and ask him, in justice to indigenous Americans, "to recall these dire Destroyers."[35]

---

on this subject, see Peter Hulme, *Colonial Encounters: Europe and the Native Caribbean 1492–1797* (London: Routledge, 1986).

[33] Anthony Pagden, *Lords of All the World: Ideologies of Empire in Spain, Britain and France c. 1500–c. 1800* (New Haven: Yale University Press, 1995), 76–86, discusses British considerations of the legitimacy of colonial acquisition of Indian lands.

[34] Troy O. Bickham, *Savages within the Empire: Representations of American Indians in Eighteenth-Century Britain* (Oxford: Oxford University Press, 2005), 68. See also Tim Fulford, *Romantic Indians: Native Americans, British Literature, and Transatlantic Culture 1756–1830* (Oxford: Oxford University Press, 2006).

[35] John Shebbeare, *Lydia, or Filial Piety. A Novel*, 4 vols. (London, 1755), 1: 6–8, 10, 12–13. Although Cannassatego quickly disappears from Shebbeare's convoluted narrative, he makes a brief reappearance in Volume 3 when he finally gains an audience with the Crown's first minister but fails to enlist him in the project of placing before the king "the Ill-usage of his Subjects, who live on our Shores, towards the *Indian* Race" and ultimately concludes that Britons in the home islands and the colonies had all been "formed in one Mould" and that "the same Perfidy which went Companion with those who left this Land, yet dwells amongst the others which remain." Ibid., 3: 264, 266.

Nor was Shebbeare's sensitivity to the many injustices British colonization had wreaked upon Amerindians unique.[36] In 1759, the lexicographer and political writer Samuel Johnson provided, in one of the *Idler* essays, an even fuller and more explicit critique of British colonial mistreatment of America's indigenous inhabitants. Johnson imagined an incident in the American woods during the Seven Years' War in which a chief, watching a British army moving toward Quebec, spoke to his followers of the "time when our ancestors were absolute lords of the woods, the meadows and the lakes," changing habitations with the seasons and living "in plenty and security." With the arrival of "a new race of men . . . from the great ocean," however, the Indians found themselves unable to cope with these "invaders," who "ranged over the continent slaughtering, in their rage, [both] those that resisted, and those that submitted." Some of them enslaved Indians in mines and on farms; others, "boast[ing of] their humanity," contented "themselves to seize our chases and our fisheries" and "to drive us from every tract of ground where fertility and pleasantness invite them to settle," and otherwise ignored the natives "except when we intrude upon our own lands"; and still others insolently "pretend[ed] to have purchased a right of residence and of tyranny."[37]

Depicting these unwelcome invaders as usurping and plundering "sons of rapacity" who in their greed for land had, despite their professions, violated all norms of common humanity, the chief expressed the hope that the Anglo-French conflict would turn out to be an occasion "when the pride of usurpation shall be crushed, and the cruelties of invasion shall be revenged." He called upon his auditors to "look unconcerned upon the slaughter, and remember that the death of every European delivers the country from a tyrant and a robber; for what is the claim of either nation, but the claim of the vulture to the leveret, of the tiger to the fawn? Let us endeavour, in the meantime," he urged, "to learn their discipline, and to forge their weapons; and, when they shall be weakened with mutual slaughter, let us rush down upon them, force their remains to take shelter in their ships, and reign once more in our native country."[38] Johnson's dark passages on the injustice of dispossessing the Indians and his unflattering portrait of British settlers conveyed a deep skepticism about the legitimacy of the colonial process and included an early invocation of the languages of humanity and justice as standards for British behavior overseas of the sort that Opposition writers would use to condemn the efforts of St. Vincent planters to seize Black Carib lands.

The paucity of discussion about settlers' injustice to Amerindians makes it difficult to assess how far such ideas penetrated into British evaluations of

[36] For instance, an author signing himself "J. B." in the *Gentleman's Magazine* (London), 27 (June 1757): 253, protested against British Americans' offering bounties on enemy Indian scalps, pointing out that "these cruelties" were undertaken "against free people . . . in their own country" who were guilty of nothing more than defending "their country, . . . their liberties, and [their] lives."

[37] Samuel Johnson, *The Idler*, #81.

[38] Ibid.

empire, yet a few pieces elaborated on the themes articulated by Shebbeare and Johnson. Thus did an anonymous author in the *London Chronicle* in 1770 lament the pernicious effects of European contact upon indigenous Americans. "The arrival of Europeans in this new world has been productive of the most ruinous consequences to the old inhabitants, who have lost their ancient habitations, and the best of their lands, either by force of arms, or of trifling presents made to them," he observed, "but this is not the worst of their misfortune." "However agreeable it may be to the selfish and all-grasping Europeans," the indigenes had suffered such great losses by virtue of the diseases and vices they had acquired from the Europeans that many "populous tribes had become extinct," and the "few that remain[ed] daily decrease[d] in their numbers."[39] Such powerful testimony to the ill effects of the rapacity and inhumanity of American settlers provided an early foundation for a new evaluation of the legitimacy of empire and strongly suggested that Britons overseas lacked the moral capacity of their metropolitan forebears and counterparts.

But such analyses were exceptional. Primarily stressing the benefits, not the liabilities, of empire, British analysts tended to ignore the costs of empire to indigenous peoples, captured Africans, and conquered settlers of European descent in favor of the many advantages it brought to colonial settlers and metropolitans alike.

Perhaps the most dramatic illustration of this tendency was the response to the expulsion of the Acadians from Nova Scotia in 1755, just eighteen years before the Carib War in St. Vincent. For more than four decades after the Treaty of Utrecht placed them under the jurisdiction of the British in 1713, the status of these French "neutrals" remained ambiguous. With their religion and property guaranteed by the treaty, the Acadians had achieved a modest prosperity, become almost entirely self-sufficient, and expanded to number more than 10,000 by the 1750s. Moreover, until the metropolitan government sponsored large-scale immigration to Nova Scotia in the late 1740s, the small size of the British population allowed French speakers a considerable degree of self-government within their respective communities. Although most of the Acadians made every effort to maintain their neutrality, "resolutely," in the words of one modern historian, "disassociating themselves from the international rivalries" of the Anglo-French conflict in America, their refusal to take an oath of allegiance to the British government became the pretext for expelling them. In 1755, Nova Scotia officials rounded up more than 7,000 of them for transport to the continental colonies to the south.[40]

---

[39] *London Chronicle*, September 1770, as quoted by Bickham, *Savages within the Empire*, 99.

[40] John Bartlett Brebner, *New England's Outpost: Acadia before the Conquest of Canada* (New York: Columbia University Press, 1927), 164–65, 180, 255, 257; Geoffrey Plank, *An Unsettled Conquest: The British Campaign against the Peoples of Acadia* (Philadelphia: University of Pennsylvania Press, 2001), 122–39; John Mack Faragher, *A Great and Noble Scheme: The Tragic Story of the Expulsion of the French Acadians from Their American Homelands* (New York: W. W. Norton, 2005), 279–364; N. E. S. Griffiths, *From Migrant to Acadian: A North*

The once happy Acadians found themselves suddenly reduced to penury and exile. As one sympathetic observer of the plight of those sent to Maryland observed, they "were at once stripp[e]d of every thing but the Cloaths on their Backs," sent off to unfamiliar and often inhospitable places where they were a religious minority, and faced with a future of only "want and Misery." Moreover, as this same observer, using the language of justice, appreciated, Nova Scotia authorities had committed this inhumane act wholly without concern for due process of law. "Sacrificed to the security of Our Settlements in that part of the World," the expelled Acadians, he pointed out, had been subjected to a form of summary justice that was appropriate for neither subjects nor enemies. As subjects, he noted, they "were intitled to the Benefit of our laws and ought to have been tried and found Guilty before they could be punished and to punish them all, All to have been tried and convicted." As enemies, he thought, they ought to have been "treated as such and maintained as Prisoners of War." "The Case of these poor unhappy People is so hard," he concluded in a telling remark, "that I wonder it has not been taken notice of by some of Our Political Writers in England."[41]

In striking contrast to the response to the Carib War in St. Vincent, however, the response in Britain to the expulsion of the Acadians was a pointed silence. Except for William Burke's brief complaint in *An Account of the European Settlements in America*, published in 1757, that the expulsion was a measure that, if "not impolitic," was "certainly such as an humane and generous mind is never restrained to but with regret,"[42] it seems to have produced no objections, no concerned political tracts or newspaper essays, and no parliamentary debate.[43] That the expulsion had occurred during the early stages of a full-scale war with France and involved a suspect Roman Catholic population that might be expected to assist the French in this struggle may explain this absence of moral outrage in Britain. Yet it may also be taken as evidence that the metropolitan British public had yet to be sensitized to the moral costs of overseas empire and that the languages of humanity and justice had yet to penetrate deeply into metropolitan evaluations of empire.

American Border People 1604–1755 (Montreal and Kingston: McGill University Press, 2005), 404–64.

[41] Charles Carroll of Annapolis to Charles Carroll, July 26, 1756, in Ronald Hoffman, Sally Mason, and Eleanor Darby, eds., *Dear Papa, Dear Charley: The Peregrinations of a Revolutionary Aristocrat, As Told by Charles Carroll of Carrollton and His Father, Charles Carroll of Annapolis...*, 3 vols. (Chapel Hill: University of North Carolina Press, 2001), 1: 30–31.

[42] William Burke, *An Account of the European Settlements in America*, 2 vols. (London, 1757), 2: 272.

[43] Indeed, the two anonymous pamphlets that did touch on the expulsion described it as an "exterpation" that, by removing a "herd of perfidious wretches" from the best lands in the province, would encourage immigration and thereby prevent the colony from "falling to destruction" and "forever" constitute a "memorable" event in ushering in "the area of *Nova Scotia's* prosperity." *An Account of the Present State of Nova Scotia: in Two Letters to a Noble Lord* (London, 1756), 23, 25–26; *A Letter From a Gentleman in Nova Scotia, to a Person of Distinction on the Continent* (London, 1756), 7.

By 1772, when war was declared on the Black Caribs, this situation had changed dramatically. Ongoing revelations, beginning in the mid-1760s, of the plundering of India by servants of the East India Company, and mounting depictions after 1765 of the iniquities of the American slave system and the African slave trade had furnished metropolitan Britons with abundant evidence of the misbehavior of overseas Britons and had thereby contributed to the development of a national sense of ambivalence about empire. In the debates over the Carib War, Opposition spokesmen heightened this ambivalence by publicly exploring the deep tensions between, on the one hand, the languages of colonization, commerce, imperial grandeur, civility, savagery, otherness, security, and English rights and liberties, and, on the other hand, the languages of humanity, justice, and natural rights.

As metropolitan Britons increasingly endorsed the principles of humanity circulating throughout the Western world and assured themselves that Britain was a civil and humane society, more and more of them would confront the dilemma of considering how far they could continue to embrace an imperial project that, for all the obvious economic and strategic benefits it brought to Britain, involved such inhumane and unjust dimensions. In coming to terms with what modern scholars would all recognize as the undesirable by-products of colonialism, would metropolitan Britons, having fully identified those by-products in many sites of imperial activity, try to remedy them, distance themselves from the people most directly responsible for them, or simply accept them as the necessary costs of empire?

I

"The Principal Cornucopia of Great-Britain's Wealth"

The Languages of Commerce, Liberty, Security, and Maritime Supremacy and the Celebration of Empire

I

The British Empire, suggested the Barbadian John Ashley, a prolific writer of tracts on the economic aspects of British overseas activities, in 1743, ought to be thought of as "one Body, *viz. Great Britain, Ireland*, and the *Plantations and Fishery* in *America*, besides its Possessions in the *East-Indies* and *Africa*."[1] Ashley's definition of the empire as the home island *and* its many outlying polities had been standard since the 1720s and 1730s, and increasingly for at least another half-century most metropolitans and colonials using the term were similarly inclusive.[2] Thus Governor Francis Bernard of Massachusetts echoed Ashley when he sought, in a memorandum written for metropolitan authorities in London in the early 1760s, to bring some clarity and precision to the way those authorities thought about the empire. "The kingdom of *Great Britain*," Bernard wrote, "has, belonging to and depending upon it, divers external dominions and countries; all which together with *Great Britain* form the *British Empire*. Let, therefore," he recommended, the term *"British Empire* signify the aggregate body of *British* dominions, and [the term] the *Kingdom of Great Britain* the island which is the seat of government."[3]

Ashley and Bernard were only two of many writers who suggested the utility of thinking about the British world in this expansive way, as a world that included both Britain and its overseas territories. "No Nation in the World,"

[1] John Ashley, *The Second Part of Memoirs and Considerations Concerning the Trade and Revenues of the British Colonies in America* (London, 1743), 94.
[2] Richard Koebner, *Empire* (Cambridge: Cambridge University Press, 1961), 61–275, is the classic work on British conceptions of empire during the eighteenth century. For suggestive recent analyses, see David Armitage, *The Ideological Origins of the British Empire* (Cambridge: Cambridge University Press, 2000), 170–98, and Marie Peters, "Early Hanoverian Consciousness: Empire or Europe?," *English Historical Review*, 107 (2007): 651–54.
[3] Francis Bernard, "Principles of Law and Polity, applied to the British Colonies in America," [1764], in *Select Letters on the Trade and Government of America and the Principles of Law and Polity, applied to the American Colonies* (London, 1774), 72.

declared Ashley, was "more commodiously situated for Trade or War than the *British* Empire, taking all together as one body." That Ashley, in this passage, mentioned trade ahead of war is significant. Except perhaps briefly in the late 1730s around the outbreak of the War of Jenkins' Ear, before the Seven Years' War the association of empire and trade was far more common in the languages of empire than the association of empire and war. Before the British military successes in America and in India in the late 1750s, the central figure in imperial thought was, notwithstanding the lionizing of Admiral Edward Vernon in the wake of his victory over the Spanish at Porto Bello in 1739,[4] not the general or the admiral, but the overseas merchant. If among the vast benefits of empire few commentators failed to mention the military and the naval, they nonetheless gave first place to the commercial. And if among the several discursive languages that metropolitans used to speak about the empire, the language of commerce and the combined languages of national security, maritime supremacy, and imperial grandeur were symbiotic, the former was consistently more prominent.[5]

II

Increasingly during the eighteenth century, commentators attributed Britain's expanding wealth to the extraordinary rise in British overseas commerce. To mark the importance of this development, Adam Anderson, a Glasgow merchant, published in 1764 a multivolume work entitled *An Historical and Chronological Deduction of the Origin of Commerce, From the Earliest Accounts, containing An History of the Great Commercial Interests of the British Empire.* As the title implies, this work reached for comprehensiveness.

---

[4] Ashley, *Second Part of Memoirs and Considerations*, 94. See Kathleen Wilson's superb article, "Empire, Trade and Popular Politics in Mid-Hanoverian Britain: The Case of Admiral Vernon," *Past & Present*, 121 (1988): 74–109.

[5] Many of the best historians of domestic Britain do not share this interpretation. While Bob Harris acknowledges that "common notions of empire" were "closely framed by notions of commerce, liberty, and the security of the metropolitan power" [Bob Harris, "War, Empire, and the National Interest in Mid-Eighteenth-Century Britain," in Julie Flavell and Stephen Conway, eds., *Britain and America Go to War: The Impact of War and Warfare in Anglo-America, 1754–1815* (Gainesville: University Press of Florida, 2004), 21] and that "considerations of national prosperity and national security were . . . usually viewed as inseparable," he argues that "it was security which was, in the last resort, viewed as most important" [Bob Harris, *Politics and the Nation: Britain in the Mid-Eighteenth Century* (Oxford: Oxford University Press, 2002), 336]. Peter N. Miller, *Defining the Common Good: Empire, Religion and Philosophy in Eighteenth Century Britain* (Cambridge: Cambridge University Press, 1994), 150–79, and Stephen Conway, *War, State, and Society in Mid-Eighteenth-Century Britain and Ireland* (Oxford: Oxford University Press, 2006), seem to share a similar priority. But see Marie Peters's masterly survey of recent literature on the eighteenth-century empire, "Early Hanoverian Consciousness: Empire or Europe?," in which she notes that the literature "about external trade" was "by far the largest category of writing dealing substantially with British overseas interests" (p. 655) and calls "for greater recognition of the many ways in which Britain's commerce – having become a god for so many and an 'affair of state' from the late seventeenth century – drew British interests and the British state out from Europe and its peripheries into overseas empire" (p. 667).

In Anderson's words, it aspired to be "not only an historical and chronological, but, likewise, a systematical and political Survey of Commerce." As the title also suggests, however, Anderson meant for the work to be a celebration of Britain's commercial development. Its "principal scope," he observed, "has a more especial and immediate regard to the Commercial History of the British Empire," and his central thesis was that commerce – broadly defined, as was characteristic of the era, as "navigation, colonies, manufactures, fisheries, mines, agriculture, and money concerns, viz. Banks, exchanges, coins, interest of money, the various rates or purchase money of lands, houses, provisions, and other necessaries" – was the primary source of Britain's national prosperity. "To the instrumentality of Commerce alone," Anderson declared unequivocally, "the Britannic Empire is, most peculiarly, indebted for its opulence and grandeur; its improvements in arts and knowledge; and, in general, for the great bulk of its solid comforts and conveniences."[6]

When Anderson here used the term "Britannic Empire," he was writing about, not the wider British Empire to which Ashley and Bernard alluded, but the island of Great Britain itself, the spectacular economic growth of which over the previous century was the obvious inspiration for his work. "Whoever reads attentively our elder writers on commerce, before our heavy customs, excises, and other taxes were laid on, and particularly the judicious writings of Sir Josiah Child" from the 1690s, Anderson wrote, "will with pleasure see the large strides we formerly took in the increase of commerce and wealth, more especially from the year 1640 downwards." Despite the fact that, as he put it, "the firm establishment of the nation's liberties, civil and sacred," had "since the ever memorable Revolution, in the year 1688, occasioned several very expensive foreign wars, which have very much retarded the rapid increase of our wealth," the country, he thought, had "since that most happy period" experienced a solid and "gradual increase of our commerce, wealth, and people." Anderson used not only the language of commerce but also the associated languages of improvement and maritime supremacy to lay out the "various infallible marks" of this development, citing "the accession of great numbers of industrious foreigners, chiefly from France, since the revocation of the edict of Nantes, in the year 1685"; the "natural augmentation of our own people"; the tremendous increase "in magnitude and splendor" of the nation's "trading cities and manufacturing towns"; the manifest growth in shipping and in "the number of our quays, wharfs, warehouses, and docks" in both London and the outports; the rise in "the number of merchants, as well as of wholesale and retail dealers"; the "vast increase of all kinds of merchandize, with which our warehouses and shops are always filled"; the continuous expansion of London suburbs through the addition of "new and finer built streets"; the rise in both rural and urban rents; the obvious increase in the size of the money supply and

---

[6] Adam Anderson, *An Historical and Chronological Deduction of the Origin of Commerce, From the Earliest Accounts, containing An History of the Great Commercial Interests of the British Empire*, 4 vols. (London, 1787), 1: vii, ix, xiii, xvi. This work was originally published in 1764.

the decline in interest rates; the "immense increase of our personal estates . . . in plate, jewels, furniture, paintings, equipages, libraries, medals, coins, shipping, horses, and other cattle"; the visible improvement of lands, mines, fisheries, and, particularly, manufactures; the conveyance of "greater portions given by all ranks to children"; the general improvement in living standards among "people of all degrees, both in town and country"; and the doubling in size of the royal navy. That these many happy developments had been, not "sudden, but gradual" was to Anderson an indication that they represented, not just a prodigious "influx of national wealth," but "solid and rational marks of prosperity." "So universally," they were all, in Anderson's view, "benefit[s] accruing from our increased commerce," and he had no doubt that Britain had long been and was "now undoubtedly in possession of an extensively active and very gainful commerce, beyond what any nation in Europe at present has, or perhaps ever had."[7]

As Anderson himself acknowledged, he was by no means the first analyst to appreciate the role of commercial expansion in Britain's rising wealth. A long line of other writers, stretching from Sir Josiah Child, Sir William Petty, and Charles Davenant in the 1690s, to William Wood and Joshua Gee in the early decades of the eighteenth century, to Malachy Postlethwayt, Thomas Mortimer, Arthur Young, John Campbell, and Adam Smith during the third quarter of the eighteenth century, had published tracts or treatises emphasizing and endeavoring to explain or to accelerate Britain's spectacular economic growth, and all had stressed the agency of commerce in this development.[8] By the mid-1770s, the idea that, as the petitioner Richard Glover testified before

---

[7] Ibid., xxxviii–xxxix, xli–xlii.

[8] The most impressive modern general discussions of eighteenth-century British economic literature are Terence Hutchinson, *Before Adam Smith: The Emergence of Political Economy, 1662–1776* (Oxford: Basil Blackwell, 1988), and Lars Magnusson, *Mercantilism: The Shaping of an Economic Language* (New York and London: Routledge, 1994). Each devotes some space to the writings of Child, Davenant, and Adam Smith; Hutchison mentions Postlethwayt, and Magnusson has a brief reference to Gay, but they neglect the other writings discussed in this chapter. Nor do these works engage with the extensive contemporary discussion of the relationship of overseas empire to British economic and social development and maritime expansion. A search of the two indices yields no references to *empire* or *plantations* and only two references to *colonies* in Hutchison. Both volumes have a few references to the *East India Company*, but pay little attention to eighteenth-century discussions about the effects of the Asian trade upon domestic British development or on ideas about empire. Julian Hoppit, "The Contexts and Contours of British Economic Literature, 1660–1760," *Historical Journal* 49 (2006): 79–110, provides a rich and suggestive survey of the range of economic writings published in Britain during the years covered. The most comprehensive study of the economic literature remains Klaus E. Knorr, *British Colonial Theories 1570–1850* (Toronto: University of Toronto Press, 1944), 63–151. Of course, by no means all Britons celebrated commercial expansion as an unmixed blessing. The critique of commerce, centered on its deleterious social and moral effects, can be followed in J. G. A. Pocock, *Virtue, Commerce, and History: Essays on Political Thought and History, Chiefly in the Eighteenth Century* (Cambridge: Cambridge University Press, 1985), and Istvan Hunt, "The Early Enlightenment Debate on Luxury and Commerce," in Mark Goldie and Robert Wokler, eds., *The Cambridge History of Eighteenth-Century Political Thought* (Cambridge: Cambridge University Press, 2006), 756–833.

the House of Commons in March 1775, Britain's extraordinary "influx of wealth" was "the creature of commerce" and that it was commerce that had "raised us so high among modern nations" and "solely" constituted Britain's "envied power and rank in the world" was commonplace. Britain's "strength and resources," Glover asserted, "wholly derived from trade."[9]

Nor was this appreciation limited to commercial writers. With so many benefits arising from trade, poets, playwrights, novelists, and observers of all sorts found it irresistible to depict the merchants who organized and presided over it as the progenitors of the new economic order.[10] Thus, in his popular play *The London Merchant*, a sad tale of the seduction and corruption of a young counting house clerk, first produced in 1731, the playwright George Lillo held up the honest and benevolent merchant Thorowgood as at once a model of virtue and personal behavior, a contributor to national greatness, and an agent in a far-flung civilizing project. The "Method of Merchandize," Thorowgood informed his faithful assistant Trueman in one scene, was not "merely...a Means of getting Wealth" but a "Science...founded in Reason and the Nature of Things" by which the merchant, operating on a global scale, unlocked the mysteries of trade and promoted humanity by opening "up an Intercourse between Nations, far remote from one another in Situation, Customs and Religion; promoting Arts, Industry, Peace and Plenty; by mutual Benefits diffusing mutual Love from Pole to Pole." "On every Climate and in every Country," he observed, "Heaven has bestowed some good particular to itself," and the "industrious Merchant's Business" was "to collect the various Blessings of each Soil and Climate, and, with the Product of the whole, to enrich his native Country." "Those Countries, where Trade is promoted and encouraged," agreed Trueman, using the language of civility often employed in tandem with the language of commerce, made discoveries, "not...to destroy, but to improve Mankind, – and by Love and Friendship, to tame the fierce, and polish the most savage, – to teach them the Advantages of honest Traffick, – by taking from them, with their own Consent, their useless Superfluities, and giving them, in Return, what, from their Ignorance in manual Arts, their Situation, or some other Accident, they stand in need of." In these lines, Lillo identified overseas merchants not only as the principal agent in enhancing Britain's national wealth, but also as national benefactors and agents of civility, whose collective discoveries in the science of commerce were, he suggested, of an importance nearly equivalent to those of the great natural philosophers Isaac Newton and John Locke.[11]

[9] Richard Glover, speech, March 16, 1775, in R. C. Simmons and P. D. G. Thomas, eds., *Proceedings and Debates of the British Parliaments Respecting North America 1754–1783*, 6 vols. (White Plains, N.Y.: Kraus, 1982–86), 5: 569.

[10] Perry Gauci, *The Politics of Trade: The Overseas Merchant in State and Society, 1660–1720* (Oxford: Oxford University Press, 2001), treats the emergence of the merchant as a prominent public figure.

[11] George Lillo, *The London Merchant: or, the History of John Barnwell* (1731), act III, scene I, in James L. Steffenson, ed., *The Dramatic Works of George Lillo* (Oxford, 1993), 178.

When Malachy Postlethwayt put together his enormous and ambitious two-volume *Universal Dictionary of Trade and Commerce*, first published in 1750–51, he could underline the national importance of commerce by drawing, in his introduction, upon lines from the poet John Gay's "To His Native Country":

> O Britain, chosen Port of Trade,
> May Luxury ne'er thy Sons invade;
> Whenever neighbring States contend,
> Tis thine to be the gen'ral Friend.
> What is't who rules in other Lands?
> On Trade alone thy Glory stands.
> That Benefit is unconfin'd,
> Diffusing Good among Mankind;
> That first gave Lustre to thy Reigns,
> And scater'd Plenty o'er thy Plains;
> Tis that alone thy Wealth supplies,
> And draws all Europe's envious Eyes.
> Be Commerce then thy sole Design;
> Keep that, and all the World is thine.[12]

III

To acknowledge the centrality of trade in Britain's meteoric rise, however, was merely to beg the prior question of why the country had been so successful in expanding its trade, and this question intrigued commercial writers and other analysts throughout the eighteenth century. One school of thought argued that commercial expansion was one of the many beneficent effects of the Glorious Revolution. Thus, as the title announced, the anonymous author of *The Advantages of the Revolution Illustrated, by a View of the present State of Great Britain*, a tract published in 1753, endeavored both to inform readers of the many developments that since the Revolution had served to put Britain in such a "thriving Condition" and to link those developments directly to the Revolution. Inviting his readers to "cast their Eyes around this Island, [to] let them behold our Seas covered with Ships of Trade, our Barns bursting with increasing Harvests, our Flocks multiplying and bending beneath their fleecy Burdens," and to "see the *Plough, Loom*, and *Sail*, those inexhaustible Fountains of Prosperity, pouring forth their Treasures in a more copious Abundance since this auspicious Aera [of the Revolution], while our *Colonies* are making richer Retribution to their Parent Country [for] the Nourishment and Support afforded in their Industry," he challenged them to deny that "*this Nation*" had "*received real Advantage[s] from the Revolution.*" In doing so, he effectively employed the language of liberty that had, for more than a century and a half, been the principal language Britons used to define what was

---

[12] Malachy Postlethwayt, *Universal Dictionary of Trade and Commerce*, 2 vols., 4th ed. (London, 1764), 1: caption on opening print. This work was first printed in 1750–51.

distinctive about themselves.[13] By freeing British "Minds... from [the] igno-minious Bondage of Ecclesiastical and State Slavery," by extinguishing "the flaming Brands of Bigotry," and by dissolving "the frozen Doctrines of Pas-sive Obedience," the Revolution, he contended, had secured British liberty and thereby excited British industry. "Industry," he declared, was "a Characteri-stick of Liberty," and industry, according to this interpretation, was principally responsible for stimulating the trade and internal and behavioral developments that underlay Britain's subsequent rise to prosperity. Commerce and liberty went hand in hand, supporting one another in ways that led ineluctably to national wealth.[14]

Far more common, however, was the view that Britain's economic growth and visible social improvement were principally the results of its expansion overseas. "If we take a view of our own Kingdom," declared the economic writer Joshua Gee in a 1720 tract, "we shall find our Trade and Riches came in but very slowly till our Plantations began to be settled, and as they throve, our Trade and Riches encreased, our Lands rose in value, and our Manufactures encreased also."[15] "Before we had plantations," agreed Malachy Postlethwayt in the early 1750s, "the condition of this country... was very low and dispica-ble." Under Elizabeth, he observed, most of what modern analysts would call economic indices were unimpressive. "But, as soon as we began to extend our trade, and to make plantation-settlements abroad," he wrote, "the face of our affairs changed; the inhabitants of the city of London doubled" during the first half of the seventeenth century and doubled again during the second half; "our shipping increased in a still greater proportion; we coined, within twenty years after the queen's death, above five millions in the Tower; in 20 years after that seven millions, and in the next 20 years eight millions," developments that, to Postlethwayt, all served "as indubitable proofs, that we had gained a prodi-gious ballance of trade in our favour." "Since we have established colonies and plantations," he asserted

our condition... has altered for the better, almost to a degree beyond credibility. – Our manufactures are prodigiously increased, chiefly by the demand for them in the plantations, where they at least take off one half and supply us with many valuable commodities for re-exportation, which is as great an emolument to the mother-kingdom as to the plantations themselves.[16]

By the 1760s and 1770s, this view extended well beyond commercial writ-ers such as Postlethwayt. Marveling at "the astonishing turn this kingdom has

---

[13] Lee Ward, *The Politics of Liberty in England and Revolutionary America* (Cambridge: Cam-bridge University Press, 2004), 1–350, explores some of the roots of the language of liberty but neglects its important origins in English jurisprudential thought.

[14] G. B., *The Advantages of the Revolution Illustrated, By a View of the present State of Great Britain* (London, 1753), 4–6, 17, 20–21.

[15] Joshua Gee, *A Letter to a Member of Parliament, Concerning the Naval Stores-Bill* (London, 1720), 18.

[16] Postlethwayt, *Universal Dictionary of Trade and Commerce*, 1: entry under "Colonies."

taken to commercial adventure, since the reign of Henry the Seventh," a political pamphleteer writing in 1766 was absolutely certain that it had been "occasioned by a most unexpected event, the discovery of a new world," and the consequent "emigration of colonies to this new world."[17] "The growth of our national prosperity," Edmund Burke announced in Parliament in March 1775, "has happened within the short period of the life of man. It has happened within 68 years," and the "American trade," he declared, had served as "the very food that has nourished every other part into its present magnitude."[18] That the colonial trades had "been one of the mainsprings of our opulence and splendour," said the political philosopher Richard Price in 1776, "is undeniable."[19]

Perhaps before the 1760s only the most enthusiastic proponents of empire would have endorsed this assessment of the relationship between Britain's rising economic power and its overseas expansion, but nearly all analysts of the country's commercial development recognized that the trading factories in India and Africa and the fisheries and colonies in America had been, as Joshua Gee remarked in 1729, "*one* great Cause of enriching this Nation."[20] Already by the early 1690s, economic writers knew that the plantation trades were getting to be, as Sir Josiah Child put it, "of as great Bulk" and employed "as much Shipping as most of the Trades of this Kingdom."[21] What made this achievement so remarkable was that it had been accomplished, as Charles Davenant noted in 1698, largely "without expence to the crown." As the Board of Trade acknowledged to the House of Lords in 1730, all "the British colonies in America . . . except that of Jamaica" had been "originally settled by private adventurers at their own expence" and "by degrees" had, as Davenant affirmed, "raised themselves by their own charge, prudence, and industry, to the wealth and greatness they are now arrived at."[22] By the 1690s, according to Davenant, English exports amounted to about two million pounds sterling per annum, more than two-thirds of which was accounted for by trade with the American plantations and the East Indies, the American trade amounting to £600,000, the East Indian trade to £500,000, re-exports of American products to £120,000, and re-exports of East Indian commodities to £180,000. Less

[17] *Application of Some General Political Rules, To the Present State of Great Britain, Ireland and America* (London, 1766), 82–83.
[18] Edmund Burke, speech, March 22, 1775, in Simmons and Thomas, eds., *Proceedings and Debates of the British Parliaments*, 5: 602–03.
[19] Richard Price, *Observations on the Nature of Civil Liberty, the Principles of Government, and the Justice and Policy of the War in America* (London, 1776), in D. O. Thomas, ed., *Richard Price: Political Writings* (Cambridge: Cambridge University Press, 1991), 57.
[20] Joshua Gee, *The Trade and Navigation of Great-Britain*, 2d ed. (London, 1730), 98. Italics added.
[21] Sir Josiah Child, *A New Discourse of Trade*, 2d ed. (London, 1694), 178.
[22] Board of Trade Report to House of Lords, April 8, 1730, in Leo F. Stock, ed., *Proceedings and Debates of the British Parliaments Respecting North America*, 5 vols. (Washington, D.C.: Carnegie Corporation, 1924–41), 4: 69; Charles Davenant, *Political and Commercial Works*, 4 vols. (London, 1771), 2: 3–4, as quoted by Thomas Day, *Reflections upon the Present State of England, and the Independence of America*, 5th ed. (London, 1783), 3–4.

than a third of the whole, £600,000, was accounted for by trade to Europe, Africa, and the Levant.[23]

This voluminous trade left little room to dispute William Penn's 1701 assessment that Britain's overseas possessions had "considerably Contributed to" the nation's "*Wealth* and *Greatness*."[24] One important indication of the growing metropolitan recognition of the nation's "great Increase in Wealth by our Colonies" was the historian John Oldmixon's publication in 1708 in London of a substantial two-volume work, *The British Empire in America, Containing the History of the Discovery, Settlement, Progress and Present State of All the British Colonies, on the Continent and Islands*, the first volume covering the thirteen continental and island colonies from Carolina to Newfoundland, plus Hudson's Bay, and the second, the ten island colonies in the West Indies and western Atlantic.[25] A second manifestation of the awareness of the economic significance of the overseas segments of the empire was the publication, two decades later, of two treatises: Joshua Gee's *The Trade and Navigation of Great-Britain* in 1729, and Fayer Hall's *The Importance of the British Plantations in America to this Kingdom* in 1731.[26] These works, each more than one hundred pages long, were among the most extensive and systematic treatises on the plantation sector of British overseas trade published since Child's study in 1694.

Arguing that Britain's plantations ought to be "more valued, and a greater Care taken [by metropolitan administrations] to improve and preserve them," both Gee and Hall wrote to explain to their "Countreymen . . . the vast Importance of our Colonies in America" and how much metropolitan Britain was "indebted to" the trade "of our Plantations," a point that, as Hall remarked, was "generally confess'd, tho' I believe, not universally understood."[27] Gee, in particular, lamented the fact that "the present Age" was "so far-unacquainted with the Cause of the Increase of our Riches, that they rather interrupt, than encourage it, and instead of enlarging, lay hold of some small trifling Things which they think may touch their private interest, rather than promote the general Good." He called for a revival of the "*English* Industry and Frugality" that "in the Days of Queen Elizabeth" had laid the foundations for the nation's rising trade, noting that during the late sixteenth and early seventeenth centuries "worthy Patriots" had found ways to entice the woolen manufactures from

---

[23] Charles Davenant, *On the Plantation Trade* (London, 1698), in *Select Dissertations on Colonies and Plantations, By those Celebrated Authors, Sir Josiah Child, Charles D'Avenant, LL.D. and Mr. William Wood* (London, 1775), 40.

[24] William Penn, *Allegations Against Proprietary Governments Considered, and Their Merit and Benefit to the Crown Briefly Observed* (London, 1701), 4.

[25] John Oldmixon, *The British Empire in America, Containing the History of the Discovery, Settlement, Progress and Present State of All the British Colonies, on the Continent and Islands of America*, 2 vols. (London, 1708), 1: xxxi.

[26] Fayer Hall, *The Importance of the British Plantations in America to this Kingdom; with the State of their Trade, and Methods for Improving it* (London, 1731).

[27] Ibid., dedication.

Flanders to England, to find markets for English woolens and other products in the Levant and in Asia, and, most important of all, to establish "Settlements both in the *Sugar* and *Tobacco Plantations*, which were indeed the Cause of the Encrease of our Shipping and Navigation."[28]

Gee acknowledged that the African and East Indian trades had been "of great Advantage to this Nation," and he particularly singled out the latter destination as a place where private merchants with licenses from the East India Company had engaged in a lucrative "coasting Trade" that had "enabled them not only to pay Debts here, but also put themselves into the Way of raising Fortunes for themselves and Families." But his principal objective, like Hall's, was to explain the many ways in which the American plantations had contributed and continued to contribute to the economic well-being of the metropolis.[29]

The first way was to provide a place where those with poor prospects in Britain or elsewhere in the Old World could become useful contributors to the national wealth. These ranged from younger sons who had before been "grievously burdensome to their Families," to those industrious souls who, in both Britain and Europe, were "uneasy under their present Circumstances" and happy to embrace the opportunity for a new start in America, to a multitude of "vagrant indolent Wretches" who in Britain had no liberty "but the liberty of starving" and "whose Time" was "spent in corrupting the industrious, or roving about the Kingdom, or begging from Door to Door." By emigrating to America, many such people had put themselves in a position at once to acquire through "their Bravery and Industry" competence, independence, and even "great Estates," to render themselves "serviceable" to the nation, and to help "enrich their Mother Country." By transplanting themselves to America, such people had, in effect, transformed themselves from parasites into producers. That "an immense Wealth had accrued to us by the Labour and Industry of those People who have settled in our Colonies," Gee had no doubt.[30]

The second way in which emigrants to America helped to enhance British wealth was through their production of valuable commodities that were commercially useful to the metropole. As James Oglethorpe remarked in Parliament in February 1732, the colonies sent every year "vast quantities" of commodities to Britain.[31] Colonial sugar, rice, tobacco, naval stores, lumber, fish, iron ore, and a host of other products augmented Britain's prosperity in two important ways. First, they relieved the nation of dependence on foreign rivals, the substitution of American for Baltic naval stores providing the classic example. Second, they enabled the country to maintain a favorable balance of trade with its European neighbors by supplying the materials for a valuable re-export

---

[28] Gee, *Trade and Navigation of Great-Britain*, 98–99, 126.

[29] Ibid., 25, 30.

[30] Ibid., preface, 59, 126; Postlethwayt, *Universal Dictionary*, 1: "Colonies"; G. B., *Advantages of the Revolution Illustrated*, 8–9, 14–17.

[31] James Oglethorpe, speech, February 23, 1732, in Stock, ed., *Proceedings and Debates of the British Parliaments*, 4: 143.

trade. Sugar and tobacco had long served this function, albeit the re-export market for sugar was declining precipitously by the early 1730s in the face of competition from the French sugar colonies. The message of Gee and Hall was that not only these traditional commodities but also many new ones, including copper, hemp, flax, silk, olives, indigo, cochineal, potash, and perhaps even the spices of Asia, could with proper encouragement from the parent state be added to the list of American products. "There is nothing can grow in any Climate," wrote Hall, "which some [one] of our Plantations is not very capable of producing."[32]

The third way in which the colonies contributed to Britain's economic development – and, as contemporaries saw it, infinitely the most important – was through their consumption of British manufactures. Already in the early 1690s, Sir Josiah Child was aware that American settlers were consuming "our *English* Manufactures, and those of all sorts almost imaginable, in egregious quantities," and he took care to inform his readers of the effects of such consumption on the nation's internal economy. Earlier writers, like Roger Coke in 1676, had worried about the ominous effects of England's having "peopled our Plantations, and repeopled *Ireland*," since the Restoration. He fretted that the flight of fishermen, tradesmen, and other "poor people" to Ireland and the colonies was robbing England "of all the growing Youth and Industry of this Nation, whereby it" was becoming "weak and feeble, and the Strength, as well as Trade" of the country was becoming "decayed and diminished." The nation's trade, he warned, would necessarily be depleted in proportion to "how many men shall be withdrawn from it." Such fears of depopulation and economic stagnation would periodically resurface whenever there were shortages in the labor market.[33]

By Child's calculation, however, emigration to colonies had had precisely the opposite effect. By providing a vast new market for English products, the colonies had given *"a constant Sustenance to"* the British economy, employing, he thought, as many as *"two hundred thousand persons here at home."* Every plantation owner in America with his slaves, Child estimated, made "employment for four men in *England*." Because this additional work was a stimulus to population, he concluded that England had *"not fewer, but the more people . . . by reason of our* English *Plantations in* America."[34] Over the next three to four decades, colonial demand for British goods increased exponentially to the point that, as Oglethorpe remarked in Parliament, "vast quantities of British manufactures and produce" were "sent from hence every year to our several settlements" in America.[35] By the 1720s, Gee reported, there were "very few

[32] Hall, *Importance of the British Plantations*, 19; Gee, *Trade and Navigation of Great-Britain*, 20–25.
[33] Roger Coke, *A Discourse of Trade* (London, 1670), 10, 46.
[34] Child, *New Discourse of Trade*, 188, 215–16.
[35] James Oglethorpe, speech, February 23, 1732, in Stock, ed., *Proceedings and Debates of the British Parliaments*, 4: 143.

trading or manufacturing Towns in the Kingdom but have some Dependance on the *Plantation* Trade," and he emphasized the extent to which "every Person employ'd in Manufactures for Exportation, adds a considerable yearly Value to the publick Stock of the Nation."[36]

Britain's overseas possessions did not merely help to enhance the manufacturing sector. Indirectly, at least, a fourth way in which they contributed to the growth of the British metropolitan economy was, as Gee pointed out, by stimulating both urban and agricultural expansion. Increasing commercial activity and a rising demand for manufactures led to the growth of an urban population that had to be fed. This expanding urban demand for provisions operated to the direct benefit of "the Landed Interest," underwriting a rise in land values and providing owners with the wherewithal for "improving and enlarging their . . . Estates."[37] The results of what modern analysts would call a multiplier effect were prodigious. As a later writer observed, "Millions of Acres" had "been recovered and improved by draining, liming, marling, burning, and other Methods of Manuring, to the great Increase of Pasturage and Tillage, and consequently of Husbandmen, Smiths, Carpenters, with various other Kinds of Artificers" – all developments that could, at least in some part, be traced back to the rise in trade with Britain's overseas plantations and factories.[38]

According to Gee, yet a fifth way in which the colonies contributed to Britain's economy was by providing a field for nurturing English mercantile development and opportunities for capital investment. The colonies, he wrote, had become

a Receptacle for young Merchants who have not Stocks of their own; and therefore all our *Plantations* are filled with such who receive Consignments of their Friends from hence, and when they have got a sufficient Stock to trade with, they generally return home, and other young Men take their Places; so that the continued Motion and Intercourse our People have into the Colonies may be compared to Bees of a Hive, which go out empty, but come back again loaded, by which Means the Foundation of many Families is laid.

At the same time, those with money to invest who preferred to stay in Britain could put their money to work earning "high Interest" from "the Mortgages on the Planters['] Estates."[39]

The sixth and last way in which the overseas empire contributed to Britain's economic benefit was through an augmentation of shipping and sailors. Child had early estimated that the plantations employed "near[ly] two thirds of all our *English Shipping*,"[40] and more than three decades later William Wood agreed that, together with the Newfoundland fisheries, the American colonies

---

36 Gee, *Trade and Navigation of Great-Britain*, 100; Gee, *Letter to a Member of Parliament*, 19.
37 Gee, *Trade and Navigation of Great-Britain*, iv.
38 G. B., *Advantages of the Revolution Illustrated*, 9–10.
39 Gee, *Trade and Navigation of Great-Britain*, 100–01.
40 Child, *New Discourse of Trade*, 188.

had "been the chief [impetus for the] Encrease of our Navigation and Sea-men, and the greatest Encouragement to both."[41] Gee elaborated upon this point. "'Tis generally agreed," he wrote in a 1720 tract, that "the Sugar and Tobacco Plantations only, employ 300 Sail of Ships, which may be allowed to find Employment for 6000 Sailors; and [that] they and their Families are all maintained by this Navigation." He estimated that if each ship was worth £2,000 "fitted out to Sea," then £600,000 "of the National Stock [was] employ'd in this Shipping, beside their Cargoes." The "Advantages of vict-ualling such a Number of Ships must be very considerable," he wrote, as the "Dependants on this Trade, and their Families," were "all supported and maintained thereby; such as Ship-Carpenters, Joiners, Caulkers, Sail-makers, Rope-makers, Anchor-Smiths, Block-makers, Ship-Chandlers, Bakers, Brew-ers, Butchers, Lightermen, Wharfingers, Porters, and Carmen, beside many other Employments."[42] By stimulating the expansion of such a complex infra-structure of navigation and by supporting "so great a Number of the best of Sailors" and ships, the plantation trade, Gee contended, using the language of maritime supremacy, had obviously helped greatly to strengthen Britain's naval prowess. The "Multitudes of Seamen" involved in the colonial trade, he wrote, meant that, "upon a War, the Nation [would be] better provided with a greater Number of Sailors than hath hitherto been known."[43] Was there any longer "a Maritime Power on the Globe that we need to fear?" asked Hall, rhetorically. The "Strength and Security of our Island," he declared, "depend principally on our Shipping, and those brave Fellows who man them," and shipping had been generated principally by the plantation trade. "While we mind our Trade and Plantations, which are perhaps the greatest Nurseries for Sailors in the World," he asserted, Britain would continue to be "by far the greatest of any other Powers in *Europe*."[44] In the view of writers like Gee and Hall, Britain's naval preparedness and security, like its prosperity, was based on the colonies.

In all these ways, commercial writers and other analysts of the British world emphasized, Britain's overseas possessions had made substantial contributions to the nation's wealth and power. In 1701, William Penn had predicted that, with expert guidance, "*America* cannot fail in time to make *England* the Glory and Mistress of *Europe*."[45] To people of the generation of Gee and Hall it appeared as if Penn's prediction had been fulfilled without such guidance. Just as the Spaniards and Portuguese had been made "rich and powerful" by the mines they had exploited in their colonies, so Britons, Gee explained, had drawn "a boundless Wealth . . . by Supplying our Plantations with every

---

[41] William Wood, *The Great Advantages of our Plantations and Colonies to Great Britain* (London, 1728), in *Select Dissertations on Colonies and Plantations*, 87.

[42] Gee, *Letter to a Member of Parliament*, 18.

[43] Gee, *Trade and Navigation of Great-Britain*, 101–02.

[44] Hall, *Importance of the British Plantations*, 6.

[45] Penn, *Allegations Against Proprietary Governments Considered*, 4.

Thing they want, and [keeping] all manufactures within our selves."[46] By the 1730s, Hall confidently claimed, Britain was gaining a "clear Profit by our *American* Colonies yearly... of one Million Sterling, exclusive of what we get by any Trades for Negroes or dry Goods by the *Spaniards*; and... in and by our Colonies only" it was "maintain[ing] and employ[ing] at least eighteen thousand Seamen and Fishermen."[47]

By the late 1730s and early 1740s, members of Parliament routinely acknowledged that the plantation trades were, as Earl Cholmondeley said in 1739, "the most valuable branch of our commerce,"[48] the source, said Sir John Barnard a year later, of "all our wealth, and that power which is the consequence of wealth."[49] Clearly, declared Samuel Sandys, "our trade to America" was "of the utmost consequence to this kingdom."[50] By midcentury, few could have disputed Postlethwayt's declaration, in his article on "Colonies" in his *Universal Dictionary of Trade and Commerce*, "that our trade and navigation are greatly increased by our colonies, and that they really are a source of treasure and naval power to this kingdom, since they work for us, and their treasure centers here."[51]

Britons congratulated themselves on the fact that the benefits of overseas empire were not limited to the metropolis. If, as the trade writer John Ashley observed in 1743, the "large Surplusage that arises from the Profits of the *junior* Branches of the *great Empire*, and particularly from its *Plantations* and *Fisheries* in *America*," yielded "a large Annual Addition to the Stock and Wealth of this elder Branch of the whole Body,"[52] colonial settlers had clearly done extremely well. Without "Mines of Gold or Silver," in "Climes less temperate and kind [than that of England], on Lands less luxuriant and fruitful," they had, in Hall's words, "enjoy[ed] more Happiness and Pleasures," were "comparatively more wealthy," were "justly esteemed more considerable, their Productions from their Labour infinitely more valuable, and their Trade more beneficial to their Native Kingdom, as well as themselves" than would ever have been the case had they remained in the Old World.[53] That the plantation trade had been what the cleric and political economist Josiah Tucker in 1749 called "a mutual benefit"[54] seemed to be proven by the fact that the colonies

[46] Gee, *Trade and Navigation of Great-Britain*, preface.
[47] Hall, *Importance of the British Plantations*, 114.
[48] Earl Cholmondeley, speech, March 4, 1739, in Stock, ed., *Proceedings and Debates of the British Parliaments*, 4: 689.
[49] Sir John Barnard, speech, February 5, 1740, in Stock, ed., *Proceedings and Debates of the British Parliaments*, 5: 25.
[50] Samuel Sandys, speech, November 16, 1739, in Stock, ed., *Proceedings and Debates of the British Parliaments*, 5: 4–5.
[51] Postlethwayt, *Universal Dictionary of Trade and Commerce*: "Colonies."
[52] Ashley, *Second Part of Memorials and Considerations*, 96.
[53] Hall, *Importance of the British Plantations*, 25–26.
[54] Josiah Tucker, *A Brief Essay on the Advantages and Disadvantages Which Respectively attend France and Great Britain, with Regard to Trade* (London, 1749), 35.

were themselves, as Oglethorpe pointed out, "daily increasing...in riches and power."[55] "In less than Three hundred Years," as the economic writer John Campbell would declare in 1774, using the language of improvement, "a great Part of the Wilds and Wastes of America [had] become rich and well cultivated Countries, settled and improved, as well as possessed by Multitudes of British Subjects."[56]

This emphasis upon the spread of British culture over parts of the Americas underlined the extent to which among eighteenth-century British commercial writers the languages of colonization, commerce, and civility reinforced one another. The conviction that commerce, as Postlethwayt remarked in 1757 in his treatise *Great-Britain's True System*, had "greatly civilized the human Race" was ubiquitous among such writers. Indeed, many of them believed that the civility associated with well-developed mechanical arts of the sort found among the Chinese and Europeans were, as Postlethwayt wrote, "the basis of all Commerce." The "daily improvements made by their Artificers, and Manufacturers," he insisted, were in great measure responsible for the "Commerce and Navigation of trading states" and were the principal feature that distinguished them from those states that "subsist on their natural Productions, and by bartering them against those of other Countries, make no Figure as a Trading People." For Postlethwayt, the absence of commerce, navigation, and mechanical arts principally explained the savage "Dispositions" of "the wild Africans, or the American Indians."[57]

How far European colonization had been an agency for civilizing the aboriginal inhabitants of the Americas was not a question that much interested these commercial writers, but Postlethwayt was an important exception. "Civilizing the American savages, who inhabited the countries on the back of the European colonies in North America," he claimed in an extended discussion of this subject in his *Universal Dictionary of Trade and Commerce*, represented one "of the greatest scenes of Improvement in the world." "Before the Europeans came among them," he explained with typical cultural myopia, the

Indians or natives...had neither houses, cattle, clothes, tools, weapons, ammunition, or hous[e]hold stuff; their cattle were beasts of the forest; their clothes were the skins of bears; their weapons, bows, wooden swords, clubs, javelins, and darts, pointed with teeth and bones of fishes; their ammunition, arrows and stones; their houses were wigwams, hovels and huts; and their hous[e]hold stuff earthen-pans hardened in the sun; their beds, matts and skins, laid on the ground; they could strike no fire, but by rubbing two sticks together; they had neither edged tools or other tools, for they had

[55] James Oglethorpe, speech, January 28, 1732, in Stock, ed., *Proceedings and Debates of the British Parliaments*, 4: 125–26.
[56] John Campbell, *A Political Survey of Britain: Being a Series of Reflections on the Situation, Lands, and Inhabitants, Revenues, Colonies, and Commerce of this Island*, 2 vols. (London, 1774), 2: 1634.
[57] Malachy Postlethwayt, *Great-Britain's True System* (London, 1757), 275.

neither iron, steel, brass, or lead; no grind-stone or mill-stone; their meat was flesh dried in the sun, and their drink no other than cold water.[58]

With colonization and its attendant commerce, Postlethwayt was persuaded, Indians had been able to improve their material lives and in the process had become more civil. "The same Indians," he reported, "even those remaining wild and savage almost as before," had quickly become convinced of the superior convenience of European goods "for the abundant accommodation of life" and, turning their energies to production and trade, exchanged processed skins and furs for British woolens and clothing, for firearms and ammunition, cutting tools, implements to provide themselves with food and fuel, and other metalware, utensils, and furniture for their dwellings. For Postlethwayt, their transformation in material culture made it clear that colonization and commerce with Europeans had caused the Indians to "grow more civilized" and that in order to civilize "the barbarous nations in all our colonies, factories, &c.," Europeans needed to do "little more than to instruct and inure" them "in the arts of living: clothing with decency, not shameless and naked; feeding with humanity, and not in a manner brutal; dwelling in towns and cities with oeconomy and civil government, and not like savages."[59]

For that reason as well as because it promised greatly to expand demand for British products, Postlethwayt was a strong advocate for extending British colonization into Africa and other "southern lands," where, he predicted, settlers on the seacoast would quickly "spread the commerce into the inland nations, and employ and enrich the inhabitants, by instructing them in the arts of living, as well as of trade." By establishing "colonies of their own nation in all the remote parts where it is proper and practicable," he thus contended, British people could at once expand their trade and wealth and "civilize and instruct the savages and natives of those countries, wherever they plant, so as to bring them by the softest and gentlest methods to fall into the customs and usages of their own country, and incorporate among our peoples as one nation." In these passages, Posthlethwayt provided a perspective on overseas expansion that obviated any necessity for apologies to indigenous communities for encroaching upon their territories, undermining their cultures, and decimating their populations.[60]

Although most writers agreed that the overseas empire had operated to the advantage of both Britons and aboriginal inhabitants, their argument during the second quarter of the eighteenth century was that it was "still improvable," whether by expanding colonization to new areas, as Postlethwayt recommended, or, more often, by adding new products in colonies already established.[61] Indeed, Gee thought that if Parliament would take steps to

[58] Postlethwayt, *Universal Dictionary of Trade and Commerce*, 1: "Guinea."
[59] Ibid.
[60] Ibid.
[61] Tucker, *Brief Essay on the Advantages*, 35.

encourage the colonies to produce a wider range of raw materials, the plantation trade could be "so improved as to be twice as good to this Kingdom as it now is." Expanded colonial production, he predicted, would open up an entirely "new Scene" in which rising colonial demand would raise the volume of exports, stimulate "additional Manufactures," and turn Britain into an even busier hive, with workmen flowing into areas of new employment and themselves generating more consumption, the result being that "Gentlemen would find new Houses built upon their Estates, Towns encrease, and Lands rise about them; [and] Corn, Cattle, and all sorts of Provisions, go off quick, and at a better Price."[62] Ashley agreed. If "the junior Branches of this *Empire*, the *Plantations*," were properly "succoured and encouraged by the elder Branch," he asserted, they would invariably "thrive and increase in People, Property and Power, and consequently add to the Wealth, Strength, and Happiness of the Whole in Proportion to such Increase."[63]

IV

The focus of the economic analysts of empire during the first half of the eighteenth century was upon the British colonies in America and, more specifically, on why they had done so well. One obvious explanation was the resolution of the labor problem through the importation of massive numbers of African slaves. As Davenant remarked in 1698, the "labour of these slaves is the principal foundation of our riches" in the plantations.[64] This is a subject we will return to in Chapter 5. But most analysts seemed to agree that, as Fayer Hall wrote, the most compelling explanation was "the Excellence of our Oeconomy and Government,"[65] what Sir John Barnard in Parliament in 1737 referred to as "the artificial advantage . . . handed down to us by our wise ancestors," by which, he explained, he meant "the superior excellence of our constitution, laws, and customs."[66] To what extent – how fully – that "artificial advantage" transferred to the colonies, and whether, as Davenant phrased it in 1698, "the people in the Plantations have a right to the privileges of English subjects," was never entirely clear. Complaining that "the contrary notion" was "perhaps too much entertained and practised" in the metropolis, Davenant contended that as long as the colonists had "English blood in their veins, and have relations in England, and while they can get [necessities] by trading with us, the stronger they [will] grow" and "the more the crown and kingdom" will "get by them," and, in language that would be repeated for another seventy-five years, he suggested that "nothing but such an arbitrary power as shall make them

---

[62] Gee, *Letter to a Member of Parliament*, 19–20.

[63] Ashley, *Second Part of Memorials and Considerations*, 96.

[64] Davenant, *Political and Commercial Works*, 1: 2, as quoted by Day, *Reflections upon the Present State of England*, 37.

[65] Hall, *Importance of the British Plantations in America*, 25.

[66] Sir John Barnard, speech, March 30, 1737, in Stock, ed., *Proceedings and Debates of the British Parliaments*, 4: 330.

desperate" would ever excite them to throw off their allegiance to the parent state. Warning against "any innovations, or breach of their original charters," he therefore urged the metropolitan government to keep "sacred and inviolate" those "conditions, privileges, terms, and charters... by which they were first encouraged, at their great expence, and with the hazard of their lives, to discover, cultivate, and plant remote places, where in truth they labour as well for us as for themselves."[67]

Davenant's conjoining of the languages of liberty and commerce was a harbinger of things to come. Frequently quoting him, later writers took up and elaborated his themes, emphasizing metropolitan encouragement, mild government, light taxation, and guarantees of settler enjoyment of English laws and liberties as the best way to keep trade flowing and to retain settler good will. Addressing those who were "in any Degree jealous lest the Plantations should throw off their Subjection to us," Fayer Hall thus assured his readers that in a residence of fourteen years he had found not the least sign of disaffection and denied that plantation settlers would ever "seek or desire Change, while they are treated like *Britons*." Though he acknowledged that, "in Proportion to their Numbers," they were "perhaps as knowing as any, and as jealous of their Rights," he assured metropolitans that the settlers were far "too sensible of the Blessing of Liberty, and the Privileges they enjoy above other nations to desire a Change." They were, he reported, "in love with our own Constitution, and hate[d] and despise[d] none but its Enemies." As "*Britons*, or the Descendants of such," he noted, they were "as useful and loyal subjects as any other" and "deserved the same Esteem with the rest of his Majesty's Subjects." Such valuable adjuncts, he recommended, must be treated with leniency.[68]

Whether the West Indian or the continental colonies were more valuable to Britain was a subject of recurrent debate within the empire from the early 1690s on. For the first half of the eighteenth century, John Oldmixon's *British Empire in America* provides one measure of the relative importance of the island and continental colonies in metropolitan eyes, the former taking more space than the latter in both the 1708 and 1741 editions.[69] The West Indian settlements produced the most valuable commodities, showed the quickest and highest returns on investments, bought the largest quantities of British manufactures, were the chief support of the African slave trade, and down to the mid-1720s accounted for a significant amount of Britain's re-export trade. But the continental colonies, too, sent valuable commodities to Britain, tobacco continuing to be a major re-export long after the decline of British sugars on foreign markets. They supplied the West Indian colonies with provisions, lumber products, and other necessities, and they brought in bullion through

---

[67] Davenant, *Political and Commercial Works*, 1: 2, as quoted by Day, *Reflections upon the Present State of England*, 10, 32, 34–35.

[68] Hall, *Importance of the British Plantations in America*, 21–22.

[69] The West Indian colonies took up 50.2 percent of the first edition and 50.9 percent of the second, and the continental colonies the remainder, just under half.

their trade with the Spanish main and, increasingly after 1740, their direct trade in rice, wheat, lumber, and provisions to southern Europe. Most important, the expanding free population and rising wealth of the continental colonies meant that they consumed large quantities of British manufactures. By 1750 it was possible to mount a strong case that their superiority in numbers and their high level of consumption of British goods contributed more "to the wealth and benefit of Great Britain, in its trade, navigation, and revenues" than the West Indian settlements ever had.[70]

Whatever the relative commercial value of the West Indian and continental colonies, metropolitan recognition that, as one anonymous writer put it in the early 1750s, "the *Colonies in America*" were "the principal *Cornucopia* of *Great-Britain's* Wealth"[71] became increasingly evident in rising government expenditures for imperial defense, which doubled between 1728 and 1748. From 1728 to 1734 parliamentary grants for military pay in the overseas empire averaged £36,438, of which a quarter went to regiments in Gibraltar and Minorca. With the expansion of the number of troops in Jamaica from two to eight companies in 1735, in response to the need to protect the settlers from incursions by the Maroons, this figure jumped to an average of £48,700, and with the establishment in 1738 of a regiment of troops in the new colony of Georgia, exposed to attacks from Spanish Florida, it rose to £58,928. In the early 1740s, during the War of Jenkins' Ear, the figure hovered around £66,827, rising to £72,054 in 1744, the first year of the War of the Austrian Succession, and averaging £84,286 a year until the war ended in 1748. In 1746, 1747, and 1748, moreover, Parliament granted more than £70,500 a year to pay the New England forces that captured and retained Cape Breton. With the conclusion of the war in 1748, peacetime military salary expenses leveled off to £72,054, where they remained for the next six years – a figure almost double the annual amount the metropolitan government had spent for military pay in the overseas empire between 1728 and 1734.[72]

Along with these escalating sums, the establishment of a buffer colony in Georgia at the southern end of the continental chain in 1734 and the development of Nova Scotia in 1749 at the northern end,[73] the first state-sponsored and state-supported colonies in the British Empire, heralded a growing recognition of the vulnerability of Britain's overseas settlements to attack from Britain's principal imperial rivals, Spain and France, and in association with Britain's long-standing fears of French aggrandizement in Europe contributed to the

---

[70] Richard Partridge, petition, April 16, 1751, in Stock, ed., *Proceedings and Debates of the British Parliaments*, 5: 476–77.

[71] G. B., *Advantages of the Revolution Illustrated*, 30.

[72] See the annual estimates in Stock, ed., *Proceedings and Debates of the British Parliaments*, 4: 2, 51, 84, 123, 175, 226, 239, 270, 316, 346, 657; 5: 17, 77, 131, 161, 178–79, 188, 227, 240, 254, 288, 370, 443, 513, 575.

[73] During Nova Scotia's first four years of parliamentary funding, from 1749 to 1752, Parliament lavished £336,707 upon Nova Scotia. Ibid., 5: 535.

coming to prominence of a language of national security in metropolitan discussions of empire. Just as Spain's "possessions in America" were "the source of" its "wealth," remarked Earl Cholmondeley in 1739 in Parliament, so was "the trade we carry on with our settlements there . . . the most valuable branch of our commerce." In the War of Jenkins' Ear, he declared, "the preservation of that trade, and these possessions, free and entire," was what Spain and Britain each had "principally in view."[74] The war with France between 1744 and 1748 helped to focus attention upon that nation's growing capacity to rival Britain as a colonizing and maritime power. Since 1700, expansion in the sugar islands and in Louisiana, in the African and East Indian trades, and in the Canadian fur trade and Newfoundland fisheries had made France into a formidable imperial state that, as British observers became ever more acutely aware, could challenge Britain in every sector of its overseas empire.[75]

Indeed, the diminution of British trade with the Continent as a consequence of France's rise as a maritime and commercial rival tended to increase awareness among metropolitan Britons of the significance of the colonies for their own economic and strategic well-being. So rapid had been their "progress . . . since their settlement," said one anonymous writer in reviewing the national state of mind on the eve of the Seven Years' War,

the shipping they employed, the manufactures they consumed, the returns they were capable of making in various articles and commodities that were supplied us by foreign nations; the treasures they were capable of acquiring upon a due encouragement being given to their trade, which would ultimately circulate home: all these, and the great capacity they had of enlarging and extending all these,

he observed, made the colonies

an object preferable to all others, . . . of such essential importance, that the nation might continue to grow rich and great and powerful, by her intercourse with them only, [even] were she deprived of every other means of commerce.

Such thinking easily led metropolitan sentiment to accept the propositions that "our colonies in this new world of our own were our only and best refuge," that "our future happiness depended upon improving them," and that, therefore, "our colonies in North America merited the first and chief attention and care of the mother country." With their extraordinary commercial benefits, the colonies had become an important object of national security.[76]

When the French sought to consolidate their hold on the Ohio River valley in the years after the Peace of Aix-la-Chapelle, they thus seemed, as an anonymous speaker in Parliament charged, to be endeavoring "to strip us of our most valuable properties." Knowing "that the source of power lies in riches, and that the source of English riches lies in America," the French, he charged, understood that by weakening the British in North America, they would be

---

[74] Earl Cholmondeley, speech, March 1, 1739, in ibid., 4: 689.
[75] Postlethwayt, *Great-Britain's True System*, 257–58.
[76] *A Full and Free Inquiry into the Merits of the Peace* (London, 1765), 17–18.

undermining the very foundations of Britain's imperial ascendancy.[77] For this reason, French activities in the Ohio country, as the author of a London tract entitled *State of the British and French Colonies in North America* reported in 1755, were genuinely alarming, opening "the eyes of the whole nation" and making "some people think of *American* affairs more than they ever intended." To be sure, he admitted, some metropolitans "remain[ed] deeply regardless and insensible" of the fortunes of the colonies, while others even went so far as to lessen and depreciate them, depicting them as sources of "unnecessary and expensive wars" and as "depopulators and weakeners of [metropolitan] *Britain*." But such insensibility and deprecation, he declared, neither made "the extreme danger which now threatens our *American* colonies one jot the less" nor changed the unfortunate fact that any activities that threatened them also threatened "the mother country, since, in whatever fate betides them, she must herself inevitably be involved."[78]

On the surface, the British colonies seemed to have all the advantages. They constituted "an immense" and "well cultivated country" with as many as ten times the settler population of the French colonies.[79] As the author of *State of the British and French Colonies in North America* made clear, however, several factors combined to undermine the defensive capacities of the British colonies. First, in contrast to the French colonies, they were composed of many "distinct government[s]," each of which "was wholly independent of the rest, pursuing its own interest and subject to no general command." Second, the large number of slaves so weakened many British colonies that they were incapable of defending themselves against a foreign enemy. For such colonies, military conflict constituted an open invitation to slave revolt. Third, such a high proportion of the free population were landholders that the colonies had few potential soldiers. "Where property is so easily secured," the author noted, there were "Many masters and but few servants," who were perhaps the largest source of recruits in Britain itself. Finally, he conceded, quoting the French writer Charlevoix, the British colonists applied themselves so completely "to the cultivation of their lands and commerce" that they were "wholly . . . unfit for war."[80]

If for these and other reasons the colonies could not defend themselves, then, many people agreed, Britain would have to assist them. Of such "infinite present advantage" were "our colonies and plantations in America," asserted Horace Walpole in Parliament in 1754, "that many thousands, in both islands [Britain and Ireland], owe[d] their subsistence to" them. "For them," he declared, reiterating two generations of metropolitan opinion, "we must fight as if we

[77] Anonymous, speech, February 21, 1757, in Simmons and Thomas, eds., *Proceedings and Debates of the British Parliaments*, 1: 195–96.
[78] *State of the British and French Colonies in North America, With Respect to Number of People, Forces, Forts, Indians, Trade and other Advantages* (London, 1755), 2, 130.
[79] Tucker, *A Brief Essay*, 35; Horace Walpole, Sr., speech, in Simmons and Thomas, eds., *Proceedings and Debates of the British Parliaments*, 1: 19.
[80] *State of the British and French Colonies in North America*, 19, 22, 29, 140.

were fighting *pro aris et focis* [for plow and hearth]; for it is to them [that] we owe our wealth and our naval strength. Our trade thither is the chief nursery for our seamen; and the imports from thence by being again exported, is what alone keeps the balance of trade in our favour."[81]

In a 1755 pamphlet, *The Present State of North-America*, John Huske, a longtime American merchant and later a member of Parliament, systematically and succinctly distilled for his metropolitan audience a half-century of thought about the benefits of American empire for Britain. "It is from the *American Colonies*," he wrote, that the British navy and the merchant fleet "in a great Measure" were supplied with masts and naval stores. The colonial trades had produced "vast Fleets of Merchant-Ships" with a consequent "increase of seamen." Colonial trade with foreign colonies in America and with southern Europe produced "most of our *Silver and Gold*." Colonials produced enough "*Tobacco, Rice, Rum*, and most of our *Sugars, Dying* and other valuable *Woods, Cotton-Wool, Pimento, Ginger, Indico, Whale and* [*cod*] *Liver Oil and Whale-bone, Beaver* and other *Furs, Deer Skins*, and innumerable other Articles" to meet British demand and to support a thriving re-export trade that shifted the balance of trade in Britain's favor. Colonial demand for labor was the source of both a "vast Assistant Profit" and a lucrative "*African* Trade" in which "vast Quantities of the Produce and Manufacture of the Country, and *East-India* Commodities" were exchanged "for *Gold-Dust, Ivory, Gums*, and several Sorts of *Dying Woods* imported into *Great Britain*." From the colonies, Huske argued, Britain derived a "great Part of the Revenue of these Kingdoms" as well as a "great Part of the Wealth we see" and "that Credit which circulates" to support the nation's thriving commerce.[82]

"What will your *Landholders, Manufacturers, Artificers, Merchants, &c.* Say of the Importance of your Colonies, and the Necessity of going to War to regain and preserve them entire, if it cannot be done by other Means," Huske inquired,

when they reflect that if they are lost, they will lose one Third of their Property and Business in general; for it is certain, that full one Third of our whole Export of the Produce and Manufactures of this Country is to our Colonies, and in proportion as this diminishes or increases, their Estates and Business must increase or diminish.

For all these reasons, Huske insisted, "the Mother Country" needed to attend closely to "the Security and Prosperity of every one of her Colonies, because it is her own Security and Prosperity; and the Colonies are to her as the Feet are to the Natural Body, the Support of the whole Political Frame." It was the American colonies, he insisted, that had "enabled us to make the Figure we do at present, and have done for upwards of a Century past, in the Commercial World, from whence we have derived Wealth, Power, and Glory, and the

---

[81] Horace Walpole, Sr., speech, November 15, 1754, in Simmons and Thomas, eds., *Proceedings and Debates of the British Parliaments*, 1: 19.

[82] [John Huske], *The Present State of North-America* (Boston, 1755), 56–57.

greatest Blessings given to Man to know. Consider then," he advised, "if you ought not to direct the whole of your Counsels and Arms to support a War wherein, with the Being of your State, you assert the Dignity of your Reputation, the Safety of your Friends, the best Branches of your Revenue, and the Properties of your Fellow Subjects." So high were the stakes, Huske declared, that resistance to French encroachments in North America called for "the most vigorous Efforts of the combined Nerves of the whole *Empire.*"[83]

Still later, an anonymous writer reviewing public sentiment in Britain "before and during the war" made it clear how far the British political nation had taken up such arguments. "Environed as they were by French encroachments, French forts and French communications; cut off as they were from the fairest riches and best part of the country by French settlements and garrisons on the Ohio, the Mississippi, and the lakes; these very colonies, our last resource," this writer observed, seemed "to be in the most imminent danger." As a consequence, he noted, metropolitan Britons had come to believe "that nothing too great, nothing too expensive, nothing too hazardous could be undertaken in their relief: everything," he added, "was to be attempted; for the time was now come to trial, and a trial not to be avoided, whether Great Britain or France excelled as a naval power."[84]

The expansion of metropolitan public awareness of the importance of America to the European state system was strongly suggested in 1757 by the publication of William Burke's remarkable two-volume *An Account of the European Settlements in America*, the earliest effort to write a transnational history of early modern European colonization in the Americas. Burke freely acknowledged that his work was an effort to capitalize on the rising interest in America generated by the war with France. Despite the fact that the colonies were so *"extremely interesting to us as a trading people,"* only a very few individuals *"before the present war"* had *"made the history"* of America *"any part of their subject."* But the *"affairs of* America," Burke announced in his preface, had *"lately engaged a great deal of public attention."* Although Burke devoted the first volume to Spanish and Portuguese settlements and one of three parts in the second volume to the French and Dutch, he designed the entire work to illustrate his central proposition: that the British had "derive[d] more advantage, and of a better kind from our colonies, than the Spaniards and Portuguese have from theirs, abounding as they are with gold and silver and precious stones." Arguing that "industry... alone [was] the parent of any solid riches," he praised the British colonies and the proliferating intercourse between the colonies and Britain as "an emulation in industry; they have nothing that does not arise from theirs, and what we receive enters into our manufactures, excites our industry, and increases our commerce." For that reason, he argued, the "great point of our regard in America ought... to be... the effectual peopling, employment,

---

[83] Ibid., 56–58.
[84] *Full and Free Inquiry into the Merits of the Peace*, 17–19.

and strength of our possessions there" and only "in a subordinate degree, the management of our interest with regard to the French and Spaniards."[85]

If the Seven Years' War helped to intensify metropolitan British appreciation of the American colonies, French military successes in North America during the early years of the war raised the specter that the French might actually succeed in depriving Britain of those colonies, and some observers pondered whether Britons could "long... maintain ourselves [as] an independent people" if Britain were once "reduced to this state."[86] "With universal concurrence," Lord Royston said in Parliament in December 1757, during one of the darker hours of the war, Britain had engaged in war "for interests the most essential to this country, the protection of its colonies, and the removing those encroachments which had been made upon them. From the turn which affairs have taken," he lamented, invoking the language of imperial grandeur, it had "become a struggle, if not for our independency as a free, and a Protestant people, yet certainly for our significancy and figure as a powerful, a respected nation."[87]

Such fears, of course, turned out to be unfounded. Under the leadership of William Pitt, the fortunes of war began the very next year to swing heavily in favor of the British. Throughout the remainder of the war, declared an anonymous writer in reflecting upon Britain's achievements in 1765, two years after the war had concluded, Britain had run

a career of glory, transcendently superior to every former period of her duration. Victory and conquest attended her arms in every quarter of the world: for in Europe, in Asia, in Africa and America, the enemy and his allies were not only baffled, but vanquished. Her subjects became immensely enriched; her trade and commerce vastly extended; joy, confidence and exultation sat on every countenance; and pleasure, luxury and dissipation reigned with an unbounded sway throughout all her triumphant dominions.[88]

V

The years following the Seven Years' War witnessed a remarkable proliferation of substantial treatises exploring the nature of Britain's extraordinary economic rise. Adam Anderson's 1764 *Historical and Chronological Deduction of the Origin of Commerce* was only the first of many such works.[89] Also in 1764, Malachy Postlethwayt published the fourth edition of his *Universal Dictionary of Trade and Commerce*. In 1768, Oliver Goldsmith issued *The Present State*

---

[85] William Burke, *An Account of the European Settlements in America*, 2 vols. (London, 1757), 1: i; 2: 293–95.

[86] Malachy Postlethwayt, *The History of America: Containing The Geographic, Political, and Commercial State of that Continent* (London, 1771), 127. This work was originally published in 1757 as *Britain's Commercial Interest Explained and Improved*, 2 vols. (London, 1757).

[87] Lord Royston, speech, December 1, 1757, in Simmons and Thomas, eds., *Proceedings and Debates of the British Parliaments*, 1: 236.

[88] *Full and Free Inquiry into the Merits of the Peace*, 1.

[89] Anderson, *An Historical and Chronological Deduction of the Origin of Commerce*.

of the British Empire in Europe, America, Africa, and Asia, a massive tome that devoted 486 pages to a detailed description of the geography, products, and value of the several parts of Britain's extended empire.[90] In 1771, Postlethwayt reissued his 1757 two-volume study, *Britain's Commercial Interest Explained and Improved,* under a new title: *The History of America, Containing the Geographical, Political, and Commercial State of that Continent.*[91] In 1772, the agricultural improver Arthur Young published his *Political Essays Concerning the Present State of the British Empire,* an extended meditation upon the constitution, agriculture, manufactures, colonies, and commerce of the larger British world,[92] and Thomas Mortimer, who conducted a school for aspiring merchants in London, issued *The Elements of Commerce, Politics, and Finances, in Three Treatises on those Important Subjects,* which contained a systematic analysis of Britain's widespread transoceanic commerce.[93] In 1774, the economic writer Sir John Campbell produced his massive two-volume work, *A Political Survey of Britain: Being a Series of Reflections on the Situation, Lands, and Inhabitants, Revenues, Colonies and Commerce of this Island,*[94] and in 1776 Adam Smith, the Scottish moral philosopher and political economist, published *An Inquiry into the Nature and Causes of the Wealth of Nations.*[95]

All of these commercial writers agreed that, as Campbell put it, "our foreign Commerce" had been the instrument that made Britain "considerable." "It is to this," Campbell wrote in summarizing more than three-quarters of a century of thought on this subject,

> that we owe the Improvement of our Lands, the Increase and Variety of our Produce, the Rise of Rents, and that Spirit of Cultivation, for which, as a People, we are distinguished. It is no less evident from the Increase of our Cities, Towns, and Ports, the Beauty, Convenience, and Elegance of private as well as public Structures, and the rich Furniture with which they are adorned. It is conspicuous in our Magazines of costly Goods, in the Quantity of our Plate and Jewels, as well as in the Treasures we possess, and the low Rate of Interest.

All of these manifestations of growing wealth and growing civility, wrote Campbell, were "the gradual Consequences derived from, or Benefits continually furnished by Our Commerce."[96]

[90] Oliver Goldsmith, *The Present State of the British Empire in Europe, America, Africa, and Asia* (London, 1768).

[91] Postlethwayt, *The History of America.*

[92] Arthur Young, *Political Essays Concerning the Present State of the British Empire* (London, 1772).

[93] Thomas Mortimer, *The Elements of Commerce, Politics, and Finances, in Three Treatises on this Important Subject* (London, 1772).

[94] Campbell, *Political Survey of Britain.*

[95] Adam Smith, *An Inquiry into the Nature and Causes of the Wealth of Nations,* ed. R. H. Campbell and A. S. Skinner, 2 vols. (Oxford: Oxford University Press, 1976).

[96] Campbell, *Political Survey of Britain,* 2: 794.

The beneficial effects of foreign commerce, in Campbell's view, extended well beyond the enhancement of Britain's "national Wealth" and civility. It had also, he thought, produced a "general Change of Circumstances in respect to Individuals." "No longer," he observed, were the British people "divided into great Lords and mean Vassals. Riches acquired by Traffic, being more equally dispersed," he explained, were "better employed, and consequently make more people happy." In elaborating upon this point, Campbell emphasized what he regarded as a direct link between commerce and liberty: "The Support of Commerce is Industry," he declared, and "the Spirit of Industry is the Result of Freedom." "The Security of Property" produced by the British system of law and liberty, he observed, "produces Independency, and the Consciousness of this, and that it is derived from and depends on our Constitution, is the genuine Characteristic of public Spirit." Campbell admitted that "this great Fabrick" did "not rest entirely upon foreign Trade," but he argued that it derived "no inconsiderable Strength from that which results from the Intercourse between the Inhabitants of the different Parts of our own Dominions." Linking them through the languages of commerce, civility, and liberty, Campbell thus suggested that all three of these characteristics of modern British life were powerfully and mutually reinforcing.[97]

The relationship of empire to the expansion of British commerce, civility, and liberty was a subject to which, without exception, authors of postwar commercial writings devoted extensive attention, and in so doing, not one of them failed to include a substantial section on Britain's numerous extra-European territories. Thus Campbell, whose *Political Survey* consisted primarily of lengthy reflections on the geography, lands, peoples, revenues, and commerce of the home islands, also included a detailed 350-page section on Britain's "Possessions, Colonies, and Settlements in all the different Parts of the Globe." Obviously, he remarked, any "Political Survey of Britain" that did not include an account of places that had made such a significant contribution "to the Grandeur and Opulence of the British Empire" would "be indeed otherwise very incomplete."[98]

In stressing the contributions of empire to British wealth, these writers all put special emphasis upon the role of the American colonies and thereby powerfully reinforced the widespread belief previously articulated by writers such as Child, Davenant, Gee, Hall, and Postlethwayt that Britain's remarkable prosperity was strongly related to, if not a direct function of, American colonization. "Before England had foreign colonies and factories," Anderson wrote in 1764, "our general commerce was comparatively inconsiderable," the "great bulk of our exportations" consisting "of our woolen drapery, lead and tin." "How happy then is the change in our national circumstances," he continued, "since we have had American plantations." If, Anderson remarked, the colonies "were indeed, for a long time, mere unprofitable drains of our people

---

[97] Ibid., 2: 794–95.
[98] Ibid., 1: iv; 2: 567.

and substance," their steady growth and development had gradually turned them into "a real and great benefit, the means of employing, increasing, and enriching their fellow-subjects at home." By the 1760s, Anderson reported, the colonies had "at length become an immense market for our woolens, linens, and metallic manufactures: for household furniture of all sorts, apparel, plate, pictures, jewels, books, armory, medicines, some material for buildings, toys, and other curiosities," while at the same time providing "rich returns" in a variety of products that could be substituted for goods formerly purchased from European rivals and used to stimulate new manufactures and new export trades. "The commerce we now carry on with our American plantations," he conjectured, "is so vast, as probably already to equal in quantity, and to exceed in profit, all the other commerce we have with the rest of the world," and, as colonial populations grew, that commerce was "incessantly increasing." Anderson estimated that the colonial trade, including the slave trade to Africa, provided work for "no less than one million of our own people at home" and "probably employ[ed] one thousand two hundred sail more of our own British shipping, and twenty thousand sailors." "In every view," he concluded, it was "easy to conceive how vastly profitable our plantations" had been "to us."[99]

Young made the same point even more emphatically in 1772: "What was the amount of manufacturing for trade before the discovery of America?" he asked rhetorically: "A mere trifle; sufficient to enrich and employ a few paltry Hanse-towns, a city of Antwerp, or a State of Genoa." Considering "the progress made since the event," the "trade of Europe before and since" and "the exportation of British, Dutch, French, and other manufactures, nine-tenths perhaps of which are consumed in America, or in Africa as a consequence of America," Young asked his readers to compare "the riches of Britain now and in the time of Queen Elizabeth." If "we examine the matter," he concluded, "we shall find the superiority of the latter times to the former, to be chiefly owing to the discovery of America."[100]

Writing in the same year, Thomas Mortimer, whose *The Elements of Commerce, Politics, and Finances* contained an extensive section "On Colonies," agreed that the colonies had been "a principal cause of enriching this nation." Encouraged by Elizabeth and James I, various adventurers, he explained, had "in the process of time . . . effected settlements in every part of the American world; which increased our shipping, extended our navigation, and" served as

one of the sources of that immense power and opulence which has enabled Great Britain, within these last twenty years, to establish a most formidable marine, to raise supplies for carrying on the most expensive wars; and yet, even in the midst of the vast operations of hostile enterprize, to extend and improve that commerce to which she is indebted for her national strength.

[99] Anderson, *An Historical and Chronological Deduction of the Origin of Commerce*, xlv–xlvi, xlix–l, liv–lv.
[100] Young, *Political Essays Concerning the Present State of the British Empire*, 466.

By serving as "an inexhaustible fund of riches and strength to the British Isles," the colonies, he concluded, had transformed England "from a little kingdom, of reknown only for valour and freedom," into "a mighty empire."[101]

Two years later, John Campbell wrote at length upon the same theme in his massive two-volume chorography. Like most earlier commercial writers, Campbell was impressed by the growth of the colonies and their contribution to Britain's economic development. Although he acknowledged that during the sixty years between the reigns of Elizabeth and Charles II the colonies had acquired such "Strength and Consistency" as to render "them of so much Consequence, and so justly an Object of national Concern" that they invited national action to channel their growing trade to the metropolis, Campbell thought that only over the subsequent century had "the Value, Utility, and Importance of the Colonies in respect to this island . . . been by the Evidence of Facts put beyond all Dispute." Supplying the settlers with "some of the Necessaries and many of the Conveniencies of Life from hence," he explained, echoing his predecessors stretching back to Child and Davenant, had turned out to be "a new and very great Source of Industry, which by affording Employment to Multitudes" had both stimulated population growth and contributed "to the Ease and Happiness of our People at Home." At the same time, he observed, "having a certain, constant, regular, and increasing Market for our Commodities" had "had a very visible Effect on almost every Branch of" Britain's "domestic Trade," while "the Returns" settlers made for British imports enabled metropolitan Britons, "after furnishing our Home Consumption, to manufacture and export immense Quantities of their Produce to other Countries," which was "a farther Addition to our Commerce, and swells not a little the Profit that arises from it." Moreover, by adding "amazingly" to the volume of shipping and the number of seamen, the colonial trade, he observed, using the languages of national security, maritime supremacy, and imperial grandeur, had also helped to increase Britain's naval power. That the colonies had "contributed greatly to increase our Industry, and of course our Riches, to extend the Commerce, to augment the Naval Power, and consequently to maintain the Grandeur and support the Prosperity of the Mother Country" seemed to Campbell "incontestably evident."[102]

Characteristically, Adam Smith in *The Wealth of Nations* operated from a broader perspective in his assessment of the contribution of overseas empire to national wealth. The discovery, not just of America, but "of the passage to the East Indies by the Cape of Good Hope" at the end of the fifteenth century, he announced in an extensive discussion of modern colonization, had turned out to be two of the "greatest and most important events recorded in the history of mankind." As a result of these discoveries, he observed, "two new worlds," each "of them much greater and more extensive than the old one," had been opened to European industry, providing "a new and inexhaustible market to

---

[101] Mortimer, *Elements of Commerce, Politics, and Finances*, 17, 21, 148.
[102] Campbell, *Political Survey of Britain*, 2: 564–65, 567.

all the commodities of Europe," giving rise "to new divisions of labour and improvements of art, which, in the narrow circle of ancient commerce, could never have taken place for want of a market to take off the greater part of their produce," and improving the "productive powers of labour . . . in all the different countries of Europe, and together with it the real wealth of its inhabitants." With these developments, he noted, Europeans had quickly "become the manufacturers for the numerous and thriving cultivators of America, and the carriers, and in some respects the manufacturers too, for almost all the nations of Asia, Africa, and America."[103]

Smith differed from many earlier commercial writers in his insistence that England had had an extensive commerce even before the colonial trades became "very considerable." Already by the mid seventeenth century, he observed, "England . . . was a great trading country," with a "mercantile capital" that "was very great and likely to become still greater and greater every day." But he did not deny that the nation's wealth had increased enormously as a result of its involvement in the imperial trades to India and America. Potentially, he thought the East Indies offered "a market both for the manufactures of Europe and for the gold and silver as well as for several other productions of America, greater and more extensive than both Europe and America put together," but he had to acknowledge that as of the mid-1770s Europe had "derived much less advantage from its commerce with the East Indies, than from that with America" and that the American trade had been "more advantageous to Great Britain than any other." No wonder that, as he reported, the "expectation of a rupture with the colonies" had "accordingly . . . struck the people of Great Britain with more terror than any ever felt for a Spanish armada, or a French invasion."[104]

Smith was not alone among contemporary commercial writers in his appreciation of the contribution of the East Indian trade to Britain's wealth. Only Young seemed to be uncertain about whether that trade had actually been beneficial. Anderson, Mortimer, and Campbell had all preceded Smith in pointing out that the East Indian trade had been, as Anderson put it, "a beneficial one for Great Britain."[105] They were quick to point out that the "Advantages arising from" that trade, as Campbell wrote, had been of "vast Importance" and "great Consequence . . . to Great Britain."[106] No less than Smith, however, they regarded it as far less significant in the expansion of national wealth than the American trade. The American colonies, wrote Mortimer, were "the primary sources of the maritime strength, riches, and prosperity of Great Britain," while the "East India factories" were only "the second efficient cause of her immense opulence."[107]

---

[103] Smith, *Wealth of Nations*, 1: 448; 2: 626–27.
[104] Ibid., 1: 448–49; 2: 597, 600, 605, 633.
[105] Anderson, *An Historical and Chronological Deduction of the Origin of Commerce*, lxi.
[106] Campbell, *Political Survey of Britain*, 2: 613, 623.
[107] Mortimer, *Elements of Commerce, Politics, and Finances*, 170.

For these post–Seven Years' War commercial writers, as for their predecessors earlier in the century, the empire's importance continued to reside primarily in the extensive commercial benefits it brought to metropolitan Britain. The opening of trade to the east had obviously been commercial from its beginnings, but, these writers suggested, so also had the colonization of America, which, as Campbell said, was the direct result of "the Idea of fixing Settlements in distant Countries for the Sake of Commerce." This orientation, as Campbell explained, had made the British Empire a most peculiar one. "Whereas other great Empires have been founded in Violence, and the Success of Armies," the British Empire had "been acquired and united to us" through "the Influence of Commerce and maritime Power" and "the Ties of mutual Interests and a reciprocal Communication of Benefits." Whereas from the circumstances of their foundation other empires had "carried in themselves the Seeds of their own Destruction from the natural Repugnance of human Nature to a slavish Subjection," the "Subjects of Britain wherever seated," in the home islands or in distant possessions, were "free."[108] It was as if, in Adam Smith's familiar formulation, the British had "found[ed] a great empire for the sole purpose of raising up a people of customers."[109] How could metropolitan Britons possibly refrain from fully embracing such a magnificent national achievement? At the same time, most analysts appreciated that the nation's trades to its vast overseas possessions and spheres of influence, in combination with the system of navigation laws that theoretically framed them, had, as the lawyer Thomas Parker phrased it in 1775 in his compendium of British maritime law, "had the greatest share in the foundation and support of" Britain's "naval power" and that the "safety of the state so much depends on this part of its strength" that any "interruption" to those trades, such as "the present unfortunate controversy with our colonies," might well "lay the foundation of a decrease in the demands for those manufactures, which are not only the support of the landed interest, but the first spring of the navigation act which furnishes so great a part of the strength of our marine."[110]

---

[108] Campbell, *Political Survey of Britain*, 1: iv; 2: 561.
[109] Smith, *Wealth of Nations*, 2: 613.
[110] Thomas Parker, *The Laws of Shipping and Insurance with a Digest of Adjudged Cases* (London, 1775), vi.

2

Outposts of "*Loose Vagrant People*"

The Language of Alterity in the Construction of Empire

I

During a House of Commons debate in November 1775 over what, in light of its army's misadventures in Massachusetts the previous spring, Britain should do to deal with colonial resistance to metropolitan authority, William Innes, M.P. for Ilchester, spoke at length in favor of strong coercive measures. Emphatically questioning whether the colonists were even "the offspring of Englishmen, and as such entitled to the privileges of Britons," he denounced them rather as a promiscuous "mixture of people" who consisted "not only . . . of English, Scots, and Irish, but also of French, Dutch, Germans innumerable, Indians, Africans, and a multitude of felons from this country." Few members of such a population, he insisted, could possibly have a legitimate claim to status as full Britons deserving of the rich inheritance and identity enjoyed by independent people in the home islands. Colonial Americans, he charged, had created and continued to live in societies that bore little resemblance to that of the home island, citing in particular the massive importation of enslaved Africans and the "despotic" exploitation of them. Societies thus drawing their very "sustenance from the very bosom of slavery," he declared, "surely [had] nothing in them similar to what prevails in Great Britain."[1]

In these remarks, Innes built upon a well-established, if diffuse, language of alterity that dated back to the earliest days of English overseas enterprise. In metropolitan Britain, the celebration of empire as an enormous stimulant to Britain's wealth and a major element in its international stature, and the conception of colonization as a noble enterprise to bring civilization to savage and rude new worlds had never been unqualified. If the colonies themselves had been an obvious boon to Britain, the settlers who inhabited them often seemed,

---

[1] William Innes, speech, November 8, 1775, in R. C. Simmons and P. D. G. Thomas, eds., *Proceedings and Debates of the British Parliaments Respecting North America 1754–1783*, 6 vols. (White Plains, N.Y.: Kraus, 1982–86), 6: 203.

to people who remained at home, far less worthy of praise. The discourses of empire that took shape in the late seventeenth and early eighteenth centuries often involved expressions of a heavy-handed skepticism about the character of the settlers who inhabited the plantations and the character of the societies that they created. From very early on, a significant strand of metropolitan imperial thought used what modern analysts would call the language of alterity or otherness to depict the colonies as receptacles for those who had failed at home: the poor, the unemployed, the unwanted, the outcasts, the very dregs of English society. Throughout the seventeenth and eighteenth centuries, this widely circulated language ran as a strong undercurrent in metropolitan conceptions of empire. The colonial process thus involved not just enlightening encounters with indigenous and imported others but also the creation of an entirely new category of others into which colonial participants could be lumped and thereby distinguished from the more successful and refined populations of the metropolis.[2]

While by no means universal, this unfavorable image of colonials and the social spaces they created was ubiquitous in British publications – in commercial tracts, critiques of colonial slavery, imperial histories, travel memoirs, fake chorographies, novels, poetry, plays, magazine and newspaper essays, political pamphlets, and parliamentary speeches. Rooted in a conviction that no one would leave England unless compelled to, this image stressed the lowly social origins of migrants and their religious and social deviancy. Furthermore, the malignant and distinctly non-English places that colonials chose to settle, sharing the wilderness with uncivil, savage peoples, and the questionable societies created in the process, seemed to put these overseas English people in a separate and inferior category. With little learning or religion (or a deviant form thereof), and with few of the other cultural amenities of English life, colonial societies were so crude that cultural degeneration over the generations, not a few metropolitans thought, was inevitable, especially when most colonial populations had started from such a low base. Moreover, their lowly origins, unsavory characters, and narrow pursuit of economic gain, metropolitans charged, produced societies deeply dissimilar to what they had left behind, societies characterized by vicious labor systems, sharp business practices, and legal regimes that catered to the self-interest of the dominant socioeconomic groups, subverted metropolitan efforts to regulate them, and showed little concern for traditional English social mores. These provided metropolitans a

---

[2] Although this chapter concentrates on metropolitan attitudes toward American colonials, Irish colonists got much the same treatment. See David Hayton, "From Barbarian to Burlesque: English Images of the Irish c.1660–1750," *Irish Economic and Social History*, 15 (1988): 5–31. For a perceptive study of the English/British encounter with the non-European worlds of others, see P. J. Marshall and Glyndwr Williams, *The Great Map of Mankind: Perceptions of New Worlds in the Age of the Enlightenment* (Cambridge, Mass.: Harvard University Press, 1982). Martin Daunton and Rick Halpern, eds., *Empire and Others: British Encounters with Indigenous Peoples, 1600–1850* (Philadelphia: University of Pennsylvania Press, 1999), is a collection of illuminating case studies on this subject.

sturdy foundation on which to construct a language of alterity. Less harsh than the well-developed languages of savagery and barbarity that were only occasionally applied to the colonies and less comprehensively exclusive than the language of alienization used to identify foreigners, this language lacked a contemporary name to encompass all of the many elements that combined to form a language of social derision or condescension that expressed metropolitan misgivings about the genuine Englishness of England's overseas offshoots and at every level deeply affected metropolitan-colonial relations.

II

The stereotype of the colonies as receptacles for those who had failed at home was already deeply entrenched by the middle of the seventeenth century. A visitor's report about Barbados, then England's most economically successful colony, was typical. That island, wrote Henry Whistler, a member of the expedition to capture Spanish possessions in 1654, "is the Dunghill whareon England doth cast forth its rubidg[e]: Rodg[ue]s and [w]hor[e]s and such like peopel are those which are generally Brought heare. A rodg[u]e in England will hardly make a cheater heare," he wrote in treating the islanders as little more than an agglomeration of social pariahs who had taken advantage of the loose texture of new societies to advance their social standing, so that "a Baud brought over puts one a demuor comportment, a whore if han[d]sume makes a wife for sume rich planter."[3]

By the early 1690s, when the economic writer Sir Josiah Child took up the subject in some detail, this stereotype was commonplace. Child was interested in countering the argument, then circulating around the metropolis, that colonial expansion weakened England's productive capacities, and in arguing that colonial migration had made it possible for many unproductive people in England both to save their lives and to contribute to the economic well-being of the nation, he elaborated in some detail upon the view that colonists scarcely came from the cream of old English society. Rather, he wrote, most of the colonies, singling out Virginia and Barbados as examples, had been

first peopled by a sort of loose vagrant People, vicious and destitute of the means to live at home (being either unfit for labour, or such as could find none to employ themselves about, or had so misbehaved themselves by whoring, thieving, or other debauchery, that none would set them on work), which Merchants and Masters of Ships, by their Agents, or Spirits, (as they were called) gathered up about the Streets of London, and other places, cloathed and transported to be employed upon Plantations.

"Had there been no English foreign Plantations in the World," Child contended, such people "could probably never have lived at home to do service for their Country, but must have been hanged, or starved, or died untimely

---

[3] "Extracts from Henry Whistler's Journal of the West India Expedition," 1654, in C. H. Firth, ed., *The Narrative of General Venables* (London, 1900), 146.

of some of those miserable diseases, that proceed from want and vice; or else have sold themselves for soldiers, to be knocked on the head, or starved, in the quarrels of our neighbors."[4]

Nor, in Child's view, were subsequent emigrants to the colonies of much higher social standing. He admitted that after the Civil War, some people of a better sort on the losing side, "having been deprived of their estates" and never having "been bred to labour" or "made unfit for it by the lazy habit of a soldier's life," "betook themselves to . . . Plantations" and that a similar exodus on the other side occurred in the wake of the Restoration, when those who had fought against the Crown suddenly found themselves dispossessed of their estates, "impoverished and destitute of employment" and without any "way of living at home," as well as those "who feared the re-establishment of the ecclesiastical laws, under which they could not live" and thus had "to transport themselves, or sell themselves for a few years, to be transported by others to foreign English Plantations." But Child insisted that

the constant supply that the said Plantations have since had, has been by such loose vagrant people, as I before described, picked up, especially about the streets and suburbs of London and Westminster, and by Malefactors condemned for crimes, for which by the law they deserved to die; and some of those people called Quakers, banished for meeting on pretence of religious worship.[5]

Champions of the colonies labored to counter this image of the origins of their settler populations and the use of the language of otherness to characterize them. As residents of England's most densely populated and wealthiest seventeenth-century American colony, Barbadians and their supporters in England were especially sensitive to such negative characterizations. Thus did the anonymous author of a 1666 history of the English settlements in the West Indies adamantly deny that the early settlers "consist[ed] only of a sort of Vagabonds and persons of mean condition, as some fondly imagine[d]" in England. This author admitted "that, in peopling those Plantations, many persons of obscure Births and very indifferent Characters went, or were, from time to time, sent and transported thither, as Occasion required." But he insisted that "some thousands of Persons of very creditable Families, good Education, and loyal Principles, went thither likewise; some through Narrowness of their Circumstances; some to avoid the Miseries of the Civil War at home; and others to improve such paternal or acquired Fortunes and Estates, as they thought convenient to carry along with them, at the time." Following the success of sugar culture in the mid seventeenth century, he claimed, Barbados in particular had "tempted [many] Gentlemen of good Families and moderate Estates" to migrate to the colony.[6]

---

4 Sir Josiah Child, *A New Discourse of Trade*, 4th ed. (London, 1695), 197–98.
5 Ibid., 198–99.
6 J. Davies, comp., *The History of Barbados, St. Christopher, Mevis . . . and the Rest of the Caribby-Islands* (London, 1666), dedication pages, 198–99; *The Groans of Jamaica Express'd in a Letter from a Gentleman Residing There, to His Friend in London* (London, 1714), v.

Similarly, the Virginia planter Robert Beverley addressed Child's remarks directly in *The History and Present State of Virginia*, published in London in 1705, one of the earliest and most substantial efforts by a colonial to write a civil history of one of England's American plantations for metropolitan readers. Beverley granted Childs' point that "at first" the plantations were "for the most part . . . peopled by Persons of low Circumstances, and by such as were willing to seek their Fortunes in a Foreign Country" and acknowledged that no person who "cou'd live easy in *England*" or had there a "plentifull Estate" would "voluntarily abandon a happy Certainty, to roam after imaginary Advantages in a New World" and confront "the infinite Difficulties and Dangers, that attend[ed] a New Settlement." For those reasons, the earliest settlers of Virginia were "chiefly single men" and began to seek wives only after "they were set[t]led there in a comfortable way of Subsisting a Family." But he insisted that once a regular constitution had been "firmly established" and "after the advantages of the Climate, and the fruitfulness of the Soil were well known, and all the dangers incident to Infant Settlement were over, People of better Condition retir'd thither with their Families, either to increase the Estates they had before, or else to avoid being persecuted for their Principles of Religion, or Government," including many "good Cavalier Families" who "went thither with their Effects to escape the Tyranny of the Usurper" during the Civil War and, following the Restoration, a few people of the "opposite Party" who sought refuge in Virginia "from the King's Resentment." Surely, Beverley suggested, people of this stamp did not deserve to be regarded as outcasts or others or derided for their lowly English origins. And he was careful to point out that Virginia had "always receiv'd very few" criminals or "malefactors condemn'd to Transportation," insisting that Virginia's laws had "been severe against them."[7]

III

But it was not just the suspect origins of the colonists that contributed to their poor reputation in England. While promotional writers hailed the colonies as inviting places of opportunity, and while chorographers and historians such as Beverley reported on their steady development as improved and anglicized social and political spaces, other writers, employing a variety of other genres, limned portraits of them as societies so oriented toward the pursuit of economic gain as to be viciously exploitative of all dependent peoples and barren of most traditional amenities of metropolitan English life. The callous mistreatment of servants and slaves was a prevalent theme. From the experiences of Marcellus Rivers and Oxenbridge Foyle, two men who were accused of royalism and rebellion and shipped to Barbados for sale as servants in the mid-1650s and who published a tract in 1659, English readers could learn that Barbadian planters were the "most inhuman and barbarous persons," who worked their

[7] Robert Beverley, *The History and Present State of Virginia*, ed. Louis B. Wright (Chapel Hill: University of North Carolina Press, 1947), 58, 286–88.

servants hard, fed them meagerly, and in general reduced them to the "most deplorable, and (as to Englishmen)... unparalleled condition" in which they were "bought and sold... from one planter to another, or attached as horses and beasts for the debts of their masters,... whipped at the whipping-posts (as rogues) for their masters' pleasures," forced to sleep "in sties worse than hogs in England, and [in] many other ways made miserable, beyond expression of Christian imagination."[8]

If Christians had to endure such a harsh labor regime, the enslaved Africans who after 1650 comprised a steadily growing share of the labor force, first in Barbados and the other West Indian colonies and then on the mainland in Virginia, Maryland, and the Carolinas, reportedly fared even worse. For a small but highly vocal group of critics writing between 1670 and 1710, the system of chattel slavery that was developing in the colonies and the social and cultural systems that supported it constituted Exhibit A in an emerging portrait of the colonies as places of cultural regress and social deviation from English norms. The Puritan devotional writer Richard Baxter inaugurated this barrage with a brief section in his monumental *Christian Directory*, published in London in 1673. The lack of any first-hand experience in America did not deter Baxter from denouncing the slave trade as a form of piracy and American planters who used the enslaved "as beasts for their meer commodity" as "fitter to be called incarnate Devils, than Christians." Slave-owning colonists might "vilifie" those they were enslaving "as Savages and barbarous wretches," but, Baxter observed, nothing was "more savage, than to use... men[']s bodies as beasts" and "their souls, as if they were made for nothing, but to actuate their bodies in your worldly drudgery."[9] To attack their credentials as Christians and to decry them as savages was, of course, to question the quality of their Englishness.

By contrast, the Anglican minister Morgan Godwyn had lived in both Virginia and Barbados for extended periods before publishing a series of substantial works criticizing the societies taking shape in the West Indies and Virginia.[10] Godwyn was careful not to challenge the legality of slavery, his principal concerns being to awaken the consciences of American slaveholders

---

[8] Marcellus Rivers and Oxenbridge Foyle, *England's Slavery, or Barbados Merchandize* (London, 1659), 1–7.

[9] Richard Baxter, *A Christian Directory, or, A Summ of Practical Theologie and Cases of Conscience*... (London, 1673), 558–59.

[10] Morgan Godwyn, *The Negro's and Indian's Advocate* (London, 1680); idem, *A Supplement to the Negro's [and] Indian's Advocate* (London, 1681); idem, *Trade prefer'd before Religion and Christ made to give place to Mammon represented in a sermon relating to the plantations* (London, 1685); idem, "A Brief Account of Religion, in the Plantations, with the Causes of the Neglect and Decay thereof in those Parts," in Francis Brokesby, ed., *Some Proposals towards Promoting of the Gospel in our American Plantations* (London, 1708). Citations here are to the second edition, published in the same year. The most perceptive analysis of Morgan's writings is Alden T. Vaughan, "Slaveholders' 'Hellish Principles': A Seventeenth-Century Critique," in Vaughan, *Roots of American Racism: Essays on the Colonial Experience* (Oxford: Oxford University Press, 1995), 55–81.

to the harsh usage that the enslaved endured on the plantations, to persuade slave owners that the enslaved could be instructed in Christianity and converted without material prejudice to their property interests and without subverting colonial societies, and to alert metropolitan readers to the disturbing character of the societies that were taking shape in the English slave colonies.

Godwyn did not scruple to "lay open to the view of the World" what he called the "*mystery of Iniquity*" embedded in the form it had taken in the West Indies. Applying the contemporary language of humanity as a standard for assessing colonial societies, he contended that the planters treated "their Slaves with far less Humanity than they do their *Cattel*" or horses and spelled out many "other *Inhumanities*" and "unmerciful Correction[s]" that they visited upon their slaves in the name of discipline. To Morgan, such practices constituted "a reproach to Humanity" and turned the colonies into nothing less "than the *Devil's Mint*, purposely designed for the *murthering* of Souls." Even more shocking, he reported that planters remained entirely "unashamed at the committing these Abominations," instead justifying their cruelties on the grounds that "*Negro's were Beasts, and had no more Souls than Beasts, and that [the enslaved's] Religion did not concern*" the planters, who went to the colonies "*not... to save Souls, or propagate Religion, but to get Money*" – an attitude, Morgan declared, that was founded on "Hellish Principles" and, he lamented, precisely captured the very "*sense and opinion of the [entire] place.*"[11]

That this ethos had produced in the Americas monstrous distortions of English society, Godwyn was certain. Whereas God had been "pleased to discover unto us, and possess us of those many rich and fruitful Countries," English settlers had impiously repaid Him not by "spreading the Gospel amongst the first Inhabitants and Natives there" or among the heathen Africans they imported to labor for them but by creating societies in which "every one" was "given to Covetousness," economic interests invariably came first, and religion and education "had to be contented with such favours and kindnesses, as the Devil and Mammon shall at last please to afford her." By subordinating religion to trade, West Indians, he charged, had effectively made religion "a Patroness of the grossest Immanities, for filthy Lucre." By neglecting schools, they were heedlessly creating conditions that would eventually reduce even the settler population to a degree of "*Barbarity*" not far above that displayed by the enslaved, whom they deliberately kept in the dark in regard to the rules of civilized and Christian behavior.[12]

Indeed, in the fraternization between the free and the enslaved Godwyn found evidence to suggest that Christians were already being barbarized. They not only permitted but participated in "all manner of Licentiousness" carried

---

[11]   Godwyn, *Negro's and Indians Advocate*, 39–41; idem, *Supplement*, 10; idem, *Trade preserv'd before Religion*, 15, 24; idem, "Brief Account of Religion," 3.

[12]   Godwyn, *Trade preserv'd before Religion*, 16–18, 21, 23; idem, *Negro's and Indians Advocate*, 2–3 137, 154, 156, 160; idem, *Supplement*, 5.

on by their slaves, especially the "*Idolatrous Dances* and Revels... with other such *Recreations* and *Customs*, by them brought out of *Africa.*" Even more disturbing, the presence of many mulattos, "whose Parents on the one side" were "*English*," was only the most visible sign of the contamination of the English population by what Godwyn referred to as "those *Debouches*" with enslaved women that masters and other free men, in "slavery to" their own "*Lusts*," did "so frequently... make use of... for their *unnatural* Pleasures."[13]

Godwyn was somewhat less critical of Virginia, which he complimented for having advanced from its "*Infancy* and *Non-Age*" to the point where it was "now almost grown adult," but he found that in many respects it still fell far short of English standards. He was especially disturbed by the fraudulent methods, including kidnaping, used to lure people to Virginia, where many were then "miserably destroyed" by hard labor and by settler failure either to promote Christianity "amongst the *Heathen*, both *Natives* and *Slaves* also brought from other parts" or to support religion even among the English. While parishes stretched over vast distances, many of them were vacant or presided over by unqualified laymen or unordained clergymen, and the settlers so scattered over the countryside that few people had access to church service. Even worse, the few qualified ministers in the colony lived a precarious existence, being "most miserably handled by their *Plebian Junto's*, the *Vestries*," which had absolute control over the terms and conditions of their appointment and which, not being legally obliged to appoint one, often "either resolve[d] to have *none at all*, or reduce[d] them to their own *Terms*; that is, to *use them how they please*, pay them *what they list* and to *discard* them *whensoever they have a mind to it*." In a word, Godwyn declared, "all things that concern the *Church* and *Religion*" in Virginia were left "to the Mercy of the People," who had little interest in devoting much of their resources to religious matters. These conditions, Godwyn claimed, betrayed not merely "the great Neglect" but also the total "contempt of *Religion*" in Virginia. The situation in Virginia, Godwyn subsequently wrote, was emblematic of the rest of the colonies, "both Islands and Places upon the Continent," where "there is almost an Universal Declension of Christianity, and a Decay of all Religion" and where in some places it seemed to have been totally "laid Aside."[14]

Godwyn was aware that these many deviations from English norms would "*seem strange to people in* England," but he noted that English immigrants adapted to them every bit as quickly as they did to the hot climate. In "a short time after their setting foot in Barbados," he said, they "discover[ed] a very discernible alteration, not only from *those at home*, but from *themselves* also as to what they were at their first arrival." If, moreover, "*the same Persons going thither*" were so "*suddenly changed*," they became so used to the changes so quickly that they made "*nothing of it*," displaying no shame and dismissing all

[13] Godwyn, *Negro's and Indians Advocate*, 30, 37, 39–40, 142, 144, 146; idem, "Brief Account of Religion," 3.
[14] Godwyn, *Negro's and Indians Advocate*, 167–72; idem, "Brief Account of Religion," 1, 3.

criticism as blatant "*Calumny* and *Slander*." Yet, if their practice and opinions were known to the outside world, Godwyn was persuaded that they would be "*ashamed to own [them] amongst better People*," and, given their "extraordinary Ambition to be thought well of" in England, he hoped that exposing their deviations in the metropolis and getting them "decryed here" might eventually "shame them into better Principles."[15]

Noting that the metropolitan English were "wholly blind and in the dark, as to Affairs" in the colonies, Godwyn had sought in his early pamphlets to enlighten them. Notwithstanding his efforts, he complained in his 1685 sermon, "no one" in England "hath hardly ever yet opened his Mouth" against colonial labor practices and religious policies. "Our profound Silence," he declared, was "no better than a constructive approbation; and our Connivance a consenting thereto," evidence, he suggested, that seemed to indicate that metropolitan English people, as well as West Indians, were "Zealous of Trade and Gain, but not of good Works." By overlooking the social and religious transgressions of overseas colonies in the interest of the profits they brought to England, the metropolitan English, Godwyn declared, had joined plantation societies in "a confederacy with Hell itself," and he called upon metropolitans to recognize that colonial societies were "a reproach and dishonour to the *English* Nation, and Government" and to join in measures that would force them into social behavior more compatible with English and Christian norms.[16]

Also during the 1680s, the tradesman, merchant, and social reformer Thomas Tryon, who resided in Barbados through most of the late 1660s, added considerable weight to Godwyn's depiction of the colonies as places of social and cultural regress.[17] Indeed, in the first of three tracts he published on the colonies, Tryon implicitly used Barbados and the other older colonies as a model for what the new colonies in Pennsylvania and New Jersey should *not* become and thereby helped to reinforce the negative image of the American plantations in metropolitan English eyes. The existing plantations, Tryon declared, were replete with many "odious Examples of . . . all kinds of Debauchery continually committed with greediness." The vicious habits of the settlers, he reported, had made them "Brutish, Sottish and Ignorant, even like *Swine*." Instead of shaping their societies to promote virtue and happiness and to bring the enslaved "to a state of *Civility*," they had done precisely the opposite, and the results were depraved societies characterized by "perpetual Crimes, Confusions and Disorders." Nor was it only the West Indian colonies that exhibited such features; even New England, which Baxter and Godwyn had treated as an

---

[15] Godwyn, *Negro's and Indians Advocate*, 13, 22, 39–40; idem, *Supplement*, 8.

[16] Godwyn, *Supplement*, 6; idem, *Trade preserv'd before Religion*, 7, 19, 21, 23, 25–26; idem, *Negro's and Indians Advocate*, 160.

[17] Philippe Rosenberg, "Thomas Tryon and the Seventeenth-Century Dimensions of Antislavery," *William and Mary Quarterly*, 3d ser., 61 (2004): 609–42, provides the fullest analysis of Tryon's writings on the colonies.

exception to the disordered political societies in America, had recently, Tryon wrote, had many of the "same Inconvenience[s]" befall it.[18]

In two additional writings, Tryon spelled out what he meant when he accused overseas English colonists of "Crimes, Confusions and Disorders." He did not deny that the English had, in the short space of sixty or seventy years, "settled many great Collonies and Plantations [in America], as *New England, Jamaica*, the Island of *Barbadoes, Virginia*, &c," nor that the "natural goodness" of its soil and the "extraordinary Diligence and Industry of the Planters" and their slaves had made Barbados "the chief of them" all. Yet the view he imparted throughout his writings made clear that these achievements had been built on a brutal labor regime. If a few planters were "Just and Merciful" in their treatment of their enslaved laborers, they were the exception that proved the rule, and the societies they were creating in America, according to Tryon, were a veritable "Babel" of vice and discord that thoroughly justified the "black Character of Oppression and Violence" the "Plantations do now lye under" and the use of the language of social denigration or otherness to describe them.[19]

Through African voices, Tryon explored both the severity of the colonial system of enslavement and its many deleterious effects upon settlers and the societies they were creating. Thus, without the social stigma that would have befallen exhibitions of such conduct in England itself, did colonial masters treat the enslaved with such "violent Oppressions, and hard Usages" that they died in great numbers, without reproducing themselves. As Tryon emphasized, this "vast Consumption" of the enslaved effectively rendered them a human sacrifice to the planter's greed and turned colonial societies into "cruel and inhumane" entities. The callous treatment of the enslaved was only the most flagrant violation of English – and Christian – norms. Drawing upon his experience in Barbados, Tryon portrayed the colonies as social quagmires in which a self-indulgent population of independent masters wallowed in excess on the produce of their laborers and lived in constant strife with one another, where settlers endeavored "to out-try and exceed each other, meerly for State, Pride, and vain Glory, and to be honoured of men," where families were "plagued with Vexations and Discords between Man and Wife, and with disobedient and rebellious Children" so willful that parents could neither "rule nor keep them in Order," where even the women would "Swagger and Curse, and Rant" at their servants, and children got only "loose and extravagant Education[s]."[20]

[18] Thomas Tryon, *The Planter's Speech To His Neighbours & Country-Men of Pennsylvania, East & West Jersey* (London, 1684), 6–9, 14–15.

[19] Thomas Tryon, Friendly Advice to the Gentleman Planters of the East and West Indies (London, 1684), 75, 136, 140, 142; idem, *Tryon's Letters, Domestick and Foreign* (London, 1700), 186–88.

[20] Tryon, *Friendly Advice*, 93, 123–25, 136–37, 142–45, 165–66, 170–72, 200, 209; idem, *Tryon's Letters*, 184, 187, 195, 199–200.

Nor was it only in family and social relations that colonial societies deviated sharply from metropolitan standards. In Tryon's words, the mere presence of so many slave women threw "open the Gates of Venus to many lewd Practices," as masters and white managers, evidently unable to resist the temptation "to gratifie their raging Lusts" by taking the wives and daughters of slaves for concubines, came to regard such adulteries as "no greater a Crime... than Fornication, & both of them but Venial Sins, Tricks of Youth, or Modish Gallantries," in the process "beget[ting] mungril Children, that are neither White nor Black, but between both, which therefore are called Molatto's." This "brutish Uncleanness, Adulteries, Whoredoms, &c." was so common, even among the "better sort" of planters, that, Tryon reported, those who engaged in it openly gloried in it and regarded chastity as "an object of... Scorn and Derision." For Tryon, the most offensive result of this sexual commerce was that fathers showed no "natural Affection" for "their own Seed" and routinely consigned them and their posterity to perpetual slavery. The "vile hard hearted Wretches" who would do such things, not the enslaved over whom they ruled, Tryon thus implied, were the true beasts – the true others – in the colonial equation.[21]

In short, according to Tryon, the plantations, especially in the West Indian and other colonies using substantial amounts of slave labor, had generated societies that were out of control and with cultural and moral standards that were well outside the bounds of English norms. In his words, as expressed through the voice of his enslaved character, white colonists lived and "walk[ed]... wide from, and contrary" to the "Christian Spirit." If the original settlers, as conventional metropolitan images had long suggested, had been people of low social origins and "small Stocks," some of their descendants had "grown wonderfully rich," but they had not improved their characters along with their fortunes, and, as presented in the works of Morgan and Tryon, the societies they had built did nothing to alter metropolitan conceptions of colonists as the dregs of English society. At the close of the seventeenth century, many metropolitans yet held, in Tryon's words, "but an indifferent Opinion of those Settlements" and the people who inhabited them.[22]

A few early eighteenth-century tracts objecting to aspects of the slave systems in the American colonies also provided support for such opinions in the metropolis. An anonymous writer who identified himself as a merchant trading to Jamaica provided the most scathing indictment of Jamaican society in *A Letter from a Merchant at Jamaica To a Member of Parliament in London, Touching the African Trade*, published in London in 1709. Calling for the British Parliament to override the self-interested "Laws of particular Societys" in America and to substitute a system of justice and humanity for the "rotten

[21] Tryon, *Friendly Advice*, 128–29, 140, 164, 177.
[22] Ibid., 122, 160; idem, *Tryon's Letters*, 188, 192.

Foundations" on which colonial slave societies had been built, he anticipated most of the objections antislavery writers would make later in the century, challenged the legality of purchasing the enslaved, and questioned the humanity, civility, and Englishness of free Jamaican settlers. Slave owners might "call themselves *Men, good-natur'd Men* and *Christians*," he wrote, but, "forgetting all Humanity," they had devised modes of punishment that "were as endless as what *Avarice* and *Iniquity* can suggest, or what the Caprice and *Cruelty* of Men *bounded by no* Fences of *human Law*, can invent and execute." Indeed, he strongly implied that in the slave colonies, Europeans, not Africans, were the ones who displayed base and brutal natures and that the system of slavery in the New World represented a reversion to earlier and less civilized norms. If in the modern world only "barbarous Nations" still sold captives as slaves, what could be said of the people who traded in and owned them or of the societies that the enslaved sustained?²³

Five years earlier, in a March 1704 sermon arguing that both Christianity and English law were compatible with servitude and assuring colonial slaveholders that conversion would not deprive them of the services of the enslaved, the Reverend Anthony Hall, a lecturer at Stratford-le-Bow in Middesex, similarly denounced the colonial practice of treating the enslaved "like Creatures of an Inferior Order, and" using "them no better than . . . *Beasts*." He condemned this practice as "a lamentable way of growing Rich" and deplored the settlers' failure to evangelize the enslaved as a blatant example of their feeding upon the "Souls of Men," a sin to which "No Circumvention, no Rapine, no Barbarity" could "come up to," a sin that made the settlers "the worst sort of Cannibals."²⁴

Hall's sermon inspired Bernard Mandeville, the Dutch social commentator who resided in London for much of his adult life, to write a short admonitory poem that he published in London in 1704 under the ironic title *The Planter's Charity.* Expressing his distaste at "*the Miserable Condition of those Heathen Wretches, that being captivated in Africa, are hurried up and down the World, and sold to cultivate the American and other Plantations*" and are there "*being used both in their Labour and Diet, like so many Heads of Cattle,*" Mandeville, in this effort, sought to condemn the existing system of slavery, "*rouse the Conscience[s]*" of American planters, and expose the shallowness and self-serving character of their rationalizations for depriving the enslaved of access

---

²³ *A Letter from a Merchant at Jamaica To a Member of Parliament in London, Touching the African Trade; To which is added, A Speech made by a Black of Gardaloupe at the Funeral of a Fellow-Negro* (London, 1709), 4, 9–14, 23, 25, 27, 29–31. For further discussion of this pamphlet see Jack P. Greene, "'A Plain and Natural Right to Life and Liberty': An Early Natural Rights Attack on the Excesses of the Slave System in Colonial British America," *William and Mary Quarterly*, 3d ser., 57 (2000), 793–808, which reprints the pamphlet in full.
²⁴ Anthony Hill, *Afer Baptizatus: or, the Negro turnn'd Christian* (London, 1704), dedication, 31, 39–40, 42–43.

to Christian teachings. At bottom, he charged, planters were motivated by nothing more than the fear of "the loss of Right and Estate":

> The Estate is the Concern, tho' you would hide
> Your Thoughts, and deck your Avarice and Pride
> With *Right* and *Lawfulness*, the poor Pretext
> That may serve in this World, not in the next.
> How dares a *Christian* make the Impious Plea,
> For robbing Christ to feed his Luxury.[25]

At the same time that they condemned the excesses of the colonial slave system, all these early eighteenth-century commentators on American slavery appreciated, in the words of Mandeville, the "*vast Benefit which* Europe, *but more especially* England, *receives from*" the plantations and granted the validity of settler claims about "*the impossibility of maintaining 'em without the Hands of those* Unhappy Savages." In consideration of the economic benefits of the American staple colonies, even those metropolitans who abhorred slavery thus seemed slowly to be coming to terms with it during the early decades of the eighteenth century. If, however, writers of Mandeville's generation accepted the economic utility of colonial slavery, they emphatically did not exempt slave owners and their societies from condemnation as deviants from English social norms.[26]

As slavery became ever more entrenched in the American colonies and the slave trade ever more voluminous and profitable to Britain during the first half of the eighteenth century, overt criticism of slavery and American slave societies became more muted in metropolitan Britain. But the conception of the plantations as places of exceptional cruelty and of the Europeans who presided over them as a category of others was kept alive by the repetition of the touching story of Inkle and Yarico, first told by Richard Ligon, a visitor to Barbados, in his *A True and Exact History of the Island of Barbados*, published in London in 1657,[27] and repeated and substantially elaborated by the Irish writer Richard Steele in *The Spectator* in 1711. In this story, Thomas Inkle, a young Englishmen on his way to Barbados "to improve his Fortune by Trade and Merchandize," escaped an Indian ambush "on the Main of *America*" and subsequently received shelter, sustenance, and affection from Yariko, a young Indian maiden "of Distinction." The two of them fell deeply in love, with Inkle proposing to take Yariko off to England to lead a civilized life with him, and when they finally managed to hail an English ship, Yariko willingly accompanied him to Barbados, where Inkle, a young man bred up on "an early Love of Gain" and worried about the monetary losses he had sustained during his long stay with Yarico, betrayed his lover and, despite the fact that she was pregnant, sold her to a Barbadian merchant as a slave.[28] In the 1720s, the poet

[25] Bernard Mandeville, *The Planter's Charity* (London, 1704), 2–3, 5–7.
[26] Ibid., 2.
[27] Richard Ligon, *A True and Faithful History of the Island of Barbadoes* (London, 1757), 55.
[28] Richard Steele, *The Spectator*, #11 (March 13, 1711).

Frances Seymour kept this story alive with her two short poems "The Story of Inkle and Yarico," and "An Epistle from Yarico to Inkle after he had left her in Slavery," the first of which was published in *The New Miscellany* in 1726 and both together in 1738.[29]

As the popularity of this story reveals, metropolitan unease with chattel slavery in the empire never disappeared and could be easily reanimated, as happened in 1735, when during the first set of Maroon Wars in Jamaica an anonymous speech purportedly written by Moses Bon Sàam, identified as a learned Jamaica Maroon, appeared in several London magazines. A powerful call for slave resistance, this speech revived images of American planters as cruel and "insolent *Enslavers*" who lived in pomp and wantonness on the sweat of the enslaved, whom they kept as "darkly ignorant" as possible.[30]

Reverend Robert Robertson, a longtime resident of Nevis, produced the most extensive response to Sàam. In *The Speech of Mr. John Campo-bell, a Free Christian-Negro, to His Countrymen in the Mountains of Jamaica*, published in London in 1736, he used the persona of Campo-bell to provide a history of the rise and perpetuation of African slavery in the broader Atlantic world, his principal goal being to show that if slavery was an evil, it was a national evil, and not just a colonial one. No defender of the slave trade or slavery, he acknowledged that the slave system within the colonies, which he thought had become less cruel over time, and the structures that supported it were characterized by many undesirable social and moral results. Indeed, he wrote, "the Nature and Circumstances of this Trade throughout, the Maxims of Interest on which the whole of it is founded, how the principal Nations professing Christianity are one way or other embarked in it, the many Lives it destroys, and the little Care that is or can be taken of" the enslaved's "Souls" made it clear that "very few such Pieces of Wickedness have ever been acted on the Face of the Earth." But he denied that responsibility for slavery could be laid entirely at the door of the American planters who bought and used slaves. Rather, he insisted, African traders, British traders, and the British government, which had done nothing to discourage such a profitable trade, were all equally culpable.[31]

Robertson was aware that some people in Britain opposed slavery on both religious and legal grounds. But, he asked, why, if the English were "Enemies

---

[29] Frances Seymour, "The Story of Inkle and Yarico" (1726) and "An Epistle from Yarico to Inkle, After he had left her in Slavery" (1738), as reprinted in Thomas W. Krise, ed., *Caribbeana: An Anthology of English Literature of the West Indies 1657–1777* (Chicago: University of Chicago Press, 1999), 141–46. Krise usefully provides a publishing history of these poems. On the frequent repetition of this story in British prose throughout the eighteenth century, see Wylie Sypher, *Guinea's Captive Kings* (Chapel Hill: University of North Carolina Press, 1942), 122–37.

[30] "The Speech of Moses Bon Sàam," 1735, as reprinted in Krise, ed., *Caribbeana*, 101–07. Krise provides a succinct publishing history of this piece.

[31] Robert Robertson, *The Speech of Mr. John Campo-bell, A Free Christian-Negro, to His Countrymen in the Mountains of Jamaica* (London, 1736), 72–73.

to *Slavery*," Britain would "*protect and encourage the Slave-Trade?*" and why the metropolitan government would take no measures questioning "the Justice of Legality of the Trade itself"? Noting that other European and Christian nations were just as "deep, and some of them deeper in" the employment and trade in slaves without showing any of the scruples displayed by the English, Robertson also raised the question of why English people were so anxious about it. Robertson found an answer to his last question in "the Spirit of *Liberty*" that ran so "high in *England*," and this spirit, he observed through Campo-Bell, meant that, relative to other nationals, Britons were more anxious about their involvement with slavery. If, however, Britons were "certainly one of the freest People in the World," and "*Liberty*" was "so much their *Darling*, and *Slavery* so much their *Dread*," why, Robertson asked through the words of Campo-bell, would "it join with Countries whom they call *Slavish* and *Tyrannical*, in" enslaving Africans? "Or, admitting them to have done it at first incautiously," he continued, "What had hinder'd them, for above Seventy Years together, from contriving a Retreat, or so much as once at some Project or Expedient of a Cure? To fall into an Error," he observed, "is consistent enough with Humanity, but to persist in it after Conviction, or to shun the Means of Conviction is not so." Such behavior, he said, could only be explained by Britain's unwillingness to relinquish its "Share of the Profits" from the slave trade.[32]

What annoyed Robertson was that, notwithstanding metropolitan Britain's complicity in the imperial system of slavery, "the Part" American planters had taken in its development had "brought, and daily brings them under the severest Censure in *England*," where, as he complained in another publication six years later, they were invariably stigmatized "as *Enemies* to the *Negroes, Oppressors, ungrateful* and *merciless Masters, insolent Enslavers, imperious Torturers, Insulters* of the *Negro Colour, and proud Spoilers of the Work of God, who dare make Beasts of human Forms.*" The ubiquity of this "Way of thinking or speaking on this Subject" revealed how profoundly colonial involvement with slavery contributed to serve the entrenched view of the inhabitants of the colonies as unworthy to call themselves Britons and the social entities they had created as distorted and inferior versions of the free society from which they came.[33]

IV

Perhaps no body of literary work was more important in cementing the metropolitan image of colonists as others and of colonial societies as only marginally English than the scatological "travel" accounts of the magazine

---

[32] Ibid., 18–20, 35–38; see also "A Review of the Argument for the Truth of *Revelation*, deduced from *Prophecy* and *Miracles*: On occasion of two Treatises lately published," *Present State of the Republic of Letters*, 4 (September 1729): 186.

[33] Robertson, *Speech of Mr. John Campo-bell*, 73; *Gentleman's Magazine*, 11 (March 1741): 145.

editor and humorist Edward (Ned) Ward. In 1698, he published his widely read *A Trip to Jamaica*, which went through at least seven editions over the next quarter-century, and, seeking to build on this volume's popularity, in 1699 he published, with more modest success, *A Trip to New-England*. That Ward ever visited either of these places is highly doubtful. Rather, he probably picked up the substantial amount of information purveyed in his *Trips* in London's Jamaican and New England coffee houses, from merchants and others who had been in America or knew about it. The appeal of these volumes was not their accuracy but their satiric bite, which left the reader with a vivid sense that the areas Ward purported to describe were crude, provincial, socially dysfunctional, and populated by the outcasts of England. Whatever of a favorable nature Ward had to say about either Jamaica or New England, no reader could have left these texts without a profound sense of the extraordinary cultural distance between the American colonies and England.

As Ward told it, down on his luck in England and "having often heard such extravagant Encomiums of that Blessed Paradise Jamaica, where Gold is more plentiful than Ice, Silver than Snow, Pearl than Hailstones," he determined "to make a trial of my Stars in that Island" and had no sooner gotten on board his vessel than he began to sketch out his unfavorable view of the colony and its inhabitants. Like him, his "Fellow-Travellers" seemed to be driven to make the voyage by "incontroul'd Necessity" and "despair of Fortune." He found one

Cherubimical Lass, who, I fear, had Lost her Self, two more, of the same Gender, who had lost their Husbands; two Parsons who had lost their Livings; three Broken Tradesmen, who had lost their Credit; and several, like me that had lost their Wits; a Creolean Captain, a Super annuated Mariner, an Independant Merchant, an Irish Kidnapper, and a Monmothean Sciths-Man, all going with one Design, to patch up their Decay'd Fortunes.

One Unfortunate Lady was in pursute of a Stray'd Husband, who, in Jamaica, had Feloniously taken to Wife (for the sake of a Plantation) a Lacker-Fac'd Creolean, to the great dissatisfaction of his Original Spouse, who had often declar'd (thro' the sweetness of her Disposition) That if he had Marri'd another Handsomer than her self, it would never have vex'd her; but to be Rival'd by a Gipsy, a Tawny Fac'd Moletto Strumpet, a Pumpkin colour'd Whore, no, her Honour would not suffer her to bear with patience so corroding an Indignity.

Yet another turned out to be "an Irish-man going over a Servant, who I suppose was Kidnap'd," and when Ward "ask'd him whose Servant he was," he professed ignorance, replying only that he had been "looking for a good Mashter" when "a brave Gentleman came to me and ask'd me who I wash; and I told him I wash myn nown shelf, and he gave me some good Wine and good Ale, and brought me on Board, and I have not sheen him sinch." In these passages, Ward managed both to convey the necessitous and shady character of the "Sinful Congregation" among whom he found himself and to call attention to the looseness of Jamaican marriage practices, the racial mixing among its population, and the unscrupulous practices of the servant trade.[34]

Nor did Ward find much to praise once he had arrived in Jamaica. Hot, with strange, repulsive (to an English palate), and expensive foods, Jamaica had a sickly population that suffered much from a peculiar American disease known as "Dry Belly-Ach," which in a few weeks cost people the use of their limbs. So prevalent was this disease that Ward proposed that the colony seal be reconstructed so that "A Man under this Misery" would become "the Scutchion of the Island . . . and Death the Crest, Argent." The capital of Port Royal, recently destroyed by an earthquake, was totally bereft of its reputed "former splendour" and contained few of the amenities of English life, the houses being so "low, little, and irregular" that "the Best of their Streets" were no better than those at "the Fag-End of Kentstreet, where the Broom-men Live[d]" in London, and a church that was "built rather like a Market-House," whose congregation included "more variety of Scare-Crows than ever was seen at the Feast of Ugly-Faces" in London. To make the town even less pleasant, the inhabitants placed "their stinking Dunghills" to "the Windward of the Town" so that afternoon sea breezes carried "the Nauseous Effluvia" throughout the town, thus "ingratefully pervert[ing] by their own ill management" a natural blessing into a social detriment.[35]

Ward found the inhabitants equally unappealing. The "generality of the Men," he reported, "look as if they had just nock'd off their Fetters, and by an unexpected Providence, escap'd the danger of a near Misfortune, the dread of which, hath imprinted that in their Looks, which they can no more alter than an Etheopian can his Colour," while a

little Reputation among the Women, goes a great way; and if their Actions be answerable to their Looks, they may vie Wickedness with the Devil: An Impudent Air, being the only Charms of their Countenance, and a Lewd Carriage, the Studi'd Grace of their Deportment. They are such who have been Scandalous in England to the utmost degre[e], either Transported by the State, or led by their Vicious Inclinations, where they may be Wicked without Shame, and Whore on without Punishment.

In short, Ward declared, Port Royal was "the very Sodom of the Universe," where the inhabitants had no "veneration for Religion," virtue was "Despis'd, and all sorts of Vice Encourag'd, by both Sexes."[36]

In this social milieu, the inhabitants "regard[ed] nothing but Money, and value[d] not how they got it, there being no other Felicity to be enjoy'd but purely Riches." So unscrupulous were they that they were invariably "very Civil to Strangers who bring over considerable Effects; and will try a great many ways to Kill" them "farely, for the lucre of" their "Cargo: And many have been made Rich by such Wind-falls." Indeed, the inflation of honors

34 Edward Ward, *A Trip to Jamaica: With a True Character of the People and Island*, 3d ed. (London, 1708), 7–11, 13.
35 Ibid., 15–16.
36 Ibid., 16–17.

and status was a fixed feature of Jamaican society, most of the prominent men being "Colonels, Majors, Captains, Lieutenants, and Ensigns." In this distorted society, Ward wrote, a "Broken Apothecary will make ... a Topping Physician; a Barbers Prentice, a good Surgeon; a Bailiffs Follower, a passable Lawyer, and an English Knave, a very Honest Fellow."[37]

Entirely "without Malice or Partiality," Ward, as he said, summed up the "Character of JAMAICA" in a short paragraph as

THE Dunghill of the Universe, the Refuse of the whole Creation, the Clippings of the Elements, a shapeless pile of Rubbish confus'dly jumbl'd into an Emblem of the Chaos, neglected by Omnipotence when he form'd the World into its admirable Order.... The Receptacle of Vagabonds, the Sanctuary of Bankrupts, and a Close-stool for the Purges of our Prisons. As Sickly as an Hospital, as Dangerous as the Plague, as Hot as Hell, and as Wicked as the Devil. Subject to Turnadoes, Hurricans, and Earthquakes, as if the Island, like the People, were troubled with the Dry Belly-Ach.[38]

New England fared only slightly better at Ward's pen. His trip there was allegedly stimulated by an urge "to forsake Ungodly London, for Religious Boston in New-England, hoping," he wrote, "to Purifie my self by the way in an Ocean of Brine, That when I got thither, I might find my Condition, as well as my Conscience ... fitted for the Conversation of the Saints in so Holy a land." Assuring his readers that his account was "free from Prejudice or Partiality," he acknowledged that Boston houses, in contrast to those in Port Royal, were "Neat and Handsome" and "in some parts [even] joyn[ed] as in London," with the "high Street" containing some "stately Edifices" worth as much as £3,000. "To the Glory of Religion and the Credit of the Town," it also had four churches "Built with Clap-boards and Shingles after the Fashion of our Meeting-houses." As well, New England was a land of opportunity for artisans of all kinds and now had "plenty of good Provisions." Moreover, he reported that over the eight decades since the first English settlement at Plymouth, "the Possessions of the English" in New England had "so greatly improv'd, That in all their Colonies, they" had "above a Hundred and Twenty Towns" and had become "one of the most flourishing Plantations belonging to the English Empire."[39]

For all their social improvements, however, New Englanders, in their own way, turned out to be almost as deviant from English norms as the Jamaicans. Ward did not depict them as a bunch of recently transported felons, vagrants, and immigrants down on their luck, albeit he did note that the fathers of the men who had built the fine houses of Boston had been no more than "Tinkers and Peddlars" when they arrived in the colony. Instead, he emphasized their roots as religious deviants who "all pretend[ed] to be driven over by Persecution" in England and whose population yet contained "more Religious

[37] Ibid.
[38] Ibid., 14.
[39] Edward Ward, *A Trip to New-England. With a Character of the Country and People, Both English and Indians* (London, 1699), 3, 5, 9, 12.

Zealots than Honest-men." They had strict laws against all forms of immorality and lived in a surveillance culture in which they were all, as Ward put it, "very busie in detecting one another[']s failings, and he is accounted, by their Church Governors, a Meritorious Christian, that betrays his Neighbour to a Whipping-Post." Although they lived "upon the Bounty of their Hearers," the clergy, wrote Ward, were "as ridiculously Proud, as their Communicants" were "shamefully Ignorant." Nor were ministers always of the best quality, only one among four in Boston being a scholar, "the second a Gentleman, the Third a Dunce, and the Fourth a Clown," and the "Saints," those who were members in full communion in "one of their Assemblies," denied baptism to those who were not, "for which reason, there are Hundreds amongst them, at Man[']s Estate, that were never Christened."[40]

Yet, if the "Inhabitants seem[ed] very Religious, showing many outward and visible Signs of an inward and Spiritual Grace," they were in many ways, Ward endeavored to show, profoundly hypocritical. "Notwithstanding their Sanctity," Ward reported, "they are very Prophane in their common Dialect. They can neither drive a Bargain, nor make a Jest, without a Text of Scripture at the end on't." They had severe laws against adultery, fornication, even kissing in public, yet "the Levity and Wanton Frolicks of the Young People" on "Lecture-Days" were such that they were commonly called "Whore Fare," while "Husking of Indian-Corn" proved to be "as good sport for Amorous Wag-tailes in New England, as Maying amongst us is for our forward Youths and Wenches," "more Bastards" being "got in that Season, than in all the Year beside; which occasions some of the loosest Saints to call it Rutting Time." Similarly, while they railed against the persecution that had driven them from England, they "us'd the Quakers with such severity, by Whipping, Hanging, and other Punishments," that they could escape "the Savage Fury of their Unchristian Enemies" only by fleeing Massachusetts for Rhode Island, where, finding "a Fertile Soil" that made it "the Garden of America," they "happily Planted themselves, making great improvements" and flourishing "like a Bay-Tree under the Noses of their Enemies." Similarly, Ward reported, New Englanders had until recently persecuted witches so severely that they managed to hang "the best People in the Country" on very slim evidence, thereby raising questions about the legitimacy of their legal system.[41]

Where New Englanders showed their hypocrisy most clearly, however, was in their business practices. If they wore "in their Faces the Innocense of Doves," Ward wrote, "you will find them in their Dealings, as Subtile as Serpents." "The Gravity and Piety of their looks," he continued,

are of great Service to these American Christians: It makes strangers that come amongst them, give Credit to their Words. And it is a Proverb with those that know them, Whosoever believes a New-England Saint, shall be sure to be Cheated. And he that knows how to deal with their Traders, may Deal with the Devil and fear no Craft.

[40] Ibid., 5–6, 11–13.
[41] Ibid., 5–6, 11–12.

"Some Years ago," wrote Ward in providing a dramatic example of New Englanders' craftiness, when they were behind in their returns to English merchants, Boston factors disposed of their goods and then "set Fire to their Ware-houses, burning them down to the Ground" and subsequently pretending that they "were all undone, their Cargos and Books all destroy'd, and so at once Ballanc'd their Accounts with England." One of the victims of this deception vowed that "if he ever trusted a New-England Saint again for three Pence, the Devil shou'd have a Title to him and his Heirs for half the Money." For such people, Ward declared, only "Interest...was their Faith, Money their God, and Large Possessions the only Heaven they know."[42]

Ward also charged that New Englanders were the victims of Creolian degeneration, having "contracted so many ill habits from the Indians, that it is difficult to find a Woman cleanly enough for a Cook to a Squemish Lady, or a Man neat enough for a Vallet to Sir Courtly Nice." Among the many such habits was laziness, the men being "such lovers of Idleness, That they are desirous of being thought Old, to have a better pretence to be Lazy." Although the fruitfulness of the women showed that men were "industrious in Bed," New England farmers, he said, were "very Lazy." "One Husband-man in England...will do more Labour in a Day, than a New England Planter will be at pains to do in a Week. For every Hour he spends in his Grounds, he will be two at an Ordinary." If they ate "like Plough-men," they "Plough[ed] like Gentlemen." "Four parts in five of their Time," Ward claimed, they spent "Eating, Drinking, Smoking, and Sleeping,... Four Meals a Day, and a good Knap after Dinner, being the Custom of the Country." Notwithstanding this leisurely existence, according to Ward, men turned "Grey at Thirty, and look[ed] as Shrivel'd in the Face, as an old Parchment Indenture pasted upon a Barber[']s Block," while the women were "Soon Ripe and soon Rotten," marrying in their early teens, becoming barren by their midtwenties, and losing their teeth soon after. Indeed, in terms of their physical characteristics Ward compared them unfavorably to their Indian neighbors, albeit both were given to drunkenness, the Indians having learned it from the English.[43]

By English standards, Ward found both the people and the landscape to be thoroughly uncongenial. He "Characteris'd" the former as "Saints without Religion, Traders without Honesty, Christians without Charity, Magistrates without Mercy, subjects without Loyalty, Neighbours without Amity, Faithless Friends, Implacable Enemys, and Rich Men without Money." For the most part, he wrote, the country was still "Wilderness, being general[l]y Rocky, Woody and Mountainous, very rarely Beautiful with Valleys," while the climate was subject to wide fluctuations and great extremes between hot and cold, to which he traced the people's propensity to be "always troubled with an ague and fever."[44]

[42] Ibid., 5, 7–8.
[43] Ibid., 10–11, 15–16.
[44] Ibid., 8–9, 11.

In these largely unflattering assessments of Jamaica and New England, Ward catered to, confirmed, and vivified ancient metropolitan English stereotypes about the deviant character of the people and the societies of colonial English America. At his hands, Jamaican and New England colonists appeared every bit as exotic as the native American Indians and Africans among whom they lived. Treating two colonies at the end of a geographic and social continuum that stretched from the wealthy and slave-rich, tropical and staple-producing island colony of Jamaica to the well-settled (with Europeans) farming, trading, and religiously oriented northern continental colonies of New England, these volumes might, had the second volume been as successful as the first, have led to a series of Wardean *Trips* to all of England's prominent colonies. Ward appreciated that the colonies were distinctive, one from another, but his larger point was the more important distinction between England and the colonies as a whole, each of which, he suggested, represented a peculiar and shocking deviation from metropolitan England. Indeed, in Ward's text, whatever social continuities existed between metropolis and colonies involved the very worst features, the underside, of English society.

V

To the extent that Ward's *Trips* were fictional, they were precursors of the emergence in the 1720s of the American colonies as an appropriate setting for belletristic literature. Of course, these novels were not the first English novels to be set in English America. Aphra Behn's *Oroonoko: Or, the Royal Slave, A True History* (London, 1688) had been set in Surinam when it was briefly an English colony in the early 1660s. A tale of romance about a royal African and his wife who wound up as slaves in Surinam, Behn's novel was principally an account of how Oroonoko's royal heritage equipped him to withstand his enslavement, and it neither condemned the institution of slavery nor showed much interest in using Oroonoko's tale to elucidate the character of England's new American world. Although Behn did describe the members of the governing Council, who condemned Oroonoko to death for inciting slave discontent, "as such notorious Villains as *Newgate* never transported and possibly originally were such, who understood neither the Laws of *God* or *Man* and had no sort of Principles to make 'em worthy of the Name of Men" and thereby called attention to the suspect English origins of colonial leaders, she presented the local planters and merchants who encountered Oroonoko as civilized gentlemen sympathetic to his plight and willing to help him and his wife, Imoinda, out of slavery.[45] The dramatist Thomas Southerne, who used Behn's novel as the basis for his play *Oroonoko* in 1696, was similarly inclined, although through his characters he did express his concern with the cruelties of the slave system and, like Behn, noted the lowly English social origins of

[45] Aphra Behn, *Oroonoko: Or, The Royal Slave. A True History* (London, 1688), 214–15.

some of the planters, one of them being described as "an Upstart to Prosperity, one that is but just come acquainted with Cleanliness, and that never saw five Shilling of" his "own, without deserving to be hang'd for 'em."[46]

The American colonies, specifically Virginia, Britain's oldest colony, and its neighbor, Maryland, figured heavily in two Daniel Defoe novels published in 1722: *The Fortunes and Misfortunes of the Famous Moll Flanders* and *The History and Remarkable Life of the Truly Honourable Colonel Jacque*. The first told the story of a child born in Newgate Prison to a mother who had been sentenced to transportation to Virginia. Moll grew up, married several times, became a highly successful shoplifter, and was eventually caught and sentenced to transportation to Virginia, where she used her ill-gotten gains to buy herself and her highwayman husband out of service, establish a successful tobacco plantation, and finally achieve the status of a gentlewoman.[47] The second was a tale of an unwanted child of gentle parents, who turned to a life of crime after his foster mother died, and in his late teens was kidnaped and sold as an indentured servant in Virginia, where he soon came to look upon his kidnaping as a deliverance from the desperate life he had been leading, worked hard, caught his master's eye, got promoted to overseer, and after being discharged from servitude became a successful planter and in a few years acquired enough wealth to indulge a desire to see the larger world, spending his next quarter-century in Europe as a soldier and absentee before retiring to his plantation in Virginia.[48]

In these two novels, Defoe treated Virginia and Maryland as places of opportunity and redemption. Six characters, three in each novel, found themselves transported or kidnaped to Virginia, where they put their lives of poverty and crime behind them and became respectable property holders with large independent resources. Thus did Moll's mother, having "been both Whore and Thief" in London, "very luckily" fall "into a good Family [in Virginia], where behaving herself well, and her Mistress dying, her Master married her, by whom she had" two children, and, "by her Diligence and good Management" during sixteen years of widowhood, had "improv'd the Plantations to such a degree as that they then were" profitable enough to enable her to send her son to England in search of a wife and to turn herself into not only a prosperous but also "a very Pious sober and religious Woman." Thus, contrary to the anonymous street ballads inspired by the novel, Moll was not "condemned for life" as a "slave at Virginia," where

> ... she handled the Hoe,
> Amongst West Indian Negroes she suffered many a blow,
> An Eye witness to the cruelties that was inflicted there....

[46] Thomas Southerne, *Oroonoko: a Tragedy* (London, 1698), 10–11, 39–40, 59.

[47] Daniel Defoe, *Moll Flanders*, ed. Albert J. Rivero (New York, 2004).

[48] Daniel Defoe, *The History and Remarkable Life of the Truly Honourable Colonel Jacque, in The Works of Daniel Defoe*, 16 vols. (New York, 1925), volumes 10–11.

Rather, Moll and her last husband followed a course similar to that of her mother with a like fortunate result, during their eight years' residence after their transportation to the Chesapeake. Thus, in *Colonel Jacque*, did the colonel and the indentured tutor who educated him both become independent planters; his wayward first wife, who turned up a transported servant on the colonel's plantation and remarried him, like him found in Virginia a way out of the life of misery and crime she had fallen into in England. In his own words, the colonel progressed from being "a pickpoket to a kidnapped, miserable slave in Virginia," "from a slave to a head-officer or overseer of slaves, and from thence to a master planter."[49]

Indeed, in *Colonel Jacque*, Defoe explicitly touted Virginia and Maryland as places where English felons and unfortunates could replicate the colonel's experience, explaining how the customary system of land grants and credit offered to servants upon expiration of their terms provided them with a start on the road to independence and respectability and expressing the opinion that "every Newgate wretch, every desperate forlorn creature, the most despicable ruined man in the world, has here a fair opportunity put into his hands to begin the world again, and that upon a foot of certain gain and in a method exactly honest, with a reputation that nothing past will have any effect upon." "Some of the most considerable planters in Virginia, and in Maryland also," the colonel declared, had

raised themselves – namely, from being without a hat or a shoe to estates of £40,000 or £50,000; and in this method, I may add, no diligent man ever miscarried, if he had health to work and was a good husband; for he every year adding more land and planting more tobacco, which is real money, he must gradually increase in substance, till at length he gets enough to buy negroes and other servants, and then never works himself any more.

Moll's mother, with whom she was reunited in Virginia, told her daughter much the same, recounting how "many a *Newgate* Bird" had become "a great Man" in Virginia. "Several Justices of the Peace, Officers of the Train Bands, and Magistrates of the Towns they live in," she said, had "been burnt in the Hand" as transported fellows.[50]

Yet, if Defoe presented Virginia and Maryland as lands of opportunity for European felons, servants, and free people, his accounts did little to undermine the metropolitan image of the American colonies as places of excessive cruelty and cultural deviance and of American colonists as people of low social origins. Although Moll's mother and Colonel Jacque were fortunate in being bought by men "of humanity," the colonel noted that most "masters in Virginia" were "terrible things," that white servants "worked hard, lodged hard, and fared hard," and that "the cruelty so much talked of, used in Virginia and Barbadoes, and other colonies, in whipping the negro slaves" was "the accustomed

---

[49] Defoe, *Moll Flanders*, 72–73, 371; idem, *Colonel Jacque*, 1: 234.
[50] Defoe, *Colonel Jacque*, 1: 234–36, 2: 4–5; idem, *Moll Flanders*, 70–71.

severity of the country." Indeed, the colonel's claim that his reforms in treating slaves with mercy and as rational beings rather than beasts had rendered Chesapeake slavery "less cruel and barbarous" as well as less dangerous than it was in Barbados and Jamaica testified to the continuing prevalence of violence and cruelty in the slave systems of the British American world. Similarly, the colonel's description, following his acquisition of a little knowledge, of himself as being "buried alive in a remote part of the world, where I could see nothing at all, and hear but a little of what was seen, and that little not till at least half a year after it was done, and sometimes a year or more," and his reluctance to return to America for the same reason, further underlined, for readers, the cultural distance between Britain and its American colonies. Furthermore, both Moll's and the colonel's American histories and, more explicitly, Moll's mother's observation that

the greatest part of the Inhabitants of the Colony came thither in very indifferent Circumstances from England: that, generally speaking, they were of two sorts, either (1.) Such as were brought over by Masters of Ships to be sold as Servants . . . Or, (2.) Such as are Transported from *Newgate* and other Prisons, after having been found guilty of Felony and other Crimes punishable by Death

could only underline and confirm for metropolitans the appropriateness of the language of otherness for describing Britain's American colonists.[51]

Throughout the early eighteenth century, other works of fiction continued to cater to these views. Thus, in 1720, two years before Defoe published the two novels just discussed, William Pittis published in London a popular fictional narrative entitled *The Jamaica Lady: or, the Life of Bavia: An Account of her Intrigues, Cheats, Amours in England, Jamaica, and the Royal Navy*, which represented an elaboration of the themes earlier marked out by his friend Ned Ward in his *Trip to Jamaica*. Pittis's titillating account focused on the shipboard amours and histories of "two notorious Women" during a crossing from Jamaica to London in 1713, and he used them to display the entire range of parvenu Jamaican womanhood. Bavia, who had come to Jamaica as a dishonest immigrant servant in flight from those she had cheated in England, there developed a profitable career from her reputed ability to predict the future. Holmesia, the consequence of a shipboard liaison between a woman being transported to Jamaica for shoplifting and "a *Mullatto* belonging to the ship," was "at best but a *Mustee*" who had made her way to wealth and respectability through prostitution and an informal alliance with an immigrant British doctor.[52]

The unnamed captain of the vessel on which Holmesia and Bavia crossed the Atlantic had a low opinion of Jamaica and the people who lived there. When Bavia's agent sought passage for her as a wealthy gentlewoman of England, the

---

[51] Defoe, *Captain Jacque*, 1: 198, 204, 231–32, 265; 2: 97–98, 130; idem, *Moll Flanders*, 70.

[52] William Pittis, *The Jamaica Lady: Or, the Life of Bavia: An Account of her Intrigues, Cheats, Amours in England, Jamaica, and the Royal Navy* (London, 1720), 8–9, 42, 64, 69.

captain pointedly questioned why a woman of such high social status would ever come "into that cursed Country" of Jamaica, "for he said [that] none but mad People and Fools, when possess'd of a plentiful Fortune, or even a moderate Competency in *England*, in Paradice, would leave it, to go into *Jamaica*, the Sink of Sin, and Receptacle of all manner of Vices: A Place so intolerably hot and suffocating, that he swore there was only a brown Paper betwixt it and Hell."[53]

Unsurprisingly, when a fellow passenger spun out the tale of Holmesia's rise, it provided the occasion for an extensive and highly critical discussion of the looseness of the female members of the free segment of the Jamaican population. Expressing his opinion that prostitution was a "Vice, which was natural to all the Inhabitants" of Jamaica, the captain averred that he saw "no Reason" to single Holmesia out for condemnation. His informant agreed. "Should such a Prodigy happen, as a virtuous Woman to land, and reside in the Island," he observed,

she is sure to be the Subject of the whole Sex; shall have Amours and Meetings made for her, and reported in all Companies; and the more her Innocence, the more Scandal shall be heap'd on her, till they have brought her to be like themselves; and then she may sin on as quiet, and as undisturb'd, as the rest of the frail, frippery Fry of Satan's Emmissaries.

Nor was sexual promiscuity the only fault of Jamaican ladies, according to Pittis, who observed through the voice of the ship captain that they sometimes disciplined their female slave attendants in great "Furies with Whips of Steel, and Hair of Serpents" and declared that "a Negro had better live in Hell than with a *Jamaican* Termagant."[54]

Pittis missed no opportunity to explore the roots of all these social deviations that, as he put it, were "new and unmannerly Invention[s] of the *Americans*, unknown to, and not practis'd by *European* Countries," and through a passenger who was worried that his wife might have been caught up in the sexual adventures occurring on the voyage he speculated about the effects of climate upon behavior. Having already "caught her tripping" while she was in Jamaica, he decided that her transgressions were "not so much the Fault of the Woman as of the Climate." Considering that she had never acted that way in England but had been a faithful wife, he decided that her infidelity was "not her natural Inclination, but" the result of "that cursed malevolent Planet which predominates in that Island, and so changes the Constitution of the Inhabitants, that if a Woman land there chaste as a Vestal, she becomes in forty-eight Hours a perfect *Messolina*, and 'tis impossible for a Woman to live at *Jamaica* and preserve her Virtue." "Having liv'd five Years in *Jamaica*," he despaired, "was time long enough, not only to tincture, but to change her whole Mass of Blood, and totally alter her Nature, and that a Disease so long growing was not to

53 Ibid., 10–11.
54 Ibid, 38, 44–45.

be presently eradicated." Even people of less lowly English social origins, Pittis thus suggested, were in the plantations quickly altered for the worse by the physical climate and the social environment they there encountered.[55]

Nearly three decades later, in 1748, an anonymous author identifying himself only as "a CREOLE" also played upon the association in British minds between the colonies and transportation in a short novelette that was sufficiently successful to be followed by a sequel later in the same year. *The Fortunate Transport; or the Secret History of the Life and Adventures of the Celebrated Polly Haycock, alias Mrs. B –, The Lady of the Gold Watch* told the story of a woman who, according to the author's succinct summary, was "begot by Chance, came into the World with Life in spight of her Mother, nursed by Charity, brought up among Pickpokets, transported for Felony, and in spite of all that now rolls in Ease, Splendor, and Luxury." The heroine, Polly Haycock, got her name from the circumstances of her conception on Hampstead Heath, where her father ravished her mother who, asleep at the foot of a hayrick, was at that very moment dreaming of the consummation of her marriage in Jamaica to its deputy governor. The couple, each of gentle family, did not survive her birth, and the illegitimate Polly grew up among "Charity Children" at St. Martin's in the Field and there learned all the "little low Tricks of a Parish Girl," including thievery, which prevented her from living an upright life even after her paternal grandmother had discovered and adopted her. After her grandmother's death, Polly soon "commenced Whore," becoming a proficient pickpocket and winding up in Newgate, from which she was sentenced to transportation to Virginia.[56]

Virginia turned out well for Polly. After two years of hard service with a master who beat her, she was rescued by and became the mistress of a magistrate who at the end of her term gave her a substantial annual annuity. Resentful of his refusal to marry her, however, she repaid him by forming a liaison with a ship captain trading to Jamaica and, with two other freed convict servants, robbed the magistrate when he was away at quarter sessions of all his valuable moveables and about a hundred and fifty guineas from his strong box, and they all sailed off to Jamaica, where the captain soon died, making her heir to his sloop and leaving her some shares in ships and a small plantation. This transaction provided Polly with "some Character in the Island" as "Captain *Wilton's* Widow" and enabled her to pass "pretty well... in the World." Taking up residence at her new plantation, she built a new house, bought an adjacent plantation, "behaved with great Decency, and gain'd the Esteem of the Neighbouring Planters, from many of whom she received Overtures of Marriage." But Polly, setting considerable value upon "her Person and Beauty, which was by no means contemptible," determined not to settle for "any Thing below those of the first Rank in the Island" and finally married, in a ceremony of "great Splendor," Mr. Ferguson, who, as the

---

[55] Ibid., 3, 35–36.
[56] "A Creole," *The Fortunate Transport* (London, 1748), 4, 7, 18–19.

highest-ranking councillor, was in effect the deputy governor of Jamaica. At
his death a few years later the former transport "was now the greatest Fortune,
as well as the Lady of the first Rank in the Island," and a second marriage
brought her still more wealth that she used to retire to England, where she
lived "in great Splendor and Affluence."[57] A sequel to the *Fortunate Transport*
traced Polly's adventures for the last twenty years of her life and wound up
with her discovering a son she had borne in Virginia a few months after her
transportation. Now a doctor who was the "most eminent of his Profession in
all *America*," he looked after her for the rest of her days.[58]

Polly's experience with a cruel master in Virginia provided the author with
an opportunity to confirm to his readers the accuracy of the long-standing
stereotype of British colonial planters as tyrannical and inhuman disciplinari-
ans. Her master, observed the author, "was a meer Planter, consequently, cruel,
haughty, and mercenary, without any soft Sentiment of Humanity in his Breast;
and his Years had laid the Fever in his Blood so much that" Polly held no sexual
attraction for him, and "he had no Thoughts but how to work the Value of
his Money out of the Slaves, and make the most of them, without regard to
their Happiness or Misery. In a Word, like most of the Tribe of Planters, he
had no Appetite but for Money; nor Pleasure in any pastime but torturing the
unhappy Wretches in his Power." Polly's rescuer was the exception who proved
the rule, possessing "a great deal of Humanity, and really [having] as little of
the Planter in him as it is possible for any Man to have who had lived forty
Years in the Country." By contrast, however, his son, whom Polly encountered
several decades later, reverted to form, turning out to be nothing but a "greedy
Creolian," "a meer Planter" who "loved nothing but Money."[59]

Similarly, the author used Polly's relations with her servants to sharpen
the unfavorable contrast he drew throughout between social dispositions in
England and in Virginia and Jamaica. In his view, Polly had "unhappily"
acquired habits during her Jamaican tenure that made it difficult for her to
keep servants in England and thereby embittered "the Sweets of her present
Grandeur." Notwithstanding the misery she had endured during her "Servitude
with the *Virginian* Savage," the author observed, she "brought Home with her
too much of the Spirit of the Planter; that is a Disposition to use her Servants
with great Severity, and scarce any Share of Humanity." By "no means famed
for her Lenity to her own Slaves in *Jamaica*," he complained, she used her
English servants, "as far as the Laws will permit . . . with the same Harshness."
Lamenting that "all Creolians complain of their *English* Servants with great
Warmth, as if there were no such Thing as good or honest Servants in the Island

[57] Ibid., 36–40, 42–43.
[58] *The Second Part of the Fortunate Transport. Being a Continuation of the Lady's Adventures,
From the Time of her Arrival in England, to her Death* (London, 1748). The quotation is from
p. 39.
[59] "A Creole," *Fortunate Transport*, 32–34; idem, *Second Part of the Fortunate Transport*, 36–37.

of *Britain*," he condemned them for treating "free-born *Englishmen* as they do Negroes and Felons in the Plantations, and expect[ing] the same Submission from the one as the other." But, he noted, "good, honest, and faithful Servants in England," used to being treated "with Candour and Humanity" by their English and Christian masters, would "not put up with such Usage here," so that only knaves would work for Creoles.[60]

Nor did the author fail to reinforce the image, earlier limned by Ward and Pettis, of the colonies as places in which English rules of sexual morality were openly violated. Thus, in commenting on Polly's stint as a mistress to her kind master in Virginia did he observe that the master's female relations treated Polly "very civily, for there a kept Mistress is no such scandalous Matter, as to give Umbrage to the married Part of the Sex." Thus, when her Jamaican ship captain designated Polly as a wife so that she could inherit his estate did the author make it clear that there had been no legal marriage by observing that "the Church had no Hand in the Match."[61]

Like Defoe, the author of the *Fortunate Transport* presented the colonies – in this case, Virginia and Jamaica – as places with opportunities for enterprising or unscrupulous former felons to rise to the top of society, while at the same time reinforcing the old metropolitan conception of colonists as people of lowly English social origins, fixated upon material wealth, without humanity, unconscionably cruel to their servants and slaves, and sexually loose. Those few who, like Polly, gained enough wealth to resettle in England proved themselves to be social misfits unable to adjust to and operating outside of the social norms of British society. And they were also socially naïve, easily imposed upon by social adventurers. An example was Polly's youngest son, Jack, who, arriving in London, was quickly "smitten with all the Vices of the Town," without "Brains enough ... to pursue them without making himself ridiculous, and the Sport of the Wenches and their Cullies," who at coffee houses and taverns diverted themselves "at the Expence of" such "Creolian[s]." Jack even picked up "one of the Ladies of the Town ... in a Bagnio," took her back to Jamaica, where she evidently fitted in well with the rest of the female population, and married her.[62]

The association of the American plantations with transported criminals and impecunious British people was further reinforced by other published accounts of people transported to the colonies for crimes. Thus in 1730 the "noted Street-Robber" James Dalton published, just before he was hanged in London, an autobiographical account of a life of crime that included three sentences of transportation to the colonies, each followed by his return to England, where he continued his life of crime. Dalton told his readers little about the details of his tenure in America, but the ease with which he there found other runaway

[60] "A Creole," *Fortunate Transport*, 42–44.
[61] Ibid., 35–40.
[62] Ibid., 41.

transports to join him in his criminal escapades suggested that the colonial population was full of such people."[63]

James Revel, another transported felon, told his story in verse in a pamphlet first published in London in 1750 and reprinted in many editions over the next half-century. Having renounced his early life as a thief and returned to England to be reunited with his parents and son after fourteen years as a convict servant in Virginia, Revel wrote to warn young people of the hard lot that awaited those who chose a life of crime.

> Forc'd from your country for to go
> Among the negroes to work at the hoe,
> In different countries void of relief
> Sold for a slave because you prov'd a thief

Bought by a master who had himself been a transport, he was worked hard for twelve years on a tobacco plantation until his master died. His master's widow sold the remaining two years of his contract to a cooper who, much to his surprise, used him "tenderly and well" and, when his time was up, paid his passage back to England. Riding with his new master around the countryside, Revel reported that he "often griev'd to see"

> So many transport felons there to be,
> Some who from England had liv'd fine and brave,
> Were like horses made to drudge and slave.

Notwithstanding the kind treatment he had received during the last two years of his indenture, Revel made clear that Virginia had been for him "a barbarous place" indeed, characterized by inhumanity and cruelty and populated by past and present felons.[64]

VI

Works from other genres published in Britain also spoke to the question of metropolitans' lack of esteem for colonists and colonies. In 1708, John Oldmixon produced the first comprehensive history of the British American Empire, which he published in two volumes in London and in 1741 revised and expanded in a new edition. Until 1755, when a London publisher reprinted William Douglas's *A Summary, Historical and Political of the First Planting Progressive Improvements, and Present State of the British Settlements in North America*, first published serially in Boston beginning in 1749, it was the only such history. In this detailed colony-by-colony history, Oldmixon sought to call attention to "the great Increase in Wealth" enjoyed by Britain as a result of its successful and expanding empire and predicted that "the *British*

---

[63] *The Life and Actions of James Dalton (The Noted Street Robber)* (London, 1730).

[64] *The Poor Unhappy Felon's Sorrowful Account of His Fourteen Years Transportation at Virginia, in America* (London, 1750), 5–8.

Colonies...may be much more advantagious to" modern Britons "than the *Roman* Colonies...were to the Romans." As he wrote in his dedication, however, he also conceived of his work as an attempt to show the falsity of the "Scandal which the Enemies of the Plantations maliciously throw upon them," including especially charges about the "the vulgar Descent of the Inhabitants," which he denounced as both "ridiculous" and "unjust." Arguing that some colonists were "descended from...the most ancient and honourable Families in *England*," he pointed out that many other colonists of lesser descent had "by their Prudence and Industry...rais'd Fortunes" and "acquire[d] Estates" in America sufficient to "ennoble them" had their achievements occurred in Britain, observing that such achievements were the essence of "true Nobility" and infinitely more impressive than titles derived merely from "a long Roll of *Ancestry*" without respect to either "Reason or Merit."[65]

Over the next half-century, many other analysts acknowledged the justice of Oldmixon's protest. Malachy Postlethwayt, for example, affirmed that, even though the colonies were "much frequented by unfortunate persons," such people "oftentimes" eventually became "wealthy there."[66] But these and similar protests or acknowledgments that the colonies provided opportunities for both metropolitan outcasts and ambitious settlers did little to transform the negative metropolitan image of the colonial world. Throughout the eighteenth century, metropolitan publications continued to depict the colonies as receptacles for the waste population of Britain who would never overcome the stain of their social origins and had created in America social milieus that in many respects fell short of even those lowly origins. Even analysts who, like Robert Robertson, acknowledged that many "People of the better sort went, or were sent to" the colonies during the English Civil War and the Restoration, often followed Josiah Child in insisting that the vast majority of "the Hands that came" to both "the *Northern* or *Southern* Colonies of *England*, were none of the Best, and such as otherwise must have starved at Home, or fled to foreign European Countries for Bread or Shelter, as very many did at that Time to *Holland*, and elsewhere."[67] Routinely, metropolitan commentators continued to show that they thought "meanly of the Colonies,"[68] to "spread the grossest Misrepresentations, and wickedly toil to make the World believe" that American settlers were "a Clan of *Kidnappers, Pickpockets, Knaves*, and *Villains*," and to stigmatize them with "*the black characters of* Unhospitable, Brutal, Savage, Covetous *and* Barbarous" people. By "*freely bestow[ing]*" such "*Epithets*"

---

[65] John Oldmixon, *The British Empire in America, Containing the History of the Discovery, Settlement, Progress and Present State of All the British Colonies, on the Continent and Islands of America*, 2 vols. (London, 1708), 1: iv, xxxi, xxxvii.

[66] Malachy Postlethwayt, *Universal Dictionary of Trade and Commerce*, 4th ed. (London, 1764), entry, "Plantations."

[67] Robertson, *Speech of Mr. John Campo-Bell*, 10–11.

[68] [Jonathan Blenman], *Remarks on Several Acts of Parliament Relating more especially to the Colonies abroad* (London, 1742), v.

upon settlers,[69] metropolitans effectively continued to categorize colonials as others who, despite their mostly British descent, were something less than genuine Britons, "a lower order of men in the scale than Europeans," who, protested one American, deserved little more than "the sovereign contempt of their countrymen" in Britain.[70] "Nothing is more certain, or better known," declared a political writer in 1766, "than that necessity has been the cause of almost every emigration that has happened, and that the beginnings of most American properties were remarkably slender."[71]

Even Adam Smith subscribed to this image in his *Theory of Moral Sentiments*, published in London in 1759. In a section on the differences in customs between a savage and "a humane and polished people," Smith observed that there was "not a negro from the coast of Africa, who does not," in respect to fortitude, "possess a degree of magnanimity, which the soul of his sordid master is scarce capable of conceiving. Fortune never exerted more cruelly her empire over mankind," he added, "than when she subjected those nations of heroes to the refuse of the jails of Europe, of wretches who possess the virtues neither of the countries which they come from, nor of those which they go to, and whose levity, brutality, and baseness, so justly expose them to the contempt of the vanquished."[72]

Five years later, in 1764, the young Virginian Arthur Lee, a student in Edinburgh, sought to answer this charge in *An Essay in Vindication of the Continental Colonies of America*. Perhaps more fully than any other writer published in London up to that time, Lee laid out the elements of the language of otherness that had long been used in the metropolis in reference to the colonies and expressed the depths of colonial resentment at the pervasive metropolitan application of that language to the American colonies and their inhabitants. By implying that American colonists consisted of "the refuse of their respective countries" and "that they were utterly destitute of every virtue, or abandoned to the influence of every infamous and detested vice," Lee complained indignantly, Smith had, without "the least shadow of truth," at least in reference to Britain's American "continental colonies," debased the Americans "into Monsters" who "should be treated with reproaches more rigorous than the severest justice, unmitigated by the least humanity, would utter against the most perfectly vicious."[73]

Such slurs, Lee declared, were "as bitter an invective as ever fell from the tongue of man." In specific reference to his native Virginia, he contended that

---

[69] "Roscommon," *To the Author of those Intelligencers printed at Dublin* (New York, 1733), 2, 8.

[70] "A Friend of Liberty, this Colony and all Mankind" to Mr. Hall, August 20, 1767, *Providence Gazette* (Providence), September 5, 1767.

[71] *Application of Some General Political Rules, To the Present State of Great-Britain, Ireland and America* (London, 1766), 75.

[72] Adam Smith, *Theory of Moral Sentiments* (London, 1759), 402–03.

[73] Arthur Lee, *An Essay in Vindication of the Continental Colonies of America, From the Censure of Mr. Adam Smith, in his Theory of Moral Sentiments* (London, 1764), iii–iv.

"no colony had ever a nobler foundation," its founders being "distinguished, even in Britain, for rank, for fortune, for abilities," and pointed out that the subsequent increase of free inhabitants had consisted mostly of emigrants "from Britain, and other countries, who chose to seek their fortunes in a new and rising world." He did not deny that Virginia had received its share of transported felons, but insisted that such people, when "transported to a country where there is little opportunity, and still less necessity for stealing," usually reformed and became honest settlers. Moreover, he emphasized, "such persons" had "been rarely the founders of families which became afterwards eminent," and few such families in either Virginia or any of the other American colonies could "be traced from so mean an original." In short, Lee concluded, "the inhabitants of the colonies" were "descended from worthy ancestors, from whom," contrary to Smith, they had not "degenerated." To support this contention, Lee observed that many analysts had acknowledged the colonists "to be, at this period, a humane, hospitable, and polished people" entirely undeserving of "the ignominy of being styled, the refuse of jails, inhuman, brutal, and base." How "the mind of a man of sense, a philosopher, a moralist," could "be so strangely perverted," Lee could explain only by his gullibility in being imposed on by "the reports of wretches" designed "to catch the ear of vulgar credulity."[74]

Although Lee expressed a low opinion of the moral and intellectual abilities of Africans and challenged Smith's characterization of them as heroes, he made no apology for slavery as an institution and expressed his revulsion at the slave trade; nevertheless, he vigorously challenged the "common creed" in Britain "that negro slaves" were "very barbarously treated" throughout the colonies. He admitted that the enslaved in the West Indian colonies underwent "a very severe labour," but cited travellers' reports that on the continent "a more moderate labour, better food, and a more healthy climate" enabled them to reproduce themselves through increase, and he turned to his own travels in the British Isles to support his contention that "the habitations of the negroes are palaces, and their living luxurious; when compared with those of the peasants of either" Scotland or Ireland.[75]

VII

If the legalization of slavery, which was common to all British colonies, was the most glaring deviation from metropolitan British social norms in the American colonies, a variety of other characteristics operated throughout the early centuries of empire to sustain a negative image of them as not quite British or even as foreign entities populated by people who, even if they had originated in Britain, were far from being recognizable reproductions of British society. Living in exotic places among the strange peoples whose land they had taken or

[74] Ibid., 10, 18, 22–23, 25, 30–31.
[75] Ibid., iv, 15, 24–25, 37, 42–42, 45–46.

who had been imported to labor for them, colonial settlers, as depicted from the metropolitan perspective through the language of alterity, themselves seemed to be a separate breed, a mixture of people unable to make it in Britain, including poor laborers, former servants, transported felons, economic and social adventurers, and religious deviants who had been demographically and culturally contaminated through their sexual liaisons with native peoples and imported Africans.

That such people would create deviant societies presided over by the social upstarts who rose to the top and, driven largely by material objectives, would be characterized by shady business practices, vicious labor regimes, immorality and suspect sexual mores, religious deviancy or neglect, social crudity, neglect of civility, extreme provinciality, and long-term cultural degeneration was, for metropolitans, only to be expected and entirely credible. When metropolitans spoke of empire, they thus frequently used a language of alterity in reference to colonial free populations that significantly qualified the enthusiasm evident in the languages of commerce and liberty that they also used in connection with the empire.

During the long debate over how Britain should respond to colonial resistance to metropolitan authority beginning with the Stamp Act crisis of 1764–66, those who condemned that resistance found it easy to slide into the language of alterity as a device for expressing their anger and outrage and to denounce colonials "as the posterity of independents and anabaptists, presbyterians and quakers, convicts and felons, savages and negro-whippers."[76] Despite the insistence of those more sympathetic to the colonial point of view that Parliament had an "essential duty not to despise the colonies, but to attain the best knowledge of them in" its "power" and "not to consider them as a set of vagabonds and transports, but an industrious, honest and free people,"[77] nor to give in to the tendency of Britons "to form the most unfavorable impressions of every people except themselves,"[78] the language of alterity proved to be a useful device in mobilizing parliamentary and public support for a coercive policy against the colonies and continued to be used in reference to Americans from the first year of conflict through the last year of the war, the philosopher Richard Price complaining in 1777 that Britons had "all along acted as if we thought the people of *America* did not possess the feelings and passions of *men*, much less of *Englishmen*."[79]

Nor did this habit of speaking go out of fashion following the loss of the thirteen colonies. Deploring the continued use of the "word Creole" as

---

[76] *The Justice and Necessity of Taxing the American Colonies, Demonstrated* (London, 1766), 23.

[77] *The Late Occurrences in North America, and Policy of Great Britain Considered* (London, 1766), 5.

[78] "A Friend to both countries" [Charles Garth], *America Vindicated from the High Charge of Ingratitude and Rebellion* (London, 1774), 2–3.

[79] Richard Price, *Additional Observations On the Nature and Value of Civil Liberty, and the War with America* (London, 1777), 86.

"a term of reproach," the political writer John Williams in a 1786 pamphlet advised his readers to "reflect on the loss of America" and "the disgrace of that dismemberment" and come to an enhanced appreciation of the colonies as "the cradles of your commerce and navigation" and thereby "to silence all such illiberal tongues for ever" and "change [such] terms of contempt for others of friendship and brotherly endearment to the remaining colonies" in America.[80]

[80] John Williams, *The Crisis of the Colonies; with Some Observations How Far They may be Saved from any Detriment by the French Treaty*, 3d ed. (London, 1786), 32–33.

3

"A Fabric at Once the Dread and Wonder of the World"

The Languages of Imperial Grandeur, Liberty,
Commerce, Humanity, and Justice and the American
Challenge to Empire

I

Success in the Seven Years' War altered the ways in which metropolitans spoke about empire. No longer was the emphasis so heavily upon trade. Defenders of the treaty that ended the war signaled the change in parliamentary debates in December 1762. "The value of our conquests . . . ought not to be estimated by present produce, but by their probable increase," one speaker explained, and "neither ought the value of any country to be solely tried on its commercial advantages." "Such ideas," he said, were "rather [more] suited to a limited and petty commonwealth, like Holland, than to a great, powerful, and warlike nation" such as Britain. "Extent of territory and a number of subjects," he argued, were "as much consideration to a state attentive to the sources of real grandeur, as the mere advantages of traffic."[1] No longer merely a powerful maritime trading nation, Britain, as a result of the war, had become an *imperial* nation attentive not just to commercial considerations but also to the "real grandeur" it had achieved through its overwhelming victories during the war.

In this new situation, Britain's extensive overseas possessions became important, not only for the great wealth they brought, but also for the extraordinary power they conferred upon the nation. When speaking of empire, the language of imperial grandeur now seemed to be as appropriate as the language of commerce. "By the additional wealth, power, territory, and influence . . . now thrown into our scale" as a consequence of the war, Adam Anderson asserted in 1764, Britain would be forever "enabled to preserve our dearest independence with regard to the other potentates of Europe; some of whom," he reminded his readers, had, "in little more than one century past, so increased in power and territory, as to have long since given alarming apprehensions to all their

---

[1] Anonymous, speeches, December 9, 1762, in R. C. Simmons and P. D. G. Thomas, eds., *Proceedings and Debates of the British Parliaments Respecting North America 1754–1783*, 6 vols. (White Plains, N.Y.: Kraus, 1982–86), 1: 422–23.

neighbours." Now that the French had been routed throughout the globe and almost entirely removed from North America, Anderson looked forward to the creation on the North American continent of a "vastly more extensive empire" than Britain had previously enjoyed, one "where our kindred and fellow-subjects" would pave "the way for the comfortable settlement of many more millions of people than the whole British Empire now contains."[2]

Many other writers offered similarly sanguine predictions. Thus, also in 1764, Thomas Pownall, former governor of Massachusetts Bay and soon-to-be member of Parliament, envisioned in his widely circulated tract, *The Administration of the Colonies*, the creation of an interdependent British transatlantic polity, "A GRAND MARINE DOMINION CONSISTING OF OUR POSSESSIONS IN THE ATLANTIC AND IN AMERICA UNITED INTO ONE EMPIRE, IN ... ONE CENTER, WHERE THE SEAT OF GOVERNMENT IS," a development, he was persuaded, that would "build up this country to an extent of power, to a degree of glory and prosperity, beyond the example of any age that has yet passed."[3] "Through a tract of ages, and through all the progressive steps of encreasing greatness," exclaimed an anonymous contemporary, "the whole structure of the British Empire, vast as it is," could be expected to "stand with security."[4]

From this new postwar perspective on the empire, the colonies could thus be exhibited not merely, in the tradition of earlier analysts, as the prolific seedbeds of a thriving overseas commerce and an amazing stimulus to metropolitan British manufactures and industry, but also as fields for the exertion and display of Britain's expanding, and infinitely expandable, imperial grandeur. Thus, when the chorographer John Campbell composed his massive two-volume *Political Survey of Britain*, published in London in 1774, he proudly included more than three hundred pages on "the Establishments we have made in all Parts of the World." Heralding those establishments as "so many distinguishing Testimonies" to "the commodious Situation of this Island [that is, Great Britain], the Superior Genius of its Inhabitants, and the Excellence of our Constitution, ... so many shining Trophies of our maritime Skill and naval Strength," Campbell touted them, not just for "support[ing] the Commerce," but also for "extend[ing] the Fame" and "display[ing] the Power of Great Britain."[5] Especially in view of the fiscal and physical exertions made by the metropolis on behalf of its overseas possessions during the Seven Years' War, these many emblems of British fame and power no longer appeared to be the

---

[2] Adam Anderson, *An Historical and Chronological Deduction of the Origin of Commerce, From the Earliest Accounts, containing An History of the Great Commercial Interests of the British Empire*, 4 vols. (London, 1787), 1: xliv–xlv.

[3] Thomas Pownall, *The Administration of the Colonies*, 4th ed. (London, 1768), 9–10. The first edition of this work appeared in 1764.

[4] *The Political Balance, In which the Principles and Conduct of the Two Parties are Weighed* (London, 1765), 48.

[5] John Campbell, *A Political Survey of Britain: Being a Series of Reflections on the Situation, Lands, and Inhabitants, Revenues, Colonies, and Commerce of this Island*, 2 vols. (London, 1774), 2: 567, note i.

virtually spontaneous and largely self-sustaining products of settler initiative and industry, as so many earlier analysts had suggested, but the consequences of Britain's own careful nurturing and protection, the glorious examples of Britain's own commercial, political, maritime, and military genius.

II

As they pondered the relationship between empire and imperial grandeur in the years immediately following the war, however, many metropolitan analysts of empire worried that the empire might lack the internal cohesion and guidance necessary for Britain to fulfill this bold and flattering destiny.[6] If overseas empire was so obviously an essential ingredient in Britain's rise to international power, should it any longer be permitted to function with so little supervision

---

[6] P. J. Marshall, *The Making and Unmaking of Empires: Britain, India, and America c. 1750–1783* (Oxford: Oxford University Press, 2005), 1–118, 158–206, 273–352, provides the most comprehensive and penetrating treatment of both the imperial context of and the issues in the metropolitan debate over the American question considered in this chapter. Marshall provides a more detailed look at some of the themes developed in this book in his indispensable collection of essays, *"A Free though Conquering People": Eighteenth-Century Britain* (Aldershot, U.K.: Ashgate Variorum, 2003), especially essays II ("Empire and Authority in the Later Eighteenth Century"), V ("A Nation Defined by Empire, 1755–1776"), and VIII ("The Case for Coercing America before the Revolution"). As H. T. Dickinson, "Britain's Imperial Sovereignty: The Ideological Case against the American Colonists," in Dickinson, ed., *Britain and the American Revolution* (London and New York: Longman, 1998), 64–96, has observed, the metropolitan side of the debate on the American question has never been explored in the same detail as the American side. Along with Dickinson's essay, Eliga H. Gould, *The Persistence of Empire: British Political Culture in the Age of the American Revolution* (Chapel Hill: University of North Carolina Press, 2000), 106–07; Julie Flavell, "British Perceptions of New England and the Decision for a Coercive Colonial Policy, 1774–1775," in Julie Flavell and Stephen Conway, eds., *Britain and America Go to War: The Impact of War and Warfare in Anglo-America, 1754–1815* (Gainesville: University of Florida Press, 2004), 95–115; Stephen Conway, "From Fellow-Nationals to Foreigners: British Perceptions of the Americans, circa 1739–1783," *William and Mary Quarterly*, 3d ser., 59 (2002): 65–100; and Jack P. Greene, *The Constitutional Origins of the American Revolution* (New York: Cambridge University Press, 2011), 67–186, this chapter represents little more than an early foray into this rich subject. To be sure, the relationship between the American question and the emergence of British radicalism has been explored far more fully in John Brewer, *Party Ideology and Popular Politics at the Accession of George III* (Cambridge: Cambridge University Press, 1976), 201–16; Colin Bonwick, *English Radicals and the American Revolution* (Chapel Hill: University of North Carolina Press, 1777); Robert E. Toohey, *Liberty and Empire: British Radical Solutions to the American Problems 1774–1776* (Lexington: University Press of Kentucky, 1778); and Jerome R. Reich, *British Friends of the American Revolution* (Armonk, N.Y.: M. E. Sharpe, 1998). Readers interested in the identity of those who opposed the Administration's turn to coercion will find John Sainsbury, *Disaffected Patriots: London Supporters of Revolutionary America 1769–1782* (Kingston and Montreal: McGill-Queen's University Press, 1987), very useful, while James E. Bradley, *Popular Politics and the American Revolution in England: Petitions, the Crown, and Public Opinion* (Macon, Ga.: Mercer University Press, 1986), provides an authoritative study of the public response to the debate considered here. Quite recently, Troy Bickham, *Making Headlines: The American Revolution as Seen through the British Press* (DeKalb: Northern Illinois University Press, 2009), 57–88, usefully explores the newspaper debate.

and control? Did not, as Anderson declared, the many valuable extensions of British power overseas now "demand . . . the first and highest regard"?[7] Did they not, as another writer suggested, "require new regulation"?[8] "Formerly," Arthur Young explained in 1772, "it mattered little, whether our statesmen were asleep or awake [in regard to the colonies]: And why? Because the increase of the colonies did the business for them: their increase caused the national trade to increase, and all went on silently, but prosperously." With the continuously rising *national* significance of the colonies, however, this "old dilatory sleeping plan," Young declared, would "no longer do."[9] As the Administration apologist William Knox had observed four years earlier, the "Prodigious extent of the British dominions in America, the rapid increase of the people there, the great value of their trade, all unite in giving them such a degree of importance in the empire, as requires that more attention should be paid to their concerns, by the supreme legislature."[10] In this view, metropolitan passivity in regard to overseas empire needed to give way to metropolitan activity.

Recalling the disunited and parochial behavior of Britain's North American colonies during the early years of the Seven Years' War, some analysts were anxious lest such fissiparous tendencies ultimately dissipate all the advantages the metropolis derived from the empire. Now that the war and the peace had "freed [them] from all those terrors of a foreign enemy which so lately agitated" them, such people fretted, the colonists, reflecting upon "their efforts, during the war, the [new] sense of their security, [their growing] confidence in their own power, [and] the mistaken opinion that independence [was] . . . freedom," might exhibit, as one observer said, "a restless spirit, which will become more dangerous in proportion as the people who feel it become more powerful." For an imperial nation to have unruly or uncontrollable colonies was unbecoming. For that reason, he thought, it seemed "expedient, . . . even necessary[,] to lay" the colonies under some appropriate "restraint now, while" it could still "be made binding." To this end, several writers called for measures that would at once maintain "the dominion of Great Britain" over the overseas empire, secure "to her the dependence of her colonies," and mold "the loose texture of that empire . . . into that form which is best calculated for the common good."[11]

For people with such views, the American Plantation Duties Act of 1764 and the Stamp Act of 1765 represented steps in the right direction. As one contemporary interpreter pointed out, the function of those and other metropolitan regulations adopted in the years immediately after the war was not simply to *"regulate the commerce, and improve the revenue of the* British *empire,"* but

---

[7] Anderson, *Historical and Chronological Deduction of the Origin of Commerce*, xlv.

[8] *Political Balance*, 39.

[9] Arthur Young, *Political Essays Concerning the Present State of the British Empire* (London, 1772), 552.

[10] William Knox, *The Present State of the Nation: Particularly with Respect to Its Trade* (London, 1768), 39.

[11] *Political Balance*, 44–45.

also to achieve still a third "great" purpose of empire: to "*secure the domin-ion*" of the parent state over the colonies. "By uniting these three objects," he thought, the American Plantation Duties Act became "at once a *Bill of Police, Commerce,* and *Revenue.*" As such, it promised to lay a "deep and broad foundation" on which to reconstruct the empire.[12]

The problem with this strategy was that from the beginning it met mas-sive resistance from the North American colonies. Obviously uncertain about how the colonies might react to this legislation, the Grenville Administration commissioned Thomas Whateley and Soame Jenyns, among others, to pro-duce pamphlets to justify it in constitutional terms. Responding to the new legislation and its supporting pamphlet literature with countering pamphlets, newspaper essays, legislative resolutions and petitions, an economic boycott, and a general congress, and finally resorting to riots and intimidation to prevent the enforcement of the Stamp Act, the colonists drew upon the traditional lan-guage of liberty, as it had emerged over the previous century and a half of their existence, to claim colonial exemption not only from parliamentary taxation, but also from laws relating to their internal polities.[13] Dismissing metropolitan arguments in favor of the legislation as naked expressions of a language of might or state power that ignored their status as free polities within the empire, they argued that, as Britons, they were entitled to all British liberties, that by right they were subject to no laws to which they had not consented through their representatives, and that their representatives sat in their several colonial assemblies, not in Parliament. This response set the terms for a decade-long debate within the metropolis over whether Britain's imperial grandeur required the British Parliament to hold an incontestable authority over the entire empire.

As the colonists continued, for a decade, to resist such claims and to employ the language of liberty to support their case, most of the British political nation seems to have agreed that the authority of the king-in-Parliament, the locus of sovereignty within Britain, extended over all places British. The staunchest adherents of this belief, who were in power for all but a few months between 1764 and the early 1780s, tended to conflate the language of imperial grandeur and the post–Glorious Revolution idea of parliamentary omnipotence. They found it impossible to imagine an imperial structure for a *British* Empire that did not vest ultimate authority in the *British* Parliament. Without questioning Parliament's authority, a significant Opposition, relying heavily on the lan-guages of liberty, commerce, and humanity, argued that Parliament, in the interest of the economic well-being of the empire and, more especially, of the parent state, should refrain from exerting its colonial authority in ways unpalatable to the colonies and pursue a policy of conciliation rather than confrontation. After 1766, the American question steadily functioned, as a writer complained in 1775, as "the leading ... subject of controversy amongst

---

[12] Ibid., 46, 48.
[13] See Craig Yirush, *Settlers, Liberty, and Empire: The Roots of Early American Political Theory, 1675–1775* (New York: Cambridge University Press, 2011).

us."[14] The languages of imperial grandeur, security, liberty, commerce, and humanity were intricately woven into the evolving debate between Administration and Opposition over the appropriate strategy for retaining the colonies in the empire and cementing the imperial grandeur that Britain had so recently achieved and displayed during the Seven Years' War.

Of course, few metropolitan advocates of imperial reconstruction thought for a moment that, as one of them put it, "American [demands] for pure natural liberty, and absolute uncontroulable independence" of the kind that erupted in the protests against the Stamp Act should weigh very heavily in comparison to considerations of metropolitan "British trade, glory, and influence."[15] Rather, they agreed with the principle that Charles Yorke set down in Parliament in 1766, that one of the central "maxims" that formed the basis for "a mighty empire" was "that the dominions of the Crown wherever they lie are bound by Act of Parliament of Great Britain, either expressly named or manifestly included." "This universality of the legislative power," claimed Yorke, expressing a sentiment widely shared among members of the metropolitan political nation, "is the vital principle of the whole Empire, and it has been confirmed at the Revolution that wherever the sovereignty of the Crown extends, the legislative power extends likewise."[16]

From this point of view, colonial demands for exemption from parliamentary taxation in response to the Stamp Act seemed to represent a blatant display of ingratitude and the epitome of American cheek. Having "been increasing in Riches for these Thirty Years... and having obtained immense Territory, and a Security from those Enemies, the *French* and *Indians*, who served to keep them in awe," complained one writer, "they are become at our Expence, and for which we are now starving, proud, lordly, and ambitious; or rather," he charged, "from their former Circumstances, and their vain Persuasion that we are in no Condition to dispute their Wills, have suffered these Seeds of Rebellion to break forth, and discover their long smothered Inclinations and Designs of setting up an Empire, independent of *Britain*." To give in to colonial demands, said another analyst, would "make *Americans* our Masters"[17] and Great Britain nothing more than "a province to her own colonies."[18] What did mere colonists situated so far from the center of such a great empire know about the way it should be run? Why should they have any say in its management?

This situation provoked widespread indignation among metropolitans who resented colonial resistance and invited them to employ the traditional and

---

[14] *An Answer to a Pamphlet, Entitled Taxation no Tyranny, Addressed to the Author, and to Persons in Power* (London, 1775), 49.

[15] *Application of Some General Political Rules. To the Present State of Great-Britain, Ireland and America* (London, 1766), 76–77.

[16] Charles Yorke, speech, February 3, 1766, in Simmons and Thomas, eds., *Proceedings and Debates of the British Parliaments*, 2: 137.

[17] *A Short and Friendly Caution To the Good People of England* (London, 1766), 8, 12.

[18] H. Hamersley to Horatio Sharpe, December 17, 1765, in Simmons and Thomas, eds., *Proceedings and Debates of the British Parliaments*, 2: 566.

pejorative language of alterity that Britons had long used to identify those who had left the home islands for America and other places overseas. This existing language made it easy for resentful Britons to condemn the colonists as the descendants of "a set of vagabonds and transports," an "obstinate, senseless, and abandoned set of convicts," to deplore their "baseless ingratitude," to charge them with treason, and to label them as rebels.[19] Many talked boldly about executing the Stamp Act "by Force of Arms."[20] One writer even fantasized that the Indians would seize the occasion to drive the colonists out of North America, incorporating a long passage from a 1759 essay in which Samuel Johnson, calling attention to the inhumanity and injustice of the European invasion of America and to the possibilities of historical retribution, had envisioned a situation in which the Indians would drive a colonial population weakened by war into "their ships, and reign once more in our native country."[21] By standing up for their liberty, the colonists, lamented one writer, seemed to have unleashed "BRITTANIA's hate" so thoroughly that "[A] golden fury . . . rages in each breast."[22]

Underlying such sentiments, of course, was not only the pride of imperialism in relation to colonial possessions but also the fear that, as a speaker in Parliament would declare in 1774, Britain could not "subsist without the advantages which are derived from our commerce with America." "So much beyond our natural power," the "situation we hold in Europe," he said, was entirely the result of "our commercial advantages," which in turn were largely a consequence of the colonial trade.[23] Once the colonists had "become independent," these analysts were certain, they would "trade where, and with whom they please." "Where then will be our trade?" asked one opponent of the repeal of the Stamp Act. "Where will be your Employment? And how will you get Bread for yourselves, your Wives, and Children? And where will Money be found to pay Taxes, for the Interest of our Debt? Or where shall we find Money to lessen our Debt, ease our Taxes, and by that means lower the Price of the necessaries of Life?" "The Moment we give up our Right and Power," this writer declared, "our Interest and Trade are gone."[24] Sharing the opinion of the former Jamaican planter William Beckford, who told his colleagues in Parliament, "You are not an empire without America,"[25] such writers seemed to have little doubt that Britain's commercial advantages and international standing could

[19] *The Late Occurrences in North America, and the Policy of Great Britain Considered* (London, 1766), 7–9, 29.
[20] *The General Opposition of the Colonies to the Payment of the Stamp Duty; and the Consequences of Enforcing Obedience by Military Measures; Impartially Considered* (London, 1766), 16.
[21] *Some Strictures on the Late Occurrences in North America* (London, 1766), 21–22.
[22] *Oppression: A Poem by an American, with Notes, by a Briton* (London, 1765), 19, 21.
[23] George Rice, speech, March 7, 1774, in Simmons and Thomas, eds., *Proceedings and Debates of the British Parliaments*, 4: 37.
[24] *Short and Friendly Caution*, 12–13.
[25] William Beckford, speech, December 7, 1768, in Simmons and Thomas, eds., *Proceedings and Debates of the British Parliaments*, 3: 34–35.

"never be maintained if we [do not] keep up the sovereign authority of this country" over the colonies.[26] For that reason, they called upon the "*British Senate*," as one anonymous author said in 1766, not to "suffer *English* Glory to fade, to be blasted by *American* breath; their Trade to be ruined by rebellious Subjects, nor *Englishmen* to become Slaves to *Creoles*."[27] Such dire developments, in their view, could only destroy the imperial grandeur Britain had so recently achieved.

III

Parliament endorsed this view in 1766 in the Declaratory Act that accompanied its repeal of the Stamp Act, and as colonists renewed their resistance when Parliament acted on the principles of the Declaratory Act with the Townshend measures of 1767–68 and in virtually every measure taken in reference to the colonies under the North Administration between 1770 and 1776, the Administration, supported by a substantial majority in Parliament and defended by a large pamphlet and newspaper literature, made its case for a coercive posture in terms, not of the languages of liberty and commerce, but of the languages of state power and imperial grandeur. Goaded by an articulate Opposition within Britain that advocated a more conciliatory policy, Administration spokesmen in Parliament and in the press were at once thoroughly alarmed by the implications of colonial resistance, absolutely determined to put an end to it, and deeply engaged in the effort to supply intellectual underpinnings for the Government case.

Virtually every Government writer, relying heavily on the language of imperial grandeur and operating on the assumption that the colonies were essential to Britain's international standing, emphasized the high stakes involved for metropolitan Britain. "The question which has been for some time agitated, *Whether the legislative power of Great Britain has a right to tax its American colonies?* is of all questions the most important that was ever debated in the country," declared the Scottish thinker Allan Ramsay in a pamphlet written during the Stamp Act crisis but not published until late 1768:

Those who compare it to that which was discussed at the [Glorious] Revolution, do not sufficient justice to its importance: for it is not concerning the forms of our constitution, or the share which this or that man, or this or that family, should have in the supreme government; but whether there should be any supreme government at all, and whether this, which is now a great and independent state, should, all at once, fall from its greatness, and perhaps cease to be reckoned among the least.[28]

"At this very momentous point of time," observed the author of another pamphlet published a few weeks earlier, after Britain had "carried her commerce all

---

[26] George Rice, speech, March 7, 1774, in ibid., 4: 37.

[27] *Short and Friendly Caution*, 19.

[28] [Allan Ramsay], *Thoughts on the Origin and Nature of Government. Occasioned by the Late Disputes between Great Britain and her American Colonies* (London, 1769), 1.

over the world; and acquired immortal glory by her arms: – now that her apparent felicity and power, her grandeur, dominion, and riches," had "attract[ed] the attention of all Europe, fill[ed] all nations with envy; and fire[d] their imperial monarchs with the high ambition of emulating her unequalled fame," the nation seemed "ready to fall into the Blackest contempt, and oblivion, from the base degeneracy of her sons at home, and the unbounded ambition of her offspring abroad."[29]

Not until 1774, when during the early stages of the crisis over the Coercive Acts an anonymous author published a pamphlet entitled *Colonising, or a Plain Investigation of That Subject; with the Legislative, Political and Commercial View of the Colonies*, did any writer systematically endeavor to explore and make theoretical sense out of the assumptions underlying the Government position. Beginning with a definition of "COLONISING" as "the act of a powerful and parental people," being "to a state what propagating is to a family," this author explained that if the entire population of a country were to move, it would establish not a colony but a state. Owing "their establishment to the conception, maintenance, or protection of a parent government," colonies, by contrast, were merely offshoots of their sponsoring state and as such had no "other political ground or national object, than the good of the *common weal*," which he defined narrowly as the "advantage of that government, to which all their enterprises should point." "As the *branches* grow from the *Stock*," he said, using the metaphor of a tree, "so do Colonies from their parent state, bearing its fruit and constituting its glory. While too they are spreading themselves to the sun, imbibing the element, and wrestling with the Wind," he continued, "the *Stock* makes them substantial returns and both grow together." Pursuing the logic of his metaphor, the author averred that Britain and the colonies constituted "ONE people, ruled by ONE constitution, and governed by ONE King." "Well regulated colonies" could bring "their Parent . . . nothing less than increase of numbers and possessions, extension of commerce, multiplication of manufactories, and the perfection of the arts." Perhaps equally important, by supplying commodities formerly provided by rival states, they brought "nothing more than prevention, impediment, and dependence" to those states, to the national advantage of their parent state.[30]

To do full "justice to this work of colonising," however, this author contended, a parent state had systematically to engage in "minute inquiry, deep investigation, essential distinction, and steady observation." Any "relaxation of government," he warned, could result in the colonies' acting "like *Suckers*, that would destroy the Tree, for they are truly a work of culture, where great rewards await on the science and attention [of the cultivator], and want and weedy mischief on ignorance and neglect." He classified Britain's colonies into

---

[29] *The Constitutional Right of the Legislature of Great Britain to Tax the British Colonies in America, Impartially Stated* (London, 1768), 2.

[30] *Colonising, or a Plain Investigation of That Subject; with the Legislative, Political and Commercial View of the Colonies* (London, 1774), 7–8.

two broad categories, colonies with *"muneral* Effects," yielding commodities such as sugar, tobacco, rice, coffee, and indigo that Britain did not produce, which served as "the riches and glory of Britain," and colonies that were "State Nurseries" of peoples and materials in climates similar to that of Britain, which functioned as Britain's "weapons and her armour." "Effecting constant order among so many new, various, wide-settled, differently occupied, and differently circumstanced Communities as our Colonies consist of," he observed, required the "nicest attention of policy," particularly in those colonies most similar to Britain, where he thought the "Fibres of Government" should never "be relaxed" and "the Laws should erect awful Authority." Alas, he concluded, Britain's "reflexion" and attention had not "kept...pace with" the colonies' "improvement," which, he implied, was the cause of the nation's colonial troubles.[31]

Colonising's author, in his efforts to supply a theoretical foundation for stricter metropolitan controls over the colonies, thus assumed, as did virtually all of those who spoke or wrote in behalf of the Administration, that the colonies were merely subordinate extensions of the metropolitan state. The Opposition – those "libertines of policy" and "clamorous and hardy vindicators," in the words of Samuel Johnson, the lexicographer and political writer[32] – might talk about the colonies, as did one anonymous writer in 1774, as "constituent parts of the British Empire," thereby implying "an idea of perfect equality, so far as interest is concerned," between them and the metropolis and suggesting that "every province" should "form a little empire within itself, subject to its own laws." But in the Administration view such formulations merely represented an unpersuasive effort to ignore the fact that the very word *colony* implied "a subjection to the power, and...a subserviency to the interest of the ruling state."[33] Britain's imperial grandeur thus required maintaining its supremacy over all segments of its empire.

Administration apologists did not deny that the colonies had been treated liberally and allowed a large measure of self-government. "Ever since they could be called a People," wrote Ambrose Serle in 1775, "they have enjoyed...all the Advantages and Immunities of *Britons.* Not the nearest Subjects to the Throne in *England,* nor the remotest Members of the State in *Asia*," he observed, "have had a wider Field of Freedom to range in, than the once happy Sons of highly-favored and indulged *America.*"[34] Even Samuel Johnson agreed that "an English Colony has very liberal powers of regulating its own manners and

---

[31] Ibid., 7–8, 13–16.

[32] Samuel Johnson, *Taxation no Tyranny: An Answer to the Resolutions and Address of the American Congress* (London, 1775), 15.

[33] *A Letter to Doctor Tucker on his Proposal of Separation between Great Britain and Her American Colonies* (London, 1774), 6–7.

[34] [Ambrose Serle], *Americans against Liberty: or An Essay on the Nature and Principles of True Freedom, Shewing that the Designs and Conduct of the Americans Tend Only to Tyranny and Slavery* (London, 1775), 27.

adjusting its own affairs."[35] In the Administration view, however, this experience did not exempt the colonies from metropolitan authority, and, as Johnson wrote in a 1774 pamphlet, it seemed absurd to "suppose that by sending out a colony, the nation established an independent power."[36] If the colonies and their inhabitants were "entitled to all the rights of Englishmen," were "governed by English laws, [and] entitled to English dignities," he declared, they were also "regulated by English counsels, and protected by English arms; and it seems to follow by consequence not easily avoided, that they are subject to English government, and chargeable by English taxation," and he denounced those who would try "to deprive the nation of its natural and lawful authority over its own colonies."[37]

In the emerging political atmosphere of the 1760s and 1770s, it was easy for writers enamored of the language of imperial grandeur to conflate the nation's authority and parliamentary authority. The Glorious Revolution had laid the groundwork for the slow development of the idea of Parliament, composed of the Crown and the two houses, as the locus of British sovereignty, a view that the constitutional debate with the colonies helped to enshrine, and in this atmosphere it was easy to assume, contrary to actual fact, that "the legislature," and not merely the Crown, had been an active participant in the formation of the colonies, even in the granting of "charters for their security and protection in trade." What could be more outrageous, Administration spokesmen asked, than for colonies so "entirely dependent" on the British legislature in their origins and so recently benefitted by British arms in the removal of the French from North America now to offer such profound resistance to metropolitan measures and even to "aim at independency, and endeavour to form an internal government among themselves, to the prejudice of the state to whom they owed their very being."[38]

As colonial resistance continued into the mid-1770s, many metropolitan defenders traced it not just to incipient colonial desires for independence and loose metropolitan management but specifically to the repeal of the Stamp Act in 1766. "Great Britain and her Colonies derive their present dispute, and its consequent misfortunes from the PATRIOTISM of the motley Junto who formed the appearance of an Administration, in the end of 1765 and beginning of 1766," and who pushed through the repeal of the Stamp Act, James Macpherson lamented in early 1776. "From that moment," he complained, "may be dated . . . the commencement of . . . an Aera of Public Ruin."[39] By emphasizing short-term commercial considerations over the long-term objective of keeping

---

[35] Johnson, *Taxation no Tyranny*, 24.

[36] [Samuel Johnson], *The Patriot* (London, 1774), 22–23.

[37] Ibid., 22; Johnson, *Taxation no Tyranny*, 29.

[38] *A Full and Circumstantial Account of the Disputes between Great Britain and America* (Glasgow, 1775), 2.

[39] [James Macpherson], *The Rights of Great Britain Asserted against the Claims of America* (London, 1776), 21.

the colonies tightly under the thumb of the metropolis, such concessions, Government writers were persuaded, undermined the very foundations of empire. Following the advice of merchants during the Stamp Act crisis, Samuel Johnson declared in 1775, was an enormous mistake. Because the concern of merchants was "not of glory, but of gain, not of publick wealth, but of private emolument," he thought that they should "rarely be consulted about war and peace, or any designs of wide extent and distant consequences." Suggesting that concessions to mercantile interests could preserve the colonial trades only "for the moment" and that only political leaders attuned to the possibility of national "glory" and "wealth" were competent to manage the empire in ways calculated to maintain that "superiority" by which they alone could ensure the "continuance of those trades," Johnson in this single sentence provided a succinct example of the Administration's tendency to subordinate the language and interests of commerce to the language of imperial grandeur, with its emphasis upon metropolitan political superiority. Britain's political standing, Johnson emphasized, could "be most effectively preserved, by being kept always in our own power." Indeed, Government supporters argued that metropolitan political superiority within the empire was the essential precondition for imperial commercial success and for international military and naval supremacy.[40]

To maintain Britain's superiority and its imperial grandeur, it appeared to Administration supporters in 1774–76, required a firm hand. They pointed out that the New-York Restraining Act of 1767, passed by Parliament and suspending the New York Assembly until it had complied with an act requiring assemblies to provide for the costs of quartering British troops stationed in their colonies, had worked, the New York Assembly having "recovered the just sense of" its "duty" so that it could be "restored to [its] ... authority."[41] Colonial resistance to the Tea Act of 1773 and the Coercive Acts now rendered beyond "a single doubt," asserted an anonymous writer in December 1774, that

the loose situation of things in our American Colonies requires a speedy reformation, and demands the full exertion of the Legislature of this Kingdom to remedy subsisting evils before they grow rooted and confirmed, by bringing the Colonies into so good and sound a state, that every part of those distant territories may enjoy its due proportion of nutriment, and be fitted and disposed to promote the interest, honour, and dignity of Great Britain, their Head, Mother, and Protectress.[42]

"To bring its refractory Offspring back again to that Duty and Allegiance they so boldly disavow," William Allen wrote in April 1774, Britain needed a plan that would then "be enforced with all its collective Power." "On such a measure as this," he added, employing the language of imperial grandeur,

[40] Johnson, *Taxation no Tyranny*, 8.
[41] *Full and Circumstantial Account*, 7.
[42] *A Letter to a Member of Parliament on the Present Unhappy Dispute between Great-Britain and Her Colonies, wherein the Supremacy of the Former is Asserted and Proved* (London, 1774), 43–44.

"depends our Existence as the happiest, most free, and greatest People on the Face of the Earth."[43]

Nor, added another writer in November 1775, did the fact that the colonies had enjoyed a large measure of British liberty over the previous century and a half present any obstacle to coercive measures. "The fact indeed is that most states do follow the plan of their own government in settling colonies; because it is what they are best acquainted with themselves," he pointed out, but for a colony to "*claim* its own laws, and choose its own mode of raising a revenue" seemed to him absolutely "contrary to the principles of [imperial] government, and acting in open defiance of that state from whence the colony derived its being." Because those principles dictated that colonies should always "be controuled by such laws as a parent-state judges most conducive to the joint interest of both," however, it followed that "Right . . . to a particular form of government," no matter how long established, could not "be pleaded by any colonies. Expedience may, but of that expedience the legislature of the parent-state must judge." When it came to colonial governance, he suggested, British libertarian traditions and decades of practice counted for nothing in competition with considerations of state as defined by the metropolis, and the language of imperial grandeur trumped the language of liberty.[44]

That force might be necessary to carry out the repressive measures they were advocating did not give such people pause. "Violent remedies," said one analyst in late 1774, "must sometimes be applied to obstinate diseases." "For my own part," he declared, "I think it far more honourable for this Nation to run even the risque of losing her Colonies in asserting her just Rights . . . than to retain them on base and ignoble terms. This Kingdom holds nothing under a weak, contested title," he proudly announced;

there is not a single ray that adorns the Imperial Crown of England, but what has been obtained by the noblest kind of purchase. We enjoy no casual advantages under grace and favour. The spirit and swords of our ancestors have made us the terror of Nations; and it will be a prodigy indeed, if their posterity should crouch and tamely yield to those who owe the Kingdom allegiance and dutiful submission.

"Let it be remembered," he wrote, drawing upon the example of the most extensive empire in antiquity, "that when the ancient Romans had occasion to establish regulations in their Provinces, it was not a mob in Italy or Gaul that dictated the terms; it was the powerful thunder of the Forum, and the Capital of Rome, that bellowed obedience and submission through all the Empire."[45]

For the many metropolitans of similar views, the massive colonial resistance to the Coercive Acts in 1774 and 1775 represented such a blatant challenge to

---

43 William Allen, *The American Crisis: A Letter, Addressed to the Earl Gower, Lord President of the Council* (London, 1774), 5.

44 *A Plain State of the Argument between Great-Britain and Her Colonies* (London, 1775), 9–11.

45 *A Letter to a Member of Parliament on the Present Unhappy Dispute between Great-Britain and Her Colonies*, 38, 45–46.

Britain's imperial pretensions that the use of force seemed to be the only appropriate response. Mocking the Opposition's suggestions that Americans might put up a formidable defense, they dismissed American claims that they could muster three million "Whigs fierce for liberty, and disdainful of dominion" as nothing more than empty bravado that, as Samuel Johnson put it, "instead of terrifying the English hearer to tame acquiescence," rather disposed "him to hasten the experiment of bending obstinacy to attack a nation thus prolific while we may [yet] hope to prevail." "Men accustomed to think themselves masters," Johnson said in reference to the majority of the British political nation, "do not love to be threatened."[46] "Notwithstanding... all their boasted numbers and disciplined provincials," said another Government writer in 1775, they were "but in a poor situation to engage in a war with us," and in proceeding to spell out their weaknesses he made a compelling case that it would be "an easy matter for Britain to ruin her Colonies."[47] Who could doubt, as another writer said, that the success of colonial arms was "an event little to be dreaded!"[48]

III

Not all metropolitan Britons agreed with this drift of thought about the empire. Indeed, during the long-running debate over how to respond to colonial resistance during the dozen years after 1764, a variety of spokesmen in Parliament and in the press subjected this view to a penetrating examination and developed an alternative interpretation that privileged commercial returns over imperial grandeur and state power, and colonial affection and liberty over colonial obedience and submission. This interpretation was an extension of an old intellectual tradition. Ever since Davenant in the late 1690s, some analysts of empire had emphasized the relationship between colonial loyalty and mild metropolitan governance. Repeatedly, they had pointed out that the colonists did "not think themselves aliens, or the less a-kin to those in *Great Britain*, because separated by a vast ocean, and dwelling in a distant part of the globe." They stressed the degree to which the colonists "insist[ed] that they" were "branches of the same *British* tree, tho' transplanted in a different soil" and that they had "not forfeited their *British* rights by that removal, because they [had] removed with consent of the government, and sincerely acknowledge[d] themselves to be subjects of the same King."[49] Restated, elaborated, and refined, this interpretation, which at its heart relied heavily on the languages of liberty and commerce, provided most of the intellectual support for the agitation that led to the

---

[46] Johnson, *Taxation no Tyranny*, 7.

[47] *Full and Circumstantial Account*, 11–12.

[48] *A Letter to a Member of Parliament on the Present Unhappy Dispute between Great-Britain and Her Colonies*, 46.

[49] *State of the British and French Colonies in North America, With Respect to Number of People, Forces, Forts, Indians, Trade and Other Advantages* (London, 1755), 63–64.

successful repeal of the Stamp Act in 1766 and to metropolitan opposition to subsequent measures that colonists found objectionable.

The principal threat to the continuing utility and unity of the empire, according to the holders of this view, was not colonial desires for independence but what a later writer referred to as "this new mode of governing the colonies."[50] People of this persuasion agreed with their opponents that a firm connection with the colonies was essential to Britain's ongoing economic success and international power. Indeed, harking back to all those early eighteenth-century writers who had stressed the commercial benefits and foundations of the empire, they emphasized the enormous annual "profits to *Great Britain* from the trade of the colonies."[51] They pointed to the fact that before the new measures of 1764–66, Britain, as Isaac Barré told Parliament, had been "at the head of the world," with both the "East and the West Indies... in your hands,"[52] and, said Edmund Burke, "North America was... indeed a great strength to this nation," a "sound, an active, a vigorous member of the empire,"[53] the whole of which, said Sir William Draper, was bound together by "one common language, descent, and affinity,... one common affection and interest" that promised to "*unite* us for ever."[54] Under the old system, said Burke in his speech on American taxation in April 1774, "whilst England pursued trade, and forgot revenue," the colonies had experienced unparalleled growth and developed a "flourishing commerce," while Britain had "not only acquired commerce but... actually created the very objects of trade in America; and by that creation... raised the trade of this kingdom at least four-fold."[55] Calling for conciliatory measures and making extensive use of the language of commerce, Opposition writers counseled those in power to take a practical view, recommending that "A Commercial Nation... act like a Commercial Individual, and weigh profit and loss in important scales."[56]

The Opposition's underlying contention was that the Government and its supporters had utterly failed to comprehend the historical foundations and conditions for Britain's imperial success. They started from the argument that early modern European empires had no historical parallels. "Arms, not Commerce, was the chief Employment of" the Romans, one writer pointed out

---

[50] *Plan of ReUnion Between Great Britain and Her Colonies* (London, 1778), 154.

[51] William Pitt, speech, January 14, 1766, in Simmons and Thomas, eds., *Proceedings and Debates of the British Parliaments*, 2: 89.

[52] Isaac Barré, speech, March 5, 1770, in ibid., 3: 227.

[53] Edmund Burke, *Observations on the Late State of the Nation* (London, 1769), in Paul Langford, ed., *Party, Parliament, and the American Crisis 1766–1774* (Oxford, 1981), 128.

[54] Sir William Draper, *The Thoughts of a Traveller upon our American Disputes* (London, 1774), 27.

[55] Burke, "Speech on American Taxation," April 19, 1774, in Langford, ed., *Party, Parliament, and the American Crisis 1766–1774*, 429.

[56] Draper, *Thoughts of a Traveller*, 14.

during the Stamp Act crisis; their principal objects,[57] added another, were "the glory of the Roman name, and the plunder of the rest of mankind, for the benefit of the Roman people," and they extracted "tribute and servility" from their conquered colonies. By contrast, this last writer explained, the "colonies established by the modern European nations . . . in uncultivated and uncivilized countries" had "two apparent views; the establishment of the Christian religion, and the increase of dominion." In the British case, the increase of dominion did not entail the establishment "of an uncontrouled power over slaves," as the Romans sought, "but a dominion founded on freedom; and not founded for the purposes of ambition and vain glory of a monarch, or a partial regard to this or that country, but for the establishment and extension of the commerce of the British dominions." Unlike the Roman colonies, the English had thus been founded by "freemen, leaving their native home to extend its commerce for the public good" and providing "a liberal obedience, filial affection, and those advantages which the balance of trade gives" in return for "that protection which the colonies have a right to expect from" the mother country.[58]

In a tract published in 1776, Samuel Estwick, the London agent for Barbados, elaborated on this point at considerable length. Modern colonies, he observed, had evolved out of and were characterized by what could only be understood as an entirely "new species of colonization." Unlike either the Greek colonies, which, Estwick explained, were the products of "excursions of people to ease a country surcharged with inhabitants," or the Roman colonies, which had "been planted among vanquished nations to over-awe, and hold them in subjection," the modern colonies established during the "last two centuries" were "*colonies of commerce,*" with trade as "the *sole* object and occasion of them." This modern form of "*commercial* colonization" differed "essentially from every other species of colonization that is known," said Estwick, and it followed that the principal concern of the managers who presided over the new commercial empires arising out of this form of colonization should be to promote the colonial trades as the principal instruments for national prosperity and economic growth.[59]

As Opposition spokesmen never tired of pointing out, the British experience with this commercially driven form of empire building had by the end of the Seven Years' War produced "a fabric at once the dread and wonder of the world,"[60] the envy of all other European imperial powers. Calling upon his

---

[57] *The General Opposition of the Colonies to the Payment of the Stamp Duty; and the Consequences of Enforcing Obedience by Military Measures, Impartially Considered* (London, 1766), 29.

[58] *The Late Occurrences in North America, and Policy of Great Britain Considered* (London, 1766), 34–35, 37.

[59] Samuel Estwick, *A Letter to the Reverend Josiah Tucker* (London, 1776), 93–94.

[60] *A Letter to Sir William Meredith, Bart. In Answer to His Late Letter to the Earl of Chatham* (London, 1774), 8.

readers, as did one Opposition writer in 1769, to compare Britain's "present elevation with that mediocrity which marked its condition in the reign of the former Stuarts," he insisted, borrowing one of the central themes of commercial writings on the empire, that "the happy difference" was entirely "owing to the colonies" and that the "advantages... derived from their commerce have more especially contributed to raise the kingdom to its present meridian of wealth and power."[61] By the 1750s, the American trades, Opposition writers contended, were bringing Britain a clear "profit of two millions a year,"[62] and they reminded their readers that "the centre of government" in Britain received not just riches "from the detached parts of its dominions, but likewise" power, "credit and honour in the world."[63] "It is by the American continent only," an Opposition author asserted in April 1775, "that the balance of power in Europe can be any longer in your hands." "Your great superiority in numbers there," he continued, enabled Britain to "command both the Americas, command Spain and Portugal, [and] influence France and other powers of Europe."[64] If the "grandeur of the Roman Empire" had long since been "annihilated," declared another writer during the Stamp Act crisis, "this island, formerly a province to" Rome "and looked upon as almost out of the world," had through the agency of the colonies acquired "a greater dominion than Rome ever prided itself in, and" was "now the centre of riches and authority."[65]

Opposition analysts traced this success to the gentle mode of British colonial governance. "It was a happy idea," said Jonathan Shipley, bishop of St. Asaph and an articulate and perceptive opponent of the Government measures taken during the crisis that precipitated war and American independence, "that made us first consider" the colonies "as instruments of commerce than as objects of government." "Had they been planted by any other kingdom but our own," Shipley declared, invoking both the language of liberty and a language of British exceptionalism that stretched back at least as far as the English legal theorist Sir John Fortescue in the mid fifteenth century, "the inhabitants would have carried with them the chains of oppression, to which they had been inured at home" and at "best... could only have hoped to be considered as the live stock upon a lucrative farm, which might sometimes be suffered to thrive for the sake of their produce." "From the beginning," however, Shipley insisted in 1773 in a sermon preached to the Society for the Propagation of the Gospel in Foreign Parts, Britain had "treated her colonies in a very

---

[61] *A Letter to the Right Honourable the Earl of Hillsborough. On the Present Situation of Affairs in America* (London, 1769), 116.

[62] [John Erskine], *Reflections on the Rise, Progress, and Probable Consequences of the Present Contentions with the Colonies* (Edinburgh, 1775), 25.

[63] Matthew Robinson-Morris, Baron Rokeby, *Considerations on the Measures Carrying on with respect to the British Colonies in North America* (London, 1774), in Paul H. Smith, ed., *English Defenders of American Freedoms 1774–1778* (Washington, DC: Library of Congress, 1972), 103.

[64] *Answer to a Pamphlet, Entitled Taxation no Tyranny*, 39.

[65] *Late Occurrences in North America*, 28–29.

different manner." Always giving priority to commercial considerations, they had provided their colonies with "liberty . . . to use their own judgment in the management of their own interest." By permitting the colonies to enjoy "the form and the spirit of our own constitution" through the instrument of representative assemblies, moreover, they had effectively placed colonists "on the same equal footing" with Britons at home and then "joined with them in fairly carrying on one common interest." "There is no instance in the records of time," Shipley declared, "where infant colonies have been treated with such a just and liberal indulgence."[66]

Making extensive use of the language of liberty, metropolitan protagonists of the colonies, throughout the late 1760s and 1770s, took pride in the fact that, in the best British tradition, "the blessings of liberty and good government" had been "diffused in a most unexampled manner . . . through our remotest provinces." "Look, Sir, into the history of the provinces of other states, of the Roman provinces in ancient time; of the French, Spanish, Dutch and Turkish provinces of more modern date," George Dempster told Parliament in October 1775, "and you will find every page stained with acts of oppressive violence, of cruelty, injustice and peculation."[67] "In America," agreed Arthur Young, "Spain, Portugal and France have planted despotism; only Britain liberty."[68] "Whereas other great Empires have been founded in Violence, and the Success of Armies from whence they carried in themselves the Seeds of their own Destruction from the natural Repugnance of human Nature to a slavish Subjection," added John Campbell, the British Empire had "been acquired and united to us by the Ties of mutual Interests and a reciprocal Communication of Benefits." "Wherever seated," he exclaimed, "the Subjects of Britain" were "free."[69] That Britain's American colonies "enjoyed a degree of happiness and liberty, which, in provinces distant from the seat of Government" had "no example in any former age," William Pulteney was persuaded, was the principal reason why they had "gone on encreasing in wealth and population, in a manner never before experienced in the world."[70] All Britons could be proud, said Dempster, that they had "sown the seeds of liberty over [such a] great part of the world." That fact, it seemed to him, was "the most meritorious part of the conduct of Great Britain."[71]

---

[66] Jonathan Shipley, Bishop of St. Asaph, *A Speech Intended to have been Spoken by the Bishop of St. Asaph, on a Bill for Altering the Charters of the Colony of Massachusetts Bay* (London, 1775), and *A Sermon Preached before the Incorporated Society for the Propagation of the Gospel in Foreign Parts* (London, 1773), in Smith, ed., *English Defenders of American Freedoms*, 19, 32, 34.

[67] George Dempster, speech, October 27, 1775, in Simmons and Thomas, eds., *Proceedings and Debates of the British Parliaments*, 6: 140.

[68] Young, *Political Essays*, 20.

[69] Campbell, *Political Survey of Britain*, 1: iv.

[70] William Pulteney, *Thoughts on the Present State of Affairs with America*, 5th ed. (London, 1778), 12.

[71] George Dempster, speech, May 6, 1774, in Simmons and Thomas, eds., *Proceedings and Debates of the British Parliaments*, 4: 339.

The phenomenal success of this liberal approach to imperial management, it seemed to Opposition spokesmen, constituted a strong argument for its continuance. "Perhaps the annals of history have never afforded a more grateful spectacle to a benevolent and philosophick mind, than the growth and progress of the British colonies in North America," Shipley observed.

We see a number of scattered settlements, formed at first for the purposes of trade, or from a spirit of enterprize; to procure a maintenance, or to enjoy the exercise of their religion, *which in those unhappy days was refused them at home*, growing by degrees, under the protection of their mother-country, who treated them with the indulgence due to their weakness and infancy, into little separate commonwealths. Placed in a climate, that soon became fruitful and healthy by their industry; possessing that liberty which was the *natural growth of their own country*, and secured by her power against foreign enemies, they seem to have been intended, as a solitary experiment, to instruct the world to what improvements and happiness mankind will naturally attain, when they are suffered to use their own prudence, in search of their own interest.[72]

Shipley was only one of many people who admired colonial achievements within the framework of this loose imperial governance. With little direction and even less financial help from the metropolis, colonial settlers, as Matthew Robinson-Morris, Baron Rokeby, noted in a 1774 pamphlet, had

divided themselves into several different governments; they have according to certain rules or laws agreed upon among them allotted every man his own; they have felled the forests; they have cleared and tilled the land, they have planted it, they have sown it, they have stocked it with cattle; they have built themselves houses; they have entered into exchange and commerce; they have spared and saved for a future day or for their families; they have by many and various means acquired many and various sorts of property.[73]

As Rokeby pointed out, this wide scope for action on the part of British colonists betokened the enjoyment of a high degree of political liberty. "As to their internal constitution," he observed, "Our North American colonies are . . . a very free people, as free as the Venetians, the Dutch or Swiss, or perhaps more so than any of them." "Certainly true and genuine," this liberty, he thought, proceeded "from their Assemblies['] being not only the nominal but the real representatives of those whom they govern. They are elected, fairly, fully, and often."[74] As the Scottish writer John Erskine explained in a 1776 pamphlet that showed considerable understanding of the nature of constitutional development in the British Empire, metropolitan authorities and colonists alike had ever "considered [the colonists] as having quitted the realm," and while the colonists "incorporated [themselves] into distinct communities," the Crown granted them the "*jus regalia*" and encouraged them

---

[72] Shipley, *Sermon Preached before the Society for the Propagation of the Gospel*, in Smith, ed., *English Defenders of American Freedoms*, 17–19.

[73] Rokeby, *Considerations on the Measures*, in ibid., 5.

[74] Ibid., 56.

to establish "their own peculiar legislatures, free, uncontrouled and complete, in conjunction with the king's deputy." "For a century and a half," he continued, "the course and practice of government" had operated according to a division of authority and responsibilities between metropolis and colonies, with the metropolitan government "imposing external and port duties, but never directly laying internal taxes on the Colonies for their lands, &c. or on their transactions within the precincts of the jurisdiction of their several territories."[75] "In all her internal concerns," Edmund Burke declared in 1774, America "had every characteristic mark of a free people."[76]

This long-term experience with the existing division of authority had accustomed colonists, as Rokeby declared, to think of themselves as

entitled to welfare and happiness, and to seek and pursue those blessings, by all the methods not attended with fraud or violence towards others, which they shall conceive and believe the most probable to procure and ensure them; that they have for that end a right to freedom in their government and to security in their persons and properties.[77]

In Erskine's words, they believed that they were "entitled to a constitution of the same political liberty as that which they [had] left" behind in Britain and that "their constitutions" could not "be new modelled and reformed, or suspended and taken away at the will of the sovereign," as the Administration tried to do in the case of Massachusetts with the Massachusetts Government Act of 1774.[78]

Such free subjects, Opposition writers insisted, could not be treated as inferiors who had to bend to the commands of superiors, one writer in early 1775 complaining of those many metropolitans who were "so intoxicated with folly, as to conceit that these Plantations are our *farms*, and the colony-subjects our *tenants.*"[79] The author of a wide-ranging analysis of Britain's relationship with the several components of the British Empire, published in London in 1766, went right to the heart of the British use of the language of alterity in reference to colonials. "It is difficult," he declared, "for a people" like the metropolitan British, "who behold themselves superior to others in arts, in arms and industry, not to give way to an over favourable opinion of self; and not to bear an haughtiness of deportment to those, whom they look upon as far beneath them;" or to develop an "insolence" that confirmed them in the opinion "that other countries are made for their sole use and gratification."[80] As another anonymous writer noted in 1768, however, such ideas were "certainly mistaken." The colonies, he argued, could not be considered "in the light of

---

[75] Erskine, *Reflections*, 8–9, 12.

[76] *Speech of Edmund Burke, Esq. On American Taxation April 19, 1774* (London, 1774), 23.

[77] Rokeby, *Considerations on the Measures*, in Smith, ed., *English Defenders of American Freedoms*, 52.

[78] Erskine, *Reflections*, 9.

[79] *Three Letters to a Member of Parliament on the Subject of the Present Dispute with our American Colonies* (London, 1775), 51.

[80] *Application of Some General Political Rules*, 10–11.

factories, who are only to contribute to our wealth and aggrandizement, and are wholly to be regulated and controulled by ourselves, in such manner as we . . . think will best answer our present designs and purposes." "The increase of dominions and subjects" through the colonies, he averred, should be recognized as "a proportionable increase of wealth and power to the whole empire, and not" considered merely for the "aggrandizement of one part of it at the expense of the other.[81]

As far as Opposition spokesmen were concerned, the roots of Britain's difficulties with the North American colonies lay, not in the colonies, but in the metropolis, and by the mid-1770s, Opposition writers could provide a long history of alleged Administration misdeeds towards the colonies that violated both Britain's traditional emphasis upon commerce in imperial matters and its libertarian heritage. The "resentment that appears among us, at the late misbehaviour of the Americans," insisted one anonymous pamphlet writer in 1774, was entirely misdirected,[82] and Shipley in the same year sought to encourage in his readers a consciousness that "we were the aggressors, that we gave the provocation, and that their disobedience is the fruit of our own imprudent and imperious conduct."[83] The American disturbances, another writer succinctly declared, were directly attributable to "want of Capacity and misconduct of Administration themselves."[84] Already in 1769, at the height of the controversy over the renewed attempt to tax and otherwise regulate the colonies through the Townshend Acts, Gervase Parker Bush, an Irishman publishing in London, had warned that "these further efforts to deprive Americans . . . of a liberty, which they have possessed, many years, under the tutelage of Great Britain" represented such a violent change in the traditional mode of British imperial governance that colonial resistance was inevitable,[85] and many additional and prospective missteps over the next few years caused Shipley and many others in 1774 to despair over the results.

No nation has ever before contrived, in so short a space of time, without any war or public calamity (unless unwise measures be so called) to destroy such ample resources of commerce, wealth and power, as of late were ours, and which, if they had been rightly improved, might have raised us to a state of more honourable and permanent greatness than the world has yet seen.[86]

---

[81] *An Inquiry into the Nature and Causes of the Present Dispute between the British Colonies in America and their Mother Country, and Their Reciprocal Claims and just Rights impartially examined and fairly stated* (London, 1769), 5–6.

[82] *A Letter to Dr. Tucker on his Proposal of Separation between Great Britain and the American Colonies* (London, 1774), 32.

[83] Shipley, *A Speech Intended to have been Spoken*, in Smith, ed., *English Defenders of American Freedoms*, 38.

[84] "A Friend to Both Countries" [Charles Garth], *America Vindicated from the High Charge of Ingratitude and Rebellion* (Devizes, 1774), 4.

[85] Gervase Parker Bush, *Case of Great Britain and America, Addressed to the King, and Both Houses of Parliament* (London, 1769), 38.

[86] Shipley, *A Speech Intended to have been Spoken*, in Smith, ed., *English Defenders of American Freedoms*, 42.

These were common themes among Opposition writers in the mid-1770s. Before the present reign when Grenville and other like-minded ministers "seized the helm" and "high-flying maxims regulated the state," declared an anonymous pamphleteer, one of many answering Samuel Johnson's *Taxation No Tyranny*, most ministers "were satisfied with America, because she purchased our goods, encreased the revenue *by that purchase* – enriched our merchants – employed our men – raised seamen for our fleets." In return for these "solid benefits," ministers "never dreamed of" taxing the colonies or of depriving "them of those liberties, which they enjoyed by inheritance, as Englishmen – and" the colonists "looked with love, reverence, and gratitude to Britain – as the Country which gave birth to their ancestors – and protected them from the assaults of their enemies." Under these arrangement, he observed, "We never imagined them independent – and they never termed us tyrannical." Rather, metropolis and colonies "went hand in hand to greatness, a mutual reciprocation of kind offices...strengthened the social bands of friendship," while Britain's "arms extirpated the French – and brought the Indians into subjection – and in return, the Americans poured in their gold by Millions into Britain. Blessed moments of unanimity – grandeur, wealth, strength, happiness, how are ye fled!," he lamented. "What pestilential hand has blighted such fair blossoms with its political touch? What cankered worm has destroyed the fruit which might have been reaped in luxuriant abundance, to nourish, and enrich both countries?" "If losing America, or resigning it, is the present alternative," this writer asserted, Britain had only the Administration "to thank...for having forced us, *wrong-headedly*, into so shocking a dilemma."[87]

Almost to a person, the Opposition was committed to preserving the empire intact. Rejecting suggestions by Adam Smith and Josiah Tucker in behalf of a voluntary separation that would spare Britain all costs of colonial administration and defense while not alienating colonial trade,[88] they agreed with their opponents that retention of the colonies was necessary for the preservation of metropolitan prosperity and imperial greatness. Both sides were animated by deep fears about how Britain would cope in a world without the American colonies.[89] In contrast to the Administration, however, Opposition writers

[87] *The Pamphlet, Entitled, 'Taxation No Tyranny,' Candidly Considered, and Its Arguments, and Pernicious Doctrines, Exposed and Refuted* (London, 1775), 4–5, 98–99.
[88] See Josiah Tucker, *An Humble Address and earnest Appeal to Those Respectable Personages in Great-Britain and Ireland, Who, by Their Great and Permanent Interest in Landed Property, Their Liberal Education, Elevated Rank, and Enlarged Views, are the Ablest Judges, and the Fittest to Decide Whether a Connection with, or a Separation from the Continental Colonies of America, be most for the National Advantage, and the Lasting Benefit of these Kingdoms* (Gloucester, 1775).
[89] See, among many examples, the anonymous *Private Letters from an American in England to his Friends in America* (London, 1769), which consisted of fictional letters "written towards the close of the eighteenth century" by "a young American" visitor to the "country of his ancestors" after the "seat of government" had been "transferred to America[,] and England" was "an almost deserted depopulated nation." The quotations are taken from the blurb at the front of the pamphlet.

advocated conciliation and the avoidance of force and other irritating measures. The route to imperial grandeur, they thought, was emphatically not
through repression and coercion. "Instead of checking their encrease by a jealous and hostile policy, you ought to encourage it by every just and generous
institution," advised one anonymous pamphleteer in April 1775;

instead of exasperating them by system, you should bind them by every demonstration of
liberal attachment; and . . . you should leave to them to conduct themselves to prosperity,
without the alarming interposition of imperial authority, except where it is *bona fide*
essential to preserve Great-Britain at the head of a united empire.[90]

Surely, said Shipley, "there are methods of making reasonable concessions, and
yet without injuring our dignity."[91]

Indeed, few Opposition thinkers had much patience with the Government's
preoccupation with metropolitan dignity, "the point of honour," and several of
them directly addressed the argument emphasized by Administration defenders
that "We must not let down the dignity of the mother country, but preserve
her sovereignty over all the parts of the British Empire." That this argument
had "something in it that sounds pleasant to the ears of an Englishman," they
did not dispute. But, making extensive use of the languages of commerce and
liberty, they argued that it "otherwise" carried "little weight" in comparison to
the commercial losses and the restrictions on colonial liberty that resulted from
the Administration's continuing commitment to a coercive colonial policy.[92]
"Many members of both houses will doubtless talk high of the honor of Parliament, and under the influences of this idea, strenuously insist that vigorous
(by which I suppose they mean violent) measures should be pursued," Charles
Garth observed before the passage of the Coercive Acts in the spring of 1774.
"But in the midst of their wrath, it would perhaps be wise and prudent to consider, that the true honor and dignity of both houses can never be supported
by enforcing claims destructive to the rights and interests of humanity." The
question confronting Parliament, he said, was

not Whether we shall maintain his Majesty's authority, which has been injudiciously
enforced, or exert the false honour and dignity of Parliament, in Opposition to the
undoubted rights of an injured people; but, Whether *Great-Britain* shall, by pursuing
the maxims of a sound and upright policy with respect to the Colonies, *forever* establish a
permanent and solid foundation for a just constitutional Union between both countries.

The question, he continued, was

Whether the honor and dignity of Parliament can be better maintained by obstinately
persisting in measures destructive to the interest of both countries; or whether that

---

[90] *Answer to a Pamphlet, Entitled Taxation no Tyranny*, 39–40.
[91] Shipley, *A Speech Intended to have been Spoken*, in Smith, ed., *English Defenders of American Freedoms*, 37.
[92] Ibid.

honor [of] which, when their own benefit is concerned, they affect to be so scrupulously nice, can be better maintained, than by extending the broad hand of Justice over the *Americans* who never disputed their authority, until Parliament herself set up claims . . . subversive of the principles of the constitution itself.

"What wise nation in pursuit of a *false notion of honor*," Garth asked, "would in an unnatural contest with her own children, inconsiderately adopt violent measures, at the risk of a civil war, one third of her commerce, one third of her revenue, and that too at a time when she is groaning under the weight of great army and naval establishments, and an immense national debt at her back"?[93] Imperial grandeur, Opposition writers thus suggested, depended upon trade, not upon constitutional niceties designed to protect British pride from the ignominy of being unable to exert full political mastery over the colonies.

In brief, the Opposition argued, the central question confronting the empire was not why the colonies were resisting, but, in Shipley's formulation, "by what steps we first gained their affection, and preserved it so long; and by what conduct we have lately lost it." From the perspective of Britain's long history of imperial success and the difficulties following from its attempts at imperial reconstruction after 1763, it seemed evident, as Shipley said, resorting to the language of liberty, that the "true art of government" consisted "in *not governing too much*."[94] "Unlucky for" Britain, added the pamphleteer Hugh Baillie in 1774 in expanding upon this same point, the "party in power have imagined, that by encouraging" the colonies, "as our fathers have done for about 200 years, we may lose their subjection to us; which, by the bye, we can never keep, except by using them well, and making it their interest to be subservient to us. In short, our conduct of late, with regard to America, puts me in mind of the man, who in a storm, for fear of being drowned, threw himself into the sea." The continued alienation of the American colonies through such measures as the Coercive Acts, Baillie warned, lapsing into the language of national security, could only lead to the loss of "the greatest branch of our trade, and our greatest nursery for sailors" and the exposure of Britain to French conquest, "whereas, by preserving our colonies there, and the affection of the inhabitants, we must become the greatest nation in Europe."[95]

With such high stakes involved, "prudent management," in Burke's words, seemed to the Opposition to be the wisest policy. No longer, Burke emphasized to the House of Commons in March 1775, could the colonies "be considered as one of those *Minima* which are out of the eye and consideration of the law, not a paltry excrescence of state, not a mean dependant, who may be neglected

[93] [Garth], *America Vindicated*, 5–8, 13.

[94] Shipley, *A Speech Intended to have been Spoken*, in Smith, ed., *English Defenders of American Freedoms*, 31; idem, *Sermon Preached before the Society for the Propagation of the Gospel*, in ibid., 22.

[95] Hugh Baillie, *A Letter to Dr. Shebeare: containing a refutation of his arguments concerning the Boston and Quebec Acts of Parliament* (London, 1774), 19–20, 22.

with little damage, and provoked with little danger." Rather, he advised, "the handling" of "so large a mass of the interests and feelings of the human race" required "some degree of care and caution."[96] So rapid had been the rise of the colonies in "population, strength, and spirit," said an anonymous writer the following October, echoing Burke's sentiments, that it would "be prudent in us to treat [them] with more respect."[97] Burke's prudential formula was simply "to revert to your old principles," avoiding all "metaphysical distinctions of rights" and leaving "the Americans as they antiently stood" to tax themselves, as they had done "from the beginning." "Whilst we held to this happy course," he said, "we drew more from the Colonies than all the impotent violence of despotism ever could extract from them."[98] "Surely no man can doubt," declared an anonymous writer in April 1775, "but that system of colony government is best by which you will derive the greatest benefit from your Colonies, with the least disquietude and discomfort to them and to yourselves."[99]

But many other Opposition writers, spelling out the implications of the English language of liberty for the organization of the empire, moved well beyond the prudential argument to mount a powerful case in behalf of colonial entitlement to English liberties. The "peculiar excellence" of "the English constitution," they noted, was that it proclaimed "to all a liberty and freedom unknown in other countries,"[100] and they pointed out that Britain could not deprive the colonists of traditional English liberties without violating its own principles and acting out of character. "Let Englishmen, who have been admired for ages, for their regard to liberty blush, when it is now said, that, by superior force, they would deprive three or four millions of their fellow-subjects of those rights and privileges to which they are so attached themselves," the political radical John Cartwright declared in the fall of 1774:

Is that the people, foreigners will say, who are so fond of liberty? No; we have always mistaken them: they are selfish, arbitrary, and tyrannical, fond of the privileges they enjoy; but they would exclude the rest of the world, nay, their fellow-subjects, from the same advantages – advantages which they have hitherto enjoyed in common with Englishmen. Is this the people so celebrated for their humanity?"

he asked rhetorically. "No; they are most inhuman: they invade the most precious rights a human being can enjoy, and would render the rest of mankind miserable servile wretches: 'Tis really strange, the national character of Englishmen should have been so much mistaken!"[101]

[96] *Speech of Edmund Burke, Esq. On Moving His Resolutions for Conciliation with the Colonies, March 22, 1775,* 3d ed. (London, 1775), 15–16, 26.
[97] *A Defence of the Resolutions and Address of the American Congress* (London, 1775), 7.
[98] *Speech of Edmund Burke,* 1775, 52, 55.
[99] *Answer to a Pamphlet, Entitled Taxation no Tyranny,* 41.
[100] *An Inquiry into the Nature and Causes of the Present Dispute,* 24.
[101] John Cartwright, *American Independence The Interest and Glory of Great Britain* (London, 1774), 11.

By raising the issue of humanity, Cartwright was invoking a language that, during the course of debate over the American question, had become increasingly manifest in Opposition discussions of the incongruity between the Government's treatment of the colonies and what East Apthorp, a loyalist cleric who had fled from Massachusetts, would refer to in a fast day sermon in December 1776 as "the boasted humanity of this nation."[102] Cartwright's characterization of the English as "the people . . . celebrated for their humanity"[103] followed upon the claim then taking hold of the English historical imagination that the English had been at the forefront of most of the "Discoveries, in the Cause of Humanity, which so distinguishes the [early modern] Era in the Annals of English History." Among "many other[s]," these discoveries, an Opposition writer noted in January 1775, included the knowledge "that the Popes of Rome were not . . . the Key-Keepers of Heaven, to let us in or shut us out as they pleased," a lesson learned at the Reformation, and that "our Kings . . . were not the indefeasible Key-Keepers of our Constitution," that "all those claims *de jure divino, &c.* were the mere Insignificancies of metaphysical Jargon," and "that Prerogative was not Absolute Power," all of which were learned at the time of the Glorious Revolution.[104]

Relatively recently, the languages of humanity and justice had entered British politics in a deep and pervasive way in connection with the debate throughout much of the early 1770s over the rapacious behavior of the East India Company and its servants, a subject that will be treated at length in Chapter 4. Commentators on the American question were quick to draw parallels between the Government's harsh measures toward the colonies and the inhuman behavior of Britons in India, where, as Erskine remarked, a "history of some battles fought and fortunes acquired" had made it clear that Mexico and Peru were "not the only countries, where professed Christians have cast off compassion and humanity."[105] Motivated by avarice, "those shameful triumphs over unwarlike and defenceless nations, which have poured into the laps of individuals the wealth of India . . . and driven us to plunder and destroy harmless natives," declared Apthorp, had already "fixed so deep a stain on the English name, as perhaps cannot be expiated."[106] The "recourse to arms . . . against our fellow subjects,"[107] the verbal abuse and othering of Americans as *graceless subjects, trans-Atlantic sectaries, and religious ingrates,*"[108] among other opprobrious

---

[102] East Apthorp, *A Sermon on the General Fast, Friday, December 13, 1776* (London, 1776), 14.

[103] Cartwright, *American Independence*, 11.

[104] *An Address to the Right Honourable L–d M–sf–d in which the Measures of Government Respecting America are Considered in a new Light: with a view to his Lordship's Interposition Therein* (London, 1775), 19.

[105] John Erskine, *The Equity and Wisdom of Administration, In Measures That have unhappily occasioned The American Revolt, Tried by the Sacred Oracles* (Edinburgh, 1776), 5–6.

[106] Apthorp, *A Sermon on the General Fast*, 14.

[107] *The Present Crisis, with Respect to America Considered* (London, 1775), 45.

[108] [Joseph Towers], *A Letter to Dr. Samuel Johnson: Occasioned by his Late Political Publications* (London, 1775), 53.

epithets, and "the virulent spirit" of the Government supporter who could "calmly contemplate the idea of savages turned loose upon the friends of freedom," and "imagine himself the huntsman of the Indian pack – hallowing forward his blood-hounds to carnage,"[109] made it easy for Opposition writers to link the coercive strategy of the Administration against the Americans with the inhumanity of the British in India and to present themselves as the champions of humanity and justice.

"Not content with innovating charters," one Opposition writer asserted in the wake of the failure of the Coercive Acts to stem American resistance, "you advise that the Americans universally should be subjugated by [yet] stricter laws and stronger obligations. You exhort that national *vengeance* may be poured on the contrivers of mischief, and that no *mistakes of clemency* should prevent abundant forfeitures. Lest this should not be sufficiently harsh and humiliating," he continued, "you suggest... that their slaves may be taken from them, though by your laws, their property, and settled, with arms for their defence, in some... arbitrary form of government." The effect of these measures, he complained, would be to "establish a Saturnalia of cruelty," to subject the colonists "to the brutality of their own slaves, enflamed and irritated to retaliate traditionary wrongs, and to wreak a barbarous vengeance on their degraded masters... and as far as you can" to "degrade" the colonists "below the rank of humanity." Thus, he charged, the Administration, with utter disregard for the principles of humanity, was, through its ever harsher coercive measures, endeavoring "to ripen tumult into anarchy, and dissatisfaction to rebellion; and to transform punishment into waste and extirpation."[110]

Decrying the idea that Britain, the land of liberty, should ever "desire to hold her empire under a forced subjection,"[111] Opposition writers insisted that the very "idea of governing provinces by force" was "visionary and chimerical."[112] Stressing the pitfalls of a coercive approach, they urged negotiation and conciliation throughout the crisis over the Coercive Acts and even after the outbreak of hostilities at Lexington and Concord in April 1775. "The very idea" of subduing the Americans "by naval or military force," said Charles Garth in early 1774, was "absurd," nothing more than "a palliative, shuffling, temporary expedient, which may for some time controul, but never can strike at the root of the disease." "A dominion founded on *Fear*, and maintained through *Compulsion*," he wrote, could "last no longer than 'till the controuling power is distressed by a general war." Not force, but only "the gentle cords of Humanity and Love," he insisted, could draw the colonies into a permanent attachment

---

[109] *The Pamphlet Entitled, 'Taxation No Tyranny,' Candidly Considered*, 102.
[110] *Answer to a Pamphlet, Entitled Taxation no Tyranny*, 60–62.
[111] *Letter To Tucker*, 27.
[112] Shipley, *A Speech Intended to have been Spoken*, in Smith, ed., *English Defenders of American Freedoms*, 36.

to Britain.[113] "If for ten thousand reasons you cannot govern by the sword," counseled another writer in April 1775, "you have but one thing left, and that is, to govern by justice, and if this proposition revolts you, it is clear that you are not in a temper to govern."[114]

Besides, exponents of this view submitted, the use of military force seemed to be at variance with the very spirit of British colonization. How could such a draconian "system" of coercion and force "be reconciled to the principles of your empire, which is free and commercial, and which cannot be either of these without being both?," asked a writer speaking in the languages of both liberty and commerce in the spring of 1775.[115] "Measures of severity may increase our power for a season," cautioned Erskine, "but the affection of the colonies alone can render it permanent."[116] "Whilst the Colonies derive from Great Britain the inestimable blessing of liberty, they will strain every nerve, in support of a power, by which that blessing is to be secured," asserted Bush. "But if we reduce them to a situation more deplorable than the French colonies, from that moment our interests will separate."[117]

As they reviewed Administration policies during the crucial years 1774–75, Opposition thinkers had no doubt that those policies had failed on every count and that, far from preventing, were actually operating to produce colonial independence. The Coercive Acts had led not to American submission but to increased resistance, and that resistance had given the lie to Administration claims that it was the product of a small coterie of malcontents who had duped an unthinking multitude into following their lead. Only widespread discontent, the Opposition pointed out, could have supported a "*ten-year's* agitation" and driven "so many provinces, with so many principles of discord among them to keep them asunder," to unite "against a parent country so powerful, and to which the moment before they were so cordially attached,"[118] and they predicted that proposals to close colonial ports and interdict colonial trade would simply "add fuel to the flame" and "make it rage the fiercer." "The dissensions which distracted the Colonies internally," one writer observed, had been "insurmountable obstacles to their independence" that might have continued for decades "if ministry had not reconciled their differences, and cooled their animosities, by forcing them to have one common interest, which has united them in one common cause." Thus had the "*ministry . . . cemented their union*" and thereby "hasten[ed] their independence." In effect, he charged, the Administration had "set fire to the house they were to protect – and now complain of being scorched by the flame!"[119]

---

[113] [Garth], *America Vindicated*, 30–31.
[114] *Answer to a Pamphlet, Entitled Taxation no Tyranny*, 43.
[115] Ibid.
[116] Erskine, *Reflections*, 51.
[117] Bush, *Case of Great Britain and America*, 35.
[118] *Answer to a Pamphlet, Entitled Taxation no Tyranny*, 49.
[119] *The Pamphlet Entitled, 'Taxation No Tyranny,' Candidly Considered*, 100, 105.

IV

As the conflict with the colonies degenerated into a bloody fratricidal war in
1775 and American leaders opted for independence in 1776, their dire predictions about the effects of ministerial policy seemed to Opposition spokesmen
to have been fully vindicated, with the result, as one writer put it in the fall of
1775, that "this unfortunate country, once the terror," had now become "the
derision of all the world."[120] "For twelve years," reported a writer using the
pseudonym "Janus" in February 1776, the Administration in its dealing with
the colonies had "shifted from expedient to expedient; from every species of low
cunning to outrage."[121] Having "determined on rigor and subduction" following the American resistance to the Tea Act of 1773, the Administration, they
charged, had sponsored a series of "shameful Acts of Parliament . . . *infringing
on Magna Charta,*"[122] acts that even the Administration "acknowledged to
be oppressive and severe." Yet, deeming "it inconsistent . . . with their dignity
to retract their measures, till obedience" had been "enforced," the Administration had steadfastly "refused to alleviate them, because the Colonists did
not pay implicit obedience to their power, in submitting to acts, which" the
colonists regarded as "inconsistent with humanity and the usages of countries,
and which, in effect, would have been a total annihilation of all their rights,
as a free people."[123] Eschewing any efforts at conciliation and "talk[ing] much
of the national honor and dignity,"[124] the Administration had then taken
refuge in the language of imperial grandeur to build a case for the resort to
the "force of arms" to coerce the Americans into acknowledging metropolitan
authority.[125]

The gravity of this situation led the Opposition to a number of important
reflections. First, the failures in America seemed to indicate that, if the retention
of the empire was the objective, the Administration had been both pursuing the
wrong policy and using the wrong tactics. Ignoring both the commercial and
libertarian principles upon which the empire had been constructed, one Administration after another, the Opposition charged, had undertaken "new plans for
our old Colonies" that revealed a total "unacquaintance" with "the true spirit
of commerce"[126] and could "be seen" by the colonists only "in the invidious
light of innovations" that would deprive them of the traditional liberties they

---

[120] *The Conduct of Administration with regard to the Colonies* (London, 1775), 15.
[121] "Janus," *The Critical Moment, on which the Salvation or Destruction of the British Empire
       Depends; Containing the Rise, Progress, Present State, and Natural Consequences of our
       American Disputes* (London, 1776), 38.
[122] Manasseh Dawes, *A Letter to Lord Chatham Concerning the Present War of Great Britain
       Against America* (London, 1777), 7.
[123] *The Conduct of Administration with regard to the Colonies,* 14–15.
[124] "Janus," *The Critical Moment,* 115.
[125] *A Prospect of the Consequences of the Present Conduct of Great Britain towards America*
       (London, 1776), 7.
[126] "Janus," *The Critical Moment,* 18.

had all along enjoyed.[127] Before "the aera of the fatal stamp-act," said Henry Cruger in Parliament, restating a line of argument to which the Opposition had long adhered, "No country" had "been more happy in its colonies than Great Britain." "Connected by mutual interests," the empire had "flourished in an intercourse of amity, protection, and obedience" and had exhibited "no instances of disobedience to your laws, no denial of the jurisdiction of Parliament; no marks of jealousy and discontent."[128] But the principal precondition for colonial obedience, the Opposition insisted, was the enjoyment of a considerable measure of British liberty in managing colonial affairs. "So accustomed" were "the people of each government to have its interior oeconomy settled, and its taxes laid on by its own representatives, to look upon its own assembly as its own legislature in either, and even to regard its sister colony as a separate state," declared one Opposition pamphleteer in May 1776, "that to turn any of those matters into another channel," invariably, "in their eyes," appeared to be "bringing about a revolution, a thing seldom attempted where the people are not better disposed to it than [were] the Americans."[129]

If the Administration's policies had been misguided, its efforts to enforce those policies after 1774, the Opposition thought, had been wholly ineffective. As "Janus" and other Opposition adherents observed, the Government's measures had severely underestimated the breadth, depth, and character of American resistance. After the colonists had continued their protests for a dozen years and were now so obviously "unanimous in their Opposition to government," declared "Janus," only the most "strangely infatuated" people in Britain could persist in believing "that such a universal dissatisfaction could prevail in the colonies" unless the colonists "sensibly felt some real cause; unless they labored under some grievances unredressed."[130] "Is it reasonable or just to conceive," asked another writer,

that a body of people, of at least three millions, many of them of distinguished and acknowledged abilities and genius, whose commerce was in the most thriving situation, whose internal resources were great and valuable, whose families enjoyed peace and plenty, affluence and ease, should, deliberately, without the utmost provocation, without the most hostile invasion of their liberties and properties, resist the authority of the parent state, and lift arms against her power?[131]

Only "one common principle, and a persuasion of right," said "A. M.," could have brought "a people so divided" and "living most happily, and sensible of it," to "make so general an Opposition to a nation which they loved, expose an extended sea coast to the most formidable naval power" and "a straggling

[127] "A. M.," *Reflections on the American Contest: in which the Consequences of a Forced Submission and the Means of a Lasting Reconciliation are pointed out* (London, 1776), 46.
[128] Henry Cruger, speech, December 16, 1774, in Simmons and Thomas, eds., *Proceedings and Debates of the British Parliaments*, 5: 254–55.
[129] "A. M.," *Reflections on the American Contest*, 48–49.
[130] "Janus," *The Critical Moment*, 36–38.
[131] *The Conduct of Administration with regard to the Colonies*, 22–23.

frontier to savages and Canadians, and the habitations of the most wealthy to the ravages of their own slaves."[132]

The Administration's failure to comprehend the nature and extent of American resistance, the Opposition charged, had caused it both to underestimate the costs of its policy and to ignore completely the effects of their efforts upon the colonies. David Hartley spoke eloquently on this subject in the House of Commons on April 1, 1776. "We are now told with great composure, by those very Men who but a few Months ago laughed to Scorn every foreboding Word of Prudence, that the whole Power of this Country is unequal to the Undertaking" of "subduing the colonies . . . but that we are now dipt in, and must wade through[.]"

If an Army of Fifty thousand Men and one hundred Ships of Force, are now found necessary, the Word to Parliament is, you must go through, there is no Retreat: It must be done. Every Corner of the Three Kingdoms is to be ransacked for Recruits; every Power in Europe is to be solicited for mercenary Aid; every trading Vessel heretofore employed in the *American* Commerce, is now destined to be transport [to] all the means of destroying the commercial Wealth of *Great Britain*, and all the Sources of Naval Empire.

This war, he declared, "must feed upon, and exhaust every vital Source of this Country, at the certain Expence of Ten or Twelve Millions for this Year," and the "Enormity of the Expence," he emphasized, was "but the least Part of the evil. Even what the Administration would call Success, would be mere irrecoverable Ruin, by destroying the very Source of Wealth and Strength to this Country."[133]

In such passages, Opposition spokesmen used the language of economy in their vain effort to turn the tide of the war, but not all the costs were fiscal, and they turned to the languages of humanity, justice, liberty, and commerce to call attention to the other heavy expenses of the war. "To what frozen region . . . has our national honor and humanity flow[ed][[?]" asked "Janus." Noting that atrocities by the Indians "and many more such inhumanities . . . must be the inevitable consequences of war," indeed, that "Our passions, our resentments, our intended cruelties to each other would disgrace the most uncultivated nations of heathens," so that "even the cruel uninformed Indian would be shocked at our intended massacres," he predicted that the "present war will disgrace the honor of the country" and "fill the historic page with a melancholy tale . . . of the unequalled massacres performed in the reign of a prince, who has ever been considered" to be "remarkable for humanity" and "a prodigy of goodness."[134] A violation of Britain's vaunted "humanity and justice," another writer declared, the "sanguinary measure[s]" then "prosecuting . . . along the

[132] "A. M.," *Reflections on the American Contest,* 17.
[133] David Hartley, *Substance of a Speech in Parliament. Upon the State of the Nation towards America* (London, 1776), 1–2, 3, 7.
[134] "Janus," *The Critical Moment,* 53, 66, 68, 72–73.

sea-coasts of America, where inoffensive and defenceless little towns and villages are fired, the inhabitants destroyed, and desolation marks the destructive
ruin of the grand and awful navy of Great Britain as far as its ships can
proceed," represented nothing but "a piratical employment for a navy which
should awe the world, and give the law to the real enemies of Britain!"[135] Such
measures, wrote "A. M.," were "as unbecoming the power, as unworthy of
the magnanimity of Great Britain."[136]

If the Administration's program for the colonies was thus a stain on Britain's
aspirations to be a humane nation, it was also, Opposition writers complained,
wholly incompatible with British ideas of liberty. "Compared to the present
measures of Administration" with regard to the liberty of British subjects,
said one writer, the "unconstitutional conduct of James the second, which
brought about the glorious revolution, was moderate and mild."[137] "However
we disregard" the opinions of the colonists, advised "A. M.," "let us regard
our own. The asserting of liberty has been the boast of Englishmen," he said,
and "to make a people we look on as brethren, even ideally slaves, must hurt
our own pride; to be enraged at them, for being as jealous of their rights as we
are," he contended, was "inconsistent." Whenever "the Parliament of Great
Britain decides in favour of liberty," he continued, "it does so consistently, and
with honour, for such decision has always the appearance of a compliance to
its own, and to the principles of the nation." "Take the matter in any light we
please," he observed, "our principles, our honour, and our interest, forbid our
forcing them." "Let us not," he pleaded, "let a mistaken pride betray us into
a conduct, the most flattering consequence [of which] is to enslave so many
valuable members of a state, which we wish to call free."[138]

Equally appalling from the Opposition's point of view, the Administration's
actions seemed to have completely ignored traditional commercial considerations. Complaining that "the wild projects of Administration" had "driven
those provinces[,] the foundations of our wealth and of our modern power,
into revolt, to renounce their allegiance to the Crown, to meet us in arms, and
even to shew they have power or prowess sufficient to baffle all our force by
sea and land," they expressed dismay that the Government continued to pursue the same "passionate, absurd plan... without seeming to perceive that we
are hurrying on headlong to our ruin."[139] Repeatedly invoking the language
of commerce, Opposition spokesmen pointed out that the British Empire had
always stressed "commercial colonization," and argued that through commerce
alone Britain had been elevated from "its own insignificancy, in point of size, on
the face of the globe" to prosperity and a position of international grandeur.[140]

[135] *A Prospect of the Consequences of the Present Conduct of Great Britain*, 24.
[136] "A. M.," *Reflections on the American Contest*, 3.
[137] *The Conduct of Administration with regard to the Colonies*, 35.
[138] "A. M.," *Reflections on the American Crisis*, 37, 41, 49.
[139] *The West Indian Merchant. Being a Series of Papers Originally Printed under that Signature
in the London Evening Post* (London, 1778), 136–37.
[140] Estwick, *Letter to the Reverend Josiah Tucker*, 28, 92–93.

"If Britain has been aggrandized by her connection with the colonies," they insisted, it was by its "trading connection, and not by dominion."[141] The Administration seemed to have forgotten, complained "Janus," that "the glory of this country, nay, all its interests depend on trade: and that neither a ministerial army or navy" could "exist without the merchants' assistance. But it is become fashionable," he continued, "to treat every proposal for the true interest of the country with contempt. The ministry and their superficial friends already insinuate, that the American trade is unimportant; that there are new channels of commerce, which will be equal to [those] that we are likely to lose with America. If this is true," he asked, joining the languages of economy and humanity, "why do we arm? Are we to expend the national treasure; are we to murder thousands for the amusement of some invisible enemy to the country? If the Americans and their trade are useless to this country, let us relinquish our present claims; and leave those obstinate republicans, as they are unjustly called, to their own situation."[142]

This extended critique did not persuade the majority of the British political nation and had little effect on the drift of Government policy. As "Janus" complained, whenever "violent measures are proposed" in Parliament, they continue to be "received with joyful acclamations," and whenever "a conciliatory plan is offered," it is met "with court Opposition."[143] *Aristocratus*, a fictional character in a mock dialogue published in April 1776, effectively expressed the sentiment that animated Government supporters. Shall we give in or shall we "act with a vigour that becomes the dignity of Great Britain, her immense resources, the might of her invincible fleet, the irresistible bravery of her troops, and conduct of her generals and those troops who have traversed the world with victory," he asked, "and shall not that arm which has subdued the power of two of the most formidable monarchies of Europe united against her, chastise the mad insurrection of her infatuated provinces, who owe all their strength to the power they resist, and who must learn that duty by force, which they will not otherwise be taught[?]"[144] The stakes were too high, it seemed to Government supporters, to back down. As one writer declared in March 1776, they had concluded that "the sword alone must decide . . . whether Great Britain shall hereafter in fact give laws to her transmarine provinces, or perhaps even retain her own proper empire in Europe."[145] The ignominy arising from Britain's inability to control its own colonies was too great to permit conciliation. No man who had "the welfare of his country at heart," wrote Israel Mauduit, a government contractor, in a February 1776 pamphlet, could "reflect on the exertions of it, to secure the happiness of her Colonies, and their

---

[141] "A. M.," *Reflections on the American Contest*, 21.
[142] "Janus," *The Critical Moment*, 70–71.
[143] Ibid., 73.
[144] *A Dialogue on the Principles of the Constitution and Legal Liberty, Compared with Despotism; Applied to the American Question* (London, 1775), 1.
[145] *Reflections on the Present State of the American War* (London, 1776), 2.

ingratitude, without glowing with a spirit of revenge, superior to, what he feels at the insults of a foreign enemy."[146]

Government supporters dismissed Opposition proposals for conciliation out of hand. "Proud of empire purchased with their blood (for Canada was dearly bought), proud of their valour and ancient glory in war," an anonymous author claiming to be a retired officer writing to his son in Parliament asserted in 1776, the "People of England" could never "give their confidence and love to an Opposition, whose conduct and principles manifestly tend to humble their pride, to diminish their empire, to stain their glory, and prostrate England at the feet of America."[147] "Will any Man dare to say, that it is consistent with Honour, or the Interest of Great-Britain, to withdraw her Forces from *America*, and in so doing prostrate herself at the Feet of the Congress?," asked another Government spokesman in May 1776. "Shall *Britain* submit to Terms of Peace, dictated by Subjects in Arms against the established Government?" "Can it be thought that *Great-Britain*, whose Government has been insulted, whose constitutional Supremacy has been denied, whose Dominions have been invaded," he continued, "will crouch to Subjects in Rebellion? Can *Englishmen* wish to see their Country so far degraded as to make ignominious Concessions under such multiplied Instances of Provocation?" Nothing less than Britain's international standing, its imperial grandeur, was at stake, and Britain must quell the revolt in order to preserve its standing as the preeminent imperial power and to save face among its European rivals. "The Eyes of all *Europe* are upon us," the author noted, concluding that "*France* and *Spain* would no doubt be well pleased" to "behold a rival State disarmed, by the Partizans of a rebellious Congress."[148]

The deepening of war in America and the circulation of reports that Americans were cheering British losses helped to create an atmosphere that encouraged Government supporters to continue to demonize Americans and draw ever sharper distinctions between them and metropolitan Britons. Turning the language of humanity against the Opposition, Government supporters powerfully suggested that it was not metropolitan Britons but American colonists who were guilty of affronts to "Humanity."[149] Already in early 1775, when Josiah Tucker was making his case for British separation from the colonies, he had endeavored "to rouse the indignation of" his "countrymen" by calling attention to the inhumanity involved in colonial treatment of enslaved Africans and Indians. Mocking American claims to the *"immutable Laws* of Nature," Tucker asked why "the poor Negroes and the…Indians" were not "equally entitled to the like Rights and Benefits." "Most certainly," he continued, "they

---

[146] [Israel Mauduit], *Considerations on the American War. Addressed to the People of England* (London, 1776), 8.
[147] *A Letter from an Officer Retired to his Son in Parliament*, new ed. (Edinburgh, 1776), 26–27.
[148] *Independency the Object of Congress in America, or, An Appeal to Force* (London, 1776), 5–6.
[149] *A Letter from an Officer Retired*, 26.

never ceded to you, the Right of disposing of their Lives, Liberties, and Properties, just as you please," and "yet what horrid Cruelties do you daily practice on
the Bodies of the poor Negroes, over whom you can have no Claim, according
to your own Principles? What shameful Robberies and Usurpations are you
daily guilty of in respect to the poor *Indians*, the only true and rightful Proprietors of the Country which you inhabit?"[150] Clearly, people who practiced
customs "so disgraceful to humanity" had no resemblance to the free subjects
who populated Britain itself.[151]

In this debate, both sides used the languages of commerce, imperial grandeur,
and humanity in arguing their positions. In assessing the grandeur and "strength
of the nation," the Opposition favored an approach to empire that stressed the
traditional primacy of commercial considerations and the perpetuation of the
libertarian traditions of empire, while the Administration placed much more
emphasis upon maintaining central political control over the "magnitude of"
Britain's extensive "dominions."[152] Not many in the Opposition could conceive
of an empire in which Parliament would not have at least nominal sovereignty.

The radical thinker John Cartwright was one of the few who could imagine
a way out of the dilemma posed by this tension between the languages of
commerce, liberty, humanity, and justice, on the one hand, and the language of
imperial grandeur, on the other. Asking whether *"his countrymen"* were not
still *"the brave sons of freedom? Lovers of justice, and by nature generous"*
they had long prided themselves to be, he lamented, in two pamphlets published
in 1775, that *"Britons of all parties, and of almost all denominations, seem
too unanimous in wishing to tyrannize over their brethren on the other side
of the Atlantic,"* and sought to *"inspire his countrymen with more generous
sentiments."* Although he acknowledged that Parliament's claim to sovereignty
over America gratified "the pride of Englishmen in general, to think that that
legislature, in which they feel themselves to have a share, should govern half
the world," he argued both that the "rights of sovereignty reside[d] in the
people themselves," and not in Parliament, an institution, he implied, that was
merely a creature of the people, and that the "rights of Englishmen" were
"not confined to this little spot of land" but "follow[ed] a person as a shadow
follows the substance, however it may vary its situation, whether it goes North,
West, East, or South."[153]

To deny English rights to Britons not resident in the realm, Cartwright went
on to declare, was to "invade the most precious rights a human being can enjoy,

[150] Josiah Tucker, *Tract V. The Respective Pleas and Arguments of the Mother Country, and
the Colonies distinctly set forth and the Impossibility of a Compromise of Differences, or a
Mutual Concession of Rights, plainly Demonstrated* (Gloucester, 1775), v–vi.
[151] *The Duty of the King and Subject, on the Principles of Civil Liberty: Colonists not intitled to
Self-Government; or to the same Privileges with Britons* (London, 1776), 41–42.
[152] *Some Reasons for Approving of the Dean of Gloucestor's Plan of Separating from the Colonies
For a Further Improvement* (London, 1775), 6.
[153] John Cartwright, *American Independence The Interest and Glory of Great-Britain*, 2d ed.
(London, 1775), i, 6, 9–10.

and" to "render the rest of" the Anglophone world beyond the metropolis little more than "miserable servile wretches." Was this appropriate behavior for a "people so celebrated for" liberty?, he inquired. "It is high time," he declared, "that we opened our eyes to the unconstitutional encroachments we have been making upon the liberties of mankind," including the Irish and the West Indians, as well as the North Americans, "and to the necessity of setting bounds to our dominion." "Swollen indeed must we be with the pride of dominion and drunk with the fumes, if we can foolishly imagine" that forceful measures could ever do more than produce "a precarious tyranny over the Americans for a while." Arguing that Britain was "*not a conquering*, but a commercial state," he called upon Britons to "pluck from our hearts that deep-rooted love of rule" and those "flatulent ideas of our own dignity and importance," the beguiling attributes of the language of imperial grandeur. "Let not the breath of anger or resentment sully your councils," he advised, "let not jealousy or ambition poison your breasts, nor hang upon your tongues."[154]

Cartwright wrote with the intention of persuading his readers that now was the time "to discover, and to establish a principle of lasting union between our colonies and the mother country." But he correctly assessed the situation when he expressed the fear "that passion and prejudice, pride and self-interest, have evidently too much influence over the minds of men, to suffer them to decide impartially and equitably in such delicate conjunctures as the present" and despaired that "the measures of administration, the deliberations in parliament, the sentiments of political writers, and the language of the people at large, all tend[ed] to prove, that the most probable event will be mutual jealousy, animosity, and strife."[155] By 1776, this proud empire was indeed, as the political writer Catharine Maccaulay said, in a "dangerous state," enduring a revolt of some of its principal components with nothing less than the imperial grandeur of Great Britain hanging in the balance. Ironically, the very measures that the Administration was taking to preserve that grandeur were instead increasing the probability of its loss.[156]

[154] Ibid., 1, 9, 30–31, 48, 66; John Cartwright, *Letter to Edmund Burke, Esq; Controverting the Principles of American Government, Laid down in his lately published Speech on American Taxation* (London, 1775), 13.

[155] Cartwright, *American Independence*, 2nd ed., 1.

[156] Catharine Maccaulay, *An Address to the People of England, and Scotland on the Present Important Crisis of Affairs* (London, 1775), in Smith, ed., *English Defenders of American Freedom*, 122.

4

Arenas of "Asiatic Plunder"

The Languages of Humanity and Justice and the Excesses of Empire in India

I

The outcry against the Carib War, discussed in the Prologue, was not the first such massive public condemnation of developments in the broader overseas empire as an affront to metropolitan British standards of humanity and justice. Almost a decade earlier, reports of the misbehavior of East India Company employees in India had evoked an even more spirited, intense, and sustained public debate in which critics had used the languages of humanity and justice as the principal foundation for mobilizing a powerful critique of the operation of empire in the East. Inaugurating a wide-ranging political discussion about the conduct and legitimacy of empire that persisted for the next quarter-century, this critique, in turn, supplied the context for and helped to stimulate similar examinations of the behavior of Britons in other situations in the overseas empire – in American plantations, in the American war, and in Ireland, each of which will be pursued in a separate chapter of this volume.

To be sure, the language of humanity had always to some extent colored earlier discussions of empire – as a supplement to the languages of commerce and imperial grandeur, envisioning trade and empire as devices for extending the civility and humanity of Britain to the unbelieving and savage worlds of America, Africa, and Asia; as a late seventeenth-century condemnation of slave traders and slaveholders for their inhumane treatment of enslaved Africans and Amerindians and their failure to evangelize enslaved and indigenous peoples in the Americas; and even, after the middle of the eighteenth century, as a reproof to settlers for their unjust expropriation of Amerindian lands. But in the wake of the Seven Years' War, the language of humanity, in association with the language of justice, acquired a new prominence as one of the principal languages employed by metropolitan Britons to speak about empire. For the first time on a wide scale, a series of problems, identified and intensely canvassed by analysts in the press and Parliament and first arising in reference to the situation in the new territorial acquisitions in India, forced metropolitan Britons to confront and endeavor to come to terms with the darker side of British colonialism. In this process, as Britons considered how to react to the evident violation of national norms by overseas Britons and the widespread complicity of metropolitans in the larger British imperial world, these languages quickly came to supply the central vocabulary for what amounted to a fundamental reevaluation of empire. In terms of the scale and intensity of their use, the languages of humanity and justice – and the symbiotic languages of rapacity, plunder, injustice, oppression, and barbarism – thereafter rapidly became some of the main languages Britons used to comprehend and represent the empire.

II

"Who could have imagined three hundred years ago," Adam Anderson wrote in 1764,

that those parts of the Levant from which, by means of the Venetians, England, and almost all the rest of Christendom, were supplied with [the] spices, drugs, &c. of India and China, should one day come themselves to be supplied with those and other articles by the remote countries of England and Holland, at an easier rate than they were used to have them directly from the East.[1]

With these words, Anderson marked the steady growth of British commerce with India under the auspices of the East India Company over the long era since Elizabeth I had chartered it on the last day of the year 1600. By the early 1750s, Malachy Postlethwayt could describe the Company as

the most flourishing trading company in this kingdom, as likewise one of the greatest of Europe, for wealth, powers, and immunities; which appears by the ships of burden they constantly employ, the beneficial settlements they have abroad, their large magazines and storehouses for merchandizes, and sales of goods at home, with the particular laws and statutes made in their favour.[2]

At the date of Postlethwayt's writing, India, insofar as metropolitan Britain was concerned, was still principally a site for gainful commercial transactions, and the East India Company that presided over those transactions was a lucrative opportunity for investment.[3]

[1] Adam Anderson, *An Historical and Chronological Deduction of the Origin of Commerce, from the Earliest Accounts, containing An History of the Great Commercial Interests of the British Empire*, 4 vols. (London, 1787), 1: xliv–xlv.

[2] Malachy Postlethwayt, *Universal Dictionary of Trade and Commerce*, 4th ed. (London, 1764), article on *East India Company*.

[3] Philip Lawson, *The East India Company: A History* (London: Longman, 1993), provides an excellent and commendably succinct history of the Company. For a more detailed treatment of the years covered by this chapter, see the classic study by P. J. Marshall, *Problems of Empire: Britain and India, 1757–1813* (London: Allen & Unwin, 1968); idem, *East Indian Fortunes: The British in Bengal in the Eighteenth Century* (Oxford: Oxford University Press, 1976); idem, *The Making and Unmaking of Empires: Britain, India, and America c. 1750–1783* (Oxford:

Nor, in the national mind, did this situation immediately change in response to the Company's conquest of Bengal in 1757, when, in response to the capture of the Company factory at Calcutta by a new nawab, Siraj-ud-Daula, Robert Clive and his troops, hastily summoned from Madras, defeated the nawab's forces at the Battle of Plassey and brought the rich territories and revenues of Bengal, then the most impressive principality in India, under Company control. Indeed, within metropolitan Britain, Clive, whom George II knighted for his exploits, became a figure of national acclaim, the valorous prototype for British military and naval commanders from Bengal to Quebec in the late 1750s.

As late as 1764, Adam Anderson could speak glowingly about the East India Company and its activities. It enjoyed "an extensive trade" and was "seemingly in a very prosperous condition, having many fine forts and factories, and a considerable territorial property, in India"; it also made "at home considerable dividends, and such immense sales, too, as were never known in former times, having also, of late years," built a fine office and extensive warehouses in London and provided the commodities for an extensive re-export trade to Europe and Africa. Upon the whole, Anderson concluded, "our East India trade, under its present circumstances, is really a beneficial one for Great Britain; and . . . moreover . . . it is highly for the nation's as well as for the Company's interest, to support, and increase our East India commerce as much as possible."[4]

Even as Anderson wrote, however, it was becoming clear that the expansion of British activities in India after Clive's conquest of Bengal was producing consequences that, over the following thirty years, would powerfully reinforce the image of colonial degeneracy in metropolitan Britain. A writer identifying himself only as "a Gentleman long resident in India" first brought these consequences to British public attention with a 1764 pamphlet, *Reflections on the Present State of our East India Affairs*. A sober analyst deeply critical of the new regime, the author succinctly distinguished the old regime from the new, ruminated on the causes of the change, and carefully explained the deleterious effects that had already resulted and might still be expected from it.[5]

According to this author, the contrast between the old and the new regimes could not have been more pointed. "Till a few years ago," he wrote, the business of the directors of the East India Company in London "was only to

Oxford University Press, 2005), 207–72; idem, '*A Free though Conquering People': Eighteenth-Century Britain and Its Empire* (Aldershot, U.K.: Ashgate Variorum, 203), Chapters 1 ("A 'Free though Conquering People': Britain and Asia in the Eighteenth Century"), 9 ("The Moral Swing to the East: British Humanitarianism, India and the West Indies"), and 15 ("Britain and the World in the Eighteenth Century: Britain and India"); H. V. Bowen, *Revenue and Reform: The Indian Problem in British Politics 1757–1773* (Cambridge: Cambridge University Press, 1991); and Lucy S. Sutherland, *The East India Company in Eighteenth-Century Politics* (Oxford: Clarendon Press, 1952).

[4] Anderson, *Historical and Chronological Deduction of the Origin of Commerce*, 1: lxi.
[5] "A Gentleman Long Resident in India," *Reflections on the Present State of our East India Affairs* (London, 1764).

answer letters of commerce, to load ships with their indented cargoes, and to vend the returns," tasks that might easily be accomplished by people of "an ordinary genius," while the chief duties of "their servants in India, as living like merchants under the protection of the prince in whose dominions they resided," was nothing more than "to barter a little broad cloth, silver, lead, iron, steel, &c. for piece-goods of certain fabricks, or for other commodities wanted in Europe," functions that also required no "extraordinary talents." While these duties "remained the sole business of the company in India," he explained, "matters went very well. Fair trade being in these times the only path to riches," the Company's employees "were induced to apply to and study" trade, fortunes were "but slowly and gradually acquired," and promotions were therefore also "but slow and gradual." People waited twenty years to "reach the dignity of a counsellor" and another ten to twelve years to achieve a more prominent position of trust, with the result that the Company's affairs in India were managed "by a set of gentlemen mature in years, and masters of their business." Under these conditions, trade flourished, the Indian economy remained vigorous, and peace "reigned without interruption."[6]

By contrast, under the new regime that had arisen in the wake of Clive's conquest of Bengal, the East India Company had

been changed, contrary to the intention of its institution, from a commercial, into a military corporation; from a body of merchants peaceably trading in the dominions, and under the protection of princes, into sovereigns of those very princes, whom, with their great and opulent countries, they hold in more absolute vassalage, than ever did the monarch of France the meanest of his feudatories.

As the "proprietor of large tracts of lands, populous and rich, from which it" drew "kingly revenues" amounting altogether to a million and a half pounds sterling per annum, the Company maintained "its power by great and expensive armies" and "noble fortresses," the annual cost of which equaled as much as half of the annual revenue of Britain, and demanded "almost the whole profits" of the Company's trade.[7]

Acknowledging the new sense of imperial grandeur that had swept Britain following the conquests of the Seven Years' War, the author did not deny that "this power and dominion of a trading company" sounded "extremely grand" and that it "must no doubt excite pleasure in every English breast, to think that not only the name, but the puissance of his country, has been in glorious degree extended to the far corners of the earth, by its merchants." But he warned his audience "not [to] let this glaring show of grandeur dazzle the eye of their understanding." For his part, he was persuaded that it would have been "Happy ... for this company, happy for the nation," if "commerce had still been at this day the sole business of Englishmen in India," and he expressed

[6] Ibid., 14–16, 34.
[7] Ibid., 20–21.

confidence that when metropolitans came to understand the excessive costs of "all this pageantry, they will surely think it too dearly bought."[8]

The author expressed his discontent with the new regime of Indian relations through two related concerns. The first was the opportunities it had opened up for the acquisition of private wealth, and the second the possibilities it provided for the aggrandizement of political power. As for the former, he complained, "the old slow, though sure tract of trade" had "fallen into universal contempt" as "new roads to wealth" had enabled people to acquire "mighty fortunes... by one stroke, and as soon as acquired, the field of India appearing too confined for the display of such opulence, the possessors... changed it for the more elegant scene of Europe." A particularly unfortunate result of this "change of measures," he observed, was that it produced "a quick rise, and consequently a quick shift of [Company] servants in India," this rapid turnover leaving administration in the hands of inexperienced young men unable to discharge efficiently the old duties associated with trade, much less the "additional, weighty charge of governing kingdoms and nations." Among this cadre, he noted, Clive "was a *rara avis*," a striking exception. With the prospect of great private fortunes before them and little commitment to the Company's commercial interests, Company servants neglected trade, "which formerly was the sole" objective of such people, regarding it as "but a secondary concern of little moment" and "greatly below the dignity and notice of sovereigns," as "such are now the company's governors in India."[9]

Still worse, this author charged, the "enormous extension of" the Company's "political power and connections in India" had already produced many undesirable results and, he predicted, was likely to "prove destructive of the very being and existence of that [important] trade." "Ever since the English re-entered Bengal by force," he reported, "the peace of that country has been continually and most thoroughly embroiled" in "a continued scene of war" verging on civil war, "the seeds" of which had been "sown by our own hands alone" and the results of which could only be "a most plentiful harvest of blood, slaughter, famine and destruction to these countries. Where the manufacturer, where the labourer used to rise undisturbed and unknowing of fear," he lamented, "there at present is heard nought but the sound of the trumpet, and the dreadful alarms of war." The results had already been devastating, as a "country, late so famous for commerce, whose rich manufactures brought to it immense wealth from every quarter of the tributary world, and whose fertile plains supplied millions of its neighbours with grain," was "unable now to yield itself the bare necessities of life. The loom is unemployed, neglected lies the plough; trade is at a stand, for there are no manufacturers to carry it on," and large numbers were "perishing... for want of food."[10]

---

[8] Ibid., 17, 21–22.
[9] Ibid., 14, 16–17.
[10] Ibid., 22, 34–35.

"But even this [development], tho' heavy," the author continued, employing the languages of oppression and rapacity, was

but a part of the misery, that this harmless oppressed people have and do suffer more immediately from the English. They have seen their fundamental laws and customs subverted, the persons of their princes most grossly insulted, the frame of their government prostituted to the lawless insolent lust of rapacious foreigners. The wantonness of power, vested in even young raw boys,

he reported, "hath trampled on the dignity of their most respectable personages. In a government thus unhinged, thus harrassed," the "unhappy subjects" found themselves "without protection, without order, nothing prevailing but anarchy, confusion and despair," while the British violated solemn oaths and treaties and overturned the government without "the smallest pretext of Authority, saving that of present force." Through "such baseness," by acting licentiously, as if "a present view of advantage" could absolve them "from the bond of oaths and treaties," the author protested, Company servants in India had not only shown themselves to be void of faith but had also delivered a powerful blow to "the faith of the English nation." In violation of traditional British ideas of humanity and justice and to the dishonor of the British nation, British rapacity, oppression, and treachery, he charged, had turned a peaceful and bountiful country into a war-torn wasteland.[11]

The author did not lay these dire developments at the door of the East India Company. Rather, he traced them to William Pitt's insistence on driving the French out of India during the Seven Years' War, which he likened to opening "a gate which mortal powers cannot shut again." "Finding a body of European troops at their command and disposal," Company governors in India soon "perceived that this [force] put it in their power to acquire an influence among the unwarlike natives," which encouraged them to begin "to interfere in the political government of those countries, in which they had till then peaceably traded." Opposed by the French, the Company soon found itself, "to the destruction of trade, and the misery and ruin of the wretched natives," involved in an active war that brought to the British victory, a large accession of territory, vast new revenues, unbridled political control, and a plethora of opportunities for the acquisition of private wealth. At the same time, however, these developments so affected the traditional Indian economy that, as the author put it, "these countries" had become "useless to us." "Trade and agriculture being entirely stopped," he asked, "what revenues can we draw from them, or what profit on commerce?" How, he asked, invoking the language of humanity, could Britain, "a nation blest themselves, and truly sensible of the happiness of a regular and well established government, remain insensible to the inexpressible anguish of their fellow-creatures" in India? Because overseas Britons had been responsible for that anguish, this question seemed to the author to bear a special poignancy for Britons who remained at home

---

[11] Ibid., 35–37, 41–43.

and to demand redress in order to vindicate the reputation of Britain from the execrable excesses of its sons overseas.[12]

III

Notwithstanding this early warning, the wide-ranging public debate over Clive's entitlement to the *jagir*, or annual subsidy of £28,000, which Mir Jafar, the new nabob of Bengal, indebted to Clive for his position, had settled upon him in 1759, seems to have been the central event in bringing the new conditions in India to the attention of the metropolitan political nation. Indeed, the fabulous private wealth acquired by Clive and many of his successors among the Company officers in India and the suspicion that much of that wealth had been gained through plunder, rapacity, and villainy gave rise in the mid-1760s to the creation of a new social type, the Asiatic plunderer, who violated all metropolitan standards of morality and decency in a frenetic and totally unprincipled quest for gain, and then brought his ill-gotten wealth back to Albion, where it resided as a symbol of the betrayal of British values beyond the line in the voluptuous East. To this new social type, metropolitans, during the last half of the 1760s and increasingly thereafter, applied the name *nabob*.[13]

Initially an Indian title of rank, the term *nabob* rapidly became, as an anonymous contemporary later complained, "a general term of reproach, indiscriminately applied to every individual who" had "served the East India Company in Asia" and implying, as "every body" understood, "that the persons to whom it is applied, have obtained their fortunes by grievously oppressing the natives of India." Insisting that "In no part of the British Empire" had "Englishmen served with more honour to themselves, and advantages to their country, than in the East Indies," and lamenting that "in no part of the British Empire" had their actions been "so much misrepresented," this writer argued that Clive was the "only *real* and *genuine English Nabob*" and took his readers through an elaborate deconstruction of the term, distinguishing among "Spurious Nabobs," those who had served many years in India and were too generous with their money when they returned; "Reputed Nabobs," those who had served long in India, returned home, and lived moderately; and "Mere Adventurous or Mushroom Nabobs," who had acquired riches quickly during a short stay in India and behaved scandalously when they returned, but whose total numbers were few. Caring not for such distinctions, however, the British public, much to this author's disgust, treated the term *nabob* as an earlier generation had

---

[12] Ibid., 17–20, 36, 44.

[13] Philip Lawson and Jim Phillips, "'Our Execrable Banditti': Perceptions of Nabobs in Mid-Eighteenth Century Britain," *Albion*, 16 (1984): 225–41, provides a brief treatment of this phenomenon. Tillman W. Nechtman, *Nabobs: Empire and Identity in Eighteenth-Century Britain* (Cambridge and New York: Cambridge University Press, 2010), provides an intriguing analysis of the nabob and covers some of the same ground considered in this chapter but with rather different objectives.

used the term *Jacobite*, as a term of extreme social opprobrium. "Rapacity, or greediness or plunder," he objected, were the terms that immediately arose "in the mind of almost every man and woman in the kingdom, on their hearing any person called a Nabob."[14]

The great wealth of some of these nabobs and their own flamboyant behavior drew public attention to them. In the sort of revolution that occurred in Bengal during the decade after 1757 "it was impossible but that a number of individuals should have acquired large property," the philosopher Richard Price remarked in 1777: "They did acquire it; and with it seem to have obtained the detestation of their countrymen, and the appellation of *nabob* as a term of reproach."[15] Although both nabobs and returned West Indian Creoles were the "common subject of envy and declamation," remarked the proslavery West Indian writer James Tobin in 1785, "their enormous riches" gave the "*Nabobs* of the East . . . a very material advantage over the *comets*," that is, the Creoles, "of the West."[16]

In the first instance, this negative conception of the nabob seems to have arisen out of the debate over Clive's behavior in India and, more especially, his entitlement to the *jagir*. Given the enormous wealth Clive brought back with him from India – it exceeded £300,000 – a faction in the Company opposed his receiving this private present, and his right to it remained under challenge until, following a series of uprisings in Bengal, he agreed to return to India as governor of Bengal on condition that the Company confirm his *jagir*, which he thenceforth enjoyed for the rest of his life.

In the wake of this contest, the political maneuverings within the Company over Clive's *jagir* became the butt of ridicule in the mid-1760s. One example, published anonymously in 1767, was an extended and heavy-handed satire on the Company meeting that confirmed the *jagir*, entitled *Debates in the Asiatic Assembly*. In this piece, an ignorant and self-interested group of supporters with names like Sir Janus Blubber, Shylock Buffaloe, the Jew, Skeleton Scarecrow, Jaundice Braywell, Caliban Clodpate, Sir Judas Venom, and Donald Machaggies made fatuous speeches praising Lord Vulture, that is, Clive, for his service in India and supporting his claim to the *jagir*. Throughout this meeting only the independent George Manly rose to expose the other speakers as "a troop of desperate banditti," to denounce their efforts as "a scandalous confederacy to plunder and strip" the Company, and to demand "an enquiry more deeply into" Clive's "avarice and oppression and tyrannical management of our affairs; his insolence, inhumanity, and breach of order." "What shall we think of a man, who is at this hour in our own service, possessed of an income

---

[14] *The Saddle put on the Right Horse; or, an Enquiry into the Reasons Why certain Persons have been denominated Nabobs* (London, 1783), 1, 7, 22–23.

[15] Richard Price, *Tracts*, 2 vols. (London, 1777), 1: 13, as quoted by Michael Edwardes, *The Nabobs at Home* (London: Constable, 1991), frontispiece.

[16] James Tobin, *Cursory Remarks upon the Reverend Mr. Ramsay's Essay on the Treatment and Conversion of African Slaves in the Sugar Colonies* (London, 1785), 33 note.

more than double that of the most ancient families in England, all which he has acquired in our service, and who shall yet demand more?" asked Manly:

Who shall insist on a continuance of this enormous j–g–re, in defiance of every independent and impartial Proprietor? Shall we tamely behold all his engines employed in every dark practice of promises and threats, of corruption and prostitution, to procure a majority of votes on his favour, to establish a precedent that strikes at the very root of our existence? Shall we exalt the destructive engineer so high above us, as to place him out of the reach of law, and inaccessible to the scourge of justice? – Shall we fall prostrate, and adore the rapacious idol we have formed?

Labeling Clive a person who was "utterly deaf to every sentiment of justice and humanity," the author, through the persona of Manly, called upon Company directors "to rescue" the Company's "effects from the luxury, the extravagance, the wanton profusions of this insatiable harpy, whose ambition is unparalleled, and whose avarice knows no bounds."[17]

IV

Such criticism became even more biting after Clive, during his second stint in India, accepted Company responsibility for collecting public revenues in Bengal. This action involved the Company in the governance of an Indian state to a degree previously unprecedented and led to calls for a parliamentary inquiry in 1766–67. The Jamaican William Beckford was one of several M.P.s to issue such a call. Pointing out that the Company had "a revenue of two millions in India, acquired God knows how, by unjust wars with the natives" and that "their Servants came home with immense fortune[s] obtained by rapine and oppression," he contended that Parliament was obliged to look into "how these revenues were consumed," why stockholders had "received no increase in dividend[s]," and "whence those oppressions so loudly talked of" derived.[18]

Over the next four years, the discussion that followed such calls identified a complex variety of issues arising out of the Company's expanded role in India. Whether the East India Company was constitutionally capable of holding and governing territory; whether Britain should have political jurisdiction over any territory in Asia;[19] whether Parliament could take over the governance of India without violating the charter rights of the Company; whether the Government could siphon off part of the vast revenues of the Company for state purposes; whether, if Indian territorial revenues were collected by the Crown, it would

---

[17] *Debates in the Asiatic Assembly* (London, 1767), 26, 32–33, 37, 39.

[18] As quoted by Edwardes, *The Nabobs at Home*, 54–55. For the general inquiry that followed, see Huw V. Bowen, "A Question of Sovereignty? The Bengal Land Revenue Issue, 1765–66," *Journal of Commonwealth and Imperial History*, 16 (1988): 155–76, and Philip Lawson, "Parliament and the First East India Inquiry, 1767," *Parliamentary History*, 1 (1982): 99–114.

[19] *A Letter to a Late Popular Director, L[aurence] S[ullivan], Relative to India Affairs, and the Present Contests* (London, 1769), 4, 9.

upset the balance of power within the British constitution;[20] whether it was either possible or desirable to establish a system of British laws in ancient and highly civilized polities such as those then existing in India;[21] and whether a government bureaucracy in India would subject the Indians to even "a higher degree of despotism" than they then suffered under the jurisdiction of the Company[22] – were all questions raised and canvassed during the years between 1767 and 1771. The issues defined during this period continued to shape the debate over what to do about the East India Company for the next fifteen years. But while Parliament conducted its first inquiry into Indian affairs in 1767, it made no recommendations for resolving any of these questions after the Company agreed to provide the Government with an annual subsidy of £400,000 and to endeavor "to correct all the abuses which" had been "felt in Bengal from Lord Clive's mistakes."[23]

As several of the questions raised during this period suggest, a recurring theme in these discussions was that Britain's problems in India, like those it faced in America, were attributable at least in part to metropolitan neglect. From "the little concern" Britain had bestowed on India, complained one writer, one could "imagine that she regards it rather like an adventitious excrescence, or as an encumbering burden unadvisedly taken up, from which she would willingly disengage herself." However, for just "a small share of her attention," this writer contended, Bengal alone was "capable of yielding to Britain...not only more riches, but also more durable benefit, than all her other foreign possessions." In contrast to the situation with the American colonies, moreover, that benefit was entirely secure, because Britain now possessed "the unlimited power of imposing, collecting and applying the revenues of that country." "Whereas the commerce with America, not being the effect of free choice or of necessity, will," he predicted, "most probably prove the cause, that Britain will, one day, lose her dominion over that country," the commerce with India could "ever [be] preserve[d] to Britain" through its complete "dominion" there.[24]

A few analysts were less certain that British control in India was so secure. Indeed, the anonymous author of *An Address to the Proprietors of East India Stock, Shewing the Necessity of Sending Commissioners to Regulate their Affairs Abroad*, published in London in 1769, argued that the East India Company, by forgetting that it was "a trading Company," turning "Politicians," and considering itself "as vested with the cares of empire," had, at the expense

---

[20] Alexander Dalrymple, *Vox Populi Vox Dei, Lord Weymouth's Appeal to a General Court of India Proprietors Considered* (London, 1769), 12–13.
[21] Idem, *A Second Letter Concerning the Proposed Proprietorship* (London, 1769), 8–12; *The National Mirror* (London, 1771).
[22] George Johnstone, *Thoughts on our Acquisitions in the East Indies, particularly respecting Bengal* (London, 1771), 26.
[23] Dalrymple, *A Second Letter*, 13.
[24] *The Importance of the British Dominions in India, Compared with that in America* (London, 1770), 6–7, 17–18, 21–22.

of "the defrauded widows and orphans of those Britons, who have lost their lives in the Company's Service," succeeded only in raising a broad coalition of "Asiatic enemies, whom the iniquity of your servants has made inveterate" foes and whose "impudence" was steadily becoming more "formidable." Moreover, he observed, that impudence had been reinforced by growing military power. No longer docile trading partners, "the oppressed princes of the East," he reported, were endeavoring to build upon the ruins of the old commercial system "Distinct and powerful states," while the "subjects of those states," having as a result of the numerous transgressions of Company servants become thoroughly acquainted with British "sentiments of liberty, to which they formerly were strangers," were deeply resentful "of the indignity of being in subjection to a few diseased and profligate natives of a distant country." "The rapid introduction of European arts," he predicted, would turn these nascent states into "formidable and lasting establishment[s]." Unless the Company stopped trying to exert political authority from London and followed the Dutch example of giving full authority to governors in India, he suggested, "luxury and the disproportionate fortunes of individuals" would soon be "the only advantages" Britain would reap from India.[25]

Notwithstanding all the Company's failures in controlling its servants in India, however, many writers were skeptical that turning Indian affairs over to the Government would solve India's problems. Thus in 1769 did Alexander Dalrymple, one of the most prolific defenders of the East India Company during these years, express doubts about the wisdom of turning to a Government that had not been "successful at home or in America" for counsel on "the management of our affairs in India, which have hitherto been managed *successfully* without them."[26] Similarly, in the same year, an anonymous writer who expressed his dismay that the Government would risk the commercial benefits of the American trade in return for the "very trifling" returns that might be expected from the Townshend taxes, laid it down as "an observation founded on experience, that commercial business can never flourish under ministerial controul, or restraint," warning that "in the present situation of our affairs, when our colony trade is in a dangerous state, the decline of the *East-India* trade" that could be expected from Government interference in East Indian Company affairs "might be attended with very fatal consequences."[27]

Yet the public engagement with Indian affairs seems to have raised awareness of the value of the Indian trade, which the more optimistic analysts were persuaded could only improve with more effective cultivation. Notwithstanding the fact that, as an anonymous writer claimed in 1770, India, through re-exports and the "two channels of revenue and private fortune[s]," was

---

[25] *An Address to the Proprietors of East India Stock, Shewing the Necessity of Sending Commissioners to Regulate their Affairs Abroad* (London, 1769), 6, 8–10, 13, 24, 27.

[26] Dalrymple, *A Second Letter*, 7.

[27] *An Essay on the East-India Trade, and Its Importance to this Kingdom, with a Comparative View of the Dutch, French, and English East-India Companies* (London, 1769), 5–7.

providing Britain with an estimated £2,400,000 per year,[28] its vast potential as a source of wealth was far from being realized. As Adam Smith would later point out in the *Wealth of Nations*, the civilized "empires of China, Indostan, Japan, as well as several others in the East Indies, without having richer mines of gold or silver, were in every other respect much richer, better cultivated, and more advanced in all arts and manufactures than either Mexico or Peru," much less than the "mere savages" who "inhabited the rest of America." "Rich and civilized nations," said Smith, could "always exchange to a much greater value with one another, than with savages and barbarians." Still, he acknowledged that Britain, like Europe as a whole, had "hitherto derived much less advantage from its commerce with the East Indies than from that with America."[29] Smith was among those writers who did not advocate Government intervention as a way of exploiting Asia's vast potential for trade.

The identification of issues that occurred during the late 1760s did little to allay the feeling that the East India Company was presiding over the wholesale plunder of India. Both the servants of the Company and the Company itself seemed to be guilty. "No officers should have the means either clandestinely, or by connivance," declared a writer signing himself "An *untainted* ENGLISHMAN" in 1767,

> to make sudden princely fortunes, and return, after a few years absence, to their own country with millions, or half millions; which are sums too large for particular persons, too vast and unreasonable for them to acquire at the expence of their employers; and give great room to think that such servants...make every thing subservient to the accomplishment of their own views.

Advocating the expropriation of Indian revenues to pay off Britain's vast national debt and thereby help "the rest of the nation to share in the future emolument of that extensive commerce," this writer asked "whether it is not a great reproach to the understanding of the British state, to suffer a few of her subjects *only*, to acquire the greatest opulence, and suddenly make as great fortunes as eastern princes, while the state itself is *sinking*, for want of money to pay off only the interest of her debt."[30]

Samuel Foote's popular play *The Nabob*, first performed in 1768, helped, as one reviewer noted, to bring the "depradations committed abroad" to the attention of those who "did not know a great deal about East India affairs,"[31] at once encapsulating and reinforcing popular resentments about the behavior of Britons in India. The nabob of the title is Sir Matthew Mite, one of those "new gentlemen, who from caprice of Fortune, and a strange chain of events, have acquired immoderate wealth, and rose to uncontrouled power abroad,"

---

[28] *Importance of the British Dominions in India, Compared with that in America*, 21–22.
[29] Adam Smith, *An Inquiry into the Nature and Cause of the Wealth of Nations*, ed. R. H. Campbell and A. S. Skinner, 2 vols. (Oxford: Oxford University Press, 1976), 1: 448–49.
[30] "An *untainted* ENGLISHMAN," *An Attempt to Pay off the National Debt, by Abolishing the East-India Company of Merchants* (London, 1767), vii, 25, 28–29.
[31] "Theatrecus," *The London Chronicle*, July 16–18, 1776.

and returned to England determined to marry into an ancient family and, using the familiar connection "between Bengal and the ancient corporation of Bribe'em," to buy election to Parliament. In pursuit of these objectives, Mite endeavors, with "so much contrivance and cunning" that he is "an overmatch for a plain English gentleman, or an innocent Indian," to gain control over the debts of the Oldhams, a gentry family, in order to coerce them into marrying their daughter Sophy to him. "Preceded by all the pomp of Asia," complains Lady Oldham, Mite "came thundering amongst us; and, profusely scattering the spoils of ruined provinces, corrupted the virtue and alienated the affections of all the old friends of the family" until the Oldhams had no one to whom to turn to fend off Mite's attack. Nevertheless, Lady Oldham stubbornly refuses to give in, accusing Mite of "voluptuously rioting in pleasures that derive their source from the ruin of others," and her steadfastness pays off when her merchant brother-in-law agrees to assume the Oldhams' debts in return for Lady Oldham's permission for Sophy to marry his son, the man she truly loves.

In the course of the play, Foote uses the negotiations between Touchit, an election broker, and the mayor of Bribe'em to drive home his larger point about the corrosiveness of empire in India. In response to the mayor's question about the character of the Indian settlements, Touchit recounts how, in the beginning, "a body of merchants... beg[ged] to be admitted as friends," took "possession of a small spot in the country, and" carried "on a beneficial commerce with the inoffensive and innocent people, to which they kindly" gave "their consent... Upon which, Mr. Mayor, We cunningly encroach, and fortify by little and little, till at length, we growing too strong for the natives, we turn them out of their lands, and take possession of their money and jewels." When the mayor asks if Touchit does not think such behavior "a little uncivil in us?," Touchit replies, "Oh, nothing at all: These people are but little better than Tartars or Turks." At another point in the play, an old school chum, whom Mite refuses to recognize, pointedly takes Mite's measure as a man who has "grown rich by robbing the heathens." "Nabobs," declares Putty, "are but a kind of outlandish creatures, that won't pass current with us."[32]

As this negative stereotype was being fashioned in the metropolis, the East India Company was failing in its efforts to bring its servants under control. As George Johnstone, an M.P., complained in a 1771 pamphlet, *Thoughts on our Acquisitions in the East Indies, particularly respecting Bengal*, the Company had sent a series of "secret and select committees, armed with plenipotentiary authority," which had only substituted new "monopolies and depradations" for the old and, in the process, crushed "every honest spirit, who might be daring enough to oppose their iniquitous acts, or give intelligence of them to the public" and in just three years brought Bengal into a "ruinous state," while metropolitan Britons saw "with astonishment, the immense fortunes that have been amassed under the distresses of the inhabitants, by those very members

[32] Samuel Foote, *The Nabob; A Comedy* (London, 1769), 4, 11, 17–18, 39–40, 42, 58, 60, 65.

to whom the [Company] directors had intrusted the absolute management of their affairs."[33]

An anonymous writer reinforced Johnstone's opinons in another 1771 pamphlet, *Observations on the Present State of the East India Company.* Noting that the excessive powers the Company had extended to its officers accounted "for all those various fortunes, from twenty thousand up to two hundred thousand pounds, brought home within these fourteen years past, the greatest part of which have been acquired within short spaces of time," this writer acknowledged that Britain could not expect people to serve in India "without the prospect of some considerable reward, especially surrounded as they are on every side with wealth . . . Fortunes," he thought, "should by all means be attainable; but neither so rapidly, nor with so much ease as of late years." Rather, he insisted, "they should be acquired by fair and open traffic, by the legal ample emoluments to be annexed to the higher offices, and to great trusts; not by the servile mode of presents, and by vile monopolies." The existing measures, he declared, had "only tended to thin the country, by driving the natives, through distress, to seek subsistence elsewhere; to reduce the revenues; to encrease the price of manufactures; and to make us feared, hated, and despised."[34] Nor, Edmund Burke asserted in 1772, was Parliament itself free of responsibility. The bargain it had struck with the Company in 1767 to look the other way in return for a share of the spoils, he charged, revealed that, while the ministerial authors of this arrangement "pretended reformation," they "meant nothing but plunder," looking "on the Companies['] unfaithful Servants in India" "not with resentment, but with Envy . . . and instead of punishing their delinquency they imitated their conduct."[35]

V

The continuing difficulties in Bengal, a severe famine in many parts of India, and a disastrous liquidity problem for the East India Company led in 1772 to a second round of public inquiry and passage of the Regulating Act of 1773, which empowered the metropolitan government to appoint a governor and to establish a supreme court in Bengal with jurisdiction over all cases that could come under British law throughout British India.

In the debates and print exchanges that swirled around this problem, most participants realized that the economic stakes for the metropolis were high, and the East India Company did not lack for defenders. Employing the language of commerce and writing at the very time when Company affairs were in highest agitation, John Campbell in his *Political Survey of Britain* sought to put the most positive possible spin on the situation. Although he acknowledged "that

---

[33] Johnstone, *Thoughts on our Acquisitions in the East Indies*, 23–25.

[34] *Observations on the Present State of the East India Company* (London, 1771), 32–34, 37.

[35] Edmund Burke, speech, December 18, 1772, in Paul Langford, ed., *Party, Parliament, and the American Crisis 1766–1774* (Oxford: Oxford University Press, 1981), 378.

the several Revolutions that gave us the Possession [of Bengal], and certain Measures that either were or were supposed necessary to preserve it since, have for the present brought some Distress on this Country by diminishing the Quantity of Silver that circulated therein, discouraging Industry, and lessening Commerce," he argued that the situation in India had never been more favorable for metropolitan Britain than it had been since the conquest of Bengal in 1757. "Instead of that uncertain and precarious State in which our Commerce remained here for many Years," he wrote,

we enjoy now the most certain and ample Security from the Nature of our Fortifications, and particularly the extensive and highly improved Fortress at Calcutta, the large Body of Troops that we maintain and pay, who from that Circumstance it is hoped may be depended upon, as the Natives, to use their own Expression, have hitherto been faithful to those whose Salt they eat.

Together with "the Experience of our Officers and their Knowledge of the Country, with the Reputation arising from our Success," Campbell reported, this new "Security hath enabled and disposed us to acquire a very large Property in these Parts, for such our Fortifications, Magazines, and in general all our Effects there may be considered," while the

territorial Income arising from the Rents of Lands, Duties on Cattle, Inland Trade, Customs, &c. amount to an immense Sum, from which all Deductions being made there may, or at least ought to remain in the Company's Treasury what is sufficient for the Purchase of the Company's Investments without sending an Ounce of Silver from hence. To all this,

he noted, "we may add the Capacity the Company is in to furnish a comfortable Subsistence, and in a reasonable Space of Time, without either Fraud or Oppression, ample Fortunes to British Subjects whom they employ in their several Establishments."[36]

These developments, in Campbell's opinion, illustrated "the vast Importance of the East India Company" and the considerable extent to which it was a significant "Benefit . . . to this Nation." Moreover, he suggested that the "Profits accruing to the Nation from the Shipping and Seamen in the Service of the Company, the Price of Freight, the Provisions they consume, the Stores they carry with and are sent to them, and the Commodities and Manufactures of this Country exported thither," the "raw Goods, especially Silk and Salt Petre, imported from thence, that give Business and Bread to Multitudes here, the annual Produce of the Company's Sales, which bring in great Sums from foreign Countries, the Customs and other Emoluments that accrue to Government, and in that respect operate in Diminution of our National Expence" would all "continually increase" in the future. Any difficulties in India, Campbell was sure, could easily be remedied by applying the wisdom and authority of

[36] John Campbell, *A Political Survey of Britain: Being a Series of Reflections on the Situation, Lands, and Inhabitants, Revenues, Colonies, and Commerce of this Island*, 2 vols. (London, 1774), 2: 613–14.

Britain to the establishment of "a mild and settled Government, under which all Europeans in general" could "enjoy the Protection of our Laws and the Natives be permitted to live according to their own Customs, free in all respects from Constraint and Oppression."[37]

In a similar vein, Burke argued that most of the problems of India could be explained by circumstances and necessity, rather than by moral decay. He did not deny that in "such a multiplicity of affairs, and in a government without laws, some enormities must have been committed." But he was persuaded that the main problem was the absence of "a comprehensive and well-digested code of laws, for the rule of every man's conduct" and the lack of appropriate institutions to enforce them. "When discretionary power" is "lodged in the hands of any man, or class of men," he declared, "experience proves, that it will always be abused. This was the case with the East-India company," whose "charter . . . was well enough calculated for the purposes of a factory" but was "totally insufficient upon the acquisition of extensive territories. Hence," Burke explained,

unlimited authority fell necessarily into the hands of their governors. The directors, attentive to the extension of their trade, had not time, nor perhaps capacity, to make general regulations sufficient for the good government of so great an empire; and, had they been possessed of these requisites, yet they wanted the power to exert them.

Because the Company found it impossible "to keep in awe" its "servants, who knew that" they "did not derive" their "authority from law, and that they could not be punished for disobedience beyond the ditch of Calcutta," the servants themselves, just "to preserve some kind of subordination," were in turn "forced occasionally to act the despot, and to terrify the refractory by the arm of power or violence."[38]

But such arguments did little to deflect parliamentary and public attention from the long catalogue of the misdeeds of the East India Company and its servants in India that came to light during the extensive consideration of Indian affairs both in and out of Parliament in 1772 and 1773. In 1772, William Bolts, a former Company servant in India whom the Company's select committee had removed from his position and deprived of his income, published the most extensive and systematic exposé of the situation in India yet issued. His *Considerations on Indian Affairs; Particularly Respecting the Present State of Bengal and its Dependencies*, which ran to 228 pages, was, as Burke later said, the first full-length book to turn "the national attention to the state of our affairs in the East Indies."[39]

---

[37] Ibid., 613–15.

[38] Edmund Burke, speech, April 13, 1772, in Langford, ed., *Party, Parliament, and the American Crisis*, 372–73.

[39] Edmund Burke to _____, in Holden Furber and P. J. Marshall, eds., *The Correspondence of Edmund Burke* (Cambridge: Cambridge University Press, 1965), 5: 263, as quoted by P. J. Marshall, *Problems of Empire*, 59.

Bolts began his volume with a compelling summary of the nature of the problems with British rule in India. "From a society of mere traders, confined by charter to the employment of six ships and six pinnaces yearly," he wrote, "the Company are become sovereigns of extensive, rich and populous kingdoms, with a standing army of above sixty thousand men at their command. In this new situation of the society," he complained,

there is scarcely any public spirit apparent among their leaders, either in England or India. The loaves and the fishes are the grand, almost the sole object. The questions, How many *lacks* shall I put in my pocket? Or, How many sons, nephews, or dependents shall I provide for, at the expense of the miserable inhabitants of the subjected dominions? are those which of late have been the foremost to be propounded by the Chiefs of the Company on both sides the ocean. Hence,

he charged, employing the languages of rapacity, barbarism, and injustice,

the dominions in Asia, like the distant Roman provinces during the decline of the empire, have been abandoned, as lawful prey, to every species of peculators; in so much that many of the servants of the Company, after exhibiting such scenes of barbarity as can scarcely be paralleled in the history of any country, have returned to England loaded with wealth,

and, "intrenching themselves in borough or East-India-stock influence," have "set justice at defiance, either in the cause of their country, or of oppressed innocence."[40]

Point by point, Bolts made his way through an extensive catalogue of the Company's many crimes. First was its adventures in "*Nabob-making*," in substituting for legitimate Indian rulers people who were beholden to the Company for their positions. The Grand Mogul and "the pretended NABOBS of Bengal and Bahar" were "the actual stipendiaries of the said Company, and the DEWANNEE, under which title" the Company "pretend[ed] to hold those territorial possessions," was

a mere fiction, invented for the private purposes of the Company and their servants; and particularly intended, if possible, to screen their seizing on the sovereignty of the country, by imposing on the British nation; though the disguise was too flimsey to deceive either the inhabitants of Hindostan or other European nations who have settlements in those countries.

"The Nabobs of Bengal," he declared, were

no other than the tools of the East India Company and their representatives in Asia, through whom not only the natives, but even Englishmen, in those remote parts, are exposed to every species of oppression; for so grievous is the present situation of British subjects in those countries, that it is in fact now easily in the power of the Governor

---

[40] William Bolts, *Considerations on Indian Affairs; Particularly Respecting the Present State of Bengal and its Dependencies* (London, 1772), iv–v.

of Bengal, whenever he pleases, to deprive any one of so much of his property as lies within the *Nabob's* dominions, or even of his life.[41]

The Company's second crime was the complete abolition of "freedom in trade" in Bengal, "though by that alone it can be made flourishing and importantly beneficial to the British state." "All branches of the interior Indian commerce," he wrote, were, "without exception, entirely monopolies of the most cruel and ruinous natures; and so totally corrupted, from every species of abuse, as to be in the last stages towards annihilation." The "baneful effects of" this "continued scene of oppression," he contended, had been "severely felt by every weaver and manufacturer in the country, every article produced being made a monopoly; in which the English, with their Banyans and black gomastahs," (terms for the Indian agent who mediated between Company servants and Indian society) "arbitrarily decide what quantities of goods each manufacturer shall deliver, and the *prices* he shall receive for them."[42]

The Company's third crime was the eradication of civil justice, which left

millions... entirely at the mercy of a few men, who divide[d] the spoils of the public among themselves; while, under such despotism, supported by military violence, the whole interior of the country, where neither the laws of England reach, or the laws and customs of those countries are permitted to have their course, is no better than in a state of nature,

"a state of the most deplorable anarchy, under the despotic sway of one, or at most a very few English gentlemen, and their Banyans." In India, he proclaimed, there was no justice, no "right but that of the longest sword, nor any law except the will of the conquerors." Under these conditions, Bolts charged, the Company had "exercised such unbounded despotism as was wholly incompatible with the laws of this kingdom, those of humanity, or such as would be thought intolerable even in Turkey or Barbary."[43]

The effects of these deficiencies upon India, according to Bolts, had been catastrophic. "While the poor industrious natives" were "oppressed beyond conception, population" was "decreasing, the manufactories and revenues" were "decaying, and Bengal, which used not many years ago to send annually a tribute of several millions in hard specie to Dehly," was "now reduced to so extreme a want of circulation, that it" was "not improbable [that] the Company" would "soon be in want of specie in Bengal to pay their troops, and in England seen pleading incapacity to pay the very annual four hundred thousand pounds which is now received from them by Government." Not just Bengal, but all British possessions in eastern India, "Bahar, and part of Orissa," were, to "the disgrace of the British government," in "every way exhausted by plunder and oppression; and while this nation is gazing after the fruit, the Company and their substitutes" were being "suffered to be rooting up the

---

[41] Ibid., vi, xii, 48.
[42] Ibid., vii, 191.
[43] Ibid., vii, 49, 91, 217.

tree." Bolts likened this behavior to "the ideot-practice of killing the prolific hen to get her golden eggs all at once."[44]

Bolts did not leave his case on this general level. Rather, he recited in chapter and verse incident after incident in which the East India Company, to which had been entrusted "the British dominions in Bengal," had, through its own immoral and exploitative behavior rendered its government "hateful to the natives by oppressions." By such behavior, the Company had both "occasioned desertions of many of the people" and generally made itself "odious in India, disgusting to and envied by many of the powers in Europe, and tyrannical in the extreme towards resident fellow-subjects." Indeed, contrasting the situation in Britain with that in India, he professed to know of "Many other instances" that would provide additional proof of "the badness of the government, police, and administration of justice in those distant dominions; some of which, though there looked upon as trifles, would in this country be considered as matters of the most serious consequence." To illuminate "all the facts of that nature which have come within the writer's knowledge," he wrote, "would be to fill a large folio volume. It would moreover be a task shocking to humanity."[45]

Bolts directly linked considerations of humanity to the national honor of Britain, recommending that Britain

never . . . consent, for the paltry consideration of a short-lived pecuniary emolument to effect the devastation of such rich and fertile countries, and the extirpation or ruin of so many millions of civilized, inoffensive and industrious inhabitants; or to sacrifice those solid and permanent advantages which might be derived to this country from a proper System of Government.[46]

In less detail, several other writers made many of the same points. Thus did the anonymous but obviously well-informed author of *General Remarks on the System of Government in India*, published in London in 1773, also trace problems in India to the British conquest of Bengal, which he regarded as an open invitation for the rampant diffusion of despotism throughout the province. From that moment, he wrote, the "authority of the prince in Bengal declined," permitting "the chiefs of the different districts under his command" to become "more and more oppressive on the subject," so that "instead of having one regular and avowed tyrant to maintain," the country now had

such a number of petty ones to support, that, by the ruinous condition into which they have reduced the province, they have almost defeated the ends for which men are so solicitous after power; for every nabob, zemindar, and rajah, are now become real tyrants within their own jurisdictions, governing on the principles of their former masters. The oppression of mankind,

[44] Ibid., vii, ix–x, 192.
[45] Ibid., 12, 110.
[46] Ibid., 228.

he observed, "must of course increase in proportion as the number of tyrants increase in the same extent of country."[47]

Under these conditions, this author explained, "a few Englishmen," with "the whole revenue of Bengal and Bahar entrusted to their care, the rest of the empire so torn by factions, as rendered it incapable of molesting them, and the king of Hindostan a fugitive from his thrown," had "been left for these ten years past, by the rulers of the British nation, to the free and uncontrouled disposal of the lives and properties of some millions of mankind." "Sensible of their power, with scarce any rules to guide them," and "under no fear of punishment for oppression committed through their neglect by the natives in office, and tempted by the easy attainment of wealth," Company servants rapidly made personal fortunes – the powerful, such as Clive, either from "presents from the duan, or from the principal farmers of the different districts, or else by the chiefs and residents who have engrossed the various manufactures, and the different produces of the earth," and lesser officials through "extortion, or plunder, secretly taken from individuals." The result was a system of extortion and monopolies that discouraged industry and siphoned off vast sums from Company revenues and that kept Bengal "in the same anarchy and confusion" created by the wars that had led to its conquest by the British.[48]

Many other writers and speakers in Parliament expressed outrage at the revelations of Bolts and others. "It is universally allowed," said Colonel John Burgoyne, who spearheaded the move in Parliament to bring India under metropolitan civil authority, in November 1772,

and indeed it is clearly proved, that the East India Company is rotten to the very core. All is equally unsound; and you cannot lay your finger on a single healthy spot whereon to begin the application of a remedy. In the east the laws of society, the laws of nature, have been enormously violated. Oppression in every shape has ground the faces of the poor defenceless natives; and tyranny has stalked abroad. The laws of England,

he continued, "have lain mute and neglected, and nothing was seen but the arbitrary caprice of despotism. Every sanction of civil justice, every maxim of political wisdom, all laws human and divine, have been trampled under foot, and set at nought," while at "home, there has been egregious mismanagement and variety of roguery."[49]

How this malignant system could have taken such a deep hold in India, how India had become a place "where lordly traders, impatient of controul" and concerned with nothing more than the gratification of their "own sordid avarice,"[50] had been able to divert such vast sums from the "great Terretorial

---

[47] *General Remarks on the System of Government in India; with farther Considerations on the Present State of the Company at Home and Abroad* (London, 1771), 40.

[48] Ibid., 23, 40–42.

[49] John Burgoyne, speech, November 26, 1772, in William Cobbett, ed., *Parliamentary History of England from the Earliest Period to the Year 1803*, 36 vols. (London, 1806–20), 17: 535.

[50] Harry Verelst, *A View of the Rise, Progress, and Present State of the English Government in Bengal* (London, 1772), 130.

revenues in Bengal" into "the coffers of private men"[51] was a question to which metropolitan analysts had many answers. "If the public enquires after the cause to which this wretched state is owing," observed Thomas Pownall in 1773,

they are told of the want of wisdom and power in the company at home; of mischievous errors in the directors; of factions in general courts; of ungovernable disobedience in their servants abroad; of peculation of public treasure; of frauds in expenditures; of fals[e]hoods in accounts; of plundering, pillaging, and rapine, both public and private; of rapacious extortions in trade, which have ruined the commerce and manufactures of the country; of tyranny, in every exertion of the cruel spirit, which had absolutely destroyed the country itself.

In Pownall's view, all of these problems were the "necessary effects of a prime original evil," the fact that the territorial acquisitions of the late 1750s and the fiscal responsibilities of the mid-1760s had required the merchant to "*become the sovereign*; that a trading company have in their hands the exercise of a sovereignty, which the company by its direction within the realm is not adequate to, and with which its servants... should not be trusted."[52]

Other observers agreed with this point and elaborated it. A writer signing himself "A. B." offered a more detailed diagnosis in a 1773 pamphlet, *A Letter to the Right Honourable Lord North, on the Present Proceedings Concerning the East-India Company.* "As the possessions of the Company were extended in India," he pointed out, "the Directors [of the Company in London] increased in importance, and became after their acquisition of the territorial revenues one of the great objects of avarice, ambition, and party; artifice, fraud, corruption, means usual and natural to them, were employed to operate upon the body of electors." As a result, "the sober, honest, and discreet Proprietors" who had previously dominated the Company retired, "satisfied with a large and unexpected increase of fortune; and were succeeded by adventurers and gamesters, a fluctuating set, who bought in or sold out as their overvarying speculations directed them." These new people made "the plunder of the Indies... the reward and wages of corrupt service; while the uncertainty of tenure spread quicker and wider the scenes of cruelty and devastation." With no law to restrain them, Company servants had no restraints upon their "avarice and rapacity" and, "in the pursuit of their objects," created "scenes of villainy and horror" that "surpass[ed] all the creative powers of invention."[53] The principal Company officers in each Indian presidency, declared another writer, were each one, "probably, the greatest Criminal in their several Provinces; for their power" was "unbounded, both in conferring benefits, and inflicting

---

[51] *An Enquiry into the Rights of the East-India Company* (London, 1772), iv–vi.
[52] Thomas Pownall, *The Right, Interest, and Duty, of the State, as Concerned in the Affairs of the East Indies* (London, 1773), 7–8.
[53] "A. B.," *A Letter to the Right Honourable Lord North, on the Present Proceedings Concerning the East-India Company* (London, 1773), 8–9, 12.

punishments, [so] that none of those frauds and oppressions" could have been committed without their connivance.[54]

In retrospect, "A. B." was certain that India had

become lawless from the moment she passed under our government; the sceptre, wrested from the gentle grasp of Asiatic despotism, was thrown aside, and rods of iron put into the hands of British barbarians: No rule for direction, no sanction for punishment, no interest in the rulers for the protection and preservation of the governed, prevailed there. The harvest was abundant, but the season short and precarious: not a moment was lost in gathering, not an art was omitted that could expedite the hoarding. Pride and emulation stimulated avarice; and the sole contest was, who should return to that home, which they almost all quitted beggars, with the greatest heap of crimes and of plunder.[55]

Noting that Clive had described "the inhabitants of Indostan . . . 'as servile, mean, submissive, and humble, in inferior stations; yet in superior, luxurious, effeminate, tyrannical, treacherous, venal, cruel,'" this author inquired whether "the contrast . . . between the servants of the Company and the Indians in superior stations" was "so great as he would have us believe" and "whether those *English Gentlemen* had not adopted and improved upon the last set of Eastern qualities?" "By all laws human and divine," this writer declared, the "miserable actors who started up into Nabobs in India" had "since become Lords of no inconsiderable possessions in Great Britain; and some . . . become legislators here, who . . . would for far less crimes committed in any civilized country, be punished there with imprisonment, confiscation, and death." "Nabobs black with crimes of the deepest dye," he observed in an obvious reference to Samuel Foote's comedy, were emphatically "not objects to excite laughter: the magnitude of" their crimes demanded "a more solemn audience, and" pointed "them out as proper persons in a more serious drama." Emphasizing the negative effects of such crimes upon the international reputation of Britain, he reminded his readers that the splendor in which the nabobs lived in Britain had been purchased with "the destruction of India and the infamy of Great Britain."[56]

The most visible defender of the East India Company and its servants in parliamentary debate, Clive traced Indian problems to the guiles of the East. He did not deny that corruption was rampant among the Company's servants in India. In his view, however, it was principally traceable to their youthfulness and the artfulness of the Indian *banyans* under whose sway they came almost immediately upon their arrival in India. Using these fine British lads as a front behind which they could line their own pockets, these *banyans* seduced them by providing them with the funds to "live in splendid apartments or have houses of their own, ride upon fine prancing Arabian Horses, and in Penqueens and Chaises," and to "keep Seraglios, make Entertainments, and treat with Champagne and Claret," while they simultaneously tutored them in

[54] *A Plan for the Government of Bengal* (London, 1772), 30.
[55] "A. B.," *A Letter to the Right Honourable Lord North*, 12–13.
[56] Ibid., 12, 26–27.

eastern ways of bribery and chicanery. Through these *banyans*, Clive admitted, many of these young servants became virtual "Nabobs and Sovereigns in the East" and acquired impressive fortunes. But he insisted that they left their abandoned ways in India and that when they returned home, they behaved so honorably that there had "not yet been one character found amongst them sufficiently flagitious for Mr. Foote to exhibit on the theatre in the Haymarket." The unspoken assumption underlying Clive's remarks was that the crimes of nabobry were merely youthful excesses committed in a land far outside Britain where corruption was already an entrenched system. Profligate and rapacious behavior by Britons, he suggested, was not damnable if it occurred in the overseas empire.[57]

Whether corruption was endemic to Asian societies, as Clive suggested, or was the fault of the East India Company and its servants, as most of his opponents thought, many analysts believed that the prospect of the rapid and extensive accumulation of wealth was difficult even for virtuous people to resist. "The degree of integrity, and strength of mind, which is sufficient to carry a man blamelessly through life in England, where the laws are many, and the temptations few," said one analyst, "may not be of sufficient proof to encounter the assaults of India, where . . . *the temptations are such, that flesh and blood cannot withstand them*, and must still be more dangerous when that flesh and blood is trusted entirely to its own legs, without any stay to keep its feet from sliding," a "Scheme of Government," he added, "which cannot be executed but by men of perfect virtue and moderation."[58]

A search for a political solution accompanied the search for blame. What seemed to be needed, as one anonymous writer put it in 1772, was a solution that would provide "an impartial administration of justice in India, without its being subject to the controul of those who are most likely the greatest delinquents"; that would put "an end to those cruel monopolies, carried on by the Servants of the Company, in the necessaries of life, and to which the wretched natives are obliged to submit, with the bayonet at their throats"; and that would make "those Servants once more attentive to the commercial interests of their employers; without attempting to equal, in riches and splendor, the first nobility of the Kingdom." The most ambitious and extreme solution called for the metropolitan government to abolish or modify the Company's most recent 1758 charter, "commonly called" by Company critics "*the Charter of Plunder*,"[59] and take over the full task of governance, establishing a British-style polity in India with British-style laws. This position had powerful support in Parliament.

But many people worried with Henry Verelst, a former governor in Bengal, that the "nature of the people, and the relation in which they stand to us," rendered "impossible a free government in Bengal," and that British laws

---

[57] Robert Clive, *Lord Clive's Speech in the House of Commons, 30th March 1772* (London, 1772), 45–46.
[58] *Plan for the Government of Bengal*, 36–37.
[59] *An Inquiry into the Rights of the East-India Company*, iv–vi, 7.

were entirely "inadequate to the controul of distant governors armed with such extensive authority as must ever be upheld in India."[60] The colonies in America offered no model for British governance in India. "Nothing of the Constitution of Great Britain or her Colonies," said one writer, could possibly "be transplanted to Bengal, where there can be no Council, no Assembly of the native proprietors of the lands to check any set of tyrants which their hard fate may bring upon them."[61]

Opponents of extensive reform were eloquent in their cautions against adopting any system that relied for its effectiveness upon any significant interference with customary Indian modes of governance. "The Indians," said Alexander Dalrymple, were "so devoted to their own Customs, which they enjoyed many ages before we had even *painted Ancestors*, that the English Laws" were "not suited to them; and although in criminal Cases they may *in general* be introduced, they are not by any means applicable to common government. Every Conqueror of India," he said, "must follow the example of former Conquerors and leave the Indians to themselves, who have existed as a civilized and polished People many thousand Years *without any laws but religious, and without* ONE *Lawyer amongst them*." Professing his deep veneration for British liberties, he insisted "that *Freedom*" could "be enjoyed only by men *who enact[ed] their own Laws, or who live[d] under equal laws of ancient usage*." It was impossible, he said, "for that state to be *free*, where the inhabitants, in *general*, have no share in the government; and therefore no plan, to be executed by *Europeans only*, can convey the *smallest portion* of *freedom* to the Indians; abuses may be corrected, their persons and properties may be secured. But these are very compatible with an *absolutely despotic government*." An "*Englishman*," he declared, was "the fittest to enact laws for *Englishmen*: He knows their wants, and he feels their grievances. But *he* is unfit to form laws for the *Indians*. He can never conceive that *eating a piece of beef* can be sufficient reason for driving a man from society as a monster of impurity."[62]

For that reason, Dalrymple observed, the Company had "never had the most distant view of introducing a code of laws, which should regulate the manners and minds of the Indians; establish a new religion amongst them," or "by destroying the casts, attempt a new mode of awakening industry, and impressing motives of action." Rather, the "Idea of the Company's Government" takes

up the Indians where it finds them, under a regular system of civilization, secured by casts [sic] and religious ceremonies, and leaves them perfectly free in the exercise thereof; not assuming the power of enacting general laws, it can never promulgate the institute of destruction, by subverting the manners and customs of the Indians.[63]

---

[60] Verelst, *A View of the Rise, Progress, and Present State of the English Government in Bengal*, 145.

[61] *Plan for the Government of Bengal*, 40–41.

[62] Alexander Dalrymple, *Considerations on a Pamphlet entitled Thoughts on our Acquisition in the East Indies, particularly respecting Bengal* (London, 1772), 30–31, 85.

[63] Ibid., 10–11.

Other writers less favorable to the Company conceded Dalrymple's point. Because the "bulk of mankind" were "governed in their opinions not by reason, but by authority; and [because] the strongest of all authorities" was "that which" had "the stamp of antiquity upon it," advised an anonymous exponent of a plan for governing Bengal, a "nation which would preserve its conquest, with the will of the conquered, must carefully preserve the old forms of government" and "affront in nothing the old manners." "Conquests... not accompanied with extirpations," he observed, "have in all ages been secured or lost, according as these rules have been observed or neglected." Still, he thought it possible for Britain to introduce into India "new laws, which new circumstances require," without depriving the "inhabitants... of their old ones."[64] Whatever system was introduced, agreed still another analyst, the facts remained that Britain had "acquired the actual government of this Country by force" and that it could acquire "the *rightful* Government" of it only "by exercising our power over the inhabitants, according to the laws of God and Nature, with justice and humanity, that they who have the best *right* to dispose of themselves, may voluntarily acknowledge the King of Great Britain as their *lawful* Sovereign, and become anxious to retain his protection." No government that was not informed by principles of humanity, he implied, would be suitable for India.[65]

As it became clear that the Government would not press for a thorough reformation of the problems in India, critics of the Company, with General Burgoyne as their principal spokesman, endeavored to introduce resolutions that vested all military or negotiated conquests in the hands of the state, declared illegal private acquisitions of wealth by people "entrusted with any civil or military power of the state," and forced all those who had profited from such acquisitions to "make restitution" to the state.[66] Sir William Meredith explored the rationale behind these proposals. The previous year's report of the parliamentary committee appointed to investigate the problems in India, he declared, had found, as the Government had acknowledged in letters to Company directors, "that every spring of this government" in India was "smeared with corruption; that principles of rapacity and oppression universally prevailed; and that every spark of public sentiment and public virtue" had been "extinguished in the unbounded lust of unmerited wealth." While Lord North, the first minister, had suggested that pushing this inquiry further "would discover actions that cannot bear the light," that would bring "dishonour on the English nation, and disgrace and misery on many worthy families in England," Meredith argued that to ignore this evidence was effectively to sanction and "establish this corruption," to "give line and scope to this spirit of rapacity," and to endorse "this unbounded lust of unmerited wealth."[67]

---

[64] *Plan for the Government of Bengal*, 13.
[65] Ibid., 8.
[66] Burgoyne, speech, May 10, 1773, in Cobbett et al., eds., *Parliamentary History*, 17: 855–56.
[67] Sir William Meredith, speech, May 10, 1773, in ibid., 17: 856–60.

"From all that we read in tales or history," Meredith said, "never did such a system exist as that" in British India, "where mercantile avarice was the only principle, and force the only means of carrying on a government. Comparisons of other tyrannies," he declared, gave "no idea of English tyranny in Bengal," where, in contrast to most tyrannies, the tyrants "use[d] their rod of iron," not just upon the rich, but upon "rich and poor . . . alike. They who have lands are dispossessed; if money, it is extorted; if the mechanic has a loom, his manufacture is cut out; if he has grain, it is carried off; if he is suspected of having treasure, he is put to the torture to discover it." Moreover, unlike most tyrants, whose behavior is moderated by fear of popular revolt, Meredith said, "our country men in Bengal" were "free from all" such

apprehensions; they have no resistance to fear from a poor disarmed people, inured to slavery and broken to oppression. And so much in reverse are they in fear of shame, that their ambition is spurred on by knowing that they are to secure honour, love, importance, dependents and friends, in proportion to the riches they bring home.[68]

Outside Parliament, other observers also complained that the new regulatory act was insufficient to set things right in East Indian affairs. In India, an anonymous essayist told the readers of *The London Chronicle* in May 1773, the "scenes of villany and horror, described in Fielding's Life of Jonathan Wild the Great, had been realized and heightened." From the moment this once "flourishing state" that was "the work of ages" fell under British government and into the "hands of British barbarians," he complained, it became "lawless." Unchecked by any superior power, those who had "started up Nabobs in India" used "rods of iron" to enrich themselves "by fraud and rapine" in a contest to see who "could return to that home, which they had all quitted beggars, with the greatest . . . plunder." In this pursuit, he charged, these "miscreant actors" had committed crimes that "in any civilized country" would have been severely punished and had thereby proven themselves to be "a race of ignorant and wicked barbarians, offensive to heaven and earth." Far from being brought to justice, however, they continued to live unmolested in Britain on large properties, with a few even becoming legislators.[69]

Difficulties of devising a different political system for India, along with the problem of assigning blame and the widespread reluctance to interfere extensively with the Company's charter rights, dictated that the reforms undertaken by the Regulating Act of 1773 should be limited, while the extraordinary economic and political clout of the East India Company, an early example of a highly successful special interest group, meant that none of the perpetrators of the troubles in India was punished. That "Great Crimes" had been charged on "the Servants of the India-Company, from a *National* Inquiry, and yet no one has suffered" had, one deeply disappointed observer complained, "stained

---

[68] Ibid.
[69] "Letter to the Right Hon. Lord North, on the present Proceedings concerning the EAST-INDIA COMPANY," *London Chronicle*, May 18–20, 1773.

the very Name and Annals of our Country with Crimes scarce inferior to the Conquerors of *Mexico* and *Peru*." Predicting that the "Historians of other Nations, (if not our own) will do Justice to the oppressed Subjects in *India*, and will hand down the Memory of the Oppressors to the latest Posterity, loaded with the Infamy due to the Magnitude of their Cruelties, Extortions, and new modes of Murder," he called upon metropolitan Britons "to perpetuate an honest Indignation against the[se] Enemies of Mankind, Tyrants clothed with civil Authority, and abusing their sacred Trust" and to continue "to call down *National* Justice on their Heads."[70]

This writer drove this point home in a long satirical poem entitled *The Nabob: or Asiatic Plunderers*. In this work, he expressed his amazement that in Britain,

> ... Laws will punish ev'ry petty knave;
> Hang low-born pilf'rers; – scourge the toil-worn slave;
> While greater villains all their threats despise,
> And by strange crimes to highest honours rise.

Trying to awaken public consciousness to the enormities of British behavior in India, he asked,

> Concerns it you who plunders in the East,
> In blood a tyrant, and in lust a beast?
> When ills are distant, are they then your own?
> Saw'st thou their tears, or heard'st th' oppressed groan?

Although he emphasized that from Britain's oppression in India,

> My Country's honor has receiv'd a blot,
> A mark of odium ne'er to be forgot,

he was also concerned that the excesses of empire be confined overseas and not tarnish metropolitan Briton's shining reputation as a land of civility, humanity, and liberty:

> All are not slaves; nor has curs'd thirst of Gold
> Our Liberty, our Lives, our Children sold:
> In *Asia's* realms let slavery be bound,
> Let not her foot defile this sacred ground,
> Where Freedom, Science, Valour fix'd their seat,
> And taught all Nations how they should be great[,]
> An hireling group in this great realm is grown
> High Lords o'er millions, whose worn hands supply
> Their pride, their pomp, and feast of luxury.
> I feel my bosom rise at this sad thought,
> By public wealth the public's foes are bought:
> While all its motion, life is sweat and toil,
> That lazy drones may banquet on the spoil.[71]

---

[70] [Richard Clarke], *The Nabob: or Asiatic Plunderers. A Satyrical Poem* (London, 1773), iii.
[71] Ibid., 3–4, 15, 38.

In a footnote and almost as an aside, the poet introduced into East Indian affairs the language of virtue, a language seldom used by metropolitan Britons when they spoke about empire. The despotism and the plunder that seemed to be so rife throughout the British overseas world appeared to this writer to be a direct function of commerce, and he pointedly refused to join in that celebration of commerce that informed so much metropolitan British speech about empire during the eighteenth century. Rather, quoting Montesquieu's remark "that commerce refines the manners, but always corrupts morals," he suggested that trade invariably drove out humanity. "What idea of christianity must Indians conceive from our traders?," he asked his readers to consider. "What notions must the Africans entertain of our humanity in purchasing slaves of such who never injured us? What Religion...can [be]...seen in *Madras*, and particularly in *Bengal*, or in the *West-Indian* Islands?" Social and moral corruption, he lamented, was "the fruit of commerce every-where."[72]

Nor was this poet the only analyst to link excesses in India to other disturbing problems in empire. In a pamphlet entitled *Britannia Libera, or a Defense of the Free State of Man in England* and published in London in 1772 at the time of the Somerset case, William Bollan, formerly agent for Massachusetts Bay, was principally concerned to express his support for the prohibition of slavery within metropolitan Britain by encouraging Parliament ever to "be solicitous to preserve the kingdom entirely free." Devoting most of his pamphlet to a broad survey of "the institution or admission of *slavery* by various ancient nations, ... the abolition of it in *Christendom*, and the partial revival of it by the *European* states concerned in the modern marine discoveries" and "the consequent acquest of foreign dominions and settlements," he also included an extended lament on "the defenceless state and sufferings of the numerous subjects in *India* lately reduced under his majesty[']s obedience, by whose labours the kingdom, and many *British* subjects have been so much enriched," sufferings that "loudly called upon the wisdom, justice, and humanity of the nation" to remedy them.[73]

In the course of his ruminations on this subject, Bollan expressed his deep regret that in the construction of overseas empire Europeans had forsaken Prince Henry's initial intention of enlarging and securing Portugal's acquisitions beyond Europe through "amity and prudence, rather than by acts of violence." He reviewed the process by which the Spanish had first violated that intention in America and then the English, despite joining "other nations in censuring the *Spanish* severities," had followed their example, using the flimsiest of excuses to take control of foreign territories and to deprive the "the natives [of] the enjoyment of their own country," actions for which "discovery could give no right, it being apparently repugnant to reason, common sense, and the nature of property, to suppose that the knowledge of the property of others transfers

---

[72] Ibid., 42 note.
[73] [William Bollan], *Britannia Libera, or a Defense of the Free State of Man in England* (London, 1772), 1, 47.

the same from the owner to the discoverer." The result was that Europeans had "destroy[ed] eleven millions, and distress[ed] many more in *America*," while Britain had "starve[d] or distress[ed] twelve millions in *Asia*." Such atrocities, Bollan declared, with their accompanying "injustice, oppression, murder, rapine, or devastation," were not only thoroughly "[in]compatible with the spirit of natural and revealed religion" but also an unpromising strategy for promoting "the dignity, strength, and safety of empire, but to draw down the Divine vengeance on the offenders, for depriving so many of their fellow creatures of life, or the common blessings of the earth, and to secure their disgrace among all good men." "It is notorious," he remarked, that if Prince Henry's "noble example had been followed by others, *America* and *India* would have been in a far more happy and secure state than they are at present, infelicity and danger being the natural offspring of injustice and cruelty, and the most powerful governments when void of justice mere *magna latrocinia* [bandits]." Because "Law and Liberty, justice and equity" were "the proper foundations of the *British* government, and humanity the most amiable characteristic of the people," he observed, "it certainly behooved those . . . concerned in the late acquest of large dominions in *Asia*" to eschew the Spanish example and "in the exercise of their power to observe the dictates of equity and goodness" and endorse no "specious pretense, the common disease of modern policy," to justify reducing "the dead and the living . . . into a state of misery."[74]

In calling attention to the moral deficiencies of early modern empire, Bollan, notwithstanding his opposition to slavery, did not call attention to the thousands of Africans caught up and similarly killed or distressed through the slave trade and the slave labor systems in the European Americas, but he could not resist calling attention to the "erroneous conduct" of ministers and Parliament in refusing to consider American petitions against metropolitan initiatives. Quoting Montesquieu on the despotic character of every government in which power was "immoderately exercised," he argued that "the refusal of freemen their right of free defence" was thoroughly "incompatible with that love of justice which ever was and ever will be the . . . lasting source of public felicity, strength and safety" and that government denial of this right to colonials in the contest over the American question had "caused great mischief, of which I can see no end, especially considering the perseverance in some of our errors, and the addition of others." "The arts of empire," he noted, "require[d] the knowledge and consideration of the state and condition of the several parts of any dominion, in order to [permit] their regulation and improvement for the common good of all, and the more extensive and divided the parts are the more necessary this knowledge becomes." For Bollan, the problems with India and America, as well as the overflow of colonial slavery into Britain, suggested that the British imperial project was deeply flawed.[75]

---

[74] Ibid., 39–42.
[75] Ibid., 38–39.

VI

Consideration of the Indian problem lost momentum in Britain during the early stages of the American War for Independence, but it was much too deeply impressed on British political consciousness to be forgotten. Thus when John Inglis wanted to delineate the full range of the unsavory types who opposed the American war, he included "a loquacious East-Indian Nabob, instructed in the principles of liberty, in the famous *Academy*, the *Bay* of *Bengal*." "Happy is the man who is initiated there . . . under the care of those faithful votaries of the adored Mammon, the wealth-creating *Nabobs*," he wrote,

Banished from their native land by poverty or dissipation, they seek in those regions of barbarity, an asylum which was denied them in that society which unfortunately gave them existence. When wasted to a climate more concordant to their habits of life, rapine, villany, and murder . . . are the shameful and horrid means they employ of amassing wealth. Thence, returning loaded with the spoils of the East, by venal methods they creep into our councils, poison our deliberations, and embroil our society; and must harangue, forsooth, in a barbarous eloquence, on liberty, and the states of Greece and Rome, which they know only by reading the Roman History by way of question and answer, or other such childish baubles.[76]

That the political and legal reforms provided for by the Regulating Act of 1773 were insufficient to stem the tide of corruption in the East India Company's regime in India was, however, apparent by the late 1770s, when public complaints again caught the attention of the metropolis. The crescendo of criticism began to rise in 1779 when James Macpherson, a Government pamphleteer and a historian, produced a detailed history of the Company.

This hostile account revived most of the earlier charges against Company mismanagement in India. "Wading through the sink of East-India corruption and mismanagement," Macpherson announced in his preface, was "a task, which adds disgust to toil." Having "industriously, and, till lately, very successfully, covered" its commercial "transactions with a veil of secrecy," the Company, he charged, had since its territorial acquisitions in 1757 "multiplied" its "acts of injustice, in proportion to the extent of" its "power" and then applied its traditional policy of silence "to a still more necessary business, the concealment of plunder." The results were that Bengal had become "a fruitful scene of peculation, injustice, and even death; and the Northern Circars, though scarcely twelve years, in our hands, present[ed] oppressions proportionable to their extent and our time." "Following the example of their superiors, or obeying their orders," the Company's "principal servants abroad" had thus turned India into a sink of "tyranny and pillage," committing acts "of treachery to the natives . . . and . . . acts of cruelty, injustice, and oppression to their fellow-subjects." As well as "the spoils," he charged, returned Company servants brought home with them "the manners of the East" and "frequently took arms against the [Company] authority, to which they owed their power;

[76] [John Inglis], *The Patriots: Or, An Evening Prospect on the Atlantic* (London, 1777), v.

till by force, by negotiation or compromise, they obtained seats at the Board"
in Leadenhall Street, where the "first use they made of their power was to cover
the retreat of their own fortunes from India; and to support, in some friend,
favourite, or partner in plunder, the same system of venality and corruption,
which had enriched themselves."[77]

In seeking remedies for these problems, Macpherson found the fate of earlier efforts to remedy mismanagement and corruption instructive. When the
"plunder of Asia, in a manner, brought the first authentic accounts of Asiatic revolutions to Europe" in the mid-1760s, he recalled, the "distance of the
scene of iniquity naturally diminished the impression made by vague reports
of crimes." But when "some writers of spirit and information took arms in
the cause of humanity and justice" and, thinking "that national indignation
might produce national justice, unveiled some of the fountains of corruption
in the East," their "discoveries were heard with attention by the nation," and
people "began to enquire, 'how, and whence such splendor came,'" and to
observe "that persons of mean parts had amassed great and sudden riches"
and, "upon their return from the provinces, flew in the face of nobility itself;
rivaled it in the possession of lands, outstripped it in dissipation, ostentation,
and luxury; and sometimes overcame it in parliamentary influence." Although
these discoveries evoked a public demand for revenge and an "ardour . . . for
restoring public honour, by exhibiting examples of public justice," Macpherson
lamented, "a benumbed state" shrank from effective action. As a consequence,
public enquiry had, "instead of repressing vice," merely produced "a larger
crop of delinquency," as the Company, spared by the failure of serious Government regulation, "flew in the face of a state, which, from its inactivity," its
members "had great reason to despise," while its servants in India proceeded
to seek new modes of "insolence and oppression" to enrich themselves. In
Macpherson's view, these problems mostly derived "from radical defects in the
constitution of the Company" and called "aloud for the correcting hand of
the legislature, to prevent future mischiefs by new regulations, if not to punish
former delinquents."[78]

In the pay of a rival faction, William Burke, assisted by his cousin Edmund,
challenged Macpherson's account of the traditional constitutional structure
of India but did not deny that "the spirit of British oriental politics" had
developed into a "scandalous shuffle of prevarication and mutual connivance"
among many Company servants and Muslim princes who had "made sport of
the faith of the British nation," introduced "a series of wars," and set up "new
despotisms" that had resulted in the deaths of many and adversely affected the
lives of many other "miserable Indians."[79] Debates in Parliament invariably

---

[77] James Macpherson, *The History and Management of the East-India Company* (London, 1779),
preface, 161, 234, 238.

[78] Ibid., 234–36, 239.

[79] William [and Edmund] Burke, *Policy of Making Conquests for the Mohometans* (London,
1779), in Peter J. Marshall, ed., *India: Madras and Bengal 1774–1785*, Volume 5 of Paul
Langford, ed., *The Writings and Speeches of Edmund Burke* (Oxford: Oxford University Press,
1981), 5: 75, 119.

produced complaints about "the mismanagements and oppressions committed by the nominal servants of the Company, who were countenanced and supported by the government at home." In forwarding a motion for parliamentary consideration of the situation in India in March 1780, Attorney General Alexander Wedderburn took up the subject of oppression at length, charging that the Company "had copied the barbarous policy of those to whose possessions they succeeded" and thereby had unintentionally "defeated the only end such a system could answer, that of enormous sums drawn from the sweat and toil of the inhabitants." "Where such a policy prevails," Wedderburn declared, a country must "in the end be ruined, or depopulated." Observing that these conditions "called most loudly for the interference" of Parliament, he called upon his fellow M.P.s to reform such "shameful abuse." Unless Parliament regarded the East India Company with a "jealous eye," said William Hussey, the Company might very well "lose all our acquisitions in India."[80]

Also in 1780, Henry Frederick Thompson, a former seeker of fortune in the Company's service in Bengal, entertained the public with a lurid tale of seduction and corruption in the East. In a substantial volume entitled *The Intrigues of a Nabob: or, Bengal The Fittest Soil for the Growth of Lust, Injustice and Dishonesty*, Thompson exposed the amours, chicanery, and dishonesty of Richard Barwell, a high Company official and later a British nabob and member of Parliament, who had seduced Thompson's paramour, a former prostitute who had been passing as Thompson's wife, and lived openly with her without benefit of matrimony, while he got Thompson cashiered from his post and refused to honor a contract in which he had agreed to pay Thompson a yearly annuity in return for leaving India quietly. Thompson's depiction of Barwell as a man who had two great vices, a "lust of power, and a lust of pleasure," and who cared "not at what expence he acquires his power" so long as he could govern "the eastern world as he pleases," confirmed the public impression that an East Indian adventurer was "more arbitrary to his province, than a British sovereign dare to be in this Kingdom," and that, as Thompson charged, an Indian "governor with all the power of an eastern monarch, and much more pride," could make "justice, law, and equity, bend beneath his will" and, with "breath more pestilential than the plague," could "blast the fairest character with impunity, and mar the fortunes of an honest man."[81]

At roughly the same time that Macpherson published his history, other critics were raising serious objections to the judicial arrangements implemented by the Regulating Act of 1773, contending that the introduction of British law and the establishment of a supreme court in India had been a disaster – except for the British lawyers, who found new ways to plunder India by encouraging Indians to file lawsuits. So bad was the situation that some of the "*British* Inhabitants of *Bengal*, and many of the native *Indians*" sent over to Britain formal

---

[80] George Rous, Alexander Wedderburn, and William Hussey, speeches, March 21, 1780, in Cobbett et al., eds., *Parliamentary History*, 21: 315, 317–19.

[81] Henry Frederick Thompson, *The Intrigues of a Nabob: or, Bengal The Fittest Soil for the Growth of Lust, Injustice and Dishonesty* (London, 1780), 14, 112, 169.

complaints and remonstrances "founded," reported the anonymous author of *Observations upon the Administration of Justice in Bengal*, a substantial tract issued without place or date of publication, probably in 1779, "in Grievances which they have long suffered, and could no longer suppress."[82]

This author had no doubt that "these Evils all flow[ed] from One Source, the Introduction of *English* Laws and Customs" into India by the Regulating Act of 1773 and their subsequent diffusion through "innumerable Channels over the whole Country" until they had "pervaded every Connection of Life, publick and private, domestick and social." Intended to preserve Company revenues "from depredation," bring Company servants under judicial control, facilitate legal redress, and provide regular justice "for the permanent Security of Liberty and Property," the "new System of Jurisprudence," the author observed, seriously blundered by providing for the wholesale transplantation "into the Opposite Quarter of the Globe" of a complex set of laws "without any Restrictions or Modifications whatever, to accommodate them to the Climate and Manners of *Asia*, without any Regard to religious Institutions or local Habits, or to the influence of other Laws handed down from the remotest Antiquity, and fixed in the Hearts of the People," and to be administered by judges "wholly unacquainted with the Religion, Character, or Manners of the People over whom they were to preside." Among the most serious of the incongruities of English law with Bengali manners, according to this author, was the introduction of "a Levelling Principle among People accustomed to the most rigid Subordination of Rank and Character." By "confounding Distinctions which have been always held sacred and inviolable" in Indian society, the new system, the author declared, had at once violated the manners and shocked the "feelings of the People." Even worse, by "breaking through the established Rules of Order" it had occasioned "a total Disrespect of the Magistrate and the Laws."[83]

To compound this error, the author further reported, the judges sent to preside over this system were accompanied "by a Number of Adventurers, who were allured by the Hopes of enriching themselves under the new Establishment." "Some of these people," he announced, drawing upon the language of alterity that had long been applied to British overseas adventurers, "were of the lowest Sort of People, and of the lowest Description of these, whose Vices had rendered them unfit to thrive in this Country by the Means of an honest Industry, and who could find no Refuge from Distress but in a Flight to the other End of the Globe. Many of them," he continued, were the domestics or dependents of the judges who, "having passed through the Purgatory of the Ocean, were permitted to assume the Forms of Attorneys, Court Officers, Under Sheriffs, and Bailiffs, or any other doubtful Shape, in which they were let loose upon the Inhabitants in search of Prey" and then, using "all the Artifice which low

---

[82] *Observations upon the Administration of Justice in Bengal* [London, 1778], 4.
[83] Ibid., 3–4, 6, 8.

Cunning could suggest," proceeded to excite "a litigious Spirit among the People, for which their Ignorance afforded...an ample Field." "Characters thus finished," he continued, "afford the most fruitful Soil to the Suggestions of Fraud and Oppression, which if they do not find, they are sure to raise; and if not made the Tools of Injustice, never fail to make Injustice theirs." Their behavior, he affirmed, showed "that no Oppression can be more severe than that which is systematical, and carried on under Forms of Justice; and presents to our View a Scene similar to that which Scripture gives us of a Country labouring under the Plagues of Divine Vengeance. The Locusts of *Egypt*," he asserted, "were not more destructive than the Vermin that spread themselves over the fertile Provinces of the *East*, upon the arrival of this *English* system."[84]

Citing recent British experience in Quebec, where popular resistance had forced the metropolitan government to permit the inhabitants to live under their own "former customs," and reminding his readers of Montesquieu's dictum that conquered polities should always "be left in their ancient State of internal Government," with the same judicatures, laws, customs, privileges, and manners they had traditionally enjoyed, this author pointed out that the advocates of the Regulating Act of 1773 had concentrated so intently on creating a new structure of governance for India that they had not fully considered the cultural and social implications of the wholesale transfer of English law to Bengal. For that reason, he contended, none of the measure's objectives had been secured. Instead of protecting Company revenues from depredation, it had "involved them in greater confusion." Instead of eliminating oppression of indigenous people, it had introduced new forms of it. Instead of securing liberty and property, it had only "served to loosen the Ties of Society, and introduce an arbitrary uncertain Standard for Government." Both policy and standards of "Humanity and Justice," he insisted, demanded that a system that was so "radically defective, and [so] founded in wrong Principles" had "to be entirely new modelled, or altogether suppressed."[85]

When the House of Commons took up these and other petitions in February 1781, two members, Nathaniel Wraxall and Charles Boughton Rouse, each of whom had begun his working life as a Company servant in India, spoke in favor of further parliamentary intervention. Contrasting "the splendour of our arms" in India "with our losses and disgraces in America," Wraxall expressed his conviction that India was "a country on which the future glory, grandeur, and permanent greatness of England must ultimately depend." But he warned that behind the "flattering and dazzling exterior" it presented "lurked a thousand hidden seeds of political disease and death," including especially Indian discontent with the effort to apply British laws. For an island situated 5,000 miles away and in such a different climate to endeavor, "in the insolence of conquest, or the ignorance of misinformation," to impose its legal system upon "a country totally dissimilar in religion, in laws, in customs and in feelings

[84] Ibid., 6–9.
[85] Ibid., 4, 6, 23, 35.

of every nature, and which had been so from the most remote antiquity," he declared, was the height of "folly and absurdity," and he expressed the fear that without a change of course Britain might find itself with "popular violence and insurrection" that would turn India into "a scene of massacre." Although he deplored the public clamor that had for so long "prevailed against every man connected with the East Indies," expressed his skepticism about the charges "that men born of respectable families, and educated like themselves, should discard every principle of morality the moment they felt the Asiatic sun," and observed that, as the "offspring of violence... sudden conquest must always occasion some oppression, some injustice, some rapacity, and rapid acquisition of wealth to its conductors," Boughton Rouse agreed that the legal reforms of 1773 had represented "a barbarous attempt to force a foreign law upon a conquered people" and called upon his colleagues "to devise some eligible plan for the good administration of our Asiatic territory." Employing the languages of humanity, he announced that this undertaking was in "the cause of humanity and national honor" and expressed his desire "to introduce among that industrious and submissive people, a system of legislation, which may be congruous to their feeling and dispositions; to conciliate them to the supremacy of our distant country; to render that" fruitful "territory a permanent appendage of the British empire; and finally, to do justice to its inhabitants, to my nation, and to my fellow-subjects."[86]

VII

The airing of Indian excesses starting in the mid-1760s first brought the languages of humanity and justice intensively to bear upon the evaluation of empire in metropolitan Britain, and the continuing intrusiveness of those excesses in Britain's national affairs over the following decades effectively contributed to sustain a process by which considerations of humanity became a standard for evaluating overseas empire and the new social types associated with that empire. As those involved with the empire looked farther afield, critiques of the behavior of Britons overseas extended well beyond India. In previous pages, we have already seen how analysts used the languages of humanity and justice to condemn settler efforts to deprive Black Caribs of their property in St. Vincent and Government insistence upon trying to quell American resistance to British authority by force. Also after the mid-1760s, the standard of humanity and justice increasingly became an important part of the calculus for evaluating the moral costs of empire in other areas of the globe: in Africa, on the Atlantic and other oceans, in America, and even in Ireland.

This extended and broad-ranging humanitarian critique contributed to a growing ambivalence about whether or how warmly metropolitans should embrace empire. Whatever the extent to which empire had been responsible

---

[86] Nathaniel Wraxall and Charles Boughton Rouse, speeches, February 12, 1781, in Cobbett et al., eds., *Parliamentary History*, 21: 1194, 1202–03, 1205–07.

for Britain's rising commercial vigor and its increasing imperial grandeur during the long period after the Glorious Revolution, however essential its contributions had been to the economic well-being and international standing of Britain in the contemporary world of overseas imperial affairs, the inhuman, uncivil, and tyrannical behavior of Asiatic plunderers in the East had brought home to a wide and increasingly knowledgeable public some of the deleterious effects of empire upon those most directly involved. Critics had made a powerful case that such behavior was not just embarrassing but thoroughly reprehensible, far below the standards metropolitan Britons expected of themselves. The Indian scandals thus unleashed a powerful dissociative impulse, an impulse to distinguish genuine Britons in the metropolis from those unsavory types who sought their fortunes beyond the civilized and humane shores of Britain in imperial projects that tempted them into acts of brutality, rapacity, and oppression that would have gained them nothing but scorn had they occurred in Britain itself. Of course, some critics recognized the complicity of metropolitans in so long turning a blind eye to the distasteful aspects of empire. But the intense light thrown upon the brutal character and effects of British excesses in India left many metropolitans convinced that a great social and cultural gulf existed between the metropolis and Britain's overseas possessions and that, by all measures of civility, humanity, and justice, Britons overseas were demonstrably inferior to Britons at home.

5

Sites of Creolean Despotism

*The Languages of Humanity and Justice and the
Critique of Colonial Slavery and the African Slave Trade*

I

Contemporaneous with the emergence of metropolitan concern with the plunder of India, analysts of overseas empire also produced a compelling critique of the systems of enslavement that had long powered the economic development of so many of Britain's American colonies. Quickly broadening to include the entire transatlantic commercial complex involved in the African trade that supplied the colonies with slaves, this critique focused on yet another area to which the languages of humanity and justice could be appropriately applied to assess the social and human costs of British overseas empire and the misbehavior of those Britons who participated in it. Condemning as barbarous and inhuman the planters and traders who, in quest of their own economic betterment, were the primary agents in and benefactors from the enslavement and destruction of so many thousands of people, these analysts focused on the *Creole* slave owner as a villainous social type every bit as antithetical to metropolitan British social and moral standards as the Indian nabob. In contrast to the situation with the Indian problem, however, this critique did not arise out of an entirely new development within the empire. English participation in the slave trade dated to the sixteenth century, while colonial use of enslaved Africans was already widespread in Barbados by the 1650s. Rather, the building condemnation of the British overseas slave system had its basis in an ancient English disquiet, manifest in the strictures of Morgan Godwyn, Thomas Tryon, and others around the turn of the seventeenth century, that had resurfaced briefly in the 1730s and, as argued in Chapter 2, still functioned to sustain the metropolitan impulse to apply a language of alterity to American colonists.

Indeed, the conception of the Creole as a deviant and distinctive social type within the English-speaking world was already relatively pervasive by the time East Indian problems came to the attention of the British public in the mid-1760s. As early as the late 1740s, the anonymous author of *The Fortunate*

Transport had endeavored to lend authenticity to his unflattering portrait of the colonial societies of Virginia and Jamaica and the morally deficient and cruel populations who dominated them by signing his production with the name "A Creole."[1] Written in the Defoevian tradition of *Moll Flanders* and *Colonel Jacque*, in which adventuresses and adventurers, the social flotsam and jetsam of Britain, found in the sordid settings of overseas empire opportunities to employ their genius to their own advantage, acquire the trappings of respectability, and return to England, *The Fortunate Transport* was only one of many publications in mid-eighteenth-century Britain that reinforced and gave concrete shape to the stereotype of the American Creole as a social type inferior to the stay-at-home Briton.[2]

So pervasive and powerful had this image of British American colonists as Creole despots become by the early 1760s that the Massachusetts lawyer James Otis, Jr., indignant at the metropolitan Administration's preferential treatment of the West Indian over the North American colonies in the Sugar Act of 1764, found himself in a tract (subsequently reprinted in London) compelled to try to dissociate North Americans from their West Indian counterparts. The metropolitan British might indiscriminately apply the term *Creole* "to all Americans of European extraction," he complained, "but the northern colonists apply it only to the islanders and others of such extract under the Torrid Zone." Otis joined in the metropolitan denunciation of that "ferocity, cruelty, and brutal barbarity that has long marked the general character of the sugar islanders," which he attributed to the fact that they "every day," either "in person or by an overseer, the joint and several proper representatives of a creole and of the d[evi]l," acted as "unrelenting taskmasters" over "thousands of slaves," and he insisted that North Americans, in contrast to West Indians, were mostly "freeborn *British white* subjects" who had far more in common with metropolitan Britons than with the "creolean planter."[3]

II

Throughout the early and middle decades of the eighteenth century, however, this image of the colonies as sites of Creolean despotism remained largely latent in British public life and coexisted with broad acceptance of the utility of the African slave trade. In speaking of this trade, the language of commerce still predominated over the languages of humanity and justice. Especially after the English had begun to employ slave labor to a significant degree, first in the West Indies and then on the North American continent during the last half

---

[1] A Creole, *The Fortunate Transport; or, the Secret History of the Life and Adventures of the Celebrated Polly Haycock, alias Mrs. B_____. The Lady of the Gold Watch* (London, 1748). This work and its sequel are more fully discussed in Chapter 2.

[2] *The Adventures of Mr. George Edwards, A Creole* (London, 1751), 19–20, offer a somewhat more sympathetic assessment.

[3] James Otis, Jr., *The Rights of the British Colonies Asserted and Proved* (Boston, 1764), 24–25, 29–30.

of the seventeenth century, a few commentators such as Godwyn and Tryon raised powerful questions about both slavery and the slave trade on religious, humanitarian, and even legal grounds. As slave systems became more and more prevalent and more deeply entrenched in the English Atlantic world, however, such protests became less common, and economic writers had no compunction about evaluating those systems purely in terms of their economic utility to metropolitan Britain. Thus did the Royal African Company during these years frequently appeal to Parliament for support on the grounds that, as it said, using the language of utility and without fear of moral reproach, in a 1748 petition, the African trade was "known to be highly beneficial to this nation, as well on account of the many valuable commodities which it naturally produces, as of the supply of negro servants, seasoned to such climates, with which it yearly furnishes the British colonies and plantations in America."[4]

During the years from 1725 to 1750, every major economic writer touted the commercial and utilitarian benefits of the African trade. "Our trade with *Africa*," explained Joshua Gee in 1730, was of "extraordinary Advantage" and "very profitable to the Nation in general." Not only did it bring in some commodities such as "Gold Dust, . . . Red-wood, Teeth, *Guinea Grain*, &c.," much of which could be re-exported to Europe, it also supplied the colonies with the slaves who were essential for the production of the commodities that formed the bulk of the plantation trade and could be sold "to the *Spanish West-Indies*" for "a great Deal of Bullion."[5] The slave trade and the plantation trades, declared William Wood, were entirely interdependent, "the *African* Trade" being both "the Spring and Parent whence" the plantation trade "flows."[6] Making an explicit connection between "the Labour of Slaves, and our Profit" from the plantation trades, Gee was certain that "our Improvements in the Plantations," the "Planting of Sugar and Tobacco, and [the] carrying on Trade there," all of which depended on slave labor, "would soon decline" unless the slave trade were "push[ed] . . . with all imaginable Vigour" so that planters had "not only very great Numbers of Slaves brought in, but" were "also afforded them at moderate prices."[7] Indeed, Gee and Fayer Hall both looked forward to the expansion of the slave trade and slavery as a result of the production of new commodities, including silk, hemp, flax, pot-ash, and iron. "In all Cases where Labour is principally required," said Hall, in citing the case of iron production

---

[4] Petition of the Royal African Company, February 16, 1748, in Leo F. Stock, ed., *Proceedings and Debates of the British Parliament Respecting North America*, 5 vols. (Washington, D.C., 1924–41), 5: 264. On Parliament's involvement in the trade, see the important essays by William A. Pettigrew, "Parliament and the Escalation of the Slave Trade, 1690–1714," and Christopher L. Brown, "The British Government and the Slave Trade: Early Parliamentary Enquiries, 1713–83," in Stephen Farrell, Melanie Unwin, and James Walvin, eds., *The British Slave Trade: Abolition, Parliament and People* (Edinburgh: Edinburgh University Press, 2007), 12–41.

[5] Joshua Gee, *The Trade and Navigation of Great-Britain*, 2nd ed. (London, 1730), 25.

[6] William Wood, *The Great Advantages of Our Colonies and Plantations to Great Britain* (London, 1728), 113.

[7] Gee, *Trade and Navigation*, 25.

in the colonial Chesapeake, blacks were "as useful as any white Men, when they are instructed."[8]

Writing as "A British Merchant" in 1745, Malachy Postlethwayt produced the most extended dilation upon this theme, in a pamphlet entitled *The African Trade, the Great Pillar and Support of the British Plantation Trade in America*. "Our *Plantation Commerce*," observed Postlethwayt, was "not only first founded on" the African trade but was "still daily upheld thereby" and could not possibly "stand alone without" that "fundamental Prop and Support." That "*White* Men" were "not constitutionally qualified to sustain the Toil of Planting in the Climates of our *Island Colonies* like the Blacks" and that "the Business of *Planting* in our *British Colonies*, as well as in the *French*," had therefore to be "carried on by the Labour of *Negroes*, imported thither from *Africa*," was "notorious to the whole World." Britons, he said, were entirely "indebted to those valuable People, the *Africans*, for our *Sugars, Tobaccoes, Rice, Rum*, and all other *Plantation Produce*," and, he announced, "the greater the Number of *Negroes*, imported into our Colonies," the larger would be the "Exportation of *British* Manufactures" to pay for them in Africa. "The more likewise our Plantations abound in *Negroes*," he explained, the "more Land [would] become cultivated" and the "*better* and greater *Variety* of *Plantation Commodities* [would] be produced." "As those Trades are subservient to the Well Being and Prosperity of each other," he wrote, "so the more either flourishes or declines, the other must be necessarily affected; and the general Trade and Navigation of their *Mother Country*, will be proportionately benefitted or injured." "That the general NAVIGATION of *Great Britain*" owed "all its *Encrease* and *Splendor* to the Commerce of its *American* and *African Colonies*; and that it" could not "be maintained or enlarged otherwise than from the constant Prosperity of both those Branches, *whose Interests [were]...mutual and inseparable*," he said, using the language of maritime supremacy, were facts so obvious "that it would be as impertinent to take up" the reader's "Time in expatiating on the Subject as in declaiming on the common Benefits of Air and Sun-shine in general."[9]

By the time Postlethwayt published his *Universal Dictionary of Trade and Commerce* in the early 1750s, he had significantly enlarged the British agenda in Africa. No longer praising it only for its seeming capacity to generate unlimited supplies of slaves for European plantations in America, he depicted Africa as a site for a massive civilizing project that would convert much of the continent into a gigantic mart for British manufactures. Using the languages of civility and improvement that Europeans had long employed to justify their exploitation of peoples who lived in societies seemingly less sophisticated or developed than those of Europe, Postlethwayt explored the relationship between civility and

---

[8] Ibid., 126; Fayer Hall, *The Importance of the British Plantations in America to this Kingdom* (London, 1731), 76.

[9] A British Merchant [Malachy Postlethwayt], *The African Trade, The Great Pillar and Support of the British Plantation Trade in America* (London, 1745), 2–3, 6, 14.

trade and used the example of the American Indian to make his case that "civilizing nations...increase[d] commerce." He noted that Indians traded with the British for "an infinite number of things" that contributed "to improve their lives and civilize them," and he predicted that as they grew "more civilized, and" came "into the European way of life, the more of our product and manufactures will they stand in need of," and "as these demands increase, the trade and commerce of Europe must increase; for increase of the civilized people is an increase of commerce in its necessary consequences, let the degree of their demands be more or less."[10]

What was good for American Indians, in Postlethwayt's view, was good for Africans, and, projecting from the American example, he envisioned "numbers of European people,... settled on the sea coast" of Africa and rapidly spreading "commerce into the inland nations" and thereby "employ[ing] and enrich[ing] the inhabitants by instructing them in the arts of living, as well as of trade." In his view, Africa had the potential for "the greatest scenes of improvement in the world."[11] Although he feared that "while the slaving trade" continued "to be the great object of Europeans, it" would "ever spirit up wars and hostilities among the negro princes and chiefs, for the sake of making captives of each other for sale," and thereby frustrate the peaceful and civilizing operations of commerce, he was persuaded that "a fair, friendly, humane, and civilized commerce with the Africans" was the best way to eliminate the slave trade, enable Africa to rise above "its present rude, unimproved state," and make it possible for Europeans to penetrate into the African interior to develop new markets. To reap the economic benefits of the "vast ocean of improvement in view upon the African coast" and in the interior, Postlethwayt declared in laying out this grandiose and nakedly imperial project, Britons had to do little more than "increase the colonies of their own nation, in all the remote parts where it is proper and practicable, and to civilize and instruct the savages and natives of those countries, wherever they plant, so as to bring them by the softest and gentlest methods to fall into the customs and usages of their own country, and incorporate among our peoples as one nation."[12]

If Postlethwayt couched his ambitious scheme for the colonization of Africa in the symbiotic languages of commerce and civility, he also used, if only little more than as an aside, the language of humanity. Part of the motivation behind his concern to eliminate the slave trade within Africa may have been related to his conclusion that it might be better for the British Empire "to have no Negro slaves at all; for with all submission to better judges," he confessed, he could not "help thinking of the slave trade as nationally disadvantageous, as it is inhuman, cruel, and unchristian-like."[13]

[10] Malachy Postlethwayt, *Universal Dictionary of Trade and Commerce*, 4th ed. (London, 1764), "Guinea."
[11] Ibid, "Africa."
[12] Ibid.
[13] Ibid., "Colonies."

Postlethwayt's admission that colonial slavery was "nationally disadvantageous," his suggestion that its inhumanity, cruelty, and seeming incompatibility with so many Christian precepts was a violation of national norms, heralded a revival and deepening of ancient metropolitan reservations about colonial slavery and the slave trade. Initially, this revival grew out of the imperial conflicts with France and Spain beginning in the 1730s and, more especially, British misfortunes during the early years of the Seven Years' War and was expressed in the language of national security. Metropolitan authorities had long been aware that wherever slavery existed on a large scale it seriously weakened the defensive capacities of the colonies, and the unsuccessful effort to prohibit slavery in the new buffer colony of Georgia in the early 1730s represented an early expression of this awareness. But the conflict with France brought this problem more fully into the consciousness of analysts of empire in the metropolis. In case of invasion by France, predicted one anonymous writer in 1755, the southern North American colonies, where there were "three or four blacks to one white," would be in great "danger... from these poor unhappy wretches... (who provoked by even a worse than *Egyptian* slavery, have two or three times [previously] formed dangerous conspiracies to destroy their masters)."[14]

Two works published in London between 1746 and 1757 made this same point even more emphatically. In the first, *An Essay Concerning Slavery*, which may have been the work of longtime Jamaican governor Edward Trelawny, the author's principal concern was the security of Jamaica's white settlers. He condemned the "Rage that Planters have for buying Negroes" and their careless management of them, which, he feared, would "sooner or later lead to the island's being over-run, and ruined by its own Slaves." Noting that Jamaican whites were "not only alarm'd by every trifling Armament of the Enemy, but under the greatest Apprehensions frequently from their own Slaves," he appealed for parliamentary action to save the settlers from themselves and Jamaica for the British Empire.[15]

Recommending the same solution, William Burke's *An Account of the European Settlements in America* expressed similar fears. The "alarms we are under at the news of any petty armament in the West-Indies," he wrote, were "a demonstrative proof of the weakness of our condition" in the colonies, particularly in the sugar islands. The disproportion of blacks to whites, he noted, showed "clearly at the first glance how much the colonies are endangered, both from within and without; how much exposed to the assaults of a foreign enemy, and to the insurrection of their own slaves." Tracing "this dangerous

[14] *State of the British and French Colonies in North America, With Respect to Number of People, Forces, Forts, Indians, Trade and other Advantages* (London, 1755), 22.
[15] [Edward Trelawny], *An Essay Concerning Slavery, and the Danger Jamaica Is expos'd to from the Too great Number of Slaves, and the Too little CARE that is taken to manage THEM, And a Proposal to prevent the further Importation of Negroes into that Island* (London, 1746), v, 1–11, 18, 22, 37.

irregularity" to the planters' inattention to attracting white settlers and their choice "to do every thing by negroes, which can possibly be done by them," he argued that this pattern of behavior had grown so "inveterate, and to such a degree," that colonists would never administer a remedy themselves. Without metropolitan intervention to encourage white emigration, he predicted, the island colonies would soon "consist of little more than a few planters and merchants; and the rest will be a despicable, though a dangerous, because a numerous and disaffected, herd of African slaves." Only an infusion of a large population "of low and middling men of a free condition," Burke said, would "effectually intimidate a foreign enemy, and take away all hope of liberties from the negroes."[16]

But the authors of both of these works moved, if somewhat cautiously, beyond such security concerns to what the author of the *Essay Concerning Slavery* referred to as "the moral one." Denouncing the slave trade as a trade "in human flesh, in the Lives and Liberties of our own Species," he drew a parallel between the fictitious country in Montesquieu's *Persian Letters*, in which the inhabitants "caught hold of every Foreigner that came near them, and kill'd them for the sake of the Grease, which" they used "in boiling their Soap," and Jamaica's use of slaves. "To kill a man for the sake of his Grease, or to make him melt it away in hard Labour for another's Profit," he observed, was "not so very unlike." By actively encouraging and sanctioning the slave trade and such a brutal violation of the rights of humanity, he suggested, invoking natural rights theory, the British nation – including Parliament, "All the merchants, all the trading towns, and all the makers and dealers in goods sent to Africa or the West Indies" – had effectually indulged white settlers with a liberty based upon the slavery of others, a "Liberty [that was] contrary to the Laws of God and Nature." "Are the Lives of human Creatures . . . to be play'd with in such a Manner, just as a giddy thoughtless Planter thinks fit?," he asked rhetorically. That English people should employ such a system of trade and labor, the author suggested, using the language of liberty, seemed to be totally out of character. "That the generous Free Briton, who knows the value of Liberty, who prizes it above Life, who loves and enjoys it, and loves it the more he does enjoy it," he asserted in an early effort to distance Britishness from slavery, "that he should for vile Lucre make a Traffick of Liberty, that he should be instrumental in depriving others of a Blessing he would not part with but with Life," he declared, "doth surprise, grieve and torment me."[17]

To explain this contradiction between British self-conceptions and British willingness to enslave other peoples, the author of the *Essay Concerning Slavery* turned to the peculiar nature of the slave societies that had developed in early modern plantation America. Settler "*West-Indian[s]*," he observed, seemed to "know no Medium in Things; a Man with you must be either absolutely a

[16] [William Burke], *An Account of the European Settlements in America*, 2 vols. (London, 1757), 2: 117–18, 132.
[17] [Trelawny], *Essay Concerning Slavery*, v, 24–27, 31, 38.

Slave, or licentiously free, free [even] from all Restraints of Law." In a society composed mostly of enslaved people, he suggested with this observation, the need to draw a sharp distinction between free men and slaves provided an especially powerful impulse for settler claims, of the most extreme variety, to an identity as free-born Britons. But such claims, the author appreciated, required settlers to justify enslavement on other than legal grounds. They could be founded only on the assumption that the enslaved were incapable of achieving such an identity. "One would imagine," he observed in articulating the implicit cultural assumptions that underlay slavery and the slave trade, "the Planters really think the Negroes are not of the same Species with us, but that being of a different Mold and Nature, as well as Colour, they were made intirely for our Use, with Instincts proper for the Purpose, having as great a Propensity to Subjection, as we have to command and loving Slavery as naturally as we do Liberty."[18]

Burke displayed a similar revulsion at the colonial slave system. "The negroes in our colonies," he said, "endure[d] a slavery more compleat, and attended with far worse circumstances, than what any people in their condition suffer in any other part of the world, or have suffered in any other period of time." The "prodigious waste," brought on by "excessive labour" and requiring annual exportation of thousands just to keep the slave population in the West Indian colonies at the same size, reflected, Burke thought, a very different mentality than could be found among metropolitan Britons. West Indian slave holders seemed not "to understand what every English wagoner clearly comprehended: that, if he works his horse but moderately, and feeds him well, he will draw more profit from him in the end, than if he never gave him an hour's respite in the day from his work, and at night turned him upon the commons for his subsistence." Burke acknowledged that slaves were "stubborn and intractable for the most part, and that they must be ruled with the rod of iron." But, turning to the language of humanity, he also insisted that slaves should be "ruled but not crushed with it" and recommended "a humanity exercised . . . with steadiness." Giving them more time and recreation and working them moderately, he argued, would allow slaves to "grow more honest, [and] tractable," while masters would "by degrees" learn "not to think them a sort of beasts, without souls." "From the whole course of history," he declared, "those nations which have behaved with the greatest humanity to the slaves, were always best served, and ran the least hazard from their rebellions."[19]

But Burke did not propose to sacrifice the economic and utilitarian benefits of the slave trade and slavery upon the altar of humanity. In his discussion of those institutions, the languages of humanity and injustice intruded upon but by no means overrode the language of commerce. Although he expressed "horror" at "a trade which must depend for its support upon the annual murder of several thousands of innocent men," he excused the trade by "the

[18] Ibid., 19, 53.
[19] [William Burke], *Account of the European Settlements in America*, 2: 124, 127–28, 129–30.

necessity we are under of peopling our colonies, and the consideration that the slaves we buy were in the same condition in Africa, either hereditary or taken in war." Admitting that the form of enslavement he proposed would operate as a "prejudice... to the African trade," he speculated that the same demand that was then "produced by the havock made of the people" might be kept up merely "by extending our colonies" and, of course, the institution of slavery.[20]

Over the following decade, many observers, often citing and building upon Burke's remarks about slavery, denounced slavery and the slave trade as thoroughly inhuman and un-British. Adam Smith's unfavorable comparison of British American slaveholders to the people they enslaved in his 1760 *Theory of Moral Sentiments* has been discussed in Chapter 2.[21] Four years later, when Arthur Lee, scion of an old Virginia Creole family and then a student in Edinburgh, sought in a pamphlet betraying the deep racism of his native society to defend his countrymen from Smith's "opprobrious" reflections and to refute Smith's characterization of Africans as heroes, he argued that North American slavery was far less severe than the West Indian variety but, significantly, thoroughly denied both the necessity and the legitimacy of the rationale that supported the slave system as it had developed in Britain's American colonies. His defense of North American slaveholders did not extend to the institution that brought them into disgrace. Using the languages of humanity and justice, he denounced slavery as "absolutely repugnant to justice," "highly inconsistent with [sound] civil policy," inimical to "all improvements in arts and sciences," detrimental to the development of "feelings of virtue and Humanity" in "freemen," dangerous to society, "shocking to humanity, violative of every generous sentiment," and "abhorrent utterly from the Christian religion." Even as he called for metropolitan appreciation of colonists for their efforts "to expand the dominion of their country," for having "braved the dangers of an unknown sea and savage land, to enrich" its "commerce, and exalt its power," Lee questioned why "a civilized, a Christian nation" should "encourage slavery" merely "because the barbarous, savage, lawless Africans have done it," why Americans should "persist in a conduct which cannot be justified; or persevere in oppression, from which their hearts must recoil." "How long," he asked, "shall we continue a practice, which policy rejects, justice condemns, and piety dissuades?"[22]

Writing in the same year, the Edinburgh divine Robert Wallace also addressed the desirability of slave labor in Britain's American empire in his long and ambitious *View of the Internal Policy of Great Britain*, a work premised upon the idea that Britain and Ireland together were capable of "great Improvement... in respect to Numbers, Riches, and Power" without dependence on

[20] Ibid., 2: 128–29.
[21] Adam Smith, *Theory of Moral Sentiments*, 2nd ed. (London, 1760), 316.
[22] An American [Arthur Lee], *An Essay in Vindication of the Continental Colonies of America, From a Censure of Mr. Adam Smith, in his Theory of Moral Sentiments* (London, 1764), iv, 18–19, 42–45.

either foreign or colonial connections. Although Wallace advocated investing in Ireland in preference to expanding trade with India, he was not hostile to the American colonies. Indeed, he expressed his admiration for "the amazing growth of the British colonies" in America and praised "the British system" of empire as "undoubtedly the best and strongest now subsisting, formed for increase, and spreading the blessings of liberty." So far from being "the scourge and destroyer of mankind," he waxed eloquent, employing the languages of colonization and improvement, "it has already planted the seeds of mighty nations of free people in the new-found America, to keep up an eternal Memorial," and he predicted that the union of Ireland and Britain "into one compleat compact Empire, well filled with people," would provide the superstructure that, in association with its American branches, would "form the greatest nation of free-men that ever subsisted."[23]

Yet "the general use of Negro Slaves" from Maryland south on the continent and in the West Indies represented for Wallace a serious blemish on this emerging scene. Although he did not challenge the idea that slave labor might have been necessary to overcome the "first difficulties" of settlement, he stressed the superior productivity of free labor and increased security for whites as the principal reasons for stopping "the further introduction of slaves." Especially in the sugar islands, where the population of slaves exceeded that of free people by a ratio of from six to ten to one, he reported, settlers lived "in constant terror from the Slaves" and everywhere except Barbados, where the ratio was only four to one, "put the government to the expence of troops, even in time of peace, for security against the slaves," and he called upon West Indian proprietors "to encourage as much as possible the breed and labour of white people."[24]

But Wallace also thought that a turn to free white labor would remedy other evils in the slave system. The first was Creole barbarism. Like Lee, he deplored the effects of slavery upon settler society. "The custom of treating and governing of slaves," he observed, introduced "a tyrannical and barbarous disposition" and an unfeeling familiarity with cruelty that children early learned from their parents. The second was casual destruction of human life among both whites and blacks in the slave trade, which annually killed thousands of Africans, while nearly one-third of the whites employed in the slave trade died or were "rendered useless." All the economic benefits and other virtues of sugar, he concluded, could not "answer for the destruction the producing it creates."[25]

III

Such discussions registered an enhanced awareness of the moral deficiencies of Creole slave owners and African slave traders and perhaps also a growing

[23] [Robert Wallace], *A View of the Internal Polity of Great Britain* (London, 1764), 252–53.
[24] Ibid., 265–68.
[25] Ibid., 265, 267–68.

unease over the pervasiveness of a system of slavery in an allegedly free empire, but at the close of the Seven Years' War they did not yet amount to a comprehensive challenge to that system or even signal a widespread revulsion against it. Emanating from the Pennsylvania Quaker community, early works calling attention to the incompatibility of Christianity and slavery by John Woolman[26] and Anthony Benezet[27] seem not immediately to have created extensive resonance in Britain. To be sure, Maurice Morgann, a colonial advisor and the author of a number of important papers on various aspects of the state of the British Empire following the peace of 1763, prepared a plan to abolish slavery in the British colonies, but he neither circulated it nor published it for nine years.[28]

Indeed, so far from raising the possibility of a public assault on the British colonial slave system, the successful outcome of the war created the potential for a massive expansion of that system. The Proclamation of 1763 called for the organization of six new colonies out of territories acquired from Spain and France as a result of the peace: East Florida and West Florida on the continent and Dominica, Grenada, St. Vincent, and Tobago in the West Indies, every one of them suitable for tropical production by slave labor. From the start, promoters envisioned them as extensions of the staple-producing slave societies of the kind that had evolved in the older island colonies and on the southern mainland, while slave traders regarded them as vast new markets for the expansion of the slave trade. In the short run, Indian dominance prevented colonial expansion into the new territories west of the Appalachians over which Britain had acquired nominal jurisdiction as a result of the war, but the potential for an eventual extension of slave regimes into that area did not escape the attention of expansionist land developers in the seaboard colonies.

In the dizzying rush to expand areas of effective occupation in the new acquisitions, few people paused to worry about the social and moral results. The most notable exceptions involved the Society for the Propagation of the Gospel in Foreign Parts, which had for many decades owned and operated a slave plantation in Barbados that it had inherited from Christopher Coddrington, a successful sugar magnate. In the late 1760s, two of the Society's annual anniversary sermons, the first by William Warburton, bishop of Gloucester, in 1766, and the second by John Green, bishop of Lincoln, in 1768, brought up the subject of colonial slavery as part of a broader assessment of the Society's

---

[26] John Woolman, *Some Considerations on the Keeping of Negroes* (Philadelphia, 1754), and *Part Second* (Philadelphia, 1762).

[27] Anthony Benezet, *Observations on the Inslaving, Importing and Purchasing of Negroes with Some Advice Thereon* (Germantown, Pa., 1759). Benezet's *A Caution and Warning to Great Britain and Her Colonies, in a Short Representation of the Calamitous State of the Enslaved Negroes in the British Dominions* (Philadelphia, 1766) was however quickly reprinted in London in 1767.

[28] [Maurice Morgann], *A Plan for the Abolition of Slavery in the West Indies* (London, 1762), i.

overseas endeavors.[29] Also in 1768, William Knox, formerly provost marshal and still a slave owner in Georgia, who well before his appointment to the metropolitan colonial bureaucracy in 1770 was making his mark as a well-published spokesman for Administration colonial policy, addressed the Society on the question of why "so little" had "been done towards instructing the free Indians or Negro slaves in the colonies," devoting two of three tracts, all published together in London, to issues involving the enslaved.[30]

Both Warburton and Green were concerned that the Society use its plantation as a model for the Christianization and mild treatment of its enslaved residents, but neither recommended freeing them or challenged the larger system of which they were a part. While noting that the gospel nowhere expressly forbids slavery, Green, in measured rhetoric, did however assert the humanity of slaves, remarked on the difficulty of justifying such "a very unnatural kind of traffick" or of treating slaves "contrary to the allowed and unalterable rights of humanity," and even suggested that "the severity of their task-masters, or the rigour of their service" might be responsible in part for the "great consumption of this human stock" in the colonies.[31]

Warburton was demonstrably less circumspect. By classifying the reduction of human beings to the legal status of property as just one of an "infinite [number of] *abuses* of Society" that shocked "all the feelings of humanity, and the dictates of common sense" and by acknowledging that "TRADING IN MEN" was "very ancient," Warburton fell considerably short of proposing to end colonial slavery. Making extensive use of the language of humanity as a standard by which to judge colonial involvement with slavery, however, he fully showed his abhorrence of the entire system. Charging that African slave traders had turned "the most remote Coasts of Africa" into a "desert" for no other purpose than "to enrich the Planters of the *new World*," he emphatically condemned as a direct infringement of "both divine and human law" the annual theft of "vast Multitudes" of Africans and their subsequent sacrifice to the colonists' "great Idol, the God of Gain." He ridiculed colonial rationalizations for enslavement. Particularly ludicrous, Warburton thought, was the colonial suggestion that "these forced migrations" saved Africans from "being perpetually hunted down like beasts of prey for profit, by their more savage and powerful Neighbours." Who but their future masters in America, with their incessant demand for slave labor, Warburton asked pointedly, if also rhetorically, were behind "this general HUNTING?" Similarly, Warburton regarded as completely absurd the colonial claim that enslavement in America had improved the condition of "these miserable Outcasts of Humanity" and

---

[29] William Warburton, *A Sermon Preached before the Incorporated Society for the Propagation of the Gospel in Foreign Parts* (London, 1766); John Green, *A Sermon Preached before the Incorporated Society for the Propagation of the Gospel in Foreign Parts* (London, 1768).

[30] William Knox, *Three Tracts Respecting the Conversion and Instruction of the Free Indians and Negroe Slaves in the Colonies* (London, 1768), 6.

[31] Green, *Sermon Preached*, 19–20.

made them happier. Tearing them "from their homes and native Country," confining them to a life of unremitting toil under a cruel labor discipline, and making them live in misery so that their "haughty Masters" could revel in a "grandeur" in which they could never hope to share was scarcely a recipe for either social improvement or individual happiness.[32]

Warburton had little respect for American colonists in general, using the language of rapacity in the early part of his sermon to denounce them for turning away from religion in their "*rapacious pursuits*" of all "the *Vices* of improved life" and, instead of promoting the Christianization of Indians, subjecting them to various "false and inhumane" policies that turned them against the British. But he reserved his deepest contempt for the many Creolean tyrants who participated in the iniquitous institution of slavery. The "*cruelty* of certain Planters, with respect to the temporal accommodations of these poor Wretches, and the *irreligious negligence* with regard to their spiritual," he declared, had "become a general scandal" in the wider British world, and, joining the language of oppression to the language of humanity, he condemned colonial slave owners as "cruel Task-masters," "petty tyrants over human freedom," "sincere Worshippers of Mammon," and "civilized violaters of humanity," whose "singular Legacy" powerfully revealed the shameful "inhumanity and impiety" of their own "tyrannous" conduct.[33]

An American plantation owner himself, Knox was far less critical of colonial slave owners. Indeed, he made security concerns primary by fretting that if Warburton's charge that masters were "*infringing both divine and human laws*" by keeping slaves should ever be sanctioned by the Society and circulated among the enslaved, "the next ships" would bring news of "a general insurrection of the Negroes, and the massacre of their owners." No less than Green and Warburton, however, Knox favored religious instruction for slaves and amelioration of their condition, and he was the only one of the three explicitly to concern himself with the problem of providing the enslaved with effective protection for their rights as established by custom and law.[34]

Before trying to make any progress toward these objectives, however, Knox thought that metropolitan religious and civil leaders needed to determine the legitimacy of Warburton's assertion that purchasing slaves was "an *infringement of divine and human laws*," and he devoted his first tract on the enslaved to this issue. In his examination of this rarely asked yet unresolved question, Knox seemed to place himself on the side of those who favored recognition of the status quo and explicit legalization of the slave trade and slavery. If the purchase of slaves was illegal, he asked, "why is such a trade permitted? A few words in an act of parliament prohibiting the importation or sale of Negroes in our colonies," he observed, would "destroy the practice in future," while "a few words more declaring the offspring of Negroes already imported to

---

[32] Warburton, *Sermon Preached*, 6–7, 25–30.
[33] Ibid., 11–13, 24–25, 27–30.
[34] Knox, *Three Tracts*, 17–18.

be free" would "prevent slavery['s] extending into the next generation." As recently as 1766, he noted, passage of an act to open free ports in the West Indies had "furnished an occasion [in Parliament] for asserting the rights of the Negroes, and displaying the infamy of trading in them." Yet, Knox wrote, by declaring "Negroes a *lawful commodity*... to be imported and sold there upon paying a certain duty," that act provided parliamentary sanction to the slave trade and colonial systems of enslavement. Moreover, as he pointed out, neither "the passing that act, nor... any former one for the encouragement of the African trade" had evoked "a single protest in abhorrence of that trade, or *of treating rational creatures as property.*"[35]

Nor was the Privy Council any different. "Framed under the king's instructions, and afterwards transmitted for his approbation in his privy council," every one of the colonial acts that provided the legal foundation for the rights of slave owners, he noted, had been subject to review by the king and council, which might have disallowed them and thereby entitled "every Negro born in the colonies... to all the privileges and franchises of the natural born subjects of this realm." "How then does it happen," he asked, "that these acts, so *repugnant to all divine and human laws* are suffered to exist? Are there no lords of the council sufficiently zealous in the cause of liberty and religion to procure their repeal? Or, are there none others to make application to the council for that purpose?" Clearly, then, he contended, "the perpetual servitude of the Negroes in our colonies is not the act of their masters, nor is it the mere effect of their power over those wretches." If purchasing "Negroes for slaves be a *violation of the law of nature and humanity*," he concluded, "it is pretty evident that the American planters do not *alone* bear the weight of that iniquity, nor are they only to be called upon to remove the evil."[36]

If, as Knox suggested, the failure of Parliament and the Privy Council to take action against these long-established colonial systems of enslavement made it clear that "the purchasing Negroes for slaves be consistent with divine and human obligations," he also thought that "care should be taken to secure the property of the slave to his owner under all circumstances, and such a plan of instruction should be digested as might best conduce to the Negroes['] eternal welfare, without making them uneasy in their present condition, or encouraging them to revolt against their owners." At the same time, he thought, many regulations would be necessary to secure "good usage to these unhappy people," which, he contended, "no authority, but that of parliament, can enforce." Knox was one of several people, including John Pownall and Maurice Morgann, who endeavored in a series of colonial state papers written over the decade following the Treaty of Paris in 1763 to develop doctrines of metropolitan supremacy that would authorize central control over an empire that had long been characterized by a diffusion of authority to its peripheries, and these doctrines involved a new and expansive concept of subjecthood that included

---

[35] Ibid., 19.
[36] Ibid., 19–20.

all inhabitants of territories politically connected to Britain, no matter what their local legal status, and placed them under the immediate jurisdiction of Parliament. Estimating the number of enslaved colonial subjects at "more than five hundred thousand," Knox declared it "most reproachful to this country" that Parliament had "never shewn the least regard" for them. Should "the servitude of these people be [ruled] unlawful," he added, it would be "still more reproachful to this country that so great a number if its subjects" had been "unlawfully made slaves." Before the British religious establishment had declared its opinion on whether slavery was contrary to divine law, Knox concluded in the first of his tracts on slavery, there was no point in proposing any regulations to Parliament. Once the bishops had acted, Parliament would be able to "decide what will be human law."[37]

The Society's decision on the religious prohibitions came quickly in its February 1768 response to Anthony Benezet, who, emboldened by Warburton's sermon, had written to the Society seeking to enlist it in his campaign to "condemn the practice of keeping slaves as unlawful." The Society refused, its secretary replying that it "found the contrary very plainly implied in the precepts given by the apostles, both to masters and servants," and, invoking the language of security, even urging Benezet to cease spreading his opinions, lest they encourage masters to become more cruel and tempt the enslaved "to rebel against their masters." This emphatic endorsement of the existing situation both made it clear that British revulsion against the profitable and by then ancient British imperial slave system did not yet run very deep and prompted Knox to compose an additional tract offering "some considerations which may lead to a humane and christian system, for the civil government and religious instruction of those unhappy people." If slavery was legal, he assumed, it could be made humane. Considerations of humanity and justice could thenceforth be reconciled with enslavement.[38]

Knox's detailed proposals need not concern us here. They required a suspension of the conventional British idea of slaves as people without rights, their labour, property, and lives being at the discretion of their masters, and the recognition that the same colonial laws that made them slaves also gave them rights, including protection from cruel usage and the provision of sufficient nourishment and days of rest, with legal remedies similar to those of English apprentices. Although he acknowledged that "the ignorance of the Negroes" concerning their rights and "the partiality of the magistrates" resulted in "the tyranny of the planter" being "much seldomer punished in America, than is the rigour of the master in England," Knox invited the Society to think of "the slavery of the Negroes in our colonies" as "no more than a legal, perpetual servitude or hereditary apprenticeship" in which, as "subjects of Great Britain in their particular capacity or circumstance," they would enjoy the rights prescribed to them by law. Calling upon "the venerable society" to try to "obtain

[37] Ibid., 27.
[38] Ibid., 29, 32.

for those people" what they, deprived of any political voice, could never hope to gain for themselves and "what it has been the disgrace of every administration since the revolution to have neglected, an impartial dispensation of the laws" that would force planters to learn that their authority over their slaves was "not absolute and unconditional" but confined by law and that "their Negroes have rights as well as they," he predicted success in this effort. Surely, he declared, in a passage that could only have reinforced metropolitan images of American slaveholders as inhuman and unfeeling despots, a benevolent prince who wished "the felicity of all mankind," such as George III, would, once he had been informed of them, never suffer "so vast a multitude of his own subjects to be inhumanely scourged, lacerated by whips, nourishment denied, and the task of labour exacted, racked by every species of torture the most wanton tyranny can invent, and either forced to expire under them, or their lives shortened by their severity," and "all this in the teeth of laws, to which his majesty, by his representative, has assented." Even as these castigations of slave traders and owners as social misfits in a benevolent British world continued to circulate, the foundations of the slave system appeared to be secure.[39]

IV

Knox's proposed compromise, whereby parliamentary legalization on the existing slave system would be followed by metropolitan-supervised amelioration of the excesses of the slave trade and colonial slavery, neither got beyond the suggestion stage nor long went unchallenged. In 1769, Granville Sharp carried this discussion to an altogether different level with the publication of his *A Representation of the Injustice and Dangerous Tendency of Tolerating Slavery; or of Admitting the Least Claim of Private Property in the Persons of Men, in England*, certainly the most systematic, learned, and powerful attack on the colonial slave system issued up to that time in the entire British world. Drawing upon legal precedents and earlier metropolitan writings about colonial slavery by Morgan Godwyn and William Burke, Sharp was principally concerned to head off the creeping spread of American slavery into Britain itself and, as he announced in his title, to make sure that the metropolitan legal community rejected all arguments for making human beings private property in England. To that end, he devoted Part I of this four-part work to raising doubts about the legitimacy of a 1729 ruling by the attorney general and solicitor general that slaves brought by their owners to Britain did not become free, and Part II, a third of the total pages, to arguing that the "obsolete Laws and Customs" formerly associated with the ancient English institution of villeinage could not, as some colonial slaveholders had evidently tried to contend, "justify the Admission of the modern West Indian Slavery into this Kingdom."[40]

[39] Ibid., 32–34.
[40] Granville Sharp, *A Representation of the Injustice and Dangerous Tendency of Tolerating Slavery; or of Admitting the Least Claim of Private Property in the Persons of Men, in England*

Scholars have paid somewhat less attention to Part III of this work, which took up almost two-fifths of the volume. An astonishingly systematic effort to delve deeply into colonial slave and servant laws, particularly those of Virginia and Barbados, it concluded with a devastating condemnation of the overseas British societies that depended upon and nourished the institution of slavery. As Sharp developed his case, he sought to persuade the reader that those societies were indeed Creolean despotisms sustained by laws and social practices that represented "gross infringement[s] of the common and natural rights of mankind" and were "plainly *contrary* to the laws and constitution" of Britain. Colonial slavery, he insisted, was "a foreign institution" that was thoroughly un-British and had no place in a polity that prided itself on being both free and humane.[41]

Sharp's examination of colonial laws revealed a plethora of practices that violated metropolitan standards of justice, liberty, and humanity. "American provincials," he found, made "no scruple to deprive poor Indians of their just rights," reducing them to "English bondage in the West Indies" and on the continent. They rendered "white servants and labourers...much more abject than the ancient slaves." They subjected free blacks and mulattoes to cruel punishments without due process of law and, under certain conditions, took them up and sold them as slaves. They put the enforcement of laws relating to servants and slaves in the hands of local justices who had "the same prejudices...and...a similar interest" as those of the masters. They permitted masters to kill their slaves and then screened them from punishment, in effect providing "a sanction...by law" to "the horrid crime of *wil[l]ful murder*." They routinely classified their slaves, along with "CATTLE, COPPERS AND STILLS, AND OTHER GOODS," as chattel, thereby dehumanizing them and signifying that they ranked them "with their beasts." They eliminated trial by jury in capital cases for free blacks and mulattoes as well as for slaves. They denied slaves instruction in Christianity. They prohibited slave marriage and manumission. The catalog of departures from British norms and traditions was endless.[42]

Such measures, Sharp exclaimed, betrayed such a "deplorable *Hardness of Heart*," such an "abandoned *Spirit of Injustice*," and "such a shameful depravity of mind in the law-makers" as was "scarcely to be equalled in Barbary itself." Schooled in what he called "the prejudices of a West Indian education" that left them "capricious and depraved," "plantation legislators," animated

---

(London, 1769), title page. For a full discussion of Sharp's confrontation with slavery issues, see Christopher Leslie Brown, *Moral Capital: Foundations of British Abolitionism* (Chapel Hill: University of North Carolina Press, 2006), 155–206. This volume is the most thoughtful, thorough, and deeply contextualized study of the origins and early history of British abolitionism. See also the perceptive recent study of the role of the debate over the slave trade in the formation of British national identity by Srividhya Swaraminathan, *Debating the Slave Trade: Rhetoric of British National Identity* (Farnham, U.K.: Ashgate, 2009), esp. 46–170, where the author usefully examines some of the texts considered in this chapter.

[41] Sharp, *Representation*, 40–41, 132–33.

[42] Ibid., 45, 49–50 note, 59 note, 67–69 note, 70–71, 99, 146–47.

by an "arbitrary, cruel and inhuman spirit," had, in his view, contrived a system that reeked of the "most consummate wickedness...that any body of people, under the specious form of a legislature, were ever guilty of." "To the indelible disgrace of the British name," these patently "self-interested dispensers of law" had established "tyrannical constitution[s]" that had turned Britain's American colonies into "countries where arbitrary power" was "exercised with...*intolerable* cruelty," the "plantation laws and customs" having encouraged "every petty planter, who avails himself of the service of Slaves," to become "an arbitrary monarch, or rather a lawless Basha in his own territories." The result, Sharp charged, was that these "Slavemongers" were "the most cruel and abandoned tyrants upon earth, or perhaps, that ever were on earth." "The epithet '*irreligious*'" was far "too mild a term to be applied" to such people and to the polities they had created. They "ought rather," Sharp declared, "to be called *diabolical*, or by any other epithet, which is capable of expressing *the most consumate wickedness*."[43]

Sharp, who often included the heavily slave colonies of North America within the term *West Indies*, explicitly eschewed in this pamphlet any consideration of the question of whether the supposed incapacity of white people to labor in hot climates made "a toleration of Slavery...necessary or justifiable in the West-Indies." But he was persuaded that the climate of the North American colonies was "in general...so wholesome and temperate, that it" could never "authorize this plea of necessity for the employment of Slaves, any more than in our own." Yet, he lamented, "the pernicious practice of Slave-holding is become almost general in those parts." His examination of slave sale advertisements in a New York newspaper, for instance, persuaded him that the "infringement of [the] civil and domestic liberty" of the enslaved in that colony had become so "notorious and scandalous" that it merited "the name of New Barbary, rather than of New York."[44]

From Sharp's point of view, the entrenchment of slavery in the colonies made American pretensions "to be very zealous in the cause of liberty" a total sham. "Notwithstanding that the political controversies of the inhabitants" were "stuffed with theatrical bombast and ranting expressions in praise of liberty," he charged, they seemed thoroughly hypocritical. "Howsoever elegant in itself," he exclaimed, "no panegyrick on this subject" could possibly

be graceful or edifying from the mouth or pen of one of those Provincials; because men, who do not scruple to detain others in Slavery, have but a very painful and unjust claim to the protection of the laws of liberty: and indeed it too plainly appears, that they have no real regard for liberty, farther than their own private interests are concerned; and (consequently) that they have so little detestation for despotism and tyranny, that they do not scruple to exercise them with the most unbounded rigour, whenever their caprice excites them, or their private interest...seems to require an exertion of their power over their miserable Slaves.

[43] Ibid., 40, 45, 47–49, 53 note, 62 note, 63 note, 65 note, 67 note, 72, 182; *An Appendix to the Representation* (London, 1772), 28.
[44] Ibid., 80–81, 87.

The freedom of the American colonies was thus only "imaginary." Censuring Americans "for their notorious violation of civil liberty," for "their shameless infringement upon it by an open profession and toleration of Slaveholding," Sharp concluded that the

> *boasted liberty* of our American colonies, therefore, has so little right to that sacred name, that it seems to differ from the arbitrary power of despotic monarchies only in one circumstance; viz. That it is a *many-headed monster of tyranny*, which entirely subverts our most excellent constitution; because liberty and slavery are so opposite to each other, that they cannot subsist in the same community.[45]

The central message that Sharp sought to convey was that the colonists, by creating polities that departed so radically from the fundamentals of the British constitution, had shown themselves to be "unworthy to be esteemed either Christians or Englishmen." "A toleration of Slavery," he declared, citing William Burke's discussion of the excessive labor of slaves and invoking the language of humanity, "is, in effect, a toleration of inhumanity." By "wearing out their Slaves with continual labour and a scanty allowance, before they have lived out half their days" and condoning such "barbarous treatment and inhuman insults," he thought, colonial slaveholders had turned themselves into "barbarians and heathens," "unworthy Englishmen" who had "entirely debauched their former principles of humanity and brotherly love." The native Indians, he suggested, were correct in thinking that England must surely "be inhabited by a better sort of people than those sent amongst them." Citing Robert Wallace's remarks on the "severity of modern Slavery" in Turkey, Algiers, Tunis, Tripoli, Morocco, "and other African countries," Sharp doubted that it could "possibly in any place be more severe, than it is even in our own colonies." No people who participated in a system of such "detestable injustice," including those who sold and transported slaves as well as those who bought and exploited them, he declared, could be anything more than "nominal Christians" or could "deserve to be esteemed a *civilized* people." In Sharp's view it would "have been better for the English nation, that these American dominions had never existed, or even that they should have been sunk into the sea, than that the kingdom of Great Britain should be loaded with the horrid guilt of tolerating such abominable wickedness."[46]

Sharp called on the king to use his prerogative to relieve his "oppressed and much injured subjects in the British colonies" by extending "the British constitution to the most distant colonies, whether in the East or West Indies." Not to do so, he feared, "must inevitably" make metropolitan Britain deeply complicitous in such an oppressive social system and bring a "great share of" the "*enormous guilt*" associated with slavery to "rest on this side [of] the water." "That the *British* constitution and liberties should be excluded from

---

[45] Ibid., 50 note, 81–82.

[46] Ibid., 69 note, 70–71, 73, 79–83, 97–98, 104–05, 147, 149; Robert Wallace, *A Dissertation on the Numbers of Mankind in Antient and Modern Times* (Edinburgh, 1753), 206–08.

any part of the *British dominions*," it seemed to him, was "a shame to this nation." But he was principally concerned to keep colonial slave systems out of Britain altogether. If Britain already had been dishonored and tainted by the vile practices of its American colonies, Sharp was determined that it should not be thoroughly infected by the spread of slavery and Creolism into the metropolis itself. He expressed his powerful opposition, as he wrote three years later in an *Appendix to the Representation*, to "the introduction of the *diabolical* Tyranny and Injustice of our West Indian Colonies, whereby *human Nature is vilifyed and degraded to the Rank and level of brute Beasts;* for not only the grossest oppression of our *fellow man* but even *murder* is there tolerated, and *Marriage* excluded." "With respect to their source, temper and necessity," he wrote, the "plantation laws and customs . . . must certainly be esteemed as different *and distant* from our own, as the *climate itself.*" If ever "the customs of *uncivilized* nations, and the *uncivilized customs* which disgrace our own colonies" became "so familiar, as to be permitted among us with impunity," he warned, "we ourselves must insensibly degenerate to the same degree of baseness, with those from whom such bad customs were derived, and may too soon have the mortification to see the *hateful extremes of tyranny and Slavery fostered under our very roof.*"[47]

Sharp's treatise did not immediately stimulate a broad public discussion. Yet it was sufficiently successful to provoke Benjamin Franklin, then a resident colonial agent in London, to counter Sharp's portrait of Americans as a people who were "such Enemies to Liberty, such absolute Tyrants, where" they had "the Opportunity," as to be unmatched by any other "People upon Earth." In "*A Conversation between an* ENGLISHMAN, *a* SCOTCHMAN, *and an* AMERICAN, *on the Subject of* SLAVERY," published in the London *Public Advertiser* in January 1770, the American protested Sharp's indiscriminate condemnation of "*all Americans*" as slave owners having no regard for liberty and exerting "unbounded Rigour over their miserable Slaves." Pointing out that the colonies from Pennsylvania north had "very few Slaves," most of whom were domestic servants, and that even in the southern colonies slavery was mostly concentrated among a few "old rich Inhabitants, near the Navigable Waters" and was uncommon among the far more "numerous Families of Back-Settlers, that have scarce any Slaves among them," the American argued that in the North American colonies as a whole not more than one free family out of a hundred had slaves and condemned Sharp for stigmatizing all Americans "with the Crime." Furthermore, the American denied that all American masters were "Tyrants and Oppressors," arguing that many treated "their Slaves with great Humanity, and provide[d] full as well for them in Sickness and in Health, as your poor labouring People are in England."[48]

[47] Sharp, *Representation*, 50 note, 73, 104–05, 134; *Appendix to the Representation*, 22–23.
[48] Benjamin Franklin, "Conversation on Slavery," *Public Advertiser* (London), January 30, 1770, in Verner W. Crane, ed., *Benjamin Franklin's Letters to the Press* (Chapel Hill: University of North Carolina Press, 1950), 187–88.

In response to the Englishman's charge that Sharp had quoted many "severe laws . . . for the Government of your Slaves (and even of your white Servants)" that could give metropolitans "no good Opinion of your general Humanity, or of your respect for Liberty" and to the observation that such laws were "not the Acts of a few private Persons" but made "by your Representatives in your Assemblies, and" were "therefore the Act of the whole," the American had to admit that some laws in colonies "where the Slaves greatly out-number the Whites, as in Barbadoes now and in Virginia formerly," might "be more severe than necessary" because of white fears that only "extream Severity could keep the [numerically superior] slaves in Obedience and secure the Lives of their Masters." But he contended that in most colonies where the enslaved constituted a smaller proportion of the population the laws were "milder, and the Slaves in every Respect, except in the Article of Liberty," were "under the Protection of those Laws." The American also denied that white servants were treated any differently in America than in Britain, except in those "Colonies to which you send your Convicts," many of whom, he said, were such "Villains" that they had to "be ruled with a Rod of Iron." Denouncing the metropolitan government's insistence upon emptying "your Gaols into our Settlements" as "an unexampled Barbarity," the American cited many examples of British severity toward miners, soldiers, and sailors and, in anticipation of a theme that would soon become powerful in the writings of both pro- and antislavery spokespeople, called attention to British metropolitan complicity in the imperial slave system through merchant participation in and government protection of the slave trade. If Americans were to be condemned for participating in that system, Franklin asked through the persona of his American participant in this conversation, "be so just as to take a Share of the Blame to yourselves."[49]

V

Of course, Sharp's negative portrait of American planters as Creolean monsters was not the only view of them circulating in the metropolis, where, like the returning nabobs of India, they continued to hold a certain fascination as wealthy and exotic Britons. Thus, as late as 1771, when Richard Cumberland's play *The West Indian: A Comedy* was first performed in London, the "Creolian" could still be depicted as a social type with many redeeming features. Thus Cumberland characterized Belcour, the youthful hero of the play who has just come to London for the first time, as "a fine West Indian." "Hot as the soil, the clime, which gave him birth," he might be "A brave, unthinking, animated rogue, / With here and there a touch upon the brogue," as *Belcour* says of himself, "an idle, dissipated, unthinking fellow, not worth your notice: in short, I am a West Indian." If, as his open benefactor and secret father, the London merchant Stockwell, says, he was a little "wild perhaps, as the manner

[49] Ibid., 188–92.

of his country is," with "an education, not of the strictest kind, and strong animal spirits" that were "apt to betray him into youthful irregularities," he was certainly "not frantic or unprincipled" but had "an high principle of honour, and an uncommon benevolence" that "atone[d] for any faults."[50]

Such indulgent depictions were commonplace. Thus did Edmund Burke in an aside in a newspaper essay in 1768 comparing the "phlegmatic" nature of the English to the "national Temperaments" of "the several kindred Tribes, which compose the great Mass of the British Empire," include, without condemnation, "the head-long Violence of the Creolians" in a list with the "Heat of the Welch, the Impetuosity of the Irish, [and] the Acrimony of the Scots."[51] Ten years later the lawyer William Russell in his *History of America* would similarly depict the "Creole" as a distinct social type having many "good qualities," including generosity, frankness, and vivacity, but also "restless in temper, and inconstant in taste," with a "warm imagination perpetually" hurrying "them into new pleasures and projects, to which they sacrifice both their fortunes and their health."[52]

Nevertheless, disquiet about the British slave system was in the air and found voice in many places, including John Fothergill's *Considerations Relative to the North American Colonies*, published in 1765, in which the author, a merchant with extensive knowledge of America, sought to enlighten his countrymen about the social and emotional differences between colonists who lived by their own labor in the northern and central colonies of North America and those who lived by slave labor in the southern mainland colonies and the West Indies, where labor systems and excessive heat combined to produce a distinctive social type. Enabled by the slave trade "to procure . . . vast Wealth, at the Expence of [a] People" who had been "torn from the tenderest Tyes of Nature, by Violence and Fraud, to drudge in Servitude during the Residue of their Days, without Hope of Redemption," Creoles, Fothergill wrote, lived lives "of Idleness and Extravagance." Surrounded from infancy by "dark Attendants" and inured to the harsh treatment meted out to the enslaved, they early became "habituated by Precept and Example, to Sensuality, Selfishness, and Despotism" and ever after avidly pursued "Splendor, Dress, Shew, Equipage, everything that" could "create an Opinion of their Importance" – all "at the Expence of the poor Negroes, who cultivate their Lands."[53]

John Millar took a broader and more penetrating view in his *Observations Concerning the Distinction of Ranks in Society*, published in London in 1771. A professor of law at the University of Glasgow, Millar recounted the decline

---

[50] Richard Cumberland, *The West Indian: A Comedy*, 2nd ed. (London, 1771), iii, 5, 6, 53, 54.

[51] Mnemon [Edmund Burke] to the *Public Advertiser*, February 24, 1768, in Paul Langford, ed., *The Writings and Speeches of Edmund Burke*, Volume 2: *Party, Parliament, and the American Crisis 1766–1774* (Oxford, 1981), 76.

[52] William Russell, *The History of America, From Its Discovery by Columbus to the Conclusion of the Late War*, 2 vols. (London, 1778), 1: 593.

[53] [John Fothergill], *Considerations Relative to the North American Colonies* (London, 1765), 40–42.

of slavery in Europe, remarked on the extent to which the "laws and customs of the modern European nations have carried the advantages of liberty to a height which was never known in any other age or country," and called attention to the "infallible tendency" of the abandonment of slavery and the "introduction of personal liberty . . . to render the inhabitants of a country more industrious; and therefore, by producing greater plenty of provisions," to "encrease" the "populousness, as well as the strength and security of a nation." That "the practice of slavery was no sooner extinguished by the inhabitants in one quarter of the globe, than it was revived by the very same people in" America, "where it has remained ever since, without being much regarded by the public, or exciting any effectual regulations in order to suppress it," struck Millar as lamentable. "Considering the many advantages which a country derives from the freedom of the labouring people," he observed, using the language of liberty, "it is a matter of regret that any species of slavery should still remain in the dominions of Great Britain, in which liberty is generally so well understood, and so highly valued."[54]

Millar found the explanation for why slavery had been so resistant in two conditions peculiar to the "institution of slavery" in the colonies. The first was the abundant supply of slaves and the tight labor discipline masters had devised, which together relieved masters of the necessity to reward labor and encourage industry. The second was the lucrativeness of the slave trade itself, which thrived on the existing system. Expressing his astonishment that so little attention had been paid to making improvements that had had such "good effects . . . in the case of the villains of Europe," Millar expressed the conviction that "the interest of our colonies seems to demand that the negroes should be better treated, and even that they should be raised to a better condition." "At the same time," he observed in language that revealed his assessment of the character of American Creoles,

it affords a curious spectacle to observe, that the same people who talk in so high a strain of political liberty, and who consider the privilege of imposing their own taxes as one of the unalienable rights of mankind, should make no scruple of reducing a great proportion of the inhabitants into circumstances by which they are not only deprived of property, but almost of every right whatsoever. Fortune,

he concluded, "perhaps never produced a situation more calculated to ridicule a grave, and even a liberal hypothesis, or to show how little the conduct of men is at bottom directed by any philosophical principles."[55]

By generating enormous public interest in the British engagement with slavery, the Somerset case, which dragged on through the winter and spring of 1772, strongly tended to reinforce Sharp's, Millar's, and others' characterizations of American planters. Indeed, while the case was in its early stages, Sharp

---

54 John Millar, *Observations Concerning the Distinction of Ranks in Society* (London, 1771), 232–34, 237.
55 Ibid., 232, 240–42.

published an *Appendix* to his earlier pamphlet reiterating his views of the horrors of the slave trade, "West India Slavery," and the "*diabolical*" people who presided over them.[56] The widespread impact of the case had far less to do with Chief Justice Lord Mansfield's carefully delimited decision than with the rhetoric of Somerset's lawyers in court and his defenders in the press, which operated to draw a sharp line between British liberty in the home islands and colonial slavery. Worrying that the "horrid cruelties, scarce credible in recital, perpetuated in America, might, by allowance of slaves amongst us, be introduced here," John Alleyne, one of the lawyers representing Somerset, asked whether Britons, "exercised, as they are now, to far different sentiments" and "feelings of humanity," could possibly "endure in the fields bordering on this city, to see a wretch bound for some trivial offence to a tree, torn and agonizing beneath the scourge?" and called on the court "to guard and preserve that liberty by which we are distinguished by all the earth" and to "be jealous of whatever measure has a tendency to diminish the veneration due to the first of blessings."[57]

Alleyne's colleague Francis Hargrave similarly insisted on the incompatibility of slavery and British legal and cultural traditions. He pointed out that domestic slavery had been in an "expiring state... in *Europe* at the commencement of the sixteenth century, when the discovery of *America* and of the Western and Eastern Coasts of Africa gave occasion to the introduction of a new species of slavery." First used by the Spaniards in Hispaniola and elsewhere, Hargrave explained, slavery was then adopted by other Europeans as they acquired American possessions, with the unfortunate result that enslaved Africans had "become a very considerable article in the commerce between *Africa* and *America*; and domestic slavery" had "taken so deep a root in most of our *American* colonies, as well as those in other nations, that" he despaired "of ever seeing it suppressed." Although Hargrave admitted that Parliament, in various statutes, had by authorizing the African slave trade "*impliedly* authorize[d] the slavery of negroes in *America*," he emphatically denied "that permitting slavery *there*" included "a permission of slavery *here*. By an unhappy concurrence of circumstances, the slavery of negroes is thought to have become necessary in *America*; and therefore in *America* our Legislature has permitted the slavery of negroes. But," he contended, "the slavery of negroes is unnecessary in *England*, and therefore the Legislature has not extended the permission of it to *England*." Colonial slavery, Hargrave suggested, following Sharp, was an American institution and should be confined to the colonies, and he called on the court not to permit it to pollute the free world of metropolitan Britain.[58]

---

[56] Granville Sharp, *Appendix to the Representation*, 22, 27–28.
[57] Remarks of John Alleyne, May 14, 1772, in Thomas Bayley Howell, comp., *A Complete Collection of State Trials*, 21 vols. (London, 1816), 20: 69.
[58] Francis Hargrave, *An Argument in the Case of James Sommersett A Negro* (London, 1772), 17, 47.

VI

For the powerful slave-trading and planting interests in Britain, this was frightening talk, and they responded quickly and forcefully. In the wake of the Somerset case, African traders found themselves, for the first time, on the defensive. Two writers associated with that trade, John Peter Demarin, writing anonymously as "An African Merchant" and claiming to be presenting, "not the reverie of a single person, but the joint sentiments of the best writers on trade, and . . . the united opinions of the most capital," experienced, and knowledgeable merchants engaged in the African trade, and Thomas Thompson, who addressed his treatise to the "Company of Merchants Trading to Africa," turned to the languages of commerce and imperial grandeur to combat the languages of humanity, liberty, and justice on which critics of the British imperial slave system so heavily relied.[59]

Starting with the familiar claim that foreign commerce had been responsible for Britain's "present greatness," Demarin boldly and unapologetically contended that the African trade was "the first principle and foundation of all the rest; the main spring of the machine, which sets every wheel in motion," and that for "both . . . exports and imports, the encouragement of industry at home, the supply of our colonies abroad, and the increase of our navigation" it was "so very beneficial to Great Britain, so essentially necessary to the very being of the colonies, that without it neither could we flourish, nor they long subsist." In view of the importance of this trade as "the first cause of our national industry and riches," those who, "under the specious pleas of establishing universal freedom," tried to strike "at the root of this trade" were nothing less than the "enemies of their country." "What vain pretence of liberty," he asked, could "infatuate people to run into [such] licentiousness, as to assert [that] a trade is unlawful, which custom immemorial, and various acts of parliament have ratified and given sanction to?" Denying that his protagonists could find support for "their enthusiastic arguments from scripture, antient usage, or the laws of the land," he assured his readers that "the richest adventurers" in the African trade were "such men, as would scorn to be engaged in any trade, but what the laws of God and man would fully sanctify" and called on Parliament to abolish the African trade "at once" if it was "in reality so contrary to law and humanity as some have set forth."[60]

Demarin's main objective, however, was to put the case to Government for an act to "set the African trade on a fair and respectable footing," one that would be "humane and equitable to the Africans, advantageous to every private free British trader, and conducive to the prosperity of our commerce, [and] the benefit and support of our colonies." To this end, Demarin proposed

[59] An African Merchant [John Peter Demarin], *A Treatise upon the Trade from Great Britain to Africa, Humbly Recommended to the Attention of Government* (London, 1772), 64; Thomas Thompson, *The African Trade for Negro Slaves Shewn to be Consistent with Principles of Humanity and the Laws of Revealed Religion* (Canterbury, 1772).

[60] African Merchant [Demarin], *Treatise upon the Trade*, 3–5, 7–8, 11.

a bill, not to abolish the African trade, but to legalize it, to authorize the sale of slaves as property, and to guarantee the property rights in slaves of their purchasers. To supervise the trade and adjudicate disputes on the African coast, he proposed to create an imperial bureaucracy and to impose large fines on any merchants or ship captains caught kidnaping and enslaving people in Africa. To prevent mistreatment of slaves in the colonies, he proposed that slaves "be secure[d] in their lives and limbs" and automatically freed in cases of "wanton cruelty," including maiming or defacement, on the part of "any planter or other of his majesty's free subjects," that anyone who killed a slave be held legally accountable in the same manner as would have applied to "the loss of any other of his majesty's subjects," that masters who provided insufficient food and clothing be fined, and that the punishment of slaves for idleness or running away be put entirely in the hands of magistrates. Certainly for critics of the slave system, however, Demarin's list of proposed reforms and the implicit acknowledgment they represented of the misbehavior of overseas Britons tended rather to confirm than to dispute existing images of inhumane traders in Africa and on the Atlantic and despotic planters in America.[61]

Whereas Demarin showed little appreciation for the claims of humanity over those of profit and national prosperity, Thompson conceded that the slave trade was a subject that was "generally considered with feelings of tenderness, and but seldom spoken of without great humanity." He even acknowledged that while men engaged in other unpleasant trades eventually became inured to them, they did not always do so with the slave trade. "There is something very affecting and disagreeable," he admitted, "in the appearance and notion of human creatures . . . being treated like mere beasts or cattle." "For the negroes so to misuse one another" was far from admirable, but "that christians maintain[ed] a commerce with those people for the numberless poor wretches, which they enslave, and drive down from the country to the factories and landing-places on the coast, to be sold like bullocks at a fair" was "a fact that seems hardly capable of a defence, notwithstanding the impossibility that our plantations can be cultivated without them."[62]

"As ill a face as it" presented and "as strong as the objections . . . commonly made against it," however, Thompson ultimately pronounced it "really as vindicable as any species of trade whatever." Against those who considered "the sale of human creatures as a violation" of the "natural distinction of the species, and levelling men with beasts," he argued "that every person is treated as a human being, who is treated according to his lawful state and condition. The buying of a slave," he wrote, was merely "taking him as what he is; and the sale does but signify, that his owner is willing to part with, and another has a mind to have him. Here then is no violation of humanity; and the property in such individual is transferable, like all other property." To the extent that traders were guilty of "Spiriting up the blacks to war . . . in order

[61] Ibid., 55–56, 58.
[62] Thompson, *African Trade for Negro Slaves*, 8–10.

to make a trading advantage by it," Thompson agreed that it was "a thing to be detested." But he insisted that the trade was usually "conducted upon true mercantile principles." "The buying and selling negroes," he declared, was "not... a clandestine or piratical business, but an open, public trade" in vendible commodities that had been "encouraged and promoted by acts of parliament."[63]

West Indian spokesmen took much the same position in two substantial pamphlets published in the immediate wake of the Somerset case, one by Edward Long, a Jamaican who just two years later would publish his three-volume *History of Jamaica*,[64] and a second by Samuel Estwick, a Barbadian.[65] Both Long and Estwick marshaled learned and sophisticated arguments that explored the legal, historical, and cultural foundations of slavery, not just in the *colonial* but also in the *metropolitan* world.[66]

They were principally concerned to show that slavery and the slave trade were not simply colonial aberrations in an otherwise free British world. It was not very difficult. The "whole nation," Long emphasized, had been "in some way or other interested in the advantages drawn from this trade" and from the many plantation commodities produced "principally by means of [enslaved] Negroe labour." For that reason, he thought, not only the colonies but also the home islands had, as he put it, "participate[d] a benefit from the sweat of the Negroe's brow." Whatever was "the state and condition of Negroes" in the greater British world, declared Estwick, "responsibility for it... [was] therefore a British and not [simply] an American question; as well it might be, since, if I may be allowed to reason chymically upon this occasion, whatever property America may have in its drugs, it is Great Britain that receives the essential oyl extracted from them." Because the home islands had been so deeply involved in both the slave trade and slavery, it seemed to settler propagandists profoundly hypocritical for the metropolitan British to suggest that "English feelings were to revolt at American punishments," and they vehemently expressed their objections to the "horrid and frightful picture[s] of the barbarity, and cruelties, that were exercised on" the enslaved "in the colonies."[67]

Estwick expanded upon this point. America, he wrote, did "not afford that scene of barbarity, which misrepresentation would have painted upon it." To

---

[63] Ibid., 11–12, 28–29, 31.

[64] A Planter [Edward Long], *Candid Reflections Upon the Judgement lately awarded by The Court of King's Bench in Westminster-Hall, on what is commonly called The Negroe-Cause* (London, 1772).

[65] A West Indian [Samuel Estwick], *Considerations on the Negroe Cause Commonly So Called, Addressed to the Right Honourable Lord Mansfield, Chief Justice of the Court of King's Bench* (London, 1772). Under his name, Estwick published a considerably expanded second edition of this work in London in 1773.

[66] These pamphlets are analyzed in considerably more detail in Jack P. Greene, "Liberty, Slavery, and the Transformation of British Identity in the Eighteenth-Century West Indies," *Slavery & Abolition*, 21 (2000): 1–31.

[67] Long, *Candid Reflections*, 40, 69; [Estwick], *Considerations on the Negroe Cause*, 29; Estwick, *Considerations on the Negroe Cause*, 2nd ed., xvi, 58, 60.

expose the moral hypocrisy of the metropolitan British, he pointed to the situation in the new British colony of St. Vincent, where at that very moment "*English troops, trampling on the laws of God and man,*" were "*slaughtering even to extirpation a guileless race of Caribs, the aborigenes of the country.*" Indeed, Estwick insisted, citing the impressment of seamen and the frequent imposition of martial law in metropolitan Britain, "cruelties and distress" were "to be found in much greater excess even in this elysium of liberty."[68]

In making their case for metropolitan complicity in slavery and metropolitan hypocrisy in condemning the imperial slave system, these writers used the language of security to underline the dangers inherent in the circulation of the "enthusiastic notions of liberty" advocated by Granville Sharp and others. Not only, wrote Long, might they "operate as a direct invitation to *three hundred thousand blacks*, now scattered over our different colonies, to mutiny, and transport themselves . . . into this land of *Canaan*," where they could enjoy British freedom, but they also threatened, Long added, "Nothing less . . . than a total sacrifice of our *African trade* and *American possessions* to their fantastic idea of *English liberty*."[69]

The destruction of slavery, they predicted, would also ruin the economies of the colonies, which, they believed, could produce nothing of value without slave labor. Without the advantages Britain obtained from the colonies, they said, echoing the sentiments of Demarin and Thompson, "Britain itself," as Samuel Martin, Sr., an Antiguan noted for his earlier treatise on agricultural improvement in sugar culture, put it in still a third proslavery pamphlet published in Antigua and circulated in London, would "become a poor, wretched, defenceless country, and very soon a province of France." By cautioning against those "pretended reformers of the age; who, under a cloak of furious zeal in the cause of religion and liberty, do all they can to throw down those essential pillars, commerce, trade, and navigation, upon which alone must depend our enjoyment of any freedom, civil or religious," and by raising the fear that, "by setting free the Africans, Britons" would open themselves to French subjection and thereby themselves become "wretched slaves to arbitrary power," these writers sought to call attention to the extent to which, not just in the colonies, but in Britain itself the wealth of the nation and the freedom of whites rested on the enslavement of blacks.[70]

That West Indians and African traders used the language of commerce in opposition to the language of humanity testifies to the continuing power of utilitarian considerations throughout the years immediately following the rise of antislavery sentiment. Except for Adam Smith, every major writer on Britain's foreign commerce continued to emphasize the value of the African trade in slaves. Thus in 1764 did Adam Anderson, echoing earlier writers such as Gee

---

[68] Estwick, *Considerations on the Negroe Cause*, 2nd ed., xvii, 51–52.

[69] Long, *Candid Reflections*, 41–42, 58–60.

[70] Samuel Martin, *A Short Treatise on the Slavery of Negroes in the British Colonies* (Antigua, 1775), 11.

and Postlethwayt, stress the economic value of "the great and constant supplies we get from" Africa "of negro slaves for our American plantations";[71]
thus in 1772 did Arthur Young declare the slave trade to be a "most beneficial
commerce";[72] and thus in 1774 did John Campbell emphasize the extent to
which the African trade had been "highly... advantageous to this Nation."
To that trade, Campbell wrote, "we owe the greatest Part of the Advantages
derived from our Plantations in America, in which Labour is chiefly performed
by Negroes. To be convinced of this," he added, "we need only consider that
the clearing of Woods, the Cultivation of Sugar, Rice, and Tobacco, can in
those sultry Climates be performed only by them. If any Thing farther be necessary," he concluded, "we may compare the State of those Colonies and the
Returns made by them to the Mother Country before and since the Introduction of Negroes, which will very clearly demonstrate that both their Subsistence
and their Extension depends and must depend on this Commerce."[73]

VII

As Gilbert Francklyn, a later proslavery writer, would lament in 1789, however, immediately following Mansfield's decision in the Somerset case, "the
imaginations of the populace of London were as much heated by the cry of
liberty, as they were a few years" before, during the Seven Years' War, "by the
name of the *Protestant religion*,"[74] and the political fallout from the Somerset
case energized not only those who wished to preserve the existing British slave
system but also those who found it shamefully incompatible with British values of liberty and humanity. In contrast to Sharp and Millar, however, most of
these writers had had extensive colonial experience.

That was certainly true of Maurice Morgann, the colonial advisor, who in
1772 published anonymously as *A Plan for the Abolition of Slavery in the
West Indies* a manuscript he had written about the slavery question in 1763.
No critic of British overseas colonization, Morgann rather praised the American colonies, founded on the principles of the British constitution, as "solid
and lasting acquisitions of industry and virtue; not the transitory fruits of violence and injustice." Unlike India, whose wealth was "paid into the rapacious
hands of a few unprincipled Nabob-hunters and oppressors, producing excess,

---

[71] Adam Anderson, *An Historical and Chronological Deduction of the Origin of Commerce,
From the Earliest Accounts, containing An History of the Great Commercial Interests of the
British Empire*, 4 vols. (London, 1787), 1: lx–lxi. This work was first published in 1764.
[72] Arthur Young, *Political Essays Concerning the Present State of the British Empire* (London,
1772), 526.
[73] John Campbell, *A Political Survey of Britain: Being a Series of Reflections on the Situation,
Lands, and Inhabitants, Revenues, Colonies, and Commerce of this Island*, 2 vols. (London,
1774), 2: 624, 632–33.
[74] Gilbert Francklyn, *Observations Occasioned by the Attempts Made in England to Effect the
Abolition of the Slave Trade* (London, 1789), x–xi.

venality, and inequality of condition," the American colonies had produced "equality, strength, public spirit, and virtue." Whereas "every other empire" had ultimately "weakened [itself] by extending," the British Empire in the Atlantic had "alone...taken root at every step." "It has not subdued but generated nations," he declared. "It has multiplied itself in America, and in every distant province has renewed a constitution, of which the most distant subject receives the *immediate* advantage and protection, and the actual enjoyment of every priviledge and right, without [any] other distinction between him and a resident Briton but that of *place*, and in return he transmits to his mother-country" the produce of "a generous commerce, the willing tribute of his wealth and possessions."[75]

Nevertheless, Morgann regarded the slave system as a serious blemish upon this proud achievement, and his pamphlet proposed a scheme that, he hoped, might at once expand British concepts of "liberty and justice" to include non-British peoples, restore "the integrity of the British government," and vindicate "the credit and honour of our common natures." Denouncing the slave trade as a violation of "every idea of justice and morality" and utterly destructive "of every principle of faith, honour, and humanity," Morgann reviewed many of the cruelties of colonial slavery and, stressing security concerns, warned that "the blacks of the southern colonies on the continent of America" might eventually become "numerous enough to throw off at once the yoke of tyranny to revenge their wrongs in the blood of their oppressors," to "carry terror and destruction to the more northern settlements," and to excite "in the islands...a general and...merited carnage." Yet he did not propose "to liberate the present race of slaves." Even if emancipation was "in other respects practicable," he wrote, the "ignorance and...bad habits" of those blacks who had been inured to slavery made them "[in]capable of receiving freedom." Rather, attributing the existing slave system, not to the traders or the colonial planters, but to "the state," he called upon the state to seek a remedy that, with "time and management," would eventually "eradicate" slavery in the colonies.[76]

Specifically, catering to the broadly accepted idea that whites could not work in hot climates, Morgann proposed that the metropolitan government sponsor a plan to purchase young Africans, civilize them in special schools, and use them as free British subjects to settle portions of the new British colonies in Florida. "In the process of time," he predicted, this scheme would "extend itself over the neighbouring colonies in America, and, by degrees, over the islands themselves; and...thereby all slavery" would "be at length compleatly extirpated." Waxing ecstatic on the virtues of this inclusionary scheme, and in the process betraying the grandiose extent and totalizing potential of some Britons' imperial dreams, the author suggested that it could lead to "the black

---

[75] [Maurice Morgann], *A Plan for the Abolition of Slavery in the West Indies* (London, 1772), 29–30.
[76] Ibid., 12, 13–15, 32.

subjects of Britain," lifted "up to an equality with Englishmen," first forming "extensive settlements in, and drawing home by commerce all the wealth and products of South America" and then turning their attention

to Africa, where, instead of seeing a few whites languishing and piddling for gum in Senegal, we might behold the whole coast colonised, and our commerce pushed through the very heart of the continent. Thus wisely availing herself both of moral and physical causes, no longer weakened and disgraced by slavery or restrained by climate, but rising upon the sure foundations of equality and justice

Great Britain, "aggrandized and invigorated at home," the author fantasized, combining the languages of commerce, civility, and imperial grandeur, might "stretch forth, with irresistible power, her sable arm through every region of the Torrid Zone; and (to compleat the climax) the whole world become at last civilized, and an universal language be obtained by the same means as should lift Great Britain into the seat of unenvied and unlimited Dominion." Through this "chimerical" plan, which the author admitted fell into the category of what the "world is pleased to call Projects," he thought, Britain thus could convert "evil into good" by drawing "out of slavery, weakness, and injustice, an energy... of irresistible power," could build a mighty empire composed of "colonies of different growth, climate, temper, *and, let me now add, of complexion*," and could remove and transcend the stain of slavery and expand its imperial hegemony throughout the southern Atlantic.[77]

The Somerset case also inspired William Bollan, a prolific pamphlet writer and former London agent for Massachusetts, to produce an extended analysis of the history of slavery from antiquity to "the partial revival of it by the European states concerned in the modern marine discoveries" and "the consequent acquest [sic] of foreign dominion and settlement." Published anonymously and entitled *Britannia Libera, or a Defence of the Free State of Man in England*, this work was principally concerned to keep slavery out of metropolitan Britain. But the author paused along the way to condemn the European introduction of slavery into the American colonies and its proliferation therein as a union between "human pride" and "the lust of domination, avarice, injustice, and cruelty." Together with the slave trade, Bollan estimated, slavery had destroyed eleven million people and "distress[ed] many more in *America*." Linking this carnage with the recent sufferings of twelve million Asians under the aegis of the East India Company, he pointed out that "depriving so many of their fellow creatures of life, or the common blessings of the earth" was "not the way to promote the dignity, strength, and safety of empire," but a sure route to suffer "disgrace among all good men" forever. Such excesses, in Bollan's view, cried out for remedy through the national exertion of "wisdom, justice, and humanity." "Law and liberty, justice and equity," he contended, were the only

77 Ibid., 1–2, 16, 26–28, 31.

"proper foundations" for British governance, abroad as well as at home, and "humanity the most amiable characteristic of the people."[78]

The following year, in 1773, Thomas Day and John Bicknell found, in the moving story of the suicide of a runaway slave who on the eve of his marriage to an English servant woman had been captured by one of the gangs of slave hunters who roamed London streets and confined to a ship destined for America, inspiration for a poetical epistle entitled *The Dying Negro*, which, according to the publisher of the last of its five editions, was over the next two decades "much celebrated." Beginning with the second edition in 1774, Day, a Quaker moralist, included a long prose dedication that fully expressed his abhorrence of colonial slaveholders. Emphasizing the miseries of slaves in antiquity and calling upon his readers to remember that there was at that very moment "a people who share the government and name of Britons; among whom the cruelty of Sparta" had been renewed without its virtue, he denounced American Creoles as nothing more than "Inglorious soldiers, ... seditious citizens; sordid merchants, and indolent usurpers," men "whose avarice" had "been more fatal to the interests of humanity," and had "more desolated the world than the ambition of its antient Conquerors!" For these lowly Americans, he said contemptuously, "the Negro is dragged from his cottage, and his plantane shade; – by them the fury of African tyrants is stimulated by pernicious gold; the rights of nature are invaded; and European faith becomes infamous throughout the globe." Expressing not puzzlement but resentment that such people should be the authors of the "clamours for liberty and independence" that were then being "heard across the Atlantic Ocean," Day, picking up a theme earlier articulated by Millar and Sharp, suggested that Creole protests would be more credible if they were "unmixed with the clank of chains, and the groans of anguish," pointedly reminding his readers that it was "in Britain alone, that laws are equally favourable to liberty and humanity."[79]

The arguments of the African traders, American planters, and other defenders of the existing slave system in the immediate wake of the Somerset case inspired a second wave of antislavery tracts. In 1773–74, the young Pennsylvania doctor Benjamin Rush, who had just returned from studying medicine in Edinburgh, published anonymously two of these.[80] In 1774, the Methodist

---

[78] [William Bollan], *Britannia Libera, or a Defence of the Free State of Man in England* (London, 1772), 1, 39–40, 42–43.

[79] [Thomas Day and John Bicknell], *The Dying Negro, A Poetical Epistle, supposed to be written by A Black, (Who lately shot himself on board a vessel in the river Thames;) to his intended Wife* (London, 1773). The quotations are from p. i of the fifth edition, published in London under Day's and Bicknell's names in 1793, and from pp. viii–ix of the third, published in 1775.

[80] [Benjamin Rush], *The Address to the Inhabitants of the British Settlements in America on Slave-Keeping* (Philadelphia, 1773); A Pennsylvanian [Benjamin Rush], *A Vindication of the Address to the Inhabitants of the British Settlements, on the Slavery of the Negroes in America, in Answer to a Pamphlet entitled "Slavery Not Forbidden by Scripture"* (Philadelphia, 1773). The second was a response to A West-Indian [Richard Nisbet], *Slavery Not Forbidden by Scripture. Or a Defence of the West-India Planters* (Philadelphia, 1773).

divine John Wesley, who had been a missionary in the colonies, produced another,[81] and in 1776, Granville Sharp issued three more.[82] All of these works were intended to confront and refute the principal claims of the proponents of slavery: that Africans were a savage and inferior people, that British slave traders bore no responsibility for stimulating the wars by which people were made captive, that the trade was a regular one without violence, that slaves were not treated badly during the Atlantic crossing, that most masters dealt with their slaves generously and kindly, that tropical places could be cultivated only by Africans, that colonists' rights as Britons guaranteed slave owners their absolute property in their slaves, that Parliament's endorsement of the slave trade and the Crown's allowance of colonial laws sanctioning slavery made it legal, and that any interference with the slave system would destroy the African trade and the value of the slave colonies and bring great economic loss and declining international status to Britain.

Together, these writers made a powerful case for the monstrous moral and social effects of the entire British slave system. Not African incapacity, they contended, but slavery itself was responsible for debasing "the moral faculties" and "understanding" of the enslaved and rendering them "torpid." "All the vices which are charged upon the Negroes in the southern colonies and the West-Indies, such as Idleness, Treachery, Theft, and the like," Rush declared, were "the genuine offspring of slavery." The "stubbornness, cunning, pilfering, and divers other vices" that slaveholders so frequently attributed to their slaves, echoed Wesley, were "the natural, necessary fruits of slavery." As Rush explained, "Domestic Slavery," like "Despotic Governments," invariably required "severe laws." "The natural Love of Liberty which is common to all Men, and the Love of Ease which is peculiar to the Inhabitants of Warm Climates," he wrote, could "only be overcome by severe Laws and Punishments." As long as slaves were "treated with [an] Inhumanity, unknown to former Ages," Rush predicted, "nothing but the Whip, melted Wax, Brine, the Gallows, the Stake, and the Gibbet" would "long prevent Insurrections among them."[83]

Nor, in the opinions of these writers, could any credible apology be made for the people who profited from it. "For a long time past," Sharp complained in a sweeping condemnation of early modern European colonialism, "the Europeans have taken upon themselves ... *to attack, destroy, drive out, dispossess, and enslave,* the poor ignorant *Heathen,* in many distant parts of the world, and may, perhaps, plead custom and prescription (to their shame be it said) for their actions, yet," in Sharp's view, Europe's many "offenders" in these

[81] John Wesley, *Thoughts upon Slavery* (London, 1774).
[82] Granville Sharp, *The Just Limitations of Slavery* (London, 1776); *The Law of Liberty, or, Royal Law, by which All Mankind will Certainly be Judged!* (London, 1776); and *The Law of Retribution; or, a Serious Warning to Great Britain and her Colonies* (London, 1776).
[83] [Rush], *Address to the Inhabitants,* 3–4; Wesley, *Thoughts upon Slavery,* 47–48; [Rush], *Vindication,* 20–21.

outrages could "no otherwise be esteemed than as *lawless robbers* and *oppressors*, who" – articulating a new theme that was also present in the Rush and Wesley pamphlets – had every "reason to expect a *severe retribution* from God for their tyranny and Oppression." Rush used similar language in calling for the dissolution of the "British African Company," which he regarded as "an incorporated band of robbers."[84]

Nor, despite the slaveholders' objections to being "represented . . . as a set of hardened monsters, who . . . wantonly indulge[d] themselves in every species of cruelty,"[85] did they fare any better at the hands of these writers. Rush expressed admiration for the "first settlers of Barbadoes" who had "fled from the Tyranny of Cromwell," but, he remarked, "what a Change has Negro-slavery made in some of their Posterity." "How often do they betray, in their sudden transports of anger and resentment," he asked in a long passage cataloguing their vicious treatment of slaves, "the most violent degree of passion and fury" and their degeneration into nothing more than "impure and hardened monsters." In Wesley's opinion, colonial masters had devised the "vilest" form of enslavement that ever existed, that ended only with death and was worse than that "found among the *Turks* at *Algiers*." No wonder, declared Rush, that West Indians sent their children for education to Britain and away from social environments that were so "exposed to Vice from every Quarter, and where they" could "breathe nothing but the polluted Atmosphere of Slavery."[86]

On one point, at least, Sharp and Wesley agreed with their antagonists – that Britain itself was deeply complicitous in the overseas slave system. "The careless Inhabitants of Great-Britain and her Colonies," Sharp charged, were alike responsible "for the notorious *Oppression* of an almost innumerable multitude of poor *African Strangers*, that are harrassed, and continually wearing out, with a most shameful involuntary Servitude in the *British Colonies!* Nay," he lamented, "and that by a public Toleration, under the sanction of Laws to which the Monarchs of England, from time to time, by the advice of their Privy Counsellors, have given *the Royal Assent*, and thereby rendered themselves Parties in *the Oppression*, and . . . Partakers of the Guilt!" What could be more wicked than "the AFRICAN SLAVE-TRADE, now carried on chiefly by our *Liverpool* and *Bristol* Merchants?," he asked. What "*bloody crime*" could be "more notorious, and more wickedly premeditated," he observed in pressing deeper into the evident iniquities of British colonialism, "than the late *Invasion* and *Conquest* of the poor innocent CARRIBBES at ST. VINCENT'S?" "The Inhabitants of *Great Britain* and the Inhabitants of *the Colonies*," Sharp observed, "seem to be almost equally guilty of *Oppression!*" The colonies "*protest* against the Iniquity of the SLAVE-TRADE," he observed, referring to the unsuccessful legislative efforts of some North American colonies to ban

---

[84] Sharp, *Just Limitations*, 13; [Rush], *Address to the Inhabitants*, 21.
[85] [Nisbet], *Slavery Not Forbidden by Scripture*, 15.
[86] [Rush], *Vindication*, 12–13, 17; Rush, *Address to the Inhabitants*, 17–18; Wesley, *Thoughts upon Slavery*, 51.

further importations, "but, nevertheless, continue to hold the poor wretched *Slaves* in the most *detestable Bondage*." Britain "indeed, keeps *no Slaves*, but publicly encourages the *Slave-trade*, and contemptuously neglects or rejects every petition or attempt of the *Colonists* against that notorious wickedness." Wherever they lived, said Wesley, directly addressing the many British residents who had "estates in our *American* plantations," "*Men-buyers*" were "exactly on a level" with "*men stealers*" on the coast of Africa. "You are the spring that puts all the rest in motion," he told them. "*You* therefore are guilty, yea principally guilty of all these frauds, robberies and murders" connected with the overseas slave system. "Thy hands, thy bed, thy furniture, thy house, thy lands are at present stained with [the] blood" of the enslaved. The "horrible Guilt, therefore, which is incurred by *Slave-dealing* and *Slave-holding*," Sharp concluded, could "no longer be confined to the few hardened *Individuals*, that are immediately concerned in those baneful Practices, but alas! The WHOLE BRITISH EMPIRE is involved."[87]

Notwithstanding Britain's complicity in the overseas slave system, however, Rush, Wesley, and Sharp all agreed that, as Wesley put it in calling upon Britons to contemplate "your grandeur, of which" the colonial enslaved's "misery makes so large a part," and reiterating a point emphasized by earlier antislavery writers, the "inhumanities" of slavery were "certainly contrary to the genius and disposition of the *British* nation, and quite abhorrent of its laws."[88] Clearly, these writers thought, it was no longer enough, as Sharp wrote, "that the Laws of England exclude *Slavery* merely *from this island*, whilst the grand Enemy of mankind triumphs in a toleration, *throughout our Colonies*, of the most monstrous *oppression* to which human nature can be subjected!"[89]

Neither Rush nor Wesley thought the returns anywhere nearly sufficient to justify enslavement in the colonies. "No manufactory can ever be of consequence enough to society," Rush asserted, "to admit the least violation of the Laws of Justice or humanity." Denying that wealth was "necessary to the glory of any nation," Wesley asked whether the enslaved did not have "a better right to their liberties and their happiness, than our *American* merchants have to the profits which they make by torturing their kind? Let therefore our colonies be ruined, but let us not render so many men miserable." "It would be better that all those islands should remain uncultivated for ever, yes, it were more desirable that they were altogether sunk in the depths of the sea," Wesley said, paraphrasing a remark from Sharp's 1769 pamphlet, "than that they should be cultivated at so high a price as the violation of justice, mercy, and truth."[90] "This Country," as an anonymous writer signing himself "W. S." succinctly

[87] Sharp, *Law of Retribution*, 16–17, 35, 305; Wesley, *Thoughts upon Slavery*, 54–55; Sharp, *Law of Liberty*, 49.

[88] Wesley, *Thoughts upon Slavery*, 26 note, 81–82.

[89] Sharp, *Just Limitations*, 2–3.

[90] [Rush], *Address to the Inhabitants*, 3; Wesley, *Thoughts upon Slavery*, 39–40, 44, 77.

declared in *The Public Ledger* in July 1772, "can support its dignity without dealing in *human Carcasses*."[91]

Neither Wesley nor Rush had to look far for an explanation of the erosion of traditional British values in the slave societies of the Americas. "How *Britons*" could "so readily admit of a change in their disposition and sentiments, as to practice in *America* what they abhor[red] and detested in *Britain*" was explainable to Wesley "on no other principle, but as being the natural effect of slave-keeping, which as the celebrated *Montesquieu* observes, 'insensibly accustoms those who are in the practice of it, to... become haughty, hasty, hard-hearted, passionate, voluptuous, and cruel.'"[92] While even "Spaniards blush[ed] at the Recital of the Massacre of the Indians in South America, and wish[ed] to blot it out of their Histories," lamented Rush,

Britons, once famed thro' every quarter of the Globe for their love of Justice, Humanity and Liberty – nay more, British Americans, the descendants of those illustrious Men of whom Britain at one period of her History was not worthy – British Americans, who a few years ago risked their all in opposing the claims of the British Parliament; these very Americans have fallen into a trade more destructive to their fellow Creatures than the Spanish tortures; they have pursued it upwards of an hundred years, and what is more – they defend it as lawful.[93]

Like Sharp, both Wesley and Rush found the hypocrisy of colonials deplorable. Wesley repeated virtually verbatim John Millar's 1769 characterization of Americans claiming liberty for themselves while wholly denying it to their slaves as "a curious spectacle." There was no difference, announced Rush, "between the British Senator who attempts to enslave his fellow subjects in America, by imposing Taxes upon them contrary to Law and Justice; and the American Patriot who reduces his African Brethren to Slavery, contrary to Justice and Humanity."[94]

VIII

Not merely pamphleteers and radical tractarians but also prominent political writers and members of Parliament picked up on this theme of colonial hypocrisy, repeatedly using it to score rhetorical points in the American controversy from the mid-1770s until the recognition of American independence in 1783. The pointed question of Dr. Samuel Johnson, the metropolitan critic and lexicographer who deplored any sign of a lenient attitude toward Americans, is well known. "How is it," Johnson asked in March 1775 in his pamphlet *Taxation no Tyranny*, "that we hear the loudest yelps for liberty among the drivers of negroes?"[95] Josiah Tucker, the dean of Gloucester, had made much the same

[91] "W. S.," *The Public Ledger* (London), July 17, 1773, as cited in F. O. Shyllon, *Black Slaves in Britain* (London: Oxford University Press, 1974), 161.

[92] Ibid., 26 n.

[93] [Rush], *Vindication*, 39–40.

[94] Wesley, *Thoughts upon Slavery*, 42; [Rush], *Vindication*, 30.

[95] Samuel Johnson, *Taxation No Tyranny* (London, 1775), in Donald J. Greene, ed., *Samuel Johnson: Political Writings* (New Haven: Yale University Press, 1977), 454.

point at far greater length two months earlier. "Can it be affirmed," he asked in addressing himself to the American Congress, "that you are...strenuous Advocates for Liberty" in all cases? Noting that the Congress had claimed colonial rights "by the *immutable Laws* of Nature," he asked why the "poor Negroes, and the *poor Indians*" were not "entitled to the like Rights and Benefits." "How comes it to pass, that these *immutable Laws* of Nature become so very unstable, and so very insignificant in respect to them? They probably never ceded to any power – most certainly they never ceded to you, the Right of disposing of their Lives, Liberties, and Properties, just as you please," he declared. "And yet what horrid Cruelties do you daily practice in the Bodies of poor Negroes, over whom you can have no Claim, according to your own Principles? What shameful Robberies and Usurpations are you daily guilty of in respect to the poor *Indians*, the only true and rightful Proprietors of the Country you inhabit?" For "whilst you, and your Constituents, are chargeable with so much *real* Tyranny, Injustice, and Oppressions," Tucker asserted, "you declaim with a very ill Grace against the *imaginary* Tyranny, and the pretended Oppression of the Mother Country."[96]

Throughout the crisis for independence of 1775–76, Government polemicists continued to elaborate upon this theme in both the press and Parliament. "The grand claims of the Americans is [sic] liberty," M.P. William Innes declared in Parliament in November 1775, "but it appears to me absurd to say, that a people who import slaves, and are despotic over them, nay,...many of whom draw their sustenance from the very bosom of slavery, have a right to [the] freedom which the inhabitants of this country enjoy. The North American spirit and practice in this respect, have surely nothing in them similar to what prevails in Great Britain."[97] Ambrose Serle, another advocate of military coercion to put down colonial resistance, agreed. In contrast to the colonies, he wrote, slavery was "no Part of...[the British] Constitution. We have no Idea of it in our Law. It is not to be Found in our Country. Negroes here, wherever they have been slaves before," he declared, putting an expansive gloss on Mansfield's decision in the Somerset case, "are emancipated in a Moment by setting Foot upon our liberating Shores."[98] That "People should be enslaved because of their complexion," asserted William Allen, a prominent Philadelphian resident in London and no friend to rights-claiming Americans, in a

---

[96] Josiah Tucker, *Tract V. The Respective Please and Arguments of the Mother Country, and of the Colonies distinctly set forth and the Impossibility of a Compromise of Differences, or a Mutual Concession of Rights, plainly Demonstrated* (Gloucester, 1775), iv–v.

[97] William Innes, speech, November 8, 1775, in R. C. Simmons and P. D. G. Thomas, eds., *Proceedings and Debates of the British Parliament Respecting North America, 1754–1783*, 6 vols. (White Plains, N.Y.: Kraus, 1982–86), 6: 203. See also *A Calm Address to Americanus. By a Native of America* (London, 1775), 4.

[98] [Ambrose Serle], *Americans against Liberty; or an Essay on the Nature and Principles of True Freedom, Shewing that the Designs and Conduct of the Americans tend only to Tyranny and Slavery* (London, 1775), 33–34.

1774 pamphlet, was "an *American* Logic, unknown to the generous *Briton*, who detests the Idea and execrates the Practice!"[99]

As much as they disapproved of such self-conscious distancing of metropolitan Britain from British overseas colonies and emphasized the brotherhood of all Britons, Opposition advocates of a rapprochement with the colonies had difficulty in wrestling with the problem of the incongruity of the Americans' libertarian claims and their entrenched system of slavery. Edmund Burke was a case in point. In his speech on conciliation in Parliament on March 22, 1775, he stressed the presence of "a vast multitude of slaves" as the principal reason why free people in Virginia and the other southern continental colonies were "much more strongly, and with a higher and more stubborn spirit, attached to liberty than those to the Northward." "Freedom is to them not only an enjoyment, but a kind of rank and privilege," he explained in expressing his opposition to proposals to reduce "the high aristocratical spirit of Virginia and the Southern Colonies ... by declaring a general enfranchisement of their slaves." "Such were all the ancient commonwealths; such were our Gothick ancestors; such in our day were the Poles; and such will be all masters of slaves," he observed. "In such a people the haughtiness of domination combines with the spirit of freedom, fortifies it, and renders it invincible." Unable to condone slavery, however, Burke chose instead to stress metropolitan involvement in the imperial slave system, suggesting that slaves might "not a little suspect the offer of freedom from that very nation which has sold them to their present masters." "An offer of freedom from England would come rather oddly," he remarked, if it were "shipped to them in an African vessel, which is refused entry into the ports of Virginia and Carolina, with a cargo of three hundred Angolan negroes. It would be curious," he added, "to see the Guinea captain attempting at the same instant to publish his proclamation of liberty, and to advertise his sale of slaves."[100]

Thomas Day, another opponent of the American war, was even less compromising. In an essay written in 1776 for John Laurens, a young South Carolina slaveholder who was queasy about slavery, but not published until 1784, Day denounced "every plea" in favor of slavery as a "plea of interest and tyranny combating humanity and truth." If, in his view, no "West Indian"could possibly be a "man of honour, sense, and humanity," North Americans bore major blame for participating in "a crime so monstous against the human species" and so subversive of "the foundations of all humanity and justice" that "all those who practice[d] it deserve[d] to be extirpated from the earth." He acknowledged that slave purchasers were not the original enslavers, but he charged

---

[99] William Allen, *The American Crisis: A Letter addressed by permission to the Earl Gower* (London, 1774), 13–14.

[100] Edmund Burke, speech on conciliation, March 22, 1775, in Warren M. Elofson and John A. Woods, eds., *Party, Parliament, and the American War 1774–1780*, Volume 3 of *The Writings and Speeches of Edmund Burke* (Oxford, 1996), 119–20.

that by encouraging "an infamous, pitiless race of men to do it for you" and then "conscientiously" receiving "the fruits of their efforts," they bore ultimate responsibility for the horrors of war and enslavement in Africa, the mortality of the Middle Passage, and the inevitable sacrifice of the enslaved to what he mockingly referred to as "the candour and humanity of American patriots." That those pretended patriots and devotees of liberty and independence could claim "rights from which they totally exclude more than a fourth part of the species" seemed to Day entirely incompatible with American claims for self-government. "If there be an object truly ridiculous in nature," he observed, "it is an American patriot, signing resolutions of independency with one hand, and with the other brandishing a whip over his affrighted slaves." Day called upon Americans to reconcile principle and practice and "admit the whole human species to a participation of your unalienable rights."[101]

The Scottish divine John Erskine, another critic of coercion, was less condemning, insisting, in the vein of the proslavery writers who protested the Somerset decision, that the Americans did not bear full responsibility. "Where did this infamous commerce originate?" he asked. "Where is it still carried on with all the eagerness which avarice can inspire? Where, but in England? By what means can it be abolished? Surely by that power alone, which Americans acknowledge the parent state, may justly exercise over all her dominions, *viz.* The power of regulating their trade." Instead, the British government had done everything it could to protect the trade, while the "legislatures of some of the colonies" had "done what they could to put a stop to the importation of African slaves, by loading it with the heaviest duties," and others had "attempted the total abolition of it, by acts of assembly which their governors refused to pass," and "though they then petitioned for new instructions to their governors on this head, after all they failed of success."[102]

On the other side, Administration pamphleteers used the American Declaration of Independence to rachet up the attack on American hypocrisy about liberty. In his *Answer to the Declaration of the American Congress* of late 1776, John Lind considered the charge that the British had precipitated "domestic insurrections among us" and declared it ludicrous. How, he asked, could the Virginia governor Lord Dunmore's offer of "*freedom* to the *slaves* of these assertors of liberty" constitute an act "of tyranny? Is it for *them* to say, that it is tyranny to bid a slave be free? To bid him take courage, to rise and assist in reducing his tyrants to a due obedience to *law*? To hold out a motive to him, that the load which crushed his limbs shall be lightened; that the whip which harrowed his back shall be broken, that he shall be raised to the rank of freeman and citizen?" "It is their boast," he continued, "that they have taken up arms in support of their own *self-evident truths* – 'that

[101] Thomas Day, *Fragment of an Original Letter on the Slavery of the Negroes; Written in the Year 1776* (London, 1784), 24, 28–30, 33–36, 38.

[102] [John Erskine], *The Equity and Wisdom of Administration, in Measures that have unhappily occasioned the American Revolt, tried by the Sacred Oracles* (Edinburgh, 1776), 27–28.

all men are *equal*' – 'that all men are endowed with the *unalienable* rights of life, *liberty*, and the *pursuits of happiness.*' Is it for *them* to complain *of the offer of freedom* held out to these wretches?," he inquired, "Of the offer of reinstating them in that *equality*, which in this very paper, is declared to be the *gift of God to all*; in those *unalienable rights*, with which, in this very paper, God is declared to have *endowed all* mankind?[103]

In the heat of conflict, Administration and other anti-American writers found the Americans' continuing involvement with the slave system an easy target. In his ongoing argument to persuade the British public that Britain would be better off to throw the colonies out of the empire, Josiah Tucker expressed his skepticism that colonial "Tyrants over their Slaves" would, despite being "Advocates for Republicanism, and for the supposed Equality of Mankind," ever take the lead "in suggesting some...humane system for abolishing the worst of all Species of Slavery," such as the one they employed in the colonies. "All Republicans antient and modern, as far as History and Experience can inform us," he observed, "suggest no other Schemes but those of pulling down and levelling all Distinctions above them, and tyrannizing over those miserable Beings, who are unfortunately placed below them." But he speculated that an American capture of the West Indian colonies might force Britain "through *Necessity* to do *that Justice*, and to make *that Restitution*, to a great Part of our Fellow Creatures, which we ought to have done long ago by *Choice*, and through a Principle of *mere Humanity*, to say nothing of higher Motives." He lamented that, as "the boasted Patrons of Liberty...and professed Advocates for the natural Rights of Mankind," Britons "engage[d] deeper in this murderous inhuman Traffic than any Nation whatever," and to make matters worse, he complained, "we [even] glory in it." Instead of making slaves "of these poor Wretches, contrary to every Principle...of Humanity and Justice," Tucker proposed that Britain teach Africans as free people how to produce sugar and other plantation commodities to exchange for European goods.[104]

During the war, Government supporters continued to deride their American opponents on the slavery issue. "It will appear impossible," wrote M.P. William Pulteney in a 1778 pamphlet, "that a rebellion can have *liberty* for its object, which has the *proprietors of slaves* for its leaders." While they pretended in *"principle*...to be the most zealous champions of freedom; in practise they" were "the severest of tyrants." They asserted that "'all men are created equal,' yet...shamefully" made "a property of their fellow creatures, whom they purchase for gold, condemn to the most servile and laborious employments, and render completely miserable by inflicting on them the most

---

[103] [John Lind], *An Answer to the Declaration of the American Congress* (London, 1776), 107. Lind expanded on these themes in [John Lind], *Three Letters to Dr. Price, containing Remarks on his Observations on the Nature of Civil Liberty, the Principles of Government, and the Justice and Policy of War with America* (London, 1776), 157–58. See also John Shebbeare, *An Essay on the Origin, Progress and Establishment of National Society* (London, 1776), 178.

[104] Josiah Tucker, *A Series of Answers to Certain Popular Objections, against separating from the Rebellious Colonies, and discarding Them Entirely* (Gloucester, 1776), 20–22, 83, 103.

unjust and severe torments that ingenious cruelty can invent, or unrelenting tyranny can practise." "Such are the glorious assertors of American Independence," he declared, the *"philosophic, righteous, consistent* members of that August Congress," who had the nerve to "complain of the injustice of the British Government on offering *liberty* to their *slaves*."[105]

In pointedly drawing a sharp line between metropolitan and overseas Britons, some analysts of this persuasion, as the Reverend James Murray of Newcastle noted in his 1778 *Impartial History of the Present War in America*, a work deeply sympathetic to the American cause, even suggested that keeping slaves should disqualify colonials from enjoying traditional British rights of civic participation in Britain, specifically from sitting in Parliament, on the grounds that those "who have been accustomed to have an unlimited right over the lives of others" could not be safely entrusted with making laws for a genuinely free society such as Britain's, perhaps not even for themselves. People of this persuasion thus justified Britain's making laws for the colonists and its "absolute right of empire over" them because their "want of feelings of humanity" made them "unfit to make laws to themselves." But, he objected, this view had two major deficiencies. First, it assumed "that all the colonies" were "alike" in their participation in the imperial slave system, which, as Murray said, was "contrary to fact." Second, it supposed that the British Parliament should "have absolute empire over a people whom" it "encouraged in a trade that makes them subject to slavery." "It is a point to be soberly considered," Murray wrote, "whether Great Britain is not as guilty as Virginia in this particular; for amongst all the laws for regulating the trade of the colonies, the British parliament has not yet made a law against this most infamous traffic. It is no uncommon thing," he noted, "to see a British member of parliament have his *Niger slave* following him, which plainly shews that this practice is not peculiar to America."[106]

At the war's end, analysts were still passionately engaged with this issue. The American Quaker David Cooper was particularly eloquent on this subject in a pamphlet published in Trenton, New Jersey, and republished in London in 1783. Declaring that Britain's persecution of America was "no more to be equalled, with ours to negroes, than a barley corn is to the globe we inhabit," he speculated that "every generous foreigner [must] feel a secret indignation rise in his breast when he hears the language of Americans upon" the infringement of "any of their own rights as freemen . . . and reflects that these very people are holding thousands and tens of thousands of their innocent fellow men in the most debasing and abject slavery, deprived of every right of freemen, except light and air." "Unless we can shew that the African race are not *men*," Cooper

[105] William Pulteney, *An Appeal to Reason and Justice, in Behalf of the British Constitution, and the Subjects of the British Empire* (London, 1778), 76–78.
[106] James Murray, *An Impartial History of the present War in America*, 2 vols. (London, 1778), 1: 26–28.

declared, calling attention to the assertion in the preamble to the Declaration of Independence that all men are created equal,

words can hardly express the amazement which naturally arises on reflecting, that the very people who make these pompous declarations are slave-holders, and, by their legislative conduct, tell us, that these blessings were only meant to be the *rights* of *white men* not of *all men*: and would seem to verify the observation of an eminent writer: 'When men talk of liberty, they mean their own liberty, and seldom suffer their thoughts on that point to stray to their neighbours.'[107]

Cooper thought it a good sign that "the disquisitions and reasonings of the present day on the rights of men, have opened the eyes of multitudes, who clearly see, that, in advocating the rights of humanity, their slaves are equally included with themselves, and that the arguments which they advance to convict others redounds back on themselves, so that few among us are now hardy enough to justify slavery." But, he asserted, as long as Africans should be "continued in chains of slavery as creatures unworthy of notice in these high concerns [about rights], and left subject to laws disgraceful to humanity, and opposite to every precept of christianity," as long as there was not an "entire *abolition* of *slavery*" and America continued to "be polluted with slave-holders," "*justice, humanity, advocates for liberty*, and the sacred name of *christians*" could command no credibility as "the *boast* of *American rulers*," and "this crying evil" would "ever remain a stain to the annals of America."[108]

IX

Throughout the war and beyond, people who spoke both the language of commerce and the languages of humanity and justice, of whom Edmund Burke provides a prominent example, wrestled with the contradictions between the two. Recognizing the economic importance of colonial slavery, Burke, like many others, sought to rationalize it on the grounds that, as he said in Parliament in June 1777, "Africa, [from] time out of mind, had been in a state of slavery" and that "therefore the inhabitants [had] only changed one species of slavery for another," albeit he expressed regret "that in changing from African to European slavery, they generally changed much for the worse, which certainly was a matter of reproach somewhere and deserves serious consideration."[109] At the same time, however, Burke gave serious attention to formulating a "Negro Code" that, by appointing a "Protector of Negroes" for the colonies and providing slaves with basic legal rights, would, he hoped, gradually "put an end

[107] A Farmer [David Cooper], *A Serious Address to the Rulers of America, On the Inconsistency of their Conduct respecting Slavery: Forming a Contrast between the Encroachments of England on American Liberty, and American injustice in Tolerating Slavery* (London, 1783), 7, 14.
[108] Ibid., 4, 16–17, 19, 22, 24.
[109] Edmund Burke, speeches on the African slave trade, June 5, 1777, in Elofson and Woods, eds., *Party, Parliament, and the American Crisis*, 341.

to all traffic in the persons of Men" and "to the detention of their said persons in a State of Slavery."[110]

In the meantime, the Creole could not escape his unsavory reputation. William Russell wrote fully upon this subject in 1778. From their "absolute dominion over the negroes, the Creoles derive an imperious manner, which makes their company be little relished in Europe," he wrote:

Accustomed from their earliest infancy to see a number of tall stout men about them, whose business it is to conjecture and anticipate their wishes, they insensibly imbibe the most extravagant opinion of their own consequence. Seldom meeting with any opposition to their will, though ever so unreasonable, they assume a domineering air, and look down with disdain upon the bulk of mankind. No man is so insolent as he who always lives with his inferiors,

he observed. "But when these happen to be slaves, habituated to wait on children, who dread even their cries, which must expose them to punishment, what must masters become, who have never obeyed!," he asked rhetorically, supplying his own answer: "wicked men, who have never been punished, and madmen, who to gratify caprice, are accustomed to put their fellow creatures in irons!" "An exercise of tyranny so cruel and wanton, accompanied by so humble a submission" on the part of the enslaved, he declared, "gives the West Indians that arrogance which must . . . be detested in every European country." Clearly, Russell implied, the degradations inherent in slavery had spared neither masters nor slaves.[111]

Like the extensive public discussions of the plunder of India by East India Company servants and the outcry against the Carib War in St. Vincent, the attack on the African slave trade and the slave systems that powered so many of the economies of the colonies and defined their social and legal regimes directed the attention of metropolitan Britons, as never before, to the seamy side of empire, to the routine, wanton, and systematic exploitation and destruction of East Indians, Africans, and even Amerindians in the construction of empire. From the mid-1760s on, metropolitan Britons had been presented with mountains of evidence and intense discussions about the heavy costs such people paid both for the economic successes of the thousands of traders, settlers, and investors who immediately spearheaded and most directly profited from imperial enterprises and for the extraordinary wealth that those enterprises brought to Britain itself in the form of trade profits, stimulation of manufacturing and urban development, naval power, and national security within Britain itself. When the nabobs, Creoles, Guinea merchants, and other imperial enterprisers found themselves under attack for their inhumane, unjust, and mercenary behavior overseas and for bringing such behavior back to Britain, they responded by citing the many ways in which metropolitan Britons were

[110] Edmund Burke, sketch of Negro Code, [post April 9, 1780], in ibid., 563.
[111] Russell, *History of America*, 1: 594.

themselves deeply involved in and dependent upon the very activities that they condemned and in which those activities had long enjoyed government sanction. How metropolitan Britons who thought of themselves as free, just, and humane would come to terms with the extraordinary moral excesses and human costs of empire, whether by eliminating or reforming them, turning a blind eye to them, distancing themselves from the behavior of Britons overseas, or by some combination of those strategies, was in the early 1780s, after fifteen years of lively debate, still far from clear.

6

"A Fruitless, Bloody, Wasting War"

The Languages of Imperial Grandeur, Liberty, Humanity, and Commerce in the American Conflict

I

At the very same time that Britons were coming to realize that their view of themselves as a great commercial, powerful, and humane nation was in conflict with the behavior exhibited by East India Company employees, American slaveholders, and traders in African slaves, they were also confronted with the problem of retaining the revolting colonies in North America. Having committed the nation to a policy of military and naval coercion, the Administration soon discovered that this objective was far more elusive than it had expected. Rarely did military operations in America go well for more than a few months at a time, the army never managing to deal rebel military units a knockout blow. As the war dragged on, as a series of Government concessions turned out always to be too little, too late, as larger and larger metropolitan armies failed to pacify, much less to control, the countryside or destroy the American military, as France recognized diplomatically and came to the aid of the new United States, as critical defeats cost the British two armies, and as the mounting costs of the war placed British taxpayers under incredible financial burdens, the Administration found itself under sharp attack from the Opposition, which reiterated and expanded upon old questions about the decision to use force against the colonies and the feasibility of that strategy as a means for retaining an association with those colonies and raised new questions about the conduct of the war. The debate over these questions renewed and intensified the pre-war discussion over how – or even whether – the language of imperial grandeur might be reconciled with the languages of liberty, commerce, and humanity in the management of such "a wide extent of empire" as that of the British.[1]

[1] William Eden, *Four Letters to the Earl of Carlisle* (London, 1780), 67. Stephen Conway, *The British Isles and the War of American Independence* (Oxford: Oxford University Press, 2000), is an excellent study of the British context of the debate described in this chapter. See also idem, *War, State, and Society in Mid-Eighteenth-Century Britain and Ireland* (Oxford: Oxford

II

With its powerful popular and parliamentary support, the North Administration had an abundance of advocates in this debate. Both in Parliament and in the press and with many variations on the language of state power, they continued to set forth the case that the decision to use force against the American rebels was constitutionally justified, necessary for Britain's continued survival as an imperial state, and certain to bring the colonies into line. That the colonies had no right to defy Parliamentary authority they had not a shred of doubt. "Will any wisdom or reason suppose," the anonymous author of *The Duty of the King and Subject, on the Principles of Civil Liberty* asked rhetorically in July 1776, in one of the fullest statements of the Administration case,

> that in the origin of colonization, the legislative body of this country would thin its inhabitants? would send them out at a large expence? would cede to them a country of ideal advantage for no other purpose but, apostle-like, to preach and teach the spirit of the English constitution to a savage nation, to form legislatures of their own independent of the mother country, and to be free and exempt from every controuling power of the constitution?

Likening colonists to the English tenantry, he acknowledged that they could "make and direct the municipal laws of their" various localities but insisted that they were "subject to the laws of the manor, or to the supremacy of the state.... To live beyond a rivulet, or beyond the Atlantic," he declared, "makes no exemption; if it be English ground, it is English empire, and subject to the Plenitude of British supremacy."[2]

Contrary to the claim of the American Congress in the Declaration of Independence, said Thomas Hutchinson, the former governor of Massachusetts and a prominent London loyalist, in August 1776, the revolting colonists were emphatically not a "*distinct people* . . . connected by *political* bands" to another people in Britain. "*Politically* considered," he asserted, they "never were a *distinct* people from [those in] the kingdom," but with Britons at home a single people, bound by the same authority.[3] The "just idea which has ever prevailed" in governing imperial relations, declared Judah Champion, one of the Administration's most vociferous supporters, was "that the Americans are our

University Press, 2006), 227–52; Eliga H. Gould, *The Persistence of Empire: British Political Culture in the Age of the American Revolution* (Chapel Hill: University of North Carolina Press, 2000), 148–214; P. J. Marshall, *The Making and Unmaking of Empires: Britain, India, and America c. 1750–1783* (Oxford: Oxford University Press, 2005), 353–79; and Troy Bickham, *Making Headlines: The American Revolution Seen through the British Press* (DeKalb: Northern Illinois University Press, 2009), 88–182, 206–33.

[2] *The Duty of the King and Subject, on the Principles of Civil Liberty: Colonists not intitled to Self-Government; or to the same Privileges with Britons* (London, 1776), 16.

[3] [Thomas Hutchinson], *Strictures Upon a Declaration of the Congress at Philadelphia* (London, 1776), 9.

subjects, and that they ought in every thing to submit to the regular laws of
our Parliament."[4]

Administration spokesmen were similarly convinced that the maintenance
of metropolitan authority over the colonies was absolutely essential to Britain's
survival as a prosperous state and an imperial power. A few analysts, including
the author of *The Duty of the King and Subject*, professed regret that the English
had ever gotten involved in colonial expansion. Complaining "that pride and
vanity had a great share in the extension of our American empire, without
due consideration to our interest," he expressed the convictions that, although
having a "wide domain" flattered the national "imagination," a "narrow spot,
well cultivated," produced "the surest gain" and that it would have been
fortunate for Britain "if Americus had been drove to the southward and never
discovered a North American shore."[5] Writing two years later, a pamphleteer
signing himself "A Man of Candour" agreed that "extensive dominions" were
"not essentially necessary to the true interests of an insular and maritime state,
especially such vast possessions as are rendered precarious and troublesome
from their situation and remoteness," and professed himself "an enemy to the
mistaken ambition of conquest in the East Indies, where our military spirit is
like to defeat our great commercial objects." But, he stressed,

our western empire is so well established and situated for the commercial purposes of
this nation, and so suited to the genius of the people, that the sovereignty of it, together
with the exclusive rights of trade and navigation should be preserved at any rate, be the
expence and trouble what it will.[6]

Despite his reservations about American colonization, the author of *The
Duty of the King and Subject* made much the same point. Only by bringing "America to a proper state of subordination," he asserted, could Britain
"secure a durable tenure in America," retain "the benefit of an exclusive trade,
and . . . render that country formidable by our garrisons, and perpetual to our
successors."[7] The war was thus not just about restoring metropolitan pride
or enforcing metropolitan pretensions to parliamentary supremacy over the
empire. It was a fight for international standing and economic survival. We
fight, declared an officer who claimed to have served in America during the
Seven Years' War, "to reduce rebels who have brought this dilemma upon us,
of either conquering or being conquered by them."[8]

[4] Judah Champion, *Reflections on the State of Parties; on the National Debt, and the Necessity
and Expediency of the Present War with America* (London, 1776), 32.
[5] *Duty of the King and Subject*, 27.
[6] "A Man of Candour," *A Letter to Mr. Powys, on the Independency of America* (London, 1778),
29–30.
[7] *Duty of the King and Subject*, 13, 34.
[8] "An Officer, who served last War in America," *Reflections on the Most Proper Means of
Reducing the Rebels, and What Ought to be the Consequence of our Success* (London, 1776),
37.

If the stakes were high, the odds of defeat seemed low. It was inconceivable, declared Alan Ramsay, an eager partisan of the Administration, that

the power which so lately carried on a successful war, against the united forces of France and Spain, should not be able to subdue a parcel of Planters and Merchants, who have no fleet, no army, no public treasury, no artillery or military stores; and who have no respectable Head of authority to produce uniformity of conduct, or to prevent mutiny and sedition in those who, from a spirit of sedition only, take upon them to be soldiers.[9]

A decisive victory, moreover, several observers candidly admitted, would enable the metropolis to accomplish other and deeper long-range objectives. In the view of Judah Champion, Britain's efforts to tax the colonies had been "partly a trial of their allegiance, and partly an attempt to reduce, under one form of government, an empire, which was insensibly dividing into many independent polities," a tendency that military success would enable Britain to arrest.[10] A clear victory, Ramsay wrote, would finally enable Britain to establish "an executive power suitable to the present riches and extent of the British Empire."[11]

The ancient British language of alterity as applied to colonists fostered and sustained this low estimation of colonial military capacities, especially among the more virulent anti-American writers. Thus did Ramsay comfort his readers by assuring them that, however horrible the American war might be, they could be sure that "no true Englishmen" would "fall in it, except he be from amongst those brave men who have lately sailed from England with red coats on their backs, to vindicate the important rights of their countrymen."[12] Champion provided the fullest analysis of precisely why Americans could not be confused with "true Englishmen," why the parent state ought to keep them in "an inferior state" and never "place them on the same footing of power and privilege with itself." Observing that colonies had always "been settlements for poor disbanded soldiers, for fugitives, and sometimes for criminals," Champion argued that the British colonies had been no exception. In his view, the original settlers, including especially the New England puritans, had mostly been "delinquents against the state," who, "by a wise and merciful policy, instead of being exterminated, had been placed in a state but little inferior to dutiful and good subjects, in a way to become such, or to be of service to the state." Once "these people had cleared the ground a little," Champion reported, "government increased their numbers by an annual clearing of the jails of highwaymen, footpads, &c. &c. &c. who soon made good saints, and worthy members of these chartered societies," and, as the plantations

---

[9] "Marcellus Britannicus" [Alan Ramsay], *Letters on the Present Disturbances in Great Britain and her American Provinces* (London, 1777), 16. For a similar view, see *A Short Appeal to the People of Great-Britain, upon the Unavoidable Necessity of the Present War with the Disaffected Colonies* (London, 1776), 24.

[10] Champion, *Reflections on the State of Parties*, 30.

[11] [Ramsay], *Letters on the Present Disturbances*, 15.

[12] Ibid., 24.

improved, they became "desirable places of venture to" other metropolitan social rejects: "men of broken fortunes, . . . mechanics, and tradesmen out of employ."[13]

Champion speculated about the effects of this motley collection of social and psychological outcasts upon American resistance to Britain. In his view, the colonies had become "rich and flourishing" and found it increasingly possible to put "on an English appearance" principally because the metropolis had so generously assisted them. Instead of showing some "gratitude, and that attachment to the parent state, which might have been expected" from such generosity, however, Americans had "spurned at their benefactors, and aimed at the destruction of that very state, which gave them existence and power." Asserting that "Americans have ever hated those laws, and that constitution, which their forefathers had attempted in vain to destroy; and against which their lives had been actually forfeited by their repeated treasons," Champion found it unsurprising either that "every public and private act of the Americans have for many years had in view, a total independence of the English government," or that America was now trying to raise "a great empire [of its own] out of the ashes of its parent." Had the colonies "been peopled by voluntary adventurers, and not by criminals and convicts," he was persuaded, "our benefits would not have found the soil so ungrateful," and "the same honour, the same liberality, the same regard to our antient and noble constitution, would have been found in the colonies, as in the genuine sons of England." To attempt by force "to reduce them to the state of colonial subjects" seemed to Champion to be the only way to deal with such a people.[14]

Not just their allegedly lowly social origins and suspect character but also their extensive use of chattel slavery continued, as had been the case in the earlier stages of debate over the American question and as has already been extensively discussed in Chapter 5, to fuel metropolitan condescension toward the American rebels.[15] When the cleric Richard Price objected early in the war to Britain's efforts to enlist Indians and enslaved blacks to fight on its side, another anonymous writer using the pseudonym "A Member of Lincoln's Inn" sarcastically asked Price, in July 1776, whether the Virginia planter or Lord Dunmore, the British governor who had first offered freedom to any slaves who would desert their masters, more clearly and genuinely "spoke the language of liberty?" How, he inquired, could there continue to be slaves in societies that Price regarded as "land[s] of liberty?" "Why did not these sons

---

[13] Champion, *Reflections on the State of Parties*, 26, 28–29, 30–32. On this point, see also [John Inglis], *The Patriots: Or, An Evening Prospect on the Atlantic* (London, 1777), x–xi.

[14] Champion, *Reflections on the State of Parties*, 28–29, 57–59.

[15] For additional examples, see *Essays Commercial and Political, on the Real and Relative Interests of Imperial and Dependent States, Particularly those of Great Britain and Her Dependencies: Displaying the Probable Causes of, and a Mode of compromising the present Disputes between this Country and her American Colonies* (Newcastle, 1777), ii; *An Appeal to the Unprejudiced; or, A Vindication of the Measures of Government, with Respect to America* (Oxford, 1777), 41; and [Hutchinson], *Strictures Upon a Declaration of the Congress*, 9–10.

of liberty restore" liberty to their slaves? Endeavoring to co-opt the languages of humanity and justice, he questioned the very humanity of such people, asking how, consistent with their own declared principles, they could keep slaves "in the state of poor abject animals, without rights, without property, without a conscience, bending their neck to the yoke and couching to the will of every silly creature who has the insolence to pretend authority over them"? Against such people as American rebels, thought this writer, no excuse was necessary for employing either Indians or the enslaved "to support the authority of parliament. That force which is most *easily* procured, and most likely to be *effective*," he declared, "is the force which ought to be employed – Whether the instrument be a German or a Calmuck, a Russian or a Mohawk, makes, I trow, but little difference."[16] Writing at the same time, another anonymous author advocated enlisting slaves in those southern colonies where they outnumbered whites by a ratio of two to one, precisely because they were so "highly oppressed by their tyrants" that they could be counted on to be eager recruits for "any scheme to alter their miserable conditions" and because, having proven to be useful soldiers during the Seven Years' War, they would greatly assist Britain in reducing "the southern parts of America to reason and justice" and forcing them to "sever themselves from the rebellious congress."[17]

Even after the massive turnout of colonists against British forces after Lexington and Concord, the Administration and others who supported a coercive approach in Britain had difficulty in believing that American resistance was not the work of a few factious demagogues who had goaded a deluded multitude in a few urban centers into an unjustified resistance and that the bulk of the population remained loyal to the metropolitan government. After all, as John Wesley pointed out in a pamphlet published in August 1776, "English government, both in the Islands and North America," had "needed no armed force to support it, for above these hundred years" and "all the Colonies" had not only submitted to it "without any armed force to compel them" but had actually "rejoice[ed] in" it. "They knew and felt," Wesley observed, that "they were not oppressed, but enjoyed all the liberty, civil and religious, which they could desire."[18] That the mass of Americans had somehow changed their minds and become rebels seemed incomprehensible, and Administration supporters assumed that once the British army had established its superiority, "multitudes [would be] flocking to the King's standard" throughout the colonies.[19]

---

[16] "A Member of Lincoln's Inn," *Three Letters to Dr. Price, Containing Remarks on his Observations on the Nature of Civil Liberty, the Principles of Government, and the Justice and policy of the War with America* (London, 1776), 156–59.

[17] "An Officer," *Reflections on the Most Proper Means of Reducing the Rebels*, 20–21.

[18] John Wesley, *Some Observations on Liberty* (London, 1776), 22–23.

[19] "An Officer," *Reflections on the Most Proper Means of Reducing the Rebels*, 23. Examples of the persistence of this belief may be found in [James Macpherson], *A Short History of the Opposition during the Last Session of Parliament* (London, 1779), 37, and [Joseph Galloway], *Considerations upon the American Enquiry* (London, 1779), 14.

No single factor operated more powerfully to fuel hostility to Americans than reports of their political and military atrocities. In his diatribe against Americans, Judah Champion had been careful to exclude those recent immigrants who had tried to instill "English principles, and English affections" by giving "regular and permanent laws to America" but who since "the rebellion" had "been obliged to silence, as their lives were endangered by the violence of the faction."[20] The intimidation to which Champion referred seemed to Administration spokesmen to be especially brutal, reprehensible, and inhumane. They castigated "American rebels" for their savagery in "TARRING and *feathering*" those who opposed the resistance movement, "a species of torture" they denounced as both "shocking to humanity" and a blatant departure from the rule of law.[21] The "unexampled brutalities and cruelties individuals, suspected of only a mental affection to his Majesty, have suffered," lamented a writer in January 1777, could not fail to elicit the deepest "pity for the friends of government in the breast of every humane and civilized person."[22]

The early stages of the war provided a fresh catalogue of American cruelties and military deficiencies. "No history will furnish us with more barbarity and savage rage, than in the mode of the present war carried on by the Americans," complained the author of *The Duty of the King and Subject* in July 1776. "Not content with the usual destructive implements of war," he charged, they used "rifle guns and marksmen," practices shunned "by all the military powers of Europe," to pick off British soldiers at a distance.[23] During the British retreat from Lexington, observed another analyst, American soldiers revealed themselves as nothing more than "cowardly assassins" who fired at their enemies "from behind hedges and stone walls,"[24] and, protested another writer in May 1777, their "mean cruelty of destroying Centinels on their post, then lying in wait for individuals, [and] their inhumanities exercised over them" served as glaring "proofs of a mean low barbarity unequalled in the History of Human Things."[25] To cap off these irregular and un-British behaviors, American soldiers reportedly also scalped British soldiers and gouged out the eyes of their captives, the latter practice, according to John Lind, being an especially barbarous "species of torture" that was "peculiar to their selves."[26] Such examples of cruelty left no doubt, as one writer put it in August 1776, that the

[20] Champion, *Reflections on the State of Parties*, 57–58.
[21] *A Full and Circumstantial Account of the Dispute between Great Britain and America* (Glasgow, 1775), 3; John Lind, *An Answer to the Declaration of the American Congress* (London, 1776), 89.
[22] *An Appeal to the Unprejudiced*, 37.
[23] *Duty of the King and Subject*, 30.
[24] "An Officer," *Reflections on the Most Proper Means of Reducing the Rebels*, 14–15.
[25] Edward Topham, *An Address to Edmund Burke, Esq. On his Late Letter Relative to the Affairs of America* (London, 1777), 19.
[26] Lind, *Answer to the Declaration of the American Congress*, 89. See also [Sir Herbert Croft], *An Answer to the Letter from Edmund Burke, Esq. One of the Representatives of the City of Bristol, to the Sheriffs of that City*, 2nd ed. (London, 1777), 33.

Americans' "most unjustifiable Rebellion" was entirely the work "of a lawless and desperate Banditti" who could never be confused with genuine Britons.[27]

Addressing "the state of America" in the House of Lords on May 30, 1777, Thomas, Lord Lyttelton succinctly summarized Administration views on the behavior of the American rebels. Deploring "the anarchy that prevails there; the acts of violence, treachery, cruelty, and injustice, that are daily committed in the country, by our rebellious subjects upon their loyal and dutiful brethren, merely because they would not join in their diabolical schemes of overthrowing all just and legal government," he complained that the "laws [were being] trampled upon, the course of justice interrupted or annihilated, government dissolved, magistrates imprisoned or banished, [and] the faithful and obedient part of the people oppressed, despoiled of their property, or obliged to fly their native land." To "all the horrors of war," he noted, "the rebels had added the brutality of savages and the treachery of cowards."[28] In their efforts to subdue such people, Administration supporters avowed, Britain did not need to apologize for any strategies it pursued. "If in the natural progress of war their Towns have been depopulated," Edward Topham wrote in May 1777,

it is these Men who are to blame; if "the widow has wept on tears of blood" over her husband, it is the humanity of these Men which has occasioned it; if their fields have been laid waste, if Desolation stalks through the land, it is not to be charged to our cruelty, but to the tenderness of those Men who have talked loud for the welfare of America, and have been the pretended assertors of her Freedom.[29]

In view of the many deficiencies of the American colonies, Administration adherents ridiculed suggestions by some British political radicals that they were "the chosen land; that part of the world to which every thing that is truly valuable is said to be retiring" and in which "the simplicity and inno-cency of [the] paradisical states and golden ages of the ancients" would "be renewed" and, as a "consequence, there" would "be neither place-men nor pensioners, nor corruption, nor luxury, nor bribery: and as some would fur-ther add, neither monarchy, nor nobility, nor church, nor clergy" – in "short, none of those things which at present shackle and enslave us, and hinder our progression towards that estate of popular and supreme liberty, after which so many good souls seem to be panting."[30] Making fun of America's "mushroom

---

[27] *An Address to the People of Great-Britain in General and the members of Parliament, and the Leading Gentlemen of Opposition in Particular, on the Present Crisis of American Politics* (Bristol, 1776), 62–63.

[28] Thomas, Lord Lyttelton, speech, May 30, 1777, in William Cobbett et al., eds., *Parliamentary History of England from the Earliest Period to the Year 1803*, 36 vols. (London, 1806–20), 19: 332–33.

[29] Topham, *An Address to Edmund Burke*, 17.

[30] *Considerations Upon the Question, What should be an honest Englishman's Endeavour in this present Controversy between Great-Britain and the Colonies* (London, 1782), 40. For the idea of America as a land of promise, see Jack P. Greene, *The Intellectual Construction of America: Exceptionalism and Identity from 1492 to 1800* (Chapel Hill: University of North Carolina Press, 1993).

generals,"[31] they predicted that the Americans, if they held out very long, would fall under the domination of the New England "puritanical calvinistic sect," who would "rule with such unbridled fury, that the rest[,] feeling the weight of their truly despotic sway, would apply to the first power, that would offer to deliver them from their intestine oppressors."[32]

In Administration circles, comparisons between America and Britain never came out in favor of America. "Generally speaking, every inhabitant of our island is a philosopher, a merchant, a soldier, a mariner, a farmer or an ingenious artist," declared the Government pamphleteer John Knox in 1777; the "Ocean . . . is it[s] bulwark; the constitution its liberty; the law, its protection; and the whole world, its fountain of commerce and wealth." "Independent of the western continent," he declared, "this island is its own defense, and the most perfect state now existing." By contrast, he asked,

What is North America? An immense Desert. And who are the Provincials? A Medley of people composed of English, Scotch, Irish, Germans, Dutch, French, and Indians, parcelled out into a dozen or more governments; opposite in manners, religion, and political opinions: Jealous of each other, and viewing one another in the most contemptible light. The northern colonies hardy, contracted, and superstitious. Those toward the south, liberal, effeminate, gay, and luxurious; while the Indians, who worship the sun and moon, retain a implacable hatred to both, whom they consider as so many robbers or plunderers of their country.

Such a promiscuous and heterogenous blend of people and polities, Knox made clear, could not possibly hope for success against the forces of a superior culture such as metropolitan Britain.[33] Administrative writers "flatter[ed]" themselves, as an anonymous pamphleteer remarked in 1777, "that the success of his majesty's Arms in America" would soon emancipate "his loyal and oppressed subjects there, from the slavery of the demagogues, who now tyrannize over them."[34]

Administration supporters thought that the "great body of the people" in America had lost the capacity "to act or think for themselves," and hoping that a few British victories would bring them to their senses, they asked those "sticklers for liberty" to recall all the benefits they had gained as loyal subjects within the British Empire. "Hath not, during the last half century," Knox inquired, "America, under the protection of Great Britain . . . acquired immense wealth; and" do not "its inhabitants . . . live far more sumptuous[ly] than any nation under the sun?" Did not, he continued, "American commerce, her shipping and her cities . . . increase with a rapidity unparalleled in the history of nations?" and had the Americans not "enjoy'd all the blessings of religious toleration?"

[31] *The American Times: A Satire* (London, 1780), 2.
[32] Cornelius Murdin, *Three Sermons* (Southhampton, 1779), 16.
[33] [John Knox], *The American Crisis, by a Citizen of the World, inscribed to those Members of the Community, vulgarly named Patriots* (London, 1777), 18–19.
[34] *Remarks on the Evidence Delivered in the Petition Presented by The West-India Planters* (London, 1777), 49.

Had not, he asked, "their lives, their properties, their commerce, their cities, their country, their civil and religious liberties . . . been protected at the expence of British valour, and of British blood"? These many benefits, Knox declared in reiterating the logic behind metropolitan efforts to tax the colonies, and "the enormous debt contracted [by Britain] in nourishing these colonies, in defending them against the Indians, and in preserving them from falling under the yoke of France and Spain" far exceeded all the "advantages of commerce, great as they are," that Britain derived from the colonies.[35]

Notwithstanding the whinging of the Opposition in Britain, whom he derisively referred to as "those Members of the Community, vulgarly named Patriots," Knox praised the "unanimity amongst the various members of this celebrated state" on the American question and, employing the language of civility, predicted that, once the Americans had been forced back into the imperial fold, that unanimity would lead to an achievement that would be "most beneficial to the human race," as Britain developed an "empire under the mildest form of government, the wisest laws, and the most liberal system of religion." With the

sword of power falling into the hands of those who know how to use it in the common cause of mankind; giving vigour to our laws throughout every quarter of the globe, and proclaiming freedom to those regions of Asia in particular, who from the remotest periods of antiquity, have been held in fetters and in the most deplorable ignorance,

the British Empire, he rhapsodized, could not fail to rise "to pre-eminence, and to universal empire." "An union producing such beneficial results towards a considerable part of [the] world," Knox wrote, would "give a higher importance to the present aera, than all the dazzling achievements of those heroes, who in gratifying their ambition, their revenge, their avarice, or their lusts, have over-run the earth only to enslave it. An event so desirable," he continued, "will add dignity to our British councils, and it will immortalize the names of those who have been the happy instruments of its accomplishments." In the end, Knox and others were confident, Britain could turn an unfortunate war into a vehicle for the perpetuation of its commercial advantage and imperial dominion and for cementing its reputation as a benevolent nation.[36]

III

Indeed, eighteen months into the war, the Administration had reason for a positive assessment of Britain's military achievements in America. Although the British had suffered significant losses during the early battles around Boston and had soon abandoned that town, together with the whole of Massachusetts, throughout most of 1776 they managed, with a superior and better disciplined and supplied force, to rout the American army at every turn, capturing first

[35] [Knox], *American Crisis*, 16–17.
[36] Ibid., 24–26.

Newport, then New York and much of the area surrounding it. But the American army itself evaded capture and in the winter of 1776–77 won its first victories in New Jersey at Trenton and Princeton. In Britain, these unexpected defeats elicited a volley of criticism in the press and Parliament questioning the legitimacy, justice, humanity, viability, utility, and management of the war, with the Opposition again, as before the war, taking the lead, using the languages of liberty, commerce, and humanity as a foil to the languages of imperial grandeur and state power championed by the Administration and insisting that Britain's future required unrestricted metropolitan supremacy over the colonies.

Richard Price laid out many of the principal ingredients of the Opposition critique in his *Observations on the Nature of Civil Liberty*, published in early 1776 when the British army was still cooped up in Boston. Contending "that a common relation to one supreme executive head; an exchange of kind offices; tyes of interest and affection, and *compacts*" were "sufficient to give the British Empire all the Unity that is necessary," Price denounced the use of coercion to force colonials to acknowledge the supremacy of Parliament as "a gross and flagrant violation of the constitution." In his opinion the resulting war was one "undertaken not only against the principles of our own constitution; but on purpose to destroy other similar constitutions in *America*; and to substitute in their room a military force." By such measures, Price suggested, the Administration had instantly transformed the free empire in which Britons had taken so much pride into a tyrannical one. Defining the word *empire* as "a collection of states or communities united by some common bond or tye," he distinguished between "an Empire of Freemen," in which all the states that composed it had "free constitutions of government, and with respect to taxation and internal legislation" were "independent of the other states, but united by compacts, or alliances, or subjection to a Great Council, representing the whole, or to one monarch entrusted with the supreme executive power," and an "Empire of Slaves," in which "none of the states possess[ed] any independent legislative authority; but" were "all subject to an absolute monarch, whose will is their law." If only "one of the states is free, but governs by its will all the other states," he explained, then that empire, "like that of the Romans in the time of the republic," was "an Empire consisting of one state free, and the rest in slavery."[37]

Price acknowledged that some supporters of the war were "influenced by no other principle, than a regard to what they think the just authority of this country over its colonies, and to the unity and indivisibility of the British Empire," but he was convinced that for the Administration "the only object of the war" was "the extension of dominion; and its only motive . . . the lust of power." Such a war, he asserted, was "horrid!" "To sheath our swords in the bowels of our brethren, and spread misery and ruin among a happy people,

---

[37] Richard Price, *Observations on the Nature of Civil Liberty, The Principles of Government, and the Justice and Policy of the War with America*, 8th ed. (Dublin, 1776), 36, 45–46, 64.

for no other end than to oblige them to acknowledge our supremacy," he wrote, was a vivid contemporary example of "the cursed ambition that led a *Caesar* and an *Alexander*, and many other mad conquerors, to attack peaceful communities, and to lay waste the earth."[38]

But the "hateful" principles of "Pride and the love of dominion" were not the only unsavory motives that drove Administration supporters, according to Price. The "infernal principles" of "blind resentment and the desire of revenge," he lamented, also had "no small share at present in guiding our public conduct." Expressing his astonishment "at the virulence, with which some speak on the present occasion against the Colonies," Price traced that virulence to metropolitan resentment at the success of the colonial resistance. Expecting to encounter "a cowardly rabble who would lie quietly at our feet," Price explained, British forces had instead found themselves opposed by an enraged populace determined to repel "force by force," who, denying "the plenitude of our power over them," insisted "upon being treated as free communities. It is this that has provoked us," Price wrote, "and kindled our governors into rage." This virulence, Price complained, had carried over into the conduct of the war. "However common it has been among mankind," he observed, "the attempt to subjugate" the Americans "by confiscating their effects, burning their towns, and ravaging their territories" constituted "a wanton exertion of cruel ambition," while the refusal of "our own people . . . to enlist" for a war against their own brethren had driven the Administration to "disgraceful" measures, including the establishment of "the laws and religion of *France . . . in Canada, on purpose to obtain the power of bringing . . . an army of French Papists*" against the colonists, the instigation of "wild *Indians* and their own Slaves . . . to attack them," the endeavor "to gain the assistance of a large body of Russians" to be sent to America, and the hiring of "*German* troops" to defend "our Forts and Garrisons" in America.[39]

Price found these developments all the more appalling because they seemed to some extent to mimic British behavior elsewhere in the empire, and, making extensive use of the languages of oppression and injustice, he invited his readers to "Turn your eyes to *India*," where "ENGLISHMEN, actuated by the love of plunder and spirit of conquest," had "depopulated whole kingdoms, and ruined millions of innocent people by the most infamous oppression and rapacity." If, as he was persuaded, the "justice of the nation" had "slept over these enormities" in India, and if the nation had failed fully to grasp their implications for its reputation and character, its efforts "to reduce to servitude its own brethren" in America, he contended, had now made it clear that Britain, "A nation, once the protector of Liberty in distant countries, and the scourge of tyranny, [had] changed into an enemy to Liberty." By refusing to be "content with controuling power over millions of people which gave it every advantage," by "insisting upon such a supremacy over" the Americans "as would leave

[38] Ibid., 66, 70–72.
[39] Ibid., 70–72, 121–24, 133–34.

them nothing they could call their own, and [by] carrying desolation and death among them for disputing it," he declared, a formerly "great and enlightened nation" had managed only to make itself "execrated on both sides of the globe" and to invite the wrath of God for its injustice. Denying that "Freemen" could ever be "governed by force, or dragooned into compliance," Price argued that coercion was "madness" that would only make Americans "detest and avoid you forever" and called for a total change to a policy that would "reclaim them by kindness" and "engage them by moderation and equity." Without such a change, he predicted, only dire calamities could follow, with the "Empire dismembered; the blood of thousands shed in an unrighteous quarrel; our strength exhausted; our merchants breaking; our manufacturers starving; our debts increasing; the revenue sinking; the funds tottering; and all the miseries of a public bankruptcy impending." The resulting crisis, he feared, would invite Britain's "natural enemies," France and Spain, to "seize the opportunity" to complete its ruin. Thus, Price asserted, did "PRUDENCE, no less than HONOUR," require Britain to retract its offensive measures and seek reconciliation.[40]

Appealing to what Menasseh Dawes, "a Gentleman of the Inner Temple," called, in a pamphlet published in December 1776, "the tender feelings of independent men, for injured liberty, for wisdom and discretion lost,"[41] writers of various persuasions throughout the early years of the war followed Price in invoking the language of liberty to condemn the use of force against the colonies as a violation of British libertarian traditions. Following the lead of Adam Smith in the *Wealth of Nations*, George Johnstone, formerly governor of West Florida, in a speech in the House of Commons in December 1777, attributed "the flourishing state to which America had attained in a very few years before our invasion of her liberties . . . to the freedom of the laws which Great Britain had given her," which he referred to as "an epitome of our own government. This," he explained, "was a secret which England first discovered, of rendering her government in the extremities of her wide empire as compact and strong as that of other free nations had been weak and inefficient," so that while "their colonists were slaves; Britain had made hers as free as herself." To support this argument, Johnstone contrasted American development with the "weakness of our governments in the East Indies," where, "governed in Leadenhall-street" by the East India Company, there was "no freedom" but only "wars, tumults, [and] outrages."[42]

Other writers agreed with Johnstone. "The administration of government towards the colonies," declared the Edinburgh minister John Erskine in late 1776, had "been conducted on this [libertarian] plan for a century and a half," with the metropolitan government sometimes "imposing external and

[40] Ibid., 94, 115–16, 132–34.
[41] [Menasseh Dawes], *A Letter to Lord Chatham, concerning The present War of Great Britain against America* (London, 1776), 5.
[42] George Johnstone, speech, December 2, 1777, in Cobbett et al., eds., *Parliamentary History of England*, 19: 520–21.

port duties, but never directly laying internal taxes on the Colonists for their lands, &c. or on their transactions within the precincts of the jurisdiction of their several territories," a division of authority that had left colonists at liberty to manage their own internal affairs.[43] "By this species of constitution," William Pulteney observed in a pamphlet published in January 1778, "the Colonies...possessed...a controul, situated upon the spot, and placed in the hands of the representatives of the people, upon the...executive" and "the administration of justice," with the assemblies enjoying "the same sort of general superintending and inquisitorial power...for controulling public abuses of all kinds, which belongs to the House of Commons in this country," and their members claiming, and "by usage actually" enjoying, "all the political privileges within each Colony, which belong to the members of the British House of Commons." The "claim of Britain to a power of taxing them by the Parliament here, and of altering their Charter of Government, without any application for that purpose from themselves, by the sole power of our Legislature," Pulteney emphasized, was the main grievance that had "united so great a part of Americans in the present contest with Great Britain." Addressing those who doubted that the Administration was the aggressor in the American contest, Pulteney asked them to "recollect, that, before the aera of the Stamp Act, there was no instance of any general combination in America, to resist the authority of this country" and "that such a general combination did immediately take place, after the passing of that act."[44] By the Stamp Act, Willoughby Bertie, 4th Earl of Abingdon, charged in a pamphlet issued in September 1777, Britain had "flung the first *stone* at America, and so (the year 1766 excepted) Great Britain continued this *stoning* of America...to the year 1775; when by Negroes and Indians, the Americans were to be *scalped* and *flayed* alive."[45]

Following the Stamp Act crisis, Erskine noted, the Administration began to think that colonial resistance could be quelled only by "checking their growth, and abridging their liberties." Denying that the colonies were "entitled to a constitution of the same political liberty as that which they [had] left" in England, the Administration adopted policies that assumed that colonial constitutions might "be new modelled and reformed, or suspended and taken away at the will of the sovereign," and then justified its behavior by recruiting "artful and designing men [who] found it no difficult task, to excite or cherish suspicions" among the broader political nation that colonial resistance was part of an ancient colonial plan to throw off dependence upon Britain. The absurdity of this charge seemed to be obvious from the simple fact that, as Erskine pointed out, "No one colony could by itself shake off dependence on the mother country: and no two had any common magistracy or principle of association, till" the

---

43 [John Erskine], *The Equity and Wisdom of Administration, in Measures that have unhappily occasioned the American Revolt, tried by the Sacred Oracles* (Edinburgh, 1777), 12.
44 Pulteney, *Thoughts on the Present State of Affairs with America*, 4.
45 Willoughby Bertie, 4th Earl of Abingdon, *Thoughts on the Letter of Edmund Burke, Esq. to the Sheriffs of Bristol, on the Affairs of America* (Oxford, 1777), 56.

British Government's "attempting to connect them to us by power, connected them to one another in policy."⁴⁶ "If we had not endeavoured to entrench their liberty," Johnstone avowed in December 1777, "they never would have attained – they never would have sought, independence."⁴⁷ "Throughout the whole business of this unhappy contest," the radical John Cartwright lamented in February 1778, the Administration and its lackeys had deluded "the nation" with such "absurdities" as *virtual representation, external taxation, imperial rights, parliamentary omnipotence*, and such like phrases, equally in disgrace to common-sense and the constitution."⁴⁸ "*Supremacy of Parliament* on one hand, and *unconditional submission* on the other," echoed another writer, "are the dogmas and language of Turks, not of Britons."⁴⁹

Not everyone in Opposition attributed the Administration's push for coercion to such highly emotive constitutional issues, however. Some traced it simply to the Administration's "*ill grounded jealousy of the Colonies being* FREE *and* FLOURISHING."⁵⁰ More commonly, others, using the language of corruption, charged that it derived from an instrumental lust for power and patronage. By calling attention to the Crown's existing Irish revenues over which Parliament had no control, William Burke suggested that the Administration was intent on making the American colonies the new Ireland,⁵¹ and the anonymous author of *The Advantageous Situation of Great Britain on the Reduction of America*, a deliciously ironic tract published in February 1777, was also persuaded that America was being taxed for no other purpose than "to support the useless lumber of a court, to be dealt out with a destructive fervor in pensions and gratuities to the servile retainers of administration, to bribe electors, to ensure a majority, to pay tax gatherers, who from their number and dispersion are more mischievous than the tax they are to collect."⁵²

Still other writers took a more straightforward view. Thus, the anonymous author of *Reflections on Our Present Critical Situation*, published in June 1777, traced the decision to use force to national indignation following the colonies' refusal to accept the doctrine "that the authority of parliament was . . . all-powerful, through every part of the dominions of this crown." "Fired" with resentment "and confident in their power to maintain such authority," the

⁴⁶ [Erskine], *Equity and Wisdom of Administration*, 2, 9.
⁴⁷ Johnstone, speech, December 2, 1777, in Cobbett et al., eds., *Parliamentary History*, 19: 520–21.
⁴⁸ John Cartwright, *A Letter to the Earl of Abingdon; Discussing a Position Relative to a Fundamental Right of the Constitution: Contained in his Lordship's Thoughts on the Letter of Edmund Burke, Esq. To the Sheriffs of Bristol* (London, 1778), 37 note.
⁴⁹ *The Case Stated, of Philosophical Ground, Between Great Britain and Her Colonies: or the Analogy Between States and Individuals, Respecting the Term of Political Adultness, Pointed Out* (London, 1778), 26.
⁵⁰ Coriolanus, *A Conciliation with America: Adapted to the Constitutional Rights of the Colonies and the Supremacy of Great-Britain* (London, 1778), 25.
⁵¹ [William Burke et al.], *The Letters of Valens* (London, 1777), x, 127.
⁵² *The Advantageous Situation of Great Britain on the Reduction of America* (London, 1777), 11–13.

"nation," this writer explained, had forgotten, "towards their fellow-subjects[,] that justice, for which the people of this country are so eminently distinguished, and towards themselves, those principles which roused their ancestors at the end of the last century, to restore and confirm the constitution." Forgetting as well the maxim of state that it is never wise to "destroy the source from which, in great measure, our riches flow," the Administration "held forth" that "UNCONDITIONAL submission" was the only acceptable policy and "was deaf to every other idea." Then, American armed resistance "served to exasperate the nation to [such] a pitch, that" it "carried on" the war "with more virulence, than against the natural enemies of this country."[53]

However complex its origins, it seemed to those who opposed the war that, as Dawes wrote in 1776, "Americans[,] for denying obedience to the most afflictive despotism[,]" were being subjected to a war that now was being "openly carried on for *power*," as the Administration with all its "cringing, interested dependants" was holding "forth the iron rod of power, to take our money by new-invented taxes, to sport with the blood of men, to call in mercenaries, to aid in the sanguine task, and lastly, to dip their hands in innocent gore!"[54]

If the Administration's program of military and naval coercion seemed to Opposition writers to violate the principles of British liberty and a free empire, it also appeared heedless of the commercial considerations that had made the empire such an economic success. Writing in September 1777, an author calling himself "An Unconnected Whig" deplored Grenville's neglect of such considerations when he endeavored to tax the colonies. Whether Britain's old commercial system "grew up accidentally, or was the fruit of design," he remarked, "the wit of man could not have devised one more extensive, or one that so effectually answered the ends of this powerful and commercial state."[55] The previous May, Charles Pratt, Earl Camden, in a speech in the House of Lords made much the same point about the decision to employ force when he expressed his regret "that in the beginning of this war, our trade had been considered as an object only of secondary consideration, and indeed as deserving no regard, when brought in competition with the high and uncontroulable supremacy of British legislature."[56] Instead of pursuing "views of interest, with respect to commerce," charged an anonymous pamphleteer in June 1777, the Administration had been guided entirely by the "pride of conquest and [the] vanity of empire."[57] In the British Empire, Matthew Robinson-Morris, 2d Baron Rokeby, insisted in a pamphlet issued in April 1777, "Liberty and commerce" were "the two sources of riches," the symbiotic engines by which the "seat of

[53] *Reflections on Our Present Critical Situation* (London, 1777), 16, 19, 21, 24.

[54] [Dawes], *A Letter to Lord Chatham*, 5, 11.

[55] *An Unconnected Whig's Address to the Public; upon the Present Civil War, the Public Affairs, and the Real Cause of all the National Calamities* (London, 1777), 29.

[56] Charles Pratt, Lord Camden, speech, May 30, 1777, in Cobbett et al., eds., *Parliamentary History*, 19: 341.

[57] "An Officer," *A Letter to the English Nation, on the War with America* (London, 1777), 42.

empire" drew "every thing to itself; whether wealth, power or honour. The money brought by the balance of trade or by any other means into Scotland, into Ireland, the riches of our West Indies, the rapine of our East Indies and even a proportion of tribute from Africa," he pointed out, "all center[ed] in England," and he expressed his regret that, as a result of Britain's "own wantonness," the produce and commerce of North America, which had so long been "reckoned in a high rank among them," could no longer be numbered among them.[58]

IV

As well as the languages of liberty and commerce, people opposed to the American war extensively invoked the languages of familial affection and humanity to make their case. Citing the "history of some battles fought and fortunes acquired in the East Indies" by British plunderers, Erskine lamented that Mexico and Peru were no longer "the only countries, where professed Christians have cast off compassion and humanity,"[59] and Dawes similarly condemned "the savage brutality of the departed Nabob slayers, who have lain wide waste in Asiatic domains, for no other cause but rapine and riches," likening their actions to the "the cruelties practiced by the Dutch at Amboyna." As horrible as these incidents were, however, Dawes thought them "but trifling [when] compared to our dealings against America. The ravages of the former," he pointed out, "were made against aliens, for private property," while "those of the latter are making against a part of *ourselves*, for public loss both of life and treasure."[60] For those who thought of the colonial relationship as one between an imperial mother and colonial children, the Ministry's "hostile conduct," as the Bristol writer Caleb Evans charged in July 1776, resembled the behavior of "mad parents" who would "*whip* a *grown-up* child, instead of using milder and more rational methods to engage him to the performance of what they might think to be his duty."[61] If Britain was the parent of America, such writers suggested, she was, by making war on her own children, indeed acting the part of an "Unnatural mother."[62]

From the outbreak of war, those who opposed coercion condemned it not just as a violation of the civilized norms of familial attachment but also as inhumane. Dawes early decried the Ministry's "measures of Blood, distress and ruin" designed "the better to slaughter our fellow-creatures, employ our army and navy, and promote desolation in the once quiet homes of a useful

---

[58] Matthew Robinson-Morris, 2d Baron Rokeby, *Peace the Best Policy or Reflections upon the Appearance of a Foreign War* (London, 1777), 47.

[59] Erskine, *Equity and Wisdom of Administration*, 5–6.

[60] [Dawes], *A Letter to Lord Chatham*, 42.

[61] Caleb Evans, *Political Sophistry Detected, or Brief Remarks on the Rev. Mr. Fletcher's late Tract, Entitled 'American Patriotism'* (Bristol, 1776), 34.

[62] *America, An Ode. To the People of England* (London, 1776), 4.

and prosperous people,"[63] and during a debate in the House of Lords in May 1777, the earl of Shelburne denounced the Ministry for its "barbarous, unjust and tyrannical [behavior] toward their brethren and fellow subjects."[64] "You have," the earl of Chatham charged, "made descents upon their coasts; you have burnt their towns, plundered their country, made war upon the inhabitants, confiscated their property, proscribed and imprisoned their persons."[65] For Capel Loft, accusations of the inhumanity of British troops at the capture of Long Island only confirmed him in the conviction "that inhumanity ever stalks in the rear or van of war, or will have its time and place when war is gone forth."[66] War was such "a dreadful evil," Price observed, that it could be justified only by "the necessity . . . to secure some *essential* interest against unjust attacks." Without such necessity, he averred, war could only make "humanity shudder."[67] Dawes expressed his revulsion at the "avidity" with which the war's supporters cheered every "dazzling intelligence of success" in the Ministry's efforts "to butcher the Americans into the terms of government." By "stirring up a war so destructive to common humanity; so offensive to christianity,"[68] he suggested, the Ministry had proven themselves to be what the poet Thomas Day denounced as "vindictive tyrants," who wrathfully, criminally, remorselessly, and inhumanely had unleashed the "flames of vengeance, and . . . ruthless steel" against their American brethren.[69] Already apprehensive lest the Americans lure the French into the war on their side, an anonymous writer in August 1775 predicted that such a development would force Britain to bring its American army home to defend Britain, where, he suggested, they might well "practice on the inhabitants of this island that spirit of ungovernable licence, with which they have been accustomed to treat the persons . . . and properties of our American Fellow-Subjects, making no distinction of age, or of sex, nor sparing the loyal more than the disloyal."[70]

Opposition writers found proposals for the use of Indians, slaves, Russians, and Germans particularly inhumane. When in a speech in the House of Commons in October 1776 William Henry Lyttelton, a former governor of South Carolina and Jamaica, proposed to recruit slaves into the British army, Johnstone immediately rose to denounce it as a plan "too black and horrid to be adopted."[71] "Heaven forbid that slaves should ever become the masters of freemen; or that Russian ferocity should triumph over English valour

---

[63] [Dawes], *A Letter to Lord Chatham*, 10.
[64] Earl of Shelburne, speech, May 30, 1777, in Cobbett et al., eds., *Parliamentary History*, 19: 346–47.
[65] Earl of Chatham, speech, May 30, 1777, in Cobbett et al., eds., *Parliamentary History*, 19: 343.
[66] [Capel Loft], *Observations on Mr. Wesley's Second Calm Address* (London, 1777), 49.
[67] Price, *Additional Observations*, 71.
[68] [Dawes], *A Letter to Lord Chatham*, 22, 52.
[69] Thomas Day, *The Desolation of America* (London, 1777), 23.
[70] *Reflections on Our Present Critical Situation*, 10.
[71] *Johnstone's Speech on American Affairs*, 4.

in any part of the world," William Burke declared in expressing his delight that the Ministry had been unable to persuade the Russian government to supply "20,000 Calmucks and Cossacks, to lay waste with fire and sword the habitations of Englishmen, and to turn one of the fairest parts of the British dominions into one of their Tartarian desarts." Although he deplored the fact that a combination of "German penury and English prodigality" had enabled the Ministry to assemble a "vast army" that, along with Britain's Indian allies, could go on "slaughtering, burning, and plundering," Burke denied that such were the best "means of reconciling the minds of the people to our government" and called for an end to the war, even though it would mean that German mercenaries would be deprived "of the largest part of the bloody glories they are to purchase by the slaughter of Englishmen" and that "fewer English scalps were to decorate the martial dwellings of the savage allies of our humane Ministry." To continue this inhumane war, he wrote, would lead only to the "Hessians ... slaughter[ing] more men in cold blood, ... burn[ing] more ... towns," and producing still "more mutual rapine of English on English."[72] Reports from America seemed to confirm these fears, an anonymous returning officer acknowledging in a pamphlet published in June 1777 that German troops seemed far "more intent on plunder than conquest, they rob and insult indiscriminately friends and foes," he claimed, even daring "to proceed to the extremes of barbarism," with "women no longer find[ing] a security in their sex, from the lust and insolence of these human savages."[73]

When in the late fall of 1777 news of General John Burgoyne's defeat arrived in Britain along with information that he had made extensive use of Indians during his ill-fated campaign, the Opposition made the inhumanity of the war its main emphasis. "For the two years that a certain noble lord [Lord George Germaine] had presided over American affairs," charged Opposition leader Charles James Fox in opening debate on this subject in the House of Commons on December 2, 1777, "the most violent, scalping, tomahawk measures have been pursued."[74] Warning that "Great Britain never, never, can build up fame or dignity to itself, upon acts of injustice and oppression," James Luttrell, M.P. for Stockbridge, the next day denounced the employment of "savages to butcher" indiscriminately American civilians and vowed his intention "to take every opportunity of repeating my abhorrence of the mercenary and savage principles of a civil war, which has never yet held out constitutional terms of peace."[75] Five days later, his brother, Temple Luttrell, M.P. for Milborne Port, challenged the Administration's contentions that the Americans had also tried to enlist Indians on their side, contending that the American Congress had "abhorred the thought of those savages being made parties in our unhappy

---

[72] [William Burke et al.], *Letters of Valens*, xiv, 13–14, 36, 127.

[73] "An Officer," *Letter to the English Nation*, 24.

[74] Charles James Fox, speech, December 2, 1777, in Cobbett et al., eds., *Parliamentary History*, 19: 523–24.

[75] James Luttrell, speech, December 3, 1777, in ibid., 19: 535, 538.

disputes" and citing the "sanguinary proclamations" Burgoyne had issued from Canada threatening American settlers with Indian warfare as proof that "Such acts of brutal ferocity" had "been reserved for the allies of modern Englishmen and Christians, against their fellow-subjects on the other side of the Atlantic."[76]

But it fell to Britain's former great war minister, the earl of Chatham, to provide the most scathing and colorful review of ministerial conduct of the war on the floor of the House of Lords on December 5, 1777. "The mode of carrying on the war," he said, "was the most bloody, barbarous, and ferocious recorded in the annals of mankind." First, by sweeping "every corner of Germany for men" and searching "the darkest wilds of America for the scalping-knife," and then by employing "Savages . . . to carry ruin and devastation among our subjects in America" and putting the "tomahawk and scalping-knife . . . into the hands of this most brutal and ferocious of the human species," he declared, the Ministry had insured that the conflict with Americans would be not "an honourable war," but one "founded in weakness, barbarity and inhumanity." Contrasting the "fame and reknown we gained in the last war with the feats and disgraces of the present," he observed that the former had taken Britain to "the highest pinnacle of glory," while the latter "had sullied and tarnished the arms of Britain for ever, by employing savages in our service, by drawing them up in a British line, and mixing the scalping-knife and tomahock with the sword and firelock." "Such a mode of warfare was," he asserted, "a contamination, a pollution of our national character, a stigma which all the waters of the rivers Delaware and Hudson would never wash away" and would so "rankle in the breast of Americans, and sink so deep into it, that he was almost certain they would never forget or forgive the horrid injury." The expectation that peace could ever "be effected, as long as German bayonet and Indian scalping-knife were threatened to be buried in the bowels of our American brethren," he said, was "absurd, mad, and foolish." "Before they consent to treat with us," he insisted, "the colonies must consider us as friends," and he declared his opinion that "a formal acknowledgment of our errors, and a renunciation of our unjust, ill-founded, and oppressive claims" would have to precede any attempt to conciliate.[77]

When Lord Dunmore, the deposed governor of Virginia, sought to counter Chatham's characterization of the savagery of British military activities in America by contending that "the Americans exceeded the Indians in barbarity" and cited a number of instances "to prove that they did not even affect humanity, but were most industriously cruel, most wantonly inhuman," the duke of Richmond, speaking in support of Chatham, "denied . . . that the assertion that the Americans had first employed and attempted to employ the Indians had been proved" and said that he "was well convinced from authentic information, that" Burgoyne, "or his army, had been contaminated from the contact of

[76] Temple Luttrell, speech, December 10, 1777, in ibid., 19: 578–79. See also the speeches by Henry Cruger and John Wilkes of the same date, in ibid., 19: 569, 585.
[77] Earl of Chatham, speech, December 5, 1777, in ibid., 19: 487–89.

Indian savages serving with them as fellow-soldiers in the field, and associating with them in other scenes of familiarity and intimacy," a result he decried "as the cursed effect of associating Christians with savages." Nor did Richmond accept the Administration's claim "that the Indians had been found useful," contending rather "that exactly the opposite was the case; for that employing of the savages was the very cause of Mr. Burgoyne's defeat. That their cruelties had excited the whole country, men, women and children, to rise upon the British army, and come upon them with staves, pitch-forks, &c. and endeavour to destroy them."[78]

Two months later, on February 6, 1778, Edmund Burke offered a detailed examination of the extent and implications of the Ministry's use of Indians as military allies, thereby breaking a long silence on American affairs that, as he had told his Bristol constituents the previous May, he had imposed on himself because he had become "convinced, that in the present state of things, all opposition to any measures proposed by ministers, where the name America appears," was "vain and frivolous."[79] In a motion for papers on that subject, Burke complained that the Ministry had provided the House with "no account... of the irregular forces, particularly those of" Britain's "savage allies; although" it had placed "great dependence... upon them, and they had been obtained at a very great expence," and argued that "it was necessary to examine into this point; because" the Ministry had lately "strenuously recommended" an "extension of" the Indian "mode of making war" by proposing in the next campaign to abandon "a war of conquest," which the Ministry "now found to be impracticable," in favor of "a war of distress and intimidation." But such a plan, Burke objected, had already been tried unsuccessfully in the Burgoyne campaign, and if, for that reason, "it did not promise to be very decisive as a plan merely military," neither, he argued, could it "be attended with" any "collateral advantages, whether considered with respect to our reputation, as a civilized people, or to our policy, in regard to the means of reconciling the minds of the colonies to his Majesty's government."[80]

Burke then turned to an examination of "the nature of a war, in which Indians were the actors against a civilized people," and observed that "the fault of employing them did not consist in their being of one colour or another; in their using one kind of weapon or another." Rather, he said, it was "in their way of making war; which was so horrible, that it not only shocked the manners of all civilized nations, but far exceeded the ferocity of any other barbarians that have been recorded either by ancient or modern history." Moreover, because the Indians had been "so entirely reduced in number and power," Burke thought that they "were now only formidable from their cruelty;

[78] Duke of Richmond, speech, December 5, 1777, in ibid., 19: 505–07, 510–11.

[79] *A Letter from Edmund Burke, Esq. One of the Representatives in Parliament for the City of Bristol, To John Farr and John Harris, Esqrs. Sheriffs of that City, on the Affairs of America* (Dublin, 1777), 12.

[80] Edmund Burke, speech, February 6, 1778, in Cobbett et al., eds., *Parliamentary History*, 19: 694–95.

and to employ them was merely to be cruel ourselves in their persons: and thus, without even the lure of any essential service, to become chargeable with all the odious and impotent barbarities, which they would inevitably commit, whenever they were called into action." Dismissing ministerial "apologies" that the army had taken "great care . . . to prevent that indiscriminate murder of men, women, and children" and its insistence that Indians "were always accompanied by disciplined troops to prevent their irregularities," he argued that "it was so utterly impossible for any care or humanity to prevent or even restrain" Indian "enormities, that the very attempt was ridiculous," and that their employment under restraint "could have answered no purpose," because "their only effective use consisted in that cruelty which was to be restrained," citing many examples "that whole nations of savages had been bribed to take up the hatchet, without a single soldier among them." The fact that the Ministry had spent £150,000 to keep "only a few hundred [Indians] in the field and only for a short time" suggested to Burke that "our ministers thought that inhumanity and murder could not be purchased at too dear a rate."[81]

Burke also took the occasion to pass "some severe strictures on the endeavour in two of the southern colonies to excite an insurrection of the negro-slaves against their masters." Insisting that "the proclamation for that purpose was directly contrary to the common and statute law of this country, as well as to the general law of nations," he "stated, in strong colours, the nature of an insurrection of negroes" and "the horrible consequences that might ensue from constituting 100,000 fierce barbarian slaves, to be both the judges and executioners of their masters." Although the "rigour and care of the white inhabitants in Virginia and Maryland had providentially kept down the insurrection of the negroes," Burke inquired what means, had they succeeded, could have been devised "for governing those negroes, when they had reduced the province to their obedience, and made themselves masters of the houses, goods, wives, and daughters of their murdered lords?," predicting that another war would have been required to subdue them, thus "adding confusion to confusion, and destruction to destruction."[82]

The only result of this wanton and inhumane deployment of Indians and slaves, Burke declared, was "that our national honour had been deeply wounded, and our character as a people debased in the estimation of foreigners, by those shameful, savage, and servile alliances, and their barbarous consequences." "Instead of any military effect or value," the use of Indians, he said, "had only led to defeat, ruin, and disgrace; serving to embitter the minds of all men, and to unite and arm all the colonies against us," while "the ineffective attempt" to incite

the negroes was the grand cause of that greater aversion and resentment, which appeared in the southern, than in many of the central and northern colonies; of their being the first to abjure the King; and of the declaration made by Virginia, that if the rest should submit, they would notwithstanding hold out singly to the last extremity: for what

[81] Ibid., 19: 694–98.
[82] Ibid., 19: 698–99.

security could they receive, that, if they admitted an English governor, he would not raise the negroes against them, whenever he thought it good to construe any occasional disturbances into a rebellion, and to adopt martial law as a system of government?[83]

The "alienation of affections, and the distrust and terror of our government, which had been brought on by these inhuman measures," Burke concluded, required that Parliament "enquire seriously and strictly into them; and, by the most marked and public disapprobation, . . . convince the world that they had no share in practices which were not more disgraceful to a great and civilized nation, than they were contrary to all true policy, and repugnant to all feelings of humanity." It "was not in human nature for any people to place a confidence in those to whom they attributed such unparalleled sufferings and miseries," he continued, "and the colonies would never be brought to believe, that those who were capable of carrying on a war in so cruel and dishonourable a manner, could be depended on for a sound, equitable, and cordial peace; much less that they could be safely entrusted with power and dominion."[84]

Other members joined Burke in using the language of humanity to criticize the Ministry's deployment of Indians in America,[85] and when the Administration ignored Burke's call for an inquiry, John Wilkes took up the cause. On March 2, 1778, he pressed for an investigation into "the horrid cruelties said to be committed on our fellow-subjects . . . both to vindicate the honour of our sovereign, and the humanity of the nation," alleging that in "the last campaign scarcely fewer women and children in some parts where the war raged with the greatest fury, expired under the tomahawk and scalping-knife, than were killed by the sword or bayonet among those who bore arms," "horrors," he said, that "not only disgraced our arms but degraded the name of Englishmen" and "fixed a foul stain on our national character."[86]

V

Critics of the war questioned not only its justice, its compatibility with English traditions of liberty, its attention to commercial considerations, and its humanity, but also, as they had done with the earliest turn to coercion, its viability and conduct. As early as June 1777, an officer returning from America published a substantial pamphlet that endeavored to make a case for the proposition "that this war has been wantonly begun, foolishly continued, and, from the melancholy prospect it exhibits at present, may have a fatal conclusion." This was a war, he declared, that "might, and ought, to have been avoided: it was folly in the extreme to engage in it; and, as an addition to our distress, it appears to be as badly conducted abroad, as it was wantonly begun at home." The Administration, this writer charged, had mishandled the war from the beginning.

[83] Ibid., 19: 699.
[84] Ibid.
[85] See James Luttrell and Thomas Pownall, speeches, February 6, 1778, in ibid., 19: 702–04, 707.
[86] John Wilkes, speech, March 2, 1778, in ibid., 19: 811–14.

First, it had completely underestimated the Americans' capacity for resistance. "The idea of the Americans taking up arms . . . was at first a subject of merriment," he wrote, the Administration affecting "to ridicule it; and, not content at laughing at it themselves, they employed a crowd of pensionary scribblers to ridicule it in print." Then, it had miscalculated the number of troops that would be required to subdue the Americans so that, "to the scandal of British arms," the Administration had been forced into the "humiliating necessity of engaging mercenary troops" from Germany in the vain effort "to recover by *violence* what was lost by *folly*." Along with British army "cruelties" against the colonists, the "abuses and irregularities of these foreigners," he contended, had "served only to invigorate the uplifted arm of the undisciplined peasant [in America], and inspire him with fortitude," with the result that the "whole Continent" of America seemed to be "animated with one soul" and to "have become soldiers and sailors" without neglecting agricultural production and with little interruption of their external trade, sending to France all those products that had formerly gone to England.[87]

"After irritating, by oppression, the Colonies, to revolt; and, after having menaced them with the penalties of rebellion," this writer pointed out, the Ministry, after nearly two years of fighting a costly war, had little to show for its efforts. "We have got New-York and Rhode-Island, where we are necessarily compelled to keep garrisons; and excepting Canada and Nova Scotia, we have no other land in America," he wrote. "It is neither easy to subdue an extent of country of 1000 leagues, nor very practicable to preserve it; and if we are obliged" to "garrison every acre of land that we subdue, which we absolutely must, if we mean to derive any benefit from it, it will require a greater force than the minister can obtain." "If he means to prosecute the war with a prospect of success," he added, "the Minister will find the aid of 20,000 Russians extremely necessary." From "the progress of our arms hitherto," he added, "we have no reason to expect that America can be conquered; and it is now become a question of importance, to enquire how long it will be adviseable to prosecute a war, which exhausts our riches, and injures our commerce, without the smallest prospect of advantage in return." What "prospect have we in the prosecution of this expensive war but ruin?" he asked. Arguing that only the "pride of conquest and vanity of empire" could drive any continuing effort "to attempt the recovery of our colonies," he lamented that "all views of interest, with respect to commerce," were "at an end" and predicted that Britain would "repent hereafter of not admitting" the colonies' "independence, and of not making a treaty with them, while they were disposed to unite with us."[88]

Along with Ireland, the West Indian colonies, as another writer said, looked upon Britain's claim of omnipotency over the colonies "with terror" and "a

[87] "An Officer," *Letter to the English Nation*, 7, 9–11, 21, 24–25, 36–37, 45.
[88] Ibid., 37, 42–43, 55, 58. For similar arguments, see *Reflections on Our Present Critical Situation*, 1, 3, 8–11, 15–17, 22, 29.

jealous eye."[89] Although the West Indian colonies had "not been able, with the northern colonies, to make the paramount power of the British parliament at present a subject of hostile discussion," warned still another, "yet too many of them," he said in singling out "the conduct of Jamaica and Barbadoes," favored "opposition, and wishfully look[ed] forward . . . to a desirable object, to an independency."[90] Contending that American successes in the war had provided "full ground to look on the whole business in a quite different light," the author of the *Reflections On Our Present Critical Situation* argued that reuniting "with America ought, and must be the first object for this country" and called for whatever "CONCESSIONS, which sound policy certainly, and which justice and reason, perhaps, equally call for," might be required to bring about the reconciliation that would terminate "the internal confusion" and "misfortune" in "this distracted empire" and "reinstate this country in its former splendor."[91]

Burgoyne's defeat at Saratoga seemed to be the last straw in ministerial ineptitude. Speaking in the House of Lords on February 16, 1778, Lord Camden "lamented the fatal counsels which had brought this nation into its present alarming situation; and the supineness of the people, in suffering themselves to be governed by such weak and destructive measures." At first, Camden said, the Ministry had been sure

that a few thousand men would look America into submission; again, that the resistance proceeded only from the ambitious views of a few individuals; and that a force sufficient to free the people from the tyranny of their leaders, would immediately put an end to the revolt; and finally when they failed in all their predictions and promises, relative to the degree and extent of the resistance, and the disposition of the people there, then, that it would be necessary to exert the full force of this country, to compel them to a full acknowledgment of the high-sounding terms and big words of the supreme rights of parliament, and unconditional submission; yet,

he despaired, "two campaigns have since passed; the whole strength of this country has been exerted; and what has been the consequence?"[92]

At the same time, however, Burgoyne's defeat raised war opponents' hopes for an end to the war, and the first half of 1778 generated an astonishing number of proposals for reconciliation. Alexander Dalrymple, who was extensively involved in East India Company affairs, was an advocate for conciliation on terms that would simply waive "the discussion of that dangerous question, 'How far the authority of this country extended over America.'"[93] Using the

[89] Willoughby Bertie, 4th Earl of Abingdon, *Thoughts on the Letter of Edmund Burke, Esq; To the Sheriffs of Bristol, on the Affairs of America*, in Paul H. Smith, ed., *English Defenders of American Freedoms 1774–1778* (Washington, D.C.: Library of Congress, 1972), 223–24.

[90] *Plan of Re-Union between Great Britain and Her Colonies* (London, 1782), 5.

[91] *Reflections on Our Present Critical Situation*, 8, 12–13, 15, 17.

[92] Lord Camden, speech, February 16, 1778, in Cobbett et al., eds., *Parliamentary History*, 19: 740–41.

[93] [Alexander Dalrymple], *Considerations on the Present State of Affairs Between England and America* (London, 1778), 23.

pseudonym "Coriolanus," another writer argued that Britain should go much further to recapture the affections of the colonies. The course of the war, he said, had made it clear that the "doctrine" of absolute colonial subjection to Parliament could never be put

> into execution, with so enlightened a people as the Americans are universally allowed to be; or indeed with any other people, except those who are conquered, or when colonies are in a state of INFANCY; and then their weakness, not their inclination, obliges them to submit to almost any thing that government may choose to impose on them.

"As all men of experience and candor allow[ed]," moreover, Coriolanus also thought that it was "absolutely impossible to restrain so numerous and so sagacious a people as his Majesty's American subjects from the free exercise of every source of industry that tends to promote their interest." Thus, he argued that Britain should "make a *virtue of necessity*, and grant them, by favor, what is really no more than their undoubted right." Only with such concessions, he believed, might "the authors of American *independency*" ever "recover from their dangerous delusion, and return to a state of peace and security" under British aegis.[94]

In contrast to Coriolanus, the anonymous author of an *Address to the Rulers of the State*, published in June 1778 and signed "A Friend to Great-Britain," proposed to acknowledge American independence. In his view, Burgoyne's loss at Saratoga had provided "the fatal and most complete experience that conquering America, by arms, is impracticable," and he asked his readers "not to indulge any farther the idle thoughts of coercive measures" and to "give up at once the imaginary *punctilo* which has hitherto deluded you, and [thereby] save the *real honour* of this great empire." "*Your first step towards the recovery of the national consequence of England*," he charged the Administration, "*must be*" to offer the "colonies a noble example, worthy of their imitation, and return to them *unconditionally*, that they may be induced to return to you." "By immediately withdrawing our troops from their coasts, repealing every obnoxious act, (either prohibitory or restrictive,) and passing one to acknowledge what we cannot deny, (the independency of America,) you may not only put an immediate end to our own misfortunes," he advised, but also create the basis for "a firm alliance to succeed to the most unnatural and hopeless war." Calling upon "England never [to] think again of employing cannon to negotiate peace with her colonies," he challenged "Englishmen and Americans, mutually embracing one another," to thereby "lay the foundations of a more glorious and lasting empire, than that of despotism, which (to our disgrace) we seemed inclined to establish in the colonies, under the pretence of taxing them." Had Britain pursued this course "four years ago," he remarked, it would not have "wasted thirty millions of money, *lost* thirteen provinces, three millions of subjects, a trade of nine yearly millions, fifteen thousand mariners, thirty thousand soldiers, the confidence of monied men, and unanimity at home!" And,

---

[94] "Coriolanus," *A Conciliation with America*, 15–16, 19, 25, 27, 54.

he suggested, Britain, "respected eighteen years ago, all over the globe, would still be so at this hour; and we should name governors, instead of *stooping* to send ambassadors to America."[95]

The Administration stopped far short of recognizing American independence and withdrawing British forces from America. Instead, it abandoned all claims to tax the colonies and pushed through the repeal of the Declaratory Act, which Camden sarcastically characterized as a program "from those who promised everything and effected nothing; confessing that we are unequal to the task; and that the only means left untried is to offer to accede to what had been so often said we never would consent to, while we had a man to fight, or a shilling to spend."[96] The Ministry also sent commissioners to America to undertake peace negotiations but forbade them to acknowledge American independence. As John Cartwright pointed out in March 1778, that effort had little chance of success because the American Congress had already, in its negotiations with an earlier commission in the fall of 1776, made such an acknowledgment the precondition for any formal negotiations with Britain.[97] If this restriction had not already doomed Britain's proposed negotiations, a commission manifesto penned by commissioner Alan Ramsay, a hard-line supporter of coercion, condescendingly offered pardons to American resistance leaders and threatened an escalation of the war if they did not immediately enter into negotiations on ministerial terms. The commission thereby insured that the American congress would dismiss its proposals, as an anonymous pamphleteer wrote, "with contempt."[98] Having "so long persisted in the mad attempt to dragoon free men into an unconditional submission . . . by the inhuman use of the tomahawk and the scalping-knife" and having thereby "sinned against America beyond forgiveness," the Ministry in its "attempt to conciliate," remarked Cartwright, now had "the folly to insult their victors with offers of their merciful pardons."[99]

With the failure of these negotiations, hopes for reconciliation dimmed, and the Ministry's orders to its American commanders "to carry on the war in such a sort, as should convince America of the determined purpose of this country to prosecute it with unremitting severity" left no doubt in the minds of the war's opponents that the Ministry fully intended, as Fox asserted in the House of Commons, "to prosecute the war in as . . . sanguinary a manner as possible."[100] In the House of Lords, the earl of Derby expressed his certainty that these orders "implied an intention of burning . . . towns, butchering . . . innocent and

95 "A Friend to Great-Britain," *An Address to the Rulers of the State* (London, 1778), 5, 21–22, 24.
96 Lord Camden, speech, February 16, 1778, in Cobbett et al., eds., *Parliamentary History*, 19: 741.
97 [John Cartwright], *The Memorial of Common-Sense, upon the Present Crisis between Great-Britain and America* (London, 1778), 21–23.
98 "Friend to Great-Britain," *Address to the Rulers of the State*, 39.
99 Cartwright, *Memorial of Common-Sense*, 19.
100 Charles James Fox, speech, June 3, 1779, in Cobbett et al., eds., *Parliamentary History*, 20: 844.

defenceless inhabitants, in cold blood; massacring old men, women, and every degree of the defenceless of both sexes, to the infant on the breast" and "relying solely on the tomahawk and scalping-knife" to do so,[101] while in the House of Commons John Wilkes declared that he fully expected a continuation of the same pattern of "plunder and cruelty" that, "since we have brought into the quarrel the mercenaries of Germany, and the savages of America," had "marked the progress of the royal army and its allies."[102] In the same debate, the duke of Richmond argued that "the war, from the commencement, had been carried on with every act of injustice that could tend to make the name of Englishmen odious in America" and cited a "regular and full account of the barbarities exercised by his Majesty's officers, and those under them in America," published by Congress and partly reprinted in the *Leyden Gazette*, to show "the ravages and rapine of the soldiery, who, following the examples set them by the Hessians, plundered the poor inhabitants, and stole every thing they could lay their hands on."[103]

In October 1776, George Johnstone early expressed the fear that the war might cost Britain its "reputation for justice and humanity,"[104] a prospect that also worried the earl of Abingdon when, on December 11, 1777, he spoke in favor of his motion to protest the "savage barbarity" of the Administration's treatment of American prisoners of war interned in British jails. "Humanity," he announced, "has ever been the characteristic of Englishmen; but, my lords, whether corruption has, with our morals, changed our very feelings, or whether it be owing to that exotic influence which has so long directed our councils, or not, it is not for me to determine; but, my lords," he continued, "instead of humanity, our national character is now stamped with inhumanity; and what is worse, we have the damning proofs before our eyes."[105]

As indeed they had. For more than a decade, metropolitans had found themselves confronted and having to come to terms with one example after another of the inhumanity of Britons overseas. To their embarrassment, they had learned of the "unpardonable avarice" of nabobs who had "plucked" most parts of India "till they could bear no more,"[106] of the planter-generated war to expropriate the lands of the black Caribs in St. Vincent, of the "barbarous" traders on the coast of Africa who were "cruel enough to" enslave their "unfortunate" purchases and sell them to planters in the West Indies and North America,[107] and of the "[in]humanity" exhibited by American Creole slaveholders in their treatment of their enslaved laborers.[108]

---

[101] Earl of Derby, speech, November 26, 1778, in ibid., 19: 1291.
[102] John Wilkes, speech, November 25, 1778, in ibid., 19: 1336.
[103] Duke of Richmond, speech, December 7, 1778, in ibid., 20: 17.
[104] *Johnstone's Speech on American Affairs*, 2–3.
[105] Earl of Abingdon, speech, December 11, 1777, in Cobbett et al., eds., *Parliamentary History*, 19: 593.
[106] "A Friend to Great-Britain," *Address to the Rulers of the State*, 35; Charles James Fox, speech, May 21, 1777, in Cobbett, ed., *Parliamentary History*, 19: 282.
[107] "A Friend to Great-Britain," *Address to the Rulers of the State*, 35.
[108] [Meredith], *Historical Remarks on the Taxation of Free States*, 4.

None of these discoveries, they knew, spoke well for British humanity. But these all involved Britons living and operating outside Britain. What was so troubling about the cruelties exhibited by the war was that they were not confined to Britons overseas but sponsored and heavily supported by Britons at home. In a speech in the House of Lords on December 7, 1778, Dr. John Hinchcliffe, bishop of Peterborough, pondered the meaning of Britain's extensive complicity in the cruelties involved in British war efforts in America. "I beg leave to remind your lordships," he said, "that it is principally owing to the mild influence of Christianity, that every nation professing the belief of it, has as it were by common consent set bounds to the savage fierceness of revenge and cruelty. Shall we, then," he asked, "be the first among the nations of Europe, to forget so very essential a part of its excellence, as the humanity and benevolence it inspires? Shall we, I say, be the first to establish desolation upon system; and to gratify an impotent resentment" and "deal fruitless destruction on the wives and children of an enemy we cannot conquer, or of friends we can no longer protect?"[109] "For some time," Sir George Yonge reportedly declared in the House of Commons in December 1778, "he had thought [that] we were a people devoted to destruction: that it now grew more certain, and we seemed resolved to deserve it: that the first capital symptom was, a total want of wisdom in our rulers; the last finishing one was, a total want of humanity in our people."[110] "We have abused and adulterated government ourselves," wrote the author of the *Case Stated*, "stretching our depredations and massacres, not only to the Eastern, but Western world," where "the guilt of murder and robbery in ten thousand instances" was "now crying aloud for vengeance on the head of Great Britain."[111] "How melancholy is the consideration to the friends to this country that in the East and in the West, in Asia and in America, the name of an Englishman is become a reproach," wrote an anonymous author in March 1779; in "Europe we are not loved enough to have a single friend," and "from such a situation there is but a step to hatred or contempt."[112] In view of these undesirable fruits, a few people even questioned the desirability of empire. Thus did Coriolanus speculate about whether "vast territorial acquisitions, especially at a very great distance," were compatible "with the true interest of a great commercial state,"[113] while Richard Price observed that efforts "to extend civil power over distant nations, and form grand unwieldy empires," had "been one great source of human misery."[114]

[109] Bishop of Peterborough, speech, December 7, 1778, in Cobbett et al., eds., *Parliamentary History*, 20: 10.
[110] Sir George Yonge, speech, December 4, 1778, in ibid., 19: 1402.
[111] *The Case Stated*, 89.
[112] "An Englishman," *Considerations upon the French and American War. In a Letter to a Member of Parliament* (London, 1779), 38.
[113] Coriolanus, *A Conciliation with America*, 5.
[114] Richard Price, *Additional Observations on the Nature and Value of Civil Liberty, And the War with America* (London, 1777), 75.

VI

Men in power had no doubts about the utility of empire and about the need for a tight dominion over that empire. Shocked by Burgoyne's defeat, the Ministry found it difficult to believe that such a numerically superior and more thoroughly trained and armed force could have been lost, and squabbled over whether, as James MacPherson would later phrase it, there had been "an error in planning at home, or a defect in the execution abroad."[115] After war advocates learned that Sir William Howe's army remained intact and that Britain still had a formidable army in America, however, they began to put Burgoyne's loss in perspective and endeavored to build public support for continuing the war. In such an extensive empire, "the occasional loss of very valuable possessions and dependencies will be the fate of every contest in which we are engaged, but these circumstances, though cruel to our feelings at the time," William Eden assured readers, "may be set right at the close of the war."[116] "The Romans themselves were not always invincible" and "frequently lost provinces and armies; yet," MacPherson announced, invoking the language of imperial grandeur, "they rose superior to all nations. The profits and losses of war can only be estimated, on the day, which concludes a peace," he wrote, assuring his readers that "that day cannot be distant" when the war would "be attended with that glory, which the spirit and exertion of a great state cannot fail to acquire."[117]

In response to demands for an end to the war, reconciliation, or even recognition of American independence, war supporters argued that the stakes were too high to give up the struggle. Such a move, Eden insisted, would lead not only to the loss of the colonies but also to that of "our islands, all our commercial establishments and distant possessions, our navy, our foreign garrisons, the free entrance and use of the different seas, and all the various parts of that complicated machine of trade, credit, and taxation" – in short, all of the imperial trappings that then made up "our position among the states of the world."[118] The loyalist Joseph Galloway insistently pressed home the same point, that the "power, the commerce, the constitution of this country, can exist no longer than America is dependent upon her." Without exception, he suggested, using the language of national security, national preservation must trump all other considerations.[119]

From this perspective, the Administration had little choice but to push on with the war, a course having wide support, albeit, as an anonymous author

---

[115] [James Macpherson], *A Short History of the Opposition during the Last Session of Parliament* (London, 1779), 10.
[116] *Four Letters to the Earl of Carlisle, from William Eden,* 3rd ed. (London, 1780), 67.
[117] [Macpherson], *Short History of the Opposition,* 58. See also "Honestus," *The Delusive and Dangerous Principles of the Minority, Exposed and Refuted in a Letter to Lord North* (London, 1778), xxxv.
[118] Eden, *Four Letters to the Earl of Carlisle,* 3rd ed., 57.
[119] [Joseph Galloway], *Considerations upon the American Enquiry* (London, 1779), 12, 52–53.

remarked in April 1778 in reviewing the Ministry's options, "more from indignation at a defeat" than from enthusiasm for the war. As, however, it became ever clearer that the metropolis could expect little revenue from the colonies, that the war was taking a heavy toll upon Britain's internal economic resources, that the Americans, "though unable to cope with our army in the field, or to hold out any place of strength against our artillery," might be able to "spin out" the war "to a great length," that Metropolitan Britons were growing increasingly tired of a war that "had produced but few laurels in its progress, and promises no advantage from its issue," and that France and Spain were likely to enter the contest on the American side, even people favorable to the Administration began to question whether it would be "prudent in Great Britain, to gratify her resentment against revolted subjects, at the risque of rendering herself incapable of resisting foreign enemies" or whether "the glory that might arise from the reduction of the Rebels" was "in any respect an equivalent, for the dishonour of being overcome by" Britain's international rivals in Europe. Hence, the Government decided to make vigorous preparations for war, while offering the Americans terms of conciliation.[120]

For many hard-line advocates of American coercion, the Ministry's conciliatory bill, passed in early 1778, seemed to be "the most pusillanimous and ruinous measure that ever disgraced the annals of any nation." By "relinquishing, implicitly and in direct terms, the power of taxation, appointing commissioners to treat with Congress, and repealing all those acts of coercion and restraint, that it had been the business of the two first sessions of this Parliament to enact," an anonymous tractarian signing himself a "Member of Parliament" asserted, the Ministry had effectively "yielded up" the "whole object of the war," and completely disregarded the heavy "expence of blood and treasure, that" had been expended during the war and "must, for ever, bear heavy on this country." Most astonishing, this writer complained, "the men who had the confidence to propose this system of absolute concession" were the very "men who were to *have America at their feet*, who were to accept of nothing less than *unconditional submission*."[121] If this "disgraceful" measure seemed to many to barter away "the honour of the nation" for the prospects of a peace of "uncertain . . . continuance,"[122] others, like General Simon Fraser, M.P. for Inverness-shire, in a speech in the House of Commons in February 1778, insisted that "if America refused the present offers, this country ought to exert herself to the utmost, and risk every thing; even to that of carrying on a perpetual war."[123]

---

[120] *The Conciliatory Bills Considered* (London, 1778), 11–15, 29–31.

[121] "Member of Parliament," *An Examination into the Conduct of the Present Administration, From the Year 1774 to the Year 1778, and a Plan of Accommodation with America* (London, 1778), 12–13, 54.

[122] *Conciliatory Bills Considered*, 29–30.

[123] General Simon Fraser, speech, February 24, 1778, in Cobbett et al., eds., *Parliamentary History*, 19: 786.

By offering terms that fell far short of American demands and by appointing commissioners "in whom the Americans could have neither confidence nor hope," the Ministry, charged one of its many anonymous opponents in a pamphlet published in December 1779 and intended to provide an account of the Ministry's repeated history of "deception" with the British public, had used the American "treatment of the Commissioners, and the rejection of the terms ... as provocatives to the indignation of the thoughtless in this country" to continue its inhumane war against the colonies with indefensible "Predatory Expeditions" designed to "spread the horrors of the firebrand." Such tactics, this author exclaimed, were "barbarous, and opposite to those rules which civilization hath introduced among Nations; and which heretofore it hath been the pride and pleasure of Britain to promote." Pursuing "such a practice in the Continent of America," he wrote, put "the conduct of Administration in a light so glaring, impolitic, and unprecedented, that the art of man cannot soften the construction of guilt."[124] Thomas Tod, a Scottish merchant, similarly condemned "the present plundering, burning, and inhuman plan of desolating the country and people" and the "unbridled barbarity" it produced. "Whoever contrived that desolating plan, and whatever success may follow," Tod observed, it was entirely "opposite to the genius and character of the British nation, who, before this unhappy dispute, were ever famed for a brave, and consequently a humane and generous people."[125] "Prompted by pride, and passion," the Quaker merchant and American expert John Fothergill lamented in a 1780 pamphlet, metropolitan Britons in this internecine war had "shut our ears, as well as our hearts, against the claims of justice and humanity."[126]

War opponents marshaled a variety of other objections to the continuation of the war. The anonymous author of a substantial treatise entitled *Principles of Law and Government* challenged the constitutional basis of the metropolitan case for coercion, flatly denying that "the supremacy of the British parliament, over the North American provinces," could "be justly vindicated, on any of the arguments, that have yet been adduced in support [of] it." Invoking the ancient language of liberty, he contended that, constitutionally, no part of the empire could have any "just right, to violate, oppress, or enslave the other[s]" without transgressing the hallowed English doctrine of consent, and he did not exclude trade regulations, which he likened to "one sister robbing another." Such restrictions, he declared, were an example of "one part of the empire" treating "the others as enemies, as tributaries or slaves, not, as fellow citizens, or fellow creatures."[127]

---

[124] *A Short History of the Administration during the Summer Recess of Parliament* (London, 1779), 6–7, 17–18.

[125] [Thomas Tod], *Observations on American Independency* (London, 1779), 19–22, 24.

[126] John Fothergill, *An English Freeholder's Address to His Countrymen* (London, 1780), 18.

[127] *Principles of Law and Government with an Inquiry into the Justice and Policy of the Present War, and most effectual means of obtaining an Honourable, Permanent, and Advantageous Peace* (London, 1781), 24–26, 53.

Where the Administration had erred so completely, many war opponents thought, was in not heeding the Opposition's call to privilege commercial considerations over those of dominion and imperial grandeur. "That many well-meaning gentlemen, did not, when the war commenced, understand the true connexion between America and Great Britain" had indeed "been a misfortune to this country," wrote John Almon in late 1780. Whereas the Government acted upon "certain notions of power; which, with respect to America, would have been found impolitic in the execution, as they have been impracticable in the attainment," the Opposition understood, he insisted, that "Trade was our proper connexion; and so long as Americans went on with agriculture, and we with manufactures, both countries were flourishing: and never was any connexion, between nations, so happily, and by nature so mutually formed, for each others benefit." While "we sent them ploughshares, protected their trade, and let alone their internal police, they were our friends." In retrospect, Almon was persuaded, it had become abundantly evident that "those noblemen and gentlemen, who deprecated the vengeance of ministers, and solicited the consideration of every measure, to avoid that of war" were "the truest friends to Great Britain; to that union and reciprocity of interests, which gave dignity to our sovereign in the eyes of all the princes of Europe; and magnanimity to our councils, by a thorough knowledge of the commercial fountains from which our strength and resources flowed."[128]

Worst of all, however, the war increasingly seemed to be hopeless – and pointless. To be sure, the advocates "for bloodshed and battery" continued to call on the nation "*to persevere*, and to *die in the last ditch*,"[129] but, despite the fact that Lord Cornwallis and his army were marching through South and North Carolina and defeating "the American arms in repeated actions," reported Almon, "the vanquished seemed to gain strength by their defeats; for after every victory he had gained, the Americans collected, and were more numerous than before."[130] As Charles Dundas, M.P. for Orkney and Shetland, observed in a speech in the House of Commons in June 1781, "the late accounts from lord Cornwallis were of a very melancholy and alarming nature; that while they announced victory, they were fraught with present disasters, and promised nothing but future defeat, and of course," he added, "pointed out the immediate necessity of desisting from the farther persecution of the American war."[131] "Every man of common apprehension," deplored Tod, "must see and confess, that, year after year, we are Burgoyned, bamboozled, and beat; whether by the fault of generals, admirals, or ministers, it is all the same to a

---

[128] "An Independent Whig" [John Almon], *A Letter to the Right Honourable Charles Jenkinson* (London, 1781), 45–46. See also *A Plan or Articles of Perpetual Union, Commerce, and Friendship between Great-Britain and her American Colonies* (London, 1780), 27.

[129] "An Englishman," *Considerations upon the French and American War*, 13.

[130] [Almon], *A Letter to the Right Honourable Charles Jenkinson*, 44.

[131] Charles Dundas, speech, June 12, 1781, in Cobbett et al., eds., *Parliamentary History*, 22: 470.

country which bleeds at every opening by the wounds that trade, commerce, and manufactures daily receive, through this unsuccessful war."[132]

"To enter into a continental war with America, supposing her to have been a natural enemy, instead of a natural friend," was "a solecism of the first magnitude," wrote the anonymous author of *A Letter from Britannia to the King*, published in London in May 1781: the "vast extent of that empire; the expence and difficulty to transport troops to such a distance, [and] a multiplicity of reasons too obvious to mention" should have determined against it. Although "Britannia" thought that an exclusively maritime war might have been more successful, he lamented that Britain had not employed the "largess of police" in dealing with America "til she was pacified." "The voyage of Orlando Furioso to the moon" was "not more chimerical, than the idea of England's keeping America in subjection," he concluded. "For an island to hold in vassallage, for any length of time, a vast empire, separated from her by a world of waters, is a supposition, that could only be entertained in minds that embrace shadows for substance, and therefore beget monsters."[133]

Henry Bankes, M.P. for Corfe Castle, succinctly summarized the war opponents' case in parliamentary debate on June 12, 1781, when he rose to challenge the views of an earlier Administration speaker who had called the American contest "a holy war." Quite the contrary, Bankes said, "it was a most accursed, wicked, barbarous, cruel, unnatural, unjust, and diabolical war" that had been "conceived in injustice" and "nurtured and brought forth in folly." Not only were "its footsteps . . . marked with blood, slaughter, persecution, and devastation" with "every thing which went to constitute moral depravity and human terpitude . . . to be found in it," he declared, it "was pregnant with mischief of every kind, while it meditated destruction to the miserable people who were the devoted objects of the black resentments which produced it. The mischiefs, however, [had] recoiled on the unhappy people of" Britain, "who were made the instruments to effect the wicked purposes of its authors," in the process draining the "nation . . . of its best blood and of its vital resources of men and money" and requiring an enormous expense that had produced nothing "but a series of ineffective victories or severe defeats."[134]

The most common explanation for this national blunder was ministerial corruption. The "Prosecution of the American War must convince every unprejudiced and dispassionate Man," a writer signing himself "An Englishman" observed in the fall of 1779, that there was "an Influence in the House of Commons superior to Reason, common Sense, and the Dictates of Humanity." The "Thirty or Forty Millions of Money squandered in this abominable Project;

---

[132] [Tod], *Observations on American Independency*, 5.

[133] *A Letter from Britannia to the King* (London, 1781), 15, 22–23; Charles Polhill, *Reflections on a Pamphlet Entitled A Short History of the Opposition* (London, 1779), 19; "An Englishman," *Considerations upon the French and American War*, 34.

[134] Henry Bankes, speech, June 12, 1781, in Cobbett et al., eds., *Parliamentary History*, 22: 488–89.

Thirty or Forty thousand English Lives sacrificed in a War upon the Subject in Behalf of the Crown, double that Number of Americans perhaps scalped and murdered, and treble that Number robbed and ruined," he wrote, constituted "so flagrant a Proof of our Corruption as no Period of our History can furnish" and left no doubt that the Ministry "wanted a Revenue, not to" contribute to

the English Treasury,... but to extend its own Influence by feeding its needy Dependents, to have Thirteen Custom Houses, Thirteen Excise Offices, Thirteen Stamp Offices, Thirteen Post Offices, with a variety of other Posts and Employments, and to devour America, with the same Train of Vermin to which this Country has so long been a Prey.[135]

Few war opponents imagined that any good could come from the continuation of the war. Thus, the author of *Considerations upon the French and American War* predicted in March 1779 that the further "prosecution of this war" would "be attended with the ruin and downfall of this country; that, instead of recovering North America, we shall lose all of which we are at present possessed there, together with the West-Indies, and all the trade depending upon them." Only by negotiating a peace with America, he thought, could Britain have any hope of securing "what by an infatuated perseverence in the war we are upon the brink of losing."[136] "Had your conduct toward the Americans been upright, politic and just; had you, in place of restraining, encouraged, cherished, and assisted their trade and industry, promoted their growing greatness, and riveted them to us by interest and affection; what an illustrious figure!," wrote the author of *Principles of Law and Government*:

What a stupendous fabrick would this empire have exhibited to the world! An empire great in arts and in arms, founded on liberty, and supported, by opulence, fortitude and justice; renowned, for wisdom and humanity, the curb of restless ambition, the support, of the Protestant interest, and the balance of power in Europe, the dread of tyrants, and refuge of the oppressed.

Indeed, he argued in stressing the free character of the British Empire in comparison to those of "other nations," "notwithstanding many unjust and impolitical measures," the "superiority of" Britain's "constitution, and the lenity of" its "conduct towards" its "dependencies" had "in a great measure" already produced such an empire "before the Americans, preferring death to servitude, had recourse to arms, and engaged, in the dreadful conflict, in the seemingly, so unequal contest; and singly opposed, the mistress of the ocean, in the zenith of her glory." But, he asked, appealing to British sensibilities of humanity, "What is it now?" "Alas, my country!," he wrote, answering his own question, it was "dismembered, distracted by internal factions, heaving under an enormous load of additional taxes, attacked by numerous foreign foes, and involved in all the horrors of a cruel civil war," the principal sounds of which were "the

[135] "An Englishman," *A Letter to the Whigs* (London, 1779), 16–18.
[136] "An Englishman," *Considerations upon the French and American War*, 43.

shrieks and groans of the wounded or the dying, the cries of the widow and the orphan, . . . and the wild whoop of the bloodthirsty savage."[137]

Administration spokesmen might dismiss such lamentations as "the language of . . . despairing Croakers" that, like the languages employed by the contemporary Yorkshire Association protests over the internal governance of Britain, "just sets forth again" the "old beaten tract and threadbare cant of bribery, – corrupt majority, – slavery, – vassalage, – taxation, – places, – pensions, – sinecures, – oeconomy, – the influence of the crown ought to be lopt, topt, cropt, and totally diminished, trienniel parliaments," and so forth, "but not a word of rebellion, . . . conflagrations deemed constitutional liberty, the rights of the people, &c. &c." What would be "inhuman," people of such persuasion argued, would be for Britain to abandon "thousands of loyal American subjects . . . to all the several cruelties that would consequently be practised on them by order of the infernal Congress."[138]

But the tide was turning in favor of peace. Following Saratoga, Sir John Eardley-Wilmont observed in November 1779, "the eyes of many independent Gentlemen, and of the Nation in general, began to open, and to see too clearly the fatal tendency of the past measures, into which they had been deceived, and the too certain prospect of future calamities."[139] The realization that the revolting colonies had been "torn from the parent stock, and engrafted on the power of France," Edmund Burke wrote in a Bristol speech in the late summer of 1780, produced a "great terror" of "an immediate invasion" that suddenly awakened the British public from its "dreams of conquest."[140] As "conviction and terror" thus took the "place of stupor and delusion," reported the author of *A Short History*, the "crimes and errors of seven years, collected and amassed, . . . broke at once on the astonished eyes of men."[141] "Excepting among a few wicked spirits, that rancour and animosity which had been excited against" the Americans, noted another author in the fall of 1780, "is now in great measure subsided, and experience has taught those who were capable of being taught, that the war has been highly injurious to this country as well as to that." "When we reflect upon the immense armaments that had for five years been employed, and consider that with all their advantages of experience, of cannon, and of discipline," the British had "not been able to subdue above a single province," he concluded, "we shall readily see the folly of attempting to subjugate such a country by mere force of arms."[142]

[137] *Principles of Law and Government*, 55–56.
[138] "Cincinnatus," *The Patriotic Mirror, or the Salvation of Great Britain in Embryo* (London, 1781), 29–30 note.
[139] John Eardley-Wilmont, *A Short defence of the Opposition; in an Answer to a Pamphlet intitled 'A Short History of the Opposition'* (London, 1779), 16.
[140] *A Speech of Edmund Burke, Esq. At the Guildhall in Bristol, Previous to the late Election in that City* (London, 1780), 39.
[141] *A Short History of the Administration*, 2.
[142] *A Plan or Articles of Perpetual Union, Commerce, and Friendship between Great-Britain and her American Colonies* (London, 1780), 5.

Notwithstanding France's entrance into the war in early 1778, many war opponents continued into the early 1780s to hope for some rapprochement. Thus, in July 1780, "An Englishman" used the language of liberty to propose the creation of a genuinely free and liberal empire in a pamphlet entitled *An Essay on the Interests of Britain, in Regard to America.* By continuing the war, he said, Britain would only drive the colonies more firmly into the hands of the French, while Britain itself would "be gradually totally exhausted, and deprived of our foreign dominions, and retain only the mortifying reflexion, that we are but the shadow of our former glory." In his view, the issue for metropolitan Britons now was "whether the new world should raise you to a degree of power you have not yet known, or deprive you of the sources of wealth you now possess." "Having laid the foundation for a vast empire," Britons, he urged, should not continue "to alienate it from us, by an attack on that liberty we taught them to revere." Counseling metropolitan Britons to recall that "freemen cannot be governed by fear, that they must be led by affection," and "to throw aside that trifling and narrow spirit which must inevitably end in your ruin," he proposed that Britain join with America to found "a confederation on equal and generous terms" that would "be for the advantage of all, let what branch soever of the confederacy become the most powerful," and in which each part of the British Empire, "as well eastern as western," should "be one people, and mutually entitled to all liberties, immunities, and privileges whatsoever," including "a free representation, the habeas corpus, trial by jury, and a free toleration of religion." With "the consent of America," he declared, this possibility was still within "our power." "It is a happiness that has never yet fallen to the lot of any nation, much less any great empire," he observed, "after the cool deliberation of years, to alter and new model their political constitution," and he enthusiastically invited Britons to rise to the occasion.[143]

But a growing number of writers realized that it was already too late for reconciliation. Long an advocate for Britain's breaking all political ties with the North American colonies, Josiah Tucker added military failure and the need to concentrate national defensive energies against France to the case for separation. "Humiliating as be the Fact," he declared in a pamphlet published early in 1780, "it cannot be controverted; circumstanced as we now are, we are unequal to the Reduction of the Colonies." "We have not only failed" in the objectives for "which at first [we] armed," he wrote, "but after amazing Expence of Blood and Treasure, we find ourselves involved in more dangerous Circumstances, than when Hostilities commenced. Great as have been our Efforts, they have all been exerted, with respect to America, without Effect." Nor, he argued, could "any Principle of Reason, Policy, or Experience on similar Occasions" justify "any Expectation of better Success, against the united

---

[143] "An Englishman," *An Essay on the Interests of Britain, in Regard to America* (London, 1780), 9–10, 13–14, 16–19, 21. See also *Renovation Without Violence Yet Possible* (Dublin, 1779), 5–6, 8–9, 15–17, 20.

Forces of France, Spain, and America, than we have hitherto obtained, when contending with America alone." "By leaving the Colonies to themselves and renouncing all Connection with them as Subjects," he thought, "we should save, not only every Expence which arises from the Prosecution of the War with them, but we shall be delivered likewise from every Charge which may accrue, by maintaining a Government among them, civil, military, and religious," and "immediately have the Assistance of our Forces, both Land and Sea, in carrying on the Contest with the French and Spaniards." Moreover, though he was certain that "Discontents and Heartburnings" fostered in American minds by those "Measures of Severity, which have occasionally been exercised among them, during the Progress of Hostilities, and the general Devastation" would not immediately dissipate, he expressed the hope that such "Prejudices, though now violent," would "by Degrees wear out" as the "Endearments of original Ancestry, and still later Connections, the Arguments of Language, Reason, and similar Manners" come to "operate in our Favour."[144]

The author of a long pamphlet entitled *Nathan to Lord North*, published in London in 1780, took a similar line. Denouncing North's "culpable and criminal conduct towards the colonies," Nathan held the minister responsible for "gradually" leading "Great Britain to that brink of national disgrace and ruin on which she now totters." When Tucker initially "proposed to give up the colonies" in the mid-1770s, he wrote, "there was scarcely a second man in the world of the same opinion." Through its misguided, impolitic, and clumsy policies, however, the North Administration – and its many adherents – had, Nathan now suggested, rendered Tucker's proposal the only solution.[145] There seemed to be no other choice. "America," agreed Opposition leader Charles James Fox in a major speech in the House of Commons on June 12, 1781, "is lost, irrecoverably lost to this country," and "we could lose nothing by a vote declaring America independent."[146] When "the dominions of an Empire be extended, while, by reason of a narrowness or weakness in the vital spring of Government, the spirit of Government cannot so extend, as to give vital union to its distant parts," the imperial analyst Thomas Pownall wrote in a treatise addressed to the sovereigns of Europe in 1780, "the extension of the dominion works not to amplitude and growth, but to the dissolution of State." Citing the British Empire as an example of this dictum, Pownall contended that the United States had already become "AN INDEPENDENT STATE *that has taken its equal station amongst the nations of earth.*"[147]

[144] Josiah Tucker, *Dispassionate Thoughts on the American War: Address to the Moderate of All Parties* (London, 1780), 9–10, 13–14, 18, 20–21, 23–24. See also [Tod], *Observations on American Independency*, 3, 5, 12.
[145] *Nathan to Lord North* (London, 1780), 26, 37–39, 44, 47, 55.
[146] Charles James Fox, speech, June 12, 1781, in Cobbett et al., eds., *Parliamentary History*, 22: 507–08.
[147] Thomas Pownall, *A Memorial, Most Humbly Addressed to the Sovereigns of Europe on the Present State of Affairs between the Old and New World*, 2nd ed. (London, 1780), 66–67.

VII

The loss of yet another army at Yorktown in the fall of 1781, growing war weariness and resentment at the high levels of taxation, and the fall of the North Ministry in 1782 finally brought the Opposition to power, and a new Ministry formed by Lord Rockingham moved to end the war and to acknowledge the independence of the American colonies in revolt. Founded "on Principles the most comprehensive, just, and enlightened," and "with a Generosity, hardly paralleled in History," the new Administration, declared Charles Polhill, a Rockingham supporter, in a 1782 pamphlet, was "disposed to redress the injuries of even the remotest Subjects of the British Empire – diffusing the Sun, their genial and propitious Influence to every Corner, to every Quarter of the Globe, where that influence can penetrate or extend," conceding independence to the thirteen American colonies and internal home rule and the removal of economic restrictions to Ireland.[148]

Of course, North's longtime supporters continued to press for a continuation of the war. "Upon the disaster in Virginia," an opponent remarked, the ministers "for a short time gave over talking big, but they soon began to change their note to the old tune: and if they had continued in office, they would have tried to wheedle the nation for this year, and for many more."[149] With a large army in America still firmly installed in New York, with control over a few other areas in the South, and with its navy still intact, Britain had no reason to submit to what one writer described as "the most degrading peace, that ever disgraced the annals of [Britain], and the most disadvantageous that ever dragged down ruin upon any nation!" To agree to a "peace dictated in the first *instance*, by the *infant, unauthoritative states of America*; without the grant of a single favourable stipulation to the mother country, a nation till then the most powerful in the world, whether considered for valuable possessions, for naval force to protect, or for resources to support them," was indeed a bitter pill. "A peace upon such terms," this writer declared, was simply "too dreadful to bear reflection."[150] Dismissing Yorktown as an "unlucky accident," Joseph Cawthorne, Pay-Master General, called for a shift to a maritime war and begged his readers not to heed "the alarming and treacherous voice of the enemies of this nation, inducing us to surrender our national honor and interest."[151]

---

[148] [Charles Polhill], *Observations and Reflections On the Act passed in the Year, 1774, for the Settlement of the Province of Quebec* (London, 1782), vi.

[149] *Thoughts on the Present War, with An Impartial Review of Lord North's Administration* (London, 1783), 66.

[150] *Consequences (Not before adverted to) That are likely to result from the Late Revolution of the British Empire* (London, 1783), 21, 32.

[151] Joseph Cawthorne, *The False Alarm. Address to the Right Honourable Richard Rigby, Esq. Pay-Master General of His Majesty's Forces* (London, 1782), 7–8. See also Joseph Williams, *Considerations on the American War* (London, 1782), 19.

But a majority of neither the nation nor the political establishment was any longer receptive to such appeals. Writing in the spring of 1782, Thomas Tod sharply attacked those who endeavored to persuade "Britannia[,] . . . now so maimed and wounded on both legs and arms, that she can scarce either work or walk, . . . to crawl out and fight on her knees, till she is wounded in the heart." Even "the most sanguine," he wrote, could now maintain "but little hope of" the American colonies' "returning to their former allegiance."[152] It was time, wrote an anonymous pamphlet author in the same year, to terminate "a dispute originating in folly – maintained on both sides by too much obstinacy – and, if longer continued, inevitably and rapidly sinking the whole British empire in one general ruin."[153] "At length," Almon observed, a "majority of the House of Commons . . . saw this situation" and finally realized that, "notwithstanding the unlimited support which they had given to the King's servants,"[154] they had succeeded only, as another author declared, in conducting "this country, from the highest pitch of political greatness to the lowest abyss of misery."[155] "The surrender of Lord Cornwallis and his army," wrote the Reverend Andrew Kippis, finally

dispelled the delusion which yet remained upon the minds of numbers who had not hith-erto been affected by a series of unfavourable events, and by all the exertions of reason and eloquence. Even those Country Gentlemen who had been the most distinguished for their attachment to *Tory* principles, and who had placed the greatest confidence in Administration, gave up the contest as hopeless.[156]

If sentiment for stopping the American war was ascendant in Britain by the summer of 1782, opinion about acknowledging American independence was much more divided. Many war opponents remained reluctant to face the loss of such valuable colonies and, hoping to salvage some of the benefits of the American empire and some national dignity for Britain, continued to hope for reconciliation, one writer calling for a "FAMILY COMPACT between Great Britain and America, like that of the House of Bourbon."[157] Given America's lack of enthusiasm for such projects, however, independence seemed to be the only option. In an extended speech to the electors of Westminster in the summer of 1782, Charles James Fox made the case that it should be seen as a measure that was both expedient and "just and honourable" – expedient

[152] [Thomas Tod], *Consolitory Thoughts on American Independence* (Edinburgh, 1782), 2, 64.
[153] *Impartial Reflections on the Conduct of the Late Administration and Opposition, and of the American Congress* (London, 1782), 78.
[154] "An Independent Whig" [John Almon], *The Revolution in MDCCLXXXII Impartially Considered* (London, 1782), 6.
[155] *The Present Hour* (London, 1782), 13.
[156] [Andrew Kippis], *Considerations on the Provisional Treaty with America, and the Preliminary Articles of Peace with France and Spain* (London, 1783), 7.
[157] *A Plan of Reconciliation with America; Consistent with the Dignity and Interest of Both Countries* (London, 1782), 47.

because it was Britain's "only security against the continuance of those evils we have already experienced, or the farther calamities we have so much reason to apprehend," and just and honorable because it would restore "freedom to a brave and generous people." Although he acknowledged that some people regarded such a step as humiliating and abject, he argued that any measure that contributed to "the preservation of a state, already at the verge of ruin" and thereby led to the "political salvation of this country" ought not to be thought of as beneath its dignity. "Without a complete unconditional acknowledgment of American independence," he exclaimed, "this country can have no safety; and why, therefore, should we destroy the effect of a necessary measure by an ungracious mode of performing it[?]." Americans, he said, "are Englishmen, – they have English habits, – English feelings," and he recommended that Parliament follow the same course with Americans that it had recently done with Ireland by "liberally" granting them "what they had an honest right to," predicting that "the same effects will follow" and that America, though independent, would in response soon learn to "trust to your generosity, and rely upon your affection."[158]

As his title suggested, the author of *An Enquiry Whether the Absolute Independence of America is not to be Preferr'd to Her Partial Dependence*, published in London in the fall of 1782, argued for independence on the grounds that it would be highly beneficial to the maintenance of Britain's own liberty. "Nothing can be more self-evident," he declared, "than that the extent of empire" was incompatible with "a free constitution." The quarrel with America (and, he might have added, the concessions to Ireland) had exposed "the Omnipotency of Parliament" (which he correctly characterized as the post–Glorious Revolution "successor of the divine indefeasible right of princes") as "a mere phantom" in relation to the larger empire. Clearly, he concluded, this principle and other vital parts of the English constitution represented "insurmountable obstacles to extensive dominion," so that "either the principles must confine the empire, or the empire subvert the principles." This author did not deny that "the absolute Independence of America" was "an evil," but insisted that it was "a necessary evil, and as much to be preferred to her partial dependence on the Sovereign as our Constitution is preferable to Tyranny, Liberty to extent of Empire, and Poverty to Slavery."[159]

Why Britain found itself in its "present melancholy situation" continued to trouble imperial analysts.[160] Those who had supported the war blamed ministerial inefficiency, bungling generals, and the divisive tactics of the

[158] *The Speech of the Right Honourable Charles James Fox, At a General Meeting of the Electors of Westminster* (London, 1782), 17, 32.
[159] *An Enquiry, Whether the Absolute Independence of America is not to be preferr'd to her Partial Dependence, as most agreeable to the real interests of Great Britain* (London, 1782), 6, 36, 38.
[160] *Impartial Reflections on the Conduct*, 26, 66.

"ranting contemptible republicans" in opposition.[161] Decrying the *"impol-icy* of" the North "Administration persisting in their absurd and impracticable plan of conquering the revolted Colonies,"[162] those who opposed the war were intent on explaining why Britain's "great men" had been "deceived by chasing a shadow, or empty name of sovereignty, and [why] the multitude" had been "inflamed in following it." They found explanations in a variety of places: in the misrepresentation of the loyalists, those "friends of despotism" who, "like vipers in the bosom of the state," propagated "abominable false-hoods, . . . misrepresented to the Ministry the true situation of America, and the real spirit of that people," and "thirst[ed] after cruel and barbarous measures" to establish parliamentary supremacy and avenge their exile;[163] in the corrup-tion of the North Government, whose "insatiable lust for emoluments, the numberless sinecures and useless places, the disgraceful pensions, and exceed-ings of the civil and military lists, the secret service money, and extraordinaries, and jobbing contracts" had motivated it to continue such an expensive and ineffective war and accounted for the enormous "debts these kingdoms labour under";[164] in the "interference of Great Britain with the internal management of her colonies,"[165] and, more especially, in the interior cabinet's uniform and unceasing commitment to "its first great object," the *"new model[ling] the government of the colonies"*;[166] and in the "unreasonable desires" of the British people, who, "dissatisfied with the blessings we possessed, and eager to obtain that *fancied* good beyond our reach," had supported "a *seven years war* in pursuit of that delusive phantom [national] independence," which, "like those predicted in Pharaoh's dream, [had] *devoured* our former plenty" and led *"justly"* to the punishment of being deprived of their bountiful colonies.[167] "The arrogance of the people, nourished by former victories and prosperity, and accompanied with an unreasonable contempt of the adversaries against whom we were engaged," Kippis thought, "hath greatly contributed to our present humiliation."[168] Whatever "the many strange causes of our misfor-tunes," wrote Tod, "the picture of our present situation" was almost "too humbling for a true Briton to paint."[169]

Particularly humbling to many writers was the fact that the war had pro-vided further evidence of British inhumanity overseas that represented a deep

[161] "Cincinnatus," *The Patriotic Mirror*, 20.
[162] *Impartial Reflections on the Conduct*, 26, 66.
[163] [Tod], *Consolitory Thoughts*, 30, 50–51.
[164] Edward Startford, 2nd Earl of Aldborough, *An Essay on the True Interests and Resources of the Empire of the King of Great-Britain and Ireland* (Dublin, 1783), 13.
[165] "A Volunteer," *Substance of Political Debates on His Majesty's Speech; on the Address, and the Amendment: November 25th, 1779* (London, 1779), 19.
[166] Joseph Williams, *An Address to the Interior Cabinet* (London, 1782), 7.
[167] *Impartial Reflections on the Conduct*, 73–74.
[168] [Kippis], *Considerations on the Provisional Treaty with America*, 5.
[169] [Tod], *Consolitory Thoughts*, 50.

stain upon the national character. Throughout the war, wrote John Almon in
the summer of 1782, the North Administration had "degraded and debased"
the "national character... in every instance of their conduct."[170] "The war
with America not having originated in laudable ambition, or in just policy,"
complained Lord John Cavendish in parliamentary debate on February 22,
1782, "had been conducted without the dignity that became the British nation.
Narrow, low, and selfish in its principle, the conduct had been mean, miserable, and defective," and without "dignified resentment." "It was begun
and carried on in pique, disgust, rancour, and narrowness," he observed,
and these "low passions," having "been fed by disappointment,... instead
of making us wise... had [only] made us foolish."[171] The British army, added
the author of *Thoughts on the Present War*, "pillaged, without distinction
of friend or enemy," used "too great severity... after some" battles, and shed
"more... blood than necessary, or usual." To the disgrace of Britain, he wrote,
"no regular army has at any time been more ready to stretch out their hands
to plunder."[172]

The Edinburgh writer Thomas Day took up this subject in a 1783 pamphlet
entitled *Reflections upon the Present State of England, and the Independence
of America*. The Americans, he wrote, had

seen their property laid waste, their towns and cities consumed, their country desolated
with all the fury that marks the last excesses of war, inflamed by civil hatred; every
insult has been offered to their women, every degree of scorn and inhumanity to those
who were taken prisoners, and every species of barbarity to those who resisted; even
the savage tribes, whose manners are sometimes quoted to express a degree of atrocious
cruelty beyond the corruption of polished nations, were not judged unworthy of the
alliance of... Britons

who remained at home. For Day, this behavior raised the question of whether
the inhumanity of the war had "extinguished even national humanity," and
he cited the Gordon riots of 1780 in London as a case in point. During those
riots, Day observed, the dire scenes of "streets heaped with the dead and the
dying, during the military fury which raged for some days uncontrouled; and
the yet more awful spectacle of promiscuous and implacable justice, served
only to gratify the stern resentment of the mildest people in Europe," who
out of "the jealousy of invaded property" had "seemed to refuse [even] a tear
for the numberless miseries that surrounded them."[173] Joseph Williams found
yet another symptom of such callousness in the plight of the loyalists, who
were "now considered by the Kingdom in general as a burden, and styled

[170] [Almon], *The Revolution in MDCCLXXXII*, 22.
[171] Lord John Cavendish, speech, in Cobbett et al., eds., *Parliamentary History*, 22: 1031.
[172] *Thoughts on the Present War*, 18.
[173] Thomas Day, *Reflections upon the Present State of England, and the Independence of America* (London, 1783), 24–25.

by the grating epithet of *Refugees.*" "Shameful contumely, and very unfair distinction!," he complained, asking "Where is the humanity of Britons? where that hospitality that was the characteristic of this island? Where that generosity which is the pride of human nature? Depraved, degenerated Englishmen!"[174]

[174] Joseph Williams, *The Criterion: Or, Disquisitions on the Present Administration. Addressed to Sir George Saville* (London, 1782), 12.

7

"This Voraginous Gulph of Hibernian Dependence"

The Languages of Oppression, Corruption, Justice, Liberty, and Humanity and the Identification of Imperial Excesses in Ireland

I

"We in *Dublin*, and you in *London*, are in the Situation of two Sets of People, who make use of the same Perspective, but at different ends of the Glass," wrote Hellen O'Roon in a 1754 tract; "we look at you through that Side which magnifies, and presents you nearer much than you really are; and you look at us through the Side which diminishes unreasonably, and throws us at an apparent great Distance."[1] *Distance* is the operative word in this remark, and the distance referred to was not physical but cultural. Indeed, members of the Anglo-Irish Protestant Ascendancy that dominated Irish public life following the Glorious Revolution frequently complained that when metropolitans did think about them, they did it in a dismissive way, regarding the Irish, as one anonymous writer said in 1754, as "ignorant and rude, awkward, blunt, and ridiculous; drunkards and cheats; combined to oppose the Government; thorough paced party-men, trained among dogs and horses, bullocks and sheep; where they are likely to lose the little good that nature has put into them."[2] The language of alterity that metropolitan Britons used in reference to overseas Britons across the Atlantic could also be – and had long been – applied to those residing just across the Irish Sea.[3]

But the use of such pejorative and demeaning language and the perception of cultural distance it implied were always to some extent mitigated by increasingly close connections between Britain and Ireland. As Britain's nearest and oldest overseas possession, Ireland was the site where the English nation had

---

[1] Hellen O'Roon, *The P——te Vindicated, and the Affairs of I——d set in a true Light, in a Letter from the Honourable Hellen O'Roon, to the Right Honourable Lady Viscountess ****** in London* (London, 1754), 6.

[2] *The State of Ireland, Laid Open to the View of His Majesty's Subjects* (London, 1754), 14.

[3] The earliest English application of the language of alterity to overseas colonists was no doubt in reference to the Anglo-Irish. See John Patrick Montaño, *The Roots of English Colonialism in Ireland* (Cambridge: Cambridge University Press, 2011), 335–85.

conducted its earliest expansive efforts to expropriate the lands and resources of an indigenous people, turn them to their own use, and replace or override indigenous culture with a transplanted English one.[4] By the eighteenth century, through intermarriage, the Anglo-Irish elite was always to some extent integrated with the English. Irish landlords could be found in both the houses of the British Parliament; Irish-born and educated political figures, such as Edmund Burke, were prominent in British politics; and the metropolitan government was far more deeply and intrusively involved in the public life of Ireland than it was in that of any of the American colonies. Notwithstanding the closeness of such ties, in the decades preceding the great controversy over Irish demands for free trade and parliamentary independence in 1778–82, Irish affairs received relatively little attention in the press or in Parliament. Indeed, it might be said of Ireland that it was the component of the overseas empire that metropolitan Britons were most likely to take for granted.

During that crisis contributors to the debate sometimes referred to Ireland as "a jewell in the British crown,"[5] demonstrating an appreciation of the many benefits that Ireland brought to Britain and underlining its importance to Britain's overseas empire. Throughout the eighteenth century, Ireland represented Britain's first line of defense against attacks from France and Spain, its principal rivals in imperial struggles, especially after 1739. Absentee Irish landlords living in Britain brought about £100,000 per annum into the British economy, while the Crown's yearly Irish hereditary revenues fell little short of that figure and provided a fund the Crown's ministers could use, without oversight from Parliament, for pensions and patronage to reward Crown favorites and to ensure that the Irish Parliament would generally shy away from the sorts of confrontations over authority and privilege with which Crown officials in the American colonies routinely had to deal. Moreover, whenever the Irish Parliament slipped its bounds, the combination of a system of close legislative review and physical proximity insured that the metropolitan Government could quash any measure it found unacceptable. Tightly restricted by British parliamentary trade regulations, the Irish economy was thoroughly subordinated to the British, and Ireland was a significant mart for British exports. Though nominally a distinctive kingdom, Ireland, from a metropolitan point of view, came close to being an ideal colony almost fully subjugated to the British polity. Because disaffected Roman Catholics composed a large majority of the Irish population, the ruling Protestant Ascendancy was wholly dependent on Britain for protection, while the monopolization of land and other resources by wealthy landlords drawn mostly from the Protestant minority rendered it by far the most thoroughly colonialized and economically underdeveloped component of Britain's settler empire.

---

[4] Ibid.
[5] *A Letter to William Eden, Esq. Occasioned by a Pamphlet Commonly Attributed to Him, and Entitled, Considerations Submitted to the People on their Present Condition, with Regard to Trade and Constitution*, 2nd ed. (Dublin, 1781), 37.

That, for all of Ireland's importance to Britain, metropolitan Britons took only occasional and sporadic interest in Irish affairs through the middle decades of the eighteenth century did not mean that they were unaware that everything was not right within Hibernia or that relations between Britain and Ireland were trouble-free. When, with the rest of Britain's overseas empire, Ireland did come under closer metropolitan scrutiny in the 1760s, the main focus, a spillover from an internal Irish debate, was upon the question of why, when Britain and the American colonies were displaying such rapid improvement, Ireland continued to be a scene of so much poverty and underdevelopment, a classic effect of what we now refer to as colonialism. Initially, discussion focused upon two subjects. The first was the vast sums drawn out of Ireland by two different groups, Irish absentees and royal pensioners. The second was the British economic restrictions that inhibited Irish demographic and commercial development and the political and constitutional arrangements that prevented Irish people from the full enjoyment of the system of British liberty, which many contemporaries believed to have been central to Britain's economic growth and military and naval prowess after the Glorious Revolution.[6] Within Ireland, a lively debate also went on about the continued legal discrimination against Roman Catholics, who, contemporaries estimated, constituted from two-thirds to four-fifths of the total population. In its early stages, this debate seems not to have created much resonance in the home island. However, as, during the 1770s, metropolitans became more sensitive to breaches of humanity by agents of British imperial expansion, first in India, then in the slave colonies and the African slave trade, a few writers directed attention to the inhumanity of Irish Protestants in their continuing discrimination against Roman Catholics. Stimulated by the debate over how to treat Roman Catholics in the formerly French colony of Quebec, this discussion added still another dimension to the critique of empire that emerged so powerfully in Britain after 1760.

II

Throughout the eighteenth century, physical proximity and cultural appeal had long attracted wealthy Irish landowners, some of whom were English, to take up more or less permanent residence in England, and the social and economic impact of such absenteeism had long been a matter of concern among Irish political analysts and political leaders. In the 1730s, following publication of Thomas Prior's *List of the Absentees of Ireland*,[7] the Irish Parliament had tried to deal with the situation by levying a special tax on absentees, but this tax

---

[6] Vincent Morley, *Irish Opinion and the American Revolution 1760–1783* (Cambridge: Cambridge University Press, 2002), is an excellent recent study of Ireland's relationship to the empire during the era considered here. Also pertinent is Martyn J. Powell, *Britain and Ireland in the Eighteenth-Century Crisis of Empire* (London: Palgrave Macmillan, 2003).

[7] Thomas Prior, *A List of the Absentees of Ireland, and the Value of their Estates and Incomes spent abroad, with Observations on the Present State and Condition of that Kingdom* (London, 1730). This work was first published in Dublin in 1729.

proved difficult to enforce and was dropped in the 1750s. But in the late 1760s, in various parts of Ireland, organized protests against economic hardship by groups calling themselves White Boys or Oak Boys once again brought this issue to the fore; in 1768 Redman Morris produced a revised and updated edition of Prior's *List of Absentees*, which he published under the direction of the Dublin Society, and a year later, a revised and amplified third edition. Whereas Prior had shown in the 1730s that absentees were withdrawing just over £600,000 per annum, Morris's initial list demonstrated that that figure had climbed to more than a million, and his revised list the next year revealed that he had drastically underestimated this figure, which he now showed reached to just over £1,500,000, or nearly two and half times Prior's estimate for the 1730s. Although this figure included pensions, salaries to placemen, mercantile traveling and education expenses, lawsuits and solicitations, military contributions, and ship expenses, about half represented remittances to absentees.[8]

As a result of this vast "Annual Remittance...to our Gentlemen Abroad," Morris wrote in spelling out in detail the connection between "this devouring drain" and Irish poverty and underdevelopment, "No Country" labored "under so wasteful a Drain of its Treasure, as *Ireland* does at present." Never meaning to live in Ireland, those "*Irish* Landlords who live Abroad," Morris charged, had "wantonly abandoned their Country" to "riot Abroad in its Ruin" and, showing no sense of civic responsibility, had routinely sacrificed "their Country's Interest" to "a luxurious Manner of Living" and "an Affectation of imitating the Nobility and Gentry of other Countries in their Expenses," a way of life, he suggested, that seemed "to have so far alienated their Affections from their Country, and hardened their Tempers towards it," that they had no other interest in Ireland beyond exploiting it as fully as possible. "Above all others," he insisted, absentees were remarkable "for letting their Estates at a Rack Rent, so as hardly to allow a Livelihood to their poor Tenants by whom they are supported." "By their constant drawing all their Rents from hence, and racking their poor Tenants," he explained, applying the language of plunder or rapacity to the situation, absentees were nothing more than "Deserters" who had proven themselves to be "the worst Enemies to *Ireland*," "laying it under a continual yearly Pillage to their Vanity and Luxury, without" making "the least Consideration or Value returned for the same" or "contributing the least Farthing towards the Support of the Government." Moreover, they paid not "the least Share of the Duties or Taxes" of Ireland and contributed nothing to the relief "of the Poor, whose miseries they never see, or" made "any Improvements."[9]

If Ireland was ever to prosper, Morris was persuaded, this situation had to be remedied, and his solution was a tax on all absentees' extractions from Ireland. If the absentees "set so high a Value on their foreign Pleasures, that

[8] [Redman Morris], *A List of the Absentees of Ireland*, 2nd ed. (Dublin, 1768), 17–18; idem, *A List of the Absentees of Ireland*, 3rd ed. (Dublin, 1769), 17.
[9] [Morris], *List*, 2nd ed., 24–25, 27, 29–30, 68; idem, *List*, 3rd ed., 63.

for the Enjoyment of them, the Kingdom must be brought into Ruin" and "the Security of the *Protestant* Religion and Interest in this Kingdom, the Prosperity of the People, and [the] Safety of the Government . . . should all give Way to the Gratifications of our Gentlemen Abroad," he wrote, appealing to Protestant concerns about domestic security against the Catholic majority, they should "not be indulged in all this, without contributing their Quota towards the Charges of the Public," and he proposed to tax "the Estates and Incomes of those [who] . . . choose to spend all the Profits thereof Abroad, to the Impoverishment and Ruin of their native Country." "There is no Way left to save us," he declared, "but obliging them to live at home, or making them pay for living Abroad."[10]

Morris's fellow Irishman Sir Hercules Langrishe brought this situation to the attention of the British public in a pamphlet published in London in 1769. An answer to William Knox's suggestion in his influential *The Present State of the Nation*, published in London in 1768, that Ireland should contribute £100,000 annually to help Britain pay off its debts, Langrishe's work was principally concerned to explain how Britain's extensive and multifaceted exploitation of Ireland, an old theme that had gained increasing currency in the context of contemporary American resistance to the metropolis in the 1760s and 1770s, made such a contribution impossible. In making this argument, Langrishe, citing the findings of Morris and others to call attention to the pauperizing effects of the absentee monetary drain, underlined the depth of Irish poverty by contrasting English with Irish riots. Whereas English riots "almost always" occurred "when the people cannot easily get the best *white* bread," he wrote, the recent "tumults" raised in Ireland by the White Boys and the Oak Boys represented "the irregular discontents of a desperate people, who through the rapacity of *landlords*, and variety of extortion exercised by *dealers in tythes*, found it almost impossible by the hardest labour to procure *potatoes*." "There is not a country in Europe, so unimproved and unpeopled – of so small a capital and limited a commerce," he said, that was "so heavily taxed as the kingdom of Ireland."[11]

Nothing came of these complaints, however, and absentee remittances continued to be an unresolved problem throughout the 1770s, with sporadic agitation for a tax on absentees. Thus did an anonymous pamphleteer, signing himself "A Real Lover of His Country" and employing the language of rapacity, seek to reopen the subject in 1773 by publishing, in Dublin, a tract complaining that absentees had "no inclination to spend more of their Time in this Country, than may be sufficient to plunder it." He argued that the rising value of their estates demanded that absentees pay a 10 percent tax on their "present nett Incomes to prevent the Ruin of the Kingdom which has so long supplied them with the good Things of Life." For any nation "quietly to permit the very Vitals

---

[10] [Morris], *List*, 2nd ed., 27, 67.
[11] Hercules Langrishe, *Considerations on the Dependencies of Great Britain* (London, 1769), 15, 42.

by which it is supported, to be entirely drawn from it by its apostate Children, for the Purpose of squandering them away in another Country," he asserted, was to "be guilty of a Kind of Self-Murder," and he predicted that the tax he proposed would "in a short Time render us a flourishing Nation, instead of being in the wretched State in which we are now plunged."[12]

The long debate over Irish demands for greater economic and political independence from Britain in 1779–82 again brought the absentee issue to the fore. In a pamphlet entitled *A Defense of Great Britain, Against a Charge of Tyranny in the Government of Ireland*, an author using the pseudonym "An Irishman" cited "the vast sums drained out of this Country by the Absentees" as one of several "domestic inconveniencies we so *loudly charge* upon Great Britain,"[13] and even those writers who attributed most of Ireland's woes to British oppression acknowledged that absenteeism was one of the main reasons why Ireland was poor and depopulated. Thus Sir John Hasler, writing anonymously and identifying himself only as a "member of the Dublin Society," in a 1779 pamphlet charged that the absentees' practice of demanding high rents drew "from the Hand of the poor Peasant, the Means which are required to produce Riches," drained "this Country of its Vitals, in Order to enrich other Nations," and was "the principal Instrument of keeping it in a State of Ignorance and Beggary." "Look at the Large trade of Land in the Kingdom belonging to that Class of People," he said, "and you will behold a lamentable Picture of the Effects of their Non-Residence." A "temporary Plague, or Famine, could not produce more pernicious and fatal Consequences unto" Ireland "than they do," he concluded, "for, independent of the Property they draw from the Country, they are principally conducive to keeping it in a State of Ignorance and Dependence." To make matters worse, he said, turning to the language of humanity, these "very Individuals who" were "the Cause of this Misery and Poverty" were "so devoid of Humanity" as to represent the tenants they were oppressing as "destitute of Gratitude, lawless, and vindictive, when they themselves" were "the sole Cause of" their "appearing so."[14] A second writer counted it a good sign that the English had begun to "reproach our absentees with injuring their tenantry."[15]

By the late 1770s, the charge that, as the duke of Chandos, himself an Irish landlord, put it in debate in the British House of Commons in May 1779, "the continual drain from the country, in order to pay the great landowners resident here" was "one principal cause of the distress felt by Ireland" seemed to be widely accepted. That many landlords, "in their whole lives, never

[12] "A Real Lover of His Country," *A Letter upon the Subject of Taxing the Estates of Absentees* (Dublin, 1773), 4–5, 7.

[13] "An Irishman," *A Defense of Great Britain, Against a Charge of Tyranny in the Government of Ireland* (Dublin, 1779), 12.

[14] "Member of the Dublin Society" [Sir John Hasler], *Cursory Observations on Ireland* (Dublin, 1779), 5, 7, 39–40.

[15] "G. B.," *The People of Ireland not a parcel of lazy, incorrigible Scoundrels* (Dublin, 1779), 10–12, 31.

spent a shilling in the country from whence they drew their incomes," he said, "was a systematic grievance, which admitted of no remedy but a tax upon absentees."[16]

Pamphlet writers publishing in Britain also took up the absentee problem. Noting that absentees held about a million and a half of the four million pounds annually charged on the Irish rent roll, the anonymous author of *A View of the Present State of Ireland* proposed in 1780 "a tax upon all lands, tenements, and heriditaments in Ireland, the proprietors of which do not reside six months in the year in that kingdom." Justifying such a tax on the grounds "that every man enjoying property in a country" was "bound to defend it" and "that every person ought to contribute a part of his property towards the expence of that government, by which the remainder is protected," this author thought that such a tax would help both arrest the outward flow of cash to the absentees, which had "debilitated the kingdom, and been one principal source of her present misfortunes," and prevent "the whole rent roll of the kingdom from" falling into "the hands of absentees and East-Indian nabobs," who would only contribute to Ireland's further oppression and exploitation.[17] If this writer explicitly equated Irish absentees with East Indian nabobs, yet another inferentially made the same point when he noted that, in terms of their susceptibility to British political corruption, Irish absentees were on a par with nabobs, Creoles, and other suspect characters in search of legitimation in the British political establishment.[18]

Notwithstanding these recurrent demands for taxing absentees, the Irish Parliament never acted to implement them, albeit in the late 1760s a bill intended to do so was only narrowly rejected. Writing in 1781, Nicholas Gay took up the cudgel for imposing such a tax. In language reminiscent of his many predecessors, he attributed Ireland's poverty to the absentees. "The absentees of this kingdom," he wrote, "have ever been, and at this hour, are the destruction of it," and if the Irish Parliament did not take "some steps . . . to put a stop to this terrible, unjust, and daily increasing evil," he warned, "we shall always continue the deserted, wretched, beggarly nation we now are." For the truth of this assertion, Gay appealed to "any man with eyes and feelings, who shall make a tour through any part of this kingdom, (two or three northern counties only excepted) which presents a picture of desolation, and woe, not easily described." Only the languages of plunder and exploitation seemed appropriate to describe this situation. Quoting Arthur Young, who in his recently published *Tour Through Ireland* had remarked that "'too many possessors of great estates in Ireland . . . wish[ed] to know nothing more of it than the remittance of their

---

[16] Duke of Chandos, speech, May 11, 1779, in William Cobbett et al., eds., *Parliamentary History of England from the Earliest Period to the Year 1803*, 36 vols. (London, 1806–20), 20: 642.

[17] *A View of the Present State of Ireland, Containing Observations upon the Following Subjects* (London, 1780), 97, 102, 104 note.

[18] *A Letter to the People of Ireland in which are Included Some Cursory Observations on the Effects of a Union* (London, 1780), 64.

rents,'" Gay insisted that "every evil" in Ireland was "altogether owing to our unfeeling, and uncharitable absentees." Thus, he lamented, "is this poor island cruelly treated; an island which, had it but its natural advantages, I will say its natural rights! and its revenue spent at home, would be one of the most flourishing and delightful spots in the world."[19] Published in 1783, the sixth edition of Morris's and Prior's *List of the Absentees of Ireland* revealed that the total annual capital drain from Ireland had by then exceeded two million pounds.[20]

III

Unlike the absentee drain, which involved the systematic exploitation of the lands and labor of Irish tenants by the most successful overlords to emerge from the British colonization of Ireland, without regard to the economic and social welfare of the kingdom as a whole, the problem with pensions and places arose mainly from the actions of the metropolitan government. As Morris's revisions of Prior's work made clear, not just "Absentee Landlords" but also "Absentee Pensioners" and absentee placemen were important sources of Ireland's capital drain and significant causes of its poverty.[21] Since the 1750s, some people had considered the "*Granting [of] Pen[sio]ns to Persons who do not reside in this Kingdom*" as "a national Grievance, demanding Redress,"[22] political analysts complaining about the "heavy drains" arising out of the Crown's awarding "Places and Pensions of Two, Three and Four Thousand Pounds annually from the *Irish* Revenues, to the Natives and Inhabitants of *Britain* and more remote Countries."[23] Funds for these pensions came from the Crown's hereditary revenues, which dated back to the Revolutionary Settlement in Ireland and were entirely at the Crown's disposal. Nothing eventuated from a 1758 proposal to substitute a fixed civil list for these revenues and thereby limit the Crown's access to Irish revenues and "prevent many a fatal Grant of Pensions,"[24] and, although no more than a quarter of the amount of absentee remittances, these pensions had exceeded £70,000 by the time Morris published his revised edition of Prior's work in 1768 – more than double the amount in the 1730s, as he pointed out.[25] In his revision of 1769 Morris raised this figure to £96,667. This "always increasing . . . Pension List,"[26] he remarked, sat particularly "heavy on

[19] Nicholas Gay, *A Letter to W. Tighe, Esq. Upon the Subject of the Absentees* (Dublin, 1781), 7–11.

[20] Redman Morris, *A List of the Absentees of Ireland*, 6th ed. (Dublin, 1783), 31.

[21] [Hasler], *Cursory Observations on Ireland*, 39.

[22] *Ireland Disgraced: Or, The Island of Saints Become an Island of Sinners* (London, 1758), 55–56.

[23] *Lysimachus: or, A Dialogue Concerning the Union of Great Britain and Ireland* (Dublin, 1760), 35.

[24] "Incognitus," *An Address to the People of Ireland, On the Present State of Public Affairs, and their Constitutional Rights* (Dublin, 1758), 14.

[25] Morris, *List*, 2nd ed., 15, 32.

[26] Morris, *List*, 3rd ed., 34.

every Body's Mind" because "the Merit of most of" the pensions was far from obvious.[27]

Morris was by no means the first to question whether this *"extraordinary Increase of Pensions on the Irish Establishment"* was of any benefit to Ireland.[28] Thus, in 1760 in a London pamphlet did an anonymous writer complain that the Irish were "obliged to support...a numberless Band of strange Pensioners, English, Scots, German, as well as Irish."[29] As this writer suggested, the strangeness of the pension list lay in the motley character of pension recipients, which early attracted considerable attention in Britain, where some people manifested an acute concern about whether the Crown and its ministers were using the Irish revenues to corrupt the British as well as the Irish House of Commons.

Writing in 1763 during the Bute Administration, Alexander McAulay, who described himself as "One of his Majesty's Counsel at Law for the Kingdom of Ireland," addressed this issue head on when he accused the Administration of having assumed an illegal and "unlimited Power of granting Pensions." McAulay did not deny Crown authority to use its private Irish revenues without restriction, but he expressed strong suspicions that British ministers and their Irish deputies were also granting without authorization pensions out of Ireland's public revenues. Employing the language of state corruption that the Opposition had long used to attack the Government in Britain, he suggested that those revenues had "been employ'd in Pensions to debauch his Majesty's Subjects of both Kingdoms," to corrupt "Men of that Kingdom to betray their Country, and Men of the neighbouring Kingdom, to betray Both. – ... to support Gamesters and Gaming-Houses," and to pilfer funds "out of the National Treasure of *Ireland*, under the Mask of Salaries annexed to Public Offices, useless to the Nation; newly invented for the Purposes of Corruption." Such pensions should, he contended, immediately "be cut off" and "the Perfidious Advisers...branded with [the] indelible Character of public Infamy; adequate, if possible, to the Dishonour of their Crime."[30]

But McAulay was also concerned with the social and economic impact of this expansive use of Irish pensions. Just as the country finally was "beginning to recover from the Devastations of Massacre and Rebellion" in the seventeenth century, he complained, this "licentious, unbounded Profusion of Pensions" was unleashing "Swarms of Pensionary Vultures" to prey upon Ireland's "Vitals" and, instead of being employed "in nourishing and improving her Infant-Agriculture, Trade and Manufactures; or in enlightening and reforming her poor, ignorant, deluded, miserable Natives," was "squandering the National Substance of *Ireland*." The result, he suggested, was that "Sloth

---

[27] Morris, *List*, 2nd ed., 32.
[28] Alexander McAulay, *An Inquiry into the Legality of Pensions on the Irish Establishment* (London, 1763), 1.
[29] [James Digges La Touche], *A Short but True History of the Rise, Progress, and Happy Suppression, of Several Late Insurrections Commonly Called Rebellions in Ireland* (Dublin, 1760), 11.
[30] McAulay, *An Inquiry into the Legality of Pensions*, 3, 21, 30–31.

and Nakedness and Wretchedness, Popery, Depopulation and Barbarism still maintain[ed] their Ground; still deform[ed] a Country abounding with all the Riches of Nature; yet, hitherto destin'd to Beggary." The Administration's profligate use of Ireland's meager fiscal resources, McAuley thus made clear, was essentially a form of imperial plunder and exploitation that showed little regard for Ireland's welfare and sacrificed Irish to British concerns – and corrupt concerns at that.[31]

McAuley's biting critique may have made British Administrations somewhat more cautious in the way they used Ireland's hereditary revenues, but the pension list remained an important source of British and Irish unease. During the early years of the Chatham Administration in 1766–77, an anonymous author with considerable Irish expertise issued a pamphlet in London predicting a thorough reformation in Irish affairs under the earl of Bristol, Chatham's appointee as Lord Lieutenant of Ireland. Among the many improvements he foresaw was a thorough examination of all public offices, the elimination of "all sinecure Employments" and "all superfluous Salaries," and the cessation of pension granting, except to those who had "done some national, some real Service." At last, he hoped, "the black Pension-list" would be "narrowly looked into" and the Irish establishment "eased from paying such large Pensions to Parasites, Whisperers, Pimps, and Concubines, those Locusts that devour the Land." Even those pensioners who had not fallen in with "such bad Company," he suggested, had probably never "done any Thing to deserve this Bounty, or to be, in any Shape, Objects of royal or national Compassion."[32] Whether or not these were realistic expectations, Bristol resigned before he ever went to Ireland, to be replaced by George, 1st Marquess Townshend, whose stormy Administration brought many Anglo-Irish issues into explicit public consideration.

Although he regarded it as only one of many ways in which Britain was systematically exploiting Ireland, Sir Hercules Langrishe similarly condemned the pension drain in a 1769 pamphlet, while also calling his readers' attention to the huge sums being drawn out of the hereditary revenues to pay "salaries to absent place-men, of which there are not a few." Whereas, according to Morris's data, pensions cost Ireland just over £90,000, "places and employment" took away a much larger sum, £143,000. Increasing the unfortunate effects of this additional drain was the fact that Irishmen rarely enjoyed much of a share of it, "the patronage of promotions, ecclesiastical and civil," Langrishe reported, being "in a great proportion applied to English purposes." "For a course of years," he complained, the "heads of the *Church, the State, the Army, and the Law*" for Ireland, "had been of another country." At the time he wrote, these included fifteen of twenty-two bishops, five of seven of the chief judicial officers, thirty-eight of forty-two commanders of Irish

[31] Ibid., 32–33.
[32] *A Letter to the Right Honourable J[ohn] P[onsonby], Speaker of the House of Commons in Ireland* (London, 1767), 35–36.

regiments, and nine of fourteen of the "great officers" of state, several of whom, holding their offices by reversionary grants, never came to Ireland so that their salaries flowed entirely out of the kingdom. To the detriment of Ireland and the expense of Irishmen, the British Administration seemed to be intent on using places as well as pensions to benefit Britain and metropolitan Britons. Wherever you "direct your observation," Langrishe lamented, "you find Ireland administering to England."[33]

With specific regard to the pension problem, Irish leaders got the impression from Townshend in the late 1760s that the British Administration had promised that, as an anonymous author remarked in a substantial pamphlet published in London in 1770, "no addition should be heaped on the load which then actually incumbered that establishment," but *authentic copies of the lists of pensions on the civil and military establishments of Ireland, returned to the [Irish] house of* commons" clearly revealed, that, "in defiance of those promises," the Administration had over the next six years added another £20,000 a year to pension disbursements. No matter how readers looked at the pension list, this writer declared, they would "find it a mill-stone about the neck of" both Britain and Ireland, "which, if not cast off in time, will sink us both in the sea." "Whether we regard the sum total, the accumulated burden," he said, in scrutinizing all aspects of the problem and combining the languages of oppression, rapacity, and state corruption, or "consider the numbers of this army of pensioners, as a band of court minions, ever ranged on the side of the minister of the day – Or" simply "view this heterogenous catalogue of English, Dutch, French, German, Scotch and Irish names, with the several sums thereunto annexed, as immediately oppressive in an extreme degree to our sister nation, [or] as eventually destructive to our own liberties," the pension list was profoundly disturbing. Drawn "from the coffers of a country whose poverty we actually hold, or at least affect to hold, in contempt, yet whose commerce we cramp, and whose manufactures in many severe instances we prohibit," and "thrown into the pockets of such worthy personages as [the] administration" wants to "gratify with yearly revenue," these pensions deprived "that miserably oppressed and exhausted kingdom" of a significant amount of its resources merely in order to reward from 200 to 250 pensioners, a privileged "*elect* . . . chosen . . . to batten on the spoils of their plundered country" at the "expence of a wretched race of savages, who live [on] butter-milk and potatoes." For participating so broadly in this largesse, he wrote, the Irish Parliament stood "stigmatized . . . with the odious epithet of the PENSIONARY parliament."[34]

Using the language of justice, this writer expressed his strong agreement with his "fellow-subjects on the other side of the water in the justice of their complaints," but he expressed "a far greater share of uneasiness when I look forward to the evil prospect which this unnatural excrescence, this overgrown wen, as I may call it, opens to the constitution of Great-Britain, than when

[33] Langrishe, *Considerations on the Dependencies of Great Britain*, 40–41, 44–46.
[34] *Thoughts, English and Irish, on the Pension-List of Ireland* (London, 1770), 3–4, 7–8, 17, 20.

I cast my eyes for the moment on her sickly sister, and observe to how low a state it has already reduced her health." Calling upon the members of the Irish Parliament to "save our constitution from being finally swallowed up by this voraginous gulph of Hibernian dependence" by closing their purses, eschewing their longtime subordination to the dictates of British ministers, and vindicating "now your dominion over yourselves," he recommended that the Irish Parliament, in its "next money-bill," include a clause for the "virtual abolition of pensions, by taxing them . . . at once to their full annual value" and thereby "effectually eradicating those noxious weeds of despotic corruption, even after they have seemed to take the deepest root in your soil."[35]

Forceful and cogent as was this condemnation of one of the most glaring excesses of British colonialism in Ireland, the Irish Parliament over the immediate future remained deaf to such arguments, and Ireland's "weighty civil establishment" continued, as the patriot Charles Lucas observed not long before his death in 1771, to be "loaded with pensions to foreigners, to aliens, and even to enemies to our constitution."[36] Remarking that Ireland notoriously had been "continually burthened with large Pensions," Josiah Tucker, in an aside to a pamphlet published on the American question in November 1775, identified one of the sources of Irish timidity on this issue by pointing out that while some pensions went "to Princes of the Blood" and ministerial favorites, some also went "to flaming [Irish] Patriots," the last of whom, he observed, would "accept of Pensions if they can get them."[37] Corruption seemingly had the capacity to stifle all opposition to reform. Ireland's chief kindness to Britain, the Barbadian Samuel Estwick bitingly observed in 1776, was in still suffering "itself to be loaded with pensions, civil and military, to the amount of 87000£. a year, and upwards."[38]

When in early 1779 and thereafter the British Parliament found itself confronted with Ireland's demands for the elimination of metropolitan trade restrictions, some members refused to believe that those restrictions were the source of Irish woes. Thus Sir George Yonge in a debate in February insisted that "the greatest part of her misfortunes arose, not from the restrictions of trade, but from the fault of her internal policy," singling out the "shameful . . . waste of their treasure in the support of pensioners and placemen" as "the great source of their calamities." Before "they came imploring the assistance of Britain," he asserted, "they should do all they could to extricate

---

[35] Ibid., 19, 26, 28–29.

[36] Charles Lucas, *The Rights and Privileges of Parlements Asserted Upon Constitutional Principles* (Dublin, 1770), 72.

[37] Josiah Tucker, *An Humble Address and earnest Appeal to Those Respectable Personages in Great-Britain and Ireland, Who, by Their Great and Permanent Interest in Landed Property, Their Liberal Education, Elevated Rank, and Enlarged Views, are the Ablest Judges, and the Fittest to Decide Whether a Connection with, or a Separation from the Continental Colonies of America, be most for the National Advantage, and the Lasting Benefit of these Kingdoms* (Gloucester, 1775), 84.

[38] Samuel Estwick, *A Letter to the Reverend Josiah Tucker* (London, 1776), 70.

themselves."[39] In these debates, Lord North denied that he had ever "thought of increasing" the "pension list" and contended that he had favored Ireland by awarding "Places in that kingdom, usually held by Englishmen...to the natives,"[40] but in a House of Lords debate the following December, the duke of Manchester reviewed a case in which North, to the great burden of Irish taxpayers and contrary to his claims in the House of Commons, had more than doubled a sinecure to his associate Charles Jenkinson.[41] In the same debate, the Irish-born Lord Shelburne, noting that the king's hereditary revenues from which pensions and salaries to placemen were drawn accounted for about two-thirds of total Irish taxes, argued that ministerial latitude in the disposition of those revenues represented a "gross defect" in the Irish constitution and "in its consequences" was "a source of endless mischief to the people" of both "Ireland and Britain; because," he said, employing the language of state corruption and repeating an old charge, "it afforded ministers on both sides the water, the means of corruption, and of rewarding those who supported them in their views and gave a sanction to their measures. It was doubly mischievous to Ireland," Shelburne added, "for while it impoverished the people there, it at the same time furnished the means of future oppression, and repeated public rapine."[42]

Writing at the same time in a London pamphlet for which Shelburne expressed high regard, Charles Francis Sheridan, a fellow Irishman who had read law at Lincoln's Inn and would soon return to Dublin to practice law, listed among the many examples of British oppression of Ireland the "band of hungry pensioners, and placemen" who "annually consume[d] in England" a considerable part of Irish revenues. The "major part of these pensioners," Sheridan declared, expressing a long-standing Irish complaint, were "so far from having any claim upon us, that the persons are as unknown to us, as their merits; and even their names we should never have heard of, but from reading them in the list of our plunderers. We cannot but think," he observed, that "the great sums expended among you by our absentees, and the monopoly of our trade, ought to satisfy you; we think it hard [that] you should *rob* a people, who have ever been so willing to give" – for British defense and other purposes.[43]

In the swirl of events in Irish-British relations after 1778, however, issues involving pensions and places were soon subsumed by more general questions involving Britain's oppression of Ireland. Thus, declared an anonymous

---

[39] Sir George Yonge, speech, February 15, 1779, in Cobbett et al., eds., *Parliamentary History*, 20: 137.

[40] Lord North's speech, March 12, 1779, in ibid., 269–70.

[41] Duke of Manchester's speech, December 1, 1779, in ibid., 1174–75.

[42] Lord Shelburne's speech, December 1, 1779, in ibid., 1161–63.

[43] [Charles Francis Sheridan], *Observations on the Doctrine laid down by Sir William Blackstone, Respecting the Extent of the Power of the British Parliament, Particularly with Relation to Ireland. In a Letter to Sir William Blackstone, with a Postscript addressed to Lord North, Upon the Affairs of that Country* (London, 1779), 81.

pamphleteer using the pseudonym "An Irishman" in a 1779 Dublin pamphlet, "pensions on the Irish establishment" were "a grievance," but, he insisted, "however they may have contributed to our distresses[,] they certainly" were "not the efficient causes of them."[44] Another Irish writer publishing in London in 1780 agreed. If "being over-burthened by a pension list" was a source of Ireland's troubles, he opined, "the fundamental cause of our distresses" were the disabling restrictions Britain imposed upon Irish commerce and upon Ireland's "internal system of government." These were the "great grievance[s]" that Britain imposed upon Ireland. Great as those grievances were, however, metropolitan Britons, as the beneficiaries of Britain's monopoly over Irish trade, had little reason to object to them, he suggested, much less even to notice the ancient and continuing "pillage" of Ireland through the misuse of hereditary revenues for purposes of making some metropolitans richer and corrupting those Irish people who might protest.[45]

IV

During the great crisis in British-Irish affairs in 1778–82, however, the most common explanation for Ireland's underdevelopment was neither the absentee drain nor the costly and undeserved pensions and places, but the systematic British economic and political discrimination against Ireland. This was an ancient Irish complaint expressed in the writings of William Molyneux and William King in the 1690s, by Jonathan Swift and Samuel Madden in the 1720s and 1730s, and by Charles Lucas from the late 1740s to the early 1770s. Indeed, Lucas, who started out as an apothecary and worked his way into public attention through his activities in Dublin city politics, played a major role in bringing a relatively long period of "imperial quiet" to an end in the 1750s. In a veritable flood of pamphlets, he showed himself to be a master of the language of liberty, a trenchant political analyst, and an irrepressible critic of British constitutional restrictions on Irish political latitude, the maladministration of the British lord lieutenants sent to oversee Ireland, and the corruption of the Irish Parliament.[46]

Threatened with imprisonment for seditious libel, Lucas in 1749 fled Dublin for London, where for several years he endeavored to bring his legal difficulties before British magistrates and, as he wrote in a pamphlet published there in 1756, to provide metropolitans with "an Idea of the Sufferings of your Fellow-Subjects, and Friends, . . . your Offspring or Brethren in the Kingdom of *Ireland*." Presenting himself as "the only man" in Ireland who "dared to assert

---

[44] "An Irishman," *Defence of Great Britain*, 11.

[45] *A Letter to the People of Ireland*, 1780, 18A.

[46] For an insightful general discussion of the writings of these and other authors, see Neil Langley York, *Neither Kingdom Nor Nation: The Irish Quest for Constitutional Rights, 1698–1800* (Washington, D.C.: Catholic University of America Press, 1994), 1–73. The quotation is from p. 53.

the natural and legal Rights of his Country" and using the traditional British language of liberty as a standard, he described how Ireland had been subjected to a "long train of ministerial Tranquility" through successive Administrations' gratification of important political leaders "with Pensions, Places, or more potent Promises" until they all became "Tool[s] of the Administration" and the Irish Parliament had been reduced in authority and rendered as impotent as contemporary French *parlements*, those "poor Remnant[s] of the *Gallic* States" that still retained "the Name without any of the essentials of a Parlement" and had no choice but meekly to register Administration edicts. With "the Leaders of the *Irish* Senate" thus "pampered by the Ministry . . . and possessed of all the Places of Profit and Trust in the State, with all their Emoluments and Perquisites," Lucas charged, that body could not give the Administration any serious opposition. Lucas's larger point was that such developments turned the Irish Parliament into an institution that little resembled the British Parliament in its much celebrated role as the guardian of British liberty. His principle contention was that the Irish Parliament, "by Law and by Right," ought to be as "free as that of *Britain*" and to enjoy "the same Authority, Privilege and Power, within that Realm, as yours has within this."[47]

As Lucas reported in a subsequent pamphlet, however, his efforts to expose "the iniquities and tyrannical measures" that were ruining Ireland found little sympathy among British officials, and only after George II's death in October 1760 had required a general election for the Irish House of Commons, the first since 1727, did the Irish political situation offer much prospect for the recovery of Ireland's inherited rights as a British polity.[48] Elected as a Dublin representative to Parliament, Lucas joined with others to pump new life into patriot aspirations to rid Ireland of the political disparities that distinguished the Irish constitution from the metropolitan. Subsequently stimulated by two intense debates in the late 1760s, one over Britain's proposal in 1768 to augment its peacetime military in Ireland by the addition of 3,000 troops and the other over the Crown's 1769 assertion of its disputed right to amend money bills, those of an independent or "patriotic" persuasion had articulated by the early 1770s a program of reform, the components of which were all of ancient vintage in Irish politics, designed to secure for the Irish polity rights and authority that would insure that members of the Irish political nation would enjoy the same liberties and rights as their equivalents in Britain. This program included a bill to limit the duration of Parliament;[49] a habeas corpus act, which, even though it had "been granted to every Colony, every Island dependent upon *Great Britain*,"

---

[47] Charles Lucas, *An Appeal to the Commons and Citizens of London* (London, 1756), 5–8, 10.

[48] Charles Lucas, *Reasonable Advice to the Electors of Members of Parliament* (London, 1760), 22–23, 68. Morley, *Irish Opinion and the American Revolution*, 68–71, provides a concise account of this episode, but see also Thomas Bartlett, "The Townshend Viceroyalty, 1767–72," in Thomas Bartlett and D. W. Heyton, eds., *Penal Era and Golden Age: Essays in Irish History, 1690–1830* (Belfast, 1979), 88–112.

[49] See, especially, Alexander McAulay, *Septennial Parliaments Vindicated*, 2nd ed. (Dublin, 1766), 9, 24–26, 43.

had "been refused" to Ireland "above forty times"; a bill to exclude placemen from Parliament; a militia bill to provide additional troops in case of a foreign invasion or a domestic uprising by the discontented majority Catholic population; an act to make judicial tenure during good behavior instead of only at the royal pleasure; the appointment of civil officials of competence and Irish birth; and the elimination of sinecures and undeserved pensions.[50]

Except for the 1768 Octennial Act providing for elections every eight years, the Patriots gained none of these objectives, and the experience left them with profound bitterness. Complaining that the Irish were being "treated, of late, not as the Children, but the Bastards of our mother country" and that the British Ministry and its Irish agents considered "all our expectations" for "an equal distribution of inheritance, ... not as claims of right, but as pretences of contumacy, and presumption," an article in the *Freeman's Journal*, subsequently reprinted in *Baratariana*, suggested that Britain's "ministerial tyranny," having found America "at too great a distance ... to fall an immediate sacrifice to the politics of despotism," had commenced "the essay ... nearer home" through, as another writer in the same journal declared, its attempts to reduce Ireland to the status of "a province only, of another kingdom." As yet another *Baratariana* essayist pointed out, such behavior was part of a pattern that dated back at least two decades. The king's viceroys, he lamented, had, one after another, "destroyed this kingdom." Having been "sent ... to govern," they instead "went to plunder," with the result that Ireland had "felt Government in the vices of its Governors, not in the protection of its King." "For a series of years," he remarked, this "Unhappy Kingdom" had "been appropriated to the bad qualities of the worst of [British] Nobility, and ... languished under the distracting vicissitudes of shifting plunderers."[51]

Still, Patriots were sure that they were in the right. They knew that Ireland "did once possess an English constitution," one Patriot wrote,[52] and had no doubt that, as another declared, the "Parliament of *Ireland*, as to its proper Jurisdiction," was "as well supported by the Principles on Northern *Gothick Government*, as that of *England*," having been "confirmed by a long prescriptive Right, even from the first Establishment of the *English* in this Island," and "prescriptive Rights" having "always been allowed one of the best Titles to particular Forms of Government."[53] Noting that Ireland had been for too long submissive "to a Tyranny, without Authority," they called upon the Irish political nation to "cast off the yoke of slavery, and vindicate our freedom and independence."[54]

[50] *A Letter to the Right Honourable J[ohn] P[onsonby]*, 4, 6, 20–37.
[51] *Baratariana: A Select Collection of Fugitive Political Pieces: Consisting of Letters, Essays, &c. Published during the Administration of His Excellency Lord Viscount Townshend; in Ireland* (Dublin, 1772), 2, 41, 87–88.
[52] Ibid., 89.
[53] *A Letter to a Noble Lord, In Answer to his Address to the People of Ireland, with Some Interesting Reflections on the Present State of Affairs* (Dublin, 1770), 18.
[54] *Baratariana*, 40–42.

Yet critics worried that Patriots were carrying their opposition too far and thereby putting "this Kingdom . . . in imminent Danger." The Commons' claims, said one Administration supporter during the money bill controversy, tended, like all "the favourite Topicks of Opposition," to "involve Us in Disputes with *Great Britain*, on Questions, which We are no more able to support by Reason, than We are able to resist her by Force of Arms."[55] Arguing that it was never "adviseable to break or quarrel" with Britain, another writer expressed his distaste "for standing upon puntilios, when there is nothing to be got, nor any good to be proposed from it."[56] "Might not a Contest between us and England, be to us most dangerous?," asked yet another author. "Can it be supposed, that they, in such a Case, would yield to us?"[57]

These discussions of imperial relations between Britain and Ireland during the 1760s and early 1770s focused intently upon Ireland's political rather than its economic grievances. An important exception was Langrishe in his 1769 London pamphlet, *Considerations on the Dependencies*. In endeavoring to make his case that Ireland was far too poor to contribute an additional £100,000 annually to help pay off Britain's debts, as William Knox had proposed in his *Present State of the Nation*, Langrishe undertook a cost-benefit analysis of what Britain and Ireland got from one another. He broke this analysis down into four main categories: civil, economic, security, and political rights, in none of which did Ireland come out the winner. Notwithstanding all the disadvantages that Ireland bore as a result of its involvement with Britain, Langrishe insisted that Ireland felt "no resentment," demanded "no recompense," acknowledged "as much dependa[n]ce as is consistent with liberty," and retained its long-standing "national loyalty" to Britain. Notwithstanding his resentment at Britain's frequent "abridgement of the natural rights of Ireland" and many other "injuries . . . done to our liberty and our constitution" and his calls for a relaxation of trade restrictions, he recommended that Ireland yield "to the circumstances of the times, and complication of the British Empire" and to the necessity for the British Parliament to exercise a "general superintending power . . . for the arbitration of commerce, and for directing, restraining, and regulating the *external* relations between the different members of the empire," even admitting that the British Parliament's "first and greatest object should be, the commerce of the *principal country*" and that "no trade should be permitted to any part of his Majesty's dominions, injurious to England."[58]

Despite Charles Lucas's complaints about the "heavy burdens" that Britain had "imposed upon a Country, deprived, as it is, of almost all the natural

55 *Letter to Sir L——s O——N. Bart. On the Late Prorogation* (Dublin, 1770), 15–16.
56 *The Principles of Modern Patriotism, Catechetically Explained* (Dublin, 1770), 27–28.
57 "Poblicola" [Gorges Edmond Howard], *Some Questions upon the Legislative Constitution of Ireland* (Dublin, 1770), 18.
58 Langrishe, *Considerations on the Dependencies of Great Britain*, 30–31, 33–38, 42–43, 48, 50–53 notes, 54–55.

resources of trade,"[59] and despite Langrishe's recommendation for easing British restrictions on Irish commerce, the hope, expressed by the latter, that Ireland and Great Britain should "be to the latest times united, by the indissoluble ties of general interest, and a constant communication of good offices" probably expressed the sentiments of the vast majority of the minority Protestant Irish establishment and inhibited the emergence of widespread demands for Britain's removal of Ireland's economic and political disabilities.[60] This situation changed following the outbreak of the American war in 1775 and a subsequent metropolitan embargo on the export of Irish provisions in early 1776. Many Irish leaders feared that this embargo would have a disastrous effect upon the Irish economy and began to construct an argument that Britain's repeated subordination of Irish economic interests to those of Britain constituted a form of systematic oppression that was itself largely responsible for Ireland's economic woes.

In a running debate that would last over twenty months, the British Parliament took up the subject of Irish commercial oppression in April 1778. Lord North alerted the House of his intention "to relax the trade laws" as they applied to Ireland on the grounds that it would both "benefit the Irish and ultimately enrich ourselves."[61] But North's proposals evoked immediate opposition from British manufacturing and trading interests, including angry petitions from Glasgow, Liverpool, Bristol, and many other commercial centers. When the House resumed consideration of the Irish question in May, these petitions sparked a vigorous debate. Speaking for the petitioners, Sir Cecil Wray predicted dire consequences for British manufacturers if North's proposed concessions went into effect and urged a detailed consideration.[62] In answer, earl Nugent decried the "illiberal sentiments" of the British petitioners as "mean, unmanly, ungenerous, despicable, and diabolical,"[63] and Edmund Burke spoke at length against delay. Using the languages of oppression and justice, he contended that the Navigation Acts had placed Ireland "under the most cruel, oppressive, and unnatural restriction," depriving it "of every incentive to industry" and shutting it "out from every passage to wealth." Although Ireland "had inwardly lamented," he continued, it "had never complained of" its "condition" but instead "had gone the most forward lengths in serving the interests, and in defending the rights of Great Britain," assisting "in conquests, from which" it "was to gain no advantage," emptying its treasury and "desolating" its "land, to prove" its "attachment and loyalty to the government of this country." For this praiseworthy conduct, Burke complained, Ireland had

---

[59] Charles Lucas, *The Rights and Privileges of Parliaments Asserted upon Constitutional Principles, Against the Modern Anticonstitutional Claims of Chief Governors* (Dublin, 1770), 72.

[60] Langrishe, *Considerations on the Dependencies of Great Britain*, 52, 90.

[61] Lord North, speech, April 7, 1778, in Cobbett et al., eds., *Parliamentary History*, 19: 1112.

[62] Sir Cecil Wray, speech, May 6, 1778, in ibid., 1116–17.

[63] Earl Nugent, speech, May 6, 1778, in ibid., 1117.

been rewarded with nothing but "restriction and bondage of the most cruel nature."[64]

In this situation, North hesitated, declaring that he thought it Britain's "duty . . . to give Ireland a degree, at least, of recompence for the exertions she had made"[65] but permitting the adjournment of debate despite warnings that, as Lord Newhaven, an Irish peer and British M.P., said, "the people of Ireland," having had their "expectations . . . raised to the highest pitch, . . . would now be plunged into the deepest despair." "Without advantage in trade," Newhaven said, "Ireland must ever remain in its present state of indigence," and postponing this matter would mean only that the arguments against it would "be the same next year as this, and so on for ever, while the poverty of Ireland and the jealousy of England existed."[66]

Parliament let a year pass before giving the question intensive discussion. In the meantime, several authors published pamphlets in London for and against Britain's taking measures to relax restrictions on Irish trade. Sympathetic to Irish demands, an anonymous author addressing the *"Merchants and Manufacturers of the City of Glasgow"* inquired why they "endeavour[ed] to intercept from the kingdom of Ireland the rays and fostering influence of the sun of commerce" and "impiously withold from its inhabitants the use of those natural advantages which God has bestowed? Why," he continued, should Ireland "remain in poverty, in dependance, in ignorance, in misery?" He urged them to consider what Scotland had been before the union and whether Scotland's "unbounded participation" in "English commerce, . . . English freedom, and . . . English favour" since 1707 had not been responsible for its overcoming of "the curse of dependence, the squalor of poverty, the grossness of ignorance, and the manners of barbarism" that before 1707 had long given Scotland an almost exact "similitude" to contemporary "Irish wretchedness," a reversal now crowning "you with riches, and" refining "you into elegance."[67]

On the other side, "T. S." favored removing all Irish grievances concerning pensions, the absentee drain, and placemen and even thought that it might "be practicable" to relax some of the trade restraints imposed by the Navigation Acts in response to Irish complaints, but he argued strongly that "it would be madness, under the stated circumstances, to annihilate them entirely." In his view, the American quarrel had proved conclusively that "detached provinces" could not "with safety, enjoy equal privileges, with that part of the state which is the seat of empire." To "cast the strength of government to a remote distance, from the centre on which it is established," he wrote, resorting to the language of imperial grandeur, was "to debilitate the power of the state" by extending

---

[64] Edmund Burke, speech, May 6, 1778, in ibid., 1119–23.

[65] Lord North, speech, May 6, 1778, in ibid., 1118–19.

[66] Lord Newhaven, speech, May 25, 1778, in ibid., 1125–26.

[67] *A Letter to the Worshipful the Dean of Guild, and the Merchants and Manufacturers of the City of Glasgow, Upon their Opposition to the Irish Bills* (London, [1779]), 8–11, 14. See also [Margaret Bingham, Countess of Lucan], *Verses on the Present State of Ireland. By a Lady* (London, 1778), 1–3.

it beyond the point at which the center could impose restraints that would effectively insure obedience to metropolitan law and discourage "attempt[s at] independency." Although he acknowledged that Ireland was "not very distant from the throne which rules it," he noted that it was still "a detached country" and one that "if at any time disposed to revolt" lay closer than America to "our natural enemy, France," which seemed to be "always ready to cherish rebellion against England." Turning to the languages of commerce and national security, "T. S." reminded his readers that trade, as regulated by the established "system of trading laws," was the source of Britain's naval and military strength alike, and of "that uncommon prosperity [that had] poured down upon the inhabitants of *every part* of the dominions of Great Britain, while concord and a peaceful adherence prevailed," and he expressed the fear "that to give it up" would make "way for invasion, devastation, and probable destruction."[68]

At the same time, in Dublin, some supporters of the Protestant political establishment, worrying that the Irish Parliament's demand for free trade had gone too far and might produce a rupture with Britain, endeavored to show both that Ireland's "present distress" did "not *principally* proceed from the restrictions laid upon our trade by Great Britain" and that the removal of those restrictions would not soon or necessarily put an end to that distress. Closely examining what he called "the real causes of the distress of our Manufacturers," a writer using the pseudonym "An Irishman," no doubt to distinguish himself from the Patriot leaders who promoted the free trade movement, denied that it was attributable to "*the Iron hand of [British] Oppression.*" Nor did he think that the Navigation Acts came "within the meaning of that hateful word Tyranny; which signifies 'despotic government, cruel, *severe, uncontrouled by law.*'" Quite the contrary. "Within the last half century, under the [alleged] tyranny of England," he wrote, Ireland had "very considerably improved." Ireland's distress, he concluded, proceeded, not "from the system of tyranny in Great-Britain," but mostly "from ourselves, and from causes incident to human nature," citing "the conduct of our landholders, manufacturers, absentees," pensioners, and placemen as being "fully sufficient to involve this country in her *present distress* without recurring to the Tyranny of Great Britain."[69] Another anonymous writer, calling himself "A Grazier" and stressing Ireland's need for British protection against France and its Catholic majority, urged readers to consider the vast benefits that Britain, through colonization, had brought to Ireland. Finding "us rude, and uncivilized, scarce a degree removed from savages," he noted, employing the languages of civility and security, "she has taught us her customs, and her manners, instructed us in commerce, improvements, and husbandry," and "spent her treasure and her blood more

---

[68] "T. S.," *Impartial Thoughts on a Free Trade to the Kingdom of Ireland, in a Letter to the Right Hon. Frederick, Lord North* (London, 1779), 9–10, 16, 20, 22–24.
[69] "An Irishman," *Defence of Great Britain*, preface, 4, 6, 11–13.

than once to prevent the bloody banners of Rome from flying triumphant in this kingdom."[70]

When the British Parliament took up the free trade question again in the late winter of 1778 and spring of 1779, the Opposition used the North Administration's inaction to become the champions of a British campaign for Irish relief, a campaign that was deeply affected by two developments within Ireland. First, Irish realization after the Franco-American alliance in early 1778 that Britain could not provide much help against a possible French invasion had prompted the formation of volunteer military units, spreading from north to south throughout Ireland. By March 1778, 11,000 men had organized themselves into local groups of Volunteers independent of state support; over the course of 1779, the number of Volunteers in arms would grow to as many as 42,000. Second, the British Parliament's failure to make significant trade concessions had stiffened Irish demands and led to the formation of Irish associations to curb British imports until Britain yielded on the question of free trade, a tactic used by the American colonies with mixed success before the outbreak of the American war.

In British parliamentary debates, the Opposition, depicting the Irish as "the most oppressed and injured people under the sun,"[71] expressed astonishment that a "great, loyal, and a brave people were" being "ruined, beggared or oppressed" for no other reason than that British producers and traders might be slightly injured by concessions,[72] reminded listeners that in 1778 the Ministry had offered much more extensive concessions to America, and accused the Administration of incompetence, duplicity, and delay. "By their clamours without doors and interest within," Lord Rockingham charged in the House of Lords in May 1779, the "manufacturers of this country had already" effectively "proscribed the trade and commerce of their brethren in Ireland," while the Ministry "had repeatedly broken" its "most solemn assurances and amused" the Irish "from session to session with promises, in order the more easily and safely to plunder them." But such delays and evasions, he charged, had only "exasperate[d] the oppressed people of Ireland, and work[ed] them up into such successive paroxysms of resentment, phrenzy, and despair, as might at length terminate in a civil convulsion, which would shake the government of these kingdoms to its inmost foundations."[73] In the face of other members' insistence that the interests of Britain as well as Ireland ought "to be considered" and that the "great body of British manufacturers had rights and claims

[70] "A Grazier," *Thoughts on the Present Alarming Crisis of Affairs: Humbly Submitted to the Serious Consideration of the People of Ireland* (Dublin, 1779), 12–13, 16. See also [Hasler], *Cursory Observations on Ireland*, 6, 28, 30–31, 34, and *Four Letters to the Earl of Carlisle from William Eden, Esq.*, 2nd ed. (London, 1779), 124, 127.
[71] Earl of Bristol, speech, May 11, 1779, in Cobbett et al., eds., *Parliamentary History*, 20: 649–50.
[72] Duke of Richmond, speech, May 11, 1779, in ibid., 20: 650.
[73] Lord Rockingham, speech, May 27, 1779, in ibid., 20: 651–52.

of their own, which they would not readily part with," North continued to waver.[74]

Only in early December, after the Irish House of Commons had threatened to withhold appropriations and both houses had, "with but one dissenting voice," expressed, as Shelburne remarked in the British House of Lords, "the united voice" of Ireland, did North finally push through a comprehensive free trade bill. Although the bill had been a long time coming, the Irish political nation received it enthusiastically; for the better part of a year this concession would have the temporary effect of defusing the crisis in Anglo-Irish relations. But the long struggle leading up to it had stimulated a general consideration of the legitimacy of Britain's claims to authority over Ireland and, as the earl of Upper Ossory phrased it in a House of Lords debate on December 1779, of Ireland's claims "to justice, and [to] the protection and rights secured by a free constitution" – the same subjects that Charles Lucas, Sir Hercules Langrishe, and other Patriot writers had previously explored during the political debates of the 1760s and early 1770s.[75]

Two pamphlets, both of them published anonymously in London in 1779 and addressed to a metropolitan British as well as an Irish audience, examined these subjects in some detail. The first, by the lawyer Charles Francis Sheridan, brother of the dramatist Richard Brinsley Sheridan, was a carefully crafted analysis intended to make the case that Britain's conduct toward Ireland exhibited "a degree of oppression" that was "totally repugnant" both "to . . . just notions of [British] liberty" and to "accurate ideas of the principles of a free constitution." His native Ireland, Sheridan wrote, had suffered "very severely from the narrow illiberal system of policy, which, with respect to that unfortunate country, has long marked and disgraced the councils of this kingdom." Declaring that it was "highly requisite, that juster notions concerning the nature of liberty; more accurate ideas respecting . . . the principles of the constitution, and particularly with regard to the extent of the *power of parliament*, should prevail in Great Britain, than those, the artful propagation, and inconsiderate admission of which, have already cost us thirteen provinces," Sheridan was primarily concerned to supply the intellectual foundations for Ireland's renewed claims for legislative independence, then being agitated in the British as well as the Irish press and Parliament.[76]

Hyperbolic and discursive, the second pamphlet took the form of a letter to the earl of Hillsborough, a major Irish landlord and secretary of state for the Southern Department, in which the author sought to explain the broader sources and nature of Irish discontent with imperial governance. He traced that discontent to apprehensions among the "people of Ireland . . . that those chains forged for America were also the models for fetters for themselves." Although they were well aware that "the encroachments of the British Legislature had left

---

[74] Earl Gower, speech, May 11, 1779, in ibid., 20: 647.
[75] Ibid.
[76] [Sheridan], *Observations on the Doctrine laid down by Sir William Blackstone*, 27–29.

but little room for any farther usurpations," they worried that "the same spirit of peculation" that had driven Britain's attempt to tax the colonies would "extend itself to Ireland" and that their right to tax themselves, "the only remaining bulwark of their liberties," would "shortly... be levelled, and... a despotic authority" erected "to preside over every branch of their civil polity." In the "universal panic [that] pervaded the nation" over this dire prospect, this author reported, and in "the despair of poverty and oppression," the Irish vainly "looked round them... for some one object of comfort," but they saw only a vast "catalogue of... woes – an encreasing debt – decreasing commerce – heavy taxes – useless pensions!," the linen trade "confined by illegal restrictions," an embargo leaving "the most valuable produce of their country rotting in their harbours," and their "unguarded coasts... hourly insulted by a triumphant enemy."[77]

In this situation, this author recounted, the Irish "recollected that a foreign Legislature had assumed over them a power of restriction" and that that "power derived from no one principle but that odious one of force." At the same time, they also recalled "that, in answer to every objection against this oppressive controlment," Britain had "answered, 'That obedience and gratitude were the necessary returns of protection and support; and that England had a right to tyrannize over Ireland, as long as she defended her from the tyranny of others.'" With the French entry into the American war, however, the Irish realized that this "argument, futile in reason," had "now become false in fact" and that Britain was "no longer able to support Ireland" or even "to defend herself – her multiplied acts of injustice" having "united the world against her" and made it impossible for Ireland to look to Britain for protection. This realization, he wrote, determined the Irish to "demand an *equality* with England," and they resolved to acknowledge "no laws but what they find in their own records."[78]

Notwithstanding the euphoria that gripped Ireland in the wake of the free trade concessions, these two pamphlets published in 1779 were the first of many published in 1780 and 1781 expressing resentment through the languages of oppression and injustice and advocating Irish parliamentary independence. Written mostly by Irishmen, these tracts were often published in both London and Dublin. "From the instant of our connexion with England, I know not the station an Irishman could place himself in, from which, until the present hour, he could look forward with sincere satisfaction," declared an author using the pseudonym "A Native of Ireland, and a Lover of the British Empire"; the "poignancy of his grief for the past sufferings of his unhappy country could only be exceeded by his fears for the future." That connection and, more particularly, Britain's claim to the power "of binding Ireland by her laws," and "that alone," he insisted, was the source of all of Ireland's economic distress.

[77] *A Letter to the Right Honourable The Earl of Hillsborough, Secretary of State for the Southern Department, on the Present State of Affairs in Ireland and an Address to the People of that Kingdom* (London, 1779), 8–10.
[78] Ibid., 11–12, 14, 19.

Denouncing the expressions of gratitude that had followed the free trade bill "as a species of idolatry" on the part of his infatuated countrymen, he inquired how any of them could possibly think that "the present revolution[,] so favourable to Ireland," had proceeded "from motives so pure, as a disinterested regard for our rights and liberties," or that Lord North, "the man . . . who [had] sported with the privileges of our American brethren," could possibly feel "a sincere affection for you." "Believe me," he asserted, "those wonderous concessions flowed not from his wishes for your welfare, but from his fears from your spirit. If praise is to be given, the volunteers of Ireland deserve the loudest applause."[79]

Indeed, in this author's opinion it was only after the Volunteers had frightened off France that the Irish had found that "there yet was one [enemy] left, "that a "more dangerous [one] . . . was lurking in our very bosom, like a canker," and had "eat[en] its way into our vitals, and was preying upon our constitution." With the confidence inspired by the military force behind them, the Irish, having "discovered that our liberty had been invaded by England, and that she had not only robbed us of our birthright, but had even tied up our hands from acquiring a compensation for so irreparable a loss," had acquired a new spirit that had enabled them to stand up to "that monster of corruption, the British Senate," and to achieve the commercial concessions that bid "fair to dispel that dismal gloom, which has so long obscured their political horizon." Yet he insisted that as long as Britain claimed "the power of subjecting" Ireland "to every restraint, which mistaken policy, narrow selfishness, or capricious tyranny may deem subservient to the purposes of oppression," the Irish had to remain wary, and he urged them to "insist upon the right of our parliament to be free from the controul of the British legislature." "Without legislative independence," he concluded, Ireland could never "flourish in commerce, become respectable as a nation, or free as a people."[80]

A London pamphlet by an anonymous Irishman used similar language to caution the Irish against attempts "to undermine our resolution, and to restore us to our antient languor upon all public subjects." Certainly, this author wrote, turning to the language of humanity, Ireland could place no confidence in Britain's humanity. If "such a thing as political humanity" ever existed, he asserted, it could never "be found in a country of commerce" like Britain. "Combining in the soul of a commercial Empire," he wrote, "JEALOUSY, monopoly, and pride" excluded "every thing, except industry, punctuality, and that species of probity which is necessary for credit." For a "mercantile empire," he observed, challenging the traditional association of commerce with liberty, questions of liberty were obviously of little importance. Beginning

[79] "A Native of Ireland, and a Lover of the British Empire," *The Usurpations of England the Chief Source of the Miseries of Ireland and the Legislative Independence of this Kingdom, the only Means of Securing and Perpetuiating the Commercial Advantages lately recovered* (Dublin, 1780), 3–4, 7, 17–18.
[80] Ibid., 3, 13–14, 20–21, 26, 31.

"by taking from the connected country her Trade," it "soon proceed[ed] to make very bold attempts upon her Liberty. – Under pretence of maintaining trade-laws," it "assert[ed] in *all* cases, and exercise[d] in *some*, the power of binding internally; and next assume[d] the right of taxing," one infringement leading to another as "the mother Country, grown insolent from Empire, and distempered from its fumes," in an effort to "to maintain a dominion [that] she has usurped," claimed "the right of taking away the liberty which she has left." "Such was the power exercised against America, and denounced against Ireland," he wrote, noting that "the resistance of the former" had "saved the latter."[81]

Still another anonymous author, this one probably English, who addressed his readers on "the eve of a revolution... in the great commercial policy of Britain towards Ireland," also thought that the source Britain's oppression of Ireland was to be found in Britain's commercial orientation. "Ruled by a principle of commerce," Britain, he wrote, had always "endeavoured to turn all her dependencies and possession into this channel of her greatness," planting "colonies in climes, where the quality of her products would afford a reciprocal advantage in the exchange of their commodities" and holding them and Ireland "under the iron rod of commercial oppression," as the "narrow illiberal temper of... trade... seemed to have reached and subdued the wisdom of the state. Instead of beholding Ireland in the light of a partner and friend," he continued, "the ruin of that kingdom, in the eye of mercantile avarice, appears to have been considered as the destruction of a dangerous rival." Thus originating "in a selfish mercantile disposition, which imposed the fetters without prescribing any terms by which the Irish might be sett free," the British, following an invasion and occupation that the author denounced as "act[s] of the highest injustice," imposed commercial restrictions on Ireland on the basis of "supposed rights from conquest and colonization," when they should have justified "this extraordinary exertion" on the "two principles" of "Justice and policy." "Against a sordid mercantile disposition," he lamented, "Humanity and justice" could never "be pleaded with success."[82]

In specific reference to the free trade issue, as Irish Patriot leaders came to understand that the British regarded their concessions as, in the words of the Ulster barrister Francis Dobbs in a pamphlet he addressed to Lord North, "a matter of EXPEDIENCY, not of right," they also realized that those concessions "rather established, than relinquished the power of British legislation over Ireland." As long as Britain treated "with Ireland under the idea of giving as little as she can, and that little from necessity," Dobbs pointed out, Ireland could "neither be thankful nor... satisfied." Using the language of liberty and defining the "boasted freedom of a subject of Great-Britain" as exemption from being "governed by laws to which he has [not] consented either by himself or his representative," and "a slave" as one who is "bound by laws, to which he

[81] *A Letter to the People of Ireland*, 1780, 6–7, 9–12, 36, 41, 71.
[82] *A View of the Present State of Ireland*, v, vii–viii, 1, 4, 8–9.

never assented, and lies at the mercy of a power over which he has no controul," he asked North directly to tell him, in terms of "these two definitions, . . . what is IRELAND?" "My Lord," he continued, succinctly spelling out the full extent of Ireland's aspirations,

we claim to be a kingdom, with every right belonging to a kingdom; governed by our own legislature, the King, Lords, and Commons of Ireland. We complain of the British legislature making laws to bind Ireland. We alledge it is without right, and we require that the legislature of Great-Britain should relinquish such a claim that we say they are not entitled to, and that they should obliterate the name of Ireland from their Statutes.

The resolution of Britain's troubles with Ireland, Dobbs thought, would require a declaration from the British Parliament that Britain had "no right to bind Ireland by British acts of Parliament" and the total repeal of "all laws hitherto made for that purpose."[83]

Writing anonymously in a pamphlet published in London and Dublin, William Eden tried to blunt such demands by reminding the Irish of their close ties to Britain and of their need for protection against both domestic and foreign enemies, appealing to their British patriotism and suggesting that Ireland's proximity to Britain and its continuing ties to the Crown would always entwine them in British affairs and inhibit their efforts to be independent of the British polity. "The kingdom of Ireland is no less appendant to the crown of England by law and constitution, than her fate is by situation to the fortunes of Great-Britain," he wrote, and "She can rise or fall but with them. This appendancy of Ireland to the crown of a *greater* country, in which country too the executive authority of both kingdoms, with its pomp and patronage, resides," he noted, "does necessarily create, without any malicious intent, a comparative inferiority; and this comparative inferiority has unavoidably appeared upon some occasions in symptoms of partiality, no less, perhaps, in point of constitution than of trade." But what other option had they? Facing a possible uprising of its oppressed Catholic majority and having been granted an open trade, Ireland, Eden recommended, needed, in its quest for constitutional change, to pursue a policy of "Prudence and kind offices," not confrontation.[84]

But prudence seemed to be entirely the wrong course to Patriot writers determined to free Ireland from its political fetters. Answering Eden, an anonymous Dublin pamphleteer contended that Eden's careful avoidance of "*the claim of right*" and his choice instead to use "that barren resource, the BOUNTY of Great-Britain," entirely misread "the present situation and spirit of the people." For to

talk of an English Parliament *allowing* a kingdom possessed of a complete legislature within herself, the *use* of her *own* ports – to talk of the representatives of the freeholders

---

[83] Francis Dobbs, *A Letter to the Right Honourable Lord North, on the Propositions in Favour of Ireland* (London, 1780), 6–10, 12, 18–19, 22.

[84] [William Eden], *Considerations Submitted to the People of Ireland on Their Present Condition with Regard to Trade and Constitution* (Dublin, 1781), 2, 4–5, 68–72.

of England, *giving leave* to the people of Ireland, who acknowledge no such authority, to export their own manufactures, or to import such merchandize as they shall think proper to import,

was, he wrote, merely "to talk *idly*." When "the people of Ireland" sought a free trade, the author informed Eden, they did not ask it "as a *favour*" but demanded it "as a *right*," and when they demanded a free trade, they did

not address the English parliament in their legislative capacity to repeal restrictive laws; – they address[ed] you as a neighbouring nation to disavow *an odious usurpation*, equally impolitic and unjust, to disclaim not laws but illegal determinations which nothing but your being possessed of a fleet, and our want of one, could have inspired you with the injustice to maintain.[85]

If the warnings of people like Eden drove Patriots to take ever more extreme positions in their quest to free themselves from the authority of the British Parliament, they gave enough people pause to prevent Patriot efforts from pushing their ideas through the Irish Parliament in 1780 and 1781. Yet the Volunteers continued to provide strong backing to such aspirations. In a 1781 pamphlet, Henry Gratton, the leading Patriot spokesman, credited them with Ireland's new resolve. "What else was it which until 1779 made the people of Ireland, with all the privileges of the British nation, afraid to resort to the benefit of their own laws?," he asked. "What, but an evident superiour strength arrayed against them? What else was it which in 1779 made the parliament and people struggle for their birthright? What, but that occult cause, a conscious strength, an inward security, an armed people?" Even though "volunteers never attempted force," he wrote, they contributed mightily to "this surprising change," in which "the nation recovered her liberty with as much tranquillity as she had lost it" by standing by and "giving a silent confidence to liberty, as an independent army."[86]

Although they made little headway in Parliament, the Patriots and their Volunteer supporters managed to articulate a program designed to bring the Irish polity to the same constitutional level as the British, a program that Grattan succinctly outlined in the same pamphlet. The first objective, he declared, was that

the power of binding Ireland by the British parliament be utterly and for ever... abolished and abjured, that there may be no seed of jealousy between the two nations, on whose heart-felt coalition their mutual happiness depends, that officious men may not traduce one country to the other, and that a future minister may not proceed, as in

---

[85] *Letter to William Eden*, 10, 34–36.
[86] [Henry Gratton], *Observations on the Mutiny Bill: With Some Strictures on Lord Buckingam-shire's Administration in Ireland* (London, 1781), 60. This pamphlet originally was published in Dublin. For a detailed account of the Irish politics in this area, see James Kelly, *Prelude to Union: Anglo-Irish Politics in the 1780s* (Cork: Cork University Press, 1992). York, *Neither Kingdom nor Nation*, 109–52, provides an excellent short account.

the instance of America, on the reserved principles of supremacy, and, unable to govern either country, embroil both.

The second objective was that "the power of the crown to alter, and of the Irish council to alter and suppress our bills, a power useless to his Majesty, opprobrious to his subjects, and founded on misconstruction of [Poynings'] law, be relinquished;" the third, that "the Mutiny Bill be here as in England, dependent on parliament;" the fourth, that "the Judges be here as in England, independent of the crown;" and the fifth, that habeas corpus be introduced so "that the mouth of the law may not be the will of power, nor the sword her instrument." If, instead of yielding on these "principal constitutional amendments," the "British minister [should] trample down America, . . . become haughty to Ireland," and meditate "a blow" against it, he noted, the Irish needed to "preserve your armed associations" in order "to keep what you have gotten already." By disbanding, he warned, the Volunteers would, to the detriment of Irish liberty, "give a silent confidence to power."[87]

The American victory at Yorktown in the fall of 1781, followed by the decline of British support for the continuation of the American war, the fall of the North Ministry, and its replacement by North's former opponents led by Lord Rockingham, set the stage for Ireland's achievement of the Irish Patriot program for constitutional reform. At the first meeting of Parliament under the new Administration on April 8, 1782, William Eden, an adherent of North's who had recently returned from Ireland, where he had been chief secretary under North's last lord lieutenant, the earl of Carlisle, rose to provide a short sketch of Irish affairs. Assuring the House that " . . . in the present state and disposition of Ireland . . . the House . . . might as well strive to make the Thames flow up Highgate-hill, as to attempt to legislate for Ireland, which would no longer submit to any legislation but its own," he announced that he planned to bring in a bill to repeal the Declaratory Act of 1721.[88] Although Eden's proposal caught the new Administration off guard, Charles James Fox, its chief spokesman in the House, agreed that Ireland deserved redress "for the oppressive treatment she had long groaned under."[89]

When the British Parliament again took up this subject on May 17, 1782, it was confronted with a resolution of the Irish House of Commons of April 16 that Ireland was a "distinct kingdom, with a parliament of her own, the sole legislature thereof."[90] Fox pushed through a bill to meet Irish demands, starting with the repeal of the Declaratory Act of 1721, and announced the

[87] [Gratton], *Observations on the Mutiny Bill*, 60, 74–75. See also Charles Francis Sheridan, *A Review of the Three Great National Questions Relative to A Declaration of Right, Poynings' Law and the Mutiny Bill* (London, 1781), 15–18, 127.
[88] William Eden, speech, April 8, 1782, in Cobbett et al., eds., *Parliamentary History*, 22: 1241–46.
[89] Charles James Fox, speech, April 8, 1782, in ibid., 22: 1247–53.
[90] Resolution of the Irish House of Commons, April 16, 1782, in ibid., 23: 19.

Administration's "intention to do away completely the idea of England legislating for Ireland." At the same time, however, he expressed regret that the North Administration had so misused Parliament's general and formerly acknowledged "power of external legislation" as "an instrument of tyranny and oppression" in both America and Ireland that "millions of subjects," feeling it "only as a scourge," had risen up against it. With these remarks, Fox left no doubt that he thought that the general "superintending power of the British parliament" over the greater British Empire was a desirable feature of imperial governance.[91]

Fox's opinion was widely shared among British legislators, and on July 5, well after the May concessions, Lord Abingdon, a steadfast friend of America throughout the American war, introduced a bill in the House of Lords asserting Britain's general superintending power over all areas of the empire. Congratulating Parliament for having disclaimed the right of internal legislation over Ireland, a right that it had never had but had "hitherto usurpedly exercised," he argued that because "the seat of the empire" was in Britain and because Britain controlled the sea, the British Parliament should have "the sole and exclusive right" to "regulate and controul the commerce of that sea for the sake of our navy" and that to give up that right would be "to abolish and annihilate your parliaments" and "to sever and totally to separate Great Britain from the rest of the British empire, leaving it as a country to stand singly, and by itself alone, for it is the only tie, it is the only bond of union that now remains to the British empire." Correctly noting that the Americans had never, before the Declaration of Independence, demanded freedom from external legislation, Abingdon was determined that Parliament should not concede such an exemption to Ireland.[92]

The sentiments of Fox and Abingdon and "*the tacit assent*" of their auditors in Parliament inspired a writer, referring to himself only as "A Student of Lincoln's Inn" and addressing himself to Edmund Burke, to publish in London a pamphlet designed to awaken the Irish from the "*the delusion of a free trade, which may be resumed at pleasure, and an independence, which exists at sufferance,*" and to "*persuade Britons that a full and unequivocal grant of what the Irish demand, as their birthright, will prove no less disadvantageous in effect, than just in principle.*" By implying "an unlimited power of imposing arbitrary regulations and restrictions on the foreign trade of Ireland; that is, of reviving, at pleasure, the odious and oppressive system of commercial monopoly," he pointed out, such claims "of external legislation" represented a vivid "*demonstration that England has not relinquished her idea of controuling the foreign trade of Ireland.*" Despite Parliament's apparent yielding to Ireland's "new-born spirit of liberty," a "*very great majority of both Houses of Parliament, and ... nine parts out of ten of the English nation,*" he estimated, retained "some remaining prejudices" that promised to be "as pernicious to this country, as they have hitherto proved fatal to Ireland." Precisely because

[91] Charles James Fox, speeches, May 17, 1782, in ibid., 23: 22–23, 31–32.
[92] Lord Abingdon, speech, July 5, 1782, in ibid., 23: 151–52.

such prejudices "still fondly linger[ed] in the breasts of Englishmen," this writer contended, nothing "short of a *total Renunciation, on the part of England, of every claim of a right to bind Ireland, in any case whatever, by the decrees of a parliament, in which she is not represented*" could "give complete satisfaction to the Irish and prove a permanent bond of union and affection between the two nations."[93]

But Fox and his associates would have none of renunciation. The Ministry's intention, Fox declared in Parliament in December 1782, was "to make a complete, absolute, and perpetual surrender of the British legislative and judicial supremacy over Ireland," but "a renunciation stating it to be a right which we never legally possessed, was what England would not be brought to agree to."[94] Such a renouncement, echoed Thomas Townshend, was what Britain "would not do, what she could not do, without recording her own shame, namely, to declare that for centuries she had usurped the rights of Ireland."[95] Britain might, under pressure, end its oppressive ways in reference to its overseas dependencies, but it could not own up to them.

In the immediate wake of the British Parliament's concessions in the summer of 1782, Francis Dobbs produced a substantial history of the course of events from October 1779 to September 1782, the "*short time,*" he said proudly, in which Ireland "*was emancipated, – a bloodless Revolution took place, and we became united with our former tyrant, by the sacred bond of equal* Freedom." Celebrating the achievements of "these extraordinary times," he invited his readers to rejoice with him in "the Modification of the Law of Poynings," the removal of the "Perpetual C[l]ause" from the "Mutiny Bill," the establishment of "the Independence of the Judges," the laying of a "Foundation . . . for the Military Establishment of Ireland, being Irishmen," and the repeal of the Declaratory Act and the restoration of "the Liberties of Ireland." With its new freedom, he observed, Ireland now seemed to be "a favoured nation," well situated "on the verge of the old" to "become the mart between it and the new world," with commodious ports and harbors, a growing interest in commerce, productive soil and seas, and an excellent climate.[96]

V

Catholics constituted a large proportion of the Irish population, and Protestant discrimination against them – the fourth and, many contemporaries thought, the most important explanation for Irish poverty – was a subject that received

[93] *A Letter to the Right Hon. Edmund Burke, Concerning the Expediency of a Total Renunciation on the Part of Great-britain of the Right to Bind Ireland by Acts of the British Parliament, either internally or externally* (London, 1782), vi–viii, 13–15, 17, 19, 22–23, 35–38.

[94] Charles James Fox, speech, December 19, 1782, in Cobbett et al., eds., *Parliamentary History*, 23: 23–24.

[95] Thomas Townshend, speech, January 22, 1783, in ibid., 23: 326.

[96] Francis Dobbs, *A History of Irish Affairs, from the 12th of October, 1779, to the 15th September, 1782, the Day of Lord Temple's Arrival* (Dublin, 1782), 6, 148–50.

considerable attention in Ireland beginning in the mid-1750s, as the anonymously published *The Case of the Roman-Catholics of Ireland* in Dublin in
1754[97] sparked a spirited debate over the continuing legitimacy of the penal
laws passed at the beginning of the eighteenth century during the early days
of the Protestant Ascendancy. Written by Charles O'Conor, a member of the
Catholic gentry, this tract argued that the present generation of Irish Catholics
had "no political crime to account for," that they had come to "revere our
Constitution," that they were loyal to the king, and that they had come to
appreciate and to "feel the Relaxation of the *penal Laws* under the Mildness of
his Government." Pointing out the many discriminations imposed by the penal
laws and their malignant social effects, O'Conor suggested that they ought to
be repealed.[98]

The anonymity of the pamphlets published in the discussion that O'Conor's
tract provoked makes it difficult to tell whether the authors were Protestant
or Catholic. An avowedly Protestant writer set forth the Protestant point of
view. On the one hand, he acknowledged that "the *public Interest* of every
Society requireth, that none of the Individuals constituting it, be laid under
any *unnecessary* Restrictions, which might *damp* their Industry, or *check* their
Application." On the other, he employed the language of national security to
argue that "if in the *Body-politic* any Members are *unsound* or *infected*, we
ought, as in the Natural Body, to apply suitable Remedies, to guard against
the Contagion spreading thro' the *whole* Body, whereby the Subversion of the
System would soon ensue," and this, he concluded, was the case in both Britain
and Ireland with respect to Catholics. It "was a glaring absurdity," he wrote,
"to expect that the Principles of *Papists* will [ever] be friendly to a Protestant
Government."[99] But a surprising number of those authors came out in support
of relaxing the penal laws. The "*Effect* of those Laws upon the Emprovements,
Wealth, and Prosperity of this Country," the "Mistake of continuing, in these
Days of Sobriety and Remission, the ACTS of querulous Times, and angry Men,"
and "the Inconsistency of such Laws with the Nature and Spirit of all free and
mixed Governments," concluded one author, invoking the language of liberty,
meant that the "Reasons *for* repealing *many* penal Laws" were "extremely
strong."[100]

These exchanges having led to no improvement in the situation of Roman
Catholics, the reformer Henry Brooke took up the subject with a vengeance in

---

97 [Charles O'Conor], *The Case of the Roman Catholics of Ireland* (Dublin, 1755).

98 *A Vindication of a Pamphlet, Lately Published, intituled, The Case of the Roman-Catholics
of IRELAND* (Dublin, 1754), 5–7. Thomas Bartlett, *The Fall and Rise of the Irish Nation: The
Catholic Question 1690–1830* (Dublin: Rowman & Littlefield, 1992), provides the fullest
discussion of the Catholic question in Irish politics.

99 *An Examination of the Case of the Roman Catholics of Ireland, Lately Published* (Dublin,
1755), 3–4, 17, 22.

100 *Vindication of a Pamphlet*, 29–30, 45–46. See also *Some Queries Relative to the Present State
of Popery in Ireland* (Dublin, 1756), 5–6, 14.

three pamphlets published in 1760. Describing himself as "a Member of the Protestant Church," Brooke pulled out all the stops in his efforts to win sentiment for repeal of the penal laws. In his first pamphlet, Brooke did little more than lay out the various exclusions to which Catholics were subjected by virtue of the penal laws, including the prohibition on having arms, owning horses worth more than £10, holding durable tenures in land, holding public office, either civil or military, hiring more than a few workers in any manufacturing establishment, serving in the army, becoming members of the professions, getting an education at Trinity College, Dublin, or having their own priests and tutors. After "setting forth the many Uses and Purposes, both real and personal, from which Papists are excluded," he said acidly, "it is hard to say *of what use they are.*"[101]

Resting his argument on the grounds of experience, social utility, and justice and pointing out that it had been seventy years "since these People have offended in Word or in Deed," Brooke argued that Ireland's impoverished and conflicted state proved that the entire system of religious discrimination was counterproductive and used the languages of justice and toleration to underline his concern about the evils of these "useless or severe laws." Surely, he observed, it was only just "to allow to others the same Latitude of Conscience that you like yourself." Even if the laws had been necessary when they were enacted, he argued, that was no reason why "they should *continue* to the End of Time." "Is no Period to be put to their State of Probation?," Brooke asked. "Must they *for ever* be kept on *Quarantine*, without Harbour or Hopes of Rest or Reconciling?" Ireland would never "put an *End to*" its "*domestic Fears,*" he declared, until it had reversed such a failed and inhuman system and granted "an Abatement or Alteration of the said disabling Laws."[102]

But such arguments did not gain sufficient currency within the Irish Protestant political establishment to effect any change. In a pamphlet published in 1762 and arguing against a proposal to raise an army of Catholics in Ireland, an anonymous author, writing under the pseudonym "Hibernicus" and emphasizing the language of security, expressed the fears that lay behind the perpetuation of the penal code. "The Condition of this kingdom," he wrote, "is, perhaps, the most peculiar on earth." Differing essentially "from other popery where it is the established religion," Irish popery, he explained, was deeply infused with the "notion of being oppressed," and with "*Two-thirds* of her people ... sworn enemies to the Constitution ... in Church and State; ever plotting to weaken the props and pillars that support it," he thought it unwise to relax any of the restrictions upon Catholics and decried the emergence of

[101] Henry Brooke, *The Case of the Roman-Catholics of Ireland: Letter I* (Dublin, 1760), 14–15.
[102] Henry Brooke, *An Essay on the Antient and Modern State of Ireland* (Dublin, 1760), 68–72, 74, 76–79; idem, *The Case of the Roman-Catholics of Ireland: Letter I*, 14–15; idem, *The Farmer's Case of the Roman Catholics of Ireland: Letter IV* (Dublin, 1760), 7–8, 18–19.

support for such measures in Britain, where, he suggested, ministers seemed to be "utter strangers to the circumstances of this Country, or else" were willing to "make light of any misery they may involve us in, to serve any purpose, however trifling, of their own."[103]

Indeed, concern with the Catholic threat to Protestant domination was a constant among Protestant political writers. "Till the *Protestant* Interest here becomes equal in Strength, if not in Numbers, to its Enemies," one anonymous author observed in 1768, identifying the most important root of Ireland's dependance on Britain, the Protestant Ascendancy remained in a "critical Situation." "We owe our present Security, and the Preservation of our happy Constitution, chiefly, if not solely, to our Connexion with *Great-Britain*, and the Privilege of taking her Forces into our Pay for our Defence," he noted, for Britain's military force was the only reason "why the Religion of the Majority is not in this Country, as well as in others, the Religion of the State; as it would soon become, if once the Protection of *Great-Britain* was withdrawn." It seemed to him obvious that in "these Circumstances our best and most secure Defence is an Army, recruited with *English* Protestants."[104] Yet another anonymous writer reminded his readers that Irish Catholics regarded Irish Protestants as "Innovators and Robbers."[105] "By the law of nations," acknowledged another writer, "the native Irish, who still make up the major part" of the Irish population, had a "right to throw off the yoke if it were in their power, for the right of conquest, certainly holds no longer than it can be maintained."[106]

But the debate over the continued existence of the Irish penal laws remained almost entirely Irish. For people in Britain at the center of empire, it seems to have had little resonance. After all, Britain had its own penal laws against Catholics. Entirely dominated by the Protestants, the British political establishment was well accustomed to Catholic exclusions. An early sign that the quiet acceptance of this situation in Britain might be open to change was the publication in London in 1764 of an anonymous pamphlet, *Considerations on the Penal Laws Against Roman Catholics in England, and the New Acquired Colonies in America*, written by a person signing himself "A Country Gentleman." As the title suggests, the pamphlet and the sentiments it contained were a direct product of a concern about how Britain should deal with populations in those colonies acquired from the French as a result of the Treaty of Paris of 1763, in particular, Quebec, which contained many thousands of people of

---

[103] "Hibernicus," *Some Reasons against Raising an Army of Roman Catholicks in Ireland in a Letter to a Member of Parliament* (Dublin, 1762), 8–9, 14–16.

[104] *Reasons for an Augmentation of the Army on the Irish Establishment, Offered to the Consideration of the Publick* (London, 1768), 14–15. This pamphlet was first published in Dublin. See also "A Country Gentleman," *Some Impartial Observations on the Proposed Augmentation* (Dublin, 1768), 5, 7.

[105] [Robert Jephson], *Considerations upon the Augmentation of the Army. Address'd to the Publick* (Dublin, 1768), 12–14.

[106] *The Principles of Modern Patriotism* (Dublin, 1770), 27–28.

European extraction who were neither British nor Protestant nor accustomed to British institutions and British law.[107]

Contending that "the benign spirit of moderation" was "gaining ground" except "in the extremities of Europe, Spain, and Sweden," this author began his pamphlet by asking "whether the religious and political reasons for enacting" British penal laws had "not entirely ceased." Before the Restoration, he noted, English authorities had enacted "many severe and sanguinary laws" in their efforts "to establish a uniformity of worship," and he acknowledged that even in recent generations, especially during the rising of 1745 and during the Seven Years' War with Catholic France and Spain, British authorities, as he put it, held "out Popery, like the Gorgon shield, to frighten away every sentiment of dissatisfaction from the minds of the people." But, he argued, using the languages of toleration and justice, "now, when sentiments of moderation prevail[ed] over [a] great part of Europe, and particularly in this kingdom, and at a time when those who profess[ed] all the various ways of thinking on [those] religious subjects which divide mankind" met "here with protection," the "hardship of such a body of penal laws remaining in force against those only who adhere[d] to the antient faith" seemed both anachronistic and unjust. Arguing that the gradual moderation of the severity of the penal laws in Britain itself had "almost worn out" the "now useless bugbear, the growth of Popery," he contended that "every circumstance which occasioned their being enacted" had long since "altered."[108]

This writer praised the Hanoverians for governing the "British empire with a glory, a display of wealth, a superiority of naval power, and an influence in the affairs of the world, far exceeding what human foresight would have conjectured," and he called upon Parliament to grant an indulgence to Catholics that, he predicted, would not only improve their situation within Britain but might also "soften the harshness of religious zeal in other parts of Europe." "The example of Great Britain in her present exalted state," he wrote, "will give a bias to the political systems, will direct the councils of other nations, and spread sentiments beneficial to human nature throughout the universe." Among "several [other] good effects which" might ensue from this action, he wrote, would be the preservation of the "inhabitants of the new-acquired colonies... from oppression," an act, he thought, that might be the best strategy for inducing "those Creolians to be as firmly attached to the English government, as they were to their former masters." "How easily might the minds of these people be conciliated to the British Government, by some degree of legal toleration," he wrote. Significantly, however, this writer did not suggest that Britain's modification of the penal laws would produce a like effect in Ireland, where, he lamented, the system contained "a vein of ingenious cruelty" that might have been "dictated by some Praetor of Dioclesian, or Spanish Inquisitor" and had

---

[107] "A Country Gentleman," *Considerations on the Penal Laws Against Roman Catholics in England, and the New acquired Colonies in America* (London, 1764).

[108] Ibid., 2–3, 7–8, 47, 65–66, 69.

continued to entail "miseries on a considerable part of the Irish nation"[109] and, as another writer said five years later, had rendered Catholics "outcasts of legislation" with a marked "similarity of their condition" to the inhabitants "of those nations, whom Britons generally thought of as slaves."[110]

Pondering the condition of his native country with his customary penetration, Edmund Burke in 1765 began writing (but never completed or published) one of the most thoughtful analyses of this problem, an analysis in which the languages of justice and oppression figured heavily. "A country which contains so many hundred thousands of human creatures reduced to a state of the most abject servitude," he observed, would be an "unhappy country." In no happy country, he posited, could the "happiness of the multitude . . . ever be a thing indifferent," and wherever, as in the case of Ireland, any law was "against the majority of the people," it was "in substance a law against the people itself: its extent determining its invalidity." As it "enlarges its operation," he wrote, such a law changed "its character," becoming not merely "a particular injustice, but [a] general oppression," which could "no longer be considered a private hardship which might be borne, but spreads and grows up into the unfortunate importance of a national calamity." He denounced the idea that, as the penal laws assumed, "indulgence and moderation in Governors" was "the natural incitement in subjects to rebel" as "a doctrine . . . repugnant to humanity and good sense," denying "that the security of an Establishment, civil or religious," could "ever depend upon the misery of those living in it, or that its danger can arise from their quiet and prosperity." Contrary to most Protestant reporters, Burke speculated that "the great [seventeenth-century] rebellions in Ireland" had not been "produced by toleration, but by persecution, that they arose not from just and mild government, but from unparalleled oppression" of the sort to which the Catholic population had subsequently been reduced by the penal laws. The lesson of those rebellions, Burke concluded, was that "an attempt to continue" Catholics in "that state" in contemporary Ireland would be "disastrous to the publick peace," rather "than any kind of security to it."[111]

Over the next few years two other Irish authors produced tracts, first published in Dublin and republished in London, arguing for the substitution of a test oath for the penal laws. In 1767, Nicholas Lord Viscount Taafe, who had spent many years in Germany, published a "short state of affairs in *Ireland*, for seventy five years past" with the "intention of opening my countrymen's eyes" to the deleterious effects of the penal laws. Taafe expressed his belief that penal laws were "absolutely necessary in every country" to preserve the

---

[109] Ibid., 41–42, 48, 57–58, 60.

[110] Gervase Parker Bush, *Case of Great Britain and America, Addressed to the King, and Both Houses of Parliament* (London, 1769), 14–15.

[111] Edmund Burke, "Tracts relating to the Popery Laws," 1765, in R. B. McDowell, ed., *The Writings and Speeches of Edmund Burke* (Oxford: Clarendon Press, 1991), Vol. 9, Part II: *Ireland*, 454, 460–61, 479.

established government from overthrow by dissident elements, but in Ireland's case, he contended, the "political fever" that had produced them "hath long been over." Over the previous eighty years, he argued, the *Irish Roman Catholics*, clergy and layety," had "no *civil guilt* to answer for." They had remained quiescent during two Jacobite rebellions, had repeatedly expressed their loyalty to the Hanoverian regime, and, despite their "long quarantine of political health," were now mostly reconciled to the existing situation. Moreover, Taafe observed, the penal laws had not worked, having neither compelled many Catholics to become Protestant nor produced anything but profound discord. Their only consequences, he declared, had been "perpetuating unrelenting animosity, multiplying legal incapacities, and preventing public prosperity, so far as it could be affected by legal restraint on so numerous a body of people."[112]

Using the language of toleration and laying it down as an axiom "that *civil punishment* without a *civil crime*, is the very essence of intolerance," Taafe called upon his readers to recognize that "*religious union* is a happiness not likely to be attained" and that the only alternative was to entertain "the possibility, that *Protestants* and *Roman Catholics* may be made as unanimous, *in one summary of civil faith, through these kingdoms*, as they are known to be, under the *Protestant governments*" among "*our German neighbours*, the Protestant States of *Lower Saxony* and *Brandenburgh*," where religious prejudice of the kind that still prevailed in Ireland "in its full and *obnoxious* force" had been completely "discarded by *experimental* knowledge." The metropolitan government's recent handling of the situation in its newly acquired colony of Quebec inspired Taafe to urge his readers to "Let *North America* be the mirror to reflect the benign face of universal indulgence to conscience." Although only recently conquered by Britain, he wrote, Quebec presented a happy scene in which

the Catholics there[,] tho' habituated to a Catholic government, have reconciled themselves to the government of a Protestant monarch, who permits them to worship God, *in their own way*, and abridges them of *no civil privileges*, for so doing. What have *Irish Catholics, born under the present political establishment, and ever obedient under it*, . . . done,

he asked, "or what *civil* guilt can be produced against them, to distinguish their case, from that of their brethren in *Canada*?"[113]

Five years later, in 1772, the Catholic political writer Charles O'Conor reaffirmed many of Taafe's points. Writing from the point of view of a Protestant and using the languages of justice and oppression, O'Conor argued that the "causes, which rendered popery of dangerous influence to the Protestant interest" were "almost wholly removed," that continued persecution could

[112] Nicholas Taafe, *Observations on Affairs in Ireland, from the Settlement in 1691, to the Present Time* (London, 1767), 22–27.
[113] Ibid., 22–23, 28–29.

"only serve to make Papists, the more obstinate," and that "in a tolerating and enlightened age, it" was "a reproach to the legislature, to continue in force, laws, which are in the highest degree oppressive." Far more powerfully than Taafe, O'Conor made the case that "the Papists of this kingdom have for seventy years past, been an insuperable obstacle to its prosperity. Cut off from the principal benefits of its free constitution," he observed, "they *necessarily* become a disease within its bowels; acting *against it*, from the incapacity to act *for it*." Invoking the languages of commerce, improvement, and toleration, he pronounced them "*the worst* kind of subjects, that can exist in a country which subsists *chiefly* by *commerce* and *useful arts*," and argued that "*As a multitude*, their inconnection, their disability, their laziness, their dependency, their beggary, must not only weaken the whole community, but affect its very vitals." The penal laws having over eight long decades entirely failed in their design to transform the Irish into "*one Protestant people*," Ireland, he recommended, should "proceed on the model of our *Dutch Neighbours*, who have long since shaken off their captivity to temporary opinion" and adopted a system of religious toleration.[114]

As during the early 1770s the metropolitan Government sought to work out a viable system for governing Quebec, various participants in the discussion directed British public attention to the plight of Catholics in Ireland. As William Knox, undersecretary for state for the colonies, said in his defense of the Quebec Act of 1774, Ireland was one of two models for "the treatment, given by our ancestors to a conquered people professing the *Roman* religion." The other was Minorca.[115] Essentially, the vocal group of Protestant traders who flowed into Quebec following the peace and may have reached as many as two thousand people by the mid-1770s were vocal advocates of the Irish model, stridently calling for the introduction of British law and representative institutions, the exclusion of Catholics from the franchise and public office, and, in the case of a few individuals, the establishment of the Protestant church.[116] From early on, as an early writer reported in a pamphlet of 1766, they advocated that "the laws of England made against Papists ought to be in force" in Quebec and "consequently that native Canadians, unless they think proper to turn Protestants, ought to be excluded from all . . . offices and various branches

---

[114] [Charles O'Conor], *Observations on the Popery Laws* (London, 1772), 1, 6–7, 11, 13–15, 49–50. On O'Conor's role in Taafe's pamphlet, see Morley, *Irish Opinion and the American Revolution*, 48.

[115] William Knox, *The Justice and Policy of the Late Act of Parliament, for Making more Effectual Provision for the Government of the Province of Quebec, Asserted and Proved* (London, 1774), 20. The standard study of the Quebec Act is Philip Lawson, *The Imperial Challenge: Quebec and Britain in the Age of the American Revolution* (Montreal and Kingston: McGill University Press, 1989). Karen Stanbridge, *Toleration and State Institutions: British Policy toward Catholics in Eighteenth-Century Ireland and Quebec* (Lanham, Md.: Lexington Books, 2003), and idem, "Quebec and the Irish Catholic Relief Act of 1778: An Institutional Approach," *Journal of Historical Sociology*, 16 (2003), 375–404, provide useful comparisons.

[116] The basic statement of the English settlers' point of view is Francis Maseres, *Things necessary to be settled in the Province of Quebec* (London, 1772).

of power." At the same time, local French leaders insisted "not only upon a toleration of their public worship, but on a share in the administration of justice, as jury-men and justices of the peace, and the like, and on a right, in common with the English, of being appointed to all offices of the government."[117] Attempting to adjudicate between these two conflicting points of view, the British Ministry took nearly a decade before it finally resolved the question through the provisions of the Quebec Act in 1774.

In the end, the Administration, having, as Knox said, investigated both the Irish and the Minorcan model "with the most critical exactness," decided to follow the Minorcan. "A comparison of the advantages with" the "mode of treatment... in *Minorca*, with what has been the result of the severe system which has taken place in *Ireland*," Knox explained, provided a considerable incentive "to adopt a plan of lenity and indulgence." Having acquired Minorca in 1713, the British Government had spent more than a hundred thousand pounds a year in times of peace to protect its harbor for commercial and military purposes, but had never tried to transform the island into a regular colony or to establish any civil government. As a consequence, civil governance remained entirely in the hands of the local Catholic population, with the result that, as Knox reported, the inhabitants had shown "no impatience under the *English* government, nor have they been found to abet an invasion by their former sovereign, or any other *Roman* catholic prince."[118]

Knox and his fellow Administration supporters defended this decision using the languages of justice and, most significantly, humanity. To deprive the French population of their own laws and governance, Knox said, would have been "cruel, arbitrary and unjust, and a violation of the solemn stipulations of" the Treaty of Paris of 1763. "Under what colour or pretence," he asked, might the "*Canadian*[s] ... have been deprived of all share in the civil offices of the province" or "their clergy" have been "stripped of their maintenance," or "the whole people [have been] made subject to laws enacted by an assembly, from which they were to be excluded, and in the election of whose members they were to be deprived of all share?"[119] The Quebec Act, declared a person of similar persuasion, employing the same languages, had been framed "upon the strictest principles of justice and humanity." From "every point of view," he declared, "we find it adapted to the genius of the people, and planned for promoting their happiness," the framers of the act having never "lost sight of the evils that would have resulted from overturning long established customs, that with" the French Canadians were every bit "as sacred from their immemorial usage, as [was] the common law with us."[120] Recommended by

---

[117] *Considerations on the Expediency of procuring An Act of Parliament for the Settlement of the Province of Quebec* (London, 1766), 4.

[118] Knox, *Justice and Policy of the Late Act of Parliament*, 26–28.

[119] Ibid., 13.

[120] *Thoughts on the Act for Making more Effectual Provision for the Government of the Province of QUEBEC* (London, 1774), 32.

"benevolence and humanity," the Quebec plan, Knox added, was thoroughly "based on justice."[121]

Not everyone was so congratulatory. Indeed, the Quebec Act encountered a firestorm of criticism in both Parliament and the press, and, although it passed by a respectable margin, Opposition writers denounced it as an unprecedented and "wonderful Phaenomenon in Politics – A FREE PROTESTANT GOVERNMENT, ESTABLISHING POPERY AND SLAVERY." By that act, they said, Catholicism was established as a state church in a formerly Protestant empire, and "a numerous...Body of People" were "cut off from, and deprived of, some of the greatest Advantages and Blessings of British Government." The Canadians, they said, were the "solitary and single Instance...of a People subjected to Laws and Institutions, so very different from, and so greatly inferior to, those Laws by which every other Part of the British Dominions" were "governed." "Instead of giving these People a free and equal Government," Charles Polhill complained, using the language of liberty, "we have settled a despotic Government, by a President and Council of Seventeen" that might "consist of Seventeen People, wholly uninterested in the Welfare of the Colony. Instead of leaving these People the invaluable Privilege of making their own Laws," he continued, "they are to have their laws made for them, by the Governor and this Council, all of whom will at best be Dependents on the Crown." "Instead of giving Liberty and Freedom to the Canadians, and thereby a Taste of the Blessings of English Government, we have not only enslaved them, but reduced many Thousand *English* now living within the Bounds of that Province, to the same Condition." Such arrangements, he declared, seemed to be poorly designed to accomplish the objective of bringing "the Canadians by insensible Degrees, to a Resemblance of the other Subjects of the Crown, in Religion, Laws, and Government."[122]

Some critics of the bill invoked the Irish case in an effort to use it to their advantage. Thus did the anonymous author of a pamphlet published in January 1775 note that "the good People of Ireland professing at one Time, almost generally, the Roman Catholic Religion...were surely as well entitled to the Establishment of their Religion as the Canadians now are," and he acknowledged that, under Protestant domination, Irish Catholics had subsequently "undergone one unremitting Scene of Persecution." Yet he thought it unavoidable, and praised "our wise Ancestors" for appreciating "for what wicked Purposes that Religion was contrived, to what wicked Purposes it has been applied. What new Circumstance then is it, that has arisen, to make us less jealous of it now, than we have hitherto been[?]" he asked rhetorically,

---

[121] Knox, *Justice and Policy of the Late Act of Parliament*, 29.

[122] [Charles Polhill], *Observations and Reflections On the Act, passed in the Year, 1774, For the Settlement of the Province of Quebec* (London, 1782), vi, ix, 24–26, 28. Although not published until 1782, when the author hoped the Rockingham Administration might move to repeal the Quebec Act, this pamphlet was written in 1774. See also Hugh Baillie, *A Letter to Dr. Shebbeare: containing a refutation of his arguments concerning the Boston and Quebec Acts of Parliament* (London, 1774), 24.

predicting that encouraging Catholicism and the establishment of a government without consensual institutions would lead eventually to a result that "all the civil and foreign Wars against this Country could never accomplish: *Make Slaves of Britons.*"[123]

Defenders of the bill answered these charges by reminding the bill's critics that it was not, as Thomas, Lord Lyttelton, said in 1775, "made for the Meridian of *England*,"[124] but, as Sir William Meredith wrote, for a country "differing from our own in her religion, her laws, her habits, and her customs."[125] Yet another anonymous writer cited "the examples of *Guernsey, Jersey, Minorca, &c*" as evidence that Britain did not have to "give our conquered states our own laws" and that such territories might "retain their obedience as well under their own laws, as they would under ours."[126] "The first principle of all law," declared Meredith, was that it "must be framed to correspond with" the "genius and temper" of the people to whom it applied, and from this perspective it seemed evident to him that the Quebec Act was entirely "consonant to justice, wisdom, and benevolence."[127] The central question, insisted an anonymous pamphleteer, was "whether the hundred thousand *conquered* Canadians, or the four hundred *colonizing* English, compose[d] the Province of Quebec." Contending that it would be unjust to put the "lives, liberties, and properties, of our subjects in Canada to the jurisdiction of the very few British Protestants settled there," this writer argued that Britain could not "empower the few Protestant settlers there under the idea of a *free representation*, to *tax* at discretion a country, of which they form a most insignificant part"; it could not, he reiterated, "enable four hundred emigrants, because they are Protestants, to erect themselves into a constitutional *aristocracy*, and tyrannize over and oppress above an hundred thousand peaceable and dutiful subjects, who first settled the country; men of property, of rank, of character." "Can there be anything more invidious – more odious – more averse, to Liberty," this writer asked,

than a system which draws a line between *settling* subjects and subjects *by treaty*; which considers emigrants from England as authorized to exercise all the tyranny, which *Roman* citizens were guilty of in their Province; and treats a Country, subjected to us by treaty, as a province acquired for the purpose of their oppressions?[128]

[123] *An address to the Right Honourable L–d M–sf–d; in which the Measures of Government Respecting America are Considered in a New Light: with a View to his Lordship's Interposition Therein* (London, 1775), 28–29.
[124] Thomas Lyttelton, *The Speech of Lord Lyttelton, On a Motion made in the House of Lords For a Repeal of the Canada Bill, May 17, 1775* (London, 1775), 2.
[125] Sir William Meredith, *A Letter to the Earl of Chatham, on the Quebec Bill* (London, 1774), 1.
[126] *An Address to the Public, Stating and Considering the Objections to the Quebec Bill* (London, 1775), 19.
[127] Meredith, *Letter to the Earl of Chatham*, 19, 35–36.
[128] *An Address to the Public*, 15, 26, 29.

This writer need not have gone to the ancient world to find such a case. Rather, he could merely have looked, but did not look, across the Irish channel to Ireland.

If this writer did not himself explicitly refer to Ireland as a place in which the descendants of the native population were subjected to precisely the sort of oppression he hoped the British would avoid in Quebec, the Quebec problem played a very important role in bringing the situation of Catholics in Ireland into public discussion in the metropolis. When Henry Ellis explained why the Administration rejected the Irish experience as a model for Quebec, he might have been drawing in part upon George, Earl Macartney's *An Account of Ireland in 1773*, published in London the year before passage of the Quebec Act. In this comprehensive report on the current state of Ireland, Macartney, describing himself as "a Late Chief Secretary of That Kingdom," took up the subject of Irish Protestant discrimination against Catholics, providing a detailed recitation of the many disabilities that the latter suffered under the penal laws. He did not condemn penal laws as a general category. Indeed, he expressed the opinion "that both justice and prudence authorize[d] penal laws against papists in a Protestant country," noting that "this has long been established opinion in England," which "early and continually guarded against the perils of popery." But, he announced, England had done so "with dignity, with judgment, and moderation," looking upon "popery as on her other foes, whose secret machinations she might apprehend, but whose assaults she defied."[129]

The Irish case, in his view, was completely different. "To the lot of Ireland," he wrote, "it has fallen to ingraft absurdity on the wisdom of England, and tyranny on the religion that possesses humanity. By her laws against popery," he declared, " the bonds of society, the ties of nature, and all the charities of kindred and friendship, are torn to pieces." In considerable detail, Macartney laid out for British readers the "multitude of . . . harsh and oppressive" clauses in these laws, leading them through a labyrinth of regulations designed to suppress Catholicism and encourage Catholics to become Protestant. "It is hardly too much to say," he concluded, "that in Ireland a Papist cannot inherit, acquire, or bequeath, for in all these cases he is liable to be disquieted or defeated" merely because of his religion. "Not the calm suggestions of reason and policy," the "laws of Ireland against Papists," he wrote, were "the harsh dictates of persecution." They "threaten[ed] the Papists with penalties in case of foreign education, and yet allow[ed] them no education at home," shutting "the doors of their own university against them, and forbid[ding] them to enter any other." Forbidden to enter the professions or the military and severely restricted in the scope of his economic activities as a trader, a mechanic, or a farmer, "a Papist" in Ireland, declared Macartney, could "be nothing but a Papist." Moreover, with their "spirit" thus "restrained from exertion" and their "industry"

---

[129] [George, Earl McCartney], *An Account of Ireland in 1773, by a Late Chief Secretary of That Kingdom* (London, 1773), 20–21.

lacking any "reward to excite it," Catholics suffered the additional indignity of being chastised for their "dullness and laziness."[130]

Condemning Protestant Ireland as an "unreasonable state," Macartney traced this situation to the early seventeenth-century Protestant immigrants, "who eagerly adopted the most harsh and oppressive measures upon those upon whose ruin they rose." If the Restoration secured these people in their property, the Glorious Revolution "armed them with power," and, "instead of using" this power "with justice and moderation," Macartney charged, "they stretched it to the utmost rigour, and seemed determined ultimately to crush, if they could not immediately destroy" the Catholic population, passing in the quarter-century after the Revolution a set of laws "Which have now for these seventy years past been the established law of the land, and which form the most compleat code of persecution that ingenious bigotry ever compiled," even at "a very recent date" adding ever more invasive restrictions. "Humanity and Justice," Macartney asserted in turning to those languages, clearly demanded a "remission of many, and an amendment of all these laws." Noting that "the dangers of popery" had largely been "removed, or [were] sufficiently guarded against," he argued that "the first principle of government ought to be to make every subject of the state as useful to it as possible." "While we are pe[r]petually awakening their regret for what they have lost, invalidating their security for what they still preserve, and withholding from them a moderate degree of permanency in what their labour might obtain," he wrote, "it is impossible for [Irish] Papists to become" good subjects. He had no doubt that this situation was "one great cause why" Ireland did "not make a more rapid progress in tillage and manufactures." He did not regard it as the only cause, but believed that if it were "removed, the rest would be less sensibly felt" and that the "exiled soldier, who now seeks bread in foreign service," would "return a loyal subject – the idle peasant" would "become a laborious husbandman – the slothful tradesman" would "be changed into a diligent artizan; and two millions of people" would "be rendered useful, flourishing, and happy," while their former oppressors would, he implied, transform themselves into the sort of humane people their British ancestors had become.[131]

William Knox made many of the same points the following year in his pamphlet defending the Quebec Act. After their uprising in support of the Catholic king, James II, during the Glorious Revolution, Knox recounted, Irish Catholics had been "absolutely at the mercy of the victorious protestants," whose dread at the superior numbers of the Catholics, who were about four-fifths of a population of around a million, and whose "resentment for the cruelties" Catholics "had inflicted on the protestants while their rule lasted" provided the motives for the adoption of the plan, which their descendants had "unremittingly pursued" to "this day," for "preventing the growth of

---

[130] Ibid., 21–24.
[131] Ibid., 20–24.

popery" in Ireland "and depriving its professors of all means of disturbing the government or abetting the enemies of the state." "It is difficult to
imagine," wrote Knox, "what more" could "be done by severe treatment to
extinguish a sect, or to deprive its followers of all spirit or ability to disturb
the government. Yet the effect of these measures, if we may believe the *irish
protestants,*" he wrote, had "not by any means answered . . . their avowed purposes." Although "the protestants now bear the proportion of two to five to the
Roman catholics, are in possession of all the offices of state, the land-owners
of nearly the whole island, and protected and supported by the whole power of
England, they think themselves in the utmost danger of being massacred by
the papists" if, in peacetime, they have fewer "than twelve thousand effective
troops" to protect them. Knox made no proposals and seems to have had no
hope of persuading Irish Protestants to support any amelioration of Irish penal
laws.[132]

By the mid-1770s, some metropolitan analysts of empire could celebrate
the empire for its generosity and humanity. "Wherever we have made an
acquisition of any foreign dominion to the British crown," proclaimed an
anonymous pamphleteer, "there is not a single instance of such a stain upon
our national humanity, as an attempt to force either our laws or our religion upon the people." But even this enthusiast had to admit that Ireland
represented an exception. In Ireland, he said, the "statutes against Roman
Catholics" were "absolutely horrible," violating both "the bonds of nature"
and the "ties of justice."[133] Indeed, throughout the last half of the 1770s, several
publications hammered home the incongruity between Irish Protestant persecution of Catholics and the new conception of Britain as a place of expanding
humanity.

A 1775 London pamphlet authored by Sir Arthur Brooke, who identified
himself as a Protestant, provided the most extensive and systematic attack
on the Irish penal laws published up to that time. "All impartial observers,"
Brooke said by way of introduction, acknowledged that "our own jealous
retention of a most grievous system of penal laws, whereby the inhabitants are
divided against each other, and a major part of them incapacitated to contribute
their help to the great scheme of national improvement," was one of "the
greatest obstructions" to Ireland's "wealth and happiness." The penal laws,
he observed, had totally failed in their objective of promoting Protestantism.
No "clearer proof of how little" they had prevented "the growth of popery"
could "be produced," he said, "than the inconsiderable number of papists who
have become converts since these laws were made." Although he argued that
most of the provisions of the penal laws, not having been "strictly enforced,"
had become a dead letter, he also showed, elaborating the case made by Henry
Brooke and other Irish opponents of the penal laws in the 1750s and 1760s,

---

[132] Knox, *Justice and Policy of the Late Act of Parliament,* 20–25.
[133] *Hypocrisy Unmasked, or, a Short Inquiry into the Religious Complaints of Our American
Colonies* (London, 1776), 10–11.

that the laws had operated to keep the vast majority of Catholics in poverty, ignorance, and slavery, to the great detriment of the nation.[134]

This writer followed earlier commentators in laying out the many ways that the penal laws had adversely affected Irish society, but he was the first to explore in detail the implications of the persecution of Catholics for a free society. Invoking the language of liberty, he asked how Protestants could "desire to live amongst beggars and slaves." By "living amongst slaves," he said, "we become insensible of slavery, and," he emphasized in a telling insight, "unworthy of liberty. Being familiarized to the former," he explained, "we may, with less reluctance, give up the latter; and receive ourselves the yoke we forged for others. There is not a more genuine mark of servitude than to be debarred the equal benefit of those laws [that] men's neighbours and fellow-subjects enjoy," he declared, "nor is ... any thing more to be regretted than that a great number of useful citizens should be reduced to a state of slavery in a land of liberty, in the midst of a nation of FREE MEN. That we should suffer it," he observed, "is inconsistent with that spirit of liberty [that] we discover upon all other occasions."[135]

If this author used the penal laws and their operation to call into question the status as a free people of Protestant Irish who were complicitous in those laws, and by implication the status of Ireland as a free polity, he also used the languages of justice and humanity to raise questions about the civility of the empowered segments of the Irish population. Noting that "Punishments, penalties, and arbitrary proceedings ... produce but a temporary and fatal security," he argued that "Nothing can work so strongly upon a generous and free people as justice and clemency." "Of all people," he said, "the English have been, for some ages past, reputed the most compassionate and just," while England took pride in the fact that "the true spirit of general and equal national liberty, and of social happiness" was "diffused through all ranks" and that an increase in "humanity and benevolence" had kept pace with its rising commerce. "Let us not, in Ireland, be behind" the English "in the practice of virtue, and the improvements of the mind," he declared. "Let it not be the reproach of this enlightened age, that we act" toward the Roman Catholics "as if we were perfectly unacquainted with the existence" of "justice and clemency" and humanity, "those delightful sweet[e]ners of society." "Let us, by a kind and charitable treatment of our own people," he recommended, "avoid the severe imputations with which we are reproached" and, he implied, thereby recommend Irish Protestants to metropolitan Britons as worthy of their British heritage and not behind them in their humanity.[136]

Informing his readers that he had heard the Irish penal laws "stigmatized ... as a system most tyrannical and absurd" in the British House of

---

[134] [Sir Arthur Brooke], *An Inquiry into the Policy of the Penal Laws, Affecting the Popish Inhabitants of Ireland* (London, 1775), 2, 75, 85–86.

[135] Ibid., 114–15.

[136] Ibid., 99–101.

Lords, he assured them that the "universal voice of Great Britain cries aloud for the repeal of them; and [that] the sense of that nation upon such a question... carries with it very conclusive evidence of the usefulness and propriety of speedily making many and great alterations in the system of penal statutes." He contended that the penal laws were "no longer necessary for the security of the present government" and that, "on the contrary, they... now serve[d] no other end than to endanger that security," while they at the same time "impede[d] the improvement of the nation, and obstruct[ed]... not the growth of Popery, but the growth of the Protestant religion." He called upon the Irish Parliament to consider the gradual amendment of those laws, assuring its members that such an action would serve as "an expiatory atonement for their past errors and mistakes." "Poverty, ignorance, and slavery," he concluded, had been "the only fruits [that] the absurd laws against the papists hitherto have produced, or probably ever will produce," asking whether it was not

the greatest madness and folly, freely and of choice, to relinquish the blessings of equal and universal liberty and property, industry, commerce, and politeness, in an improved country, and to harbour in our bosoms that frightful group – their opposites – tyranny, slavery, wretchedness, rude barbarism, and lazy idleness, in a dissolute, barren, and uncultivated territory?[137]

Dr. Daniel Magenise produced a substantial pamphlet on this subject three years later. Published in London in 1778, this tract ranged over many topics, but, employing the language of justice, the author devoted a substantial segment to explaining why the Irish penal laws were unjust and needed to be repealed. "In directing my inquiries into the situation of the distressed Irish," Magenise wrote, "I found above two millions of innocent people given up to the mercy of their natural enemies, viz. The usurpers of their properties, and lamenting the loss of their natural representatives" and "groaning under partial laws, perpetual punishment, and the severest yoke of servitude that ever was imposed on any part of the human species." This "race of [English] usurpers," Magenise argued, had first "robbed the natives of their lands and liberties" and then subjected them to a code of laws that could not "be equalled in the annals of mankind, for its barbarity and ferocity." "Under the veil of religion," he charged, "they... established so many harsh laws" that they destroyed every basis for establishing a "common interest" among all Irish people and "planted, in every heart, the fruitful seeds of ferocity, barbarity, forgery, perjury, rebellion, discord and revenge." To compound their offense, they then proceeded to "transmit to the latest posterity, an implacable rancour and enmity, not only against those that they injured in their liberty or property, but against their whole race for ever after," perpetuating "in their children, from father to son, the same act of cruelty and oppression against all the succeeding generations of the people they had ruined." "Can any one believe," he asked, "that we live in a land of liberty, where such a principle is supported [in a nearby portion

[137] Ibid., 102–03, 110–11, 117, 121–22, 125–26.

of the empire], and used as an instrument to enslave the greatest part of our fellow-subjects?"[138]

Magenise had little hope that the Irish Parliament would correct this situation. Not only were the "greatest part of the Irish Members . . . descended from the usurpers of the Irish lands," but the Irish Parliament had originally "laid the foundation" for the Catholics' "servitude" and then continued it by "their express orders and assistance." Nothing less than a moral transformation, a sudden infusion of *the love of virtue, immortal fame, and eternal recompense*," he suggested sarcastically, could ever persuade that body to restore Catholics "to the benefit of their social contracts, and to make them useful and living members of society." Rather, he suggested that the British Parliament had to take action, noting that that body and repeated British administrations had been complicitous with Irish Protestants in the continuing persecution of Irish Catholics. "*It should* be known to every Englishman," he wrote, "that the doctrine of imposing everlasting famine, with other punishments, on the posterity of the Irish, for the imaginary crimes attributed to their forefathers, has," as he put it, "got footing in England and Scotland." In "every reign," he said, the generality of Catholics had waited in vain for the British government to step in to deliver them from the "mean partialities" under which they suffered. The question now, he suggested, was whether British authorities would continue to assist the Irish Protestants "for another century, or for ever, to continue Cromwell's curse, (viz. Hunger and lice) against the distressed natives of Ireland," or whether, in the interest of "universal peace and happiness over all the British dominions," it would "abolish the penal laws," put "Roman Catholics, and all sects, upon a par, with regard to offices and every kind of literature," "punish all those who breed religious mutiny," and "compose a code of just, universal, and impartial laws, for the reconciliation of all parties."[139]

In 1778, the British Parliament passed a major Catholic Relief law for Great Britain, and during a House of Commons debate over Irish free trade demands in April of that year, Thomas Townshend rose to declare that, although he was a steadfast Protestant and "hated the Romish religion for its persecuting spirit," he "would not on that account wish to be a persecutor" and observed that "he should be glad to see some means adopted to grant such indulgencies to the Roman Catholics of Ireland, as might attach that great body of men to the present government; their affections had been alienated," he added, and he expressed his wish "to recall them by indulgent behaviour."[140] North put Townshend off on the grounds that the Irish Catholic question was in

---

[138] Daniel Magenise, M.D., *The Reformation of Law, Physic and Divinity: with Arguments to Prove That Their Spirit should be The Basis of Our Social Contracts; and That to establish Peace and Happiness, among all Parties, in Great Britain, Ireland, and America, they must be linked in a Chain of one common Interest, and the penal Laws made against Papists, dissenting Nonjurers, &c. Must be Repealed*, 2nd ed. (London, 1778), xi, xiv–xv, xxii, xxxvii, xli.

[139] Ibid., xi–xii, xv, xvii, xx, xxiv, xliii.

[140] Thomas Townshend, speech, April 7, 1778, in Cobbett et al., eds., *Parliamentary History*, 19: 1111–12.

the province of, not the British Parliament, but "the parliament of Ireland," where the laws that "were so severe against the Roman Catholics had originated" and where the "redress of domestic grievances should of right originate likewise." Observing that the "penal laws of Ireland were the consequence of apprehension, which, however groundless, always adopted the most cruel and severe policy," North expressed his opinion "that the Irish parliament would see where the grievance lay, and redress it," granting "such indulgence to the Roman Catholics as their loyalty deserves."[141]

Encouraged by the knowledge that Ireland's penal laws had been "lately regarded [as] Censurable in Speeches in *England*" and by the North Ministry's directions to the Earl of Buckinghamshire, then lord lieutenant of Ireland, to encourage the Irish Parliament to consider the question of Catholic relief, the Irish Catholic Committee drew up and published in Dublin in 1778 a *Humble Remonstrance, for the Repeal of the Laws against the Roman Catholics* seeking "to remove all objections against the Repeal of those Laws."[142] The Protestant judge and author Gorges Edmund Howard, who in 1775 had published a series of cases on the operation of the penal laws,[143] weighed in on the debate, stimulated by this remonstrance. Writing from the perspective of a judge who had "had ample Opportunities, above all others," of "witnessing the Inconveniencies which have attended these particular Laws," at a time when, as he put it, slavishness was daily wearing away "in every Country in Christendom," and members of both houses of the British Parliament had "at different and many Times" declared those laws, "as they now stand," to be "a Reproach to a civilized Nation, . . . an Affront to Christianity, . . . against common Right, and . . . totally opposite to the Principles of a Free Constitution," he urged the Irish Parliament to pass a relief act. Arguing that penal laws had become "the Disease of the [Irish] Body Politic" and that no question was "of more real Consequence to" Ireland, he rehearsed all of the pernicious social, economic, and human side effects earlier critics had attributed to those laws and laid out a strategy that by enhancing economic and educational opportunity for Catholics would make "it their Interest to live quietly with us." He admitted that his "enlarged, noble, and exalted Notions" differed "most widely from that outrageous Zeal and Fury, that almost invincible Resentment, Pique and Malevolence, which the little narrow Minds of different Sects or Parties in Society, both in Religion and Politicks do too often bear for each other," as a result of imbibing "Prejudices, Errors, and Legends . . . from their very Cradles, and" having them "confirmed to them every Day, as they grow up." "Without prejudicing in the least the Safety of the Protestant Religion, the political State, or the Community in general," he contended, there was "ample Room in this

---

[141] Lord North, speech, April 9, 1778, in ibid., 19: 1112.

[142] *Humble Remonstrance, for the Repeal of the Laws against the Roman Catholics. With Judicious Remarks for the General Union of Christians* (Dublin, 1778). The quotations are from the opening unpaginated section entitled "To the Reader."

[143] Gorges Edmund Howard, *Several Special Cases on the Laws Against the Further Growth of Popery in Ireland* (Dublin, 1775).

huge Code of Laws, for vast Relaxation, in order to give some Comfort to these dispirited People" who had already served "a long Political Quarantine" of nearly seventy years and had repeatedly "demonstrated their loyalty to the House of Hanover," and he looked forward to a time when "the first and most zealous Consideration of every Sect and every Party will be, *the Good of the Great Whole.*"[144]

The Irish Parliament did pass a Catholic Relief Act in 1778, but it only removed some restrictions on landholding and inheritance and fell far short of Catholic expectations. "Until the last sessions here... when at that time it received ministerial sanction and support," reported the anonymous author of *The Alarm; or the Irish Spy*, published in London in 1779, "every order" in the Irish Parliament "universally reprobated" the "idea of diminishing or relaxing those laws." With nothing but "the nod of the Minister" to support the bill, the Irish Parliament adopted a measure that made limited concessions and postponed the broader reforms the Catholic Committee had requested. By this measure, this author remarked, the Irish Parliament had both disappointed Catholic expectations and frittered away an opportunity to "attach that body of people to it," with the result that this numerically formidable people, whom the author estimated to outnumber Protestants by more than seven to one, remained a profoundly alienated and "dangerous" component of the Irish nation.[145]

So dangerous indeed was it that ministerial supporters in Britain did not hesitate to use the threat of an alliance between Britain and Irish Catholics to discourage Irish Protestants from going too far during the controversy over free trade and parliamentary independence. The "offer of a more perfect toleration than they" could "ever hope to obtain from an Irish parliament, and the flattering project of retaliation upon that interest to which they have been forced to crouch for near a century past," speculated William Knox in a 1778 pamphlet, would quickly bring Catholics into such an alliance, the final result of which could only be the ruin of "the Protestant Interest" in Ireland. "It is a notorious truth," he wrote, "that in all countries not under the protection or dominion of a foreign power, the religion professed by the majority of the people must finally prevail, and become the religion of the state," and he predicted that if Ireland ever succeeded in withdrawing "from the protection of Great Britain," the "Protestant cause, having lost the protection of that power who planted it in this island," would invariably have to "yield, and be glad to accept of a toleration, if its rivals are so generous as to grant it."[146]

---

[144] Gorges Edmund Howard, *Some Observations and Queries on the Present Laws of this Kingdom, Relative to Papists* (Dublin, 1778), 3–6, 11, 17, 19, 20, 22.

[145] *The Alarm; or the Irish Spy. In a Series of Letters on the Present State of Affairs in Ireland* (London, 1779), 16, 26.

[146] William Knox, *Considerations on the State of Ireland* (Dublin, 1778), 17–20. See also [William Eden], *Considerations Submitted to the People of Ireland on Their Present Condition with Regard to Trade and Constitution* (Dublin, 1781), 68–70, which was reprinted in London, and Charles Pelham, speech, May 26, 1779, in Cobbett et al., eds., *Parliamentary History*, 19: 662.

Yet a rough consensus emerged that, notwithstanding the limited concessions provided by the Catholic Relief Act of 1778, Catholics were not yet all
completely alienated from the Protestant establishment. Catholic writers such
as the Reverend Arthur O'Leary continued to counsel patient negotiation,[147]
and another writer thought that, while it may not have given Catholics everything they wanted, the Irish Relief Act of 1778, by "restoring some of the rights
of humanity to the Roman Catholics," had at the very least "contributed to
establish a broad and solid basis for national unanimity," thus making it possible for "all religious persuasions" to be "now embarked in the same cause" and
creating a prospect of the "dissipation of the cloud of prejudice... before the
rising day of concord and harmony."[148] Henry Grattan celebrated the proposition that the campaign for parliamentary independence and greater political
rights had not been "confined to one persuasion, but Protestant and Papist,
their ancient animosity in such a cause subsiding, [had] signed the same declaration of right; and those whom neither time, nor severity, nor lenity, nor
penal code, nor its relaxation, had been able to unite, in freedom found a rapid
reconciliation." It was a time, he said, "when the spirit of truth and liberty"
had descended "upon the man of the Romish persuasion, and touched his
Catholic lips with public fire," a time when he "was tried and... found faithful;... weighed in the balance and proved sufficient."[149] In Britain, Charles
James Fox subscribed to this perception of Protestant-Catholic relations during his speech in behalf of the bill to repeal the Irish Declaratory Act. "The
intestine divisions of Ireland," he informed Parliament, "were no more; the
religious prejudices of the age were forgotten, and the Roman Catholics[,]
being restored to the rights of men and citizens[,]" could not fail to "become
an accession of strength and wealth to the empire at large, instead of being a
burthen to the land that bore them."[150]

But such expectations failed to take into account either the intensity of
Catholic resentment or the depth of Protestant reluctance to share power,
subjects addressed at length by the young Catholic writer Matthew Carey
in a pamphlet printed in Dublin in the fall of 1781 but suppressed by the
Catholic Committee before it could be published. The published advertisement
for this pamphlet was sufficient to persuade the Committee that it was far too
confrontational to be helpful to the Catholic cause in the Irish political climate
of the early 1780s. The pamphlet was, however, altogether less confrontational
than the advertisement. Far from calling for an uprising, it was instead just

---

147 Arthur O'Leary, *An Address to the Common People of the Roman Catholic Religion, Con-
    cerning the Apprehensed French Invasion* (Cork, 1779).
148 *A View of the Present State of Ireland, Containing Observations upon the Following Subjects*
    (London, 1780), vi.
149 [Henry Gratton], *Observations on the Mutiny Bill: With Some Strictures on Lord
    Buckinghamshire's Administration in Ireland* (London, 1781), 35–36. This pamphlet was
    reprinted from Dublin.
150 Charles James Fox, speech, May 17, 1782, in Cobbett et al., eds., *Parliamentary History*, 23:
    27–28.

another effort to put an end to the system of penal laws in Ireland through legislative means. Announcing that "his *sole* inducement in this undertaking" was to "gain, for this Country, a REAL, *durable Peace, unattainable* between TYRANTS and SLAVES," Carey lamented that at a time "when the *Tyranny* of a British Parliament over Ireland has been annihilated by the *intrepid Spirit* of Irishmen," who had *"taken off an unjust* ENGLISH YOKE," the *"Majority of that Nation . . .* remain[ed] still" chained "by one *infinitely more galling"* in the form of the penal code against Catholics, a code, he asserted, that, "for cruelty, might shame a Turkish Divan" and by which "Every rigour, which could be devised, was exercised." Whereas a "Tarquin, a Dioclesian, or a Nero, might have professed a design of holding people in subjection, not by treating them as men, but by tyranny and oppression," he observed, invoking the language of liberty, "to behold such a system adopted in a country, boasting of its freedom, and in the vicinity of potent rivals and enemies" was "truly a political phenomenon."[151]

Carey agreed with Irish Patriot leaders that Ireland's misfortunes could be traced to Britain's "tyrannic laws." From the beginning, he charged, the "rapacity of the English adventurers," treating Ireland as a conquered country, had proceeded with "as little justice as the European plunderers in America and the East Indies," while the "trade and restrictive laws" about which Ireland was then in a state of high agitation were deeply oppressive. In his view, however, these oppressions paled before Britain's instigation of and active support for the penal code by which Irish Protestants "and others of the same complexion," acting as the "subordinate engine in the hands of England," had subjugated the vast majority of the nation's population and created "the disunion of the inhabitants of Ireland" that remained one of the "numerous distresses of a once mighty empire." This disunion, Carey argued, was the direct result of "the penal laws; and until the cause shall have been radically removed, it were in vain to hope for a removal of the effect." Only when Catholics "shall no longer be aliens, by law, in their native land; when they shall be able, without sacrificing their religion, to choose any profession, to which their genius shall lead them; then, and not until then," he predicted, would "they be well-affected towards government" and, "having an equal interest in the constitution, . . . take the usual share in its support."[152]

Expressing his fear that Irish Protestants "too well relish[ed] the Sweets of" Catholic "Slavery, to be willing to loose the horrid Fetters," and acknowledging that it would be difficult "to persuade people . . . accustomed to an iron sway . . . to resign it, however it may have been acquired," he asked why "those

[151] Matthew Carey, *Urgent Necessity of an Immediate Repeal of the whole Penal Code Candidly Considered* (Dublin, 1781), advertisement, 61, 75. Evidently the only surviving copy, including the advertisement and the bulk of the text, is in the Carey Papers at the Library Company of Philadelphia. Maurice J. Bric, who called this work to my attention, discusses it more fully in his manuscript article "Mathew Carey, Ireland, and the 'Empire of Liberty' in America" (2012), 1–7.
[152] Carey, *Urgent Necessity*, 13, 17, 73, 82.

barbarous, detestable statutes, enacted to plunder" Catholics "of their property, continued in force, to the disgrace of the nation" and, in the name of justice, humanity, and experience, called upon the Irish Parliament to "use no temporizing expedients, but totally [to] repeal a code of laws, the most iniquitous in their enactment, the most inadequate to their end, and the most ruinous and oppressive in their consequences."[153]

VI

From a discursive literature that spanned the Irish Sea and from parliamentary considerations of Irish affairs, metropolitan Britons in the decades after 1750 came to speak of Ireland not just as a valuable adjunct of empire but as a place that had to be spoken of largely through the medium of a language of oppression, a place that suffered from or exhibited a variety of oppressions that had stunted Irish economic development and social improvement and reduced the Irish kingdom to a status wherein its Protestant leaders enjoyed less autonomy than their counterparts in the distant American colonies. The oppressions about which Protestant leaders became most exercised involved Britain's systematic subordination of the Irish to the metropolitan economy, the limitations on Irish autonomy over its domestic affairs, and the British Ministry's use of Crown hereditary revenues to create pensions and places that, far from being of any obvious benefit to Ireland, drained money from the country and provided the means for the Irish Administration to corrupt the Irish Parliament and thereby to turn it into an instrument for the reenforcement of the very oppressions of which the "Patriot" opposition in Ireland had long complained in tracts published in both London and Dublin. With the exception of the pension drain, these oppressions became a widespread subject of concern in Britain only as a result of the successful agitation of Patriot Irishmen, using an economic boycott and backed by a large army of Volunteers, for free trade and the removal of Irish political disabilities between 1778 and 1782.

But still other oppressions derived most immediately, not from Britain but from the Protestant Irish establishment itself. These included the Protestant aggrandizement of Irish estates in the wake of the Protestant Ascendancy until by 1780, according to Arthur Young, in his 1780 *Tour in Ireland*, Protestants possessed 95 percent of the land. Another oppression involved the exploitation and pauperization of a numerous tenantry and the flight of hundreds of absentee landlords with their rents to the more exciting world of Britain, where their suffering tenants were out of sight and out of mind. All of these internal oppressions had long been identified as important factors in Ireland's failure to develop more quickly. Even more galling was the systematic subjugation of the majority Catholic population to the Protestant interest through the penal laws after 1700 and the enforcement of that subjugation by a dozen regiments of British troops stationed in Ireland and paid for by the Irish Parliament. The

[153] Carey, Advertisement; idem, *Urgent Necessity*, 87, 92.

very existence of this force revealed, as Young said, the continuing "strength of the oppressed, and the extent of the oppression." Young had no doubt that the "domineering aristocracy of five hundred thousand Protestants" enjoyed "the sweets of having two millions of slaves," but, he emphasized, such a system could "never advance the public interest" and "must inevitably prevent the island from ever becoming of the importance which nature intended."[154]

In Young's view, responsibility for this system of oppression fell largely on the Protestant elite but ultimately upon Britain itself. When the "gentlemen of that country" complained "of restricted commerce, and the remittance of the rentals to the absentees of England," he observed, they surely could not "be thought serious in lamenting the situation of their country, while they continue[d] wedded to that internal ruin which is the work of their own hands, and the favourite child of their most active exertions. Complain not of restrictions while you yourselves inforce the most enormous restriction," Young wrote, "and what are the absentees when compared to the absence of industry and wealth from the immense mass of two millions of subjects?" "Great and acknowledged as they are," he declared, "both these evils . . . are trifles when compared with the poverty and debility which results from the persecution of the Roman Catholics." What, he asked, "could have influenced the British Government to" continue to permit and "tolerate such a system," especially at a time when the "enlightened spirit of TOLERATION" was "so well understood and practised in the greatest part of Europe" and "making progress every day, save in Ireland alone."[155] Yet, tolerate this system it did. If Ireland was to remain "the jewell in the British crown," the British Government had no choice, no matter how many of its servants might have preferred otherwise.[156] Notwithstanding its newly won commercial and political privileges, Ireland faced the future as a divided kingdom, built on an unjust and inhumane system of religious and civil persecution, yet another shameful residue of the excesses of overseas Britons in the pursuit of empire.

[154] Young, *Tour in Ireland*, 1: 59, 64, 66–67.
[155] Ibid., 1: 67–68.
[156] *Letter to William Eden*, 2d ed., 37.

8

A "Shadow of Our Former Glory"?

The Discussion of Empire in the Wake of American Secession

I

As in the early 1780s people of all political persuasions began to face up to the probability that the American colonies were unlikely to remain within the British Empire, they had to confront the possibility that such a massive loss might leave Britain with so few overseas possessions that it would, as one writer put it in July 1780, "retain only...the shadow of our former glory" as an imperial nation.[1] Imperial analysts worried about the possible loss of Britain's imperial grandeur and the effects of such a loss on its standing in the society of European imperial nations. They considered whether and how the revolting American colonies might be retained within the empire or, if that were impossible, how Britain might reestablish a profitable economic relationship with the new United States. They also sought to take stock of Britain's remaining imperial holdings in Ireland, in the Mediterranean, on the African coast, on the North American continent, and in the West Indies and Atlantic islands. In so doing, however, they found themselves having to cope with the persistence of conditions that over the previous two decades had called into question the very humanity and justice of British ventures overseas and reflected adversely upon the national character of Britain itself.

II

Few metropolitan observers were happy about the loss of so many of the North American colonies, and several of them pondered what that loss meant for the future of the British Empire. Contending that *"the settling of"* the American *"colonies at first was unwise, and the subsequent encouragement that was given them highly impolitic,"* James Anderson, a longtime enthusiast for the war,

---

[1] "An Englishman," *An Essay on the Interests of Britain, in Regard to America* (London, 1780), 17.

produced a long and bitter treatise in March 1782 in support of the arguments *"That our American colonies instead of promoting the trade and manufactures of Great Britain, have tended in a most powerful manner to depress them,"* that *"instead of adding strength and stability to the empire, they have necessarily weakened it in a great degree, and exposed it to the most imminent danger,"* and that the British Empire would no doubt be better off without them.[2] Trying to put the best face on the situation, a writer signing himself "A Country Gentleman" pointed out that in addition to the thirteen American colonies, Britain had lost only Minorca, Tobago, and the two Floridas, and that it still retained Gibraltar, the colonies to the north and east of the United States, the West Indian provinces, the holdings in India, a continuing political association with Ireland, and "that great superiority in the African trade which she has so long enjoyed; by which many of her first ports have been sustained, and by which LIVERPOOL, particularly, from a meagre and inconsiderable borough, has become a place of infinite industry, wealth and population."[3]

But others were not so sanguine. In a pamphlet entitled *Serious Considerations on the Political Conduct of Lord North*, published in 1783, Nathaniel Buckington expressed a deep nostalgia for "the ministry of Mr. Pitt, in the latter days of King George the Second," which "had lifted the [British] superstructure to the clouds, round which the infatuated people danced in circles, crowned myrtle, like a milk-maid's garland, with spring flowers on May-day." Then, he noted,

The Powers on the Continent looked up to us with a mixture of amazement, jealousy, wonder, dread, and their constant attendant hatred; for a universal monarchy on the main, was as odious and much to be dreaded from the power of Great-Britain, at the Peace of Paris, in 1763, as a similar sovereignty on the Continent was in the beginning of the century, from the united powers of the Houses of Bourbon. We had quiet and positive possession of the whole Continent of North America, without a rival, and without an enemy. In Asia we stood possessed of a tract of country almost as extensive, four times more populous, and fifty times more wealthy; and the navy of England was at that period confessedly superior to the united maritime of all Europe besides. To such a giddy height of splendor and reknown was the nation raised at that wonderful aera,

he lamented, "that it makes sick the soul, and dims the mind's eye, with taking but a superficial transient glance back to that prodigious mass, which in a moment, as it were, is become a shadow." With heavy sarcasm he complimented North for his "consummate wisdom, unabating integrity, and matchless perseverance" in *"set[ting] down the nation* by soft, easy, almost

---

[2] James Anderson, *The Interest of Great-Britain With Regard To Her American Colonies, Considered* (London, 1782), 136.
[3] "A Country Gentleman," *Candid and Impartial Considerations on the Preliminary Articles of Peace with France and Spain, and the Provisional Treaty with the United States of America* (London, 1783), 14, 22, 32–33.

imperceptible degrees, from so dangerous a summit of grandeur, to her proper level in the scale of Europe."[4]

Still others displayed a deep melancholy over the evident disintegration of Britain's once great empire and what the writer John King referred to as "a glowing shame at the degraded name and character of an Englishman."[5] "Grasping at a toy," the Government, charged Thomas Day in 1783 in his *Reflections upon the Present State of England, and the Independence of America*, had in a mere twenty years "thrown away the noblest empire in the universe," leaving metropolitan Britons "nothing but the melancholy consolation of reflecting at leisure on what we have lost." In its misguided efforts to preserve the empire, Day complained, the Government, "assisted by the vanity, blindness, and supineness of the rest [of the nation], had succeeded" in "what the united force of all the Powers of Europe could not have effected": the loss of the very colonies that, in his view, had "been the immediate cause of" Britain's "greatness. A country prolific in all the articles either of necessity or luxury; a climate varying through every degree of heat and cold; an immense ocean every where furnished with ports, and inviting the inhabitants to industry and commerce; together with the extent of fertile soil which seemed to allow the human species liberty to expand for ages yet to come," Day reflected, "were such advantages as no period of recorded time has ever seen attached to any other people in the universe. When we add to this, an identity of manners, language, prejudices, religion, nay, of interest itself," he despaired, "it must be confessed that we have no reason to expect a similar phoenomenon" in the future.[6] Joseph Williams also wondered how American independence would affect "this nation, I will not say Empire, which name we must lose by the loss of such extensive territories."[7]

No longer, in Day's words, the "proud, imperious conqueror"[8] of the Seven Years' War, Britain now found itself, another writer lamented, with "but a very small remnant of what heretofore composed this once great empire," just "our remaining possessions in the West Indies, and British America, . . . in Newfoundland, Africa, and the East Indies." He drew a dark picture of Britain's future as an imperial power, doubting whether any of these remaining possessions would continue in a "permanent state of dependence upon Great Britain." Predicting that Britain's external commerce would thenceforth stagnate, that its naval force would decay, that its countryside would be depopulated by emigration to America, that its manufactures would be transplanted to other countries, and that its economic resources would diminish as a result of its

---

[4] Nathaniel Buckington, *Serious Considerations on the Political Conduct of Lord North* (London, 1783), 45–46.

[5] John King, *Thoughts on the Difficulties and Distresses in Which the Peace of 1783 Has Involved the People of England* (London, 1783), 22.

[6] Thomas Day, *Reflections upon the Present State of England, and the Independence of America* (London, 1783), 1–3.

[7] Joseph Williams, *Considerations on the American War* (London, 1782), 9.

[8] Day, *Reflections upon the Present State of England*, 35.

territorial and commercial losses, he was one of many who worried that *"The Sun of Great Britain"* had "set to rise no more."[9]

Moreover, the disappointment evident in such assessments did not dissipate quickly. Five years after the conclusion of the war, the pro-imperial observer Sir Nathaniel Wraxhall was still lamenting

> the loss of thirteen colonies, of both the Floridas, of part of our West India Islands, and of Minorca – The surrender of whole armies – the ignominious flight of English fleets before those of France and Spain – the expenditure of a hundred and thirty millions of pounds – the abyss of ruin into which a long train of unfortunate councils has plunged the empire – the accumulation of taxes, under which every order of the community is oppress'd and overwhelmed – and the degree of political insignificance into which a country is fallen, who once dispensed her largesses and her subsidies to half the Princes of Europe.

The mere "remembrance of that unhappy war which emancipated America, restor'd the prostrate genius of France, ... render'd back to Spain the proudest trophies of more triumphant reigns," and thereby resulted in "the Imperial Eagle, which had soar'd so high," being "trampled in the dust, insulted, and expiring," Wraxhall observed, operated as a constant reminder "of the faded glories of the English name."[10]

Not all observers were so pessimistic, however. Thomas Tod was one person who, building on the earlier insights of Adam Smith and Josiah Tucker, thought that economic loss might not be a necessary result of political separation. If Britain could "keep markets on the continent of America, open and independent of every European nation" and free from native or immigrant "artisans and manufactures," he wrote, it would continue to get the "largest harvest" of the American trade, and the loss of the colonies, "so much feared as the greatest misfortune" that could befall the British Empire, might actually turn out "to be an advantage to Britain."[11] The Irish peer Edward Startford, 2nd Earl of Aldborough, made the same point, adding that America's long-standing ties with Britain "in blood, religion, and constitution" would lead to a rapid revival of the American trade so that "the treasures spent there" during the war would "quickly flow in again, and Britain and Ireland [would] once more enjoy all the pristine benefits of America, without the expence of keeping it."[12] Day agreed. With commercial exchange restored, he predicted, "the colonies will still be ours; ours in every rational and enlightened view of interest, without infringing the rights of nature, or violating the laws of humanity." Indeed, he

---

[9] *Consequences (Not before adverted to) That are likely to result from the Late Revolution of the British Empire* (London, 1783), 19–20.

[10] Sir *Nathaniel* Wraxhall, *A Short Review of the Political State of Great-Britain at the Commencement of the Year One Thousand Seven Hundred, and Eighty-Seven* (London, 1787), 3–4, 10–12.

[11] [Thomas Tod], *Consolitory Thoughts on American Independence* (Edinburgh, 1782), 2, 14, 67.

[12] Edward Startford, 2nd Earl of Aldborough, *An Essay on the True Interests and Resources of the Empire of the King of Great-Britain and Ireland* (Dublin, 1783), 20.

continued in trying to revive the language of commerce as the principal way of speaking about Britain's overseas activities: "if we consider the true interest of this country, we shall find that it is commerce alone which had raised us to our late envied pitch of greatness; and that it is by commerce only that we can hope to preserve some political importance, and the shattered fragments of our empire."[13]

Other writers echoed this call for a return to a policy of giving primacy to commercial considerations in the operation of empire. Indeed, in a 1784 pamphlet, William Bingham, an American resident in London, expressed the hope that Britain's loss of so many colonies would transform the entire "system of European Politics" by convincing all nations "of the futility of becoming great by conquest," thus making them "more inclined to abandon the cruel system of war, in order effectually to enrich themselves by pursuing the Peaceful line of commerce."[14] Five years later, the political writer John Williams expressed the hope that the "disgrace" Britain had sustained from the loss of "revolted America" might "be a spur to" its "care of the loyal commercial colonies." Decrying the spread to America of the new "Asiatic system" that sacrificed "all the art and powers of man to raise an immense fortune in a short time" and operated on principles of "folly and wickedness" that promised to prove "fatal to a trading nation, which had originally blended profit with honor," he called for a return to "the old spirit, by which our colonies were cherished and made flourishing" and in which the system of colonial development and capital accumulation within the empire was the result, not of extensive state expenditures or oppression of indigenous peoples, but of the industry and enterprise of settlers and merchants, and both groups were "happy with a moderate" acquisition of a "hereditary estate" over several generations in an imperial context in which "the most valuable principles" had been "unwritten, and conveyed in reciprocal right, that" had bound "the mother-country and colonies, knitting together the most distant parties of the whole empire of commerce."[15]

Yet the loss of the American colonies also raised the specter of British national declension as a result of massive emigration to the new United States. This was an old concern that surfaced whenever the labor market within Britain seemed to be contracting during periods of heavy emigration, such as the era immediately before the American war. Thus, in June 1776 did an anonymous pamphleteer, contending that "Of all the evils that attended a country, a spirit of emigration is the greatest," lay out for his readers a comprehensive list of the many ways emigration brought "a certain ruin and desolation to society." By depopulating "our manufacturers," raising "the price of labour beyond the

[13] Day, *Reflections upon the Present State of England*, 43–44.
[14] William Bingham, *A Letter From an American, Now Resident in London, on the Subject of the Restraining Proclamation* (London, 1784), 2.
[15] John Williams, *The Crisis of the Colonies; with Some Observations How Far They may be Saved from any Detriment by the French Treaty*, 3d ed. (London, 1786), 4–5, 7–8, 36–37.

compass of the artist," destroying "the seminary of agriculture, and the nursery for seamen and sailors," and conveying "away our arts and sciences," he explained, emigration led directly to "our profitable fields" becoming "waste; our flourishing towns desarts; until, at last, our sovereign and our nobility must whistle after their stocks over the plain for want of shepherds; must handle the plough share for want of labourers to cultivate the soil."[16] Such concerns resurfaced toward the conclusion of the war, as a number of pamphleteers in the early 1780s wrote tracts designed to discourage emigration from Britain to North America.

The intent of these writers was to present America as a thoroughly "inhospitable land," radically different from Britain and a site of unfulfilled dreams for immigrants, and they easily lapsed into the old language of alterity in doing so. "The condition of society varies extremely in the provinces of America from that of England," John King told his readers in 1783, and he warned that immigrants would "find themselves egregiously deceived" if they went there with "expectations of ease and affluence." America was "not a country matured and grown opulent by commerce," King wrote, but "a new discovered land, occupied by ancient savages, and ravaged by late wars." In America's "present state of simplicity," he said, "farmers are the people they want, and plain mechanics, for the works of necessity," and he predicted that it would be more than a century before they would require more than "mere labour on the soil." Clearly, he concluded, America could not "suit the dainty sons of England," who would be crossing "the Atlantic for a scanty subsistence, earned by the sweat of their brow." "Nothing is so difficult," he admonished his readers, than to endeavor "to naturalize customs and foreign habits" in such a vastly different social setting.[17]

Writing as "Philodemus," Josiah Tucker in a 1783 pamphlet went well beyond King in his denigration of America. In his efforts to dissuade Britons from migrating to America and to cure them of "the *Americomania*" then sweeping the country, Tucker also played on the tropes of alterity metropolitans had always used in reference to distant settlers and places in the overseas empire, limning a picture of rural isolation, social crudeness, ubiquitous annoying insects, savage Indians, labor exploitation, and human degeneration. Unlike "British villages; where offices of assistance and civility are to be met with close at hand, and where mutual cheerfulness can sweeten manual labor," he reported, America, except in towns, had "no such thing as close habitations." Even worse, he wrote, "the innumerable millions of mosketoes, midges, and other abominable insects, which harrass by day and night... all summer long," destroyed personal comfort, while the "savage Indians," a "set of wild and barbarous people," who made "no more of cutting throats than you would to destroy a gnat," had "been known to come down and murder

---

[16] *The Duty of the King and Subject, on the Principles of Civil Liberty* (London, 1776), 40–41.
[17] King, *Thoughts on the Difficulties and Distresses*, 31.

and scalp for many miles into the plantations at once," leaving "no body, if possible to tell tales," and "sparing neither women nor children."[18]

Denouncing the system of emigrant transport as a "diabolical trade... carried on in flesh and blood, by a set of unfeeling brutes" and "carcase dealers" for the benefit of themselves and the "inhuman tyrants," all "pests of mankind, and common enemies of human nature," and drawing on the language of colonial inhumanity, Tucker claimed to know of cases in which indentured servants had been "set to labor with negroes, and other deluded unhappy people like themselves, at the arbitrary command of a hardened wretch, who," knowing "that their hardships were his profits, and their miseries his reward," forced them into "all kinds of drudgery" and showed "neither mercy nor manners." Finally, he contended, in America "Englishmen, Scots, and Irish... degenerate[d] in health and vigor," which, he implied, must have obvious "consequences... upon the mind, and [upon] how much the manly sense and open temper of the Briton is lost here." For proof of this contention, he referred his readers to the appearance of even the wealthy who came to Britain, none of whom were very English. "Do even these look like Englishmen?," he asked. "Are they not generally puny, wire-drawn, long-limbed, yankee-bodied, mortals who would be no more in the hands of one of our country-fellows, than a bundle of tatters?" "If ever [a] region can be marked for degeneracy," he concluded, it "surely is America." "Let the negro drivers and slave-buyers say what they please, let the self-interested merchants or kidnappers urge what they can," he declared, "in every point of view, whether natural, civil, or moral," America was a "cursed country" and Americans an inferior people.[19]

Still other tract writers endorsed and elaborated on these evaluations. Writing to refute the generally laudatory views of J. Hector St. Jean de Crèvecouer in his only recently published *Letters from an American Farmer*, Samuel Ayscough depicted America as a place beset by riots and boundary disputes in which every town was "less improved, civilized, and cultivated" than "every city in England." Although he acknowledged that America had "not been inhabited long enough for many persons to have amassed lordly estates" and become "great Lords," he noted that those who had "power exercise[d] it in the most tyrannical manner, both over their slaves, and those who, perhaps, are if possible in a worse situation than their slaves, the poor distressed Europeans, who may have been deluded with false pretences from their native hospitable shore, to cultivate forests for their, perhaps, inhuman masters."[20]

---

[18] "Philodemus" [Josiah Tucker], *A Plain Letter to the Common People of Great Britain and Ireland, Giving Some Fair Warning Against Transporting Themselves to America* (London, 1783), 15–17, 24.

[19] Ibid., 3, 5–8, 10, 13–14.

[20] [Samuel Ayscough], *Remarks on the Letters from an American Farmer; or a Detection of the Errors of Mr. J. Hector St. John; Proving the Pernicious Tendency of those Letters to Great Britain* (London, 1783), 16–19, 23–24.

In his pamphlet on American independence, Thomas Tod also included a section calculated to dampen the enthusiasm for emigration to America. Why, he asked, did so many "Britons so ardently wish to leave their native country in pursuit of imaginary treasures, which they vainly hope to gather in distant unhealthy climes?" In such places, he wrote, "vast numbers drag out a wretched life in the midst of debility, sickness, and poverty; ashamed to return home without riches," only to be "buried and forgot, while the few who acquire[d] fortunes come to dazzle the multitude, who, all big with the hope of such acquisitions, abandon a country where industry is certain of a comfortable and healthy livelihood, and nothing to annoy and disturb that peace and freedom, which alone produce real tranquility and happiness." In colorful language, Tod urged prospective emigrants

to consider the dreadful drawbacks of those distant territories, where the gloomy woods and wilds are haunted by lions, wolves, tigers, and horrible beasts of prey, who watch at the foot of the unwary traveller; where lakes, rivers, and sea coasts, which tempt the scorched stranger to bathe, and cool the sultry heat, are filled with alligators, sharks, crocodiles, and devouring fish, or strange amphibious animals; where the groves and forests conceal such a variety of hissing serpents and poisonous snakes; where the sultry atmosphere swarms with infectious insects, which night and day are fanned away by miserable slaves, which scenes must fill a heart of feeling with constant anguish, to behold them toiling in the scorching fields, and reaping a wretched living from their cruel rapacious masters; whose frequent chastisements fill the air with howling cries, by often requiring more work than the poor slave can perform; where the natives, driven from their natural possessions, keep the bordering inhabitants in constant alarm of making reprisals for their inequitable dealing with them.

"In short," Tod remarked, "a discerning mind would imagine, if gold and riches were to be gathered in every corner of these distant and unhealthy climes, it would be scarce a motive to desert the Paradise of Britain."[21] "God of my life! Protect me as I stray," the poet Thomas Coombe wrote in expressing the same ideas in his poem *The Peasant of Auburn; or, The Emigrant,* "Where human wolves in mur'drous ambush lay."[22]

Whether or not imperial analysts could stem the emigration by such discouraging reports, the loss of the colonies dramatically raised the question, as Startford asked, whether a smaller empire might not be a better one. "The period we are now at, the eventful changes occasioned by the late war, in the total dismemberment of thirteen of the most fertile and powerful provinces of America from the British Empire, and the emancipation of Ireland from the subjugation of the Legislature of her sister state," he observed in *An Essay on the True Interests and Resources of the Empire of the King of Great-Britain and Ireland,* published in Dublin in 1783, inevitably turned men's thoughts to the remaining resources "of the empire, in what is called its curtailed state." Arguing that "we never could [hope to] manage so distant and large an empire,

---

[21] [Tod], *Consolitory Thoughts,* 27–28.
[22] Thomas Coombe, *The Peasant of Auburn; or, The Emigrant, A Poem* (London, 1783), 7.

but at a great annual and increasing expence," he celebrated what he called "the compactness of empire."[23] "A Country Gentleman" agreed "that a very great extent of remote territory" was "seldom desireable" for an empire and urged his readers to learn from the failed "experiment of subduing America" that "as colonies on a widely-extended continent enlarge and become populous, they will, and they necessarily must, gradually recede from the controul of the original state."[24]

Still other writers addressed this theme. "Far from being beneficial to the country from which they emigrate," asserted an anonymous writer in commenting on the preliminary peace treaty, colonies could be "a real disadvantage." In this observation, he was particularly concerned to make it clear that the loss of Senegal to the French was "less to be lamented" because its unhealthy climate made it so "destructive to European constitutions" as to furnish "a miserable picture to what the avarice of a few will subject their fellow-creatures for the sake of aggrandizing themselves." But he laid it down as a general rule that by "rob[bing] the Mother-country of its inhabitants," dividing the national population, making governance "unwieldy," and rendering the defense of possessions "at such a distance... inconvenient," the "extent and separation" of national "dominions" could, as had been the case with the Roman Empire, be "one cause of the ruin of that empire."[25] But the most important insight to grow out of the loss of the American colonies, according to Tod, was that while arbitrary states could treat their colonies arbitrarily, "a free commercial country" like Great Britain had to concede the wishes of colonies "to have the same liberty" as "the parent state, and to be governed by the same laws," wishes that were in fundamental conflict with predominant contemporary metropolitan understandings of British constitutional arrangements but thoroughly compatible with the operation of a fundamentally commercial empire.[26]

Yet, for all such speculation, few people thought that Britain should relinquish the remainder of its empire. A diminished empire was still an empire, and having an empire remained an essential element in Britain's struggle to maintain its status as a major European state. Thomas Day was hopeful that Britain's immense territories in India, "a territory so vast, so fertile, so well peopled," might at least partially "compensate many of our losses, could we be but convinced of the necessity of regulating it by wholesome laws, adapted to the genius of the inhabitants,"[27] and Startford predicted that Ireland, now that it had been "emancipated... from its late absurd thralldom," would "prove, as an ally instead of a slave, of more solid advantages, comfort, and support to Great-Britain and more to be relied on in time of necessity, than when the parliament of Great-Britain [had] usurped an authority over it." Indeed, Startford

[23] Startford, *Essay on the True Interests and Resources of the Empire*, 6, 18.
[24] "A Country Gentleman," *Candid and Impartial Considerations*, 38.
[25] *Observations on the Preliminary and Provisional Articles* (London, 1783), 17–18.
[26] [Tod], *Consolitory Thoughts*, 30.
[27] Day, *Reflections upon the Present State of England*, 64–65.

declared, "I will take upon me to affirm [that] we are, and shall continue, the greatest empire, as to riches, commerce, and manufactures, in Europe, mistress of its seas, and the ballance of its power."[28]

III

The most extensive part of that empire was in India, an area that throughout the 1780s was a subject of public and parliamentary scrutiny over the continuing excesses of East India Company servants. Although Parliament renewed the Regulatory Act of 1773 in 1780, continuing reports of corruption in India generated a demand for a parliamentary reconsideration of the East India question. The result was a far more extensive parliamentary inquiry, proceeding through two changes in ministry, in which all political groups agreed that Parliament needed to make deep and effective changes in the administration of Britain's Asian empire. Carried on by a Secret Committee appointed in 1780 and a Select Committee appointed in 1781, and functioning with extensive powers after December 1781, this inquiry lasted until 1784, and the Select Committee produced a mountain of evidence and reports that provided the foundation for three separate bills for Parliament to consider over the next two years.[29]

The public and parliamentary debate that swirled around this inquiry in many ways represented a reprise of the discussions in the early 1770s. Routinely, in legislative debates, critics of the Indian situation referred to company servants as "Asiatic plunderers"[30] and declared their intention finally, as the solicitor general, James Mansfield, declared in May 1781,

to put a stop to that system of plunder practised by the subjects of this country, who, after being in India only two or three years, came home with fortunes of from one [hundred] to 500,000£, and bore themselves with such insolent triumph, and such consciousness of the superiority their ill-acquired wealth gave them that they assumed more than the first nobles of the kingdom. By their rapacity, practised under the pretence of obtaining presents from the Indian princes and nabobs,

he continued, "they had for many years been disgracing us as a nation, and making us appear in the eyes of the world, no longer the once-famed generous Britons, but a set of banditti, bent solely on rapine and plunder."[31] Speakers openly demanded not just the reform of Indian affairs but the punishment of those individuals who, having "come home rich . . . procured seats in"

---

[28] Startford, *Essay on the True Interests and Resources of the Empire*, 23, 30.

[29] This phase of the Indian problem has been perceptively analyzed by Nicholas B. Dirks, *The Scandal of Empire: India and the Creation of Imperial Britain* (Cambridge, Mass., 2006).

[30] See the debates for May 25, 1781, in William Cobbett et al., eds., *Parliamentary History of England from the Earliest Period to the Year 1803*, 36 vols. (London, 1806–20), 22: 319–21, 329.

[31] James Mansfield, speech, May 25, 1781, in ibid., 22: 333–34.

Parliament, and thenceforth rested easy with their "ill-gotten gains."[32] As Edmund Burke, the most assiduous member of the Select Committee, put it in April 1782, nothing less than "the preservation of our possessions in India, and, what was more, of our honour and reputation" demanded the most thorough investigation.[33] Burke was not the only one worried about the preservation of India as part of the empire. Precisely because India "was the brightest jewel that now remained in his Majesty's crown," Charles James Fox declared in April 1782, it "called for reformation and correction more immediately than any other part of his Majesty's dominions," albeit he was careful to add that "there was food for reformation almost in every part of those dominions."[34]

As the concerns expressed by Burke and Fox revealed, the investigation of problems in India coincided with the British capitulation in the American war and in Ireland, where the Irish Parliament had just secured home rule, and some pamphlet writers followed Fox in touting India as a place upon which Britons could focus their misdirected imperial energies.[35]

But the lamentable condition of India made others far less sanguine. Thus, the polemicist John King thought that "India, as the affairs of it" were "managed," did "not hold out any prospects of [financial] relief to this country, as a nation, in its present distressful situation." Not only was India a "country wasted by depradation," its "people impoverished by repeated extortion," he declared, using the languages of oppression and injustice, but the "impunity of peculators and criminals, the oppression exercised in trade, by the wretched instruments of an injudicious and impolitic monopoly" had so "rouzed the whole peninsula of Hindostan" that "the surviving remains of a half butchered and famished nation" were "begin[ning] to revolt against their unnatural invaders" and were now "look[ing] only for a convenient season to effectually extirpate the whole race of European monsters" and thus repay "their rapine, their ingratitude, and their barbarity," a deserving fate, he thought for those "Asiatic offenders" who had so far "not only escape[d] justice" in Britain but had added "infection to our corrupted Boroughs – dishonour[ed] our British Senate – and after acts of atrocious delinquency, and with hands yet reeking with Indian blood, take[n] their seats among the representatives of the nation." In the final analysis, King speculated, India might turn out to have been nothing more than "a receptacle for desperate and abandoned adventurers," whose nefarious activities had "injured, rather than benefitted" the "industrious and valuable part of this nation." Whether India would be "a millstone round the neck of England, or a golden basis to erect her prosperity," he wrote, would entirely depend upon whether Britain could contrive "wise . . . measures in her future plan of governing it."[36]

[32] Thomas Townshend, speech, May 25, 1781, in ibid., 22: 334–35.
[33] Edmund Burke, speech, April 15, 1782, in ibid., 22: 1304.
[34] Charles James Fox, speech, April 15, 1782, in ibid., 22: 1285–86.
[35] See Day, *Reflections upon the Present State of England*, 64–65.
[36] King, *Thoughts on the Difficulties and Distresses*, 23–24, 27–28.

"However exhausted with private oppressions and public wars," King explained, India was "still the dernier resort of all the desperate and profligate: a cheesemonger's boy metamorphosed to a general officer, Stratton, Sykes, Rumbold, and innumerable others," sprung "from filth and crimes, into elevated situations and splendid fortunes," providing models that had "maddened the brains of tradesmen and mechanics. When indolence or extravagance has reduced men to ignorance," he observed, "Asia" was "a magnet that" attracted "their hopes and views; to reach India, and to create sudden fortunes" seemed to them "but one and the same thing." Similarly, women who had "no pretensions to a settlement, from a want of beauty, of fortune, and of virtue, look there, not only for an asylum from distress, but as to a theatre of splendid success, where, with tolerable address, and a promptitude to villany, they must obtain the summit of their expectations." "The astonishing and rapid *revolutions* in Asia," he wrote, had "determined [many British] men and women to try whether they were born the children of fortune." Indeed, King lamented, whenever he thought about India he felt

a glowing shame at the degraded name and character of an Englishman; my fancy sees the sun-burnt coast swarming with the mournful spirits of the oppressed and famished natives, imprecating the vengeance on their sordid and inhuman tormentors; myriads of pale spectres, starved by artificial famine, shock my busy fancy; and the once peaceful plains, hallowed by a venerable religion and learning, seem strewed with unhappy victims.[37]

Certainly the M.P. most determined to make sure that the conditions of which King and so many others had so long complained would finally be remedied was Edmund Burke. As the principal member of the Select Committee that conducted the parliamentary inquiry of 1781–84, Burke, building on "the research of years" and "wind[ing] himself into the innermost recesses and labyrinths of the Indian detail,"[38] took a leading role in articulating the case against the East India Company's Indian regime. In April 1783, he "prepared the House to expect, in the next report from the select committee, such accounts of the cruelty, barbarity, and rapine of our government in India, as would shock every man of the least sensibility," "arraigned, in very severe terms, the conduct of governor [Warren] Hastings," whom he called "the grand delinquent of all India, to whose measures all the calamities under which that country was groaning were... to be ascribed," and "pledged himself" to bring Hastings to justice.[39]

This denunciation of Hastings followed upon publication of J. Z. Holwell's *An Address to the Proprietors of East India Stock* and testimony in the committee from Philip Francis. Both Holwell and Francis had been involved in East India Company affairs in India. "No conduct," asserted the former, "could

---

[37] Ibid., 22, 24–26.

[38] Edmund Burke, *Mr. Burke's Speech, on the 1st December 1783* (London, 1784), 3.

[39] Edmund Burke, speeches, April 25, 1783, in Cobbett et al., eds., *Parliamentary History*, 23: 797, 800.

have produced consequences more pernicious to the Company and dangerous to the nation, than that of Mr. Hastings, for these five years past." Holwell did not charge Hastings with peculation. Rather, he denounced him for disobedience to company orders. Holwell reported that Hastings, contrary to his instructions, which had prohibited "servants abroad, from employing their troops in making distant conquests, and have directed them to bestow their attention on the improvement of what they already possess," had gone "far beyond the example of even arbitrary monarchs, and involved his masters in a war from ambitious projects of his own. With gigantic imagination," according to Holwell, Hastings had, without consulting the metropolitan government, "vainly grasped at universal empire in the east" in an effort, Holwell surmised, "to compensate the severe checks received in the Western World." In so doing, Holwell contended, Hastings had at once brought the company "to the brink of ruin" and "violated and tarnished" the "faith, the military reputation, and dignity of the nation." Whether these results "proceeded from the rapacity of one man, or the *visionary and injudicious schemes* of another," Holwell added, was "of little consequence to the public." Hastings's "late transactions in India," he insisted, had "certainly... tarnished" the "national faith, and national honour" of England.[40]

Francis, who had been a member of the supreme council in Bengal under Hastings, made many of the same points, accusing Hastings of being "exclusively responsible for the war which was undertaken" in 1777–78 "for the *avowed* purpose of conquest and extension of dominion, which carried desolation with it wherever it extended, and which has ended in the ruin of the East-India Company." "So far from being difficult to find instances of disobedience" by Hastings, Francis affirmed, "the difficulty would be to point out an order of the Directors [of the company], that ever was regarded. The East India Company little know," he observed, "in what sort of estimation their Directors are held in India."[41] Such conclusions found plentiful expression in the Select Committee's *Ninth Report*.[42]

Burke also received strong support from other pamphleteers. Making extensive use of the languages of oppression and rapacity, the anonymous author of *A Brief and Impartial Review of the State of Great Britain, at the Commencement of the Session of 1783* denounced Hastings as "the *self-throned sovereign of Bengal*," who treated company directives with "contempt and haughty aversion" and whose evident "*delinquency*" was "*marked in the bankruptcy of the Company – in the disgrace of the British name – and in the desolation of the fourth part of the world.*" With "the dazzling examples,

[40] J. Z. Holwell, *An Address to the Proprietors of East India Stock* (London, 1783), 12, 51, 54–55.
[41] Philip Francis, *Two Speeches in the House of Commons on the Original East-India Bill and on the Amending Bill* (London, 1784), 15, 63, 67.
[42] *Ninth Report from the Select Committee, Appointed to Take into Consideration the State of the Administration of Justice in the Provinces of Bengal, Bahar, and Orissa* (London, 1783), 52.

of Alexander and Tamerlane, before his eyes," this *"proprietory Emperor of Hindostan,"* this writer charged, had set out "to extend his dominions by conquest." In pursuit of this goal, Hastings displayed a "conquering spirit" such as had never "been more pompously attended with all its long and dismal train of *exactions, oppressions, blood-shed, massacre, extirpation, pestilence and famine"*; he "beggared" his *"subjects* . . . to feed the war with supplies" and devastated "some of the finest countries of the world" through "the wild projects of his frantic ambition." Contrary to the contentions of his supporters, this writer declared, Hastings deserved no applause "for exacting from the wretched natives of Bengal, a temporary supply to answer exigencies created by *his own* misconduct," for "the *plunder of imprisoned princes,"* or for the *"monopolies,* and exactions, which have exhausted every source of future taxation and revenue," all of which together had ruined trade, decreased population, and virtually stopped "cultivation in the once flourishing kingdom of Bengal," formerly the "pride of Hindostan" and "the granary of the East!"[43]

But, this author continued, *"Beggary, ruin and extirpation"* were by no means the extent of Hastings's legacy to India affairs. As a result of his activities, this writer claimed, the East India Company was "no longer [even] a *commercial corporation,"* but "a *political body* raised on the ruins of commerce, and attentive only to share in the rapine and peculation of those, who are called the *Company's Servants,* but who are in truth and fact the *Despots of Asia."* No "longer composed of individuals, who have thrown their money into the Company's stock, for the sake of sharing in its *commercial* profits," the "Court of Proprietors," he contended, was now chiefly "made up of the friends, agents, dependents, and accomplices of the rulers abroad, qualified by the spoil, and attached by the patronage of Bengal." In consequence, he reported, "Instead of the Bengal investment standing in the high scale of a million sterling, the Company" had been

reduced to borrow that sum from her own servants, at an interest of eight per cent, to supply the investment of the present year. Instead of fleets crouding our ports freighted with the precious commodities of the East, the property of British merchants; we have now nothing left, but the importation of the fortunes of splendid delinquents, amassed by peculation, and rapine,

a "miserable traffic [that] must shortly have an end, as there is nothing left for farther depradation." The "state of the Company's government," he argued, demanded "the vigourous interposition of Parliament, as well to rescue the Legislature from contempt, as to secure the trade of the nation, from the dreadful shock, which threatens every moment to overwhelm it." "The security of our Asiatic trade and dominions – the safety of a million and a half of the national revenue, which depends on this trade – but above all the happiness of

---

[43] *A Brief and Impartial Review of the State of Great Britain, at the Commencement of the Session of 1783,* 3rd ed. (London, 1783), 42–44, 51.

the miserable natives of India," he concluded, called "loudly, on the national justice and wisdom, for a manly and substantial reformation."[44]

The anonymous author of *An Examination into the Principles, Conduct, and Designs, of the Minister* also used the languages of oppression and plunder to support the recommendations of the Select Committee. Condemning the Shelburne Ministry for trying to protect "the plunderers of Asia . . . from punishment," he urged the public "to pay attention to" the "authentic evidence" of "the shocking inhumanities practised by the Company's servants in India," where they had "robbed, murdered, and driven" the "great and ancient Princes of India . . . from their possessions," violated "their sanctuaries," exposed "their women . . . to shame," committed "lawless and daring insults . . . on their persons," undertaken "mean and disgraceful attempts upon their property," made "their countries [into] . . . a desart, and" driven "their subjects . . . to seek refuge in distant states." That country, he asserted, exhibited "universal distrust, detestation and horror, at the weakness, the wickedness, and the violence of our Governmernt." Indeed, he wrote, Britain had no government but that of a

lawless set of men [who] are let loose to plunder the country. The governors give the example, and not only fleece the poor people themselves, but encourage and set on their blood-hounds to encrease their spoils. The servants of the East-India Company have laid waste the country more unmercifully than the most merciless of the Mohomedan conquerors. These, though they plundered, did not ruin the country. Their avarice did not suffer them to lose sight of the policy of leaving a sufficient stock to encrease, till they could reap another harvest. But the servants of the Company have plundered without any views to posterity, and leave to their successors what alone they are incapable of carrying off. The greater the riches they bring home, the more they have it in their power to purchase protection. By these means, rich and well-cultivated lands are turned into dreary and inhospitable deserts, marking the progress of the licentious servants of a Company of Merchants.

Lamenting that "Our connection with India has been the greatest curse that country ever felt," the author argued that Britain needed to take firm steps to punish "these monsters" as well as "those who have been sharers in their spoils, and screened them from the justice due to their crimes" before it could hope "to recover the confidence of the people of India" and

convince them that we are desirous of acting as becomes good sovereigns, not as lawless tyrants; forming wise and beneficent laws, suited to the genius and the temper of the inhabitants, and suffering them to enjoy practically their good effects, before we can receive from them the proofs we seem to expect of their trusting to '*the probity, punctuality, and good order of our Government.*'[45]

44 Ibid., 40–41, 46, 51, 54.
45 *An Examination into the Principles, Conduct, and Designs, of the Minister* (London, 1783), 52–56.

Burke's long speech of December 1, 1783, in Parliament represented the culmination of nearly two decades of engagement with the Indian problem. India, he said, formed "a territory larger than any European dominion, Russia and Turkey excepted," and included about thirty million people, who, far from being "an abject and barbarous populace," were "a people for ages civilized and cultivated; cultivated by all the arts of polished life, whilst we were yet in the woods." In India, he remarked, was

to be found an antient and venerable priesthood, the depository of their laws, learning, and history, the guides of the people whilst living, and their consolation in death; a nobility of great antiquity and reknown; a multitude of cities, not exceeded in population and trade by those of the first class in Europe; merchants and bankers, individual houses of whom have once vied in capital with the Bank of England.

"All this vast mass, composed of so many orders and classes of men," Burke said, was "infinitely diversified by manners, by religion, by hereditary employment, through all their profitable combinations." This very complexity and civility rendered "the handling of India a matter in a high degree critical and delicate. But oh!," he exclaimed, "It has been handled [very] rudely indeed."[46]

"In its best state," Burke declared, "Our Indian government" was "a grievance," and, although he deemed it "an arduous thing to plead against abuses of power which" originated "from your own country, and" affected "those whom we are used to consider as strangers," he condemned, with what he called a "map of misgovernment before" him, the company's "determined resolution to continue and countenance every mode and every degree of peculation, oppression, and tyranny," denounced Hastings for his many "despotic acts," decried the fact that "the transport of plunder" had become "the only traffic of the country," and deplored "that universal systematic breach of treaties which had made the British faith proverbial in the East." He spent much of his long speech illustrating three propositions: first, that in the whole of India, from the "large range of mountains that walls the northern frontier" to "where it touches" British India "in the latitude of twenty-nine, to Cape Comorin, in the latitude of eight, . . . there is not a *single* prince, state, or potentate, great or small[,] . . . with whom" the Company's servants had

come into contact, whom they have not sold. I say *sold*, though sometimes they have not been able to deliver according to their bargain. – Secondly, I say, that there is not a *single treaty* they have ever made, which they have not broken. – Thirdly, I say, that there is not a single prince or state, who ever put any trust in the Company, who is not utterly ruined; and that none are in any degree secure of flourishing, but in the exact proportion to their settled distrust and irreconcilable enmity to this nation.

"These assertions," Burke insisted, "are universal. I say in the full sense *universal.*"[47]

[46] *Mr. Burke's Speech, on the 1st December, 1783,* 3, 12–15.
[47] Ibid., 16, 33, 51, 66, 70, 78.

For Indians, Burke was persuaded, the British conquest of Bengal and its neighboring provinces had been far more calamitous than any of the many previous invasions by other conquerors. Under the British, in his view, Indians had been the unwitting victims of all the evils associated with what modern analysts have termed colonialism. If the "Tartar invasion" had been "mischievous," he said,

it is our protection that destroys India. It was their enmity, but it is our friendship. Our conquest there, after twenty years, is as crude as it was the first day. The natives scarcely know what it is to see the gray head of an Englishman. Young men (boys almost) govern there, without society, and without sympathy with the natives. They have no more social habits with their people, than if they still resided in England; nor indeed any species of intercourse but that which is necessary to making a sudden fortune, with a view to a remote settlement. Animated with all the avarice of age, and all the impetuosity of youth, they roll in one after another; wave upon wave; and there is nothing before the eyes of the natives but an endless, hopeless prospect of new flights of birds of prey and passage, with appetites continually renewing for a food that is continually wasting. Every rupee of profit made by an Englishman is lost for ever to India. With us are no retributory superstitions, through ages, to the poor, for the rapine and injustice of a day. With us no pride erects stately monuments which repair the mischiefs which pride had produced, and which adorn a country out of its own spoils. England has erected no churches, no hospitals, no palaces, no schools; England has built no bridges, made no high roads, cut no navigations, dug out no reservoirs. Every other conqueror of every other description has left some monument, either of state or beneficence behind him. Were we to be driven out of India this day,

Burke declared, "nothing would remain, to tell that it had been possessed during the inglorious period of our dominion, by any better than the ourang-outang or the tiger."[48]

"Any one who" took "the smallest trouble to be informed concerning the affairs of India," Burke concluded, knew "that the habitual despotism and oppression, the monopolies, the peculations, the universal destruction of all legal authority of this kingdom, which have been for twenty years maturing to their present enormity, combined with the distance of the scene, the boldness and artifice of delinquents, their combination, their excessive wealth, and the faction that they have made in England" would require years to root out and destroy, and, calling upon the languages of humanity and justice, he expressed his happiness that he could cast his vote for "destroying a tyranny that exists to the disgrace of this nation, and the destruction of so large a part of the human species." "It is now to be determined," he said, "whether the three years of laborious parliamentary research, whether the twenty years of patient Indian suffering," were "to produce a substantial reform in our Eastern administration; or whether our knowledge of the grievances has abated our zeal for the correction of them, and whether our very enquiry into the evil was only a pretext to elude the remedy which is demanded from us by humanity, by justice,

48 Ibid., 31–33.

and by every principle of true policy. Depend upon it," he said, "this business cannot be indifferent to our fame. It will turn out a matter of great disgrace or great glory to the whole British nation. We are on a conspicuous stage, and the world marks our demeanour." The integrity of the British nation, he thus asserted, depended upon reining in the transgressions of those rapacious, corrupt, and inhumane Britons who had treated India as a site for their own personal plunder.[49]

Of course, by no means everyone accepted Burke's definition of the problem or agreed with his remedies. Major John Scott, Hastings's agent in Britain, published what he intended to be a point-by-point refutation of Burke's speech. Calling it "an artful, though a gross and glaring misrepresentation of all the events that have happened in India from the year 1756 to the present time" and denouncing the Select Committee's Ninth and Eleventh Reports as "the most infamous, and execrable libels, that were ever imposed upon a deluded public" and an affront "to the dignity, the justice, and the honour of the British nation," Scott asserted that "pretended patriots, and political adventurers," such as Burke, had "gulled, deceived, and cheated" the "People of England" into believing that company servants in India were "infernal monsters." He did not deny that in the days of Clive some "very glaring instances" could "be found, of men who acquired large fortunes in a short time." But he argued that Hastings had the Indian situation so well under control that "the sudden acquisition of wealth in India" was a problem that no longer existed; pointed out that no young men were in positions of authority; listed many improvements that had been made under Hastings, including erecting schools, building bridges and roads, cutting new channels of navigation, increasing trade, and turning Calcutta into a permanent and thriving urban space; and pointed to the growing economic returns Britain had received from Asia since the acquisition of Bengal. With few exceptions, Scott insisted, "the gentlemen who have served their country in India" were "men of as strict honour, and as exemplary characters in every respect, as any set of men whatsoever."[50]

John Dalrymple, Earl of Stair, was another who was unpersuaded that the Select and Secret Committees had produced "solid proofs...that excesses" still "exist[ed], or, at least, have been carried to the singular and unnatural extent each parliamentary disclaimer is pleased to assign them." He dismissed many of the charges against the company and its servants as "tedious farrago" that did "not much exceed in veracity, the Arabian Night's Entertainments," praised Hastings "as that powerful genius of resource," and suggested that the proponents of the India bill were willing to violate charters in order "to obtain the plunder of India for themselves and their adherents." Indeed, one of his principal objections to the regulating bill was that it eliminated the Company's charter rights. More importantly, he also thought that the Government was

---

[49] Ibid., 1–2, 97–98, 105.
[50] Major John Scott, *A Reply to Mr. Burke's Speech of the First of December, 1783* (London, 1783), 2, 15–21, 43.

not the proper agent to "restore the golden age in India" and that "nothing but absolute necessity, and the sure consequence of losing" the Indian "trade altogether, could justify" such wholesale Government interference, reminding his readers that "under the direction of their own proprietary, uncontrouled by parliament," the Company had risen "to an unexampled height of wealth and prosperity" and that "since the intervention of parliament, their affairs have declined." Stair agreed that considerations of "humanity, and a wish to restore India to a better and juster system of government, less rapacious, and less oppressive to the natives," was "a fair and generous object," but he thought that this goal could be achieved merely by "send[ing] out a well-chosen committee of visitation and inspection, with adequate and efficient powers from Parliament."[51]

Other writers worried about the effects of regulatory bills on the constitution. For instance, William Pulteney was concerned that such a bill would place too much power in the hands of the Ministry, and James Boswell, Samuel Johnson's companion, feared that it would "annihilate the constitutional monarchy of these kingdoms" by taking too much power away from the Crown. Usually, these writers did not dispute that East India Company servants had, as Boswell put it, "flagitiously abused" the territorial powers it had acquired since the mid-1750s.[52] Yet Pulteney acknowledged that a strong case could be made that "the Company's affairs" were "in no desperate condition," that "the Misconduct of their Servants abroad" had "been exaggerated," that it had not been "the Trading Concerns of the Company, which" had "produced malversations in India, but their power and authority over the natives," and that a new system of administration would probably also "send out a great number of new hungry Persons, with much the same sort of principles, with those who have hitherto visited that unfortunate Company."[53]

Against these positions, Company antagonists contended that the "numerous and authentic Reports of the Secret and Select Committees" contained such "ample proof of the necessity of parliamentary interference" as to override all concerns about the sanctity of the charter rights of a company guilty of such mismanagement.[54] Characterizing the attack on the committee reports as nothing more than "petulant ribbaldry," the anonymous author of a pamphlet entitled *Popular Topics* charged that opponents of the regulatory act turned to a charter defense only because they were "unable to disprove a single article contained in" those reports. The only charters that were "sacred things," he argued, invoking the standards of the British language of liberty, were those that secured "liberty against power. But is the East-India Charter

[51] John Dalrymple, Earl of Stair, *The Proper Limits of Government's Interference with the Affairs of the East-India Company* (London, 1784), 11, 13–14, 18–19, 21, 24.
[52] James Boswell, *A Letter to the People of Scotland, On the Present State of the Nation* (Edinburgh, 1783), 8, 10; William Pulteney, *The Effects to be Expected from the East India Bill, upon the Constitution of Great Britain* (London, 1783), 4–5.
[53] Pulteney, *Effects to be Expected from the East India Bill*, 5–7.
[54] *Chartered Rights* (London, 1784?), 14.

of this description?," he asked. "Is it a security for any man's liberty? Yes, says a proud Nabob, it is a security for our franchises." But these franchises, "the chartered right of Nabobs and oppressors," this author argued, involved only the "power of governing, or rather oppressing thirty millions of men." A franchise that thus conveyed "a despotic, unaccountable, and uncontroulable authority over the lives and property of mankind" seemed to him to be a "pretty kind of liberty and franchise" indeed. Even now, with the East India Company under intense investigation, he observed, "almost every dispatch received from India produces melancholy proofs of the ruin which our mismanagement has occasioned." The "repeated breach of treaties, and violation of public faith, by the Company's servants," he wrote, had "rendered the British name odious in Hindostan." "If these abuses were accidental," he continued, strong measures might have been unnecessary, but, he insisted, "they are habitual" and proceeded "from radical defects in the constitution of the Company," defects that could be remedied only by a strong regulatory bill.[55]

In the interest of protecting charter rights, the House of Lords rejected the India bill prepared by Fox and Burke in late 1783, but the following summer a new Ministry, headed by William Pitt, the younger, passed a shorter India bill. This measure left the charter intact and the East India Company in charge of its internal governance, patronage, and commercial policy. But by putting Indian affairs under the close supervision of a metropolitan Board of Control in London and Indian territories under the direction of a royally appointed governor general with veto powers over regulations in all three Indian presidencies, it provided the foundations for bringing Indian policy under much closer ministerial supervision. Subsequent parliamentary measures in 1786 and 1788 refined this arrangement, and by the 1790s, as the historian H. V. Bowen has remarked, "there was a broad agreement that the new measures had brought the Company's servants under control" and had "promoted stability and prosperity in territories now described as 'national' concerns."[56]

In 1785, the anonymous author of a pamphlet entitled *We Have been all in the Wrong; or, Thoughts upon the Dissolution of the Late, and the Conduct of the Present Parliament, and upon Mr. Fox's East-India Bill* reviewed the long controversy over the East Indian question during the previous twenty years. "From the year 1766, until the year 1783," this author declared, India "had exhibited a repetition of continual criminality in the servants of the Company, and of continual impunity. Both arose either from the collusion of the Directors with delinquents; or from their procrastination, or desire to conceal delinquencies, even where there was no collusion." As governors of Bengal and Madras, respectively, Warren Hastings and Sir Thomas Rumbold had subverted the regulatory act of 1773, in the process assuming to themselves

---

[55] *Popular Topics: or, the Grand Question Discussed* (London, 1784), 21–22, 27–28.
[56] H. V. Bowen, "British India, 1765–1813: The Metropolitan Context," in P. J. Marshall, ed., *The Eighteenth Century, Volume II of The Oxford History of the British Empire* (Oxford: Oxford University Press, 1998), 544–45.

"the most unprecedented powers . . . of making war and peace, of hiring out the
Company's troops as mercenaries to Princes of the country, of giving away the
dominions of England to other European states, of acquiring new ones from
native Princes, of delegating their own and their Council[']s powers to others,"
and many other "extravagancies." For his part, Hastings, "in a scene . . . which
the Sun never saw," in one day dispossessed all the proprietors of land in "a
kingdom larger and richer than France," put their estates up for "auction for
rack rents," permitted company servants to rent "many of them in their own
persons" or in the persons of their subordinate banyans, "who could do what
their employers durst not": establish monopolies, charge usurious rates for
loans, extort money "with impunity," traffic in "the collection and farming
of revenues," and make "war and invasions without any authority but their
own," all which "abuses" had been "proved by the reports of the East-India
Committees." As a result, by 1783, the very year America was lost, Ireland was
"hanging upon England only by a thread, the English Empire in the East [was]
tottering to its fall."[57]

By providing effective measures against all these practices and by guaran-
teeing "such of the native Princes as were under the protection of England, in
the most unbounded enjoyment of their rights," providing "reparations for the
oppressions they had suffered, or should suffer, against their English oppressors," and fixing the rents of all landholders, the India bill, the author was
hopeful, would establish "a sublime system of policy and justice, for the recovery of the Eastern empire, after the sad blow which England had so recently
received in the loss of the Western one." "By this complication of humanity,
applied to so many different objects," he observed, the framers of those bills
had at once done "all that men could do, to attach the immense body of the
natives of all dominions connected with ours, to government on which the
security of their own tenure was thus made to depend" and exhibited Britain's
commitment to a humanitarian approach to empire.[58]

But not all metropolitan Britons believed that Pitt's reform bill had resolved
all the problems that had been identified with the situation in India since
the mid-1760s. For the next decade, Burke's relentless efforts to bring Warren Hastings to justice as a final act of public repudiation of the misdeeds of
Britain's Asiatic plunderers and the seven-year impeachment trial of Hastings,
lasting from February 1788 until his final acquittal by the House of Lords
in April 1795, kept the transgressions of Britons in India constantly in the
public eye. Critics continued to condemn the Company's servants as inexperienced young men whose only objective was to acquire a fortune and return to
Britain a nabob, and to depict India as a place where the "fundamental principles of the Government" constituted "a strong incentive to every species of

---

[57] *We Have Been All in the Wrong: or, Thoughts upon the Dissolution of the Late, and the
Conduct of the Present Parliament, and upon Mr. Fox's East-India Bill* (London, 1785), 1–2,
51–52, 55–57.
[58] Ibid., 60, 63.

vice" and where that government supported an "internal policy" by which the inhabitants were "cruelly oppressed, and deprived, in great measure of those resources which might enable them to obtain ample redress." Such policies, critics contended, were not only unfavorable for the Indian population but also, because of the absence of a consensual element, "extremely prejudicial to the liberties of an Englishman." Unlike traditional British colonial governance, the government of India, they thought, was a form of despotism, "as arbitrary, in many respects, as it is impolitic and inauspicious to those who" were "unfortunately obliged to be regulated by such a system," a system, in their view, that simply added a new dimension to the long-festering problems of empire in the East.[59]

IV

Perhaps because the trade disruptions associated with the American war severely reduced the volume of the slave trade, metropolitan agitation against the imperial slave system slowed dramatically. For almost seven years after 1776, no one published any substantial tracts on this subject, and public discussion, in and out of Parliament, from then through the early 1780s, focused largely on either the propriety of British offers of emancipation to the enslaved in return for military or naval service or the incongruity of Americans' commitments, on the one hand, to political liberty for free people and, on the other, to chattel slavery. But the close of hostilities promised a rapid revival of the slave trade to meet pent-up demand in the West Indies. Before the war suspended it and "many of the Guinea-men ... turned [themselves in]to privateers," an anonymous pamphlet writer pointed out immediately after the peace in 1783, the "Guinea-trade employed several hundred sail of ships, manned by above 3000 seamen, and we used to calculate the annual exports at above two million." Because the African trade had long been of such "great extent and importance" and because it formed "a main link in the chain of our connection with the West Indies, where slaves are as much wanted as lumber," he expressed the hope and the expectation "to see this branch of commerce revive on the first dawn of peace."[60] Immediately after the war, perhaps in response to this prospect, agitation against colonial slavery and the African slave trade revived in earnest, now, given the secession of the thirteen American states from the British Empire, focused almost entirely on the West Indian colonies.

Already in February 1783, while peace was still being negotiated, Beilby Porteus, bishop of Chester, raised in the annual sermon given to the Society for the Propagation of the Gospel the problem of "that unhappy race of beings, the AFRICAN SLAVES in our West Indian Colonies." Although Porteus went out of his way to praise recent efforts of "several of the most wealthy and most

---

[59] William Humphrey Faulkner, *Rights of Man Invaded; Being an Exposition of the Tyranny of our India Governments* (London, 1792), 16–17, 55.
[60] *A Letter on the Preliminaries of Peace* (London, 1783), 25.

worthy proprietors of West India estates, resident as well in this country as in the islands[,] . . . both to mitigate the hardships and promote the instruction of their Negroes," he acknowleged that these efforts were in part a response to the interruption of the slave trade during the war and made clear that he had no illusions about the continuing severity of the colonial slave system, where too many masters continued to consider the enslaved "as mere machines and instruments to work with, as having neither understandings to be cultivated nor souls to be saved."[61]

Nevertheless, Porteus expressed the hope that the "many excellent tracts" published "within these few years . . . both in this and other countries on the subject of Negroe slavery," along with "a still more excellent one" that would "soon see the light," would eventually "remove the prejudices (if any still remain) of the West India planters, and excite the attention of government to this most important object." Using the languages of humanity and justice, he called upon the SPG to devise a plan that would make "the civilization and conversion of the Negroe slaves . . . one of the grand leading objects of our pious endeavours," predicting that such a plan would so excite "the generosity, the humanity, . . . the justice of the English nation" that people would provide the assistance necessary to extricate *"near half a million* of their fellow-creatures" from "the most deplorable state of heathenism, irreligion, and vice." "It would be glorious to Great Britain to take the lead in this benevolent and truly Christian enterprize," he declared, adding

that it is peculiarly incumbent on the people of this kingdom to exert their utmost liberality in alleviating the miseries, both temporal and spiritual, of the wretched Africans, since they have been for many years (till interrupted by the late war) more largely concerned in that inhuman merchandize of men, and have imported more slaves into the colonies, than any other nation in Europe.

"Let then," he concluded,

our countrymen make haste to relieve, as far as they are able, the calamities they have brought on so large a part of the human race; let them endeavour to wipe away the reproach of having delivered over so many of their innocent fellow-creatures to a most heavy temporal bondage, both by contributing to sooth[e] and alleviate that as much as possible, and by endeavouring to rescue them from the still more cruel knowledge of ignorance and sin.[62]

The forthcoming work to which Porteus referred was one of two important volumes published in 1784. The first was *An Essay on the Treatment and Conversion of African Slaves on the British Sugar Colonies* by James Ramsay, vicar in Teston, Kent, whose twenty-year residence in St. Kitts as an Anglican minister, a planter, and a slaveholder gave his work instant public credibility and propelled him into a prominent role as a spokesman for a steadily cohering

---

[61] Beilby Porteus, *A Sermon Preached before the Incorporated Society for the Propagation of the Gospel in Foreign Parts* (London, 1783), 7-8, 15-17.

[62] Ibid., 14, 33–34.

antislavery movement for the next decade. Fourteen years in the composition, Ramsay's substantial *Essay* ran just short of 300 pages and was remarkably comprehensive, joining a historical analysis of slavery in ancient and modern times with a vindication of the natural capacity of Africans, an analysis of how the religious instruction of slaves would both improve their lives and profit their masters, and a specific plan for converting slaves, improving their lives, and mitigating many of the worst features of the British imperial slave system.[63] Reviewers immediately recognized the power of its appeal; one of them judged it to be "unquestionably the clearest, the most rational, and the strongest appeal, that has hitherto ever been made to the wisdom of the legislature, and the humanity of the nation, relative to the slavery of the Negroes in our West India islands."[64] The second work was the much shorter but insightful *Thoughts on the Slavery of Negroes*, the first edition of which appeared anonymously, by the Quaker Joseph Woods.[65]

By providing a firsthand account by a person with extensive experience as a slave owner who had tried with modest success to bring Christianity to his slaves, Ramsay hoped to call British public attention once again to the evils of slavery, to overcome the "universal carelessness and indifference" of metropolitan Britons about those evils, and to underline the contradictions between colonial slavery and metropolitan norms. "Why," he asked, "hath the active zeal of the benevolent Mr. Granville Sharp, and a few others, in this business that we now agitate, hitherto [done little more than to make] the unfeeling indifference of our age, and nation, but the more conspicuous?" Like Sharp, Ramsay expressed the "shame and sorrow" of Britain, "that she, who" had "been raised so high above her fellows, by the influence of this heaven-descended liberty, at this day" was, "and, for more than two centuries past," had "been, striving with all the venturous energy of a commercial spirit, to establish slavery in the new world; in a region, where the curse of slavery was unknown, till, through the infernal love of gold, she introduced and fixed it," that "a nation most highly favoured of liberty" was now "viewed as taking the lead in this odious traffic, and as bending down the soul in utter darkness, the more effectually to enslave the body." "Freedom must blush indignantly," he declared, "while humanity moans over the reproachful tale."[66]

In this venture, Ramsay remarked, Britons had shown themselves to be markedly inferior to the "savages of America," who were "so wholly without the conception of the possibility of one man's being submitted to the will of another, that they" knew "no medium between roasting their prisoners, and adopting them into their families." "Settled in the same country," Europeans, by contrast,

---

[63] James Ramsay, *An Essay on the Treatment and Conversion of African Slaves in the British Sugar Colonies* (London, 1784), preface.
[64] *The Critical Review* (London), 57 (1784): 452.
[65] [Joseph Woods], *Thoughts on the Slavery of Negroes* (London, 1784).
[66] Ramsay, *Essay*, viii, 33–35, 105, 179.

could traverse the vast Atlantic to traffic for, enslave, and sell, wretches unknown to them, who never injured them; nay, could keep working in iron chains their own unhappy countrymen sent among them: while they boast[ed] of having vindicated for themselves, as the natural inheritance of freedom, a total independence on all authority not originating from themselves.

It was an ugly fact, Ramsay lamented, that "every where, in every age, the chain of slavery" had "been fashioned, and applied by the hand of liberty." "While we reflect on the state of slavery in our colonies, among the freest people in the world," he continued, it was clear that slaveholders who had liberty were "constantly restraining its blessings within their own little circle, and delight more in augmenting the train of their dependents, than in adding to the rank of fellow citizens, or in diffusing the benefits of freedom among their neighbours."[67] That Americans regarded a "large Number of healthful robust *Negroes*" as evidence of "an extensive and fruitful Estate," and the "principal Riches" of an American province, John Waring, secretary of Bray's Associates, a benevolent society dating back to the early eighteenth century, remarked earlier in the 1780s, was a national embarrassment.[68]

Both Ramsay and Woods acknowledged that success in this effort would require overcoming two extraordinarily powerful obstacles. The first was the opposition of the West Indian slave owners. "However incumbent it be on the individuals concerned in this species of property to satisfy the demands of reason and conscience by relinquishing it," Woods wrote in reference to both African traders and colonial planters, "experience has taught, that it is too deeply entangled with motives of interest and habits of power to be voluntarily abandoned, at least in any general line,"[69] and Ramsay agreed that masters would oppose and were powerful enough to defeat any "law to improve the condition of . . . slaves, or to instruct them in the principles of religion," on the grounds that it would be "an incroachment on their master[']s property, and an hindrance of their profit."[70]

Ramsay traced the colonials' excessive power in this regard back to the British constitution itself, which, as he explained, had "such an excessive bias to personal liberty, that in contradiction to the maxims of every well ordered state, it cannot, or will not, meddle with private behaviour," with the result that the imperial government in its relations with the colonies exhibited a pronounced "want of energy, vigour, and even propriety in every department of police." With regard to colonial slavery, Ramsay continued, the constitution laid "no claim to the slave, but confines its attention to the intercourse of freemen, leaving citizens at liberty, as masters, to dispose of, and treat their slaves, with the same indifference, if they please, with the same wantonness, which

[67] Ibid., 36 note, 66.
[68] John Waring, *A Letter to an American Planter from His Friend in London* (London, 1781), 4.
[69] [Woods], *Thoughts on the Slavery of Negroes*, 22–23.
[70] Ramsay, *Essay*, 280.

without controul they may exercise over their cattle," regarding slaves "as having, distinct from" their masters, "no right or interest of their own." This situation, Ramsay surmised, was the principal explanation for "the artificial, or unnatural relation of master and slave; where power constitutes right; where, according to the degree of his capacity or coercion, every man becomes his own legislator, and erects his interest, or his caprice, into a law for regulating his conduct to his neighbour."[71]

In a 1785 pamphlet, Josiah Tucker made much the same point in trying to explain why, as he put it, "English planters in general . . . treat[ed] their slaves, or suffer[ed] them to be treated, with a greater degree of inhumanity than the planters of any other European nation." "The very form of the English constitution," Tucker wrote, made "English planters . . . more their own masters, their own law-givers in their assemblies; also the interpreters, the judges (as jurymen), and the executioners of their laws, than those of any other nation," with the irony that a "constitution, originally calculated for the preservation of liberty," tended, in the case of slavery, "to destroy it."[72]

But, taking a cue from Granville Sharp's similar observations in 1776,[73] these postwar critics also pointed to a second and even more substantial obstacle to reform: the broad involvement of metropolitan Britons in the imperial slave system. Woods underlined and elaborated upon this point. "Because the revenue of the government, the profits of the merchants, and the luxury of the people, have involved the whole nation as *participes criminis*" in colonial slavery, he announced, "the burthen of restoring to the Africans their alienated rights should not press too partially on the planters, who adopted, not introduced, this iniquitous traffick, and have pursued it under the patronage of Britain." All efforts at amelioration, he pointed out, had "generally been discouraged," not just "by the narrow prejudices of the planters," but "by the illiberal policy of the governing powers." The arguments that "the scene of oppression is distant, and the hearts of those who are immediately engaged in it, are hardened by the powerful influence of avarice and habit," and that "those very sufferings are the source of public revenue and private wealth," were not, in Woods's view, sufficient reasons for Britain to refuse to grant whatever relief was in its power to give. The unspoken assumptions behind such "commercial" objections, he complained, were "that the claims of religion and morality ought to be subservient to those of avarice and luxury, and that it is better that thousands of poor unoffending people should be degraded in the most abject slavery, than that the inhabitants of Europe should pay a higher price for their rum, rice, and sugar."[74] "The *planter*, the *slave-merchant*,

---

[71] Ibid., 3, 64–65.

[72] Josiah Tucker, *Reflections on the Present Matters in Dispute between Great Britain and Ireland* (London, 1785), 10–11.

[73] See, especially, *The Law of Retribution; or, a Serious Warning to Great Britain and her Colonies* (London, 1776), 305.

[74] [Woods], *Thoughts on the Slavery of Negroes*, 6–7, 11, 18–19, 23.

the *King*, the *Legislature*" that permits the traffic, George Gregory agreed in an essay on slavery and the slave trade published in 1785, "have each their respective portion of guilt."[75]

One of the reviewers of Ramsay's *Essay* expansively defined its purpose as "the overthrow of a tyranny, the most disgraceful ever tolerated in any civilized nation,"[76] but the obstacles in the way of such a goal meant that the immediate objectives of both Ramsay and Woods were far more modest. Although Ramsay expressed his belief that "absolute freedom" was "within the plan of providence, and of man's progressive advancement in society," and fervently hoped that metropolitan Britons, "a people, who" had "risqued their own existence, frequently, as a state, to keep one continental tyrant from ridding the world of another, might," in the meantime, "at last have wisdom to render themselves rich and powerful" by breaking "the iron chain which disgraces our nature and nation, . . . restoring to liberty, and recovering to society and reason, the exiled sons of Africa," he was under no illusion that slavery might be easily or soon abolished.[77] Woods also called for the "total abolition of slavery, in every part of the British dominions," but recognized, with Ramsay, that it would have to be "gradual." In the interim, he advocated passage of "some authoritative act, to render the present situation of the slaves more tolerable, to allow them some profit from the sweat of their brow, to provide some mode of instructing them in useful truths, and rigidly to prohibit the importation of more."[78]

Woods's advocacy of a parliamentary statute constituted an endorsement of the earlier insights of William Knox, Maurice Morgann, and Granville Sharp that, as Woods phrased it, "the alteration and gradual subversion of" the imperial slave "system, can only be hoped for from the interposition of the British legislature."[79] Always the hard-headed realist, Tucker despaired that Parliament would ever act even to bar the slave trade. Notwithstanding the public outcry against it, he noted in 1785, "the same trade in human blood is still carried on, not only with impunity, but also with the consent, approbation, and even assistance of the British legislature. Nay, I will venture to foretel[l]," he lamented, "that the same will be for ever carried on, till some other method can be devised for supplying Europe with sugars, and with other produce of the southern climates, at a *cheaper rate* than what we receive through the medium of slavery. *Cheapness* alone," he declared cynically, could "work a surprising alteration in the thoughts and dispositions of mankind on such subjects. For self-interest . . . would do more towards exciting a strong aversion to the present monopoly of labour in our plantations, and to an abhorrence of the various evils attendant on slavery, than all the reasonings, moral arguments, or eloquence in the world."[80] Expressing his hope that "the great revolution which seems

[75] George Gregory, *Essay Historical and Political* (London, 1785), 302.
[76] *Critical Review*, 57 (May 1784): 381.
[77] Ramsay, *Essay*, 35, 127–28, 280.
[78] [Woods], *Thoughts on the Slavery of Negroes*, 31–32.
[79] Ibid., 23.
[80] Tucker, *Reflections on the Present Matters in Dispute*, 9.

preparing in the Western world" might "accelerate the fall of this abominable tyranny," the philosopher William Paley in 1785 remarked acidly that such a development would invite reflection on "whether a legislature, which had so long lent it's assistance to the support of an institution replete with human misery, was fit to be trusted with an empire, the most extensive that ever obtained in any age or quarter of the world."[81]

In contrast to many of his metropolitan contemporaries, Ramsay, as an ex–West Indian himself, did not see all Creoles as degenerates. "For some time past," he reported, extreme mistreatment had, among Creole West Indians, "been generally mentioned with indignation," and he acknowledged knowing many West Indians who had, because of "good sense, a regard for their reputation, and a well informed conviction of their interest," been induced "to treat their slaves with discretion and humanity." The "dictates of humanity, or even of prudence alone," he observed, could "stand in stead of a thousand laws." He even singled out one man, "a Creole of at least four descents, the friend of the author," as "a man of more considerable humanity in private, and more comprehensive generosity in public life, than . . . had ever come within my notice." Rating West Indian planters more highly than their counterparts in North America, who, in contrast to the West Indians, treated their English servants "with full as much severity as was practised only on Africans in the sugar islands," Ramsay even argued that "adventurers from Europe" were "universally more cruel and morose towards slaves, than Creoles, or native West-Indians," which, in view of the fact that the Europeans were "usually collected" from "the refuse of each man's connections, of every trade, and every profession," he found wholly unsurprising. Not, then, "the effect of the illiberal turn of the colonists, accustomed from their infancy to trifle with the feeling, and smile at the miseries, of wretches born to be the drudges of their avarice, and slaves of their caprice," he argued, but "the arbitrary unnatural relation that" existed between masters "and their wretched dependants" inherent in the slave system was the principal reason for the perpetuation and harshness of colonial slavery.[82]

But Ramsey's apologia for West Indian Creole slave masters did not prevent his audience from reading his work as an unrelenting condemnation of the imperial slave system. This was certainly true of his attackers, who, unlike Long, Estwick, and Martin in the wake of the Somerset case, professed to be not "Champion[s] of slavery"[83] but defenders of the "British West India planters" against Ramsay's "acrimonious misrepresentations" of them as "a set of illiberal tyrants." James Tobin, a former member of the Council in the colony of Nevis, was the most prominent of these. With "intemperate zeal," Tobin objected, Ramsay seized "every occasion, of stigmatizing the *English*

---

[81] William Paley, *The Principles of Moral and Political Philosophy* (London, 1785), 197.

[82] Ramsay, *Essay*, 36 note, 67–69, 91–92, 95, 99.

[83] *Remarks on a Pamphlet, written by the Rev. James Ramsay* (London, 1784), 4. While this pamphlet professed to be an answer to Ramsay, it was actually directed at Joseph Woods's anonymously published *Thoughts on the Slavery of Negroes*.

planters, as the most barbarous and cruel masters; and, indeed, as the most vicious and unprincipled of men," and Ramsay's portrait of "the West Indians . . . as a band of inhuman and unprincipled tyrants while abroad, and a set of useless, unthinking, dissipated spendthrifts when" in England, he protested, was nothing more than a "detestable caricature."[84]

Ramsay's supporters agreed that his depiction of West Indian slavery was harsh, but they thought it was deservedly so. Ramsey had provided "such a picture of insolent unfeeling despotism, and miserable servitude, as seems even to surpass the horrible condition of Spartan Helotes," declared one reviewer. The toleration of "such oppression . . . by the legislature of a civilized country," the reviewer added, was "a circumstance truly mortifying to humanity."[85] Even if Ramsay had exaggerated, wrote George Gregory, he had made it clear that colonial slavery was "a system of such complicated inhumanity, oppression, and fraud" that it was unimaginable "that a single argument or excuse could be adduced in its support" and that it was so "productive of *pride, luxury, and licentiousness*" and "dissoluteness of manners" among slave owners as to be thoroughly "shocking to humanity."[86] "From all that can be learned by the accounts of people upon the spot," wrote Paley, the enslaved lived under "a dominion and system of laws, the most merciless and tyrannical that ever were tolerated upon the face of the earth," laws that "confer[red] upon the slaveholder" an "inordinate authority," which he "exercised . . . with rigor and brutality."[87] "The question is not, *Whether the laws of those islands be always, and in all cases, put in force*," Gregory agreed, but "*Why are laws permitted to disgrace the code of any civilized community, which scandalize every sense of justice and humanity?*"[88]

Ramsay had shown conclusively, said another reviewer, that slavery invariably produced defective societies, which he affirmed "to be in the highest degree the case of our colonies. Slavery, indeed, in the manner wherein it is found there, is an unnatural state of oppression on one side, and of suffering on the other," he asserted, "and needs only to be laid open and exposed in its native colours, to command the abhorrence and opposition of every man of feeling and sentiment." "Read this, and blush," he continued,

ye Creoles, who live at ease in our land; who spend in riot and dissipation the profits of your plantations, thus earned by extreme labour, oppression, blood! Read this, ye African traders, who tear from their native country, to be thus inhumanly treated, poor, quiet, harmless beings, who, without our love of gain, and desire of aggrandizement,

[84] "A Friend to the West India Colonies, and Their Inhabitants" [James Tobin], *Cursory Remarks upon the Reverend Mr. Ramsay's Essay on the Treatment and Conversion of African Slaves in the Sugar Colonies* (London, 1785), 4–5, 33–35, 47.

[85] *Critical Review*, 57 (May 1784): 386.

[86] Gregory, *Essay Historical and Political*, 298, 312, 321.

[87] Paley, *The Principles of Moral and Political Philosophy*, 156.

[88] Gregory, *Essay Historical and Political*, 312.

would happily recline under the shade of their plantains, and enjoy the beauties of nature and of climate which kind Providence has allowed them.[89]

Some antislavery writers moved beyond questioning the Britishness of the despots who held sway in the West Indies to challenge even their commitment to Christianty. Such "cruel hard-hearted" people, Joseph Waring declared in a 1781 pamphlet, were "a Disgrace to the Christian Name" and should "be called Infidels, Heathens, Barbarians, or any thing but Christians,"[90] a theme that a number of prominent writers, including Thomas Clarkson, later picked up and explored at length. Contrasting West Indians with the "generous and brave" metropolitan Britons who were, "of all nations, the most remarkable for humanity and justice," Clarkson denounced African traders and West Indian slaveholders as men who were "not *Christians*" but "*infidels*" and "*monsters*... out of the common course of nature," who, by their example had taught the enslaved that "*Christianity*" was nothing "but a system of *murder* and *oppression*."[91]

The former African slave Ottobah Cugoano, who survived the Middle Passage and a stint in colonial slavery before his master took him to London, where he converted to Christianity, gained his freedom, and enjoyed the support of Granville Sharpe and other antislavery advocates, provided the most emphatic statement of this point in his 1787 pamphlet *Thoughts and Sentiments on the Evil and Wicked Traffic of the Slavery and Commerce of the Human Species*. "Except in the annals of the Inquisition and the bloody edicts of Popish massacres," he wrote, "nothing in history can equal the barbarity and cruelty of the tortures and murders committed under various pretences in modern slavery." Although he praised British opponents of slavery as men whose actions redounded "with great honor to themselves, to humanity and their country" and acknowledged that "since the last war, some mitigation of slavery has been obtained in some respective districts of America, though not in proportion to their own vaunted claims of freedom," and hoped that they would "yet go on to make a further and greater reformation," he forcefully complained that, "notwithstanding all that has been done and written against it, that brutish barbarity, and unparelelled injustice" was "still carried on to a very great extent in the colonies with an avidity as insidious, cruel and oppressive as ever," and he minced no words in denouncing the "Colonians," the "great and opulent banditti of slave holders in the western part of the world" as "pirates, thieves, robbers, oppressors and enslavers of men."[92]

---

[89] *Monthly Review*, 70 (June 1784): 409, 413.

[90] Waring, *Letter to an American Planter*, 14.

[91] Thomas Clarkson, *An Essay on the Slavery and Commerce of the Human Species, particularly the African* (Philadelphia, 1786), 85–86.

[92] Ottobah Cugoano, *Thoughts and Sentiments on the Evil and Wicked Traffic on the Slavery and Commerce of the Human Species Humbly Sumitted to the Inhabitants of Great-Britain* (London, 1787), 2–3, 16, 89.

A Christian country, Cugoano observed, might be expected to exhibit "the flourishing growth of every virtue, extending their harmonious branches with universal philanthropy wherever they came," and he found it "strange" that "the inhabitants of Great-Britain[,] ... who ought to be considered as the most learned and civilized people in the world[,] ... should carry on a traffic of the most barbarous cruelty and injustice, and that many, even among them, are become so dissolute, as to think slavery, robbery and murder no crimes" and see no need to "justify the deeds of their conduct towards us." But, he said, in expanding upon the insights of William Bollan in a 1772 pamphlet from which he quoted, it was a sordid fact that within the British Empire "almost nothing else is to be seen abroad but the bramble of ruffians, barbarians and slave-holders, grown up to a powerful luxuriance in wickedness." The Spaniards having begun "their settlements in the West Indies and America, by depredations of rapine, injustice, treachery, and murder" and continued them "ever since," "every other nation in Europe" had adopted "their principles and maxims in planting colonies," and, he charged, this "guiltful method of colonization" had "undoubtedly and imperceptibly ... hardened men's hearts, and led them on from one degree of barbarity and cruelty to another: for when they had destroyed, wasted and desolated the native inhabitants, and when many of their own people, enriched with plunder, had retired, or returned home to enjoy their ill-gotten wealth," they turned for laborers to Africa, where they proceeded "to rob and pillage" the continent in pursuit of "that diabolical traffic which is still carried on by the European depredators" and had resulted in Africa suffering "as much or more than any other quarter of the globe." "None, but men of the most brutish and depraved nature, led on by the invidious influence of infernal wickedness, could have made their settlements in different parts of the world discovered by them, ... have treated the various Indian nations," and created the international slave trade "in the manner that the barbarous inhuman Europeans have done," he charged. "It may be said with confidence as a certain general fact," he observed, "that all their foreign settlements were founded on murders and devastations, and that they have continued their depredations in cruel slavery and oppression to this day."[93]

Contending that the slave system was thoroughly incompatible with "civilization and the laws of justice among men" and that it could "maintain its ground" only "among a society of barbarians and thieves," Cugoano expressed his conviction that "the several nations of Europe that have joined in this iniquitous traffic of buying, selling, and enslaving men, must in course have left their own laws of civilization to adopt those of barbarians and robbers" and that, through their toleration and support of "such predominant wickedness as the African slave-trade, and the West Indian slavery ... in their colonies," the generality of their inhabitants "must be not only guilty themselves of that

[93] Ibid., 24, 77, 86, 92–93; [William Bollan], *Britannia Libera, or a Defense of the Free State of Man in England* (London, 1772).

shameful and abandoned evil and wickedness, so very disgraceful to human nature, but even partakers in those crimes of the most vile combinations of various pirates, kidnappers, robbers and thieves, the ruffians and stealers of men, that ever made their appearance in the world." Those "who can approve of such inhuman barbarities," he concluded, "must themselves be a species of unjust barbarians and inhuman men."[94]

Like their predecessors, the authors of the post–American war literature on the British imperial slave system stressed the extent to which slavery was an extra-European phenomenon. The colonies, though presided over by Britons or their Creole descendants, were, as Woods put it, "inured to scenes of oppression" that violated and showed little regard for the moral and social standards of the metropolis.[95] "Among Europeans," wrote Ramsay in a later pamphlet, slavery existed "only in the western world, where their proper religion and laws are not deemed to be in full force; and where individuals too often think themselves loosened from ties, which are deemed binding in the mother country."[96] As Ramsay said in still another pamphlet illustrating his point, it was absolutely "*shocking for an Englishman, on his first going to the West Indies, to pass a plantation where the negroes are at work*, and hear the violent strokes from the unmerciful whip."[97] "However we may boast of the more enlightened principles upon which, as far as concerns their domestic government, the statesmen of modern *Europe* appear to act," remarked George Gregory, "the feeling moralist must look with an aching eye, and with a bleeding heart, to the depopulated regions of *Africa*; to that wretched and selfish system upon which our colonies abroad are cultivated, and *peopled*."[98] In total contrast to metropolitan Britons, West Indians, a later antislavery writer declared ironically, regarded "the right of enslaving others" as "one of the most valuable of their privileges."[99] Clearly, the impulse, in the words of a 1772 writer, to "preserve the race of [metropolitan] Britons from [the] stain and contamination" of colonial slavery remained strong.[100]

From the 1760s on, critics of the British imperial slave system explicitly condemned the degenerate people who participated in that system, a system that, as a writer pointed out in 1788, had resulted in "the slaughter of five or six millions of the aboriginal inhabitants of America, and by the transportation of

[94] Cugoano, *Thoughts and Sentiments*, 77–78, 103, 114.
[95] [Woods], *Thoughts on the Slavery of Negroes*, 8.
[96] James Ramsay, *A Reply to the Personal Invectives and Objections contained in Two Answers* (London, 1785), 51.
[97] James Ramsay, ed., *A Letter from Capt. J. S. Smith to the Revd. Mr. Hill on the State of the Negroe Slaves* (London, 1786), 16.
[98] Gregory, *Essay Historical and Political*, 296.
[99] *An Address to the People of Great Britain, on the Propriety of Abstaining from West India Sugar and Rum*, 11th ed. (London, 1789), 7.
[100] "A West Indian" [Samuel Estwick], *Considerations on the Negroe Cause Commonly So Called, Addressed to the Right Honourable Lord Mansfield, Chief Justice of the Court of King's Bench* (London, 1772), 43.

as many more Africans to replace them and fulfill the purposes of slavery."[101] Increasingly, "the *African Merchant* and *West-India Planter*" had become stock figures who symbolized the violation, beyond the bounds of Britain, of every component of the sacred character of Britons.[102]

As, in the late 1780s, they increasingly made the abolition of the slave trade their first priority in the campaign to bring down the British imperial slave system, antislavery writers gloried in having brought metropolitan Britons to an understanding that, as William Leigh, using the pseudonym "Philo-Africanus," wrote in a 1788 pamphlet, the slave trade, which had been so long "talked of... with an indifference, common to other commercial considerations," was anathema to "the generally received opinion of the civilized part of mankind." They regarded it as a vast national awakening for the public to have come to appreciate that the trade had "originated in private prospects of gain; was established by violence and treachery; and has been conducted for two centuries past, even to this day, with a spirit of *cruelty* and *injustice* unknown in the history of *any other* people or *any other* country," and that, in the process, "flagitious" African traders had so "perverted" the "open, liberal, [and] ingenuous" "Spirit of English commerce" into an "instrument of the most common crimes" that it was "no longer the commerce of Englishmen, of Christians, or of Men."[103] Before Granville Sharp brought up the subject it "was never properly before us as a people," agreed Ramsay, the "whole passed unnoticed as a common speculation in commerce," and Britons "were unwittingly guilty of the iniquity interwoven in it." However, now that he and his fellow antislavery writers had "exposed [the trade] to the world in all its native horrors,"[104] any further "attempt to impose such reasoning on the publick," said Ramsay, would be "an insult to the national character," a "declaration to all Europe, that profit" was "the only idol to which we bow."[105]

Mostly as a result of this same effort, colonial slaveholders, about whom some metropolitans had long had reservations, also suffered a further fall from metropolitan grace. Repeated charges of their cruel treatment of slaves contributed to the enhancement within the metropolis of a highly negative image of colonials as Creolean despots. As James Tobin noted in his answer to Ramsay's *Essay* in 1785, this unfavorable depiction had been so "generally adopted in Great Britain" as to make West Indians "the favourite butts for the shafts of prejudice."[106] In vain did the slavery apologist Gordon Turnbull, who had lived for several years in the West Indies, protest in another 1785 pamphlet that "the

[101] "A West-India Planter," *Considerations on the Emancipation of Negroes and the Abolition of the Slave-Trade* (London, 1788), 25.
[102] Granville Sharp, *The Just Limitation of Slavery* (London, 1776), 11.
[103] "Philo-Africanus" [William Leigh], *Remarks on the Slave Trade, and the Slavery of Negroes* (London, 1788), 2, 9, 20, 42–43.
[104] James Ramsay, *An Address on the Proposed Bill for the Abolition of the Slave Trade* (London, 1788), 37.
[105] James Ramsay, *Objections to the Abolition of the Slave Trade with Answers* (London, 1788), 47.
[106] [Tobin], *Cursory Remarks*, 50, 73.

planters in general" were "not tyrants" but, "on the contrary," were "remarkable for urbanity of manners, liberality of sentiment, and generosity of disposition," traits "incompatible with those avaricious and despicable motives, which their accusers" had "falsely asserted, had influence[d] their conduct in the treatment of their slaves."[107] "It seems to be the universal aim of every author who has occasion to mention a West India planter," Tobin observed in a subsequent exchange with Ramsay, "to render that name synonymous with a cruel and relentless task master." By this "torrent of general reproach," he complained, antislavery writers had unjustly taken men who had "succeeded in the arduous task" of creating a colony and whose "indefatigable perseverence" had "proved one of the greatest sources of wealth to their mother country" and represented them "as the worst and most merciless tyrants" and "total strangers to truth and honour, and vilified [them] as nothing better than mean, sordid, and self interested broachers of fable and imposture."[108] "Authors of the paragraphs, hand-bills, newspapers, and pamphlets," complained Gilbert Francklyn, seemed to think themselves "at full liberty to abuse West Indian planters."[109]

But such protests had little effect. Tobin marveled that a gullible British public could possibly suppose that "human nature" should "be totally different in America, from what it" appeared "in Europe; that the descendents of British parents [should] have souls differently formed from those of their honest ancestors; and that every man's ideas of truth, justice, and humanity" would be "immediately obliterated as soon as he unfortunately" ventured "to pass the tropic."[110] Similarly, Francklyn professed not to understand why the British imperial slave system was any worse than other excesses of British colonialism that had come to public attention over the immediately preceding decades. How, he asked, could Britons heap so much opprobrium on "the purchase of slaves" when they themselves

patiently suffer[ed] their fellow subjects, their fellow citizens, their brethren, to be...bought and sold [as servants], and transported, not to climates congenial to those which gave them birth, but to the burning regions of the torrid zone, or to countries almost covered with perpetual snows; to be employed, not in the cultivation of the ground, in agriculture, and in the arts of peace; but, in ravaging, destroying, and depopulating the finest countries of Asia, or invading the peaceful retirement of the American savages, whose territories they usurp, whose hunting grounds they render useless, whose health they destroy, and whose morals they corrupt?[111]

[107] Gordon Turnbull, *An Apology for Negro Slavery: or the West-India Planters Vindicated from the Charge of Inhumanity* (London, 1785), 58.
[108] James Tobin, *A Short Rejoinder to the Reverend Mr. Ramsay's Reply* (London, 1787), 25–26, 112–13.
[109] Gilbert Francklyn, *An Answer to the Rev. Mr. Clarkson's Essay on the Slavery and Commerce of the Human Species* (London, 1789), 5.
[110] Tobin, *Short Rejoinder*, 112–13.
[111] Gilbert Francklyn, *Observations Occasioned by the Attempts Made in England to Effect the Abolition of the Slave Trade* (London, 1789), 10.

But the tide of sentiment was running strongly against slavery apologists. By the late 1780s, when George Colman, Jr., wrote his opera *Inkle and Yarico*, a startling variation on an old story of love, betrayal, and hard-heartedness between a young Briton and the native girl who rescued him, he also took the occasion to draw a sharp contrast between colonial and metropolitan Britons. After Inkle, the aspiring planter, had succumbed to the material temptations of the West Indies and was on the verge of selling his rescuer into slavery, a virtuous metropolitan, attuned to the moral demands of Britons' traditional concern for liberty, shamed him into changing his mind.[112]

Critics of the imperial slave system had managed to persuade large segments of the British public that, to the shame of Britain, at the same time as metropolitan Britons in an enlightened age were "pretending to the finest feelings of humanity," unsavory slave traders and morally deviant Creoles had, by planting "slavery in the rank soil of sordid avarice" and "exercising unprecedented cruelty" over the enslaved, "greatly surpassed, in brutality and injustice, the most ignorant and barbarous ages." But this effort was slow to achieve any tangible results. Evidently, as an advocate for a national boycott of sugar products explained in 1791, the "wealth derived from the horrid traffic" had "created an influence that" secured "its continuance."[113] Catering to the interest of the slave traders and honoring what one antislavery writer denounced as the "injudicious and impolitic spirit of obstinacy in the Planters," the majority in Parliament preferred to ascribe the fact that, as Tobin remarked, the British had "become the *honourable slave-carriers* for other nations," as Ramsay had chosen "sneeringly to call them," to "the *commercial*, rather than to the *unfeeling*, spirit of his countrymen."[114]

This was hardly surprising. Material considerations, considerations that lay at the heart of the vision of the empire as an instrument for the creation of national wealth and greatness, dictated that within the greater British Empire the languages of commerce and imperialism would continue to hold sway over the language of humanity. Writing in 1788, an anonymous pamphleteer who signed himself "A West-India Planter" succinctly spelled out the calculus at work. Of all the evils that had been produced by empire, he acknowledged, the British imperial slave system was "certainly not among the least." But, he explained,

as it has been established for so long a time, and is now so interwoven with our commercial system and circumstances of finance, any attempt, at this day, either to annihilate it intirely, or to restrain it as to prevent any further accession of slaves to the colonies; though it may be morally right, must be politically wrong, absurd, and impracticable; the most precious interests of the country being implicated in the measure.[115]

---

[112] George Colman, Jr., *Inkle and Yarico: An Opera* (London, 1788).
[113] *Address to the People of Great Britain*, 1.
[114] Tobin, *Short Rejoinder*, 37.
[115] "West India Planter," *Consideration on the Emancipation of Negroes*, 26.

Similarly, and in the same year, Reverend Francis Randolph, former fellow at King's College, Cambridge, called on the younger Pitt to follow his legislation "to correct the Rapacity and Avarice of the Eastern Despot" with "some salutary Regulations . . . to counteract the Tyranny and Barbarity" of "the Commercial System in our West India Islands," an establishment, he declared, that had made such a vast "Breach . . . in the System of national Virtue" in the British world. But he had to acknowledge that such a project would be extremely difficult because "the System of Revenue" had long been "so involved with the System of Slavery, the Exigencies of the State so dependant upon the Planter[']s Wealth, and the security of their Property so strongly ratified, and enforced by repeated Acts of the [British] Legislature" and because "the smallest Incroachment on personal Dominion will be deemed a Sequestration of Property, and any Endeavour to bind the Hand of Tyranny and Oppression, will be [opposed as] loosening the Band of all Order and Subjection." To overcome these difficulties and the "Variety of Interests" that lay behind them, he observed, would require a high degree of "Earnestness and . . . Zeal in the Cause of Humanity."[116]

As late as 1807, Granville Sharp, one of the founding fathers of the imperial critique that emerged during the last half of the eighteenth century and by now a grizzled veteran of the antislavery wars, complained that no official act of the British nation had ever once mentioned the colonial slave systems "as a *national* crime; nor" had "taken the least step . . . for the gradual enfranchisement of the oppressed people, or even *of their children, that have been born in the king's dominions.*" As a result, "THE SYSTEM OF COLONIAL LAW *relative to* PROPERTY" in human beings as slaves remained wholly intact, despite the fact that, as he and his colleagues had been pointing out for forty years, that system manifestly "*violate[d] the whole System of English Law,* – nay the very *foundations of Law, Justice,* and *Righteousness,* on which all *true* and *legal* PROPERTY, necessarily depends." Sharp had no doubt that "the *long continued toleration of this unnatural oppression*" was "certainly a *national crime,* most hateful and provoking to the judgment of God."[117]

Yet, in another way, Sharp and his colleagues accomplished their larger goal of defining and illustrating one of the principal negative developments of empire. By identifying the people of whose behavior they were ashamed in terms of the social stereotype of the Creole, those who used the language of humanity to talk about empire had endeavored in the 1750s and 1760s to contain responsibility for the sordid, uncivil, and inhuman aspects of colonial slave systems and the slave trade, effectively drawing a line between metropolitan Britons and those monsters of depravity who carried the British presence to American slave colonies and to the coast of Africa. Their gradual

---

[116] Reverend Francis Randolph, *A Letter to the Right Honourable William Pitt . . . on the Proposed Abolition of the African Slave Trade* (London, 1788), 5, 22, 53–55.

[117] Granville Sharp, *"The System of Colonial Law" Compared with the Eternal Laws of God* (London, 1807), 4, 14–15.

comprehension after the mid-1770s of the deep complicity of metropolitan Britain in overseas slavery was not very comforting. Despite the Somerset decision, the sordid side of empire had thoroughly insinuated itself into Albion.

V

Irish parliamentary agitation beginning in 1778 for the relaxation of metropolitan controls over the Irish economy and polity, which struck Thomas Tod as a healthy indication that "a spirit of independency" seemed to be rising "through all the British empire,"[118] was well timed to take advantage of Britain's preoccupation with the American war. Indeed, the Opposition pamphleteer John Almon was persuaded that that agitation was directly inspired by that event. "Viewing with horror, the principles and conduct of Ministers, in the creation and prosecution of the American war," he wrote in a 1782 pamphlet, Irish political leaders had "taken up the alarm respecting their own privileges and liberties" and "demanded a specific renunciation of certain claims, which had lain dormant during the Whig administrations of George the First, and George the Second," and, he thought, "would not have disturbed the happiness of George the Third, if his Tory Ministers had not sown the seeds of war and jealousy throughout all his dominions."[119] Although recent historians have persuasively insisted that the specific reforms Irish patriots sought were ones that "had occupied their attention for a generation" and long antedated Britain's altercation with America,[120] Irish demands resembled in many respects those that the Americans had made on the eve of the war, including especially legislative independence and control over internal governance and taxation, albeit the Irish demands for exemption from British trade laws went well beyond any American claims before the Declaration of Independence. Edmund Burke later referred to the reforms achieved by the Irish as a result of this agitation as "the Irish revolution of 1782."[121]

Whether this revolution could be sustained and for how long were questions that faced Britain and Ireland throughout the 1780s.[122] Four factors materially limited the scope of Irish parliamentary independence. First, the achievements of 1782 left the authority to review and reject Irish laws in the hands of the British Privy Council and thereby enabled British ministers to intervene often

---

[118] [Thomas Tod], *Observations on American Independency* (London, 1779), 23.

[119] "An Independent Whig" [John Almon], *The Revolution in MDCCLXXXII Impartially Considered* (London, 1782), 23–26.

[120] See Vincent Morley, *Irish Opinion and the American Revolution 1760–1783* (Cambridge: Cambridge University Press, 2002). The quotation is from page 332.

[121] *A Letter from the Right Hon. Edmund Burke, M.P. in the kingdom of Great Britain, to Sir Hercules Langrishe, Bart. M.P. on the Subject of Roman Catholics of Ireland* (London, 1792), reprinted in R. B. McDowell, ed., *The Writings and Speeches of Edmund Burke* (Oxford: Clarendon Press, 1991), Part II: *Ireland*, 9: 617.

[122] For a detailed treatment of this subject, see James Kelly, *Prelude to Union: Anglo-Irish Politics in the 1780s* (Cork: Cork University Press, 1992).

in Irish affairs, external and internal. "The late emancipation of Ireland; with respect to legislation," as an anonymous author emphasized in a 1787 tract, "established and acknowledged" Ireland's "rights, both externally and internally," as well as its "power of trading with every country in the world," but that emancipation by no means made Ireland "wholly independent." Given the fact that its Crown was "inseparably united with that of Great-Britain, where the Sovereign resides, and where one essential branch of" its "legislature acts," this writer explained, "the controul of the ligislative [sic] over the executive power must continue to influence the actions of the Sovereign in that country where he resides, and over that part of the united empire over where he does not reside." For that reason, he wrote, the Crown's British ministers had to "be accountable for all the measures of Government adopted in Ireland, as well as in Great Britain, and therefore must take care to exercise the negative vested in the Crown, with respect to Ireland, with a proper regard to the welfare of the empire, at the head of which is placed the Sovereign of Great-Britain."[123]

Second, the emergence in 1782–83 of a highly vocal movement among the Volunteers for parliamentary reform within Ireland had the effect of dampening the Irish reform impulse. As one writer noted, the "oppression and injustice" under which "this ill-fated Country groan[ed]" before 1782 derived not only from British restrictions but also from "a *venal* herd of sycophants" who, "living on the *spoils* of their Country, *betray[ed]* every *public trust*, and sacrifice[d] her dearest rights." People of this persuasion argued that "the period has *now* arrived, when the *rights* of the PEOPLE *may* be regained; when corruption *may* be banished; and IRELAND *may* be FREE."[124] But Irish parliamentary leadership was skeptical about giving way to popular demands and rejected proposals for reform in November 1783.

Third, the split in Patriot opinion over this issue enabled the Irish Administration, employing the extensive patronage available from its continuing control over the Crown's hereditary Irish revenues, to regain the initiative that it had enjoyed in the Irish Parliament for decades before 1778. "Think Not, Gentlemen, that Britain, stripped of her tyrannic powers," now intended calmly to yield "us a fair discussion and unimpeded resolution in public affairs," Capel Molyneux cautioned his readers in a 1783 pamphlet complaining about the misuse of the hereditary revenues.

The places, posts, and pensions of this Kingdom, wielded in an *English* cabinet by an *English* minister! – the numerous *heads* of departments replete here with Britons! – hereditary *votes* and rank in the state daily dispensed to insulting strangers! – that simpering confidence with which those alien minions of a Viceroy, *ex officio*, quarter themselves in our court on every political squabble of our sister isle! – These,

---

[123] *Considerations on the Political and Commercial Circumstances of Great Britain and Ireland* (London, 1787), 1–2.

[124] [W. W. Seward], *The Rights of the People Asserted and the Necessity of a More Equal Representation in Parliament Stated and Proved* (Dublin, 1783), 6.

he declared, were all "mortifying clogs on our boasted freedom" and "badges of [our] former slavery – unconstitutional exertions of prerogative which *must be deprecated!*"[125] But an Irish political establishment nervous about mobilizing a popular uprising could do little about them.

Fourth, no British Administration in the 1780s was comfortable with the Irish exemption from British commercial regulations, and they all sought to work out some arrangements whereby Ireland would submit to British regulation of its external policy. Pitt, the Younger, went furthest in this direction. With his "System of Final Adjustment," he offered Ireland an equal participation in Britain's colonial trade in return for Ireland's acknowledging, among other things, Britain's "*exclusive* power of legislating for Ireland in matters respecting navigation" and "Making laws to tax, to restrain, and [to] prohibit, almost every branch of" its "foreign commerce." But this arrangement met immediate and articulate Irish resistance. One writer denounced it as an arrangement that "by striking at the independence, and subverting the Constitution of Ireland" would rob the Irish "of every thing they hold most dear."[126] Another declared that it would require the "surrender of every Constitutional Right" that Ireland had acquired in 1779–82. By requiring of Ireland "a perpetual recognition of, and submission to ... British regulation, British restriction, British prohibition, and British taxation ... as Great Britain may for ever think to impose, touching all and every article of commerce," he charged, "this final adjustment" would reverse the repeal of the Declaratory Act, eliminate Ireland's exemption from British judicial proceedings, and be "radically subversive" of the independence of the Irish Parliament. These concessions, he contended, were "such as the Parliament of Ireland by her constitution" should never "accede to," and he called upon the Irish to reject this "gilded poison" and thereby maintain their recently won "constitutional rights, faculties and functions, concentred and entire."[127]

So exercised did the Irish become over Pitt's proposal that the Irish Administration was unable to push it through the Irish Parliament in August 1785 and had to withdraw it. But this victory by no means insured that Ireland would retain full control over its commerce. In the words of a later writer, Britain had "many powerful engines to controul and regulate" Ireland's commerce, including treaties with foreign states, authority to prevent Ireland from trading with other parts of the empire, and power to lay duties on Irish imports into Britain.[128] If, however, "a commercial arrangement" was "necessary to unite the two kingdoms," as, according to one Irish writer, "most people allow[ed]," it would have to be one that would not involve "trenching on the legislative

---

[125] Capel Molyneux, *A Warm Appeal to the Freemen of Ireland on the Present Interesting Crisis of Affairs* (Dublin, 1784), 4–5.

[126] *The Irish Protest to the Ministerial Manifesto, Contained in the Address of the British Parliament to the King* (London, 1785), 36–38. This pamphlet was reprinted from Dublin.

[127] *An Address to the King and People of Ireland. Upon the System of Final Adjustment* (London, 1785), 9, 26–28.

[128] *Considerations on the Political and Commercial Circumstances of Great Britain*, 3.

freedom of Ireland."[129] For the time being, Ireland had at least managed to avoid relinquishing its authority to regulate its own trade.

If the reforms of 1779 and 1782 brought somewhat less commercial and political autonomy to the Irish polity than Patriots had expected, they did not even touch on any of the three issues – absentee taxes, pensions, and Catholic persecution – that at one time or another since the early 1750s had been at the center of metropolitan concerns about Ireland. The requirement that the British Privy Council approve Irish laws before they went into effect insured that the Irish Parliament would be unable to tax wealthy absentees residing in Britain, while the Crown carefully retained control over the hereditary revenues ministers used to reward its supporters and bureaucrats, few of whom were Irish.

As for Catholic relief, the cooperation of Anglicans, Dissenters, and Catholics in achieving the reforms of 1782–83 inspired some in both Ireland and Britain to conclude that reform of the penal laws would soon follow, and the Irish made some concessions in a relief act in 1782. At least in the short run, however, Ireland's success in winning concessions from Britain was less of a boon for Irish Roman Catholics. The Irish Parliament, operating under the new constitutional provisions, did move to repeal more of the provisions of the penal laws in a 1785 bill, but used the occasion to reaffirm the basic philosophy of those laws.

In a short pamphlet, Edmund Burke, an Irish native and a steady critic of the penal laws for more than three decades, explained how this measure looked from Britain. "To look at the bill, in the abstract," he wrote, it was "neither more [n]or less than a renewed Act of UNIVERSAL, UNMITIGATED, INDISPENS-ABLE, EXCEPTIONLESS *Disqualification*." "Whether or not it was wise, for the sake of expunging the black letter of laws, which menacing as they were in the language, were every day fading into disuse, solemnly to re-affirm the principles, and re-enact the provision of a code of statutes, by which" Catholics were "totally excluded from THE PRIVILEGES OF THE COMMONWEALTH, from the highest to the lowest, from the most material of the civil professions, from the army, and even from education, where alone education is to be had," he wrote, "is not easy for me to determine." "Whether this scheme of indulgence, grounded at once on contempt and jealousy," he continued, would have "a tendency gradually to produce something better and more liberal, I cannot tell." The "whole merit or demerit of the measure," in his view, depended "upon the plans and dispositions of those by whom the act was made, concurring with the general temper of the Protestants of Ireland, and their aptitude to admit in time of some part of that equality, without which" Catholics never could "be FELLOW CITIZENS."[130]

---

[129] *A Candid Review of the Most Important Occurrences that Took Place in Ireland, during the Last Three Years* (Dublin, 1787), 51.

[130] Edmund Burke, *A Letter from a Distinguished English Commoner to a Peer in Ireland, on the Repeal of a Part of the Penal Laws against the Irish Catholics* (London, 1785), 4–7.

Describing this measure as "*an act full of jealousy*, and professing persecu-tion," Burke declared, using the languages of humanity and justice, that it was "*a piece of cruelty*, in which till very lately I did not suppose *this age* capable of persisting." "One would imagine," he wrote, "that a bill inflicting such a multitude of incapacities, had followed on the heels of a conquest, made by a very fierce enemy, under the impression of recent animosity and resentment." No man, on reading that bill, Burke stressed, "could imagine he was reading an act of amnesty." Although the bill stipulated "that CATHOLICS ought to be considered as GOOD AND LOYAL SUBJECTS to his majesty, his crown and government," Burke complained, it then provided for "an universal exclusion of those GOOD and LOYAL subjects from every, even the lowest office of trust and profit, or from any vote at an election; from any privilege in a town corpo-rate; from being even a freeman of such corporations; from serving on grand juries; from a vote at a vestry, from having a gun in his house, from being a barrister, attorney, Solicitor, or &c. &c. &c." To Burke, these exclusions gave the bill "much more [an] air of a Table of Proscription, than an ACT OF GRACE."[131]

Because, as Burke perceived, the bill "tended to finish the scheme for making the people not only two distinct parties for ever" but "two distinct species in the same land," he regarded the continued prohibition of marriages between Catholics and Protestants as "one of the worst parts of" this "truly barbarous system, if," he added, "one could well settle the preference, where almost all the parts were outrages on the rights of humanity, and the law of nature." "From what I have observed," he speculated, "it is pride, arrogance, a spirit of domination, and not a bigotted spirit of religion, that has caused and kept up these oppressive statutes. . . . It is injustice, and not a mistaken conscience, that has been the principle of persecution." That the new act amounted "very nearly to a toleration with respect to religious ceremonies" seemed to him "undoubtedly good," but, he concluded, it "put *a new bolt* on civil rights, and *rivets it* to the old one in such a manner, that neither, I fear, will be easily loosened."[132]

Burke was right, and as in the 1790s Protestants came to identify Catholicism with radical protest and revolutionary fervor, Protestant support for Catholic emancipation withered away, and political tensions ran along religious lines. No friend to revolutionary fervor, Burke nonetheless continued to protest the injustice and inhumanity of the penal laws, a subject he addressed at length and with penetration in what he called "a long dissertation" that had originated as a letter to his friend Sir Hercules Langrishe, formerly an early fellow critic of the "old code" but now himself wavering in the cause and thinking that it "ought to continue for ever." In this work, published in Dublin and London early in 1792, Burke sought to lay out the rationale for the penal system and the psychology that lay behind and sustained it, to analyze the deleterious effects

[131] Ibid., 6–7, 9, 11.
[132] Ibid., 25, 28–29.

it had produced, and to speculate on the conditions that might eventually destroy it.[133]

In this exercise, Burke certainly did not underestimate the penal system's effectiveness. Indeed, he professed to abhor it precisely because of "its vicious perfection. For I must do it justice," he declared, "it was a complete system, full of coherence and consistency; well digested and well composed in all its parts. It was a machine of wise and elaborate contrivance, and as well fitted for the oppression, impoverishment and degradation of a people, and the debasement, in them, of human nature itself, as ever proceeded from the perverted ingenuity of man." Its "declared object was to reduce the Catholics of Ireland to a miserable populace, without property, without estimation, without education," he wrote, "to deprive the few men, who, in spite of those laws, might hold or obtain any property amongst them, of all sort of influence or authority over the rest." By this strategy, he explained, the contrivers of the penal code sought to divide "the nation into two distinct bodies, without common interest, sympathy or connexion; one of which bodies was to possess *all* the franchises, *all* the property, *all* the education," while the "other was to be composed of drawers of water and cutters of turf for them." Under this arrangement, Burke lamented, the "majority of the people of Ireland (the Catholics)" effectively found themselves in "a state of *civil servitude*" in which they were "under the state, but not the state itself, *nor any part of it,*" in a "lower and degraded state of citizenship."[134]

Burke traced these measures back to the bloody conflicts between Catholics and Protestants in seventeenth-century Ireland, and particularly to "the total reduction of the kingdom of Ireland in 1691," when "the ruin of the native Irish, and in a great measure too, of the first races of the English, was completely accomplished." The new English Protestant interest quickly devised the penal system, "that unparalleled code of oppression, which" was "manifestly the effect of national hatred, and scorn towards a conquered people; whom the victors delighted to trample upon, and were not at all afraid to provoke." Its contrivers thereafter "looked to the irresistible force of Great Britain for support in their acts of power" in total certainty that no complaints "from the natives would be heard" in Britain "with any other sentiments than those of contempt and indignation." "Indeed at that time in England," Burke observed, "the double name of . . . Irish and Papists . . . shut up the hearts of every one against them. Whilst that temper prevailed, and it prevailed in all its force to a time within our memory," Burke wrote, pointedly ignoring the question of when that temper changed and why, "every measure was pleasing and popular, just in proportion as it tended to harass and ruin a set of people, who were looked upon as enemies of God and man; and

---

[133] *Letter from Burke to Langrishe,* in McDowell, *Writings and Speeches of Edmund Burke,* 9: 598, 635, 637.
[134] Ibid., 597–99, 637.

indeed as a race of bigotted savages who were a disgrace to human nature itself."[135]

Although Burke refrained from addressing the question of when people of enlightened sensibilities began to regard Catholic persecution as unjust and inappropriate for an empire whose people prided themselves on their humanity, he made a telling comparison between the situations in Ireland and in Quebec that did not come out in Ireland's favor. Whereas in Ireland "the efforts of so much violence in conquest, and so much policy in regulation, continued without intermission for near an hundred years," had driven the majority Catholic population to desperation, in Quebec the British government had insured – first in the Quebec Act of 1774, that the majority Catholic inhabitants would retain their ancient laws and religion, and then in the Constitutional Act of 1791, that they would have representative institutions without any religious qualifications for the franchise – that Catholics would, "in the utmost latitude of the description, . . . be free subjects." As a result, he said, they had become "good subjects." Burke obviously understood that the heritage of bitterness in Protestant-Catholic relations rendered the Quebec model unworkable in Ireland. Nevertheless, he queried whether "the French Canadian Catholics" were any better suited to be "citizens than the Irish of the same communion." Given his own appreciation of the humanity of people of other religions, as a result of his long involvement "in supporting the rights, privileges, laws, and immunities of a very remote people" in India, a "people," he said, "with whom I have no tie, but the common bond of mankind," Burke avowed that he could not express his conviction that "all the Pagans, all the Musselmen, and even all the Papists" were "worthy of a liberal and honourable condition" while at the same time excepting only one group, the one that formed "the majority of the inhabitants of the country in which you and I were born." If, as Irish Protestants alleged, "the Catholics of Ireland" were indeed "ill-natured and unjust people," Burke inquired, why should any one think better of the Protestants who came from the same soil, a soil that was "supposed to infuse into its sects a kind of venom unknown in other places?"[136]

Although he expressed pride that he, Langrishe, and others had been among the first to attack the penal system and cause it "to stagger, crack, and gape," he was under no illusion that Irish Protestants would relent any time soon. In agreeing to the constitutional reforms of 1782, Britain, Burke thought, had risen "above the vulgar ideas of policy, the ordinary jealousies of state, and all the sentiments of national pride and national ambition," and he was clearly persuaded that "the *Anglo-Irish*" could never build a viable state until they could act with a similar liberality toward the Catholic majority and thereby "demonstrate to the whole people, that there was something at least, of a common interest combined with the independence, which was to become the object of common exertions." But the only way he could foresee that happening

[135] Ibid., 616.
[136] Ibid., 636–37.

was through the self-destruction of "the old code." "My opinion ever was," he concluded, that that code "was so constructed, that if there was once a breach in any essential part of it; the ruin of the whole, or nearly of the whole, was, at some time or other, a certainty."[137]

Despite the insistence of other analysts that a Protestant government could be maintained in Ireland only by "a communication of *constitutional privileges*" to the entire population, the Irish Protestant establishment continued to cater to the general Protestant fear that if, in the civil realm, they gave Catholics an inch, they would take a mile. They reasoned, said one anonymous writer in a 1792 pamphlet, that

if you give them real property, they will acquire political privilege, they will acquire more property; and then, they will get into corporations; and, from corporations, into parliament; from the civil, to the military; from the law to the revenue; and then, by one great bound, there will be none but Papists; or, at least, a great majority, in the army, in the senate, in the civil administration: and then, we shall have a popish church, and a popish state, and there is an end of it.

By continuing to act on such reasoning, this writer observed, Irish Protestants continued to hold fast to a system that "perpetually remind[ed] those whom they" had "deprived" of land and governance that there was "a perpetual irreconcilable opposition between" Protestant and Catholic interests, creating a unique situation. Whereas "in England the Roman Catholics" were but "a sect," in the Ireland created by the penal laws they had become "a nation." "A Papist can reason as well as a Protestant," he warned, "and he can argue, with infallible conclusion, that if [he] is of necessity dangerous to a Protestant Government, a Protestant Government can by no possibility be salutary to him."[138]

VI

Except for the cruelties charged against the British Ministry and its supporters and British armed forces during the American war, none of the inhumanities identified in the 1760s and 1770s and associated with Britain's overseas empire had been fully resolved as the eighteenth century drew to a close. To be sure, as P. J. Marshall has emphasized, public criticism of British rule in India after 1790 softened as a result of the operation of Pitt's reforms and Cornwallis's achievement of some degree of success in extending "the essentials of civil society, secure property and the protection of law . . . to millions [of Indians] who had previously quaked under oriental despotism.[139] Yet, these reforms did not

---

[137] Ibid., 617–18, 638.

[138] *A Dissertation, Addressed to a Friend, on the Propriety of Admitting the Roman Catholics to a Share in the Elective Franchise* (Dublin, 1792), 10–11, 30, 36–37, 39.

[139] P. J. Marshall, "The Moral Swing to the East: British Humanitarianism, India and the West Indies," in idem, *'A Free though Conquering People': Eighteenth-Century Britain and Its Empire* (Aldershot, U.K.: Ashgate, 2003), Chapter 9, 69–95. The quotation is from page 83.

entirely atone for past sins, and the exposés of the previous twenty years left more than a little residue of suspicion that East India Company servants were still running amok in India and that the continuing exploitation of Indians for British profits reflected little glory upon Britain. In other areas of the empire, notwithstanding all the complaints about these imperial inhumanities and all the efforts by people of a wide variety of political persuasions to call attention to and check them, British Guiney-men were still conducting a massive trade in slaves on the African coast, slave masters in the West Indies and the Atlantic islands continued to expropriate the labor and the lives of thousands of slaves without restriction, Protestants in Ireland continued their persecution of Irish Catholics with only minor abatement, new settler colonies in British North America and in Australia were still growing at the expense of indigenous lands and lives, and even the St. Vincent Caribs were removed to mainland Central America. Notwithstanding the elimination of the worst excesses of colonialism in India, the relationship between empire and injustice, oppression, and inhumanity, like that between empire and commerce and imperial grandeur, had by 1790 been firmly established, at least in the British case, for those who deplored it. The question of whether inhumanity was a necessary consequence of empire was still in play.

Epilogue

"Against Every Principle of Justice, Humanity, and Whatever is Allowed to be Right Among Mankind"

Standards of Humanity and the Evaluation of Empire

I

During the quarter-century following the conclusion of the Seven Years' War in 1763, the discussion of empire in Britain took a new turn. Metropolitan Britons were accustomed to celebrating the British Empire as an engine for the growth of Britain's commerce, wealth, and maritime power, an arena for the extension of British liberty, improvement, and civility, an outlet for individual ambition, and a site for the displacement – and possible redemption – of metropolitan undesirables. Up to 1763, the languages of commerce, maritime power, liberty, improvement, and civility had been sufficient for metropolitan Britons to express their generally favorable assessment of empire, and the language of alterity, to express their skepticism about those who peopled and presided over those societies and their claims to a British identity. In the wake of Britain's extraordinary and worldwide victory in the Seven Years' War, metropolitans added a language of imperial grandeur to their repertoire.

Very quickly after the peace, however, a series of developments throughout the empire exposed the tensions among these conventional languages of empire and raised questions about whether they were adequate to tell the full story of Britain's imperial achievement. While the controversy with the American colonies over their status within the empire brought out the latent contradictions between the languages of commerce and liberty, on the one hand, and that of imperial grandeur, on the other, ongoing revelations about the rapacity of East India Company servants; increasingly strident protests against the systems of enslavement entrenched in many American colonies, the iniquities of the African slave trade, and those who benefitted from them both; opposition to the Carib War in St. Vincent, and a new consciousness that Britain's imperial successes in Ireland and America had been at the expense of indigenous people; full revelations during the late 1770s and early 1780s of Britain's long-standing economic and political oppression of Ireland; a growing public condemnation of the Protestant persecution of Irish Catholics; and persistent

Opposition charges of British inhumanity toward American rebels during the American war – all seemed to demand a new lexicon for speaking about empire.

Successively and in combination, these problems focused metropolitan attention on the underside of the imperial project and on the many injustices and inhumanities that overseas Britons were ready to commit in the pursuit of wealth and empire. Thinking of Britain as a just, humane, and liberal nation of free people, many metropolitan Britons judged the behaviors of nabobs, Guiney-men, Creoles, metropolitan war leaders, and Irish Protestants by metropolitan standards and found them gravely wanting. To account for these behaviors and cast the light of public attention on the underside of empire, metropolitan analysts turned to the languages of humanity, justice, and liberty and their antonyms of cruelty, oppression, rapacity, plunder, slavery, and tyranny. While they never entirely displaced the conventional languages of imperial discourse, by the mid-1780s these languages had acquired a new salience and prominence in the discussion of empire. Advocates of empire and those overseas Britons who found themselves under attack, as the new standards of humanity and justice were applied to their behaviors, aggressively used the conventional languages to defend their behavior on grounds of economic or strategic utility and to emphasize their achievements in extending the boundaries and benefits of empire and thereby contributing to the national interest. In the process, they acknowledged the force of the new standards by claiming to have acted as humanely and justly as possible, given their respective situations.

II

An appropriate time for taking stock, the end of the American war provided an occasion for reassessing Britain's imperial activities. One of the many clerics who preached sermons on a day of general thanksgiving for the peace with the United States, on July 29, 1784, Gilbert Wakefield in Surrey used the occasion not just to celebrate the end of a costly and bloody war, whose issues he thought might have been better addressed "under other Terms, by the Rules of Equity and Justice," but also to "take a short Retrospect of those" many "Devastations through the Extremities of the Globe, those horrible Achievements of Bloodshed and Destruction, that have unhappily distinguished these Times and this Country" and that "have passed *in these very Days*, and in some Respects, under our own Observation." "We have been blessed, as a Nation, with a more than ordinary Share of Favour," he told his audience:

We have enjoyed greater Opportunities of doing Service to Mankind, than any other People whatsoever. We have been able to claim for ourselves, a Degree of civil and religious Liberty, which has made us the Envy of the World and the Pride of human Nature. This little Spot of Land has sent it's Arms into every Corner of the Globe, and dispersed it's Ships through every Ocean under Heaven. Our Proficiency in Arts and Science has been commensurate to our military Reputation, and has conspired to exalt us to the highest Pinnacle of Greatness. – But, he inquired, "have we been as renowned for a liberal Communication of our Religion and our Laws, as for the Possession of them? Have we navigated and conquered to save, to civilize, and to instruct; or to oppress, to plunder, and to destroy?" To answer these questions he turned to India and Africa, saying of the first that "we have exhausted [her] of her Wealth and her Inhabitants, by Violence, by Famine, and every Species of Tyranny and Murder," and of the second that we were "daily carry[ing] off" her children

from the Land of their Nativity, like *Sheep for the Slaughter*, to return no more: we tear them from every Object of their Affection; or, sad Alternative! Drag them together to the Horrours of a mutual Servitude: we keep them in the profoundest Ignorance; we gall them in a tenfold Chain, with an unrelenting Spirit of Barbarity, inconceivable to all but the Spectators of it, unexampled amongst former Ages and other Nations, and unrecorded even in the bloody Registers of heathen Persecution.

"Reason tells us, and Experience proves, that Countries, remote from the Seat of Government, are seldom ruled with Humanity and Justice," he concluded; the "Inhabitants are too often plundered and oppressed by those, who are commissioned to protect them; eager as these are in Extortions, from a Knowledge of the Uncertainty of their Stations and from a Willingness to enjoy at Home as soon as possible the Fruits of their Rapacity." "Such is the Conduct of us, enlightened Englishmen! Reformed Christians!," he said. "Thus have we profited by our Superiour Advantages, by the Favours of God."[1]

Two years earlier, in March 1782, Thomas Parker, a lawyer at Lincoln's Inn, provided a far more detailed and comprehensive assessment of Britain's recent imperial transactions in his remarkable and substantial *Evidence of our Transactions in the East Indies, with An Enquiry into the General Conduct of Great Britain to Other Countries, from the Peace of Paris in 1763*. As the title suggests, most of the volume was devoted to India and much of that to the publication of documents concerning the misdeeds of East India Company servants between 1757 and 1772. However, in a short and trenchant preface and in an independently titled and paginated extension to the book, *An Enquiry into our National Conduct to Other Countries*, he provided in fifty-five packed pages the fullest, most penetrating, most damning critique of the effects of British imperial activities published up to that time. An evaluation of those activities over the previous twenty years from the perspective of professed metropolitan standards of humanity and justice, this work is the single most important contemporary assessment of the range and depth of metropolitan disillusionment with and misgivings about the effects of what later generations would come to term *colonialism*. Giving fullest attention to India and Africa, Parker repeated most of the gory details and standard objections that earlier writers and parliamentary speakers had been making against the plunder of India, the

---

[1] Gilbert Wakefield, *A Sermon Preached at Surry on July 29th 1784, The Day Appointed for a General Thanksgiving on Account of the Peace* (London, 1784), 4, 7–10, 15–17.

evils of the slave trade, and the inhumane treatment of the enslaved in American colonies, and he included long sections of documents from parliamentary reports to support that emerging narrative. But three features distinguished his work from that of previous writers. The first was its comprehensive scope. From India and Africa, he went on to consider the Carib War, the acquisition of indigenous lands in America, as well as Britain's treatment of its European neighbors, omitting only Ireland from the sites of British inhumanity that had come to public scrutiny in Britain since 1760. The second was its focus upon not just the misdeeds of British peoples overseas, but the effects of those misdeeds upon local peoples, bringing the enormities of British behavior home to readers by asking them how they might respond if the situation were reversed. The third was its emphasis on the complicity of metropolitan Britain in the misdeeds of overseas Britons, developing a case for the proposition that the Government's refusal to condemn overseas excesses effectively made the nation a party to them and thereby turned them into *national* excesses for which all Britons stood responsible.[2]

Parker's analysis was saturated with the languages of humanity and justice. Flatly stated in the preface, Parker's object was to show "that our conduct" abroad contained "every injury which the people of one country can well do to those of another" and to inquire "how far it may be proper to allow all these proceedings to stand under the apparent sanction of the whole kingdom, and go down to the next and all future ages with that approval they have hitherto obtained in the age in which those transactions have taken place." More specifically, he hoped that his volume would provoke an inquiry into "our national conduct," by which "British subjects... within the last twenty years" had

rendered miserable and destroyed millions of mankind, and which must lead a considerable part of the world to look forward with dread to the time when they shall hear of our recovering that state of peace, which when last in our possession, was made use of as the season wherein to plunder, oppress, enslave, and to spread war and ruin in other countries, whose inhabitants never came to do us any injury, and who never have received from us any acknowledgment or reparation for the wrongs they have suffered at our hands.

"By the plainest rules of justice," he wrote, such wrongs demanded

the abolishing of the very being of those trading societies, in whose names such enormities have been practised... and which, so long as they continue to exist in this nation, from the character they have obtained, cannot but place the whole community, in the esteem of a great part of the world, as in a state of avowed opposition to all the rights

---

[2] Thomas Parker, *Evidence of our Transactions in the East Indies, with* [separately paginated] *An Enquiry into the General Conduct of Great Britain to Other Countries, from the Peace of Paris in 1763* (London, 1782). Astonishingly, this work seems to have escaped the notice of most recent scholars of empire, with the exception of Christopher Brown.

of other nations, whenever we have the power to deprive them of their possessions or enslave their persons.[3]

India occupied first place in Parker's catalogue of sites in which the deeds of British subjects had transgressed metropolitan norms of justice and humanity. Having at first been "admitted into the East-Indies by the favour of the princes of that country, to trade with their subjects, and then to have settlements among them," he reported, East India Company servants, following the territorial acquisitions in 1757, soon discovered devious ways to acquire vast fortunes with which they returned to Britain, and Company members soon began to collude with their representatives in India in a new design "to enrich ourselves, at the expence of the people of that country; and this, not by commerce, but by war and conquest." By making "wars with the natives," Britons soon turned a country they had found as "a garden for plenty" into "a wilderness," in a mere "five or six years" transforming what had long been "the store-house of that part of India" into "a place of wretchedness and misery" as Britons "destroyed, starved, and drove away three millions of people of the country by our violence, rapine and oppression. Assisted by our public forces, we have allowed our people to make one revolution after another, till we have made ourselves masters of the dominion and of the people, said to have been fifteen million in number when we first went among them." As a result of these injuries, Parker pointed out, "the subjects of Great Britain in India" had brought away "many millions of money... from the people of that country, by means the most unjust and violent," had deprived "the princes of India" of their territories "by force, in the name of the East India Company," and, "in the course of these proceedings," had destroyed or terrified into exile "as many of the natives... as there were of inhabitants in our American colonies before the war began – that is, about three millions," about a fifth of India's total estimated population.[4]

To make matters worse, Parker complained, "Whilst all this business was going forward in India, those of our fellow-subjects that had enriched themselves with the property of this unhappy people, were, one after another, coming home among us; many of them" purchasing "great estates, and" appearing "on the seats of the legislature." Although the "managers of the company in England... made many complaints of their servants in India," they "at the same time... gave pressing orders for the collection of the revenues of the country acquired in their name." Despite "many public complaints" against these developments, Parker noted, Britain was at the very same time "receiving, as a nation, the payment of a large sum out of the common spoil." On the basis of appended documents. Parker estimated that in less than fifteen years after the East India Company "had obtained the power of absolute government over the people of the Provinces," renamed "the Territorial Acquisitions of the

---

[3] Parker, *Evidence of our Transactions in the East Indies*, iv, ix–x.
[4] Parker, *An Enquiry into our National Conduct to Other Countries*, 11, 25, 54.

East India Company," the Company and its "servants [had] received between twenty-nine and thirty millions of pounds sterling from the princes of India and their subjects, besides a sum not known, arising from the exclusive trade which the Company's civil and military servants took to themselves."[5]

Britain's record in Africa was equally dismal, and its transgressions were much older. By the 1760s, Parker wrote, British slave traders had "long been accustomed to send...ships to the coasts of Africa...to procure the people of that country" to meet the labor demands of the staple colonies in the West Indies and southern North America. Responding to British inducements, he reported, "the most unworthy" of the Africans fell "upon their countrymen, their wives, and children" and took "by force in great numbers" whomever they "found unable to defend themselves," for the sole purpose of making them "slaves to the subjects of this country." By these tactics, they had turned a formerly plentiful and peaceful country into a land of terror, where inhabitants of an "extensive coast" lived "in continual fear of being laid hold on and delivered into our hands, and sent away into endless slavery; to which they shew their unwillingness by defending themselves to the last degree; and in the desperate battles they fight, to prevent their being made our slaves, great numbers are annually destroyed, of which there is no account." In consequence of this trade, Parker lamented, "the people of that country" had "been kept in a state of war and confusion, by the people of Great Britain for many years," while "a great number, of which no account is given," had lost "their lives in the battles that are fought to force them into our hands." Through this trade Africa was losing "on an average...more than seventy thousand [people] yearly," about a third of whom perished. In "fourteen years, from 1760," Parker estimated, "above three hundred thousand men, women and children" had been thus "destroyed, and double that number taken into slavery to the subjects of the crown of Great Britain."[6]

That this trade "violated and trampel[l]ed under foot" the very "principles of natural justice" and "humanity" that Britons held dear in their own country seemed to Parker obvious. Yet, he observed in reference to the antislavery movement that had sprung to life in the 1760s, "the conduct of this country to the people of AFRICA" had "continued the same for so many years, that the most public endeavours of several individuals, to make us look upon that conduct as criminal in itself, have not produced any reformation, or removal of that sanction which is given by the state to a trade which at once produces and tolerates all the ill treatment which the Africans receive at our hands." Moreover, when a few North American colonies had tried to "to shut their ports against slaves," the British state refused to support them, "notwithstanding," Parker said, that "we had solemnly declared, that slave-holding in this nation

---

[5] Parker, *Evidence of our Transactions in the East Indies*, 281; idem, *An Enquiry into our National Conduct to Other Countries*, 12.

[6] Parker, *Evidence of our Transactions in the East Indies*, vii; *An Enquiry into our National Conduct to Other Countries*, 13, 27, 54.

was against our laws, because against natural justice and humanity, in the way in which they are now attained and used." At least temporarily, Parker wrote approvingly, the American war had "put an end to" that "merciless trade; and... given a season of peace to the people of Africa," an accomplishment that "neither individuals nor nations" had previously "been able to effect." However, because the trade had "only [been] discontinued against our consent, and for want of a power to carry it on," he observed, despite "all that these people have hitherto suffered at our hands, whenever any of our colonies or plantations may be again in a state of peace, the subjects of Great Britain" still had "the sanction of the state to enter again upon this trade, and spread all that misery among the people of Africa, which any people will live in, who are in constant fear of being forced away without distinction of rank, age, or sex, into a foreign slavery."[7]

Parker spent considerably less space in laying out in the third item in his catalogue the immoral and inhumane conditions that Africans found in the colonies to which they were transported, where they were sold "as cattle" to be "slaves for life, their offspring slaves, and all that descend from them." But he made it clear that the British settlers who presided over those societies had constructed them without regard for the humanity of the enslaved. If "the formal resolutions we have made for governing them... may be called laws," he wrote, "they are laws to place them in a condition much worse than our cattle are used for any sort of labour in this country; besides beating and whipping them to make them do our work" and subjecting them to severe corrections extending even to the "chop[ping] off half a foot," which was "among the punishments provided for the people of Africa in slavery to the people of this nation." "Wherein we have distinguished them from cattle," he wrote, "the distinction itself shews the impious length to which our oppression of them has proceeded." By "public authority," he reported, a master who murdered his slave had only to "pay but a fine of a few pounds." Parker did not deny that masters fed and took care of their slaves, "with a view to preserve them in health, and to prolong their lives," or even that a few "humane masters" – Parker thought no more than "one in ten thousand" – freed an occasional slave. But, "in general," he insisted, "the care and kind treatment which the working cattle in England meet with, from those they belong to, places them in a situation, as to all comforts of mere animal life, much superior to the circumstances under which the people we bring from Africa live and die in our service."[8]

In an unusual move, Parker reached out beyond most of contemporary critiques of empire to include, as a fourth example in his catalogue of Britons' inhumanity to and oppression of the peoples they encountered in their quest for empire, the "treatment... which the native inhabitants of AMERICA met with

---

[7] Parker, *Evidence of our Transactions in the East Indies*, viii; *An Enquiry into our National Conduct to Other Countries*, 13, 15, 27, 54.

[8] Parker, *An Enquiry into our National Conduct to Other Countries*, 14–15.

from those that went from among us." As had been the case with the Africans, however, he regretted that this example had "been so long continued, that we may have ceased to think it ever was, or is at this time chargeable as a crime, to have driven away the people of the country, which they were as much used to consider as their own, as ever the people of this country were to consider the house they lived in as their own." But the simple fact was, he asserted, that except

in a single province [Pennsylvania], where a few of our countrymen regulated their conduct to the natives by the principles of equity . . . in all the rest . . . we forced our way wherever our inclinations led us, as far as we could; and when a regard to our own safety obliged us to make terms with the poor people we had invaded, and boundaries were fixed by public contracts, we broke them whenever we saw ourselves superior to them, 'till we possessed ourselves of all that vast country, for which we have been contending as our right and dominion.[9]

Parker's fifth and final site of Britain's oppression in its overseas empire was St. Vincent and the Carib War of the early 1770s. He reviewed how the French had ceded the island in 1763 on the condition that the British would allow the Caribs to continue to possess "their lands in peace and safety," how the Caribs had subsequently resisted planters' efforts "to take their possessions from them," how the planters had succeeded in getting the Ministry to send an expedition to put down the Caribs, how this army, at the expense of many casualties, had eventually killed many Caribs and "made the rest submit to our pleasure," and how, even though the officers who "commanded in this war . . . thought it a very dishonourable one," the Ministry had "acted as if it was not only just but necessary," the sense "which, as a nation, we passed upon it." "In this transaction," Parker announced sadly, "we followed the example of those of our nation, who had before disregarded the natural rights of men, and the feelings of humanity, in possessing themselves of many parts of the provinces of America; by destroying the ancient inhabitants." Parker found it more than a little ironic that St. Vincent, "the little island in which we had made the bad use of our power over the Caribbes," was the "first of our total losses of dominion" to the French in the West Indies and that the French had restored to "those of them that survived our dishonourable war against them" the "antient rights which we invaded."[10]

But Parker's larger point in once again laying this vast but familiar panoply of transgressions before the public was to show how the nation, through its government, had endorsed every one of them. In the case of the East India Company and its servants, he wrote, "after the repeated publication of their crimes to the whole nation, the people of this country have not only, in all the variety of distinct bodies, and corporate societies, into which our nation is divided, been silent under all that has been done without a single exception;

9 Ibid., 15–16.
10 Ibid., 16–17, 28.

but several of them have selected" some of the most flagrant perpetrators "to appear in their name... to transact their part of the public business in the legislature." "We have," Parker charged,

publicly divided the spoil with those that brought it to us; and we have done all a nation could do, to give those dominions and that property which we have acquired by force against right, accompanied by "perfidy and murder," all the sanction of lawful dominions, and of property duly obtained; as if the whole proceedings had been strictly agreeable to all that is required of mankind in their conduct to each other, by the rules of natural justice, and consistent with our character as a christian state.

By its inaction, Parker explained, the nation had "made all that has been done as much its own, as that which is done by a few, can be made the act of all that participate with them in what has been obtained, and acquit them of all blame as to the manner by which they did it." To this day, he remarked, the East India Company, "in whose name all these crimes have been committed against every principle of justice, humanity, and whatever is allowed to be right among mankind," had been

suffered to have its being in the very bosom of the state, to have its name held up as honourable, and to receive the full patronage of the whole kingdom; and from the first knowledge of all the wrong done by the people of Great-Britain in India to this day, there has not been a single county, city, or incorporate body in the whole kingdom that has uttered a single complaint – All that has been done, and the impunity [with] which the whole has been allowed to pass, has been made as public as any national concern could well be made, and neither from the whole nation, assembled in its representatives, nor from any one of the elective bodies into which the kingdom is divided, has there been a single negative, but for now nigh ten years has all this conduct obtained the uniform sanction of the state.[11]

Regarding the African traders and the Creolean despots who presided over the slave-powered colonies in America, Parker made much the same argument. Their conduct also appeared "to be as much the conduct of the whole country, as any thing which is done by a few men can be made the act of all. Our national arms protect the ships that carry these unhappy people to their endless slavery," he argued;

we fight for and defend the ground on which they suffer their miserable oppressions, as much as if it was within the island in which our nation is seated. We use the things which these men, women, and children are made slaves, in order to cultivate; and as a nation, we have a constant regard to the advantages which result from their slavery.[12]

Similarly, Parker thought, in the "small instance" of the Carib War, "we set our seal to all the unjust conduct our countrymen had been guilty of against the Indians; by letting all that had been done against these poor Caribbes pass without a single censure either on those that proposed the cruel treatment of

[11] Ibid., 25–26, 54–55.
[12] Ibid., 15.

them, or on those without whose authority it could not have been carried into execution, and by leaving them at the mercy of their oppressors." By its resolution, he contended, Parliament had "acquitted the subjects of Great Britain of any crime in all they did to the Caribbes of St. Vincent, whatever were the numbers of these poor people that were destroyed in consequence of the desire to have their lands." "After the whole transaction was enquired into," Parliament's response to this "national disgrace," he wrote, "amounted to little less than a public declaration, that," with regard to British imperial considerations, "all the obligations of natural justice and humanity must give place to the present interest of our own people, in any part of the world, where they had themselves, or we could give them superiority."[13]

What should we "think of the character of that nation, whose public sentence declared, there was nothing wrong in what had been done" in the commission of acts such as those that had been committed throughout the empire, he asked his readers, "that the men who had designed and authorised all this, had done it because it was their interest and their pleasure; and that the interest of native subjects and the pleasures of men in public stations, were worthy of much more consideration, than the rights and lives [of] a few hundred" or even thousands of "people, of whom we knew nothing more than they were of foreign extraction"? For Britons to declare through their "public acts, and the reports of our national proceedings," that those who went "out from us do great and meritorious services, when they" force "tens of thousands into slavery, oppress and destroy millions; deprive foreign princes of their just dominions,... plunder whole nations of all that we can bring away from them," "bring back millions by the same right that robbers take their booty, and acquire whole provinces by perfidy and murder," Parker declared, was both to ignore the "just degree of enormity" of the crimes of British colonialism and to "proclaim to all mankind and to all future ages, the undisguised sentiments of the present," that "this or any other nation" that acted "to oppress, enslave, deceive, plunder and destroy the people of any other country but their own... [had]... the countenance," support, and "sanction of our repeated example" to excuse it.[14]

At the end of the Seven Years' War, Parker mused,

Britain was placed, as a nation, in a state of the greatest apparent safety from all foreign danger, by the superiority that had been given to our national arms, and by the moderation that was observed on the part of this country, in restoring to France and Spain some of their valuable distant dominions, that had been taken by our forces during the war; which left both nations without any reasonable cause for interrupting the peace at any future period, on account of any thing that was already past.

"With this prospect of a lasting peace, and of security from all danger from without," Parker recalled, "we seemed to possess within ourselves, as a nation, as many, if not greater advantages than perhaps the people of any other country

13 Ibid., 16–17, 53.
14 Ibid., 18, 31–32.

are favoured with. The situation and produce of different parts of the dominions, afforded all the advantages arising from useful employment, and extensive
commerce, that could be well desired. And with these advantages and apparent
safety, we then" also enjoyed the "unequalled rights and privileges which every
rank of the subjects possess in common with the members of the legislature
itself" as well as all "just and necessary religious liberties." But the "events that
have taken place in the British empire... since the peace of 1763," he wrote,
had unfortunately "include[d] in them a great and general calamity to the people of this country, its colonies and dependencies." Parker did not dwell on the
many inhumanities that many Britons associated with the "civil war" that had,
"for some years, been carried on, with a numerous division of our fellow subjects in America," but he did include the war among " the sum of the evils we
have suffered." He lamented the "many thousands" who had "fallen by each
other[']s hands," the "many more" who had been "miserably wounded," the
widespread destruction of fields, towns, and houses, "the daily toil of millions
to provide for the expence of all this misery and devastation," and "the present
difficulties, and probable dangers" that confronted "the people of this country
and its colonies."[15]

In laying out his vision for the best possible settlement of that war, Parker
also revealed what his vision of a just and humane empire might look like.
"Were the people of this kingdom and America to throw an everlasting veil
over all that is past, and to a man, from this day, consider themselves as one
people, heirs of the same privileges by which they have so long been distinguished from all mankind," and "unite as firmly, as ever they were united," he
suggested, they might then be able to grapple successfully with the gargantuan
"task which the whole empire has got to go through, to recover the situation
in which we were before our unhappy contest began" and, instead of pursuing empire without regard to British metropolitan standards of justice and
humanity, "make the whole dominions one great asylum for the oppressed and
persecuted to fly to, from under tyranny and superstition in other countries."
Parker did not consider the probability that these new dominions would be
cleared for settlement by indigenous displacement. In calling upon Britons to
eschew the pride of dominion and the avarice of conquerors and "to open to
themselves a secure and lasting commerce betwixt their several countries and
the growing continent of America," the "natural produce of many parts of
which, is so suitable to their wants, and its inhabitants calling forth supplies, as
must employ multitudes of" Britons in the parent state "and swell the streams
of their several revenues," he strongly suggested that liberty and commerce,
not dominion or imperial grandeur, were the only foundations of a just and
humane empire and the proper antidotes for the evils of colonialism overseas.[16]

Those metropolitan Britons who wondered why Parker failed to include
Ireland on his list of sites of British colonial oppression could have found the

[15] Ibid., 1–2.
[16] Ibid., 2–3.

evidence they sought in a pamphlet first published in London in 1777 and republished in Dublin in 1792. In *Remarks on the English and Irish Nations*, Thomas O'Brien McMahon, a Catholic priest from County Clare in Ireland, included a twenty-five-page footnote that made a powerful case that the excesses of English imperialism had far deeper roots, going back to the beginnings of overseas empire in the late fifteenth century. Dilating on the "burlesque irony" of the English people's persistent "flout[ing of] themselves" by "constantly boasting of [their] *good-nature*, tenderness of disposition, and humanity; qualities which they are not even acquainted with in theory," McMahon asked the "unfortunate natives of Ireland," who, to their "cost," were longer and "better acquainted with this *unamiable* people" than any other, "what marks have you after five hundred years connection, to produce of their *lenity* and *good-nature*? Alas!," he protested, the

very mention of such virtues, as are pretended to by a nation so diametrically opposite to them, is adding insult to your long and unparalleled sufferings under their yoke. – Your fertile country uncultivated, through their *industry-chilling discouragement* – your trade, notwithstanding your advantageous situation, cramped and insignificant, through their *restraining laws.* Your staple manufacture . . . marked for circumscription. Every branch of trade – particularly those beneficial to agriculture, English influence has doomed to decay. No sooner were your Breweries and Distilleries noted for promoting cultivation, than they were blighted by *experimental* laws, which must have originated in something worse than idiotism. In short all your manufactures are kept in a hectic state through their *monopolizing jealousy*, their *burthensome establishment*, and *fleecing pensions.*[17]

But that was not the sum of English iniquities against the Irish people. "After lawlessly distributing your estates, possessed for thirteen centuries or more by your illustrious families, whose antiquity and nobility" were "[un]equalled by any nation in the world," and otherwise "seizing on your inheritances," they had flung them, he charged in a humorous play on English last names, "among their *Cocks, Hens, Crows, Rooks, Daws, Wolves, Lions, Foxes, Rams, Bulls, Hogs*, and other beasts of prey; or" vested

them in the sweepings of their jails, their *Smallwoods, Dolittles, Barebones, Strangeways, Smarts, Tarts, Sterns, Churls*, and *Savages;* their *Scarlet's, Greens, Blacks, Browns, Greys, and Whites;* – their *B[lack]smiths, Carpenters, Brewers, Barbers, Bakers*, and *Taylors;* their *Suttlers, Cutlers, Butlers, Trustlers*, and *Jugglers;* their *Norths, Easts, Souths*, and *Wests;* their *Fields, Rows, Streets* and *Lanes;* their *Tom's sons, John's sons, Will's sons, James's sons, Nick's sons*, and *Wat's sons;* their *Packs, Slacks, Tacks*, and *Jacks.*

Nor had they "confined the mischiefs they inflicted on you to the temporal ones, however grievous," McMahon complained. "To complete their ingratitude and injustice, they" had "transported a cargo of ignorant hungry adventurers

---

[17] Thomas O'Brien McMahon, *Remarks on the English and Irish Nations* (Dublin, 1792), 61–64 note.

among you, impiously calling the filthy lumber, *Ministers of God's Word*," and "empowered and commissioned" them "to put in practice every species of ill-usage and persecution, with an avowed design of dragging from you the holy faith" that "you [had] preserved in its original purity, in the smoky, dreary, and comfortless hovels to which they have reduced you." "To this diabolical spirit," McMahon declared, "you owe all" the "stratagems and violences, practised by them, for two hundred years, without intermission to strip you of your orthodoxy, the *only one* of your possessions, that has hitherto escaped their appropriating hands." "Who could enumerate every wanton indignity and evil, they heap upon you – your country weekly depopulating through that accursed system of policy they adopted, of *reducing to beggary* every nation subject to their realm?," he asked rhetorically. "These and the like favours, which they dispense with a liberality peculiar to themselves, will proclaim to the whole world the equity, moderation, and *good-nature* of – Englishmen."[18]

McMahon did not, however, confine his denunciation of English imperialism to Ireland. Indeed, he used the Irish experience to underline the unsavory continuities that over time and in every possible kind of venue had characterized British imperialism. He asked the "harmless natives of the *Empire of Hindostan* and its dependencies" whether they had "become happy by falling under the Dominion of a certain *good-natured* European Country, ... I mean such of you, as are not yet – *slaughtered* or *starved*," and called upon them to "bear witness to the – *gentleness*, – aversion to *famine-creating monopolies*, – ignorance in the arts of *treachery and barbarous rapacity*, of – Englishmen." Similarly, noting that their actions had already anticipated his interrogatories by showing "abundantly the deep sense they entertain of the Moderation, freedom from tyrannical insolence, distinterestedness, *good-nature, and humanity* of – Englishmen," he inquired of the

too credulous *North American nations* ... whose dominion you felt most oppressive, and are on that account most averse to? What people have you experienced – least indulgent, – least compassionate, least kind-spoken – least sympathizing, least disposed to mitigate, by humane and heart-soothing usage, the severity of a yoke, which the Realms that are freest themselves are the aptest to press, in the most galling manner, on the necks of dependent States?

In conclusion, McMahon assured his readers that, despite English claims to have become a more humane people over time, his "sketch of English manners" proved "beyond the possibility of a reasonable attempt at refutation, that no difference subsists between the heart of an Englishman of the sixteenth, and that one of the eighteenth century, and very little between the savage mode practised by them in both periods, to express their disapprobation of persons, countries, and things."[19]

[18] Ibid., 63–66.
[19] Ibid., 66–67, 84.

III

Notwithstanding this sweeping critique of empire, its authors had relatively few concrete achievements to show for their efforts as late as the early 1790s. By the standards of humanity and justice, Britain's sole unqualified success had been in Quebec, where many metropolitan Britons regarded its concessions to the majority Catholic population as a liberal act of justice and a generous response to the religious heterogeneity of the settler empire after 1763. Wherever else one looked, however, the costs of empire – in terms of human misery and Britain's national reputation – yet seemed to many observers to be excessive – and possibly even irremediable. Demands for the abolition of the slave trade and the amelioration of the condition of the enslaved in the American colonies had not yet succeeded; Irish Protestant flirtations with the amelioration of the penal laws in the wake of Irish political emancipation in 1782 had come to little; while Catholic demands for civil space had stiffened Protestant determination to deny them. P. K. Marshall has made a powerful case that Parliament's efforts to correct East Indian excesses, including the institution of "security of property and a system of impartial justice" and the regularization of administration under Cornwallis, had by the 1790s largely provided India with "a clean bill of moral health." The metropolitan majority were persuaded that Indians were "no longer . . . suffering any injury from British rule," and nabob-bashing was on the decline.[20] Yet a number of analysts continued to doubt that metropolitan reforms had entirely satisfied objections about the humanity and justice of the Indian project and were quite certain that they had not atoned for the extensive evils perpetuated over the quarter-century after the conquest of Bengal in 1757.

Edmund Burke was, of course, one of the most prominent of these. When in 1792 he returned to the subject of Protestant persecution of Catholics in Ireland, he explained his long neglect of a subject that had concerned him deeply for over three decades by his intensive engagement, "not yet finished, in favour of another distressed people [in India], injured by those who have vanquished them, or stolen a dominion over them."[21] Burke's neglect had been entirely understandable. Over the previous three decades, he had been at the vanguard of those who had endeavored to make sense of and come to terms with the myriad excesses in the behavior of Britons pursuing empire overseas that had come to metropolitan public attention after 1763, excesses not only in Ireland and India but also in Africa and the slave colonies of North America and the West Indies and Atlantic Islands, and in the conduct of the war with America.

[20] P. J. Marshall, "The Moral Swing to the East: British Humanitarianism, India and the West Indies," in idem, *'A Free Though Conquering People': Eighteenth-Century Empire and Its Empire* (Burlington, Vt.: Ashgate, 2003), Chapter 9, 84–90.

[21] *A Letter from the Right Hon. Edmund Burke, M.P. in the kingdom of Great Britain, to Sir Hercules Langrishe, Bart. M.P. on the Subject of Roman Catholics of Ireland* (London, 1792), reprinted in R. B. McDowell, ed., *The Writings and Speeches of Edmund Burke* (Oxford: Clarendon Press, 1991), Part II: *Ireland*, 9: 635.

Although Burke had largely left the excesses in Africa and the slave colonies to other critics, he was one of the earliest to call attention to the injustices of Irish Protestants, was a prominent critic of the cruelties inflicted by British forces during the American war, and took the lead in trying to understand the magnitude and character of the misdeeds of East India Company servants in India. In this last endeavor, he was still hoping for success in the early 1790s.

But Burke was only the most prominent of a number of metropolitan analysts who, evaluating those excesses in terms of the standards of humanity and justice that Britons liked to claim for Britain itself, found them to be incompatible with the very meaning of Britishness and undertook to comprehend what this discovery implied about the nature of empire, of a nation and the peoples that it spawned. Using the pseudonym "Timothy Touchstone, Gentleman," an anonymous poet published, in 1792 in London, a poem in two cantos entitled *Tea and Sugar, or the Nabob and the Creole*. This work added nothing new to the discussion of empire but it effectively captured the spirit, the outrage, and the resentment that characterized the increasingly elaborate critique of overseas empire that had taken shape over the previous quarter-century. As the title suggests, Touchstone used two social types, the *Nabob* and the *Creole*, who had come to epitomize the moral deficiencies of empire, to emphasize the extraordinary human costs of exotic products, illustrate the lurid excesses of British behavior overseas, and distance Britons at home from the actions of Britons abroad: the Asiatic plunderers in the East and the Creolean despots in the West.[22]

"Touchstone" began by excoriating the Nabobs.

> My Country's shame, and poor Hindostan's curse, . . .
> Men, who bring *Britain's* edicts into shame,
> And make its MAGNA-CHARTA, *merely* name . . .
> Some, for love of gold, have famine caus'd,
> Nor, until thousands perish'd, ever paus'd:
> While others, fortunes make, by unjust wars,
> Or *Murd'ring* MAN! By *Ex post facto* laws.

By such men and means were

> Briton's . . . procur'd the Eastern wares,
> Your Iv'ry Cabinets, and your Iv'ry Chairs;
> Your Silks, your costly Gems, and baneful Tea,
> Pernicious DRUG! – to health an enemy!
> Which for to gain, thousand's of Indian's bleed,
> And base Corruption's ready-growing seed
> Is largely strewn, O'er *Britain's* famous land,
> By an unprincipled, a savage band.[23]

---

[22] "Timothy Touchstone," *Tea and Sugar, or the Nabob and the Creole; A Poem in Two Cantos* (London, 1792).
[23] Ibid., 1–2, 8–10.

The Creole, in Touchstone's portrait, was

> SLAVERY'S *Prime Minister*, of swarthy hue
> And sickly look; of various tints combin'd,
> A true epitome of a jaundic'd mind;
> By whom the plunder'd, from Old Afric's shore
> Are made to sweat, nay bleed through every pore;
> Whom every generous feeling hath defy'd
> To whom, sweet social love, is unally'd;
> Whose flinty heart, but more obdurate mind,
> No Woe can penetrate – No Virtue find;
> Who, under *British* Laws, – with grief I speak,
> A greater tyrant is, than *Algier's* Chief.

All this, only to provide Britons with

> that sweet ingredient, SUGAR call'd,
> Made by the sweat and blood of the enthrall'd;
> Bitter their cup, alas! Who makes this sweet,
> Poor Slaves! Whose hearts, in sad affliction beat;
> From whence, the CREOLE, with unpitying eyes,
> Remorseless draws, his large, his vast supplies,
> Nor does he deal them with a sparing hand,
> Profusion guides, and has the sole command;
> Licentiousness, with Arrogance beside,
> The staunch supporters of his giant-pride . . . [24]

Praising "Touchstone's" work for being "strongly in favour of justice and humanity," one reviewer observed that it provided "a dreadful picture – and the more dreadful, because . . . it is drawn from life[,] . . . of Eastern rapacity, and Western cruelty."[25]

Also in 1792, the Scot James Thomson Callender, who had as little respect for the British imperial undertakings as McMahon, considered at length and surveyed widely Britain's record of imperial moral offenses in his pamphlet *The Political Progress of Britain: Or, an Impartial History of the Abuse of the Government of the British Empire in Europe, Asia, and America*, first published in Edinburgh in 1792. "At home Englishmen admire liberty," he wrote, "but abroad they have always been harsh masters." "In the East and West Indies, the conduct of the United Kingdoms," he asserted, "may be candidly compared to the *trial* of Atahualpa" in Peru, but the "peninsula within the Ganges," he had no doubt, was "the grand scene, where the genius of British *supremacy* displays its meridian splendour. Culloden, Glencoe, and Darien, the British famine of four years, Burgoyne's tomahawks, Tarleton's quarters, the Jersey prison-ship, and the extirpation of six hundred and sixteen thousand Irish men, women, and children, dwindle from a comparison" with an India in which five million

---

[24] Ibid., 11–13, 15–17.
[25] *Monthly Review* (London), 9 (1792): 214–15.

had been expelled or destroyed between 1757 and 1772 "and men found themselves wading through *blood* and *ruin,* when their only object was *spoil.*" From 1758 to 1792, he reminded his readers, India had experienced a waste of more than a million people, a long-continuing tragedy that far exceeded the Spanish "massacres in Mexico and Peru" and should have made "the spoilers of Bengal ... blush for their species."[26]

"But what quarter of the globe has not been convulsed by our ambition, our avarice, and our baseness?," he inquired. "As far back as 1756," the British, "most inhumanly and upon pretences, that in the eye of an honest man are not worth a farthing, *root*[*ed*] *out*" the neutral French from Acadia, a "*poor, innocent, deserving people* whom our utter inability to govern, or to reconcile, gave us no sort of right to extirpate." By the empire's subsequent expansion, he continued, the "tribes of the Pacific Ocean" had been "polluted by the most loathsome of diseases," and "on the shores of Africa, we bribe[d] whole nations by drunkenness, to robbery and murder; while in the face of earth and heaven, our senators assembled to sanctify the practice. Our brandy has brutalized or extirpated the aborigines of the western continent; and we have lured by thousands, the survivors to the task of bloodshed" during the American war. "On an impartial examination it will be found, that the guilt and infamy of" these practices "exceed by a considerable degree, that of any other species of crimes recorded in history."[27]

This dismal record prompted Callender to ponder whether the price of empire was worth it. A few people, of course, had at various points in the post-1760 discussion asked themselves whether empire could ever exhibit much humanity. Thus in 1779, the anonymous author of the satyrical pamphlet *The Cabinet Conference, or, Tears of a Ministry* had attributed such sentiments to Lord Shelburne during an imagined ministerial discussion of the "general establishment of empire." All empires, Shelburne allegedly said, seemed to him "the child of power, and of the sword," professing that he did not know "in the history of the world, save the aboriginis, an acre of land that has not been got, and empire that has not been formed, by slaughter, devastation, cruelty, and corruption." "Whence arose the Roman right to the territories they enjoyed? – Power. – Whence the Norman, Saxon, and Danish right to England? – The Sword. – Whence England's right to Ireland? – Capitulations violated. – Whence K. William's to this Country? – Power and party."[28] But Callender's reservations about empire were more explicit in detail and more reflective of the experiences of his generation. In his view, what demonstrated "the real inutility of external territories to Britain" were "the unfathomable waste of money requisite to retain them, the injustice and guilt that constantly

---

[26] James Thomson Callender, *The Political Progress of Britain: Or, an Impartial History of the Abuse of the Government of the British Empire in Europe, Asia, and America* (Philadelphia, 1795), Part One, 109, 117, 119–20; Part Two, 13.

[27] Ibid., Part One, 117; Part Two, 96.

[28] *The Cabinet Conference, or, Tears of a Ministry* (London, 1779), 22–23.

attend such acquisitions, and the intolerable ravages we suffer from internal taxes, in consequence of national wars about them."[29]

IV

If they had not, during the closing decade of the eighteenth century, entirely succeeded, in Thomas Parker's words from a decade earlier, in "throw[ing] an everlasting veil over all that is past"[30] and sublimating an awareness of the inhumanities and injustices in the pursuit of empire, the unapologetic proponents of British overseas expansion were clearly still in the ascendance. To be sure, their continued uses of the language of alterity, with its implicit standard of British worthiness, attested to their deep reservations about the people on the front lines of overseas empire. But the long war with France after 1793, strategic considerations with respect to Britain's European rivals, the continuing profitability of empire arising out of Indian revenues and the Indian, African, and West Indian trades, and the market potential of old and new colonies in North America and Australia had once again made the interlocking languages of commerce, maritime supremacy, liberty, and imperial grandeur seem the most appropriate and resonant languages for speaking of empire, tempered only slightly by the languages of humanity and justice.

The Administration's continuing reluctance to take action, either to put a total stop to all the imperial excesses that had come to light after 1760 or to condemn and apologize for them, calls for an explanation. Certainly an important part of any such explanation can be found in the ambiguous structure of the early modern British Empire, created with a minimum of central direction by chartered companies, proprietors, traders, investors, and, above all, individual settlers, all of whom, as Adam Smith and many other contemporary analysts recognized, had wide latitude to establish and reinforce the structures of authority in overseas polities or spheres of economic activity. As those entities became viable and successful contributors to the economic and strategic well-being of the metropolis, powerful metropolitan interest groups arose to represent their interests in Britain. Limited financial and coercive resources weakened the metropolitan state's capacity to enforce any measure that these overseas polities and their metropolitan supporters might oppose. Indeed, when the metropolitan state spent those resources, it often did so to protect those polities, as it dramatically did in the wars between 1739 and 1763, or to support the requests of a specific interest group, as it did with the St. Vincent planters in the early 1770s.

Again and again, from the late seventeenth century on, critics such as Morgan Godwyn, recognizing the impossibility of persuading local power holders to remedy the problems they had identified in the overseas empire and concluding that the metropolitan government was their only hope, appealed to it

---

[29] Callender, *Political Progress of Britain*, Part Two, 19.
[30] Parker, *An Enquiry into our National Conduct to Other Countries*, 2–3.

for action, only to be disappointed. Even if the means of coercion to enforce unpopular measures in the peripheries had been available, economic considerations and the influence of metropolitan interest groups would still have constituted a powerful bar to metropolitan intervention. Far from changing, this structural situation had become even more entrenched by the last half of the eighteenth century. As a result, post-1760s critics found themselves faced with the extraordinarily difficult challenge of persuading a Government invariably resisted by such interest groups, even when it was only trying to shore up its own authority, to act against the powerful interests, colonial and metropolitan, that profited from imperial excesses.

During the last decades of the eighteenth century, this continuing failure to act left the empire precisely in the situation in which Parker had placed it in 1782, one where Government reluctance constituted a continuing and blatant "public declaration, that," with regard to British imperial considerations, "all the obligations of natural justice and humanity must give place to the present interest of our own people, in any part of the world, where they had themselves, or we could give them superiority."[31] In Thomas O'Brien McMahon's words, beyond the immediate shores of Great Britain itself, nothing was safe from the "appropriating hands" of overseas Britons.[32] It was almost as if metropolitan Britons, having been thoroughly informed about the human and ethical costs of empire by an extensive critique stretching out over a quarter-century, had decided to ignore them in the national interest.

Whether or not that was the case, Britons and their imperial agents would continue for another century and a half to spread over an amazingly large part of the globe in the pursuit of colonies of settlement, in the process displacing and marginalizing indigenous peoples in British North America, Canada, Australia, New Zealand, South Africa, Kenya, and Rhodesia.[33] As many of the critics considered in this volume fully appreciated, of course, this process was not new but an old British imperial tradition worked out in the oversettlement plantations in Ireland and the displacement settlement colonies in North America, the Atlantic islands, and the West Indies, and this tradition would be of enormous service to Britain's American descendants as they displaced and marginalized indigenous peoples throughout the rapidly expanding United States.[34] Britons would also found an expanding number of fiduciary colonies, exploiting the labor of their indigenous inhabitants and imported workers and justifying the annihilations of their cultures on the grounds that they were bringing European civility and institutions to the benighted. In both settler and fiduciary colonies, they would reduce indigenous peoples to a subordinate

---

[31] Ibid., 16–17, 53.

[32] McMahon, *Remarks on the English and Irish Nations*, 63–66.

[33] See James Belich, *Replenishing the Earth: The Settler Revolution and the Rise of the Anglo World, 1783–1939* (Oxford: Oxford University Press, 2009).

[34] Jack P. Greene, "Colonial History and National History: Reflections on a Continuing Problem," *William and Mary Quarterly*, 3d ser., 64 (April 2007), 235–50.

social status on grounds of race, religion, or cultural inferiority, subject them to an unfamiliar system of law and justice, undermine their religious beliefs, and control them by the threat or actual use of force. They would exclude indigenous "subjects" from an active voice in political life[35] and deprive all but an assimilated, co-opted few of opportunities to share in the economic profits of empire. It was a record that would not have surprised many late eighteenth-century critics. And it was no worse a record than that of other Western nations, including the ostensibly anti-imperial United States.

From the vantage point of the early twenty-first century, after a long scholarly campaign to expose the human costs of imperial and national achievements that advocates of empire wished to acclaim, these eighteenth-century critics of empire may appear naïve for imagining that any empire could operate in a humane and just way, without the callous pursuit of turf, profit, advantage, and dominance on the part of colonial adventurers, without the subjugation, exploitation, and destruction of indigenous peoples and imported laborers, and without mayhem, bloodshed, or dishonesty, cultural condescension, or legal discrimination. For all the celebration of empire as a civilizing and humanizing agent, a commercially oriented empire that had acquired the trappings of imperial grandeur, as was the case of the early modern British Empire, was ill-prepared to let considerations of humanity and justice take priority over profits and state security. The construction of empires and nations has never been pretty. But the critics studied here did not have the advantage of hindsight. Unlike modern scholars, they could neither excuse imperial excesses on the grounds that colonials had not yet developed modern sensibilities nor condemn them in the conviction that anyone, anytime should have known better. Their accomplishment was to confront, define, and expose, in the British case, the high costs of empire and to articulate a new standard based on considerations of humanity and justice against which to gauge the acceptability of behavior in imperial ventures, a standard that they would apply across the empire from India to Ireland and from Africa to America.

The result was the elaboration of an extraordinary and general appreciation of the profound costs of colonialism in its early modern guise, costs that had long escaped the attention of a public eager to embrace empire for the enormous benefits it brought to Britain. Few proposed that Britain entirely renounce these benefits, but, with the new standard that they had created, critics could weigh their costs and propose actions to check excesses that, in their view, were unjust, inhuman, and un-British, blemishing the character of the state and of all who composed it. Their efforts were integral to some important victories registered after the period covered in this book, most notably, in the abolition of the slave trade and slavery throughout the empire, the regularizing of colonial administration in India, the emancipation of Catholics in Ireland, and the working out of a peaceful process for yielding self-government to

---

[35] Jack P. Greene, ed., *Exclusionary Empire: English Liberty Overseas, 1600–1900* (Cambridge: Cambridge University Press, 2010), 50–76, 132–288.

settler colonies – all problems identified and defined between 1760 and 1790. Few historians have appreciated the full range of problems that these early critics addressed when speaking of empire or noted the ways in which their passionate efforts to understand and resolve these problems fed upon one another. By awakening and focusing national sensibilities about the underside of empire, these critics were collectively, if not effectively, the forerunners of British and modern anticolonialism.

Index